COINS, BODIES, GAMES, AND GOLD

COINS, BODIES, GAMES, AND GOLD

THE POLITICS OF MEANING IN ARCHAIC GREECE

Leslie Kurke

PRINCETON UNIVERSITY PRESS   PRINCETON, NEW JERSEY

Library of Congress Cataloging-in-Publication Data
Kurke, Leslie.
Coins, bodies, games, and gold : the politics of meaning in
archaic Greece / Leslie Kurke.
p.   cm.
Includes bibliographical references and index.
ISBN 0-691-01731-X (cl. : alk. paper). — ISBN 0-691-00736-5 (pbk.
: alk. paper)
1. Greece—Antiquities. 2. Greece—Civilization—To 146 B.C.
3. Meaning (Psychology)—Greece. 4. Coins, Greek—Greece—History.
5. Greece—Social conditions—To 146 B.C.   I. Title.
DF222.2.K87   1999
938—dc21   99-12205

This book has been composed in Sabon

The paper used in this publication meets the minimum
requirements of ANSI/NISO Z39.48-1992 (R1997)
(*Permanence of Paper*)

http://pup.princeton.edu

Printed in the United States of America

1   3   5   7   9   10   8   6   4   2

(Pbk.)
3   5   7   9   10   8   6   4   2

For Andrew

Contents

PART TWO: PRACTICES

Illustrations

Preface

I STARTED OUT to write a book about the invention of coinage as the cause of a conceptual revolution in archaic Greece, but the more I worked on the topic, the more it seemed coinage was not a cause but a symptom of a complex shift—one site of contestation within an ongoing political struggle. And the more I looked at coinage, the more I was led to other things: the imagery of metals, stories about tyrants, prostitutes, counterfeiting, and games. Hence this is a hard book to characterize. It is much concerned with Herodotus, but it is not a book about Herodotus; it considers the invention and early use of coinage in the Greek world, but it is not really a book about coinage either. It might best be described as a study of some discourses, symbols, and practices through which competing ideologies struggle to imprint the world in archaic and classical Greece. For long before elitist and egalitarian ideologies emerge into the clear light of political rhetoric and political theory in fourth-century Greece, they exist and contest each other in an "incorporated" state—in the stories people tell, the songs they sing, the games they play, and the coins they use.[1] Thus this book is an attempt to write the obscure prehistory of political theory through practices: to trace some of the ways the egalitarian ideology of the polis first emerges, as well as acknowledging the ongoing resistance of an elitist tradition to that development. As such, it attempts to produce for ancient Greece what Michel de Certeau's *The Practice of Everyday Life* and Pierre Bourdieu's *Distinction* offer for the modern world. Like the latter, I would like to provide a kind of densely textured "thick description" of the material symbols that identify and reproduce different class fractions; like the former, I am trying to unearth something of the manifold, improvisatory tactics employed by actors in social life that usually escape notice because they are "hidden in plain sight."[2]

The nature of the evidence imposes severe restrictions on such an inquiry: for any period of antiquity, we possess only 5 to 10 percent of the original literary and artistic production, while all that we do possess (at least of the literary remains) is the product of an elite of birth, wealth, and status. This makes it nearly impossible to write for Greek antiquity

---

[1] For the notion of "incorporated" practices, see Bourdieu 1977, 1990; for the relatively late appearance of explicit political theory in Greece, see Loraux 1986: 173–80, 202–20, Ober 1989: 38.

[2] For this notion, cf. de Certeau 1984: 22.

the history (or ethnography) of the "ordinary man" to which de Certeau aspires. Still, I believe there is much more evidence of ideological conflict traceable in our texts than is generally acknowledged—in the rifts and fissures left by the conflict of competing positions. There are two reasons for this. First, I follow Ian Morris in seeing the struggle of elitist and egalitarian positions as an intra-elite opposition, so that we can find both positions explicitly espoused in the literary remains.[3] Second, the peculiar conditions of production and reception in archaic and classical Greece require a reading that focuses on the receiving audience and its positionality as much as on the "author." For in this period, all poetry and also (I believe), Herodotus's prose, were composed for public performance and embedded in clearly defined ritual or social contexts. Thus the sites for literary performance ranged from the closed group of the elite symposium to the entire city assembled for the staging of tragedy and comedy. Each different performance site required a different compact of author and audience, a different agreement on the values and models espoused. But also, given their social centrality, these performance texts did not simply reflect their audience's values but in some measure also constituted audience and values in turn. It is this double action within representation (including material representations like games and coins) that I try to capture and describe.

[3] Morris 1996.

Acknowledgments

I HAVE BEEN THINKING ABOUT and writing this book for a very long time and have incurred many debts along the way. It is a pleasure to record them here. Juliet Fleming, Tom Habinek, Ian Morris, and Seth Schwartz helped me enormously with conversation, ideas, and reactions as I was first conceptualizing the project, while Deborah Boedeker, Anne Carson, Page duBois, Kathy McCarthy, and Josh Ober provided invaluable support (both moral and intellectual) at its end. There are also a few people whose encouragement, intellectual stimulation, and engagement with the work have been so constant and so sustaining that this book could not have been written without them: they are Carol Dougherty, Mark Griffith, and Richard Neer. To them I owe the profoundest debt. Many others read some or all of the manuscript at various points and gave me valuable responses in spoken or written form: for that, thanks to Danielle Allen, Karen Bassi, Paul Cartledge, David Chamberlain, Kate Gilhuly, Robert Knapp, Donald Mastronarde, James Redfield, and Sitta von Reden. Needless to say, none of them agrees with all that I have argued here, but all of them have challenged me to enrich and complicate my thinking. I owe special thanks to Chris Howgego, Henry Kim, and Jack Kroll, who over the years shared their ideas and numismatic expertise on various issues and generously read parts of the manuscript. Even when they have disagreed with my interpretations, they have consistently encouraged me in my work.

I recently observed, in response to a query by a colleague, that this book could have been written only in Berkeley—not merely because of the financial support I have received from the University of California, though this has been substantial (two years of leave in 1993–94 and 1997–98, funded by a President's Research Fellowship in the Humanities and two Humanities Research Grants, as well as generous yearly research and RA funds), but also because Berkeley provides an extraordinarily vibrant intellectual community. For that, in addition to the colleagues and students I have already named, I would thank all the participants in my "Economies and Literature" Graduate Seminar (fall 96), who listened to and argued over many of the ideas presented here, and the members of my reading group, Katherine Bergeron, Tim Hampton, Celeste Langan, Michael Lucey, and Nancy Ruttenburg, who read and improved most of the manuscript-in-progress over the years. Thanks are also due to James Ker for his superb editorial work on the penultimate version of the manuscript; in the end, he was much more of an intellectual interlocutor than a research assistant. In addition, for help with various technical matters along the way, I owe thanks to my colleagues Crawford Greenewalt Jr., Robert Knapp, Donald Mastronarde, and Ron Stroud. And, though I conceptualized and finished this book in Berkeley, I started it elsewhere; for hospitality during a leave year I spent in Austin and Cambridge, I'm grateful to Michael Gagarin and Simon Goldhill.

Brigitta van Rheinberg, Classics and History Editor at Princeton University Press, has been supportive and enthusiastic about the project from the time I first described it to her and has eased the passage from manuscript to book at every stage. Marta Steele proved an efficient and good-natured copy editor. William Fitzgerald drew my attention to Edwin Long's painting, *The Marriage Market: Babylon,* which was to become my cover. Finally, this book is dedicated to Andrew Garrett for his unfailing patience and support. Even if he has not read it all, he has had to live with this book far too long.

Earlier versions of parts of the Introduction, Chapters 1, 2, and 5 appeared originally in article form as "ΚΑΠΗΛΕΙΑ and Deceit: Theognis 59–60" (*American Journal of Philology* 110 [1989]), "Herodotus and the Language of Metals" (*Helios* 22 [1995]), and "Inventing the *Hetaira*: Sex, Politics, and Discursive Conflict in Archaic Greece" (*Classical Antiquity* 16 [1997]). For permission to reprint that material here, I am grateful to The Johns Hopkins University Press, Texas Tech University Press, and the University of California Press, respectively.

Finally, a few words about the transliteration, quotation, and translation of Greek in the text. I had wanted to transliterate Greek person- and place-names in a way that was truer to their original Greek form than the standard Latinized versions familiar to English speakers, but I have refrained from doing so when the Latinized form seemed too well established. The result, I know, is hopelessly inconsistent: thus I use Aeschylus, Herodotus, Sophocles, Thucydides, but also Aigina, Anakreon, Ibykos, Polykrates. My quotation of Greek texts may seem erratic (I do not quote the Greek on every occasion), but it follows a compromise principle. For most passages of poetry and where the individual words of the text matter, I quote the Greek original; for most passages of prose and those poetry quotations not discussed in detail, I have given only an English translation, with important Greek words and phrases included in parentheses. Unless otherwise noted, all translations are my own; they aim not at elegance, but at an accurate rendition of the Greek. Readers may find them awkward and overliteral in places, and too colloquial in others. All I can say in their defense is that my aim was demystification and defamiliarization; I have tried to capture in translation both different generic and stylistic levels as well as the pervasive strangeness of Greek texts. Thus it seemed best to translate fragments of comedy and iambic abuse (for example) colloquially, while I have tried to convey the rich texture and sudden stylistic shifts of Herodotus in English.

Abbreviations

ANCIENT AUTHORS AND WORKS

Aelian *VH*	*Varia Historia*
Aesch.	Aeschylus
Ag.	*Agamemnon*
Ch.	*Choēphoroi*
Eum.	*Eumenides*
Pers.	*Persians*
Prom.	*Prometheus Bound*
Seven	*Seven against Thebes*
Suppl.	*Suppliants*
Alk.	Alkaios
Alk. *Ody.*	Alkidamas *Odysseus*
Anakr.	Anakreon
AP	*Palatine Anthology*
Apoll. *Bibl.*	Apollodorus *Bibliothēka*
Ap. Rh. *Arg.*	Apollonius Rhodius *Argonautica*
Arch.	Archilochos
Arist.	Aristotle
Hist. An.	*Historia Animalium*
NE	*Nicomachean Ethics*
Pol.	*Politics*
Rhet.	*Rhetoric*
[Arist.]	ps.-Aristotle
Ath. Pol.	*Athēnaiōn Politeia*
Oik.	*Oikonomika*
Aristoph.	Aristophanes
Ekkl.	*Ekklesiazousai*
Lys.	*Lysistrata*
Thesmo.	*Thesmophoriazousai*
Artem. *Oneir.*	Artemidoros *Oneirokritika*
Athen. *Deipn.*	Athenaios *Deipnosophistai*
Bacch.	Bacchylides
Carm. conv.	Carmina convivalia
Carm. pop.	Carmina popularia
Dem.	Demosthenes
Demetr.	Demetrios

Din.	Dinarchos
Dio Chrys. *Or.*	Dio Chrysostom *Orations*
D.L.	Diogenes Laertius
D.S.	Diodorus Siculus
Et. Mag.	*Etymologicum Magnum*
Eur.	Euripides
Alk.	*Alkestis*
El.	*Elektra*
Herakl.	*Herakleidai*
HF	*Hercules Furens*
Hipp.	*Hippolytus*
IA	*Iphigeneia in Aulis*
IT	*Iphigeneia in Tauris*
Or.	*Orestes*
Pho.	*Phoinissai*
Suppl.	*Suppliants*
Eustathios	
Comm. Hom.	*Commentaries to Homer, "Iliad" and "Odyssey"*
Harpokr.	Harpokration
Hdt.	Herodotus
Herakleitos *Quaest. Hom.*	*Quaestiones Homericae*
Hes.	Hesiod
Theog.	*Theogony*
W&D	*Works and Days*
Homer *Od.*	*Odyssey*
Isoc. *Antid.*	Isocrates *Antidosis*
Paus.	Pausanias
Philostratos *Her.*	*Heroikos*
Pindar	
I.	*Isthmian*
N.	*Nemean*
O.	*Olympian*
P.	*Pythian*
Plato	
Alc.	*Alcibiades*
Gorg.	*Gorgias*
Phdr.	*Phaedrus*
Rep.	*Republic*
Soph.	*Sophist*
Symp.	*Symposium*
Theaet.	*Theaetetus*
Tim.	*Timaeus*

Pliny *HN*	*Historia Naturalis*
Plut.	Plutarch
Alex.	*Life of Alexander*
Lys.	*Life of Lysander*
Mor.	*Moralia*
Nik.	*Life of Nikias*
Per.	*Life of Perikles*
Pollux *Onom.*	*Onomastikon*
Polyainos *Strat.*	*Stratēgēmata*
Quintilian *IO*	*Institutio Oratoria*
Schol. *ad*	Scholiast to . . .
Seneca *Epist.*	*Epistulae*
Simon.	Simonides
Soph.	Sophocles
El.	*Elektra*
OT	*Oedipus Tyrannos*
Stes.	Stesichoros
Suet. *Tib.*	Suetonius *Life of Tiberius*
Theokr. *Id*	Theokritos *Idylls*
Theophr.	Theophrastos
Char.	*Characters*
De Lap.	*De Lapidibus*
Thgn.	Theognis
Thuc.	Thucydides
Tim.	Timokreon
Xen.	Xenophon
Hell.	*Hellenika*
Kyrop.	*Kyropaideia*
Mem.	*Memorabilia*
Oik.	*Oikonomikos*
Symp.	*Symposium*
Xenoph.	Xenophanes

EDITIONS, REFERENCE WORKS, AND JOURNALS

ABV	J. D. Beazley. 1956. *Attic Black-Figure Vase-Painters.* Oxford.
Add.²	T. H. Carpenter, T. Mannack, and M. Mendonça, eds. 1989. *Beazley Addenda.* 2d ed. Oxford.
AJA	*American Journal of Archaeology*
AJP	*American Journal of Philology*

Annales ESC	*Annales: Economies, Sociétés, Civilisations*
*ARV*²	J. D. Beazley. 1963. *Attic Red-Figure Vase-Painters*. 2d ed. Oxford.
ASNP	*Annali della Scuola Normale Superiore di Pisa*
BCH	*Bulletin de Correspondance Hellénique*
BICS	*Bulletin of the Institute of Classical Studies of the University of London*
CA	*Classical Antiquity*
CJ	*Classical Journal*
CP	*Classical Philology*
CQ	*Classical Quarterly*
CVA	*Corpus Vasorum Antiquorum*
DK	H. Diels and W. Kranz, eds. 1966–67. *Die Fragmente der Vorsokratiker*. 12th ed. Berlin.
FGrH	F. Jacoby, ed. 1954–69. *Die Fragmente der griechischen Historiker*. Leiden.
G&R	*Greece & Rome*
Gentili	B. Gentili, ed. 1958. *Anacreon*. Rome.
GRBS	*Greek, Roman and Byzantine Studies*
Greene	W. C. Greene, ed. 1938. *Scholia Platonica*. Haverford, Pa.
HSCP	*Harvard Studies in Classical Philology*
JHS	*Journal of Hellenic Studies*
K.-A.	R. Kassel and C. Austin, eds. 1983—. *Poetae Comici Graeci*. Berlin.
Kaibel	G. Kaibel, ed. 1899. *Comicorum Graecorum Fragmenta*. Berlin.
Kock	T. Kock, ed. 1880–88. *Comicorum Atticorum Fragmenta*. 3 vols. Leipzig.
LSJ	H. G. Liddell, R. Scott, and H. S. Jones. 1968. *A Greek-English Lexicon*. 9th ed., with Supplement. Oxford.
N²	A. Nauck, ed. 1964. *Tragicorum Graecorum Fragmenta*. 2d ed. Hildesheim.
NC	*Numismatic Chronicle*
Para.²	J. D. Beazley. 1971. *Paralipomena: Additions to Attic Black-Figure Vase-Painters and to Attic Red-Figure Vase-Painters*. 2d ed. Oxford.
Paroem. Gr.	E. L. von Leutsch and F. G. Schneidewin, eds. 1958. *Corpus Paroemiographorum Graecorum*. Hildesheim.
PCPS	*Proceedings of the Cambridge Philological Society*
PdP	*La Parola del Passato: Rivista di Studi Antichi*
PMG	D. L. Page, ed. 1962. *Poetae Melici Graeci*. Oxford.
P. Oxy.	*The Oxyrhynchus Papyri*, a series published under different editors.

QUCC	*Quaderni Urbinati di Cultura classica*
R	S. Radt, ed. 1977. *Tragicorum Graecorum Fragmenta.* Vol. 4: Sophocles. Göttingen. OR S. Radt, ed. 1985. *Tragicorum Graecorum Fragmenta.* Vol. 3: Aeschylus. Göttingen.
RE	G. Wissowa, ed. 1894–1980. *Paulys Realencyclopädie der classischen Altertumswissenschaft.* Munich.
REA	*Revue des Etudes Anciennes*
REG	*Revue des Etudes Grecques*
RhM	*Rheinisches Museum*
Rose	V. Rose, ed. 1966. *Aristotelis qui ferebantur librorum fragmenta.* Stuttgart.
SIG³	W. Dittenberger, ed. 1982. *Sylloge Inscriptionum Graecarum.* 3d ed. Hildesheim/Zurich/New York.
SM	B. Snell and H. Maehler, eds. 1970. *Bacchylidis carmina cum fragmentis.* 10th ed. Leipzig. OR B. Snell and H. Maehler, eds. 1975. *Pindarus. Pars II. Fragmenta. Indices.* 4th ed. Leipzig.
TAPA	*Transactions of the American Philological Association*
TrGF	B. Snell, ed. 1971. *Tragicorum Graecorum Fragmenta.* Vol. 1. Göttingen. OR R. Kannicht and B. Snell, eds. 1981. *Tragicorum Graecorum Fragmenta.* Vol. 2. Göttingen.
V	E.-M. Voigt, ed. 1971. *Sappho et Alcaeus Fragmenta.* Amsterdam.
Valk	M. van der Valk, ed. 1971–87. *Eustathii Commentarii ad Homeri "Iliadem" Pertinentes.* 4 vols. Leiden.
W, W²	M. L. West, ed. 1989–92. *Iambi et Elegi Graeci.* 2 vols. 2d ed. Oxford. (W² = second edition specifically)
ZPE	*Zeitschrift für Papyrologie und Epigraphik*

COINS, BODIES, GAMES, AND GOLD

Toward an Imaginary History of Coinage

> The Lydians use customs very similar to those of
> the Greeks, apart from the fact that they prostitute
> their female children. And first of men whom we
> know, they struck and used currency of gold and
> silver, and they were also the first retail traders.
> And the Lydians themselves claim that also the
> games that now exist for them and for the Greeks
> were their invention.
>
> (Herodotus *Histories* 1.94)

THOSE WHO READ AND TEACH Herodotus for a living have perhaps become too accustomed to him. We no longer notice how profoundly strange Herodotus's account often is—in its collocations, its assumptions, and its implicit claims. If we will ourselves to defamiliarize and denaturalize Herodotus's matter-of-fact tone, his content suddenly becomes as bizarre as a Borges encyclopedia entry. Compare Herodotus's Lydian ethnography with the following: "A certain Chinese encyclopaedia" records that "animals are divided into: (a) belonging to the Emperor, (b) embalmed, (c) tame, (d) sucking pigs, (e) sirens, (f) fabulous, (g) stray dogs, (h) included in the present classification, (i) frenzied, (j) innumerable, (k) drawn with a fine camelhair brush, (l) *et cetera*, (m) having just broken the water pitcher, (n) that from a long way off look like flies." Michel Foucault, who cites this Borgesian "Chinese encyclopaedia," observes, "In the wonderment of this taxonomy, the thing we apprehend in one great leap, the thing that, by means of the fable, is demonstrated as the exotic charm of another system of thought, is the limitation of our own, the stark impossibility of thinking *that*."[1] It is this experience of estrangement, of "stark impossibility" that I would like to recapture for the text of Herodotus. Why does Herodotus attribute to the Lydians the routine prostitution of their daughters, the first minting of coinage, the origin of retail trade, and the invention of games? Just as intriguing, why do all these phenomena form a natural class for the historian (if they do)? In a sense, the entire discussion that follows is an attempt to make this a

---

[1] Foucault 1970: xv; Foucault does not provide a specific reference to Borges.

comprehensible list: to explain why it is especially so for a mid-fifth-century writer and why it occurs in Herodotus's *Histories*. I am engaged, then, in a project of cultural archaeology, attempting to reconstruct historically a particular ancient field of symbolization—to recapture a part of the Herodotean imaginary in all its cultural specificity and strangeness.[2]

As the way in (though not the extent of the inquiry), coinage becomes the wedge—a device to pry open the seemingly guileless surface of Herodotus's narrative. My choice of coinage is deliberate, for it is both one among a number of signifying practices that emerge in the archaic period and a privileged signifier insofar as its economic and political affiliations are most obvious. Thus, in some sense, I would contend that it is coinage that generates the other terms of this list, and coinage that emblematizes a conceptual revolution in archaic and classical Greece. Herodotus is the first extant Greek author to mention coinage by name—to use the word *nomisma* (literally, "conventional measure" or "currency") in the passage cited above.[3] Yet Herodotus's explicit mention of coinage in the semiotic cluster of Lydian tyranny,[4] prostitution, retail trade, and games opens a prospect backward over the 150 or so years that separate his text from Alkaios's first reference to the "staters of the Lydians" (Alkaios, fr. 69 V).[5] Thus, this is also a book about coinage, as it figures in and shapes the Greek cultural imaginary in the first two and a half centuries of its existence, between 600 B.C.E. (the approximate date of Alkaios's fragment) and the first explicit theorization of coin by Aristotle. Approximately halfway between the first mention of coin in a Greek text and Aristotle's attempt at theorization stands Herodotus, poised between poetry and prose, between the material symbolism of practice and the Aristotelian systematization of theory.[6] It is this "between" space, its concrete discourses and its practices, that I wish to analyze.

---

[2] For a definition of imaginary, see Alan Sheridan's translator's note to Loraux 1986: 328 ("Imaginary Athens"): " 'Imaginary' is the usual way of rendering the French *imaginaire*, both as adjective and as noun. As a noun, *l'imaginaire* was given wide currency first by Sartre, then by Jacques Lacan, who incorporated it in a triad with the *réel* and the *symbolique*. From French psychoanalysis, where it corresponds to Freud's 'fantasy' but with a more flexible use, it has spilled over into other domains, notably social theory, as in 'social imaginary.' It is in this sense that it is used here, in reference to the city's 'self-image,' how it sees itself in fantasy, with a large element of idealization and wish fulfillment." For the use of the term, cf. Loraux 1986, 1993; Castoriadis 1987, and cf. also Anderson 1991 on "imagined communities."

[3] Laroche 1949; Will 1954, 1955b, 1975; Chantraine 1968-80: 743–44.

[4] Cf. Hdt. 1.93 for emphasis on tyranny—and tombs.

[5] That Alkaios is here referring to coinage, not to a unit of weight, is demonstrated by Breglia 1974. For discussion of the fragment, see Kurke 1991: 252–54.

[6] The date of Herodotus's work is still very much an open question. Traditional scholarship tended to see Herodotus's composition extending from the late 440s through the early 420s (e.g. Jacoby 1913: 229–32), since the latest datable event in Herodotus falls in the summer

This is the period of the first use of coinage in the Western world and is thus, with historical hindsight, a revolutionary moment. But did it look like a revolution to the Greeks? It is perhaps too easy to assimilate the first coinage to the entire Western tradition: we must instead force ourselves to recognize the extent of cultural difference. In this endeavor the methods and perspectives of anthropology may serve as a useful guide. Thus, we must remind ourselves, first, that like many other traditional economies, the ancient Greek economy was "embedded" in other institutions and structures (such as kinship relations, civic status, religious practices). As Karl Polanyi (who coined the term) puts it: "the elements of the economy are . . . embedded in non-economic institutions, the economic process itself being instituted through kinship, marriage, age-groups, secret societies, totemic associations, and public solemnities. The term 'economic life' would here have no obvious meaning."[7] To say that an economy is embedded, however, is not to say that its participants are unable to think and act in terms of economic advantage; as Pierre Bourdieu has demonstrated, we must simply go beyond our "narrowly economistic" understanding of what that means, recognizing the "perfect interconvertibility" of real and symbolic capital.[8] Where the economy does not exist as an autonomous sphere, strategies for gaining advantage are also imbricated in the larger network of social institutions and practices. Still, the fact of an embedded economy must make a difference to the causes for the invention of coinage and the uses to which it is put once invented (as we shall see below).

Beyond the fact of an embedded economy, which ancient Greece shared with many other cultures, we must also attempt to locate the cultural

---

of 430 (Hdt. 7.137). But this assumption has been challenged by Fornara (1971a, 1971b, followed by Raaflaub 1987): Fornara would like to push down the *terminus ante quem* of the "publication" of Herodotus' *Histories* to 414 B.C.E., based largely on what he takes to be references to the end of the Archidamian War in Herodotus's text, an extended Herodotean parody in Aristophanes' *Birds*, and the presumed influence of Herodotus's account of Helen in Egypt on Euripides' *Helen* of 412 B.C.E. Fornara's arguments have been thoroughly and methodically countered by Cobet 1977 (with response by Fornara 1981). I follow Stambler 1982: 229–31, Gould 1989: 17–18, and Miller 1997: 105 in seeing the latest elements in Herodotus's composition falling in the early 420s. At the same time, I imagine an extended process of composition and performance, since I believe that Sophocles' *Antigone* (probably performed in 441) shows direct Herodotean influence in one passage (lines 904–20, cf. Hdt. 3.119; I take these lines to be genuine).

[7] Polanyi 1968: 84.

[8] Bourdieu 1977: 171–97 (quote taken from p. 178). For a related critique of Polanyi from a Marxian perspective, see Godelier 1977: 15–69; cf. Cartledge 1983: 6: "There seem to me several flaws in 'Polanyism' as a self-sufficient theory of economic history, principally the absence of a concept of exploitation, an economic analysis based on patterns of allocation rather than relations of production, and the stress on integration at the cost of disregarding conflict and competition."

specificity of money in archaic and classical Greece. As Jonathan Parry and Maurice Bloch conclude in their cross-cultural survey *Money and the Morality of Exchange*:

> Money is accorded quite different meanings in different cultures. . . . The obvious corollary of our relativistic conclusion about the meanings of money is that it is quite impossible to penetrate these meanings without an understanding of the ways in which they are informed by the wider symbolic and social orders. . . . The general comparative lesson . . . is that the specificity of the particular symbolic system, the similarities in the solutions which different cultures provide to the same fundamental problems of human existence, *and* the way in which historical forces act on and transform an existing cultural template, all have to be taken into account if we are to begin to understand the meanings of money.[9]

My aims here are precisely to explore the "wider symbolic and social orders" within which money functions in Greece *and* to chart the impact of historical forces on the "existing cultural template" in the first 100 to 150 years of coinage. Herodotus's account of the customs and inventions of the Lydians makes an ideal starting point for such an endeavor. If we can determine a larger nexus of symbolic relations that links coinage to tyranny, monuments, prostitution, retail trade, and games, we shall have gone some way toward elucidating the "meanings of money" in archaic and classical Greece.

I. WHAT IS COINAGE FOR? NUMISMATIC AND HISTORICAL DEBATES

Our task entails the reading of literary and artistic remains against the backdrop of significant material and conceptual developments in the archaic period—first and foremost, that of coinage. Given this purpose, we must first review the current state of numismatic evidence and theory about the origins and early use of coinage in the Greek world. As we shall see, the evidence (especially for the very beginnings of the process) is extremely scanty, so that any account of the reasons for the invention and rapid spread of coinage in Greece is necessarily speculative.

Even so, there has been a kind of revolution within Greek numismatics since the 1950s and 1960s. In the first place, in the 1950s E.S.G. Robinson challenged the existing orthodoxy on the dating of the beginning of coinage, downdating the earliest electrum coins to the third quarter of the seventh century, based on a careful reexamination of the earliest

---

[9] Parry and Bloch 1989: 29.

hoard of coins and precoins found under the foundation of the temple of Artemis at Ephesus. Though some of his arguments have been challenged, recent advances in numismatic methodology (especially the analysis of die links and coin hoards) have tended to confirm Robinson's estimates or even downdate coinage still further. Thus M. J. Price has recently proposed a date in the last quarter of the seventh century for the earliest Lydian and East Greek coins found at the Artemisium, while the earliest mainland Greek coinages (those of Aigina, Athens, and Corinth) are now thought to have begun ca. 550 B.C.E.[10] Once introduced into the Greek world, coinage spread rapidly, so that by 500 B.C.E. established coinages existed in mainland Greece, Italy, Sicily, and Western Asia Minor. This downdating means that in some cases we have literary texts that are contemporary with the introduction of coinage to a region (e.g., Alkaios), or that, at the outside limit of oral tradition, can be plausibly read as recording the impact of coinage over its first hundred years (e.g., Herodotus, Pindar).[11]

Perhaps as important as this downdating is the acknowledgment within numismatics of the extraordinary historical and cultural gap that divides our understanding of coinage from that of the first Greek coiners. In a seminal article in 1964, Colin Kraay took on the pragmatic modern assumption that coinage was invented to facilitate trade, pointing out (1) that the earliest coinage existed in denominations far too large for local market trade, while (2) in most cases, the earliest currencies were too circumscribed in their areas of circulation to have functioned in long-distance trade.[12] Elsewhere, Kraay notes that the use of coinage is essentially a Greek phenomenon, "which non-Greek peoples such as

[10] Robinson 1951, 1956; Kraay 1964, 1976, 1977; Price and Waggoner 1975; Price 1983; Carradice and Price 1988: 24–46. Renewed excavation of the foundations of the temple of Artemis have confirmed Robinson's downdating by lowering the date of the structure built above the hoard to ca. 560 B.C.E.: cf. Bammer 1990, 1991. Robinson's dating seems to have become the new orthodoxy within numismatics: cf. Kiyonaga 1973; Rutter 1981; Kroll and Waggoner 1984; Karweise 1991; Howgego 1995: 1–6; von Reden 1997: 156–57. A few proponents of an early seventh-century date remain: cf. Weidauer 1975 and Kagan 1982 (the latter based mainly on late literary evidence). Finally, Vickers 1985 advocates a much lower dating of coinage (based on his radical redating of the chronology of Attic vase painting), which seems to have found no acceptance in Greek numismatic circles.

[11] On the three-generation span of oral tradition in Greece, see Thomas 1989: 123–31 (Murray 1987: 95–96 asserts more optimistically that we can see a two hundred-year span behind Herodotus's work); on Herodotus's oral sources, see Lang 1984; Murray 1987; Thomas 1989: 96–154, 171–72; Evans 1991: 89–146 (and see discussion below, 000).

[12] As an exception to point (2), Kraay (1964: 80–83) noted that bullion-rich areas such as Athens and the Thraco-Macedonian region seem to have exported coinage in large quantities throughout the Mediterranean from fairly early on. For Athens, Kraay suggested that this sizable export of bullion in the form of coin was learned from the activities of the Thraco-Macedonian cities, and may itself have motivated the shift from the earlier

the Etruscans, Phoenicians, Carthaginians and Egyptians were slow to adopt"—after all, for millennia bullion and kind had formed an adequate basis for trade.[13] With these observations, Kraay dismantled the modern "commonsense" understanding of the invention of coinage and made the motivation for the beginning and spread of coinage in the Greek world a central problem for numismatics and ancient history. We now confront the remarkable fact that we do not understand the reason for the first minting of coin in the Western world, since we cannot attribute to the earliest coiners the same "commonsense" motivations that would power us.

Recent discoveries in numismatics have modified Kraay's two essential points somewhat. First, refinements of archaeological technique and the resulting finds of small denominations have made it likely that small change was much more abundant in many Greek silver issues from the late sixth century than Kraay had thought.[14] This makes it much more plausible that silver coinage functioned from its inception within the practices of local retail trade. Second, new hoard finds reveal much more movement of the early coinages of Aigina and Corinth than Kraay had been aware of; this movement of coin contradicts Kraay's thesis that only bullion-rich cities with access to their own silver mines exported coins in quantity outside their circumscribed areas of circulation. Since both Aigina and Corinth were famous in antiquity as trading cities, it is tempting to see this movement of coin as linked to trade.[15] Even so, these modifications to Kraay's thesis seem to pertain to only a few among the very many Greek cities that minted coins starting in the sixth century, so that they do not, I think, dismantle his overarching point.[16] Kraay's argument still has value as a salutary challenge to "commonsense" expla-

---

changeable types of the so-called *Wappenmünzen* to the standard head of Athena/owl coinage approximately twenty-five years after coinage was first introduced.

[13] Kraay 1964, 1976: 317–28 (quote from p. 317). Cf. Howgego 1995: 1–2 on coinage as a "Greek phenomenon": "Coinage spread rapidly throughout the Greek world, but was slow to take root elsewhere. Within the Persian empire coinage was produced in the sixth century B.C. only in hellenized areas (western Asia Minor, Cyprus, Cyrene). The Phoenicians struck no coins until the middle of the fifth century. The Carthaginians produced their first coinage in Sicily in the second half of the fifth century. Etruscan coinage was plentiful only in the third century, although there were a few issues in the fifth and fourth."

[14] Howgego 1995: 7, citing Kim 1994; cf. Kim forthcoming: a and b. Still, Kraay 1964: 88 had already acknowledged that there was "a continuing and plentiful supply of the smallest denominations" in Athens, Aigina, and Ionia.

[15] Howgego 1995: 95–98; cf. Howgego 1990: 3 for other reservations about Kraay's argument.

[16] It is worth emphasizing in this context the extraordinary proliferation of weight standards within the unitary phenomenon of Greek coinage, for this multiplicity would seem to support Kraay's point that the earliest coins would have limited advantages for long-distance trade. Thus Kraay 1976: 329–30 (Appendix I) lists fifteen different weight standards

nations that presume the unproblematic working of market mechanisms as the motor behind coinage at its very inception. Even if trade is acknowledged as one factor involved in the invention and rapid spread of coinage, it cannot be regarded as the only factor.

Kraay's own solution to the puzzle is that the first coinage is essentially a phenomenon of the Greek polis, instituted for the standardization of payments to and disbursements by the state. Kraay observes of the era of the invention of coinage:

> This is the period during which for the first time the Greek states can be comprehended as historical entities; colonization had greatly extended the area of the Greek world, and political and economic relations between its different parts were becoming increasingly complex. One of the recurring themes of the period is the gulf between rich and poor, and the emergence of coinage is itself a sign of surplus wealth which there was no immediate need to convert into land or cattle or some other commodity. Another characteristic of the period is the first appearance of monumental public buildings. These alone imply the existence of settled and highly organized communities, and it is from this period too that there survive inscribed on stone the earliest Greek laws with penalties already expressed in numbers of coins.[17]

One problem with Kraay's thesis, as M. J. Price pointed out, is that the model of coinage instituted for the standardization of state payments and disbursements "assumes that payment for service was acceptable, and this in turn would suggest at least in part that coins were suitable for retail trade."[18] Price's solution to the chicken-or-egg quandary to which Kraay's theory leads is to articulate the development of coinage into two distinct phases: the earliest coining of electrum in Lydia and East Greece, and the adoption, about fifty years later, of silver currency by mainland Greek states. Price notes that the earliest electrum was minted in very small denominations with many different types that tended to remain "within a close radius of their place of origin" (probably

---

that would have been current in the sixth and fifth centuries in different parts of the Greek world.

[17] Ibid: 320–28 (quote from p. 321). In a note Kraay underscores the association of coined money with the Greek polis structure as such: "It is of some interest that, apart from during a few decades in the late sixth and early fifth centuries, the northern Greek tribes must have normally disposed of most of their silver in the form of bullion rather than coin. The fact that it was only in the Greek coastal cities that the bullion was converted into coin serves to emphasize the close connection of coinage with Greek city life." (ibid.: 325n.1). For a similar interpretation of the state functions of early coinage, cf. Snodgrass 1980: 134–35.

[18] Price 1983: 6.

because the electrum was overvalued in relation to its real gold and silver content). In contrast, the earliest silver coinage seems to have been minted in "recognizable issues of particular city mints," which tended to circulate more widely from their sites of origin. Price's conclusion is that the earliest electrum "coins" may have been more akin to gifts or medals, issued by states, monarchs, and even private individuals as bonus payments (for example, presented to mercenaries at the end of their stint of service).[19] With time, this circulation of electrum bonus payments made possible the institution of true (state) silver coinage by habituating receivers to metallic payment for services: "The place of such objects in the economy would grow as the practice of electrum bonus payments and gifts of coin became more widely adopted and as the coins circulated in other transactions. By the time Croesus of Sardes had brought within his kingdom the cities of the western seaboard . . . the economy was ripe for the reform which brought gold and silver coinage into existence for the first time. It is then that the view of coinage as a medium for standardising payments to the state becomes attractive."[20]

The great strength of Price's theory is that it acknowledges that the generalized acceptance of metallic payment is problematic in a premonetary economy. For in a premonetary gift economy, goods tend to be valued not cardinally but ordinally, in ranked spheres of exchange. In ancient Greece, precious metals constituted the top rank of exchange goods, and, except in extraordinary circumstances, could not be traded down.[21] Price's theory provides for an intermediate stage between "pure" gift exchange and the development of all-purpose money, in the form of electrum "coins" as gifts or bonuses. The electrum circulated within the traditional context of gift exchange, but in the case of mercenaries, for example, its circulation extended beyond the normal restrictions of top-rank goods, habituating a larger portion of the population to receive metallic payment for services. At this point, it was possible for the Greek polis to intercede, to take over the minting and issuing of "true" coinage for its own purposes.

---

[19] Ibid: 5–8. For the theory that the earliest electrum was minted to pay mercenaries, Price is following the suggestion of Cook 1958. Price's two-stage model has been convincingly applied to a reading of Hdt. 1.94 by Smith 1989: 208–12. Howgego 1995: 3–4 takes exception to Price's notion that private individuals could have been issuers of early electrum bonus payments, noting that "there is no certain case in the whole of antiquity of coins being produced by individuals" (p. 3). Howgego's modification, however, does not seem to me to vitiate Price's entire argument; we might just assume that the earliest issuers of electrum were states and monarchs.

[20] Price 1983: 7–8.

[21] On the theory and practice of spheres of exchange, see Bohannan 1959; Bohannan and Dalton 1962; Firth 1965: 341; on the application of the model to archaic Greece, Finley 1977; Gernet 1981a; Morris 1986a, 1989; Kurke 1991: 94–107.

The same problem for which Price's theory aimed to account—the gulf between a gift economy with ranked spheres of exchange and the unproblematic acceptance of metallic payment—has inspired other numismatists to suggest a more gradual development of money within Greece itself. In anthropological terms, we can define money as any object or material that functions as a store of wealth, a measure of value, or a means of payment and exchange. In primitive and archaic societies, different materials may have some (but not all) of these functions in specialized contexts; thus, we can speak about "special-purpose money" vs. "general-purpose money" that fulfilled all the monetary functions.[22] It has been suggested that various forms of money pre-existed coinage in Greece, so that we should perhaps regard coinage as the endpoint of a fairly long, gradual development, rather than a sudden new invention. Thus, in the Homeric poems, finished objects of metal and other *keimēlia* functioned as a store of wealth, while cattle served as a measure of value. But within the strictly controlled gift-exchange circuits represented in epic, there was no place for money as a means of exchange.[23] In the post-Homeric period, there is evidence that iron spits circulated in certain (top-rank) contexts, while archaic laws from Crete call for the payment of fines or penalties in specified numbers of worked metal bowls or tripods.[24] Finally, John H. Kroll has argued, based on the evidence of the laws of Solon, that silver in the form of weighed lumps or ingots may have served some— perhaps all—of the functions of money in some parts of Greece for a century or more before the adoption of coinage.[25] Such a gradual development of the money-form in Greece, though difficult to make out in detail, would again provide a context in which the slow habituation to metallic payment over a wider range of spheres could occur.

Indeed, if we accept Kroll's argument about the active circulation of weighed silver as money from ca. 700 B.C.E., a different question arises: Why did the Greeks take the final step to mint coins at all? This may seem a paradoxical (or naïve) question, but we know that many of the great empires of the Near East and Egypt continued for millennia using weighed silver as money and never felt the need to coin.[26] Kroll's own solution is purely practical: coinage streamlined exchange because it did not require weighing at each transaction, while the state profited from

<hr />

[22] Polanyi 1968: 166–90.

[23] On Homeric *keimēlia* and their restricted uses, see Finley 1977: 60–61; Morris 1986a: 8–9; Howgego 1995: 13–14.

[24] On spits, see Brown 1950; Snodgrass 1980: 135–36; Strøm 1992; on bowls and tripods as fines in Cretan law, see materials collected in von Reden 1997: 157–63.

[25] Kroll 1998; cf. Kim forthcoming.a.

[26] See Polanyi 1968: 188–89; Howgego 1995: 12–13; Kroll 1998: 229–30 with further documentation he cites in note 22.

the slight overvaluation of coin in relation to the real value of the metal. Kroll's account is itself completely speculative (since we do not have any evidence for weight standards contemporary with the earliest coins), but more than that, such a narrowly economistic explanation cannot account for the details of cultural difference and specificity.[27] Thus Kroll contends that the Greeks recognized the profit of minting coin from Lydian issues (always overvalued in relation to their variable metal content), but he cannot account for the forty to ninety year time-lag between these electrum issues and the first Greek silver coinages.[28] More problematical still: Kroll's reading of the data cannot explain why great trading states like Carthage and Phoenicia did not immediately adopt the practice of coining, given its obvious advantages and profitability. Yet again, we return to the fact that coinage is somehow intimately linked to the Greek polis form and particular to it, which suggests, at the very least, a complex interaction of causes. While acknowledging that part of the motivation for the first coinage may have been mercantile convenience and economic profitability, I would like to focus on other, social and political motivations that arguably coexisted within the Greek city.

Thus we might offer an alternative narrative behind the development of various money forms in Greece: an ongoing struggle over the constitution of value and who controlled the highest spheres of exchange, between the traditional elite and the emerging city-state. If it is true, as has been argued, that in a system of ranked spheres of exchange, the elite can maintain its status by maintaining a monopoly on top-rank goods, we might see the pattern of usage reflected in the Homeric poems and in the deposition of iron spits as conforming to such an attempt.[29] The (generally slightly later) written laws from Crete, then, might be read as the city's bid to insert itself and its juridical authority into the top-rank sphere, by exacting precious metal objects as civic penalties. Next, if Kroll is right, we might see the development of silver money before coinage as the first general-purpose money, that crosscut and thereby began to break down the rigid hierarchy of ranked spheres of exchange through which the elite maintained its authority. Finally, the minting of coin would represent the state's assertion of its ultimate authority to constitute and regulate value in all the spheres in which general-purpose money operated simultaneously—economic, social, political, and religious. Thus, state-issued coin-

---

[27] In this respect Kroll's assumptions have much in common with the economic determinism of early Marxist criticism and are open to the same kinds of critique. For the terms of this critique, see Castoriadis 1987: 115–26.

[28] Kroll 1998: 231; for the profit motive behind early electrum issues, Kroll follows Wallace 1987.

[29] For the general argument, see Morris 1986a, 1989; for the limited (and apparently elite) deposition patterns of iron spits, Strøm 1992, von Reden 1997: 159–60.

age as a universal equivalent, like the civic agora in which it circulated, symbolized the merger in a single token or site of many different domains of value, all under the final authority of the city.[30] It may be that the final stage in this development—the city's assertion of sovereignty through the minting of coinage—was adapted by the Greeks from their experience of the rulers and dynasts of Lydia.[31] However that might be, I would see this assertion of sovereignty as a double gesture, directed both inward and outside. For every Greek polis that issued its own coin asserted its autonomy and independence from every other Greek city, while coinage also functioned as one institution among many through which the city constituted itself as the final instance against the claims of an internal elite.[32]

This model has much in common with the important recent contribution of Sitta von Reden. Von Reden has revived the theory of Edouard Will, that coinage was first invented as a means of social, distributive justice within the Greek city. Both Will and von Reden see coinage arising out of a seventh/sixth-century crisis of justice and the unfair distribution of property, which they find reflected in the texts of Hesiod, Solon, and Theognis. Indeed, Will even suggested that the first minting of coinage in some cities occurred when tyrants confiscated the property of the rich and distributed it in standardized form to the demos at large.[33] Will supported his speculations with linguistic arguments: following Laroche, he pointed out that *nomisma* was an abstract form derived from the root

[30] For a similar argument, see Seaford 1994: 199–232; Howgego 1995: 13–18. Though Howgego emphasizes the role of trade and commoditization rather more than this account, I find extremely useful and persuasive his general treatment of the complex, multiple causality for the emergence of money and coinage in archaic Greece. Since my discussion focuses almost entirely on the post-coinage period in Greece, I shall henceforth use the terms "money" and "coinage" interchangeably. For the parallel (slightly earlier) emergence of the public space of the agora (dated in Athens ca. 600 B.C.E.), see Martin 1951: 261–73; Hölscher 1991: 363–68.

[31] If so, it would represent an intercultural development parallel to the category of the *turannos*, which apparently passed over into the Greek world from Lydia.

[32] For the former aspect, it has long been recognized that civic pride and self-definition played a part in the beginning and spread of Greek coinage: see Austin and Vidal-Naquet 1977: 57–58; Snodgrass 1980: 135; Howgego 1990: 20–21. The validity of this interpretation has recently been challenged by T. Martin 1985, 1996, but cf. the counterarguments of Will 1988, Howgego 1995: 40–46, 59–60.

[33] Will 1955a: 495–502; cf. Will 1954, 1955b, 1975; von Reden 1995: 4–5, 176–81. Will's arguments for the redistributive activities of tyrants in Corinth depended on the old, earlier dating of the beginnings of coinage in Greece; given the current chronology, Corinthian coinage would postdate the reigns of Kypselos and Periander. Still, it would be possible to connect the tyrants with distributions of silver money before coinage. As parallels for the public distribution of money, Will points to Hdt. 7.144 (Athens) and Hdt. 3.57.2 (Siphnos).

nem-, "to allot, to distribute." Hence, *nomisma* is etymologically the process or the result of lawful distribution, and Will wanted to see in this etymology a trace of its earliest function.[34] According to this argument, coinage is not merely a phenomenon of the Greek city, but a token of egalitarian ideology and practice within the polis.

For von Reden, the political, egalitarian context of coinage is part of a larger argument: that there existed what she calls an "embedded money economy" in ancient Greece. Modern scholarship has tended to misrepresent the invention of coinage as a destructive and revolutionary event, unproblematically identifying money with trade, commodification, and a "disembedded" economy and opposing it to a traditional nonmarket gift economy.[35] Von Reden contends that these are *our* prejudices about money, anachronistically imposed on the early Greek evidence: to understand the "meanings of money," we must situate it in its proper historical contexts. She argues instead that money in early Greece, as in many other cultures, was neutral in itself, drawing its moral charge from the context and nature of the exchange in which it participated and the status of exchange partners. According to von Reden, these contexts (and the moral charge that attended them) pre-existed the invention of coinage in the Greek world: already in Homer, Hesiod, and Solon, certain kinds of exchange were valorized as contributions to the common good (whether household or city) and the larger cosmic order, while other transactions could be branded as the individualistic pursuit of gain, ruinous for the commonality and the cosmos. Von Reden accounts for this bifurcated ideology of exchange by invoking the anthropological model of "transactional orders," recently proposed by Jonathan Parry and Maurice Bloch.[36] According to Parry and Bloch, many societies constitute the activities of exchange and economics as two separate but organically articulated transactional orders. The long-term transactional order is always positively valued, insofar as it is perceived to perpetuate and reproduce the larger social and cosmic order. The short-term transactional order, the

---

[34] Will 1954, 1955b: 9–10, 1975. Ironically, though Will claims to be following Laroche, Laroche's own etymology of the term is somewhat different: he emphasizes the lawful or customary aspect of *nomisma* more than its distributive connotation (Laroche 1949: 232; for emphasis on this aspect of the etymology, cf. Austin and Vidal-Naquet 1977: 56–58, Howgego 1995: 17).

[35] Von Reden 1995: 171–94. Von Reden singles out for criticism Gernet 1981a, Shell 1978, and Kurke 1991. The flipside of this "revolutionary" model is the assertion that the invention of coinage had the positive effects of enabling individualism and stimulating philosophical, abstract thought: for the former, see Simmel 1978, Farenga 1985; for the latter, G. Thomson 1955: 175–207, 251–70, 302–47; Shell 1978; duBois 1984: 99–103, Goux 1990; Seaford 1994: 220–32.

[36] Von Reden 1995: 3–4, 79–216. For another application of Parry and Bloch's model of transactional orders to ancient Greece, see Morris 1993 (review of Millett).

sphere of "individual acquisition," "tends to be morally undetermined since it concerns individual purposes which are largely irrelevant to the long-term order." But the short-term order retains its moral neutrality only as long as it remains separate from and subordinate to the needs and activities of the long-term cycle. As Parry and Bloch note, the "strongest censure" is reserved for "the possibility that individual involvement in the short-term cycle will become an end in itself which is no longer subordinated to the reproduction of the larger cycle; or, more horrifying still, that grasping individuals will divert the resources of the long-term cycle for their own short-term transactions."[37]

Still, the relation between the two spheres is not as straightforward as this simple moral structure might suggest. For, as Parry and Bloch observe, the two transactional orders require each other: "If the long-term cycle is not to be reduced to the transient world of the individual, they must be kept separate. . . . But if the long term is to be sustained by the creativity and vitality of the short-term cycle, they must also be related—hence the concern with the kinds of transformative processes of which the 'cooking' of money in Langkawi is just one example."[38] By the "cooking" of money, Parry and Bloch refer to one culture's system of "conversion," a ritual or symbolic practice which enables the transfer of money from the short-term cycle, where it is produced, to the long-term transactional order. Parry and Bloch insist that the possibility of conversion is a cultural necessity: "It is not that what is obtained in the short-term cycle is a kind of ill-gotten gain which can be 'laundered' by being converted into socially approved channels of expenditure and consumption. It is rather that the two cycles are represented as organically essential to each other. This is because their relationship forms the basis for a symbolic resolution of the problem posed by the fact that transcendental social and symbolic structures must both depend on, and negate, the transient individual."[39]

As von Reden applies this model to the early Greek evidence, the articulation of long- and short-term transactional orders predates the introduction of coinage into the Greek world, corresponding roughly to the spheres of human-human and human-divine gift exchange (including agriculture), on the one hand, and trade, profit, and market exchange, on the other.[40] Thus in Homer, top-rank gift exchange between aristocratic

[37] Parry and Bloch 1989: 26–27.
[38] Ibid: 26.
[39] Ibid: 25.
[40] Von Reden 1995: 8–9, 13–44, 58–76, 127–46. On the consistent mystification of the labor of agriculture as a form of human-divine gift exchange, cf. Bourdieu 1977: 175–76; Vernant 1983: 248–78. Von Reden also conceptualizes this opposition in terms of Marshall Sahlins's model of generalized and negative reciprocity existing along a cultural continuum. Cf. Sahlins 1972: 185–230.

heroes, or lavish offerings and sacrifices to the gods are always positively represented as perpetuating the long-term social and metaphysical order. But at the same time, the *Odyssey* especially reveals the coexistence of the short-term transactional order, the world of Phoenician traders and *prēkteres*, "mindful of their cargo and looking out for gain" (*Od.* 8.162–64).[41]

Coinage, when it is invented, plugs into this pre-existing structure, deriving its moral inflection from the transactional order in which it participates. Thus there are significant ideological continuities from pre-monetary to monetary systems (hence von Reden's "embedded money economy"), though there are also significant developments. Von Reden sees a shift in the nature and relation of the two transactional orders in the late archaic and classical periods, as the political community constitutes itself as the final, supra-individual instance. As a corollary to her notion of the retributive, civic function of coin, von Reden explicitly links this conceptual shift with the introduction and use of coinage:

> A crucial distinction between coinage and other wealth lay in the question of their origins. The recognition of coinage as a recompense meant the acknowledgment of the *polis* as an institution that controlled justice and prosperity. Agrarian wealth and ancestral treasure, by contrast, referred to a divine order of justice which could be controlled by humans, if at all, only by religious ritual. The introduction of coinage indicates a shift of authority over social justice from the gods to the polis. The first step towards the introduction of coinage was thus a decline of faith in the reliability of divine justice. The *polis* replaced the divine order by compensating virtue immediately and precisely rather than with . . . "indefinite certainty."[42]

Von Reden's insistence that we historicize and contextualize our reading of money in Greek antiquity is important, and I find her application of the anthropological model of transactional orders and its corollary, the "embedded money economy," compelling. Perhaps most significant, though, is her acute perception of the profoundly political nature of money and the major conceptual shift from "metaphysical" to civic order it betokens.[43] Her insight that, with the rise of the polis, a shift takes place in the definition and balance of the two transactional orders is

---

[41] On traders in Homer, see Finley 1977: 66–71; von Reden 1995: 58–79; Winter 1995; Dougherty forthcoming; on this ideological crisis-point in the *Odyssey*, cf. Humphreys 1978: 159–74; Rose 1992: 120–121, 138, 144–46.

[42] Von Reden 1995: 6–8, 91–94, 173–87 (quote taken from p. 175).

[43] One could strengthen von Reden's argument on this point by noting that other scholars have charted a similar course of development for different spheres of Greek cultural and political life: cf. Detienne 1996, on the developments in poetry and speech; Ostwald 1969 on the shift from *thesmos* to *nomos*; Vlastos 1947 on the importance of notions of egalitarian

foundational for this study, informing the readings in the chapters that follow.

Yet I feel von Reden has ignored or elided crucial elements of conflict around the civic appropriation of the long-term transactional order. The city's constitution of itself as the ultimate instance was not achieved without a struggle, for there was resistance to this ideological shift from some elements within an aristocratic elite. Between and within individual poleis, some archaic aristocrats cultivated and maintained a parapolitical system based on the interlocking institutions of *xenia* and *hetaireia*. *Xenia*, long-distance guest-friendship between families, had played a prominent part in the organization of Homeric society and endured for centuries as an important form of elite networking. Insofar as it required loyalty and commitment to other members of an inter-polis elite first and foremost, the system of *xenia* could often be in tension, if not in open conflict, with the demands of the local authority of the polis.[44] Within the individual archaic poleis, aristocratic resistance took a related form. As Oswyn Murray notes, this was the period of the organization of aristocratic *hetaireiai*, or private drinking clubs, "in response to the emergent city-state, designed to perpetuate aristocratic control of the state against the demos."[45] Like the long-distance links of *xenia*, the private drinking club constituted itself as an alternative "imagined community" that challenged and competed with the order of the city.[46] Those who participated in these sympotic clubs often vehemently opposed the city's assertion of authority *and* coinage as a token thereof. Thus von Reden herself notes,

---

justice in the thought of the Presocratics; and Herman 1987: 132–42, on proxeny as a civic appropriation of private *xenia* between aristocrats.

[44] On *xenia* in Homer, see Finley 1977: 60–66, Morris 1986b; on its endurance as an elite system in archaic and classical Greece, see Herman 1987, Kurke 1991: 87–92, 135–59, Griffith 1995: 68–69.

[45] Murray 1983: 265–66. I follow Murray in using the term *hetaireia*, though it is somewhat anachronistic since our earliest preserved usages with a clear political connotation occur in Eupolis and Thucydides. For other discussions of sympotic drinking clubs, their history and activities, cf. Calhoun 1913; Ziebarth 1913; Talamo 1961; Connor 1971: 25–32; Rösler 1980: 26–36; Murray 1990b, 1995: 224–34.

[46] For the notion of "imagined communities," see Anderson 1991; for the interconnections between *xenia* and *hetaireia*, see Griffith 1995: 68–72, Morris 1996: 34–35. Here and throughout the argument, I resort to the somewhat awkward hypostasis "the city" or "the polis" as actor and agent; this is necessitated, I believe, by our very limited real knowledge about who exactly is doing what in this period. I do not intend to suggest thereby that "city" and "elite" are mutually exclusive categories (since, throughout the archaic period, it is almost certainly the elites who are running the cities); instead, I want to signify the existence of two different authoritative regimes or imaginary allegiances (see discussion below of Morris's notion of competing "middling" and "elitist" traditions). In like manner, I shall on occasion use the terms *aristocratic* or *noble* to designate those members of the elite who self-identify with the elitist tradition.

though she cannot explain, the fact that in both visual and literary representations, "the symposium remained a sphere which was hostile to money as recompense."[47] Von Reden offers us, then, only half the picture—the positive reception and function of coinage *es meson*, at the center of the city. In order to excavate aristocratic resistance to coinage as political token, we need to explore the symposium as a kind of anti-polis and reconstruct the imaginary of the *hetaireia* through its traces in monody, sympotic elegy, skolia, and vase painting.[48]

Von Reden misses this oppositional voice partly because she focuses almost exclusively on Athens, where almost all the literary remains represent the voice of the winning side: Athens is most of all the place of civic coinage and the embedded money economy. Combined with this Athenocentric focus, von Reden often stops short of carrying through a political interpretation. Thus, in her observations on the origin of coinage (quoted above, p. 16), what begins as a political argument ("a shift of authority . . . from the gods to the *polis*") slips unnervingly into a religious or metaphysical explanation denatured of politics ("The first step toward the introduction of coinage . . . was thus a decline of faith in the reliability of divine justice"). *Whose* decline of faith? Everyone's? If so, who was perpetuating the injustice? In her bland assertion of a metaphysical moment, von Reden has effaced actors and victims in a preeminently political struggle. In this, her argument simply reenacts the strategies and rhetoric of the triumphant polis ideology she describes, rather than questioning its explanatory adequacy. On the other hand, her claim that "agrarian wealth and ancestral treasure . . . referred to a divine order of justice" likewise universalizes a tenet of Greek *aristocratic* ideology, replicating a mystification of elite control instead of analyzing it. Von Reden's argument thus tends to suppress all trace of conflict in the momentous political and conceptual shift she documents.

It is my purpose to provide the other side of the coin, as it were: to supplement von Reden's excellent analysis of the positive construction of coinage within the political order in Athens. I want to focus instead on mainly non-Athenian sources, and on aristocratic hostility to money. As von Reden's discussion has made abundantly clear, the elite opposition

---

[47] Von Reden 1995: 200, 205–6 (quote taken from p. 206).

[48] On the symposium as anti-polis, see Murray 1990b: 7: "The *symposion* became in many respects a place apart from the normal rules of society, with its own strict code of honor in the *pistis* there created, and its own willingness to establish conventions fundamentally opposed to those within the *polis* as a whole." In practice, Murray's opposition of the symposium/*hetaireia* vs. the civic sphere may be overly schematic; Schmitt-Pantel (1990, 1992) suggests that we should instead think of different, competing "rituals of conviviality" that characterized each domain. For various ways in which different forms of conviviality were distinguished by their material symbolism, cf. Cooper and Morris 1990, Luke 1994.

to money is not so much economic as political—it is part of a larger project of aristocratic resistance to the encroaching authority of the polis.[49] At least in the literary remains, I see a fierce conflict raging (through the sixth century and even into the fifth) over what constituted the long- and short-term transactional orders. The definition and balance of these two transactional orders are precisely what is being contested between different ideological positions within the Greek city.

Thus even within non-Athenian poetic sources, there are competing traditions and voices to consider. In order to restore to von Reden's developmental schema its proper frame of political and ideological conflict, I will supplement it with Ian Morris's model of the competing "middling" and "elitist" traditions in archaic Greek lyric, elegy, and iambic.[50] Morris traces out two strands in archaic poetry (both, of course, the products of aristocratic poets): on the one hand, those aristocrats who "deliberately assimilated themselves to the dominant civic values within archaic poleis," thereby forging a "middling" tradition; on the other hand, those who espoused the elitist tradition, claiming that their "authority lay outside these middling communities, in an inter-polis aristocracy which had privileged links to the gods, the heroes, and the East." Morris traces the middling tradition back to major societal upheavals of the eighth/seventh centuries, which already imposed pressure from below for a more egalitarian order, helping to form the characteristic structures of the Greek polis.[51] This middling tradition tends to be represented in archaic elegy and iambic, by poets embracing

---

[49] Von Reden 1997 seems to represent a kind of recanting of her earlier strong association of coinage with the order of the city: thus von Reden contends, "money [in Greek poleis] does not by nature signify anything particular—economic relationships, egalitarianism, the market, etc.—but is symbolised by its repeated usage in particular institutions," while she refers to the "underdetermination of money as a signifier" (p. 154). I am uncertain how to reconcile this with von Reden 1995 (especially the argument quoted above), and somewhat puzzled by the notion that the meaning of the earliest coinage is "underdetermined." Especially if we accept the existence of money before coinage in Greece (as von Reden does), the choice to shift from bullion to coinage must have been made by somebody, and for some reason (the counterexample of non-Greek cultures like the Carthaginian, Phoenician, and Egyptian that stayed with bullion, shows that the force of inertia was on the other side). Von Reden's response seems to be that "the state" did not itself have an adequately defined existence in the period of the earliest minting of coin (von Reden 1997: 157; cf. von Reden 1995: 176–81), but I find this an implausible claim for the third quarter of the sixth century.

[50] Morris 1996.

[51] Ibid: 18–36 (quotes taken from pp. 19–20, 27). Morris sees the middling tradition arising as an elite response to populist pressure dating back to the eighth century B.C.E. (for which he detects evidence in the archaeological record; cf. Morris 1987, 1996: 24–25). Akin to Morris's notion of the "middling" tradition as a response to pressure from below is Victor Hanson's model of small farmers as the mesoi, a "middle class" instrumental in

a moderate style of life under the supreme authority of the polis, rejecting both extremes of excessive wealth and aristocratic display *and* of abject poverty. The elitist tradition emerges as an oppositional voice, most clearly in monodic lyric, mobilizing the heroic past, special links to the gods, and a lifestyle of Eastern-influenced luxury (*habrosunē*) to reassert the propriety of aristocratic preeminence.[52] As Morris observes succinctly, "Much of the social history of the Archaic period is best understood as a conflict between these two conceptions of social order." Morris is not, however, claiming that the middling tradition as we find it in the literary remains championed democracy and the rights of the people. Rather,

> Both traditions were "elite" in the sense that most poems were produced by and for elites of birth, wealth, and education. The hostility between the extant traditions was primarily a conflict within the highest social circles over what constituted legitimate culture. Bourdieu suggests that such struggles are common to all elites, and that very often one group will claim to monopolize a high culture which is beyond the reach of the masses, while another fraction will assert its power by deliberately transgressing, conferring high status on values and objects excluded from the privileged aesthetics. The popular aesthetic is normally not simply a failure to grasp elitist tastes, but also a conscious refusal of them, among ordinary people and among the elite. . . . [The poets of the middling tradition] were not surrendering their claims to be elite: a wealthy symposiast insisting on the excellence of *to meson* represented a situation very different from that of a poor farmer pronouncing the same words. However, they claimed leadership as special members of the polis, not as a wholly distinct aristocratic community of the kind created by the elitist tradition. There is no reason to think that middling aristocrats struggled across the seventh and sixth centuries to create democracy. But the unintended consequence of their beliefs was that when the elitist ideology collapsed after 525, the general acceptance of middling values made democracy a real possibility; and when a ruling elite fell apart in disorder, as at Athens in 507, democratic institutions were one obvious response.[53]

Still, as these remarks show, Morris sees a crucial turning point in the period 520-490 B.C.E., when the elitist ideology had lost much of its

---

the formation of a pervasive ideology of egalitarianism among citizens in the traditional Greek polis (see Hanson 1995: 108–26, 181–219; 1996).

[52] For the elements of the elitist tradition, Morris is following Mazzarino 1947: 191–246; Arthur 1984: 37–47; Kurke 1992: 91–102.

[53] Morris 1996: 27–28.

credibility, and the prevalent egalitarianism of the Greek polis system made democracy imaginable as a response to civic crisis. It is no accident, as Morris points out, that precisely this period saw the appearance of important new genres of civic poetry—tragedy and epinikion—which functioned in context to mediate middling and elitist traditions.[54]

Clearly, Morris's notion of an ideologically charged conflict between those who predicated their preeminence on the external authorities of "the gods, the heroes, and the East" and those who built on the power base of the community of citizens has a great deal in common with von Reden's model of the civic appropriation of the long-term transactional order. The juxtaposition reveals the limitations of von Reden's analysis: (1) It depends almost exclusively on the middling tradition, largely ignoring the counterclaims of the elitist strand, and (2) it accepts the highly tendentious account of the middling tradition as if it were an objective rendition of the facts. The great strength of Morris's analysis, by contrast, is the recognition that issues of power and the contestation of legitimate authority inhere in poetic discourses of justice and divine retribution, as well as those of heroic exemplars and Eastern eroticism. Where von Reden sees metaphysics, Morris sees politics.

And yet, both von Reden and Morris, as historians, are attempting to get at issues of ideology as they are played out in the Greek city at large, beyond the intra-elite discursive struggles between middling and elitist traditions. For both, there is a domain of significant social action beyond the world of our texts, to be accessed by other means. For von Reden, the use of inscriptional and visual evidence supplements the literary remains; for Morris, intensive study of such features as burial practices, sanctuary dedications, and house size in the archaeological record reveal a Panhellenic pressure toward egalitarian uniformity beginning in the eighth century and continuing into the fifth and fourth.[55] By these means, both are grappling with the problem of accounting for the (surprising)

---

[54] Ibid: 37–40. At times Morris seems to see choral poetry and tragedy as simply extensions of the middling tradition: thus, he asserts, "Epinician poets embraced the image of the middling citizen" (p. 37). I believe the social function of both tragedy and epinikion is a more complex one of mediation and reconciliation of the two competing traditions: for particular instances of such mediation in epinikion, see Kurke 1991: 182–256, 1992: 106–14; in tragedy, see Ober 1989: 152–55; Ober and Strauss 1990; Griffith 1995; Kurke 1998; Wohl 1998.

[55] Von Reden 1995: 195–216, 1997; Morris 1986a, 1987, 1989, 1998. Both historians also, by their use of material evidence, aim to acknowledge and analyze local geographic differences (see especially von Reden 1997; Morris 1998.10-68). Given the nature of the evidence I am using (the fragmentary literary record), I have much less opportunity to produce a fine-grained and nuanced account of local differences within the large-scale ideological struggles chronicled here.

power and prevalence of egalitarian ideology in the Greek world as it emerges from the archaic period.[56] I hope to contribute to this same enterprise, but by a different route. I believe that more evidence for the struggles behind this ideological formation can be excavated from our texts, by the consideration of texts *against* material practices. By attending closely to what texts of both traditions say (and do not say) about pervasive communal practices such as coinage, game-playing, and prostitution, I hope to shed light on how practice impinges on ideology and discourse and how they, in turn, influence practice.

Coinage is a paradigm case for such analysis. If we are properly to understand the "meanings of money," we must situate coinage squarely in the frame of the political and social contestation Morris elucidates. Adopted by the cities of the Greek mainland in the third quarter of the sixth century B.C.E., coinage is a token of this struggle at its most intense. The issuing of coinage is a sign of the city's self-assertion, its constitution of itself as the ultimate instance, the supra-individual summit of the long-term transactional order. If we divide coinage conceptually into its two aspects, essence vs. function, intrinsic vs. extrinsic value, we can identify two ways in which coinage as a civic *sēma* works to break down aristocratic authority. In terms of essence or substance, it is no accident that coinage is composed of precious metal, which develops first (if M. J. Price is right) in the context of gift exchange. For by its standardized distribution of precious metal, the city appropriates the highest, aristocratic sphere of exchange. The aristocracy can no longer monopolize the circulation of precious metals and the contexts in which it occurs. The city itself becomes a key player in the circulation of precious metal as top-rank gift exchange. In terms of function or symbolic value, on the other hand, coinage serves to dismantle the multicentric gift economy and the social hierarchy it supports. For, as Paul Bohannan has observed, general-purpose money works to break down the distinctions of spheres of exchange entirely.[57] By providing a standard against which all goods and services can be measured, money symbolically makes all labor comparable, and thereby constitutes a more egalitarian order opposed to ranked spheres of goods and activities.[58] In both its aspects, then, coinage represents a civic, egalitarian challenge to the structures of elite authority—a challenge that does not go unrecognized or unopposed.

Hence, tracking coinage (and those phenomena that share its semantic sphere) in literary representations from Alkaios to Herodotus gives us a precious window into the contestation between the polis, as it attempts

---

[56] Cf. also Hanson 1995, 1996; Robinson 1997.

[57] Bohannan 1959; cf. Bohannan and Dalton 1962; Kopytoff 1986: 64–73.

[58] Will 1954 articulates this aspect most clearly in his analysis of Aristotle *NE* 1133a-b.

to establish its authority as supreme, and the elitist strand within the aristocracy. We can thus reconstruct a history of struggle, extending over a 100–150 year period, which is largely obscured within the central texts of the Athenian tradition, both because of their genre and their date.[59] We must instead turn to and juxtapose archaic poetry of both middling and elitist strands, and the text of Herodotus.

But this is a strange kind of history we are engaged in. Because coinage is itself a polyvalent symbol within a complex symbolic system, the struggle I endeavor to reconstruct is a struggle fought *over* and *in* representation. At issue is who controls signification and who has the power to constitute the culture's fundamental hierarchies of value. While these issues have "real life" implications—for example, in the sociological basis of citizenship and relative status of citizens—such a struggle over fundamental hierarchies of value can only be a discursive one, fought out in the codes of our texts, visual images, and signifying practices over the constitution of the cultural imaginary. Thus, it is not as if there is some "reality" we are struggling to get to behind the texts, images, and practices, if we can just break through their screen by patient source criticism and sifting of "facts." In this "contest of paradigms," the discursive structures of our texts (literary and visual) *are* the "facts" at issue. Hence my methodology will be more literary than historical, attuned to the texts' tropes, their rhetorical strategies, their equivocations. And, since the struggle we are charting is discursive, it has ramifications beyond the narrowly political. We shall find that, within representation, a kind of leakage or mutual reinforcement occurs from coinage as a symbolic system to other systems of signification—games, writing, language, and ultimately that symbolic system which is preeminently constituted within language, subjectivity or the representation of the self.

II. LITERARY METHODOLOGY

The nature of our topic necessitates reading obliquely. For, between Alkaios's mention of the "staters of the Lydians" and Herodotus's use of *nomisma*, the topic and language of coinage barely occur in our extant

---

[59] With the exception of tragedy, insofar as it functions to act out tensions and conflicts within civic ideology: see Vernant 1988: 29–48. Thus I am also attempting to supplement the important synthesis of Seaford 1994. Seaford seeks to document the impact of state formation on the latest stages of Homeric composition and on the origins and generic patterns of tragedy. I am attempting to construct a similar argument drawing on a complementary set of data, looking at the fragmentary literary remains from the period between Homer and tragedy for traces of ideological conflict around the issues of state formation. I do not mean to claim that ideological struggle and contestation do not go on in other

texts. Emmanuel Laroche, who noticed this absence in his study of the root *nem-* and its derivatives, suggested that it was largely an accident of genre and preservation: the lyric and elegiac poetry, which we have, is not concerned with money; the early prose and inscriptions, which we lack, may have spoken of it.[60] This explanation is predicated, however, on an outmoded conception of poetry as essentially separate from and irrelevant to real-world issues.[61] Given the profoundly political context in which coinage functions and the ongoing ideological struggle taking place in archaic poetry, we might expect coinage as a token of civic authority and a signifier of egalitarian status to be a concern to both middling and elitist strands of archaic poetry. How then to account for this discrepancy between expectation and what actually occurs in our texts? Here, I think we must take a lesson from a number of modern literary theoretical methods that have learned to read not just what texts say, but what they crucially do not say. Psychoanalysis, deconstruction, and certain versions of Marxian criticism have all become attuned to the silences or gaps in the text, attributing them variously to psychological processes, the play of difference and deferral in the signifier, or the material conditions for textual production. This last approach will be particularly useful in the present context.

Marxian literary theory posits, first, that the literary text does the work of ideology, transforming the "raw materials" of ideological values in complex ways. Because these values suppress certain possibilities, because they are incomplete and contradictory, the text incorporates those suppressions, inadequacies, and contradictions. As Pierre Macherey describes it, a "symptomatic reading" aims to identify the silences and tensions that are constitutive of the text:

> We should question the work as to what it does not and cannot say, in those silences for which it has been made. The concealed order of the work is thus less significant than its real *determinate* disorder (its disarray). The order which it professes is merely an imagined order, projected on to disorder, the fictive resolution of ideological conflicts, a resolution so precarious that it is obvious in the very letter of the text where incoherence and incompleteness burst forth. . . . The distance which separates the work from the ideology

---

texts of the Athenian tradition; only that by the late fifth and fourth centuries, democratic ideology is essentially hegemonic in Athens, so that debate goes on within a different framework. For the hegemony of democratic ideology in Athens, see Ober 1989; Hunter 1994; Yunis 1996; for ongoing critiques of democracy, see Ober 1998.

[60] Laroche 1949: 232–33.

[61] This assumption has surprising resilience: cf. Millett 1991: 46 on Pindar's use of the imagery of economic interest: "If anything, Pindar endows interest with the Hesiodic quality of something extra and unexpected, putting the borrower back on an equal footing with the lender. But this is a piece of poetry, and the point cannot be pressed."

which it transforms is rediscovered in the very letter of the work: it is fissured, unmade even in its making. A new kind of necessity can be defined: by an absence, by a lack. The disorder that permeates the work is related to the disorder of ideology (which cannot be organised as a system). The work derives its form from this incompleteness which enables us to identify the active presence of a conflict at its borders.[62]

We must read texts symptomatically, attuned to what Macherey calls the silences that structure the discourse of the text. In contrast to Macherey's reading of nineteenth-century literature as structured by the Marxian relations of production, however, I would contend that the constitutive silences of Greek texts are first and foremost political, and economic only insofar as different symbolic economies support different paradigms of social and political order. Nonetheless, the struggle over the culture's central hierarchies of value, of which coinage forms a part, crucially structures the texts both by significant presences and constitutive absences. As I shall attempt to demonstrate in the chapters that follow, even where coinage is not explicitly mentioned, a whole set of themes and tropes associated with it—metals, prostitution, games, counterfeit language and the counterfeit self—function discursively to play out this central ideological struggle. That is to say, these tropes function like photographic negatives, whose exposure reveals the outlines of a significant absence.

At a practical level, the reading process must also be adapted to the nature of our sources. First, archaic poetry presents special problems because of the largely fragmentary state of text and context. Given how lacunose the tradition is, much of my reading of archaic poetry will be perforce conjectural, but conjecture based nonetheless on certain generally recognized assumptions.[63] All Greek poetry of the archaic and classical periods was composed for public performance, whether in the closed sphere of the aristocratic symposium or at the center of the city, before the entire citizen body. Where poetry is thus socially embedded, genre depends on occasion, and poetics on the social functions the work performs in context. Thus, rather than focusing on production—the isolated

---

[62] Macherey 1978: 155. For further discussion of symptomatic reading of the text's supressions and inadequacies, see Jameson 1981: 56–57; Frow 1986: 19–29. For an application of this method to readings of classical texts, see Konstan 1987a, 1990; Rose 1992: 331–69.

[63] The point that *all* reconstructions based on archaic poetry are conjectural needs to be emphasized, for many classicists still behave as if the reconstruction of historical events from ancient texts has greater truth value than the reconstruction of *mentalités*, or ideologies. But there is no justification for this naïve empiricism—in fact, just the opposite: given that all we have in many cases are textual traces, we are in a better position to reconstruct the ideological or symbolic systems at work than the "realities" of events. Cf. Morris 1998: 4–9.

lyric poet pouring out his inmost soul (the basis of Laroche's assumption that Greek poetry has no relation to the real)—we must focus on reception: on the rhetorical strategies and moral paradigms deployed to accomplish different ends with different audiences. From the perspective of the performance and performative aspects of Greek poetry, we recognize that Morris's middling and elitist traditions tend to align along a fundamental division of occasion and audience. The iambic poetry of Archilochos, Hipponax, and Semonides; the elegiac verse of Tyrtaios and perhaps Solon; and the choral lyric of Simonides, Pindar, and Bacchylides all appear to have taken place within a civic context, and all, according to Morris, endorse the ideal of the middling citizen.[64] In contrast, the monodic lyrics of Alkaios, Sappho, Anakreon, and Ibykos, proponents of the elitist tradition, seem to have been performed within the aristocratic symposium (or the tyrannical appropriation thereof).[65]

Furthermore, as Morris notes, it is not the biographical reality of the poet but the performance context that determines the poetry's ideological alignment: "Like any artists, individual poets (or traditions) were not consistent, occupying a single point on this spectrum; they rather occupied a range of positions. Thus Alcman gives us some strikingly elitist statements in his *partheneia*, but in fr. 17 apparently adopts a middling, iambic persona, calling himself the eater of everything (*pamphagos*) who rejoices in common foods (*ta koina*) just like the people (*ho damos*)."[66] This occasion-bound shift, which implies that it is the *audience* rather than

---

[64] Morris 1996: 27; as Morris notes, the alignment of formal features with the middling-elitist divide is neither exact nor rigid. For the intimate link of genre and occasion in archaic Greek poetry, see Rossi 1971; Calame 1974; Edmunds 1985; Gentili 1988; Kurke 1991: 1–7. For the performance context of archaic iambic, see West 1974: 23–39; Miralles and Pòrtulas 1983; for that of choral lyric, see Mullen 1982; Slater 1984; Herington 1985: 20–31, 181–89; Nagy 1990b: 339–81; Kurke 1991: 6–7; Calame 1997; Stehle 1997: 3–169. The situation with elegy is more complex. Bowie 1986 contends that early elegy was performed in two different contexts: at the symposium and in aulodic competitions at public festivals. According to Bowie's schema, poems performed in the former context tend to be shorter, thematically connected to the symposium, hortatory, or erotic, while poems performed in the latter context tend to be longer (one thousand lines or more), historical and civic in their orientation. Bowie (1986: 18–21) would categorize Solon's elegies as sympotic, but I am inclined to put more stock in the traditions about their performance and see them as originally situated in some kind of civic context; cf. West 1974: 12; Tedeschi 1982; Herington 1985: 33–35; Schmitt-Pantel 1990: 25; Stehle 1997: 61–63. Finally, Bowie 1990 argues for a sympotic context for the martial elegies of Tyrtaios, but in the exceptional context of Sparta, I would contend, both the peacetime *sussitia* and the king's tent on campaign should be regarded as civic contexts (cf. Murray 1991: 96–98).

[65] On the performance context of monody, see Kirkwood 1974; Rösler 1980: 33–45; Burnett 1983: 121–81, 209–28; Herington 1985: 31–39, 195–200; Gentili 1988: 72–104, 197–215; Stehle 1997: 213–318.

[66] Morris 1996: 27.

the poet whose politics are decisive, is nowhere clearer than in the newly published fragments of Simonides. The extended elegiac celebration of the Battle of Plataia (presumably performed in a public setting, perhaps in Sparta[67]) appropriates the individual *kleos* of epic for the communal valor and endurance of the Spartan and Corinthian contingents, while the sympotic fragments 21 and 22 W² luxuriate in opulent fantasies of homoerotic gratification, the essence of aristocratic *habrosunē*.

Given the correlations between occasion, genre, and ideology within a contest of paradigms, we must go one step further and acknowledge that the formal aspects of Greek poetry also have political implications. Style, decorum, generic borrowing, and formal structure are not merely literary issues: where different genres are articulated and defined by recognizable structures and levels of style, the transgression or transposition of these formal features evokes the interaction of occasions and the social functions and audiences they imply. Thus Alkaios's use of strikingly coarse abuse for Pittakos represents an attempt to subsume the scapegoating power of iambic into the lyric medium, but by the same token, the host medium cannot avoid the popularizing destablilization of elite authority such language implies.[68] Conversely, as Morris points out, Hipponax's use of the participle *ludizousa*, "playing the Lydian," for the woman who is beating the speaker's genitals in an outhouse in fr. 92 W, alludes to and debunks the entire elitist tradition of Eastern *habrosunē*, which Anakreon was to characterize with the single word *ludopatheis*, "living like Lydians."[69] So we will concern ourselves with issues of style and decorum as well as those of content, for stylistic anomalies mark the stress-points within their texts—the moments of contradiction or contestation within ideology.

Finally, the elegiac corpus of Theognis presents special problems. As Gregory Nagy has argued, we cannot simply assume an original, authentic Theognis, whose work was then contaminated by later insertions and accretions of lesser poets.[70] Within the corpus of the Theognidea, we have what appear to be references to the tyranny of Theagenes, probably datable to the last third of the seventh century, and to the Persian invasion of 480-479 B.C.E. Within this temporal range at least, the Theognidea

---

[67] Spartan performance was suggested to me by R. S. Stroud. For discussion of possible performance contexts of the Plataia elegy, see Boedeker 1995; Pavese 1995; Stehle 1996; Aloni 1997.

[68] For extended discussion of the sociological implications of Alkaios's ruptures of lyric decorum, see Kurke 1994.

[69] Morris 1996: 35. On Anakreon fr. 136/481 *PMG* within the archaic "cult of *habrosunē*," see Kurke 1992: 93–94.

[70] Nagy 1985: 46–51, opposing the traditional model of van Groningen 1966, as elaborated by West 1974: 40–71.

represents the product of an ongoing tradition of composition in performance in which "Theognis" is simply a persona, a place from which to speak to the sympotic and civic audience. Given the multiplicity of voices that speak as "Theognis," we find also a multiplicity of points of view—specifically, a confusing spectrum of opinions that range from middling to elitist. Thus Morris has some difficulty with Theognis: he assimilates him to the middling tradition but acknowledges, "For all the antagonism between the traditions . . . , they were not rigidly separated. They should be seen as ideal types, representing the ends of a spectrum of social attitudes. Phocylides, for example, is more 'middling' than Theognis, whose complex attitudes were sometimes hostile to ordinary citizens."[71] It is my contention, then, that the multiplicity of points of view in Theognis is not the result of a diachronic development from elitist to middling values (or vice versa), but rather the synchronic reflection of a period of contestation and negotiation between the two ideologies.[72] The Theognidea is the site of multiple speakers meditating in dialogue about the relations of aristocratic *hetairoi* within the group, their relations to individual outsiders, and the relation of the entire *hetaireia* to the civic community at large. It is this multiplicity and the process of negotiation enacted in performance that give the Theognidea its dense and complex texture.

With the text of Herodotus, we confront another kind of multiplicity. As histor, Herodotus is the collector and arranger of the logoi of others, who feels it incumbent upon himself to "say what is said" even if he does not believe it (Hdt. 7.152.3; cf. 2.123.1, 3.9.2). Given the language barriers, this means predominantly the logoi of other Greeks, which Herodotus would have acquired in oral form over an extended period.[73] As Carolyn Dewald has compellingly argued, Herodotus

---

[71] Morris 1996: 27.

[72] Thanks to Richard Martin for this formulation. Cf. Stein-Hölkeskamp 1989: 57–138.

[73] On Herodotus's oral sources, see Murray 1987; Thomas 1989: 96–154, 171–72; and especially Evans 1991: 89–146; on Herodotus's techniques of oral composition and performance, see Lattimore 1958; Lang 1984; Fehling 1989: 250–51. For Herodotus's apparent ignorance of other languages, see S. West 1985: 296–97; Miller 1997: 105. While I am sympathetic in general to the approach of Fehling 1989, I cannot accept his arguments in their strong form—that Herodotus had no real sources but simply fabricated his entire narrative as a kind of historical fiction *avant la lettre*. For, while Fehling and others have argued persuasively that Herodotus makes serious errors and fabricates source attributions when dealing with non-Greek material (Fehling 1989: 12–86; cf. S. West 1985, Rollinger 1993), this kind of source criticism does not preclude the possibility of multiple *Greek* informants behind the *Histories*. After all, Herodotus also gets a surprising amount right, suggesting that he traveled and acquired information himself or got it from other Greek travelers. The issue of whether (or where) Herodotus got it right or wrong is not my concern; I want to establish only that Herodotus's text is constructed from disparate logoi

chooses not to assimilate or reconcile the different logoi into a single "transparent" account that claims veridical authority. Instead, the histor preserves, juxtaposes, and stitches together logoi while maintaining a critical distance from them: "[Herodotus] has rather presented the 'I' of the authorial persona as an alternative voice, one that goes to some lengths to distinguish itself from the logoi it recounts. For Herodotus, the way to achieve *akribeia* . . . is carefully to preserve the distinction between his own voice, as an investigator, and the voice of the logoi he investigates; Herodotus has emphasized the alternation between the two voices in order to render our reading effortful in certain ways."[74] As a result, Herodotus produces a profoundly dialogic text, which can reveal to us what the Greeks (or certain Greeks) thought, if we attend to the ripples or furrows in the narrative surface. A careful reading of Herodotus suggests that this inclusion of other voices and other logoi comprehends a broader socio-economic spectrum than is available in archaic poetry (or perhaps any other Greek literary text). For Herodotus's logoi seem to derive not just from the educated elite, but, on occasion, from other segments of the Greek population.[75] This means, I would contend, that the rifts and unevennesses of the *Histories* are of a different order from those envisioned by Macherey (whose paradigm is the seamless, apparently unitary text of the nineteenth-century novel). With Herodotus we have to deal not only with the inevitable rifts within ideology, but also with the jostlings and uneasy juxtapositions of different perspectives competing within a kind of open agora of logoi. Thus, I would add to Dewald's conception that the different traditions and voices embedded in the Herodotean text are profoundly embroiled in the political struggle we have sketched above: Herodotus's narrators and narratives are never ideologically innocent. However fairytale-like they may seem to us, the stories of Polykrates' ring (derived from the Samian aristocracy) and Amasis's rise to power (derived perhaps from the merchants of Naukratis) participate in a discursive conflict over the proper relations of power and modes of exchange.

---

of multiple informants. For critiques of Fehling, see Dewald and Marincola 1987: 26–32; Murray 1987: 101n.12; Gould 1989: 136–37n.16; Pritchett 1993; Miller 1997: 107.

[74] Dewald 1987: 141–70 (quote from p. 153). For a similar model of Herodotus's text (though with a different view of *akribeia*), cf. Darbo-Peschanski 1985: 105–28, 1987: 107–89.

[75] Murray 1987: 102–5 points out that different classes within the Greek city are likely among Herodotus's oral sources, but he does not pursue the ideological implications of this possibility. It is worth noting also that Fehling 1989: 243–45, once he has done away with Herodotus's "sources" entirely, feels the need to make Herodotus himself a "common man." Both scholars, I suggest, are responding to the strangely uneven and atypical qualities of Herodotean narrative.

More than ever before, critics have come to acknowledge the extraordinary literary sophistication of Herodotus's *Histories* and have begun to unpack his mythological, traditional poetic, and imagistic repertoire.[76] Herodotus has been read from the perspective of narratology, and quite frequently through the lens of an anthropologically informed structuralism.[77] Still, these literary approaches resolutely ignore the politics inherent in the formal and thematic patterns they analyze, while structuralist readings have rarely acknowledged the need to situate different narrators and narratives socially before subsuming them into the generic Greek imaginary.[78] The result is a dehistoricized, depoliticized emphasis on hermeneutic and interpretation, projected from the work of the critic into the text of Herodotus as its central motor.[79] This is not to deny the thematic prominence of interpretation in the *Histories*—simply to insist that it participates in a political struggle over representation, who controls it, and who constitutes the culture's fundamental hierarchies of value.[80]

In addition, I would critique Dewald's assumption that Herodotus's goal in producing his complex, uneven narrative is *akribeia*, the most accurate possible rendition of "what really happened." The very literary strategies she analyzes so well—the construction, order, and juxtaposition of logoi, and the narrator's constantly shifting distance from the logoi he recounts—enable narrative interventions, distortions, and irony. That is to say, the Herodotean narrator is no more ideologically innocent than his sources. He has his own politics, though it may not always be easy to say what they are. Given the kind of narrative Dewald describes, we

[76] See, for examples, Vernant 1988: 207–36; Nagy 1990b: 215–338; Sourvinou-Inwood 1991; McGlew 1993; Steiner 1994: 80–84, 127–85.

[77] For narratology, see Dewald 1981, 1987; Darbo-Peschanski 1985, 1987; Munson 1991; Chamberlain 1997; for structuralist approaches to Herodotus, see Rosellini and Saïd 1978; Schmitt-Pantel 1979; Konstan 1983; Redfield 1985; Hartog 1988; Vernant in Vernant and Vidal-Naquet 1988: 207–36, 1989; Detienne and Svenbro 1989.

[78] On the other hand, historical treatments of Herodotus have generally limited their political speculations to arguments about whether Herodotus was (1) pro- or anti-Athenian (Strasburger 1965; Fornara 1971b; Raaflaub 1987); (2) a friend of Pericles or not; (3) hostile to tyranny or simply a completely objective witness thereof (Ferrill 1978; Waters 1985; Gammie 1986; Flory 1987). For exceptionally synthetic and clear-sighted accounts (combining literary and historical approaches), cf. Stambler 1982; Boedeker 1988; McGlew 1993; Steiner 1994; Maurizio 1997.

[79] This emphasis on interpretation comes in many different forms: so, for example, Nagy's notion that Herodotus's genre is *ainos* (1990b: 314–38); Dewald's reading of Herodotus's treatment of objects (1993); Munson's and Christ's discussions of Herodotean kings and tyrants as investigators (Munson 1991; Christ 1994). For a similar critique of modern anthropology, cf. Bourdieu 1990: 17, 27, 34–37.

[80] Cf. Bloomer 1993, who demonstrates the centrality of evaluation to the Herodotean project.

cannot simply "read" Herodotus's politics off the surface of the text: the ideological workings of the *Histories* can only be teased out of a careful reading of its shifts, slippages, and ironic refractions.[81]

All this, which makes Herodotus such a difficult source, also makes him an invaluable one—the touchstone of our inquiry, to which we shall return again and again. For Herodotus preserves oral tradition of approximately one hundred years preceding his researches (so, 550-450?) on *both* sides of the struggle we are attempting to chronicle. Furthermore, Herodotus offers us a text that is uniquely capacious in content as well as in sources: thus he explicitly discusses many of the topics central to our inquiry for the very first time. This can be demonstrated in miniature simply by a list of relevant words that occur for the first time in Herodotus's text: in addition to *nomisma*, Herodotus gives us our earliest extant instances of *banausiē* (together with Sophocles' *Ajax*), *dokimos*, *hetaira* used for a courtesan, and *kapēlos*/*kapēleuō* (aside from a single occurrence in Hipponax).[82] Finally, Herodotus is central to this endeavor because he ironizes, problematizes, and even deconstructs the competing accounts he records, as we can see clearly from the juxtaposition of the different strands of the poetic tradition with Herodotus's playful text.[83] Reading

---

[81] My position, then, is closer to Benardete 1969; Darbo-Peschanski 1987; and Flory 1987 in its commitment to the close reading of Herodotus. But, unlike them, I am interested in reading Herodotus's text against the backdrop of a whole series of practices and discourses that emerge in the archaic period and that, I contend, participate in a contest of paradigms and transactional orders.

[82] Cf. von Reden 1997: 168: "The most complex discussion of money, exchange and systems of social evaluation can be found in Herodotus." It is worth noting in conjunction with these topics Loraux's observation that Herodotus is unique among fifth- and fourth-century sources in his clear-sighted praise and evaluation of democracy as a system: "it is not surprising if the work of the foreigner from Halicarnassus, of the citizen of Thurii, has elements of a purely democratic thought that are not to be found in the Athenian historian of the Peloponnesian War" (Loraux 1986: 204–9, quote taken from p. 205).

[83] This is not to engage in a traditional kind of *Quellenforschung*, unearthing Herodotus's poetic "sources" in a purely literary framework in the manner of Aly 1921. Instead, I believe that a political and sociological reading of archaic poetry provides the broader cultural background we need to comprehend Herodotus's symbolic codes. I should add here that I have also resisted the urge to grapple comprehensively with the text of Herodotus. The aspiration to totality I regard as one of the principal seductions of Herodotean narrative: both because of its own seemingly comprehensive coverage and its refusal to forge a definitive account, the text of Herodotus can draw the critic into a dream of totalizing order. Thus, rather than trying to account for all of Herodotus, I have been deliberately selective—proffering a style of reading rather than a comprehensive interpretation. In addition, I focus mainly on the first four books of Herodotus, where it seems Herodotus is laying out the cultural groundwork for the escalating confrontation of Greeks and Persians in the last five books (in other terms, the first four books offer a clear Newtonian mechanics of the cultural system, while the last five books put them into high-speed, Einsteinian motion).

archaic poetry and Herodotus against each other reveals a vital contest of paradigms *and* the dialectical transformations this ideological struggle undergoes in the course of the fifth century.

III. THE STRUCTURE OF THE ARGUMENT

Here it must be acknowledged that we are not dealing simply with a two-sided opposition in which money, neutral in itself, draws its moral charge from its exchange context—positively valued when it is an "embedded" long-term transaction, negatively valued when it participates in a "disembedded" context that privileges the short-term transactional order.[84] Since our literary evidence preserves at least two different ideological positions engaged in a struggle that takes place largely within representation, we are really confronted with a three-sided model. Both the aristocratic elite and the polis lay claim to the good, "embedded" economy for themselves, and both vilify the other side by representing it not as an alternate order, but as disorder—socially ruinous disembedding perpetrated by selfish economic interests. Thus in every instance we need to specify as precisely as possible *whose* representation it is and from *whose* point of view. From an oligarchic perspective, the Great King of Persia is Darius *kapēlos*, a money-grubbing small trader (Hdt. 3.89), while Polykrates of Samos is a flagrant and habitual violator of the proprieties of gift exchange, whose transgressions provoke a suitable cosmic retribution (Hdt. 3.39-60, 120–25). But from an egalitarian perspective, aristocratic gift exchange itself figures as the grotesque betrayal of the community for individualistic profit: thus the parodic portrait of Alkmeon the Athenian, given all the golddust he can carry on his person by the magnanimous Kroisos (Hdt. 6.125).[85]

To read these vignettes aright, we must understand the representational strategies through which this struggle for discursive control plays itself out. For we confront a situation in which both sides exploit common symbolic resources, wielding the same weapons against each other. Here the model of Peter Stallybrass and Allon White provides a useful tool for analysis. In discussing the uses of the carnivalesque in British literature

---

[84] For complementary representations of a two-sided opposition, see von Reden 1995 and Kurke 1991: 225–56. Together, the two interpretations offer a fuller picture.

[85] This three-sided model may account for the discursive slippage in the language of gifts and bribery, often noted by ancient historians. Thus, it is well known that the Greeks did not differentiate in vocabulary between a "gift" and a "bribe"; depending on the discursive context and the positionality of the speaker, "accepting a gift" could be either a noble act or a signal betrayal of the political community. See F. D. Harvey 1985; Herman 1987: 75–81; von Reden 1995: 94–95, 117–20, 132–34.

and culture from the early modern period through the nineteenth century, Stallybrass and White attempt to describe the symbolic uses to which a prevailing binary opposition high-low is put, through its "transcoding" in four interconnected domains—the somatic, the social, the topographic, and the psychic. That is, they contend that the high-low opposition functions to maintain cultural order through its application to the body, social class, place, and identity, and that these four categories constantly interpenetrate and reinforce each other.[86] Codes of high and low in these four spheres represent the symbolic resources through which social and political contestation are played out. One possibility is that both sides or statuses lay claim to the "high" and constitute the opposition as the "low."[87] Another possibility is that those who are marginalized or subjected choose to invert the symbolic codes by a process Stallybrass and White term *transgression,* following the lead of an anthropological definition of "symbolic inversion": "Symbolic inversion may be broadly defined as any act of expressive behaviour which inverts, contradicts, abrogates, or in some fashion presents an alternative to commonly held cultural codes, values and norms be they linguistic, literary or artistic, religious, social and political."[88]

In this symbolic contestation, the body occupies a privileged place, "for transcoding between different levels and sectors of social and psychic reality are effected through the intensifying grid of the body. It is no accident, then, that transgressions and the attempt to control them obsessively return to somatic symbols, for these are ultimate elements of social classification itself."[89] Hence Stallybrass and White are particularly

---

[86] Cf. in general, Bourdieu 1990: 200–270 (on "irresistible analogy"); for a reading of such interpenetration of spheres in Herodotus's *Histories,* see Konstan 1983.

[87] Stallybrass and White 1986: 4: "It would be wrong to imply that 'high' and 'low' in this context are equal and symmetrical terms. When we talk of high discourses—literature, philosophy, statecraft, the languages of the Church and the University—and contrast them to the low discourses of a peasantry, the urban poor, subcultures, marginals, the lumpenproletariat, colonized peoples, we already have two 'highs' and two 'lows.' History seen from above and history seen from below are irreducibly different and they consequently impose radically different perspectives on the question of hierarchy. Indeed they may and often do possess quite different symbolic hierarchies but because the higher discourses are normally associated with the most powerful socio-economic groups existing at the centre of cultural power, it is they which generally gain the authority to designate what is to be taken as high and low in the society. This is what Raymond Williams calls the 'inherent dominative mode' and it has the prestige and the access to power which enables it to create the dominant definitions of superior and inferior. Of course the 'low' (defined as such by the high precisely to confirm itself as 'high') may well see things differently and attempt to impose a counterview through an inverted hierarchy."

[88] Babcock 1978: 14, quoted by Stallybrass and White 1986: 17.

[89] Stallybrass and White 1986: 26; cf. Bourdieu 1990: 69–79 on "embodied practical logic."

interested in the opposition of the "classical" and "grotesque" bodies, and the symbolic uses to which the latter in particular is put:

> The classical statue has no openings or orifices whereas grotesque costume and masks emphasize the gaping mouth, the protuberant belly and buttocks, the feet and the genitals. In this way the grotesque body stands in opposition to the bourgeois individualist conception of the body, which finds *its* image and legitimation in the classical. The grotesque body is emphasized as a mobile, split, multiple self, a subject of pleasure in processes of exchange; and it is never closed off from either its social or ecosystemic context. The classical body on the other hand keeps its distance. In a sense it is disembodied, for it appears indifferent to a body which is "beautiful," but which is taken for granted.[90]

Though their discussion focuses on a very different period and culture, many of the categories and discursive strategies Stallybrass and White identify seem applicable to archaic and classical Greece. Specifically, we can chart the discursive use of the grotesque body to vilify the opposition on the part of *both* elitist and egalitarian traditions. Thus the grotesque body becomes a trace of ideological contestation in our texts. The fanatical aristocrat Alkaios denounces his opponent Pittakos not only as "base-born" (*kakopatridais*, fr. 348 V) but also as "blubber" (*o phusgōn*, fr. 129.21 V), while egalitarian hostility to aristocratic gift exchange transforms Alkmeon (in the Kroisos narrative referred to above) into a grotesque parody of the human form, "swollen up," mouth stuffed with golddust, barely able to walk, "like to anything more than a person" (Hdt. 6.125.4). On the other hand, in the Herodotean portrait of Amasis we detect the operation of Stallybrass and White's second strategy—symbolic inversion—this time through the transgressive valorization of the grotesque body. Amasis farts his way to power and, once pharaoh, allegorizes his own transformation of status by fashioning his footbath into a cult image worshiped at the center of the city.

Thus I shall have recourse to Stallybrass and White's model of four cultural codes—the bodily, the social, the topographic, and the psychic—

---

[90] Stallybrass and White 1986: 22; cf. 23–25. Clearly, in their interest in the grotesque body, Stallybrass and White follow Bakhtin 1968: 303–436, but as they point out, they diverge from Bakhtin's purely celebratory identification of the grotesque body with the folk, seeing instead a complex struggle over shared representational categories. It is this more analytic and strategic use of Bakhtin's categories that I find most congenial in their method. It should also be acknowledged that the value-laden characteristics of classical and grotesque bodies they analyze are culturally specific, not natural or inevitable. Still, since the entire Western tradition derives these models from Greek antiquity, their use for analysis of this period seems acceptable.

and their interaction in the analysis of the conceptual categories through which the Greeks thought and contested "the meanings of money." In this context it is worth noting the final step in their argument about symbolic appropriation and transgression. Stallybrass and White maintain that we can only understand the psychic process of identity-formation as the transposition or displacement "inward" of the culture-specific symbolic repertoires of the other three spheres. The ambiguous representations of the somatic, social, and topographic are not merely analogous to the psychological; they are constitutive of it. As Stallybrass and White put it, "Thus the logic of identity-formation involves distinctive associations and switching between location, class and the body, and these are not imposed upon subject-identity from the outside, they are the core terms of an exchange network, an economy of signs, in which individuals, writers and authors are sometimes but perplexed agencies. A fundamental rule seems to be that what is excluded at the overt level of identity-formation is productive of new objects of desire."[91] This thesis raises the intriguing possibility that in excavating the political and social struggles that fueled the archaic Greek battle over value and signification we may find ourselves unwittingly contributing to an analysis of shifting identity-formation in archaic and classical Greece.

Thus, in the chapters that follow, I will trace out an argument about political and economic contestation that is strangely shadowed by the tropes and troubles of identity-formation. This is also an attempt to describe the crystallization and workings of ideology before the emergence of theoretical discourse—as it is "embodied" in imagery, story, and practice.[92] Hence the book is divided into two main sections: the first half explores concrete discourses (imagery and narratives) through which political and economic contestation are played out; the second half turns to the consideration of practices that shape and involve the body as contributors to opposed ideological positions. The first half works out a system and a way of reading ideological contestation in the "incorporated" form of narrative; the second half then applies that method to other, interlinked domains of practice. Even here it must be acknowledged that the division into "discourses" and "practices" is somewhat artificial, for the narratives I consider are about concrete practices, while the practices of the second half—prostitution, games, and coinage—are themselves inextricably enmeshed in discourse and representation. Still, what I hope to articulate by this division is the progressive movement of the

---

[91] Stallybrass and White 1986: 25.

[92] For this attempt to read the embodied "logic of practice[s]," cf. Bourdieu 1977, 1990; de Certeau 1984.

argument toward greater materiality. This is to move out from a poetic of texts to a poetic of practices, and thereby to attempt to access the domain of popular culture and ideology.

Chapter 1 sets the scene of elitist resistance in the *hetaireia*. There, I focus on a single important image system, that of metals, as an aristocratic strategy for displacing coinage and thereby denying it autonomy and legitimacy. Three following chapters then explore competing representations of the tyrant in Herodotus that grow out of and adumbrate the archaic poetic "language of metals" and the problematics of gift exchange. The tyrant deserves our attention as a prominent figure in the Greek imaginary, a flashpoint for fantasies that transform power and value, both from above and below. Thus Chapter 2 opposes the negative elitist portrait of Darius *kapēlos*, minter of the daric, to the heroic grotesquerie of the demotic Amasis. In Chapter 3, I consider in detail the dialogic quality of Herodotus's Samian Stories, which incorporate both elitist and civic strands in their complex representation of Polykrates' violations of gift exchange. Chapter 4 turns to Kroisos and charts the divergent narratives and evaluations his legendary generosity elicits in choral lyric and in the text of Herodotus.

Chapters 5 and 6 consider competing systems of the traffic in women as another kind of currency, "an equivalent more universal than money."[93] In Chapter 5, I explore the opposition *hetaira-pornē*, which functions in elitist discourse like the binary metals-money, to differentiate the untainted *charis*-relations of the *hetaireia* from the promiscuous exchanges of the public sphere. We shall see how this representation, already unstable within sympotic poetry, is challenged and subverted by Herodotus's wry narrative of Rhodopis and her pyramid. Chapter 6 also examines Herodotus's alternative fantasy of proper political and economic relations at the center of the polis, played out through a different kind of traffic in women—the Babylonian system of bride auction.

Chapter 7 turns from prostitution to another, linked element in Herodotus's ethnography of the Lydians: games of chance and skill. Just as the binary *hetaira-pornē* helps articulate the symbolic opposition of elite symposium and agora, various games that first appear in the archaic period seem to align along the same axis, contributing to the identity-formation of their players as either elite symposiasts or proper citizens of the polis. Chapter 8, finally, shifts from the symbolic tokens of game pieces to that of civic coin, to try to analyze the ways in which the symbolism and materiality of coin help constitute the community of citizens who use it. This chapter, in a sense, brings us full circle, laying

---

[93] de Lauretis 1987: 45, quoting Lea Melandri.

bare a coherent practical response to the elitist "language of metals" described in Chapter 1.

As this summary reveals, my choice of topics has been idiosyncratic and selective at best—perhaps not what a literary critic *or* historian would expect from an exploration of the meanings of money in archaic and classical Greece. This has been conditioned partly by the surreptitious approaches of the sources themselves, and partly by my own obsessions. The first half of the book is more narrowly and traditionally literary, offering more extended readings of Herodotus and other texts. The second half is more concerned with the lowly stuff of culture that exists before and behind theory: those phenomena that are marginal, seemingly too trivial to be worth studying and yet pervasive, at the lower edge of culture. Thus it may be that the first half will be of more interest to literary scholars, especially readers of Herodotus; the second half more engaging for historians and archaeologists. The book is also designed to be read as a constellation of free-standing essays grouped around related issues (all predicated on the historical and methodological presuppositions laid out in this introduction). While this has entailed some repetition, it has seemed worthwhile to facilitate the reader's access to individual chapters. It is, of course, my hope that readers of many different stripes will persevere and find value in both halves of the book and a kind of unity in their conjunction.

Part One

DISCOURSES

CHAPTER 1

The Language of Metals

IT IS A CURIOUS FACT that for nearly two centuries after its appearance on the edge of the Greek world, coinage (that is, *nomisma*) is never named in any extant Greek text. Emmanuel Laroche, who noted this absence, suggested that it was largely an accident of genre and preservation: the lyric and elegiac poetry, which we have, is not concerned with money; the early prose and inscriptions, which we lack, may have spoken of it.[1] Sitta von Reden takes a different tack. She asserts: "The Greeks had no word for money. They had the term *nomisma* which meant currency and which is identical neither with coinage nor with money," while the most common word for money was *chrēmata*, which pre-dated coinage and maintained a range of uses.[2] From this linguistic evidence, von Reden concludes: "The absence of a name for the phenomenon of monetary exchange in Greece suggests that it gradually emerged rather than being imposed from outside. Distinct meanings and functions of coinage should therefore be analysed in relation to meanings and functions of exchange which were established before coinage appeared as a means of exchange."[3] Yet this thesis, which forms the basis for von Reden's argument for an "embedded money economy," sidesteps the issue of the peculiar absence of *nomisma* from the sources for the first two hundred or so years of its existence (of extant sources, the term first occurs in Herodotus). This absence is particularly striking, since *nomisma* (of all the terms for "coinage" or "money") is, as Will contended, a politically significant designation. For whether we etymologize it (with Will) as "process or result of lawful distribution" or (with Laroche) as "convention," the term *nomisma* points to the political function of coinage, either as a means of effecting retributive justice or as an institution of consensus.[4] This political function, as von Reden herself acknowledges, is what crucially distinguishes coinage from other forms of wealth (both of which are designated indiscriminately by *chrēmata*). Hence we must attend to the different connotations of *nomisma* and *chrēmata* in our sources and wonder all

---

[1] Laroche 1949: 232–33.
[2] Von Reden 1995: 173–74 (quote from p. 173).
[3] Ibid: 175.
[4] See discussion of etymology above, Introduction, pp. 13–14 with note 34.

the more at the absence of the former, political term throughout the crucial period of its civic adoption and implementation.[5]

Should we then accept Laroche's generic explanation? I would be content with this account, were it not for a second curious phenomenon—the repeated and emphatic mention in aristocratic poetic texts of the sixth and fifth centuries B.C.E. of the weighing, refining, and testing of precious metals. These technological processes are mentioned six times by Theognis, at least once by Simonides, five times by Pindar, and once by Bacchylides, always as images for the noble mind or self or for the authenticity of celebratory song.[6]

The image of refining metals seems to originate as a topos of didactic poetry: hence its extraordinary prominence in Theognis. For example, the poet asserts, echoing the language of the *Iliad* (22.351–52):

Πιστὸς ἀνὴρ χρυσοῦ τε καὶ ἀργύρου ἀντερύσασθαι
ἄξιος ἐν χαλεπῇ, Κύρνε, διχοστασίῃ. (Thgn. 77–78)

A trustworthy man deserves to be weighed against gold and silver, o Kyrnos, in harsh city strife.

Elsewhere, Theognis shifts the image from weighing to the testing of gold against a touchstone (in fact, the elegies of Theognis provide the earliest references in Greek to the use of the *basanos*). On one occasion, he opines,

Δόξα μὲν ἀνθρώποισι κακὸν μέγα, πεῖρα δ᾽ ἄριστον.
πολλοὶ ἀπείρητοι δόξαν ἔχουσ᾽ ἀγαθοί.
εἰς βάσανον δ᾽ ἐλθὼν παρατριβόμενός τε μολύβδῳ
χρυσὸς ἄπεφθος ἐὼν καλὸς ἅπασιν ἔσῃ. (Thgn. 1104a–6)

Reputation is a great evil for mortals, but testing is the best thing. Many who are noble have reputation when they are untried. But going to the

---

[5] In this context we should note the observation of Caccamo Caltabiano and Radici Colace (1983, 1985, 1989) that almost all the terms for coinage preserved in Pollux's *Onomastikon* highlight the issues of legitimacy and authority, rather than weight or quality of metal. This argument tends to confirm Will's claims about the political significance of the term *nomisma* and points to the fundamentally political character of the Greeks' conceptualizations of coinage. While this confirms von Reden's larger argument (see Intro., pp. 13–17), it points up the problem in simply conflating all the different terms for coinage in order to establish a picture of continuity from pre-coinage to coinage exchange systems.

[6] Thgn. 77–78, 415–18, 449–52, 499–500, 1104a–6, 1164e–h; Simon. fr. 87/592 *PMG*; Pindar *P.* 10.64–68, *N.* 4.82–85, *N.* 8.20–21, *Paian* 14.35–40, fr. 122.16 SM; Bacch. fr. 14.1–5 SM (it should be noted that within the exiguous and lacunose corpus of archaic lyric and elegiac, this represents a veritable explosion of references to metallurgy). A comprehensive catalogue of images of metallurgy, coinage, and seals in Greek literature to the time of Aristotle is provided by Hangard 1963, though he makes no attempt to analyze their patterns of occurrence or interrelation.

touchstone and [proving to] be refined gold rubbed beside lead, you will be beautiful to all.

And, in lines 415–18, the same image of gold against the touchstone is deployed in a slightly different context:

Οὐδέν' ὁμοῖον ἐμοὶ δύναμαι διζήμενος εὑρεῖν
πιστὸν ἑταῖρον, ὅτῳ μή τις ἔνεστι δόλος·
ἐς βάσανον δ' ἐλθὼν παρατρίβομαι ὥστε μολύβδῳ
χρυσός, ὑπερτερίης δ' ἄμμιν ἔνεστι λόγος. (Thgn. 415–18 = 1164e–h)

Seeking, I can find no trusty comrade like to myself, the sort who has no trickery within. But going to the touchstone, I am exposed like gold rubbed beside lead, and we have the reckoning of superiority.

As Hudson-Williams glosses this highly elliptical expression, "I am rubbed (on or with the stone) like gold side by side with adulterated gold (i.e. containing an admixture of lead)."[7]

In Pindar and Bacchylides, we see the epinikian adaptation of this didactic topos, used to figure the authenticity of poetic praise within a circuit of aristocratic reciprocity. In perhaps the most elaborate example, in *Pythian* 10, Pindar asserts:

πέποιθα ξενίᾳ προσανέϊ Θώρα-
κος, ὅσπερ ἐμὰν ποιπνύων χάριν
τόδ' ἔζευξεν ἅρμα Πιερίδων τετράορον,
φιλέων φιλέοντ', ἄγων ἄγοντα προφρόνως.
πειρῶντι δὲ καὶ χρυσὸς ἐν βασάνῳ πρέπει
καὶ νόος ὀρθός. (Pindar P. 10.64–68)

I trust to the gentle hospitality of Thorax, the very one who, bustling after my grace, yoked this four-horse chariot of the Muses, a friend to a friend, leading one who leads in kindness of spirit. And for the one testing, both gold against the touchstone is conspicuous, and the upright mind.

What all these passages have in common is that they come from aristocratic texts and specifically from contexts that mark an in-group of *hetaireia* or *xenia*. The frame of the aristocratic *hetaireia* becomes clear

---

[7] Hudson-Williams 1910: 204 (*ad* 417–18). On the technology of the touchstone, the *locus classicus* is Theophrastos, *De Lapidibus* 46: "Those concerned use streaks, starting with that which indicates the smallest amount of baser metal, this amount being [a krithe, then a kollybos, then] a quarter-obol or a half-obol. Thus the proportion of precious metal is detected from these streaks" (translation from the edition of Eichholz 1965; see his comments *ad loc.*). Cf. also Pliny *HN* 33.125–26 and Arrian *Epiktetos* I.20.8 and see the modern discussions of Babelon 1901: I.873; Graf 1903: 22–25; Hangard 1963: 14, 26, 39, 51–61; Bogaert 1968: 321–22, 1976: 8–13; Buttrey 1981: 79–80; Wallace 1987: 390–91.

when Theognis's lines are read in their larger context. Thus lines 77–78, for example, emphasize the need for a trustworthy companion in civil strife. In fact, these lines form part of an extended meditation on the difficulty of finding trusty *philoi* and *hetairoi* (73–82). Echoing the *pistos anēr* of 77, lines 415–18 turn on the lack of a *pistos hetairos*: as Gregory Nagy and others have argued, *pistos hetairos* delineates the member of the aristocratic in-group as a kind of technical term.[8] In Pindar also, the mention of *xenia* between the poet and Thorax locates these lines within the closed sphere of the aristocratic symposium.[9]

Almost certainly, the weighing and refining of precious metals did not normally go on in the privacy of the symposium, for this same period saw the invention and ideological vilification of the category of the "banausic." *Banausos* is a post-Homeric term, derived, as the ancient lexicographers inform us, from βαῦνος ("furnace, forge") and αὕω ("to light a fire, make blaze"). It is then, as Pierre Chantraine notes, properly the designation of "those who work with the techniques of fire . . . essentially, blacksmiths, metallurgists, and potters." *Banausos* and its derivatives are also, from their earliest recorded occurrences (Soph. *Ajax* 1121 and Hdt. 2.165), highly negatively charged: they designate "base" or "menial" labor from an aristocratic perspective.[10] Thus, paradoxically, elitist texts appropriate the imagery of metallurgy for themselves at the precise moment that aristocratic discourse is engaged in constructing the metallurgist as the paradigm of the vulgar menial laborer.[11] Nor can this explosion of references to the use of the *basanos*, the "touchstone," be regarded simply as an epiphenomenon of the invention and circulation of coined money. For the touchstone can only test the quality of *gold* effectively, whereas the coinage circulating in all the Greek cities where these poems

---

[8] See Nagy 1979: 241–45 and Donlan 1985: 223–44. For the aristocratic context of these images, cf. the discussion of duBois 1991: 9–18. duBois, however, makes no distinction between metals and coinage in her discussion of the texts—a distinction I believe to be crucial, as I hope to show.

[9] This context for the image of refined gold is noted by Gundert 1935: 37 and 123n.162, in his discussion of *P*. 10.64–68. See also Kurke 1991: 140–43 for an extended analysis of *xenia* elements in this passage.

[10] For the etymology of *banausos*, see *Et. Mag.* 187; cf. Aelius Dionysius p. 112 Erbse. Chantraine 1966: 43 accepts the ancient etymology, citing Hesychios's gloss on βαναυσία· πᾶσα τέχνη διὰ πυρός· κυρίως δὲ ἡ περὶ τὰς καμίνους· καὶ πᾶς τεχνίτης χαλκεὺς ἢ χρυσοχόος βάναυσος ("*Banausia*: Every craft [that works] through fire; but properly the craft concerned with furnaces or kilns; and every craftsman who fashions bronze or melts gold is a *banausos*"). Chantraine (1966: 43–47) also notes the frequently negative connotation of *banausos* and its derivatives; cf. Aymard 1967.

[11] That this same paradox permeates Greek attitudes to labor is argued by Austin and Vidal-Naquet 1977: 12: "While the work of the artisan was admired, he was neglected or down-graded as a person."

were performed (so far as we can reconstruct) was *silver*.[12] In the absence of any plausible empirical explanation, how are we to account for the prominence of the imagery of testing and refining metals in sympotic verse? It is my contention that these two phenomena—the absence of any mention of coinage and the obtrusive presence of the imagery of metallurgy—are interconnected. Indeed, it appears that in aristocratic poetic texts of the sixth and fifth centuries they stand in complementary distribution.[13] I suggest that this presence and absence in fact form a coherent system within a moral discourse of place, status, and self constructed by aristocrats. In the next section, I will attempt to map out the terms of this conceptual field. I will then turn to Herodotus to explore a few reflexes of this same symbolic system in the historian's text.

I. FORGING THE LANGUAGE OF METALS

I would like to delineate this conceptual field by triangulating on the archaic period from two texts—Aristotle's brief remarks on coinage and Hesiod's myth of the races. In his analysis of coinage in the *Politics*, Aristotle identifies two different aspects of coinage (*nomisma*) proper. First, he argues that coinage is a convenience developed to facilitate trade—a way of preweighing and measuring a certain amount of precious metal:

> For each one of the things that is necessary in nature is not easily transported. Therefore, with regard to exchanges, they have agreed to give and take some such thing between themselves, which, itself being among the useful things, had the advantage of being easy to manage for livelihood (for example, iron

[12] On the silver coinage of Aigina (Pindar *N*. 4, *N*. 8), and Corinth (Pindar fr. 122 SM), see Kraay 1976: 41–49, 78–85. Megara (Theognis's city) apparently did not mint its own coins until the fourth century; Figueira 1985: 148–49 speculates that Megara may earlier have used the silver coins of Aigina, Corinth, and Athens (all its near neighbors). For Simon. fr. 87/592 *PMG*, Pindar *Paian* 14.35–40, and Bacch. fr. 14.1–5 SM, we do not know the site of performance, while Pindar *P*. 10 was performed in Thessaly, which had no coinage of its own until some time after 500 B.C.E. (see Kraay 1976: 115–16; T. Martin 1985: 34–59). For the ineffectiveness of the touchstone in testing silver as opposed to gold, see Bogaert 1976: 11–12; Buttrey 1981: 79–80; Levine 1984: 133; for its inadequacy in testing electrum, see Wallace 1987: 391.

[13] Thus, I must disagree with von Reden (1995: 174), who offers as proof of the continuity of pre-coinage and coinage exchange systems the following argument: "The century of sympotic lyric [by which she means Theognidean elegy] was the century of the gradual introduction of coinage. Nevertheless no obvious changes in the attitude to *chrēmata* can be observed within the extant corpus." As I argue below, we can detect substantial changes in the imagistic repertoire of Theognidean didactic poetry, and we can plausibly connect those changes with the development of coinage.

and silver and if there is any other such thing). At first it was defined simply
by size and weight, but in the end they would also cast a stamp upon it, so
as to release them from having to measure it. For the stamp was put on as
the sign of how much [it weighed]. (Arist. *Pol.* 1257a31-41)

That is to say, money is simply worth the precious metal of which it is
made—this is a view we might term essentialism. But in the same context,
Aristotle offers another view:

ὁτὲ δὲ πάλιν λῆρος εἶναι δοκεῖ τὸ νόμισμα καὶ νόμος παντάπασι, φύσει
δ' οὐδέν, ὅτι μεταθεμένων τε τῶν χρωμένων οὐδενὸς ἄξιον οὔτε χρήσιμον
πρὸς οὐδὲν τῶν ἀναγκαίων ἐστί. . . . (Arist. *Pol.* 1257b10–14)

But sometimes coinage seems to be nonsense and entirely convention, but
nothing by nature, since if those using it change, it is worth nothing nor
useful toward [the purchase of] any of the necessaries. . . .

This position sees only the symbolic function of coinage, ignoring its real
metallic worth. And even in Aristotle's time, this functional or symbolic
interpretation perceived coinage as a threat, setting it under the sign
of convention as opposed to nature and associating it ominously with
arbitrary change.[14]

I suggest that precisely this dichotomy of essentialism and functionalism
is operative already in our sixth- and fifth-century texts, and that, splitting
along the lines of elitist and middling traditions, it explains the complementary distribution I've observed. That is, a whole set of aristocratic
poetic texts—those of Theognis, Simonides, Pindar, and Bacchylides—
focus only and obsessively on essence, that is on the quality of metal,
thereby eliding or repressing the existence of coinage altogether. For
coinage represents a tremendous threat to a stable hierarchy of aristocrats
and others, in which the aristocrats maintain a monopoly on precious
metals and other prestige goods. With the introduction of coinage looms
the prospect of indiscriminate distribution, exchange between strangers
that subverts the ranked spheres of exchange-goods operative in a gift-

---

[14] In a sense Aristotle's discussion of coinage in the *Nicomachean Ethics* (1133a–b)
provides the answer to the negative representation of currency as arbitrary convention in
the *Politics*. For, in *NE* as well, Aristotle acknowledges that coinage is simply a convention
that becomes useless if we change it, but goes on to valorize its symbolic function as an
"exchangeable representation of need" (ὑπάλλαγμα τῆς χρείας), which makes possible the
construction of community (κοινωνία). Hence, according to von Reden 1995: 184–87, the
difference in moral and political inflection between the two accounts reflects the difference
in context: while the *Politics* envisions trade between individuals from different communities,
NE considers only intra-polis exchange as a subcategory of reciprocity. For other significant
accounts of both of Aristotle's discussions of coinage, see Will 1954, 1955b; Polanyi 1968:
78–115; Finley 1970; Meikle 1979, 1995; Picard 1980.

exchange culture.[15] This threat, in turn, represents a social and political threat to elite control, for one of the premises of the system of ranked spheres of exchange is the complete identification of self and status with the precious metals possessed and controlled. Hence the aristocratic monopoly on precious goods within a closed system of gift exchange guarantees an absolute (naturalized) status hierarchy. Coinage represents a double threat to that system, for it puts precious metal into general circulation, breaking down the system of ranked spheres of exchange, and it does so under the symbolic authority of the polis. As stamped civic token, coinage challenges the naturalized claim to power of the aristocratic elite.[16]

In response, aristocratic poetic texts deny the existence of coinage by speaking only about metals. Thus, ironically, it is the threat of coinage, once invented, that generates these desperate affirmations of aristocratic quality in the language of metals. As a *comparandum* we might note that Hesiod's didactic poem, composed in the period before the invention of coinage, has no such obsession with the image of refined gold for the trustworthy *hetairos*. Even in a context where we might expect such a comparison, Hesiod's text is bare of metallic elaboration:

μὴ δὲ κασιγνήτῳ ἶσον ποιεῖσθαι ἑταῖρον·
εἰ δέ κε ποιήσῃς, μή μιν πρότερος κακὸν ἔρξαι
μηδὲ ψεύδεσθαι γλώσσης χάριν· εἰ δέ σέ γ' ἄρχῃ
ἤ τι ἔπος εἰπὼν ἀποθύμιον ἠὲ καὶ ἔρξας,
δὶς τόσα τείνυσθαι μεμνημένος· εἰ δέ κεν αὖτις
ἡγῆτ' ἐς φιλότητα, δίκην δ' ἐθέλῃσι παρασχεῖν,
δέξασθαι· δειλός τοι ἀνὴρ φίλον ἄλλοτε ἄλλον
ποιεῖται· σὲ δὲ μή τι νόος κατελεγχέτω εἶδος. (Hes. W&D 707–14)

Do not make a companion equal to a brother. But if you do, do not be the first one to treat him badly nor speak falsely the grace of the tongue. But if he makes a beginning speaking a word or doing [a deed] that is hateful to you, remember and pay him back double. But if in turn he leads himself to friendship and is willing to furnish justice, accept it. To be sure, a base man makes different ones friends at different times. But don't let your mind in any way shame your form.

As scholars have observed, there are powerful thematic continuities between the didactic poetry of Hesiod and Theognis which might lead

---

[15] On the system of spheres of exchange and its sociological implications, see Bohannan 1959: 491–503; Firth 1965: 336–44; Gregory 1982: 49–53; Morris 1986a: 8–13. On the threat coinage represents to the aristocracy, cf. Gernet 1981b: 286–87; Howgego 1995: 17.

[16] In Chapter 8 below, I will consider the strategies by which the city in its turn naturalizes the medium of coinage.

us to expect the use of similar language and images in similar contexts.[17] Here, at his most "Theognidean," Hesiod doles out advice about the proper behavior toward *philoi* and *hetairoi*, and with the last two lines comes very close to the parainetic sentiments we have been considering. The consistency and dependability of noble *philoi* over time, and the denial of any discrepancy between inside (*noos*) and outside (*eidos*) are precisely the themes that precipitate the obsessive imagery of testing and refining metals in the later didactic tradition. Yet neither here nor anywhere else in the text of the *Works & Days* does Hesiod resort to the imagery of metallurgy for the quality or interaction of any human group.[18]

The complete absence of figurative metallurgy in Hesiod confirms the motivated complementary distribution I have posited for texts of the archaic period. The imagery of metallurgy is present *because* coinage is absent from our texts (and vice versa)—confronted by the double nature of coinage (so dispassionately analyzed by Aristotle two centuries later), elitist texts choose to admit only the essence of precious metal, denying and excluding the symbolic or functional aspect of "currency." If this is so, the language of metals provides a textual trace that enables us to circumvent the reticence of our sources, for the mention of metals stands as a marker for the suppressed but still problematic issue of coinage behind. But it is not simply the repression of the fact of coinage that the figurative metallurgy of these texts achieves. We must read this trope positively as well as negatively, taking quite seriously the contexts in which it recurs. For the image of refining metals figures as a key term in a triple discourse of status, place, and self. Along the lines of the model of Stallybrass and White, we can discern the outlines of an elitist moral discourse that takes shape around the images of metallurgy, and in which the three spheres of social rank, topography, and identity formation consistently interpenetrate and reinforce each other. Thus, the binary

---

[17] On continuity within the tradition of wisdom literature/didactic poetry, see Friedländer 1913; Martin 1984; the essays collected in Figueira and Nagy 1985; Nagy 1990a: 36–82; Kurke 1990. On this passage of Hesiod in particular, cf. Nagy 1990a: 71–72: "Hesiod pointedly teaches that one should not make one's *hetaîros* 'comrade' equal to one's own brother (707). This negative injunction then becomes an excuse for displaying the poetic traditions available for teaching a *hetaîros* instead of a brother, since Hesiod goes on to say in the next verse: 'but if you *should* do so [make your *hetaîros* equal to your own brother], then . . .' (708). What follows in the next several verses is a veritable string of aphorisms that deal precisely with the topic of behavior toward one's *hetaîros* (708–722), and there are numerous striking analogues to the aphorisms explicitly or implicitly offered by Theognis to his *hetaîros* Kyrnos. . . ."

[18] Cf. Levine 1984: 125n.2; Levine, who traces the Semitic sources for the imagery of metals and metallurgy in Greek texts, observes, "It is surprising that Hesiod, with his extensive debt to Semitic sources, does not use the counterfeit or touchstone images with which we are here concerned."

noble metal-counterfeit coin (for, as we shall see, in this discourse there is *only* counterfeit coin) signifies the opposition of aristocratic elite vs. base demos (Theognis's *kakoi* or *deiloi*); the symposium vs. the public space outside (polis or agora); and finally the noble self vs. the tricky, deceitful nature of the outsider.[19] The image of testing and refining gold most often occurs in this last context—of self-constitution and the testing of self in intersubjective relations. The language of metals provides the medium through which the noble self and its proper relations are thought and articulated.[20] Thus, while they suppress mention of coinage, these images construct a powerfully morally charged conceptual frame. And indeed, within this discourse of self, coinage can only occupy one position. That is to say, these aristocratic texts appropriate coinage as another kind of *sēma*, as a signifier within their own moral system. In these texts coinage and metal frame a contested field for the conceptualization of self.

A good part of the moral charge invested in the language of metals derives from the invocation—in these images of refined gold—of Hesiod's myth of the races (*W&D* 106-201). This is perhaps itself a response to the paradox of bringing the refining techniques of the agora into the symposium. To offset the intrusion of artisanal labor into the aristocratic milieu, these texts appropriate the ideology of Hesiod's golden age. They thereby superimpose Hesiod's symbolic ranking of metals onto their own grid of essentialism vs. functionalism, metals vs. coinage. Thus in the

---

[19] In Chapter 2 we shall observe how Stallybrass and White's fourth level, the somatic or bodily, also plays into the metal-money binary. This is not to claim that there was in archaic Greece a unitary "self" as a prior, naturally existing concept, problematized only by the growing public sphere and exchange economy. Just the opposite: I would contend that all notions of self are constructs, and that the discourse of the texts at issue here formulates two models of self in dialectical opposition.

[20] We may perhaps detect the influence of this discursive system persisting in Plato's *Timaeus*, where, as Vidal-Naquet observes, "The demiurge is above all an artisan in the proper sense of the term . . . he uses all the artisanal techniques available in Plato's time: smelting and metallurgy, iron-working and welding, the craft of the carpenter and the potter, painting, wax-working, weaving, and agriculture. All this is clear enough. What is less understood, in my opinion, is that all these skills form a meaningful hierarchy. . . . At the peak of creation, the world-soul is produced by the finest metallurgy, with its techniques of refining, alloying, even lamination (*Tim.* 35a et seq.). The human body, by contrast, is produced by the relatively less complex work of the potter (*Tim.* 73e). The altogether humble tasks—such as the implantation of the soul in the body, deployment of the circulatory system, or grafting of skin onto the body—are consigned to the level of agricultural technique (*Tim.* 41e, 73c, 76c, 77c, 91c)." (Vidal-Naquet 1986: 235). Vidal-Naquet notes the paradox that Plato explicitly condemns and disdains artisans, even while he has the demiurge create the world by artisanal techniques. I would only add to his analysis the suggestion that the crafting of the world-soul by the techniques of metallurgy may be partly motivated by the archaic aristocratic discourse of self, in which the image of refining metals serves as a mastertrope.

myth of the races, gold had already figured as the standard of sameness over time: the members of the golden race, we are told, are "always like in hands and feet" (αἰεὶ δὲ πόδας καὶ χεῖρας ὅμοιοι, W&D 114).[21] In like manner refined gold serves as an image of the proper aristocratic self in the archaic texts *because* of its sameness: it has the same quality through and through and is not changed or damaged by time (this is, after all, why *we* call gold a "noble metal"[22]). For the former quality, consider again Theognis lines 415–18:

> Seeking, I can find no trusty comrade like to myself (ὅμοιον ἐμοί), the sort who has no trickery within. But going to the touchstone, I am exposed like gold rubbed beside lead, and we have the reputation (literally, reckoning) of superiority.

A *pistos hetairos* is by definition one who has no "trickery within" (he is the same through and through), while *homoion* in line 415 signals another kind of sameness—the *hetaireia* should be a band of the same.[23] The integrity of gold through time (another kind of sameness the aristocratic self should have) is asserted at Theognis lines 449–52:

> εὑρήσεις δέ με πᾶσιν ἐπ' ἔργμασιν ὥσπερ ἄπεφθον
> χρυσὸν ἐρυθρὸν ἰδεῖν τριβόμενον βασάνῳ,
> τοῦ χροιῆς καθύπερθε μέλας οὐχ ἅπτεται ἰός
> οὐδ' εὑρώς, αἰεὶ δ' ἄνθος ἔχει καθαρόν.

> You will find me for all deeds like refined gold, ruddy to see when rubbed on a touchstone; on top of the surface no black rust fixes nor mould, but it has always a pure bloom.

---

[21] Cf. W&D 235 with the comments of West 1978: 215–16: among the characteristics of the Just City which reprise the golden race, τίκτουσιν δὲ γυναῖκες ἐοικότα τέκνα γονεῦσιν ("and the women bear children like to their parents").

[22] Cf. Pliny HN 33.59-60 on the reasons for gold's preeminence among metals: *nec pondere aut facilitate materiae praelatum est ceteris metallis, cum cedat per utrumque plumbo, sed quia rerum uni nihil igne deperit, tuto etiam in incendiis rogisque. quin immo quo saepius arsit, proficit ad bonitatem, aurique experimentum ignis est, ut simili colore rubeat ignescatque et ipsum. . . . Altera causa pretii maior, quod minimum usus deterit, cum argento, aere, plumbo lineae praeducantur manusque sordescant decidua materia.* ("Neither because of its density nor its malleability has it been preferred to all other metals, since it yields in both to lead, but because to it alone of things nothing is lost by fire, but it is safe even in flames and conflagrations. Indeed, the more frequently it has burned, the more it advances in purity, and fire is the means of testing gold, whether it redden to a uniform color and its mass become incandescent. . . . Another, more important reason for its value is that use wears it away least of all, whereas with silver, bronze, and lead, streaks are drawn out and the hands get dirty with material that falls off.")

[23] Cf. Hes. W&D 182–84: in contrast to the golden race, Zeus will destroy the iron race when "father and sons are no longer likeminded to each other (ὁμοίιος), nor guest to host, nor *hetairos* to *hetairos*." West 1978: 199 notes that Hesiod is here using the obscure word

In contrast, the *hetairos* who is found to be false—"unlike"—is lead rubbed beside gold, as in Theognis lines 417–18. It is noteworthy that, within the *hetaireia*, even falsehood and difference are figured exclusively in the language of metals (noble and base), while coinage is never mentioned.

But more significant, perhaps, than the Hesiodic association of gold with sameness and consistency is the symbolic alignment of the golden race with sovereignty. Thus, for example, Hesiod closes his account of this *genos*:

αὐτὰρ ἐπεὶ δὴ τοῦτο γένος κατὰ γαῖα κάλυψε,
τοὶ μὲν δαίμονες ἁγνοὶ ἐπιχθόνιοι τελέθουσιν
ἐσθλοί, ἀλεξίκακοι, φύλακες θνητῶν ἀνθρώπων,

. . . .

πλουτοδόται· καὶ τοῦτο γέρας βασιλήιον ἔσχον. (Hes. W&D 121–26)

But when indeed the earth covered this race, they are holy *daimones* upon the earth, noble guardians of mortal men who fend off evil . . . givers of wealth; and they got this as their kingly honor.

Indeed, Jean-Pierre Vernant has offered an extended structural analysis of the Hesiodic myth of the races which takes as its central terms sovereignty and justice. Vernant suggests that we read each pair of races as the positive and negative versions of Georges Dumézil's three functions. Dumézil contends that the Indo-Europeans originally constructed their Pantheon around three ranked functions that reflect the social system: first, priest-magician-king; second, warriors; and third, farmers. He then proceeds to find relics of this three-tiered system preserved in the mythology of various Indo-European daughter languages. Vernant maps this system onto the Hesiodic myth of the races: thus the gold and silver races together enact the poles of *dikē* and *hubris* within the sphere of kingship and religion; the races of bronze and heroes likewise embody the violent and just aspects of the warrior function, respectively; and finally, the two parts of the iron race represent the positive and negative possibilities for the agricultural function. Vernant concludes:

We have here, not five races in chronological succession, arranged in the order of a more or less progressive decline, but rather a threefold construction, each level being divided into two opposite and complementary aspects. . . . This pattern recalls, in its main outlines, the tripartite functional classification whose important influence on Indo-European religious thought has been demonstrated by G. Dumézil (whether or not there is a direct link

---

ὁμοίος as if it were ὅμοιος (like), and interprets it in light of lines 183–84 as equivalent to ὁμόφρων (likeminded).

between these two). The first stage of Hesiod's myth does indeed describe the function of kingship where the king pursues his juridical and religious activities; the second, the military function where the brute force of the warrior imposes a lawless rule; and the third, the function of fertility and vital foodstuffs which are the special responsibility of the farmer.[24]

It is precisely the association of gold with just sovereignty and religious authority that these aristocratic archaic texts appropriate for their own ends. Thus, we might reconsider Pindar's use of the image of testing gold in *Pythian* 10. This image occurs right *after* the extended myth of the Hyperboreans (a representation of the golden race translated to the ends of the earth) and right *before* the closing lines in which Pindar affirms the just rule of the Aleuads in Thessaly:

ἀδελφεοῖσί τ' ἐπαινήσομεν ἐσλοῖς, ὅτι
ὑψοῦ φέροντι νόμον Θεσσαλῶν
αὔξοντες· ἐν δ' ἀγαθοῖσι κεῖται
πατρώιαι κεδναὶ πολίων κυβερνάσιες. (Pindar *P.* 10.69–72)

And we will praise his noble brothers, because they bear aloft the ordinance of the Thessalians, exalting it: but in the hands of good men are laid the ancestral trusty governances of cities.

The powerful political impact of this closing sequence derives, to a great extent, from the submerged echoes of Hesiod it contains. We might say Pindar's gold comes trailing glory from Hesiod's myth of the races.[25]

Of course, in *Pythian* 10 the association of the ruling house with Hesiodic gold is unproblematic, since the poem was written to be performed in Thessaly—an *ethnos* not a polis, where the Aleuads enjoyed undisputed sway. In poems written for aristocratic citizens of a polis, this appropriation of Hesiodic sovereignty and justice had to be more

---

[24] Vernant 1983: 3–72 (quotation from pp. 20, 22). I am less concerned here with the correctness of Dumézil's model for Indo-European, than with Vernant's application of Dumézil's trifunctional system to Hesiod's myth of the races, and the ways in which that system seems to inform the archaic language of metals.

[25] The implicit association in these earlier texts finds explicit formulation later. Thus Plato in the *Republic* appropriates Hesiodic metals but feels compelled to distinguish them from their real counterparts. At 415a Socrates reveals the substance of the "noble lie": all the citizens are earthborn, but "the god when he fashioned them mixed gold in the generation for those who are equipped to rule . . . and silver for their helpers, and iron and bronze for the farmers and the other craftsmen" (cf. 546e, where Socrates acknowledges the Hesiodic pedigree of his four races). A little later, Socrates adds that the guardians must be inculcated with the belief that "for those who always have divine gold and silver in their soul there is no need of human [gold and silver], nor is it holy for them to pollute [divine gold] by mixing the possession of that with the possession of mortal gold" (*Rep.* 416e4-8; on the connection between Hesiod and Plato, see Hartman 1988: 103–14).

circumspect. For example, consider Pindar's use of the image in *Nemean* 4.82-85:

ὁ χρυσὸς ἑψόμενος
αὐγὰς ἔδειξεν ἁπάσας, ὕμνος δὲ τῶν ἀγαθῶν
ἐργμάτων βασιλεῦσιν ἰσοδαίμονα τεύχει
φῶτα·

Gold when it is refined shows all its beams, and the hymn of good deeds makes a man equal in *daimōn* (in lot) to kings.

In Pindar as in Hesiod, there is a strong association of gold and kingship here. But notably in this epinikian appropriation, the one whom the hymn of praise makes "equal in his lot to kings" is not the victor himself, but his maternal uncle Kallikles, now dead (*N.* 4.80). "Dwelling around Acheron," like the Hesiodic *daimones* of the gold and silver races, he watches his descendant's activities and enjoys "royal honor" at the performance of the victory hymn. By displacing the Hesiodic association backward in time, Pindar's rhetoric avoids directly claiming sovereign status for the victor himself.

It is worth pausing for a moment here to emphasize that we really are dealing with two separate systems, though they have been superimposed or willfully conflated in the archaic texts. The first, the Hesiodic paradigm, constructs a ranked series of metals and endows them with symbolic value—gold in this system represents sameness over time and also rightful sovereignty. This model, in turn, has been overlaid on a more fundamental opposition between metals and coinage—between essentialism and functionalism in the construction of the aristocratic sympotic group and the aristocratic self. We can see that there are two systems in play because of the slight rifts or the imperfect fit between them: thus the distinctive quality of Hesiod's golden race is their sameness over time, but the archaic texts have generalized that sameness to the cohesiveness and equality of the aristocratic *hetaireia*. And thus also, the Hesiodic myth aligns gold with kingship, but its moral charge has been appropriated to validate the authority of aristocrats in general. Still, in spite of these slight rifts (to which I'll return in Chapter 2), the conflation of these two models conspires to obliterate coinage completely from the discourse of archaic elitist texts.

What right do I have, then, to claim that coinage is a signifier in this discourse at all? The answer, I think, lies in an intriguing asymmetry within Theognis's text. When speaking of untrustworthy figures outside of his own *hetaireia*, and only there, Theognis evokes the image of counterfeit coin, as in lines 117–24 and 963–66. In the former passage, befriending the *kakoi* and the *deiloi* has been the poet's theme from line 101, emphatically reiterated in lines 113–14. It is this dangerous transgression of the proper boundary of the *hetaireia* to include the others that elicits the obsessive image of counterfeiting, repeated three times in eight lines:

Κιβδήλου δ' ἀνδρὸς γνῶναι χαλεπώτερον οὐδέν,
  Κύρν', οὐδ' εὐλαβίης ἐστὶ περὶ πλέονος.
χρυσοῦ κιβδήλοιο καὶ ἀργύρου ἀνσχετὸς ἄτη,
  Κύρνε, καὶ ἐξευρεῖν ῥᾴδιον ἀνδρὶ σοφῷ.
εἰ δὲ φίλου νόος ἀνδρὸς ἐνὶ στήθεσσι λελήθῃ
  ψυδρὸς ἐών, δόλιον δ' ἐν φρεσὶν ἦτορ ἔχῃ
τοῦτο θεὸς κιβδηλότατον ποίησε βροτοῖσιν,
  καὶ γνῶναι πάντων τοῦτ' ἀνιηρότατον. (Thgn. 117–24)

Nothing is harder to know than a man who is counterfeit, Kyrnos, nor does anything require more caution [than this]. The delusion of counterfeit gold and silver is endurable, Kyrnos, and easier for a wise man to discover. But if the mind of a man who is a friend, in his breast, escapes [your] notice being false, and he has a tricky heart in his breast, this is the most counterfeit thing the god has made for mortals and this is the most grievous of all things to find out.

As B. A. van Groningen has noted, *kibdēlos* in these lines does not necessarily refer to counterfeit *coinage*: Pollux (7.99) glosses *kibdos* as an alloy of gold, so *kibdēlos* can designate simply adulterated gold or silver.[26] Yet the movement of the poet's thought and language reveals that the image implicit in these lines is that of coinage, not simply of a corrupted metallic alloy. For Theognis is not concerned with the indistinguishable mixing of good and bad qualities in the *kakos anēr*, but with a thoroughly base interior (heart or soul) concealed beneath an apparently noble surface. That is to say, the paradigm is not that of a consistently adulterated alloy, but that of a counterfeit coin, formed from a plug (or in technical terms, an "anima") of base metal (copper or lead) concealed within a slip of gold or silver.[27] This thematic paradigm finds its confirmation in the verbal structure of these verses, which reflect in their word

---

[26] Van Groningen 1966: 50–51 (*ad* 117, 119); cf. Hangard 1963: 62–66, 94; Levine 1984: 128–33; LSJ, s.v. *kibdēleia, kibdos*. On the other hand, *kibdēlos* is used to designate generically various kinds of counterfeit coin: see Stroud 1974: 171–72; Caccamo Caltabiano and Radici Colace 1983: 442–43.

[27] On Greek counterfeiting techniques (which appear to have been practiced from the earliest minting), see Babelon 1901, I: 373–74, 633–35; Graf 1903: 34–66; Regling 1931: coll. 471–74. For parallel passages that make explicit that coinage is at issue, cf. Demokritos fr. B 82 DK (where *kibdēlos* is linked with *agathophanēs*) and Eur. *Medea* 516–19 (where *kibdēlos* appears in conjunction with *charaktēr*, the stamp on a coin). The numismatic technical term "anima" (used to designate the base kernel of a counterfeit coin) unfortunately appears to have no ancient precedent.

order the poet's anxious relation to another's concealed interiority. The lines that describe counterfeit metals proceed in a lucid sequence of noun and adjective, but as soon as the poet takes up the topic of human "counterfeiting," that style changes. φίλου ... ἀνδρός encloses the suspect νόος, δόλιον ... ἦτορ hides ἐν φρεσίν, and even the god (θεός) lurks within his most counterfeit creation (τοῦτο ... κιβδηλότατον).

In lines 963–66, as in the earlier passage, it is precisely the too-hasty acceptance of a stranger into the inner circle that evokes the image of the "counterfeit nature" (κίβδηλον ... ἦθος).[28] Thus coinage only ever figures in the negative—there is only bad coinage—and it is aligned precisely with the space outside the *hetaireia* and with anti-aristocratic qualities. The counterfeit nature of the outsider is inconsistent within itself *and* changeable over time, as Theognis emphasizes in lines 965–66:

πολλοί τοι κίβδηλον ἐπίκλοπον ἦθος ἔχοντες
κρύπτουσ' ἐνθέμενοι θυμὸν ἐφημέριον.

To be sure, many having a counterfeit thieving nature hide it, putting in a spirit that varies as the day.

Thus the untrustworthy Other—just like the symbolic function of coinage in Aristotle's discourse—combines artifice (ἐνθέμενοι), trickery (ἐπίκλοπον and κρύπτουσι), and inconstancy (ἐφημέριον).[29]

---

[28] It is worth noting that in lines 967–70, the image of the counterfeit nature is extended to the treacherous beloved. I do not consider this extension a counterexample to my claim about the precise context for the image of counterfeiting; I take it instead as part of the poet's systematic assimilation of the treacherous beloved to the *kakoi*. For this strategy (which often attributes to the beloved the vulgar promiscuity of the public sphere), see Thgn. 253–54, 599–602, 959–62, 1091–94, 1099–1104, 1243–46, 1263–66, 1311–18, 1377–80, and cf. the essays by Cobb-Stevens and Donlan in Figueira and Nagy 1985. I would suggest that Thgn. 1244 also uses imagery drawn from the domain of coinage to characterize the treacherous beloved negatively. There the speaker describes the addressee as ἦθος ἔχων δόλιον, πίστεος ἀντίτυπον ("having a tricky nature, the antitype of good faith"). As Vetta 1980: 52 notes, the adjective *antitupon* is rare and difficult; the closest parallel is Aeschylus *Seven against Thebes* 521, where Typho is described as τὸν Διὸς ἀντίτυπον. I would suggest that in both contexts, the image in *antitupos* derives from the striking of coins, where the incised pattern of the die produces its exact replica *in reverse* on the flan. Thus the "antitype" exactly corresponds to, but inverts its model: an ideal image for the beloved's deceitful imitation of the *pistis* that should properly characterize the relations of *hetairoi*. For the association of *antitupos* with coining, see LSJ, s.v. *antitupos* II.2.

[29] Cf. Ferrari 1988: 50–51; Ferrari starts from different premises but comes to very similar conclusions about the asymmetry within Theognis's text: "the corresponding bad exchange [is] the spurious return that takes place when friendly behaviour is met with the mere appearance of friendship—far harder to tell from the real thing than counterfeit gold from genuine (Thgn. 119–28; cf. 1,263). And only in the case of this sort of exchange does Theognis posit the existence of a hidden self behind the social mask. . . ." See also Levine 1984: 128–33, who notes that *basanos* and *kibdēlos* never occur in the same contexts in

Another text which reveals to us that coinage occupies a very specific place in this conceptual field of self-representation in the archaic period is a fragment of Simonides embedded in a disquisition by Plutarch :

ὁ δὲ ψευδὴς καὶ νόθος καὶ ὑπόχαλκος ὤν, ἅτε δὴ μάλιστα γιγνώσκων ἑαυτὸν ἀδικοῦντα τὴν φιλίαν ὥσπερ νόμισμα παράσημον ὑπ' αὐτοῦ γενομένην, ἔστι μὲν καὶ φύσει φθονερός, ἀλλὰ τῷ φθόνῳ χρῆται πρὸς τοὺς ὁμοίους, διαμιλλώμενος ὑπερβαλέσθαι βωμολοχίᾳ καὶ σπερμολογίᾳ, τὸν δὲ κρείττονα τρέμει καὶ δέδοικεν, οὐ μὰ Δία

παρὰ Λύδιον ἅρμα πεζὸς οἰχνεύων
ἀλλὰ
"παρὰ χρυσὸν ἐφθόν," ὥς φησι Σιμωνίδης,
"ἀκήρατον οὐδὲ μόλυβδον ἔχων."
(Plut. Mor. 65b1 [How to Tell a Flatterer from a True Friend])

[The flatterer] is false and baseborn and adulterated and, since he knows very well that he is wronging friendship by making it just like counterfeit coinage, he is also by nature envious. But he uses his envy against those who are like him, vying to surpass them in buffoonery and gossiping, while he trembles at and fears the better man, not by Zeus "going on foot beside a Lydian chariot," but, as Simonides says, "having not even lead [to set] beside purified refined gold."

In propria persona, the philosopher reflects that a flatterer is "false and baseborn and adulterated" (ὑπόχαλκος), revealing his friendship "just like counterfeit coinage" (ὥσπερ νόμισμα παράσημον) in his hostility toward true friends. The flatterer fears, Plutarch tells us, quoting Simonides, that he will be exposed "having not even lead to set beside purified refined gold." What I want to point out particularly here is the slippage in decorum between the quotation and the frame. If Simonides' phrase comes (as I assume it does) from a similar context—the discussion of a false friend within one's in-group (that is, Plutarch's "flatterer")—it is worth noting the exquisite tact Simonides exercises in speaking only in the language of metals. In contrast, Plutarch's framing text, composed at least half a millennium later, knows no such fine distinctions. In a world completely at ease with a monetary economy, counterfeit coinage becomes an available image for falsehood within any social group.[30]

---

the Theognidea, though he offers a somewhat different interpretation of the kibdēlos passages. Strikingly, the same asymmetry obtains in Plato's discussion of divine vs. mortal gold (Rep. 416e4–417b): it is only when Socrates raises the specter of contaminating divine gold with its mortal counterpart (συμμειγνύντας μιαίνειν) that coinage makes its appearance in the text (416e8–417a1).
[30] Cf. the passages cited by Volkmann 1939: 100.

Between quotation and frame, we have moved from a significant absence to a conspicuous presence.

Thus archaic elitist texts seem to construct through the imagery of metallurgy a highly charged set of associations: the pair pure gold-counterfeit coin analogizes the symposium vs. the outside and the noble self vs. duplicitous "others." But Plutarch's choice of quotations may suggest another association as well, for intriguingly, he pairs Simonides' image of purified gold with a line from Pindar that describes an Eastern luxury item, "going on foot beside a Lydian chariot" (Pindar fr. 206 SM). The philosopher's association of images here may be random (and lacking the context for both fragments, we can never be sure), but other evidence suggests a strong connection between gold and the fabulous luxury of the Lydians already in archaic and classical Greek texts. Thus Herodotus reports as the single natural "wonder" (θῶμα) of Lydia the fact that golddust is carried down from Mt. Tmolus by the River Paktolus (Hdt. 1.93; cf. 5.101.2), while the historian elsewhere lingers in fascination over the extraordinary dedications of gold (and silver) by Gyges and Kroisos at various Hellenic shrines (Hdt. 1.14, 1.50–52, 1.92).[31] Kroisos in particular figures in Herodotus's narrative as the possessor and giver of vast amounts of gold (Hdt. 1.69.3–4, 6.125).[32] In all these instances, two things seem to capture the Greek imagination: that gold can occur in a relatively pure state *in nature* and that the Lydian kings are the great controllers and purveyors of this quasi-magical natural resource.[33] The former makes gold a powerful image for the natural superiority of the Greek elite, while the latter connects it with the elitist cultivation of *habrosunē*.

We should finally note that it is not just gold itself that is strongly associated with natural occurrence and Lydian provenience. The touchstone, the *basanos*, which proofs and reveals the true quality of gold, is also a natural phenomenon with quasi-magical qualities, believed by the Greeks to occur only in Lydia. Thus, according to Theophrastos:

> The nature of the stone that tests gold is remarkable (θαυμαστή), for it seems to have the same power as fire, for that also tests gold. On that account some people are puzzled by this, but not too aptly, for the stone

---

[31] Cf. Archilochos fr. 19 W, where Gyges' epithet is πολύχρυσος ("rich in gold").

[32] I shall consider these Herodotean narratives of Kroisos's dedications and gifts in detail in Chapter 4 below.

[33] It is worth emphasizing that gold, unlike silver, can occur in a relatively pure metallic state in nature (though it is usually alloyed in different amounts with silver, copper, or iron). Silver, by contrast, almost never occurs in its pure metallic state in nature, so that the earliest uses of silver require knowledge of refining techniques for silver and lead ores. See Forbes 1964: 154–56, 165–69, 194–206; Healy 1978.

does not test in the same way. But fire [works] by changing and altering the colors, while the stone [works] by friction. For it appears to have the power to bring out the essential nature of each [metal]. . . . And all such stones are found in the River Tmolus. (Theophr. *De Lap.* 45, 47)[34]

The same association of the touchstone with Lydia is confirmed by a fragment of Bacchylides, which itself was found inscribed on a gem that may have served as a touchstone:

Λυδία μὲν γὰρ λίθος
μανύει χρυσόν, ἀνδρῶν δ᾽ ἀρετὰν σοφία τε
παγκρατής τ᾽ ἐλέγχει
ἀλάθεια. . . . (Bacch. fr. 14 SM)

For the Lydian stone reveals [the quality of] gold, but wisdom and all-conquering truth prove the virtue of men . . . [35]

This strong connection with Lydia, the center of Eastern luxury emulated by the elitist tradition, may contribute to the popularity of the image of the *basanos*, like that of refined gold, in aristocratic poetry.

We have been focusing exclusively on the construction of a ranked hierarchy of metals in texts of the elitist tradition. What of those texts that represent, in Morris's terms, an opposing "middling" tradition? In fact, we can cite no text in the middling tradition that breaks the aristocratic ban on the naming of money;[36] we may, however, find a challenge to the symbolic language of metals in a fragment of Hipponax. Hipponax was a native of Ephesus, active in the second half of the sixth century

[34] It is an ackowledged scholarly problem that Theophrastos refers here to a *river* Tmolus (otherwise unknown in antiquity), instead of a *mountain* Tmolus (as in Herodotus). In any case, his geography seems to be Lydian. For the confusion, see the commentary of Eichholz 1965: 120.

[35] For the touchstone referred to as the "Lydian stone," cf. Theophr. *De Lap.* 4; Theokr. *Id.* 12.36–37; Pliny *HN* 33.126; Pollux *Onom.* 7.102; Hesychios s.v. *basanitēs lithos*, *chrusitis lithos* (though, by Pliny's time, other sources for touchstones were known). For the inscription of Bacchylides' fragment on an ancient jewel, see Daremberg-Saglio 1, 2 p. 1548A and the edition of Snell-Maehler 1970: LII, 90 (*apparatus criticus* to fr. 14 SM).

[36] With the possible exception of (the middling) Xenophanes, who, according to Pollux (*Onom.* 9.83 = fr. 4 W), attributed the first coining of money to the Lydians. Unfortunately, we have no way or knowing what term Xenophanes used, nor in what context he would have made such a claim. We should also mention Herakleitos, who in fr. B 90 DK treats gold as a universal equivalent, not as part of a ranked hierarchy of metals. Yet I do not think Herakleitos can be easily assimilated to Morris's middling tradition (though he defends the value of civic law in frr. B 44, 114 DK). Rather he seems to stand apart from both middling and elitist traditions as outlined here, a philosophical maverick pursuing his own course. For gold as the money form in Herakleitos, and its impact on his philosophical system, see Shell 1978: 49–62; Musti 1983; Riverso 1983; Seaford 1994: 221–23.

B.C.E. Morris has recently underscored Hipponax's tendency to parody the language and forms of aristocratic *habrosunē*:

> But perhaps the most effective attack on elite pretensions came from Hipponax, who abused the delicacy, eroticism, and orientalism which Sappho and others saw as sources of social power. The dung-covered hero of fr. 92 [W] found himself in a toilet with a woman who performed an obscure act on his anus while beating his genitals with a fig branch. The fragment ends with a cloud of dung-beetles whirring out of the filth. The woman was *Lydizousa*, "speaking in a Lydian fashion;" perhaps the whole episode is so down-market that it did not even involve a real Lydian. This is classic iambic abuse, making it hard to take the *habrosynē* ideology seriously, and that was surely the point.[37]

Hipponax's preferred meter, the choliambic or "limping iambic," may offer a formal analogy to his parodistic content. For, as M. L. West suggests, the poet's indecorous metrical practices may represent a deliberate attempt to characterize an uncouth speaker: "Perhaps the curious mutation that the iambic trimeter and trochaic tetrameter have undergone in Hipponax, by which the penultimate syllable is usually long, may be understood as a deliberate crashing incorrectness emphasizing the clumsy uneducated character that is being projected; it cannot be accounted for by any ordinary genetic process."[38] In a two-line fragment preserved by Tzetzes, Hipponax prays:

ὦ Ζεῦ πάτερ <Ζεῦ> θεῶν Ὀλυμπίων πάλμυ,
τί μ' οὐκ ἔδωκας χρυσόν, ἀργύρου πάλμυν; (Hipp. fr. 38 W)

O Zeus, father Zeus, Sultan of the Olympian gods,
Why have you not given me gold, sultan of silver?[39]

---

[37] Morris 1996: 35.

[38] West 1974: 30.

[39] I have followed the text of Masson 1962 (fr. 38) against those of West 1989 and Degani 1991. Both Degani and West dagger the end of line 2 as corrupt, though Degani follows one branch of the MS tradition, printing πάλμυν, while West prefers πάλμυ. Both editors therefore assume that forms of πάλμυς have intruded into the second line from the end of the first and feel that "gold, sultan of silver" is unacceptable in sense. Masson, however, defending the reading πάλμυν, notes (1) that Hipponax frequently repeats words from one line to the next, and (2) that sense can be made of the expression: "l'or est le 'roi de l'argent', c'est-à-dire qu'il est plus précieux que l'argent" (Masson 1962: 127). Indeed, Vernant's analysis of the symbolic meaning of metals in Hesiod's myth of the races adds force and point to the expression—gold is not simply "more precious than silver," it is king over silver. Cf. Vernant 1983: 11 (with n. 41): "Silver does not possess a specific symbolic meaning of its own. It is defined in terms of gold, being like gold a precious metal, but inferior to it."

On this fragment, West comments, "The gods are approached in a spirit of base materialism, with prayers that cannot be anything but deliberately comic in their juxtaposition of solemn form and banal content. . . . (38; the effect is rather like that of Belloc's 'Would that I had three hundred thousand pounds.')"[40] I would take West's reading of incongruity still further and suggest that it has a real political point, as a challenge to the elitist hierarchy of metals. For the fragment skillfully plays on the essentialist homology between Zeus, the highest god, sovereignty, and gold: into this perfectly ranked cosmic order, the speaker intrudes with the startling concreteness of the second line. With this functionalist demand for gold, framed in his trademark indecorous choliambic, the speaker ruptures the myth of perfect identity between the noble self, sovereign power, and gold, just as the materialism of the phrase "gold, sultan of silver" questions the status of Zeus and subverts the seriousness of prayer. Most striking of all is the poet's repetition of πάλμυς, a rare Lydian loanword—and the word on which the iambic stumbles into choliambic in two lines in succession. Its occurrence at the end of the first line, in the vocative addressed to Zeus, seems slightly incongruous: it is certainly not the supreme god's normal epithet. Repeated at the end of the second line, in the accusative modifying χρυσόν, πάλμυν tips the whole prayer into bathos. For it exposes not just the *speaker's* "base materialism," but also the materialistic interests that power the aristocratic homology of divinity, sovereignty, and gold. It is, finally, no accident that this pivotal term is an Eastern loanword: by its strategic deployment, Hipponax parodies elitist aristocratic claims to power based on privileged links to the gods, the East, and the reigning hierarchy of metals.

II. METALS AND OTHERS IN HERODOTUS

At this point, having sketched out an archaic aristocratic model poised between Hesiod and Aristotle and one possible "middling" response to it, I would like to turn to Herodotus. For Herodotus, at least in part, seems to incorporate the traditional aristocratic system, appropriating metals and coinage as signifiers within a moral discourse based on essentialism. Yet, while the text of Herodotus exploits the signifying value of the language of metals, the narrator tends to maintain an ironic distance from his characters' metallic forays. This Herodotean irony makes the histor difficult to place along the ideological spectrum we have traced out: his position shifts and wavers with different anecdotes and narratives. I would like to conclude this survey of the language of metals with three

---

[40] West 1974: 29.

densely coded episodes of Herodotus, where different permutations of the system serve to characterize and contrast three sets of non-Greek "others."

1. On numerous occasions, we find Hesiodic metals inscribed in Herodotus's text. Perhaps the most elaborate and unproblematic version of the Hesiodic myth of the races figures in Herodotus's tale of the burning gold of the Scythians. Herodotus recounts the Scythians' own version of their origin from three brothers: "[They say that] from some such descent Targitaos came, and that three sons were born from this one [Targitaos], Lipoxais and Arpoxais and the youngest Kolaxais. And when these were ruling, golden objects borne from heaven—a plow and a yoke, an axe, and a libation-bowl (φιάλην)—fell into the Scythian land, and that the eldest, having seen them first, rushed right out wishing to get them, but the gold burnt him as he approached it. And when this one had withdrawn, the second brother approached, and the same thing happened to him. These two indeed the gold thrust away by burning, but for the youngest coming up it was quenched, and that one conveyed it back to his own house. And the older brothers, yielding to these things, rendered the entire kingship (τὴν βασιληίην πᾶσαν) to the youngest." (Hdt. 4.5.2–4).

These gold objects fallen from heaven are precisely Louis Gernet's *agalmata*, charged with numinous and otherworldly value.[41] But they also represent Dumézil's three functions—the plow and yoke correspond to the agricultural function, the axe to the warrior function, and the phiale to the first function, kingship and religion.[42] We recall that in Dumézil's system the king himself embodies all three functions—and this is figured here in the language of metals by the fact that *all* the objects are made of gold.[43] In the redundant signifying system of this narrative, their heavenly origin, their substance, and their powerful effects mark these objects as talismans or tokens of legitimate kingship, and the two older brothers wisely recognize them as such. As part of the same system, Herodotus tells us later that the Scythian kings are buried with "libation bowls of gold; they use no silver or bronze" (4.71), and they have no slaves "bought with silver" in attendance (4.72).

2. In line with this same Hesiodic paradigm, gold often carries with it its traditional associations with justice and sovereignty, signalling the "mettle" of its owner or giver. Thus, for example, Kroisos dedicates at

---

[41] Gernet 1981a: 73–111.

[42] Benveniste 1938; Dumézil 1979: 169–211. Both Benveniste and Dumézil consider this narrative in isolation as a relic of authentic Scythian myth. The reading proposed here does not reject that attribution; it simply wishes to consider the code of metals in this narrative as it forms part of the larger signifying structure of Herodotus's text (cf. the methodological remarks of Hartog 1988: 3–11).

[43] Thus Dumézil 1979: 175.

Delphi "a statue of a lion made of refined gold," weighing 10 talents
(Hdt. 1.50.3). As archaeologists and numismatists have made abundantly
clear, the lion is the symbol of the Lydian royal house, so that the statue
of refined gold represents Kroisos himself as he wishes to appear to the
Greeks at the Panhellenic shrine of Delphi.[44] He is the perfectly just,
lawful king. In light of this identification, it is worth noticing Herodotus's
coda to this dedicatory narrative: "This lion," he tells us, "when the
temple at Delphi burnt down, fell off its base . . . and now lies in the
treasury of the Corinthians, weighing 6½ talents; for there were melted
from it 3½ talents." We might read the collapse and melting of the lion
in the fire at Delphi as symbolic of Kroisos's own fall and loss of substance,
foretold by the Delphic oracle and chronicled by Herodotus in the course
of Book 1.

Yet here already, Herodotus's narrative doubles its message. The precise
quantification of weight strikes a false note within the Hesiodic framework, calibrating the distance between the Lydian king and the noble
savagery of the uncomplicated Scythians. Thus the repeated calculation
of the exact weight of the lion subtly subverts its symbolic representation,
exposing Kroisos's obsession with counting as a failure within the terms
of the "pure" aristocratic paradigm. We remember that the Lydians are
the "first to mint and use gold and silver coinage and the first retail
traders (kapēloi)" (Hdt. 1.94), and that Kroisos himself naively equates
"blessedness" (olbos) with quantifiable riches in his famous encounter
with Solon (Hdt. 1.30–33).[45]

3. With another Herodotean narrative, we move from the symbolic
value of Hesiodic agalmata to the archaic obsession with the testing and
refining of gold. The debate by Xerxes and his advisors about whether
or not to invade Greece provides an extended example of this archaic
aristocratic paradigm in the historian's text:

Μαρδόνιος μὲν τοσαῦτα ἐπιλεήνας τὴν Ξέρξεω γνώμην ἐπέπαυτο·
σιωπώντων δὲ τῶν ἄλλων Περσέων καὶ οὐ τολμώντων γνώμην
ἀποδείκνυσθαι ἀντίην τῇ προκειμένῃ, Ἀρτάβανος ὁ Ὑστάσπεος, πάτρως
ἐὼν Ξέρξῃ, τῷ δὴ καὶ πίσυνος ἐὼν ἔλεγε τάδε· Ὦ βασιλεῦ, μὴ λεχθεισέων
μὲν γνωμέων ἀντιέων ἀλλήλῃσι οὐκ ἔστι τὴν ἀμείνω αἱρεόμενον ἑλέσθαι,
ἀλλὰ δεῖ τῇ εἰρημένῃ χρᾶσθαι, λεχθεισέων δὲ ἔστι, ὥσπερ τὸν χρυσὸν τὸν
ἀκήρατον αὐτὸν μὲν ἐπ' ἑωυτοῦ οὐ διαγινώσκομεν, ἐπεὰν δὲ
παρατρίψωμεν ἄλλῳ χρυσῷ, διαγινώσκομεν τὸν ἀμείνω. (Hdt. 7.10.1)

---

[44] See Pedley 1968: 72; Kraay 1976: 23–25; Hanfmann 1983: 6, 95; Wallace 1988:
203–7; Markoe 1989: 103.
[45] On the opposition of Scythians and Lydians, see Stambler 1982: 215–17; Redfield
1985: 109–12. On the eastern penchant for counting and quantification, cf. Konstan 1987b
and see discussions about Darius and Kroisos below (Chs. 2 and 4).

Mardonius, saying so many things to gloze over the opinion of Xerxes, made an end. And while the other Persians were silent and were not daring to reveal an opinion opposed to the one put forth, Artabanus the son of Hystaspes, being paternal uncle to Xerxes and trusting indeed to that, said, "O King, if opinions opposed to each other are not spoken, it is not possible for a man choosing to get the better one, but he must use the one spoken, but if [opposing opinions] have been spoken, it *is* possible [to choose the better], just as we do not recognize purified gold itself against itself, but whenever we rub it against other gold, we recognize the better."

Herodotus's Persian grandees here speak the language of Greek didactic poetry. We recognize the setting as a closed in-group of aristocratic *hetairoi*, and even the word translated as "opinion" (γνώμη) serves as a technical term in Theognis and elsewhere for the teachings of didactic poetry.[46] In this closed aristocratic setting, Artabanus invokes the language of metals to represent one piece of advice as "refined gold." Indeed, the only deviation from the aristocratic didactic topos we have observed is that Artabanus does not speak of gold and lead, but only of better and worse gold. This crucial change I take to be his tactful concession to the performance context, in which Mardonius's advice cannot be called *bad*, but only *worse* than someone else's. Nonetheless, it is worth noting the elitist essentialism that informs the grandee's discourse: everything depends on the quality of the opinion, spoken, as in Pindar, from an "upright mind," and the finest gold represents the truth, consistency, and timelessness of the best advice.

But into this aristocratic milieu, Herodotus has again introduced a false note in the narrative voice, subverting the metallic purity to which the speakers lay claim. In characterizing Mardonius's support for Xerxes' opinion, Herodotus uses the strange verb ἐπιλεαίνω, "to smooth or gloze over" (a Herodotean *hapax*). The verb conjures up the image of a flawed interior concealed by a prettified surface—in fact, it marks the *gnōmē* of Xerxes and Mardonius as a counterfeit.[47] And by the strategic use of this verb, the narrator marks his own ironic distance from the Persian *hetaireia*.

In all these narratives, metals function as a gauge of the culture and civility, honesty and calculation of "others" in Herodotus's ethnography. The "hard" and uncomplicated Scythians maintain the pure affinity between talismanic gold and kingship, while the Lydian king Kroisos (at the "soft" end of the spectrum) incongruously links the symbolism of

---

[46] Especially in the plural *gnōmai*; cf. Thgn. 60, 717; Herakleitos fr. B 78 DK; Soph. *Ajax* 1091.

[47] For a similar play on ἐπί in a context of figurative counterfeiting, cf. Demokritos fr. B 63 DK.

gold with the precise calculations of the *kapēlos*.[48] Finally, the Persians, enervated by two generations of luxury, prettify and counterfeit the integrity of aristocratic *gnōmai* at the precise moment that they make the fateful decision to invade Greece. Yet it is not enough, I think, to read Herodotus's use of the language of metals simply as a tool of his ethnographic characterization of "others." Given the ideological contestations around this symbolic system within the Greek community (which we have explored in the first section of this chapter), the permutations of the language of metals must have implications for "self" as well as "others"—for the Greeks who are the main sources and intended audience of Herodotus' *Histories*. It is to the functions of this symbolic system in the Greek imaginary that we turn in Chapter 2.

[48] For the workings of the anthropological distinction of "hard" and "soft" cultures in Herodotus, see Redfield 1985.

Tyrants and Transgression: Darius and Amasis

THE *HETAIREIA* OF XERXES (with which we ended Chapter 1) should give us pause, for it suggests that even when the narrative is explicitly about "others," it is in some sense also about the "same"—the Greeks who are both producers and consumers of Herodotus's logoi. This is not simply because the Greeks can only imagine the "other" in terms of categories they know ("The Great King's council is *like* a group of aristocratic *hetairoi*"), but also because, whatever tales Greeks tell, it is the tensions and contestations of fifth-century polis society that are played out through them, even if only by a dream logic of compression, condensation, and inversion. Or, if we prefer to put it in terms of Herodotus as author of his text (rather than of the insurgence of the Greek "political uncon- scious"), we might say that, like those of every historian, Herodotus's perception and representation of key issues are shaped by the prevailing concerns of his era. Thus Herodotus cannot fail to see struggles *like* the struggles in the polis as the motor of events, even when his gaze is fixed on Lydians or Persians or Egyptians. This is a truism when it comes to the level of Greek foreign policy: Herodotus's narrative is shaped by the overarching conflict of Greeks and barbarians, which (depending on the dating of Herodotus's text) may also be read as an allegory for Athenian imperialism.[1] But this kind of reading rarely allows for the internal politics of the Greek city as a shaping influence on Herodotus's narrative: it is this level that I wish to explore. And indeed, we can often detect the civic subtext of his narrative by the sudden efflorescence and clustering of terms that belong to the aristocratic symposium or the public sphere of the Greek city.

This is thus an attempt to read the political significance of the "embod- ied" discourses of story, legend, and anecdote. For readers of Herodotus still tend to split along disciplinary lines: traditional historians attempt to recuperate the "real" bits, while literary scholars focus on formal

---

[1] Thus Fornara 1971b: 75–91; Raaflaub 1987. Though I regard Fornara's dating of the *Histories* as too low (for the reasons stated in the Introduction, n. 6), many of Fornara's and Raaflaub's particular readings of Herodotus's text as implicitly anti-Athenian Empire seem to hold nonetheless (as Cobet 1977: 25–27 notes). Thus, my reading is intended not to replace, but to supplement theirs.

features or anecdotes read as fiction.[2] The attempts of François Hartog and other structuralists to fuse the two methods to produce insights into what they call the Greek "cultural imaginary" have partly healed this rift, but they, in turn, produce accounts that assume a unitary, perfectly homogenized Greek *mentalité*.[3] And yet, given Herodotus's oral sources and multiple informants, we should be able to find in his text traces of the conflicts played out *within* the different elements of the Greek city. In this chapter and those that follow, I attempt to break down the boundary between literary and historical approaches to Herodotus, taking the pattern-making literary readings and teasing out their political and ideological implications. Such a style of reading is predicated on the perception of Herodotus's text as a remarkable point of confluence, which accommodates both older, oral traditions of encoding ideology in narrative and newer, more explicit political theorizing.[4] These two forms coexist in Herodotus's rich, uneven account. Thus I start from a set of anecdotes generally regarded as "pure fiction" and analyze how they might provide insights into sixth- and fifth-century conflicts within the Greek city.

Nowhere is this confluence of different discursive forms more conspicuous in Herodotus's text than around the issue of despotic power—ranging from the astonishing array of stories about kings and tyrants to the articulated theory of the Persian "constitutional debate." As Hartog has observed, power—royal and tyrannic—is a central preoccupation of the *Histories*, where, he finally concludes, the two forms are identical. The barbarian king (whose epitome is the "Great King" of Persia) and the Greek tyrant confront and mirror each other, in a reciprocal play that allows Herodotus to think the nature of power:

> To verify the proposition that kings are barbarian, that is to say, that they have something in common with the Great King, we need to investigate the nature of his power. But if such an investigation is to prove illuminating, we are bound to introduce another figure: the tyrant. He is very much present in the Histories and, as I see it, the King and the tyrant are two of a kind.

---

[2] For examples of traditional historical treatments of Herodotus in this vein, see Waters 1971, 1985; MacGinnis 1986; Pritchett 1993; for literary scholars tracing out formal patterns, see Benardete 1969; Dewald 1981, 1993; Flory 1987; Erbse 1992.

[3] For examples of structuralist readings, see Rosellini and Saïd 1978; Redfield 1985; Hartog 1988; Steiner 1994.

[4] This confluence may be the result of Herodotus's location on the cusp between a culture that is still predominantly oral and the beginnings of literacy: see S. West 1985; Hartog 1988: 273–89; Thomas 1989: 284–86. On the need for "embodied" or "incorporated" forms of symbolic power in cultures where institutionalized structures (like writing and literate education) are lacking, see Havelock 1952, 1963; Bourdieu 1990: 122–34; on Herodotus's "concrete" style of political thought, see Raaflaub 1987; Saxonhouse 1996: 36–57.

Each provides a mirror image for the other. The image of tyrannical power is thus fashioned in relation to royal power, and the image of royal power is constituted in relation to tyrannical power. At the intersection of these two images the representation of despotic power is constructed.[5]

Thus far I would agree with Hartog, and, in the following chapters, I wish to trace out the civic implications of Herodotus's portraits of various dynasts—Darius, Amasis, Polykrates, and Kroisos—all read as versions or allegories of Greek tyrannic power. But I cannot entirely concur with Hartog's assessment of the representation of tyrannic power in Herodotus:

> Monarchy necessarily means tyranny, and the portrait that he draws of the monarch is none other than that of the tyrant. The tyrant is himself defined as the reverse of the isonomic regime. He gives no account of his actions, puts people to death without judgment, does not respect the customs of the ancestors, violates women, surrounds himself with the worst people while getting rid of the best, and so forth. This is the original portrait of the tyrant, the one repeated by tradition right down to Aristotle.[6]

This portrait of the tyrant as master of *hubris* and destroyer of *nomos* (which Herodotus certainly offers us) is the prevailing fifth- and fourth-century view, but I would contend that it is itself the result of a struggle over the construction of tyrannic power in the archaic period. For there are also remnants in Herodotus (as elsewhere) of a competing portrait of the tyrant as champion of egalitarian justice and opponent of aristocratic overreaching. Others have noted the unevenness of Herodotus's tyrannic representations: James McGlew has recently teased out the traces of a representation of the tyrant as *euthuntēr*, "straightener," the bringer of justice and law, while Karen Bassi has noted the profound ambivalence inscribed in the Athenian traditions around Peisistratos.[7] What I would like to add to this complex of issues is a consideration of the tyrant as

---

[5] Hartog 1988: 324–25. This equation of barbarian king and Greek tyrant is confirmed by Arist. *Pol.* 1285a, 1295a; for more on Herodotus's usage of the terms *basileus*, *turannos*, and *mounarchos*, see Ferrill 1978.

[6] Hartog 1988: 325–26. For similar assessments of tyranny in Herodotus, see Schmitt-Pantel 1979; Gammie 1986; Lateiner 1989: 163–86; for arguments that Herodotus is more positively disposed toward tyranny, see Flory 1987: 119–49. Waters 1971, 1985 contends that Herodotus has no bias whatsoever when it comes to kings and tyrants; he is simply reporting "the facts."

[7] McGlew 1993: 61–86; Bassi 1998: 144–91. Cf. Nagy 1985: 42–46 (on Theognis); 1990b: 274–313. McGlew 1993: 72, for example, notes that, although Herodotus generally represents the Corinthian tyrant Periander extremely negatively, he still preserves the tradition that Periander acted as mediator between Athens and Mytilene over the contested territory of Sigeum (Hdt. 5.95).

coiner, since the link between tyranny and coinage seems to haunt the Greek tradition in odd and insidious ways.[8] These traditions may perhaps derive from the fact that, in some cities at least, tyrants may have been instrumental in the introduction and early spread of coinage. Thus in Athens, numismatic and historical evidence locates the earliest coinage squarely within the reign of Peisistratos, where the institution of *nomisma* is very much of a piece with the tyrant's efforts to foster civic community and counter elite dominance.[9] And yet, no single literary text links Peisistratos with the introduction of coinage. This odd scattershot pattern, by which coinage is invisible at the center, but tyrannic coiners proliferate at the margins, invites us to look more closely. But, in order to register all the conflicts and permutations of the tyrant as coiner, we must widen the field to consider barbarian kings as allegories of Greek tyrants *and* to read the ideological struggles of coinage behind the language of metals. Thus we must read through a double screen—of "other" for "self" and metals for money.

I. DARIUS AND THE DARIC

In all the *Histories*, there are only three individuals who are said to coin money: the Great King Darius, his satrap Aryandes (4.166), and the Samian tyrant Polykrates (3.56).[10] In this chapter and those that follow, I consider the two coining dynasts, Darius and Polykrates, in each case paired with another Herodotean ruler who forms their inverse or complement. In the narratives of Darius and Amasis, the language of metals intersects in complex ways with Herodotus's preoccupation with forms

---

[8] The association of tyrants or rulers with coinage is made in the cases of Pheidon king of Argos (*Marmor Parium* lines 45–47; Ephoros *FGrH* 70 F 115, F 176; *Et. Mag.* s.v. *obeliskos*; Pollux *Onom.* 9.83); the Phrygian king Midas's Kymaian wife (Arist. fr. 611.37 Rose); Hippias of Athens ([Arist.] *Oik.* 2.1347a); Polykrates of Samos (Hdt. 3.56). We should also note that the first mention of coinage in a Greek text (Alkaios fr. 69 V) links the "staters of the Lydians" to the "cunning-minded fox" who is presumably the tyrant Pittakos. On the association of tyranny and coinage, cf. Farenga 1985; Seaford 1994: 220–32; Steiner 1994: 159–66; von Reden 1997: 170–74.

[9] For the chronology of early Athenian coinage, see Kraay 1956, 1976: 56–63; Kroll and Waggoner 1984. For Peisistratos's attempts to promote civic consciousness and community feeling while breaking the power of aristocratic patronage (including massive public building programs, promotion of civic cults, establishment of circuit judges, loans to small farmers, etc.), see Andrewes 1956: 108–14; Frost 1985; Ober 1989: 66–67; Shapiro 1989; Stein-Hölkeskamp 1989: 145–53; Hölscher 1991: 362–68.

[10] These passages represent two of the three total occurrences of the term *nomisma* meaning "coinage" in Herodotus's text; its third occurrence is 1.94 (Herodotus's ethnography of the Lydians), where no particular individual is associated with the "first coining of gold and silver."

of tyrannic power; while Polykrates and Kroisos both act and react within a dominant paradigm of gift exchange. Let us first consider Darius, who aspires to leave behind a unique memorial, as Herodotus tells us:

> But this was the Aryandes who was appointed governor of Egypt by Kambyses, who at a later time perished when he tried to make himself equal to Darius (παρισούμενος Δαρείῳ διεφθάρη). For, having learned and seen that Darius was eager to leave behind as his monument this which had been accomplished by no other king, he was imitating this one (ἐμμέετο τοῦτον) until he got his wages. For Darius, having refined gold so that it was as pure as possible, had coins struck, but Aryandes, as ruler of Egypt, was making this same quality silver coinage. For even now, the purest silver coinage is the Aryandic. But when Darius learned that he was doing these things, he brought another charge against him—that he was rebelling—and killed him. (Hdt. 4.166)

Many historians and numismatists have expressed doubt that there is any truth to this story, since no coinage of Aryandes survives, and otherwise, we know of no coinage produced in Egypt before the fourth century B.C.E.[11] By its very gratuitousness, then, this anecdote raises intriguing questions. Why should the Greeks tell such a story about the Great King? In our terms, this narrative functions in complex ways within the archaic language of metals. By this little drama, Herodotus's text exposes the uncomfortable fit between the two superimposed systems we analyzed in the last chapter, for Darius's actions signify completely different things in the Hesiodic and aristocratic registers. Within the Hesiodic paradigm, which is also the pole of essentialism, it is clear that the quality of the metal, the *substance* of which the coin is made, is of profound importance. Refined gold signifies Darius' own rightful sovereignty, while Aryandes' silver imitation precisely reenacts the originary *hubris* of the silver race. (Recall that in Vernant's analysis of Hesiod, both gold and silver races embody the first function, kingship, but in the opposing terms of justice and *hubris*. The silver race, after all, was destroyed by the gods because "they were not able to restrain violent *hubris* from each other" [*W&D* 134–35]). So here, the logic of the Hesiodic myth makes Darius's conclusion eminently comprehensible: Aryandes' silver coinage is immediately construed by Darius (and by our narrator) as a violent, unlawful bid for sovereignty—as an act of insurrection.

But Darius's actions and interpretations in this passage expose the seams, the somewhat uneasy fit between the Hesiodic paradigm and its elitist appropriation. In the first place, gold for Darius signifies kingship

---

[11] J. M. Cook 1983: 64, 240n. 23; Howgego 1995: 46–47. For an extended exposition of other theories and final affirmation of Herodotus's version of events, see Tuplin 1989.

pure and simple, rather than general aristocratic quality. In the second place (and this follows from the first), the king himself may be always the same (*homoios*), but he is decisively *different* from everyone else. In these terms Aryandes' crime is that he aspires to be like the king (notice especially παρισούμενος and ἐμμέετο). One way of explaining this rift is to say that it represents the difference between Greek and barbarian, between polis society and oriental despotism. But I am reluctant to leave it at that, because, as I have suggested, all Eastern monarchs in Herodotus serve a double function—they represent the Other, but they simultaneously furnish Herodotus and his audience with paradigms for conceptualizing the modalities of Greek tyranny.

Insofar as we can "read" Herodotus's Persians as Greeks, then, Darius's act of reconstituting the Hesiodic paradigm becomes explicable as the strategy of an aristocratic *homoios* who becomes a tyrant. That is, we can understand the narrative of the Persian conspiracy against the Magi as an oligarchic coup which is then manipulated by one member of the *hetaireia* to establish his own monarchic rule. For Herodotus's conspirators bear an uncanny resemblance to a Greek aristocratic *hetaireia*, which defines itself as a "band of the same." We are told that Otanes, who originated the plot, is "like to the first of the Persians in descent and property" (γένει δὲ καὶ χρήμασι ὅμοιος τῷ πρώτῳ Περσέων, 3.68.1), and that each of the original three "added as *hetairos* that man among the Persians whom he most trusted" (καὶ ἔδοξέ σφι ἕκαστον ἄνδρα Περσέων προσεταιρίσασθαι τοῦτον ὅτεῳ πιστεύει μάλιστα, 3.70.2). With the verb προσεταιρίζεσθαι and the concept of *pistis*, we are squarely in the semantic sphere of the *hetaireia*.[12]

The odd man out, the seventh who adds himself to the *hetaireia* is Darius, and Otanes is careful to underscore his sameness by traditional praise of his aristocratic lineage: "O child of Hystaspes, you are from a good father and you are likely to reveal yourself (ἐκφαίνειν . . . σεωυτόν) as no less than your father" (3.71.3). This articulation of genealogical sameness functions in context as an admonition to the headstrong Darius to be more like his fellow conspirators. But it is precisely difference,

---

[12] Note that the only other occurrence of προσεταιρίζομαι in the *Histories* refers to Kleisthenes' "making the demos his *hetairos*" in preparation for the institution of his reforms (Hdt. 5.66). On its significance in that context, see Ober 1993 (with earlier bibliography). Murray 1987: 111–14, following Reinhardt 1960, regards the narrative of the seven conspirators as a Persian oral tradition, deriving from elements in the high Persian aristocracy opposed to the official monarchic account. Like Gould (1989: 138–39n. 7), I am skeptical of the possibility of distinguishing Greek from Persian oral traditions, but even if we accept Murray's model, I think it likely that his "Persian aristocratic tradition" would appeal most to a Greek aristocratic or oligarchic position, and translate most comfortably into a narrative of the *hetaireia*.

rather than sameness, to which Darius aspires. Once he achieves the distinction of royal power, therefore, he reverts to the Hesiodic ranking of metals, investing his monarchy with legitimacy by aligning it with gold, while demoting his former aristocratic *homoioi* and identifying their actions with *hubris*.[13]

But even as the tyrant struggles to disentangle the two paradigms—to authorize a single interpretation and reestablish the Hesiodic golden age— the aristocratic discourse in which he is enmeshed (the narrative of the *hetaireia*) takes its revenge on him. For we have been focusing exclusively on the metals and their quality in this narrative—we must now consider the signifying value of coinage in the aristocratic register. Darius is the only character in the *Histories* who wishes to leave *coinage* behind as his monument. The formula μνημόσυνον (-α) λιπέσθαι in Herodotus usually denominates a physical monument of impressive proportions (1.185.1, 1.186.1, 2.110.1, 2.121.1, 2.148.1, 4.81.6, 7.24), an extraordinary deed (6.109.3, cf. 7.220.2), or even a brilliant or courageous saying (7.227, cf. 4.144.1–2). In contrast, Darius's ambition to make a monument of coinage gives new meaning to the functionalist or symbolic aspect of currency, while it participates in Herodotus's scathing portrait of "Darius *kapēlos*." This characterization occurs as the prelude to a lengthy account of the tribute paid by all the Persian satrapies:

> At the time of Kyros's rule and again of Kambyses', there was nothing established concerning tribute (φόρου), but they used to bring gifts (δῶρα). And on account of this assignment of tribute and other things very similar to this, the Persians say that Darius was a petty trader (κάπηλος), Kambyses a master (δεσπότης), and Kyros a father (πατήρ), because the first used to run everything like a shop (ἐκαπήλευε), the second was hard and insolent, but the third [was] gentle and contrived all good things for them. (Hdt. 3.89.3).

[13] Darius thus faces the same problem as did the first king of the Medes, Deiokes, as Herodotus describes it (Hdt. 1.96–100)—he must decisively differentiate himself from the aristocrats who were once his peers. Deiokes accomplishes this by becoming invisible— he withdraws into the innermost ring of the seven concentric circles of Ekbatana and communicates only by writing (on this strategy, see Shell 1978: 17–19, Steiner 1994: 130–32). Darius's coinage is the analogue of Deiokes' seven-tiered stronghold (and it is no accident that the two innermost circles of Ekbatana are painted silver and gold)—the king's body becomes invisible, while his seal engraved on the purest gold affirms the propriety of his rule throughout the land. In these terms, it becomes clear why Darius cannot tolerate any other coiner of the purest metal—as the narrative tells us explicitly, such activity is an attempt to "make oneself equal to" the king (*parisoumenos*). In contrast to *parisoumenos*, Deiokes' rules of royal invisibility have as their aim "that he seem to be different in kind (*heteroios*) to the men who could not see him" (Hdt. 1.99). For a similar play of sameness and difference between a new ruler and those he rules, see Arist. *Pol.* 1259b6–9 (citing Amasis as an example).

Scholars of the Achaemenid Empire have pointed out that Herodotus's summary is overly schematic and misleading: it is likely that there was "tribute" before Darius (based on much older Near Eastern systems of royal redistribution), and that "gifts" continued to be part of the system under Darius I and long after.[14] Indeed, Heleen Sancisi-Weerdenburg has speculated that Herodotus's portrait of Kyros *patēr* and Darius *kapēlos* has more to do with Greek conceptions than Persian realities.[15] So, the question is, What is the appeal of this schematic system to Herodotus and his Greek audience? I suggest that the contrast of Kyros and Darius allows Greek aristocrats to play out an ideologically charged conflict of exchange systems—gifting vs. monetary exchange, the father vs. the huckster.

In order to understand this schema, we need to contextualize both terms: what does *kapēlos* mean to Herodotus's Greek audience? And what are the contrasting features of Kyros *patēr*? In normal Greek usage, a *kapēlos* is a small-time retailer, a shopkeeper or middleman who profits by his mediating function. *Kapēlos* itself has no Greek etymology: it is, perhaps, a Lydian loanword that first occurs in Hipponax.[16] Indeed, I would suggest that the term comes to the Greeks from the East together with the concept of coinage and remains closely associated with it. Thus here, as in the account of the customs of the Lydians (Hdt. 1.94), *kapēleia*

---

[14] See Descat, Sancisi-Weerdenburg, and Zaccagnini in Briant and Herrenschmidt 1989; Howgego 1995: 46. On one occasion, Herodotus's own text suggests that "tribute" pre-existed Darius's organization of empire: see 3.67.3 (the false Smerdis gives the entire empire a three-year reprieve from "tribute" [*phoros*]).

[15] Sancisi-Weerdenburg 1989: 129–31: "But such a sharp contrast between two different systems should arouse suspicion. In its literal form, these two sentences might well say more about the Greek vision of the Persian empire current in the time of Herodotus, in which the reign of Cyrus was invariably seen as 'the good old time' when monarchic rule was still justified by so-called fatherly behaviour and the benevolent image of the king was contrasted with the later period when the empire gradually transformed into a political system where all the power rested with the king and the subjects were little more than slaves with no alternatives but to obey and pay taxes." (p. 130).

[16] Hipponax fr. 79 W, line 18 (in the verbal form καπηλεύει). On the normal meaning of *kapēlos*, see Hasebroek 1933: 1–14, Finley 1935, Smith 1989. On its etymology, Chantraine 1968–80: 494; Smith 1989: 210n.20 (suggesting that the term is borrowed from the Lydians). Smith (211) wants to argue for an exceptional meaning in Herodotus, where, he contends, *kapēlos* cannot mean "petty retailer," largely because of the scale of the transactions involved (in, e.g., 1.94, and 3.117). I am opposed to Smith's thesis on two grounds: (1) it seems methodologically dubious to claim that Herodotus gives a special meaning to a common Greek word—we must first try to make sense of his usage within the normal meaning of the term, and (2) as I shall argue, Herodotus's portrait of Darius repeatedly plays on precisely the kind of incongruity of scale to which Smith objects. That is, we can understand this vertiginous shifting of scale not as proof that the word must have a different meaning, but rather as a conscious stylistic device through which Herodotus characterizes and travesties the Great King.

is associated with the practices of a money economy. In this opposition, Kyros "the father," giver of all good things and receiver of gifts, stands as an emblem of proper aristocratic gift exchange, the willing and reciprocal exchange of goods and benefactions which operates on the household rather than the civic model. The introduction of money and accounting into the system inevitably transforms the empire into a shop and Darius into a petty trader, a middleman who produces nothing, but profits from the labor of others—that is to say, the ultimate figure of a disembedded economy.[17] In this stark contrast we trace not the reality of gift vs. commodity exchange, but the lineaments of Greek aristocratic ideology, which valorizes gift exchange between households and reduces the public sphere, the domain of money, to shopkeeping. Rather than acknowledge an alternative civic authority (whose site is the agora and whose token is coinage), this elitist mystification makes coinage simply an instrument of trade and the triumph of the short-term transactional order.[18] Within this framework, Darius's aspiration to leave behind coinage as his monument belittles the Great King, exposing him as a money-grubbing small trader.

But we have not yet exhausted the field of associations of *kapēleia* within elitist discourse. Beyond the pragmatic reasons for Darius's sobriquet—the fact that he organized the Persian empire into taxpaying satrapies—the designation *kapēlos* participates in a moral system. Once again, Herodotus's Kyros, that fantasy figure of noble gift exchange, gives us our cue. In the context of Kyros's conquest of Ionia, Herodotus narrates an exchange between a Spartan emissary and the Persian king. The Spartan Lakrines comes to Sardis to inform Kyros of the *rhēsis* of the Lakedaimonians: do not harm any city of the Greek land, since the Spartans will not overlook it (Hdt. 1.152). Herodotus has Kyros respond: "I have never yet feared such men, for whom there is a place appointed in the middle of the city for them to come together and deceive each other on oath"

---

[17] On *kapēlos* as a morally negative evaluation within the Persian system, see J. M. Cook 1983: 75–76: "Apologists of Darius . . . have seen in this remark a testimonial to his good management. But the Persian nobles were brought up in a tradition that eschewed buying and selling. The implication is that Darius was not the mirror of Aryan chivalry." The same might be said for the attitude of *Greek* nobles, so that Cook's remarks may serve as a good corrective to the rosy picture painted (e.g.) by Gammie 1986: 182 and Flory 1987: 134–35: "like Deioces and Pisistratus, Darius plots deviously to gain this throne, but once in power he rules as well and honestly as he can. His first official acts as king . . . are to divide the country into easily governable satrapies and to arrange for the orderly payment of taxes."

[18] It is a historical irony that this aristocratic mystification has been read as literal truth by certain modern scholars, who invoke Hdt. 1.94 to prove that coinage was invented by the Greeks to facilitate trade (see the scholars critiqued by Kraay 1964; more recently, see T. Martin 1985: 214–15).

(τοῖσί ἐστι χῶρος ἐν μέσῃ τῇ πόλι ἀποδεδεγμένος ἐς τὸν συλλεγόμενοι ἀλλήλους ὀμνύντες ἐξαπατῶσι. Hdt. 1.153.1). Herodotus explains that this gibe is aimed at "all the Greeks, because, having set up agoras, they practice buying and selling" (ὅτι ἀγορὰς στησάμενοι ὠνῇ τε καὶ πρήσι χρέωνται, Hdt. 1.153.2).[19] Kyros's characterization of trade, "deceiving each other on oath," has the pithiness and point of a saying. A very similar apophthegm is put into the mouth of another barbarian, the Scythian Anacharsis. According to Diogenes Laertius, Anacharsis "defined the agora as a place for deceiving each other and claiming more than one's share" (τὴν ἀγορὰν ὡρισμένον ἔφη τόπον εἰς τὸ ἀλλήλους ἀπατᾶν καὶ πλεονεκτεῖν, D.L. 1.105). The remarkable similarity of these two gibes, recorded six centuries apart, attests to the enduring power of the equation of trade with deceit. Both sayings participate in the tradition of the sage foreign observer offering wry commentary on Greek practices.[20] But of course Anacharsis, like Herodotus's Persians, spoke Greek. That is to say, both Kyros and Anacharsis (as they are represented in the biographical tradition) are the creations of Greeks, and they express Greek sentiments (or the idealization thereof) for a Greek audience.[21]

Whose opinions, then, are these wise foreigners voicing? The scorn expressed for what goes on in the agora corresponds to the scorn of the

[19] As the mouthpiece for this position, Kyros emblematizes by contrast the positive mode of gift exchange between individuals. As the noble king who can engage in "pure" gift exchange unfettered by the constraints of the polis, Kyros has an enduring appeal for Greek aristocratic ideology. Thus, in Xenophon's *Kyropaideia*, he is the perfect Greek *kalos k' agathos*, who achieves world empire by tactical skill and maintains it by his deployment of gift exchange. It is no accident that Xenophon's portrait is predicated on the Greek fantasy of the Persian "free agora," from which (as Xenophon explains) "market wares, hucksters (*hoi agoraioi*), their cries, and their vulgarities" are all banned (*Kyrop.* 1.2.3; cf. Arist. *Pol.* 1331a30–b15). In this constitutive moment of the noble Persian education, just as in Hdt. 1.153, we see a reflection of aristocratic hostility to the symbolic geography of the polis.

[20] For a discussion of this tradition in Greek literary sources, see Kindstrand 1981: 59–61; Romm 1992: 45–81, 1996; Martin 1996.

[21] Thus, Aly 1921: 54 sees in the Kyros episode not the reality of Persian customs, but certain topoi of Greek poetry and tradition. He notes that Kyros's immediately following lines, "You will be talking not of the sufferings of the Ionians, but of your own," are a near quotation of a verse of Archilochos. On Anacharsis, see Kindstrand 1981: 17: "As we have already seen . . . the historical character of Anacharsis is extremely doubtful. It would therefore be naive merely to accept the ancient tradition of a Scythian, who came to Greece for more or less private reasons, and became famous for his wisdom, as the ultimate reason for a later more legendary development . . . . As most traits in the legend of Anacharsis evolved in Greece, the Scythians having no knowledge of him, we must look for such information and ideological attitudes on the part of the Greeks, which could have invented and further developed this legend." Kindstrand would like to see much of Anacharsis's criticism of Greek customs as the invention of the archaic period. He includes Anacharsis's definition of the agora, which he compares with Hdt. 1.153 (pp. 60, 152).

Greek elite, directed against professional traders.[22] For what both gibes refer to is not *emporia*, long-distance trade (usually by sea), but *kapēleia*, local retail trade.[23] Plato defines the distinction between the two quite nicely in the *Republic*: "Or don't we call those who busy themselves with buying and selling when they are set up in the agora '*kapēloi*,' but [don't we call those] who wonder from city to city '*emporoi*'?" (Plato *Rep.* 371d5-7)[24] This distinction in function entails a distinction in status. There is some evidence that in the archaic period, at least, *emporia* was a viable activity for Greek aristocrats exporting their own produce.[25] As Bravo notes, for a nobleman to voyage *ep' emporiēn* did not make him an *emporos*; his social identity was not determined by his involvement in occasional, nonprofessional trading.[26] But *kapēleia*, retail trade in the marketplace, could not be practiced as a nonprofessional. From an aristocratic perspective, the *kapēlos* produces nothing and makes a profit only by conventionally acknowledged deceit.[27]

Two more passages in Herodotus confirm the association of retail trade with deceit. The first is the famous description of the education of the Persian nobility: "They educate their sons beginning from five years to the age of twenty [to do] three things alone—to ride and shoot the bow and tell the truth" (παιδεύουσι δὲ τοὺς παῖδας ἀπὸ πενταέτεος

---

[22] The question of aristocratic participation in and attitudes toward trade in the archaic period is a complex and controversial one. For discussions of the whole topic, ranging from Homer to the fifth century, see the classic work of Hasebroek 1933: 30–43, and recent treatments by Bravo 1977: 1–59; Humphreys 1978: 159–74; Mele 1979; Cartledge 1983: 1–15; Morris 1986a: 2–7. For the occurrence of the same gibe in the Theognidea, see Thgn. 53–60 (with discussion in Kurke 1989).

[23] On the distinction, see Hasebroek 1933: 1–14; Finley 1935: 320–36; Hopper 1979: 47–67.

[24] For the same distinction, see Plato *Soph.* 223d5–10.

[25] Thus Hesiod gives advice on sailing when the agricultural season is over, ἐπ' ἐμπορίην (*W&D* 646; see 618–96). The poet disapproves of such pursuits, but only because he perceives them as dangerous, not discreditable. According to Aristotle, Solon left Athens for ten years, κατ' ἐμπορίαν ἅμα καὶ θεωρίαν εἰς Αἴγυπτον (*Ath. Pol.* 11.1) and Sappho's brother Charaxos was probably in Egypt for the same reason (see Hdt. 2.135; Strabo 17.808; Athen. *Deipn.* 13.596b). See Hasebroek 1933: 12–14; Humphreys 1978: 159–74; Bravo 1977.

[26] Bravo 1977: 43. Another way of saying this might be to say that *kapēleia* is the marked and *emporia* the unmarked term for trade in aristocratic discourse. This would account for the fact that, though the denotations of the two terms are fairly fluid and unstable, their connotations endure.

[27] Plato *Rep.* 371c5–d3 reflects the aristocrat's complete contempt for *kapēloi*. This attitude is still reflected in the comments of Cicero on retail trade: *Sordidi etiam putandi, qui mercantur a mercatoribus, quod statim vendant; nihil enim proficiant, nisi admodum mentiantur.* ("For they must also be considered base, who buy from wholesale merchants to retail immediately; for they would get no profits without a great deal of outright lying," *De Officiis* I.150).

ἀρξάμενοι μέχρι εἰκοσαέτεος τρία μοῦνα, ἱππεύειν καὶ τοξεύειν καὶ ἀληθίζεσθαι, Hdt. 1.136.2). The second passage is Kroisos's advice to Kyros on how to make the Lydians soft and easy to rule: "command them to educate their sons to play the kithara, pluck [the lyre], and practice retail trade" (πρόειπε δ' αὐτοῖσι κιθαρίζειν τε καὶ ψάλλειν καὶ καπηλεύειν παιδεύειν τοὺς παῖδας, Hdt. 1.155.4). Kroisos' advice is clearly intended to stand in contrast to the program of Persian education: each passage uses the phrase παιδεύειν (-ουσι) τοὺς παῖδας with three bare infinitives. κιθαρίζειν contrasts with ἱππεύειν, ψάλλειν, "to pluck" replaces τοξεύειν,[28] and καπηλεύειν provides the climactic contrast to ἀληθίζεσθαι. Again, Diogenes Laertius's Anacharsis shows us that Herodotus's two programs of education have a direct bearing on Greek practices. For the biographical tradition puts into the mouth of Anacharsis the bemused question, "How is it that [the Greeks] forbid lying, when they lie openly in the practices of retail trade?" (πῶς, ἔλεγεν, ἀπαγορεύοντες τὸ ψεύδεσθαι ἐν ταῖς καπηλείαις φανερῶς ψεύδονται; D.L. 1.104).

Thus Herodotus's text exposes the aristocratic association of *kapēleia* and deceit. With the text of Aristotle, we shift from the means to the end of *kapēleia* in the aristocratic conception: the deceitfulness of retail trade functions in the service of unlimited acquisition. In the *Politics* Aristotle locates the invention of money in the need for an easily portable intermediary in the exchange of necessary goods (itself a part of κτητική ... οἰκονομική, "the household art of acquisition," Arist. *Pol.* 1256b26–1257a41). Once invented, however, coinage stimulates another kind of χρηματιστική ("expertise in acquisition") unrelated to the needs of the household:

> Once a supply of money came into being as a result of such necessary exchange, then, the other kind of expertise in business arose—that is, commerce (τὸ καπηλικόν). At first this probably existed in a simple fashion, while later through experience it became more a matter of art—[the art of discerning] what and how to exchange in order to make the greatest profit (πλεῖστον ... κέρδος). It is on this account that expertise in business is held to be particularly connected with money, and to have as its task the ability to discern what will provide a given amount [of it]; for it is held to be productive of wealth and goods. ... For the expertise in business and the wealth that is according to nature is something different: this is expertise in household management (αὕτη μὲν οἰκονομική), while the other is commercial expertise (ἡ δὲ καπηλική), which is productive of wealth not in

[28] This pairing is especially apt since ψάλλειν is often used of plucking the bowstring; see LSJ s.v. ψάλλω I.

every way but through trafficking in goods, and is held to be connected with money, since money is the medium and goal of exchange. And the wealth deriving from this sort of business expertise is indeed without limit. . . . But of expertise in household management as distinguished from expertise in business there is a limit. (Arist. *Pol.* 1257b1–31, trans. C. Lord 1984)

For Aristotle as for Herodotus, *kapēleia* is peculiarly linked to the invention of coinage and peculiarly problematic because dissociated from the household as the proper sphere of production and consumption. The very thing that makes retail trade into deceit (that it produces nothing but makes a profit) also means for the philosopher that it has no natural limit.

The objection might be made that to read Aristotle's definition of *kapēlikē* as an extension of aristocratic ideology is anachronistically to retroject a fourth-century philosophical model to the very different context of sixth- and fifth-century debates. Yet the aptness of Aristotle's reflections is proved precisely by Herodotus's characterization of Darius *kapēlos*. For there is no passage in the *Histories* that captures the two aspects of *kapēleia* we have identified from Herodotus and Aristotle— deceit and the pursuit of unlimited gain—better than Darius's speech inciting the other conspirators to action against the Magi:

> I myself have the most attractive pretext by which to pass, claiming that I have just now come from the Persians and wish to indicate some word from my father to the king. For where it is necessary to say a lie, let it be said. For we all strive after (γλιχόμεθα) the same thing, both those who lie and those who use the truth. Some men, at any rate, lie then, when they are going to profit in some way by persuading with lies; others tell the truth in order to attract some profit by the truth and in order that someone yield more to them (οἱ μέν γε ψεύδονται τότε ἐπεάν τι μέλλωσι τοῖσι ψεύδεσι πείσαντες κερδήσεσθαι, οἱ δ' ἀληθίζονται ἵνα τι τῇ ἀληθείῃ ἐπισπάσωνται κέρδος καί τις μᾶλλόν σφι ἐπιτράπηται). Thus, though we don't practice the same means, we cling to the same end (τὠυτοῦ περιεχόμεθα). But if they were not going to profit at all, the truthteller would be likewise a liar and the liar true (εἰ δὲ μηδὲν κερδήσεσθαι μέλλοιεν, ὁμοίως ἂν ὅ τε ἀληθιζόμενος ψευδὴς εἴη καὶ ὁ ψευδόμενος ἀληθής). (Hdt. 3.72.3–5)

What is remarkable in this passage is the extraordinary emphasis on desire and seduction, expressed in the strong verbs γλιχόμεθα, ἐπισπάσωνται, and περιεχόμεθα. Like almost every other tyrant in Herodotus, Darius is driven by an almost erotic lust for power.[29] But what

---

[29] Cf. Benardete 1969: 136–37: "Herodotus uses ἔρως in only two senses: sexual desire and the desire for tyranny. In every instance of sexual desire (except one) it is illegitimate. . . . ἔρως, then, designates all private and illegal desires, whether they break the law in a sexual or political way." Cf. Hartog 1988: 330.

differentiates Darius from the other rulers and would-be rulers of the
Histories is the peculiarly "kapelic" nature of his desire—expressed here
as his willingness to use deceit and his emphatic goal of maximizing
profit. As many scholars have noted, Darius's readiness to lie, and even
to break his oath (3.71.5), contravenes both Persian and Greek aristocratic
codes.[30] And indeed, Darius's last sentence here confirms his complete
disregard for the ethics of the *hetaireia*, for it transforms *homoios* from
the ideal likeness of one *hetairos* to another into the indifferent methods
of truthteller and liar in attaining their ends (ὁμοίως).

If Darius's speech to the other conspirators articulates the *theory* of
tyrannic *kapēlikē*, the ruse by which he wins the throne demonstrates
the *practice*. The conspirators (minus Otanes) have agreed that the person
whose horse first gives voice as the sun rises shall be king. Darius consults
his groom Oibares, who assures him that he has "a mechanism"—"drugs"
that will accomplish what Darius needs (3.85). The groom proceeds to
carry out his plan:

> When night came, Oibares led one of the mares (the one Darius's stallion
> most fancied) to the suburb, bound her, and led up Darius's stallion. And
> he led him around near the mare many times, letting him almost touch the
> female, and in the end he allowed the stallion to mount. Together with the
> dawning of day, the six were present, as they had agreed, upon their horses
> and, as they were riding out through the suburb, when they came to the
> spot where the mare had been bound on the foregoing night, Darius's horse,
> running up to the spot, whinnied. But together with the horse doing this,
> thunder and lightning occurred from a clear sky. And these things converging
> for Darius confirmed him just as if they had occurred by some agreement,
> and the rest leapt down from their horses and made obeisance to Darius.
>
> Some indeed say that Oibares contrived these things, but others [say] such
> things as the following (for in fact it is told both ways by the Persians):
> that, having touched the genitals of this mare with his hand, he held it
> hidden in his trousers. But when, together with the sun rising, the horses
> were about to be let loose, this Oibares raised his hand and brought it to
> the nostrils of Darius's horse, but that the stallion perceiving it, snorted and
> whinnied. (Hdt. 3.85.3–87)

Scholars have made much of the convergence of supernatural determination (thunder and lightning) with the earthy ruse of the groom in Darius's
election. Many have read this as proof of Herodotus's polyvalent narrative

---

[30] For the centrality of truthtelling to the Persian moral system, cf. Hdt. 1.136.2 and
1.138.1 ("they consider lying the most shameful thing"); for Darius's violation thereof, see
Immerwahr 1966: 45, 199, 307; Benardete 1969: 84–87; Lateiner 1984: 265, 279n.30;
Redfield 1985: 111; Flory 1987: 129–30; Erbse 1992: 57–58.

that exposes Darius's victory as a trick, even while it acknowledges the cooperation of the divine in his accession.[31] While I agree with this polyvalent reading, it is worth inflecting it slightly to acknowledge the effect of Herodotus's narrative construction of the episode. For we should note that Herodotus not only offers a second comic variant of Oibares' trick, but narrates it after the mention of the sign from heaven confirming Darius—that is, technically, out of its proper narrative sequence. We could imagine a different version of this account, narrated in the sequence: first version of Oibares' trick—second version of Oibares' trick—divine confirmation—*proskunēsis*. Such a narrative, while incorporating the same incongruous double motivation, would end on a note of divine favor and human recognition of Darius's sovereignty. Instead, Herodotus has chosen to frame the divine sign with the two versions of Oibares' ruse, thus heightening the incongruity and ending the account with a vision of equine genitals and nostrils.[32] In what should be a kind of divine ordeal (ἀγών, 3.85.3), Darius allies himself with his groom against his aristocratic cohorts, deploying trickery (σοφίην, μηχανῶ, 3.85.1), drugs (φάρμακα, 3.85.2), and sex to establish his preeminence. In the *Histories* in general, both horses and the sun are associated with royal power, so that the terms of the "ordeal" are particularly fitting. Darius and his groom, however, subvert the solar and equine symbolism of the contest by reducing it to the coarse bodily functions of one particular animal.[33] In narrating this as a collapse of decorum, Herodotus flags Darius's betrayal of the *hetaireia*: he has violated its ethic of loyalty and sameness, cheating and tricking his aristocratic *hetairoi* to achieve public power.

To return to the account of Darius and Aryandes, then, Herodotus's seemingly innocent narrative of Darius's monumental aspirations reveals the bite of satire: even as Darius strives to legitimate his rule through the issuing of refined gold, his choice of coinage as monument subverts his efforts and exposes his own debased, tricky nature. The narrator confirms the satiric bite of this little contest of metals by suppressing a key detail: in wishing to leave behind as his monument coinage of the purest gold, Darius actually *succeeded*. For two hundred years, the highest-quality gold currency in Greece and Asia Minor was the daric, the coin that

---

[31] For discussions (with different emphases), see Benardete 1969: 87; Flory 1987: 134; Köhnken 1990: 125–26, 135–36; Erbse 1992: 61–62.

[32] On the two versions, see Köhnken 1990: 128–32. Given the narrative framing of the divine sign, I cannot agree with the assessment of Flory 1987: 134: "The ruse is amusing and undignified . . . , but Herodotus ennobles the moment by having a peal of thunder confirm the conspirators' choice."

[33] For the association of horses and sovereign power, cf. Hdt. 1.189.1, 7.40.1–4; for the sun as royal symbol, cf. Hdt. 7.37.2, 7.54.2, 8.137.4–5. On Darius's exploitation of the body here, cf. the remarks of Benardete 1969: 81, 87.

carried and memorialized Darius's name.[34] Yet our narrator strangely
fails to mention this fact, pausing instead to note that "even now, the
purest silver is called the Aryandic." In these two choices—of silence
and of naming—Herodotus' narrative reveals its complicity with the
aristocratic discourse that travesties Darius as *kapēlos*. It is not just that
coinage is an absurd monument, but that Darius is robbed by the narrative
even of the lowly immortality he achieved, in a miniature *damnatio
memoriae* that suppresses name and coin alike.

II. DARIUS *KAPĒLOS*

A number of other anecdotes, peppered throughout the *Histories*, reinforce the characterization of Darius *kapēlos*. In every case Darius's defining feature is his privileging of short-term profit over the customs and
institutions on which the social and cosmic order depend. Thus, at the
close of the Persian tribute list and the lengthy account of the wonders
of the ends of the earth to which it leads (3.89–116), Herodotus transports
us to a "plain in Asia, encircled by mountains, through which there are
five gorges" (3.117.1):

> From this encircling mountain flows a great river, whose name is Akes.
> Formerly this [river], divided in five directions, used to water the lands of
> those mentioned, carried through each gorge for each people, but when they
> are under the Persian, they suffer the following: the king has walled up the
> gorges of the mountains and set gates upon each, and, since the water has
> been shut off from its exits, the plain within the mountains has become a
> sea, since the river flows in but it has no egress anywhere. And the people
> who before were accustomed to use the water, being unable to use it they
> consider it a great misfortune. For the god sends rain to them just as also
> for the rest of men, but during the summer they sow millet and sesame and
> are much in want of water. But whenever no water is rendered to them,
> going to the Persians, themselves and their wives, they stand at the gates of
> the king and howl aloud, and the king orders [his men] to open the gates

---

[34] The preeminence of the daric and the anomaly of its absence in 4.166 were pointed
out to me by J. H. Kroll. On the widespread use of the daric throughout the Mediterranean,
cf. Kraay 1976: 32–34; Riverso 1983: 218–23; Howgego 1995: 8. As an example of the
extraordinary prominence of the daric, cf. Xenophon's anachronistic references to Kyros's
receipt and distribution of gold darics (Xen. *Kyrop.* 5.2.7, 5.3.3)—the daric was so much
the standard in Xenophon's time that he felt no incongruity in retrojecting its existence
two generations to the reign of Kyros the Great (for discussion of this anachronism, cf.
J. M. Cook 1983: 70). That Herodotus was familiar with the coin and its eponym is proved
by Hdt. 7.28. On the royal iconography of the daric (also called "archers" by the Greeks),
see Root 1989.

leading to these who are most in need. And whenever their earth is sated drinking the water, these gates are closed, but he orders [them] to open other gates for others—those of the rest who are most in need. (Hdt. 3.117.2–6)

Finally, we get the punchline—the observation with which Herodotus ends this account and his entire survey of the Persian empire: "As I know having heard, he opens the gates when he has exacted a great deal of money in addition to the tribute (χρήματα μεγάλα πρησσόμενος ἀνοίγει πάρεξ τοῦ φόρου). These things indeed are thus." This single chapter, isolated at the end of the lengthy survey, gives us a vivid illustration of how Darius "used to run everything like a shop" (ἐκαπήλευε, 3.89.3)— for profit.[35] Thus the Great King's business proclivities frame the entire sweep of the catalogue of subject peoples and the wonders of the ends of the earth, pulling us up short with the incongruous juxtaposition of vast and petty.

In this case, Darius's pursuit of gain interferes with a system that is practically an emblem of a perfectly just, balanced natural order—the circle of mountains through which flows the river, evenly divided (διαλε-λαμμένος πενταχοῦ) to water the lands of five peoples amicably coexisting.[36] Into this perfectly balanced natural order, a microcosm of the order of the world as Herodotus describes it, the Great King intrudes, transforming a plain into a lake, gorges into locked gates, fertile fields into parched land, and men and women into howling beasts (βοῶσι ὠρυόμενοι).[37] In every respect Darius's intervention represents not an improvement (as his people might expect in return for their tribute), but a grotesque perversion of the natural order.

With another anecdote we move from natural to cultural justice. In his description of the movements of the Persian fleet during Xerxes' expedition against Greece, Herodotus pauses to tell us about the Persian commander:

[35] Cf. Immerwahr 1966: 171–72 and N. Smith 1989: 211 (Smith notes that 3.117 illustrates Darius's activities as *kapēlos*, which he understands to mean "middleman" rather than "petty trader"). How and Wells (1928: I.294) regard this particular narrative as fanciful but note that the idea is "quite correct; the control of irrigation is in the East one of the prerogatives of government, and great sums are charged for the use of water." Whatever the accuracy of Herodotus's account, it is his choice to use this story to round out the survey of the Persian empire.

[36] How and Wells (1928: I.294) note that Herodotus's account in this chapter cannot be squared with the known positions of the five tribes mentioned, so it may be that Herodotus has placed various tribes around the plain to enhance the symmetry and order of the picture. For Herodotus's assumption of a model of perfectly balanced cosmic order (like that expressed in Anaximander fr. B 1 DK), see Stambler 1982; Redfield 1985: 103; Darbo-Peschanski 1987: 99–101; Gould 1989: 85–109.

[37] The only other time ὠρύομαι occurs in the *Histories* is in a description of Scythians, high on hemp smoke, howling with pleasure (4.75.2). LSJ (s.v. ὠρύομαι) notes, "properly

The commander of these was the governor of Aiolian Kyme, Sandokes, son of Thamasios. Before these things, King Darius, when he caught him upon the following charge, crucified him (at that time, he was one of the royal judges): Sandokes had given an unjust judgment for money (ὁ Σανδώκης ἐπὶ χρήμασι ἄδικον δίκην ἐδίκασε). When he had been crucified, Darius discovered by calculation that he had done more good things than harm for the royal house (λογιζόμενος ὁ Δαρεῖος εὑρέ οἱ πλέω ἀγαθὰ τῶν ἁμαρτημάτων πεποιημένα ἐς οἶκον τὸν βασιλήιον). And Darius, discovering this and recognizing that he had acted more swiftly than wisely, let him go. (Hdt. 7.194.1–2)

There are two ways of interpreting this anecdote. The first is that Darius weighs Sandokes' single wrongdoing against a long career of royal service and so reverses his judgment. After all, the Persians have a custom which Herodotus singles out for praise, of not executing anyone for a single offense:

> . . . and this custom also I praise—that for the sake of a single wrong done, neither does the king himself execute anyone, nor does any of the other Persians do any irreparable harm to any of his household. Instead, if he find by calculation that his wrongdoings are more and greater than his services, in that case he indulges his anger (ἀλλὰ λογισάμενος ἢν εὑρίσκη πλέω τε καὶ μέζω τὰ ἀδικήματα ἐόντα τῶν ὑπουργημάτων, οὕτω τῷ θυμῷ χρᾶται). (Hdt. 1.137.1)

Yet, in spite of the verbal echoes between 1.137 and 7.194, the anecdote of Sandokes is open to another interpretation. Darius seems to be calculating (λογιζόμενος) not justice vs. injustice, but material benefits rendered to the royal house. That is to say, he seems to be redefining what it means to be a "*royal* judge": instead of a judge whose justice and honesty are backed by royal authority, the adjective connotes a judge whose decisions (fair or not) are advantageous for the royal house. We recall that the royal judges are men "picked out of the Persians," whose task it is to "judge cases and act as exegetes of the ancestral laws"—and Herodotus notes, "all things are referred to them." These men hold office "until they die or until some injustice is discovered for them" (ἐς οὗ ἀποθάνωσι ἢ σφι παρευρεθῇ τι ἄδικον, μέχρι τούτου, 3.31.3). Here, verbal echoes (παρευρεθῇ—εὗρε; ἄδικον—ἄδικον) condemn rather than support Darius's decision, exposing it as a perversion of justice for profit.[38]

---

of wolves and dogs; . . . of lions; . . . of animals generally." I owe these observations on the semantics of ὠρύομαι to David Chamberlain, "Herodotus, Shamans, Writing" (unpublished paper).

[38] For critics who espouse the first interpretation (citing 1.137, but not 3.31), see How and Wells 1928: I.116; Erbse 1992: 71–72.

The point is that we cannot use verbal echoes from the account of Persian customs (1.137) *or* the description of the royal judges (3.31) to establish definitively the moral evaluation of Darius's activity at 7.194. Herodotus's own language authorizes two competing interpretations, the echoes of the two earlier passages straining against each other. In this ambiguous space, there is at least the suggestion that Darius reprieves a corrupt judge whose suborning was also a source of profit for the royal house, and that by so doing, he sets at risk the *patrioi thesmoi* ("ancestral laws") of which the royal judges are caretakers.

We find support for this interpretation when we compare Darius's response to that of Kambyses in similar circumstances. When Darius appoints Otanes commander against the rebellious Greek cities of the coast, Herodotus tells us:

> His father was Sisamnes, who was one of the royal judges. And King Kambyses, because he gave an unjust judgment for money (ὅτι ἐπὶ χρήμασι δίκην ἄδικον ἐδίκασε), killed him and skinned him, and when he had flayed the skin, cut strips from it and stretched them across the seat on which he used to sit to give judgments. And when he had done this, Kambyses appointed to be judge in place of Sisamnes, whom he had killed and skinned, the son of Sisamnes, bidding him remember the seat, sitting on which he gives judgment. This Otanes, the one sitting on this seat, at that time became the successor to Megabyzos in the command and captured Byzantium and Chalcedon. . . . (Hdt. 5.25–26)

Herodotus's horrified fascination with Sisamnes' punishment clogs up his narrative: he simply can't get past the image of the son sitting on his father's flayed skin as he renders judgment. And no passage better exemplifies the pathological cruelty of Kambyses, referred to in 3.89. Still, the harshness and cruelty of Kambyses' punishment of Sisamnes set in relief Darius's cool calculation of profit and loss. The two episodes demand to be read against each other as glosses on the sequence *kapēlos*, *despotēs*, *patēr*. For, though it is obscene in its excess, Kambyses' punishment has a certain logic. The royal judges are guardians of the *patrioi thesmoi*, on which they depend in rendering judgment. The father, who has betrayed the ancestral laws, becomes the skin on which the son rests in his turn. The father is punished and the notion of ancestral remembrance as the basis of Persian justice is horribly literalized. Terrible as it is, Kambyses' punishment is an object lesson that has as its goal the reinstatement of the ancestral order. In contrast, Darius's aborted punishment of Sandokes is concerned only with the material advantage of the royal house.[39]

---

[39] For a similar interpretation of 5.25, cf. Benardete 1969: 138.

Finally, the same portrait of Darius *kapēlos* informs certain anecdotes about the Great King's encounter with burial customs—what we might call the *nomos* par excellence of each culture.[40] In his account of the city of Babylon, Herodotus relates the unusual burial of Queen Nitokris:

> And this same queen also contrived some such trick (ἀπάτην) as this. She had a tomb prepared for herself over the most trafficked gates of the city, in mid-air on top of the gates themselves, and she carved onto her tomb writing saying the following: "Of those becoming kings of Babylon later than I, if any be short of money (χρημάτων), opening the tomb let him take as much money (χρήματα) as he wishes; otherwise, if he is not in need, let him not open it. For it is not better." This tomb was undisturbed until the kingship came round to Darius. And it seemed a terrible thing to Darius not to be able to use these gates at all and, with money sitting there and the writing itself inviting, not to take it. (And he made no use of these gates on this account, because there was a corpse over his head for him as he went through them.) But having opened the tomb he found no money, but [only] the corpse and writing saying the following: "If you were not insatiate of money and greedy for base gain, you would not have opened the tombs of corpses" (εἰ μὴ ἄπληστός τε ἔας χρημάτων καὶ αἰσχροκερδής, οὐκ ἂν νεκρῶν θήκας ἀνέῳγες). And this queen now is said to have been such.[41] (Hdt. 1.187)

In a sense, Nitokris's tomb is a paradox made concrete, a "self-consuming artifact" that invites its own desecration. Yet the queen's foresight and the double inscription she leaves behind, outside and inside the tomb, appropriate the tomb's violation and transform it into her own triumph. Thus, rather than defacing her memory, the opening of her tomb triggers her enduring remembrance through her own words (γράμματα λέγοντα τάδε) and the narrative in which they are embedded (in this case, Herodotus's own account). Nitokris has the last word, and it is thus appropriate that the paragraph closes with her characterization.[42]

---

[40] For the exemplary nature of burial customs, see Redfield 1985: 104–6, Hartog 1988: 133–34. Indeed, the Greeks themselves referred to funerary practice and cult simply as *ta nomizomena* or *ta nomima* (cf. Eur. *Bacchae* 71; Aeschines 1.13; Dem. 18.243; Isoc. 19.33).

[41] Many scholars have noted the folkloric and apparently entirely Greek framing of this anecdote: see Sayce 1883: 108n.2; Aly 1921: 56–57; How and Wells 1928: I.145; Baumgartner 1950: 96; S. West 1985: 296. Dillery 1992 suggests that the story developed from an authentic feature of Darius's Zoroastrianism (his inability to pass under a gate containing a dead body), which has then accreted a Greek fantasy around it.

[42] Cf. the way Herodotus refers to her tomb at 1.185: "And this [queen], who was even cleverer than the one who ruled before, left behind memorials which I shall narrate" (linking her memorial with her cleverness).

In all this, Darius is merely the stooge, first of the clever queen and then of Herodotus's narrative reenactment of the trick. Still, as we have seen, it is no accident that of all the Persian kings, it is Darius who takes the queen up on her offer.[43] In his single-minded pursuit of gain, Darius quite cheerfully violates the memorials of the dead—their peaceful rest and the remembrance that comes to them from their tombs. By this violation he earns the designations ἄπληστος ... χρημάτων ("insatiate of money") and αἰσχροκερδής ("greedy for base gain"). In content the former reminds us of Aristotle's definition of kapēlikē as the pursuit of money without limit,[44] while in style ἄπληστος ... χρημάτων encodes a strange incongruity. ἄπληστος is a word of very elevated style, bathetically conjoined with the matter-of-fact χρημάτων.[45] This vertiginous slippage in levels of style is compounded by αἰσχροκερδής, which occurs only here in the Histories. To appreciate how striking this adjective is in context, we should compare Aristotle's remarks on aneleutheria and aischrokerdeia:

Others in turn are excessive with respect to taking, in that they take every-thing from everywhere, like those who work at servile jobs, pimps (πορνο-βοσκοί) and all such, and those who loan at interest (τοκισταί) little by little and for much. For all these people take from where they ought not and how much they ought not. And common to these appears the shameful pursuit of profits (ἡ αἰσχροκέρδεια). For all of them endure reproach for the sake of gain (ἕνεκα κέρδους)—and this little. For those who take great amounts from where they ought not, and what they ought not, we do not call illiberal (ἀνελευθέρους), for example tyrants sacking cities and looting temples, but rather [we call them] wicked and irreverent and unjust (οἷον τοὺς τυράννους πόλεις πορθοῦντας καὶ ἱερὰ συλῶντας, ἀλλὰ πονηροὺς μᾶλλον καὶ ἀσεβεῖς καὶ ἀδίκους). But the gambler and the clothes-thief and

---

[43] Cf. S. West 1985: 296; Gammie 1986: 182; Dillery 1992: 30–31; Erbse 1992: 63–64; Christ 1994: 188n.59; Steiner 1994: 136–37, who note that it is characteristic of Darius's money-grubbing to loot Nitokris's tomb.

[44] Cf. Arist. Pol. 1257b23–24: "And the wealth deriving from this sort of business expertise is indeed without limit" (ἄπειρος).

[45] For ἄπληστος, cf. Thgn. 109, Aesch. Eum. 976, Soph. El. 1336, Plato Laws 773e. The lofty tone of ἄπληστος is well illustrated by Herodotus himself at the end of Book 1, where the queen of the Massagetai twice reproaches Kyros as "insatiate of blood" (Ἄπληστε αἵματος Κῦρε, Hdt. 1.212.2; ἄπληστον ἐόντα αἵματος κορέσω, Hdt. 1.212.3; cf. Aly 1921: 31–32, who notes the elevated, "tragic" tone and style of this chapter). In many ways Darius's encounter with the Eastern queen Nitokris prefigures Kyros's conflict with Tomyris at the end of the book. As in the case of the counterpointing of Darius's and Kambyses' narratives, this pair of stories provides a gloss on the opposition Darius kapēlos-Kyros patēr. The former is "insatiate of money"; the latter "insatiate of blood" (cf. J. M. Cook 1983: 76).

the robber are among the illiberal; for they are shamefully greedy (ὁ μέντοι
κυβευτὴς καὶ ὁ λωποδύτης καὶ ὁ λῃστὴς τῶν ἀνελευθέρων εἰσίν· αἰσχρο-
κερδεῖς γάρ). (Arist. *NE* 1121b31–1122a8)

For Aristotle, the distinction between the αἰσχροκερδής and the tyrant
who "sacks cities and loots temples" is one of scale. The vastness of the
tyrant's crimes earn him grander terms of abuse, while *aneleutheria* and
aischrokerdeia are designations reserved for the pimp, the usurer, the
gambler, and the footpad. Thus the choice of the word αἰσχροκερδής
(by Nitokris *and* by Herodotus) reinforces the bathetic effect of ἄπληστος
. . . χρημάτων: just like the incongruous sobriquet Darius *kapēlos*, Nitokris's abuse exposes Darius, reducing him from Great King, lord of Babylon, to petty thief.[46]

The violation of burial customs that characterizes Darius' *kapēleia* at
1.187 sheds a somewhat different light on one of the most familiar
passages in the *Histories*—Darius's object lesson about *nomos*. Reflecting
about Kambyses in Egypt that only a madman "would undertake to
deride temples and customs" (*nomaia*, 3.38.1), Herodotus proceeds to
substantiate his claim with an anecdote:

> For if someone should put them forth (προθείη) for all people, bidding them
> pick out the most beautiful *nomoi* from all *nomoi*, having taken a good
> look, each group would choose their own customs. So much does each group
> consider its own customs to be the best. It's unlikely, then, that anyone but
> a madman would make mock of such things. But that all people believe
> thus concerning *nomoi*, is present to measure both from many other proofs,
> but especially this one: Darius at the time of his rule summoned those of
> the Greeks who were present and asked them for how much money they
> would be willing to eat their dead fathers (ἐπὶ κόσῳ ἂν χρήματι βουλοίατο
> τοὺς πατέρας ἀποθνῄσκοντας κατασιτέεσθαι). But they said that they
> would not do these things for any amount of money. And after that Darius
> summoned those of the Indians called the Kallatiai, who eat their parents,
> and asked them, with the Greeks present and learning the things said through
> an interpreter, for what price they would agree to burn their dead fathers
> with fire. But they, raising a great shout, were bidding him not to speak
> blasphemy. Thus these things now are established by custom, and rightly

---

[46] For the same issue of scale between tyranny and petty crimes, see Plato *Rep.* 575b6–c4
(where Plato differentiates between the "small evils" a few tyrannic men commit in the
city vs. an established tyranny) and 590b6–9 (*kolakeia* and *aneleutheria* transform the
thumoeidēs from a lion into an ape). That Aristotle's sociological decorum is the more
conventional one, from which Herodotus's diction deviates, is suggested by Theophrastos's
portraits of *aneleutheria* and *aischrokerdeia* (Theophr. *Char.* 22, 30). Theophrastos shares
with Aristotle the notion that these are the faults of nickel-and-dime moneygrubbers, not
of kings and tyrants.

Pindar seems to me to have composed when he said "custom is the king of all" (οὕτω μέν νυν ταῦτα νενόμισται, καὶ ὀρθῶς μοι δοκέει Πίνδαρος ποιῆσαι νόμον πάντων βασιλέα φήσας εἶναι). (Hdt. 3.38.1–3)

In context, Darius is usually read here as a hero of cultural relativism, wise in his appreciation of the sanctity of *nomoi* in contrast to his mad predecessor Kambyses.[47] But even if we can accept this parable as an unproblematic expression of Herodotus's own view (as he invites us to do in the last sentence), certain oddities in the narrative remain unaccounted for. Why, after all, is it *Darius* who stages this spectacle of cultural encounter? What is rarely noted in critical discussions of this passage is the form Darius's questions take: not "Would you eat/burn your fathers?," but *"For how much money* would you do so?"[48] The form of the question constructs Darius not as the wise and all-powerful ruler, but as the kapelic enquirer who sets the desire for gain against the sanctity of custom.

In this, Darius distinguishes himself from the narrative voice that speaks the preamble and the close of this episode. For Herodotus begins by imagining a marketplace of *nomoi*, where every culture's customs are displayed for exchange.[49] But, the narrator insists, there is no exchange— every right-thinking person prefers his own *nomoi*. The possibility of the market exchange of *nomoi* is then revived by Darius, who wants to find out exactly how much money it will take to get the Indians and the Greeks to exchange burial customs—that is, how much for each to destroy his own *nomos*. In this fantasized transaction, Darius is the ultimate middleman, the huckster of *nomoi* on the open market. On this reading Herodotus's citation of Pindar is also a rejection of Darius's huckstering experiment: "*Nomos* is king of all," while Darius, who deploys *nomisma* to destroy *nomos*, is revealed as tyrant and petty trader.[50] Thus here, as in

[47] Thus Burkert 1990: 22–24; Munson 1991: 57–63; Romm 1996: 122–23.

[48] Benardete 1969: 81 and Humphreys 1987 represent exceptions to this elision on the part of critics: Benardete observes, "Darius puts the question in terms of the body, stressed by the offer of money," Humphreys, following Konstan 1987b, suggests that the form of Darius's question is part of the general phenomenon that "Persian kings like to count" (Humphreys 1987: 218). Cf. Christ 1994: 188.

[49] For the notion of a "marketplace of *nomoi*," cf. Munson 1991: 58. Notice Herodotus's use of the verb προτίθημι, which can mean "to set out wares for show or sale" (LSJ, s.v., II.2). Powell (1938: 326) oddly defines it in this passage as "command," which makes it redundant with the participle κελεύων. For a parallel in a context of display and illicit transaction, cf. the middle προθεῖτο, Hdt. 3.148 (Maiandrios attempts to bribe the Spartan king Kleomenes by prominently displaying his gold and silver drinking cups). Christ 1994: 187–89 sees a similar bipartite structure and critique of Darius in Hdt. 3.38.

[50] For a somewhat different reading of Herodotus's use of Pindar, see Bloomer 1993: 49. At another level, Herodotus's portrait of Darius *kapēlos* might be read as a series of negative allusions to the Athenian empire: thus Darius is a tyrant who imposes tribute (*phoros,*

3.89, the point of the parable turns on the opposition between legitimate
sovereignty and tyranny exposed as *kapēleia*.

Inscribed in this famous parable is the same aristocratic bias we have
detected in a number of other stories around Darius. For, within the
sphere of *nomos*, custom, belief, and practices are constructed here as
completely unambiguous and unproblematic, by the invocation of the
culture's most sacred custom and the one most constitutive of community—the treatment of the dead.[51] What this absolute model of *nomos*
in 3.38 lacks, as James Redfield has pointed out, is the concept of political
nomos, as Demaratus will articulate it to Xerxes at 7.104. Political *nomos*
means not only custom that guides political action, but also custom that
can be changed and legislated by the civic community. As Redfield notes
of Herodotus's Greeks in contrast to the Persians: "Among the Greeks
a change in *nomoi* can strengthen *nomos*; this is because *nomoi* are not
merely traditional but are a matter of conscious design, just as they are
founded on debate and consent."[52] What we find in 3.38 is a very different
model of *nomos*: unlike the critical adaptation of others' customs characteristic of civic *nomos* (of which Herodotus heartily approves elsewhere—
cf. 2.4.1, 2.177.2), *nomos* here is purely cultural and not susceptible to
change or legislation. Whereas Herodotus as critical enquirer sometimes
praises another culture's *nomos* as *kallistos* ("most beautiful"—cf.

3.89) and jealously guards his sole prerogative to coin (4.166). This last trait might have
reminded a contemporary audience of the Athenian Coinage Decree, but we cannot be
sure, given the uncertainty about the date of that legislation (see Meiggs 1972: 167–72;
Howgego 1995: 44–46; for this style of reading individual tyrant figures in Herodotus, see
Raaflaub 1987). I would contend that (1) here, as elsewhere, the representation of Athens
as *polis turannos* mobilizes and draws its potency from older, preexistent cultural paradigms
of tyranny (cf. Connor 1987b: 257), and (2) this kind of portrait speaks most directly to
non-Athenian elites in the Greek cities of the empire (cf. Fornara 1971b: 74, Meiggs 1972:
405–11). Thus we might trace a consistent pattern of aristocratic abuse from Alkaios'
portrait of Pittakos as *phusgōn* and *kakopatridais* to Timokreon's vilification of Themistokles as "innkeeper" (πανδόκευε, Tim. fr. 1.727 *PMG*, line 10) to the caricature of Darius
as *kapēlos*.

[51] See Redfield 1975, 1985: 104–6; Morris 1987.

[52] Redfield 1985: 117. Redfield's argument is challenged by Humphreys 1987, but see
Redfield's response in the same volume: "Surely it is true that everyone (except the Canni-
bals—IV.106) has *nomoi*; Demaratus is not in this way distinguishing the Spartans from
others. It is only that the *nomos* of others—most particularly of those powerful organised
barbarians who up to now have laid claim to civilisation—is to be ruled by persons; what
characterizes the Spartans is that they are ruled by their *nomos*, it is a *despotēs nomos*.
Surely this has something to do with the idea of citizenship, of a polity which is not
organised around deference and personal loyalties, but on the common commitment to
collective action of a plurality of juridically equal persons. These people, as they are all
engaged in governance, do not need a governor continually to instruct them; they have, in
the jargon of the psychologists, 'internalized the norms.' " (Redfield 1987: 252).

1.196), the preamble here asserts that one would only ever find his own culture's *nomoi* "most beautiful."[53]

This complete suppression of the political dimension of *nomos* suggests that 3.38 is something of an elitist credo. It is only in the sphere of the polis that there might be competing *nomoi* and only in the sphere of the polis that *nomisma* exists as custom or convention (indeed, we might say that money is the political *nomos* par excellence). In contrast 3.38 represents the Greeks (like the Persians and the Kallatiai) as a community constituted by their shared, absolutely valid cultural *nomoi*, even as it sets up an absolute hierarchy of custom (*nomos*) and money (*chrēmata*).[54] Money, introduced into the system by the tyrant, can only destroy *nomos*, threatening both the human community and the divine order as it supports the social system (notice the Indians' shocked exclamation against blasphemy, implying that Darius's offer of money threatens even the divine).

As in the other anecdotes that characterize Darius *kapēlos*, Darius's failed marketplace of *nomoi* reveals by contrast what constitutes the long-term transactional order—all that is set at risk by his monomaniacal pursuit of gain. The natural order of farming (3.117), the proper adjudication of justice (7.194), burial customs and the tombs of the dead (1.187, 3.38), and finally the overarching sanctity of *nomos* that cannot be changed or legislated—all these, which completely circumvent the order of the polis, are endowed with absolute cultural primacy by Herodotus's emblematic anecdotes.

III. AMASIS THE VULGAR TYRANT

Thus with Darius, we get a highly negative aristocratic portrait of the tyrant as coiner. Can we find anywhere a complementary "middling" representation of the tyrant's activities that would correspond to the theories of Will and von Reden? After all, in Athens at least, it was the tyrants who introduced coinage initially (according to this theory, as part

[53] How do we account for this discrepancy, if we simply accept the narrative voice here as Herodotus's? Is this *nomos* for barbarians—part of a dialectic on the way to civic *nomos*? Or, to put it another way, is Herodotus acting out his own inverse debate on the constitutions? Thus here, oligarchy refutes the claims of monarchy, to be refuted in turn by the claims of *isonomia* later on (in a precise inversion of the sequence of 3.80–82). It is also worth noting that one of the foreign customs Herodotus particularly admires as "most beautiful" (and so would presumably like to appropriate for the Greeks) is a way of instituting a fair distribution *es meson*—that is to say, it is a preeminently civic *nomos* (see discussion in Ch. 6 below).

[54] It is worth noting that the narrator does *not* use *nomisma* in this context. Is this because the narrative voice does not want to dignify money with the status of "instituted custom" in a context that might suggest the equivalence or parity of *nomos* and *nomisma*?

of a process of distributive justice). Still, though traces remain of an association of tyranny with justice, and occasionally with coinage, these two strands never seem to converge in anything like this modern picture.[55] How, then, are we to account for this gap in our evidence?

The reason, I suggest, is twofold. First, of poetry contemporary with the activity of the tyrants, we might say that the elitist strand has succeeded in establishing its discourse as "hegemonic," as the only version that survives, and this entails the complete suppression of positive representations of coinage (as we have described it in Chapter 1). By the fifth and fourth centuries, we find representations of coinage within the civic sphere: as von Reden has demonstrated, historical writing, inscriptions, and the speeches of the orators are informed by a positive evaluation of money in the service of the polis.[56] Yet by this time (especially in Athens) the tyrant has become a figure for vilification, while the positive, distributive aspects of coinage are closely aligned with the democratic regime. As a result of this double suppression—first of coinage and then of the instrumentality of tyrants—Will and von Reden can cite no literary evidence for their thesis between Hesiod and Solon, on the one hand, and Thucydides and Aristotle, on the other.[57]

Is there any way to fill in this gap in our sources? I think we may do so indirectly, if we are willing to read obliquely—in the cracks and crevices of the dominant ideology. We must return to the language of metals as it shadows the suppressed workings of coinage, and examine the ways in which this system has been appropriated and inverted by certain tyrant figures. That is to say, we must accept that the elitist tradition has set the terms of the discourse (an evaluative ranking of metals not money), and that only within these terms can an opposing tradition play and challenge the dominant order. Thus we may not be able to recover a straightforward historical portrait of a tyrant empowering the demos through coining, but we may still be able to find traces of a representation of the tyrant from below, encoded in the language of metals.

Let us consider the representation of Amasis in Book 2 of Herodotus. This narrative of the commoner who becomes pharaoh operates with the

[55] On tyranny and justice, see Will 1955a: 495–502; Nagy 1985: 42–74; McGlew 1993: 61–86; on tyrants and coinage, see note 8 above.

[56] von Reden 1995: 79–104, 171–216.

[57] These are precisely the sources used by Will 1954 and 1975 to construct his argument. This gap in the literary evidence motivates von Reden, in one of her most compelling chapters, to turn to sixth- and fifth-century vase representations, which she reads as depicting money positively in the public space of agora and palaistra (von Reden 1995: 195–216). We might also note the association of coinage as a civic institution with Solon in the later tradition (cf. Dem. 24.212–14; [Arist.] *Ath. Pol.* 10.1–2; Plut. *Solon* 15.4–5); is this perhaps a displacement of the positive aspects of coinage from Peisistratos to Solon?

same system of signs—what I have termed "the language of metals"—but inverts the meaning of the terms. As others have noted, Amasis is a trickster figure in Herodotus, aligned with "cunning intelligence" and changeability.[58] Amasis is inconsistent within himself, as his parable of the bow (2.173) underscores, *and* changeable over time, shifting in the course of the narrative from thief and *dēmotēs* to Pharaoh (2.172, 174).[59]

Amasis's shifty, baseborn nature is revealed the very first time we meet him in Book 2 (Hdt. 2.162). Herodotus tells us that he was sent as emissary of the reigning pharaoh, Apries, to persuade a group of disaffected Egyptians not to revolt. But surprisingly, the narrator gives us no direct information about Amasis at this point: we are told simply, "Apries, having learned these things [that is, the incipient rebellion], sends to them Amasis in order to stop them with words." I suspect that Herodotus is deliberately uninformative when Amasis is first mentioned—part of the point of the ensuing narrative is to reveal who and what Amasis is. As Amasis is making his pitch to the rebels, "One of the Egyptians standing behind him put a helmet on his head and as he put it on, said that he was putting the kingship upon him. And the thing done was somehow not against his will, as the sequel showed" (2.162.1–2). And with that brief encounter, Amasis switches sides and becomes the leader of the rebels.

Beyond the revelation of his shifty, untrustworthy nature, this brief introduction also completely inverts the Hesiodic language of metals. It is not simply that the rebels have no authority to make Amasis king, but that they crown him with a *helmet*. And as we know from the elaborate narrative of Psammetichos which occurs just ten chapters earlier (2.151–52), the helmet must be bronze. Whatever crowning with a helmet signifies within the native Egyptian tradition, to a Greek audience it represents a radical inversion of the symbolic meaning of gold and bronze.[60] The bronze helmet, emblematic in form and substance of the warrior function, is here used as if it were a golden crown, to elevate Amasis to the status of sovereign.

The sense of impropriety created by this gesture is immediately reinforced in a different register. For Apries, getting wind of Amasis's about-face, sends another emissary whom we are told is "the most distinguished

---

[58] On Amasis as a trickster figure, see Camerer 1965: 79; Dewald 1985: 54–55 and 1993: 59–60 with n. 8. For the possibility of a class association with Greek *mētis* ("cunning intelligence"), see Brown 1947; Rose 1992: 113–19.

[59] For discussion of the Amasis episodes from a somewhat different perspective, see Flory 1987: 139–43; Chamberlain 1997.

[60] On the Egyptian tradition behind the helmet, cf. How and Wells 1928: I.248 and Lloyd 1988: 176 (*ad* 2.162). For a discussion of the function of metals in the story of Psammetichos, see Kurke 1995: 55–57.

of the Egyptians at his court" (*dokimon*, 2.162.3; *dokimōtaton*, 2.162.6),
to order Amasis immediately into the king's presence. Amasis's response,
as Herodotus tells us: "Amasis (for he happened to be sitting on a horse),
raising himself up, farted and bid him take *this* back to Apries" (2.162.3).
In pointed contrast to the soothing *words* he was sent to speak to the
rebels, Amasis sends a violent challenge in the language of the body. He
is thereby not only insulting the king's noble emissary and the king himself
by his coarse behavior, he is also arrogating the royal prerogative of
controlling the discourse and constituting the meaning of the message.
Thus Amasis's windy response perfectly emblematizes his paradoxical
relation to sovereign power: he is simultaneously the most inappropriate
king *and* the most royal, insofar as he is able effortlessly to appropriate
control of signification.

In this Amasis's rupture of decorum functions very differently from
the equivalent in the narrative of Darius—Oibares' horse trick. In that
context Oibares defiles what should be a divine ordeal, reducing the solar
and equine symbolism of sovereignty to the nostrils and genitals of two
particular horses. The introduction of the bodily into a symbolic *agōn*
subverts Darius's claim to kingship, even while the divine signs of thunder
and lightning seem to confirm it. In contrast, it is Amasis who chooses
the bodily code of the message in this narrative, in what can best be
described in Stallybrass and White's terms as symbolic inversion or transgression.[61] For Amasis valorizes the grotesque body and uses it to destabilize the existing hierarchy, challenging not his own claim to the throne,
but that of the reigning pharaoh Apries. And indeed, we can read the
sequel as an *agōn* carried out in the language of the body. The pharaoh
Apries responds to Amasis's message in the same terms, "giving no word
to [the messenger]," but simply mutilating him—cutting off his nose and
ears in his anger that his emissary has not led the outlaw Amasis to him
(2.162.5). And if Amasis and Apries are engaged in an *agōn* of the body
whose terms are set by Amasis, the judges are the Egyptian people: "But
the rest of the Egyptians, who were still on Apries's side, when they saw
the most worthy man among them treated so shamefully with indignity,
wasted no time in going over to the other camp, and gave themselves to
Amasis" (2.162.6). This defection is decisive: with the support of all the
Egyptians, Amasis easily defeats Apries and his army of foreign mercenaries (2.163–69). Thus Amasis successfully deploys the orifices of the grotesque body in his transgressive bid to become pharaoh.

Amasis enacts a similar complex subversion of the elitist language of
metals in another anecdote:

---

[61] Stallybrass and White 1986: 6–26 (and see discussion in the Introduction above).

When Apries had been brought down thus, Amasis was king, being of the Saïte nome, from the city called Siouph. And at first the Egyptians were contemptuous of Amasis and considered him in no great share, since he was a commoner before and of no conspicuous house (ἅτε δὴ δημότην τὸ πρὶν ἐόντα καὶ οἰκίης οὐκ ἐπιφανέος). But Amasis, with cleverness rather than stubbornness (ἀγνωμοσύνῃ), brought them around. He had countless other good things, and especially a golden footbath (ποδανιπτὴρ χρύσεος), in which both Amasis himself and his drinking-buddies all used to wash their feet on each occasion. Chopping this up, he made an image of a god from it and set it up in the most appropriate place in the city. And the Egyptians, going to the image, used to reverence it greatly. And Amasis, when he learned what was done by the citizens (ἐκ τῶν ἀστῶν), called the Egyptians together and made a revelation, saying that the icon came into being from a footbath, into which the Egyptians formerly vomited and pissed and washed their feet, but that at that time they revered it greatly. And then he spoke, saying that he himself fared like the footbath (ὁμοίως αὐτὸς τῷ ποδανιπτῆρι πεπρηγέναι): for if he was a commoner before, at present he was their king, and he bid them honor and respect him. In such a way he brought the Egyptians around so as to deem it just to be slaves. (Hdt. 2.172)

I suggest that this parable encodes two competing systems of signification into its "language of metals." Appropriately enough (perhaps) to mark his royal status, Amasis's footbath is gold—and yet, in many respects the golden footbath-turned-icon inverts the signification of the traditional aristocratic system. The juxtaposition of gold, that sovereign metal, with vomiting, pissing, and foot-washing is incongruous enough, but there is a more subversive level still to Amasis's object lesson. In the transformation from footbath to icon (which is also a movement from the privacy of the symposium to the center of the city), the metal of which the object is made is ultimately of less significance than the use to which it is put by the sovereign authority that endows it with symbolic meaning. That is to say, this parable rejects essentialism and valorizes functionalism, thereby turning the traditional language of metals on its head. If all Eastern despots in Herodotus can be read as versions of Greek tyrants, in this story the paradigmatic tyrant accepts the aristocratic constitution of identity through metals and (implicitly) through coinage—he simply inverts the positive and negative values of this contested field. Thus, Amasis makes virtues of the aristocratic failings of trickiness, changeability, and inconsistency, while he puts precious metal into symbolic "circulation" in the public space of the city.[62]

---

[62] Cf. the discussion of Farenga 1985 on the "numismatic strategies" of the Greek tyrants, and notice that the verb used for Amasis's fashioning of the idol is κατακόπτω, a verb

We might say Amasis's mastertrope is oxymoron—the incongruous pairing of opposites that subverts the aristocratic decorum of sameness of self and consistency over time. The message Amasis sends in the language of metals is rehearsed in several other registers by the ensuing narrative. First, we are told (2.173) that Amasis used to work eagerly from first light "until the time that the market was full," but from that time he used to drink and joke with his drinking buddies (ἔπινέ τε καὶ κατέσκωπτε τοὺς συμπότας καὶ ἦν μάταιός τε καὶ παιγνιήμων).[63] His friends reproach him for his behavior, saying "O King, not rightly do you rule yourself leading yourself forward into excessively base behavior (ἐς τὸ ἄγαν φαῦλον). For it were fitting for you sitting solemnly on your solemn throne through the day to do your work and thus the Egyptians would believe that they are ruled by a great man and you would have a better reputation. But now you behave in no kingly fashion (νῦν δὲ ποιέεις οὐδαμῶς βασιλικά)." Amasis responds with another object parable: "Those who possess the bow," he says, "string it when they need to use it, but when they have used it, undo it. For if it were strung all the time, it would break, so that they would not have it to use when necessary. Such indeed also is the constitution of a human being: if he should wish always to be serious and devote no part of himself to play, he would escape his own notice going mad or becoming senseless. Knowing this, I allot a share to each activity" (2.173.3–4).

The friends wish to eradicate all trace of the commoner in the pharaoh—to make Amasis always the same and always kingly (notice especially the iconic polyptoton ἐν θρόνῳ σεμνῷ σεμνὸν θωκέοντα, 2.173.2). Amasis responds that change and variety are essential to human nature. But here again, the object Amasis chooses to prove his point is freighted with mythic resonances. For the ability to string the bow—from the *Odyssey* to the long-lived Ethiopians in Herodotus—signifies rightful sovereignty in the logic of myth.[64] Yet again, Amasis turns this traditional system on its head, asserting that he can be a good king only by unstringing the bow—by behaving in an unkingly fashion at times. As in his parable

---

regularly used for the coining of money. Even the *narrator's* language in this episode conforms to the inversion of aristocratic virtues and vices, since Herodotus designates Amasis's tricky change as σοφίη . . . οὐκ ἀγνωμοσύνη ("with cleverness rather than stubbornness"). ἀγνωμοσύνη, a rare word in Herodotus, always designates an action (regarded by the actors themselves as noble) from a hostile perspective that condemns it as "foolhardiness" or "stubbornness" (cf. Hdt. 4.93, 5.83.1, 6.10, 7.9β1, 9.3.1, 9.4). So here it is a very negative way of describing the aristocratic cult of sameness and consistency.

[63] Notice that, in aristocratic terms, Amasis's behavior violates the proper rules and decorum of the symposium: for the norm, cf. Xenoph. fr. B 1 DK and Thgn. 481–96, 503–8.

[64] Cf. *Od.* 21.53–79; Hdt. 2.106.3, 3.21.3, 3.30.1, 3.35–36, 4.9–10; Ktesias *FGrH* 688 F 13 and see Rose 1992: 131.

of the footbath, Amasis valorizes difference and functionalism in the construction of self.

Another oxymoronic anecdote follows immediately (Hdt. 2.174). When he was an *idiōtēs*, Herodotus tells us, Amasis was a real joker (φιλοσκώμμων), who used to steal (apparently for fun). He was often caught and taken by the rightful owners of the property to various mantic shrines, to test his claims to possession. "When he was king," Herodotus continues, "he did such things: however many of the gods released him as not a thief, to these he paid no attention and gave nothing to their upkeep, nor was he sacrificing to them on the grounds that they were worthless and possessed false oracles. But however many condemned him as a thief, to these he was paying the most attention, on the grounds that they were truly gods and furnished unlying oracles" (2.174.2). Amasis behaves here as a poor man's Kroisos (quite literally), furnishing in his own person the means to test oracular truth.[65] Within this narrative, his method is paradoxical, for the oracles that find him true, he finds false, and vice versa. As a further paradox, Amasis inverts the normal (aristocratic) relations of reciprocity which obtain in the transition from private citizen to king: those oracles that benefited him as a private citizen are ignored, while those that condemned him are rewarded. For the normal pattern, we might compare Amasis's response with the tale of Darius and Syloson (Hdt. 3.139–41). When Darius was a spearbearer for Kambyses, the Samian Syloson presented him with a magnificent cloak, which Darius happened to admire in the Egyptian marketplace. When Darius later becomes king of Persia, Syloson turns up at his doorstep, claiming to be his benefactor. Reminded of the favor, Darius exclaims, "O most noble of men (γενναιότατε ἀνδρῶν), you are that one who gave to me, though I had no power yet, even if small things, still the gratitude is likewise equal (ἴση γε ἡ χάρις ὁμοίως) as if I should get something great from somewhere now. In exchange for these things, I give you endless gold and silver, so that you never regret treating Darius the son of Hystaspes well" (3.140.4). Rather than adhering to this gift-exchange model of royal reciprocity, Amasis privileges the use value of oracular shrines, testing the true and false mantic currency of his kingdom.[66]

Amidst all these oxymoronic parables, Herodotus frames his narrative of the metamorphosis of the footbath negatively: he concludes "in such a way [Amasis] brought the Egyptians around so as to deem it just to be

---

[65] Darbo-Peschanski 1987: 170–71 also notes the parallelism of Amasis and Kroisos in their testing of oracular truth.

[66] The image of "mantic currency" is not completely alien to the text of Herodotus, as his use of the expression χρησμὸς κίβδηλος ("duplicitous or counterfeit oracle") reveals (Hdt. 1.66, 1.75; cf. 5.91.2). For a discussion of the analogy between currency and oracular utterance, see Chapter 4 below. It is also worth noting that in the Samian stories of

slaves." Still, the narrative as a whole seems more ambivalent toward Amasis. As Dewald has noted, he is one of very few characters in the *Histories* who manipulates the meaning of symbolic objects and gets away with it.[67] What are we to make, then, of the narrative's apparent approval of Amasis's subversive valorization of functionalism? I would like to suggest a sociological explanation for this phenomenon. On two occasions in the account of Egyptian history from the reign of Psammetichos on (2.147 and 2.154), Herodotus pauses to tell us that he now has other sources besides the Egyptians themselves. Indeed, on the second occasion, he tells us explicitly that only because Greeks first settled in Egypt during Psammetichos's reign do "we know accurately all things [about Egypt] also later" (2.154.4). A. B. Lloyd, in his exemplary commentary on Book 2, concludes from these statements that Herodotus's sources for the latter part of Book 2 were largely oral and largely Greek.[68] We know that the Greeks who inhabited Egypt in Herodotus's time (as in the sixth century) consisted almost entirely of two groups: Greek mercenary soldiers and Greek merchants and traders. I suggest that it is in this distinctly *non*-aristocratic milieu that the folktale narratives we find in Herodotus accreted around the figure of Amasis.[69] Perhaps, what we find embedded in Herodotus's narrative is the other side of the coin, as it were—Amasis becomes a culture hero for Greek mercenaries and tradesmen. Thus, in these instances at least, Herodotus's ethnographic logos becomes a screen on which is projected another kind of otherness— that of status in the contestation of ideological discourses.

So it seems that the different relations of Amasis and Darius to Herodotus's narrative surface are the result of different sources and different status. As an aristocrat who betrays his *homoioi* to make himself tyrant, Darius becomes the butt of Herodotus's ironic narrative—we might say he is deconstructed in his bid to control signification by the text in which he is embedded. Amasis, on the other hand, as the demotic or vulgar tyrant and culture hero (and I mean vulgar in all its senses) is the perfect figure to deconstruct the elitist language of metals.[70] According to this reading, Herodotus as histor has preserved in his text precious evidence

---

Herodotus's Book 3, we find very different portraits of Darius and Amasis; on gift exchange in the Samian stories, see Chapter 3 below.

[67] Dewald 1993: 59–70; cf. Gammie 1986: 175–76 on Herodotus's untypically positive representation of Amasis.

[68] Lloyd 1975: 13–32, 1988: 115–16; cf. Murray 1987: 102–3; Fehling 1989: 86. See also Aly 1921: 60–62, 70–73: Aly insists on the basis of content and style that the Psammetichos and Amasis stories are Greek and "volkstümlich" in origin.

[69] On the non-aristocratic status of Greek traders in Naukratis, see Austin 1970: 22–37; Mele 1979: 92–109.

[70] I borrow the association of Amasis with deconstruction from Dewald 1993: 70.

of the struggle over signification which took place within archaic discourse. It is in this sense that the Machereyan "conflict at the borders" of archaic elitist texts figures at the center of Herodotus's unique narrative.

Yet, in a sense, we are still reading Amasis "from above" by focusing on the aristocratic codes and paradigms his behavior transgresses. In light of the possibility that the stories around Amasis represent the discourse of the "other," of low-status groups whose interests oppose traditional aristocratic values, it is worth rereading these narratives "from below." For it is not simply that Amasis's actions constitute a radical inversion when read through aristocratic norms (as they do), but that his accession and rule are consistently empowered by the common consent of the people at large. Thus, in radical contrast to Darius, whose story takes place entirely within the frame of the aristocratic *hetaireia*, the Amasis stories transpire in the public space of the city, where the tyrant functions as the instrument of the people's will.

The element of popular consent, of Amasis's constitution as ruler from below, is already clear in his paradoxical "coronation." The impression that Amasis is an ordinary citizen chosen by the will of the people is heightened, first by the fact that he enters the story bare of any particular characterization or even a patronymic; and second by the fact that the one who crowns him is simply τις Αἰγυπτίων, an anonymous emblem of popular will. It is then the people, as I have noted, who adjudicate his *agōn* with Apries, in stark contrast to the divine and aristocratic terms of the *agōn* by which Darius attains sovereignty. It is finally the people whose united support guarantees Amasis's success in battle (2.169.1), and the people who claim the right to judge and execute the deposed Apries (2.169.3).

Read in this light, Amasis's parable of the footbath-turned-icon becomes the climactic representation of tyrannic rule by common consent. The vast kingdom of Egypt is suddenly transformed into a single (distinctly Greek-style) city, where Amasis is a "common citizen," a "member of the demos" (δημότην, 2.172.2), and the icon is set up in public, "in the most appropriate place in the city" (τῆς πόλιος ὅκου ἦν ἐπιτηδεότατον, 2.172.3). In this context, Herodotus designates the Egyptians uniquely as *astoi*, fellow-citizens of a city (2.172.4).[71] Given this extraordinary emphasis on citizens and civic space, we can interpret Amasis's functionalist parable somewhat differently. Amasis does not dupe the Egyptians by his transformation of the footbath, nor is it *his* authority alone that endows it with meaning. Instead, his object lesson is an acknowledgment

[71] See Hartog 1988: 46–50, 258–59 for the analogous process of symbolic Hellenization which transforms the Persian army into Greek-style hoplites when they confront the nomad Scythians.

of his dependence on the will of the people: it is *their* belief and acceptance of the icon that make it into a god, just as their election and support made him pharaoh. Read thus, Amasis's performance has a great deal in common with the story of Peisistratos and Phye (Hdt. 1.60), as W. R. Connor has recently interpreted it. What Herodotus's disapproving narrative preserves there is not the duping of the demos by a manipulative tyrant, but a public performance through which the people of Athens express their support for Peisistratos by participating in his divine charade.[72] Just as their belief makes Phye Athena and Peisistratos her sidekick, the Egyptians' common consent makes a footbath into an icon. And in this case, Herodotus' evaluation is similarly disapproving: "in such a way [Amasis] brought the Egyptians around so as to deem it just to be slaves" (ὥστε δικαιοῦν δουλεύειν, 2.172.5). Yet even here, Herodotus's language paradoxically attributes a strange kind of power to the demos. As they have been repeatedly in the story of Amasis, they end as adjudicators (δικαιοῦν), even if (from the narrator's perspective) they use their power to sustain the tyrant who "enslaves them."

And if, as Karen Bassi has argued, Peisistratos's dominant mode is theatrical, Amasis's is metallic.[73] In every case, his inversion of the language of metals is linked with the will of the people as audience and judge: their choice transforms a bronze helmet into a crown and their belief legitimates the golden icon he fashions. Thus we might read Amasis's transvaluation of metals as an allegory of coinage. Even if they cannot speak directly of coinage as egalitarian token, the stories around

[72] Connor 1987a: 42–47; for a reading that attempts to account for Herodotus's disapproval and willful misunderstanding of the episode, see Sinos 1993.

[73] Bassi 1998: 145–91. Indeed, we might extend the parallel with Peisistratos still further and suggest that Amasis served as a stand-in for Peisistratos, accreting popular stories derived from the Athenian tradition. There are striking similarities in the traditions around Peisistratos and Amasis: Herodotus claims that "at the time of Amasis, it is said that Egypt was most fortunate" (Ἐπ' Ἀμάσιος δὲ βασιλέος λέγεται Αἴγυπτος μάλιστα δὴ τότε εὐδαιμονῆσαι, 2.177); cf. the remark in [Arist.] *Ath. Pol.* that "people were always saying that the tyranny of Peisistratos was the age of Kronos" (διὸ καὶ πολλὰ κλέα ἐθρύλλουν ὡς ἡ Πεισιστράτου τυραννὶς ὁ ἐπὶ Κρόνου βίος εἴη, *Ath. Pol.* 16.7—that is, both inversion of the normal hierarchy and golden age!). Cf. also Herodotus's statement that Amasis introduced a kind of census, which Solon regarded as fine legislation and took over for Athens (Hdt. 2.177.2). As How and Wells (1928: I.253) note, this is an obvious anachronism, since Amasis's rule began in 570 B.C.E., nearly twenty-five years after Solon's legislation. Another tradition, preserved by Plutarch (*Solon* 31), attributes the Attic legislation to Peisistratos. Perhaps these traditions were displaced onto the exactly contemporary figure of Amasis, once the Peisistratids fell from power and popular favor. For Athenian ambivalence about Peisistratos, see Bassi 1998: 145; for the general phenomenon of the city appropriating and reconstructing the tyrant's story after his fall, see McGlew 1993: 6–11, 124–56.

Amasis adumbrate a plausible context for such a development: a challenge to the aristocratic monopoly on signification through the combined will of the tyrant and the demos whose consensus supports him.[74]

It is worth noting, finally, how different the portrait of Amasis the vulgar tyrant is from Darius *kapēlos*. While both are associated with deceit and trickery, Darius's kapelic desire for gain is consistently represented as a threat to the cosmic and social order: the balance of the natural world, the administration of justice, and the burial of the dead. Amasis, by contrast, performs a radical inversion of elitist values which serves to reconstitute the long-term transactional order, re-routing it through the public space of the city. Where Darius perturbs the cosmic and natural order by shutting off the normal distribution of water (3.117), Amasis reorients the worship of the divine to the civic space (2.172).[75] Where Darius perverts the administration of justice to the advantage of the royal house in reprieving Sandokes (7.194), Amasis supports the true order of justice to his own disadvantage in honoring those oracles that condemned him as a thief (2.174). Finally, where Darius desecrates the tombs of the dead for profit (1.187), Amasis uses trickery to protect his corpse from violation. In Book 3, Herodotus informs us that the mad Kambyses exhumed Amasis's body, had it whipped, and finally burned it (3.16.1–4). But the histor appends an alternative account:

---

[74] Indeed, we can measure the extent of these narratives' transgressions of aristocratic norms by comparing the originals with Diodorus's précis of Herodotus's account (D.S. 1.68.3–6):

(1) In Diodorus's account, Amasis is described as a "conspicuous Egyptian man" (ἀνὴρ ἐμφανὴς Αἰγύπτιος) when he is first introduced—when Apries sends him to speak to the rebels. (Cf. Flory 1987: 182n.23.)

(2) There is no incident of farting, and no explanation of why "the rest of the natives" join Amasis (so no *agōn* in the language of the body between Amasis and Apries).

(3) Apries is captured in battle and strangled on the spot (there is no specification of who did it).

(4) Amasis's rule is represented as completely unproblematic and conventional (ἦρχε νομίμως τῶν Αἰγυπτίων καὶ μεγάλης ἐτύγχανεν ἀποδοχῆς, "he ruled the Egyptians lawfully and happened upon great favor," D.S. 1.68.5).

Thus Diodorus has consistently normalized Herodotus's anomalous narrative, suppressing all traces of Amasis's "commonness," his valorization of the grotesque body, his paradoxical behavior as king, *and* (perhaps most significantly) the prominent role played by the demos in adjudicating and supporting Amasis's rule. All that Diodorus suppresses serves as evidence for the demotic "otherness" of Herodotus's bizarre narratives.

[75] A closer parallel with Amasis's activity at 2.172 is actually 1.183, where Darius is tempted to carry off a large golden icon of a god from the city of Babylon but doesn't have the nerve (Xerxes ultimately accomplishes the desecration). Here the contrastive pattern with Amasis is quite exact: while Amasis converts the king's private gold into a public icon, Darius wants to steal a public icon to enrich the royal treasury.

Still, as the Egyptians say, it was not Amasis who suffered these things, but some other of the Egyptians who had the same stature as Amasis, whom the Persians outraged when they thought they were outraging Amasis. For they say that Amasis, having learned from a mantic shrine what was going to happen to him when he was dead, thus indeed as a cure for the future buried this man, the one who was whipped as a corpse, at the gates within his own tomb, and bid his son put him himself as far as possible into the depths of the tomb. These commands of Amasis referring to the tomb and the man do not seem to me to have been original, however: I think the Egyptians merely magnify these things (ἄλλως δ᾽ αὐτὰ Αἰγύπτιοι σεμνοῦν). (Hdt. 3.16.5–7)

According to the Egyptians, Amasis alters the normal burial *nomos*, counterfeiting a corpse to keep his tomb inviolate. But Herodotus, though he knows Amasis as a cunning trickster and manipulator of objects, draws the line at this story, expressing his opinion that it is simply a later fabrication of the Egyptians. Still, his closing words here contain the final paradox of the Amasis story. For in "magnifying these things," the Egyptians prove that they have taken to heart Amasis's parable of the footbath-turned-icon: "He said that he had fared like the footbath: for if before he was a commoner, at the present time, he was their king, and he bid them honor and respect him" (καὶ τιμᾶν τε καὶ προμηθέεσθαι ἑωυτὸν ἐκέλευε, 2.172.5). Furthermore, even if Amasis's corpse really has suffered desecration, the common belief of the people restores it. Their consensus fulfills the function of a funeral monument: they "magnify" Amasis and preserve his memory long after death. Thus in this anecdote, as in the others, the trickster tyrant reinvents the long-term transactional order with the complicity of the demos.

CHAPTER 3

Counterfeiting and Gift Exchange:
The Fate of Polykrates

I HAVE ARGUED that Herodotus's narratives of Darius and Amasis occupy the two poles of aristocratic and "demotic" representations of tyranny; that Darius is caricatured as a *kapēlos* and Amasis valorized as a trickster complicit with the common will. If these two figures offer us competing representations (from above and below) staged partly through the code of metals, two other Herodotean dynasts perform the same dialectic within the dominant signifying system of gift exchange. In the next two chapters we will consider Herodotus's portraits of the Greek tyrant Polykrates and Kroisos the Lydian king—both embroiled in complex webs of gift exchange, transgressed and respected, which shape their destinies and their stories.[1] But while they participate in the same signifying system, they seem, like Darius and Amasis, to be refracted in it through divergent ideological positions.

I. COUNTERFEITING AND VIOLATED EXCHANGE (Hdt. 3.39–60)

Let us begin with Polykrates, whose narrative in Book 3 is subtly interwoven with that of Darius. We first meet Polykrates in 3.39, right after Darius's fantasized marketplace of *nomoi* (3.38), and the story of his rise and fall (3.39–60; 3.120–28) frames the extended narrative of the usurpation of the Magi, the death of Kambyses, the conspiracy of the seven Persian grandees, and Darius's own accession and organization of empire. As Henry Immerwahr noted long ago, this framing is not accidental: a multiplicity of themes and motifs link the opportunistic tyrants Darius and Polykrates, so that their juxtaposed stories comment reciprocally on each other.[2] If Darius is a *kapēlos*, viewed through the jaundiced

---

[1] Indeed, the stories around these two figures are singled out by Gould 1991: 6–9, 17–18 as exemplary instances of the importance of gift exchange/reciprocity networks to Herodotean narrative (more on Gould below).

[2] Immerwahr 1956–57: 314–20. Cf. especially Immerwahr's summary statement: "Herodotus' work is specifically characterized by the recurrence of patterns. Each isolated tale in Herodotus bears a relation, or a resemblance, to some other story or event, and is structured to express this relationship. The difficulties in appreciating Herodotus lie not in his lack

eye of the *hetaireia*, the same view represents Polykrates as a ruthless pirate, whose aspiration to thalassocracy consistently violates the proper order of gift exchange. Indeed, the two are united by the strange combination of money and desire: just as Darius is ἄπληστος χρημάτων in the posthumous rebuke of Nitokris (1.187), we are told that Polykrates could be lured to his death because he "somehow desired money greatly" (καί κως ἱμείρετο γὰρ χρημάτων μεγάλως, 3.123.1; cf. also 3.72). Given this parallelism, it is worth noting that Darius and Polykrates are the only two rulers in the *Histories* Herodotus explicitly says coined money.

In what seems an irrelevant and almost accidental inclusion in the first Samian narrative, Herodotus reports:

> And the Lakedaimonians, when it had been forty days for them besieging Samos and they had made no headway, departed to the Peloponnese. But as a sillier/less credible story (ματαιότερος λόγος) began to be told, [it is said] that Polykrates having struck much local coinage by gilding lead gave it to them, and that they, having accepted it, thus departed (Πολυκράτεα ἐπιχώριον νόμισμα κόψαντα πολλὸν μολύβδου καταχρυσώσαντα δοῦναί σφι, τοὺς δὲ δεξαμένους οὕτω δὴ ἀπαλλάσσεσθαι). This was the first expedition to Asia the Lakedaimonian Dorians made. (Hdt. 3.56)

We shall return to this brief aside to consider why Herodotus regards it as a "sillier story" (*mataioteros logos*); for now, I would simply like to read it without the narrator's reservation and note how central this seemingly accidental report is to the structure of the Samian narratives. For in this tale of Polykrates, counterfeit coin (gilded lead) represents a single instance of an obsessive series of corrupted or transgressive exchanges. Or rather, we should say, giving counterfeit coin is paired with the deliberate and consistent violation of proper gift-exchange relations (the two form the halves of a single transgression, as we shall see). Thus, almost the first thing we are told about Polykrates (after the matter-of-fact revelation that he killed one brother and exiled the other, and has formed a bond of *xeinie* with Amasis) is that, in his drive to establish a thalassocracy, he "used to loot and pillage all, distinguishing no one; for he said that he would gratify his *philos* more by giving back what he had taken than by not taking it in the first place" (ἔφερε δὲ καὶ ἦγε πάντας διακρίνων οὐδένα· τῷ γὰρ φίλῳ ἔφη χαριεῖσθαι μᾶλλον ἀποδιδοὺς τὰ ἔλαβε ἢ ἀρχὴν μηδὲ λαβών, 3.39.4).[3] Under the sign of this Polykratean

---

of organization, but in an excess of relatedness. Herodotus reports each event as he thinks he found it in the tradition, but he proceeds at once to connect it (by affinity or contrast) with all other pertinent events, which for him coexist in a series of ideal patterns." (Immerwahr 1956–57: 319–20).

[3] Gould 1991: 6–7 rightly calls attention to this passage as Polykrates' conscious inversion of the "grammar" of gift exchange; Gould does not, however, play out the consequences

theory of friendship, the Samian narratives play themselves out as a series
of violated or interrupted gift exchanges. Thus the Spartans give as their
reason for aiding the Samian exiles two acts of Samian piracy: "the theft
of a krater, which they were bringing to Kroisos, and of a corselet, which
Amasis the king of Egypt sent to them as a gift" (3.47.1). Thus also,
the Corinthians join the expedition on the grounds of another violated
exchange: at the time of Periander, the Samians had interceded to prevent
the transfer of "three hundred sons of the first men of the Korkyreans"
to Alyattes in Sardis ἐπ' ἐκτομῇ, "for castration" (3.48.2).[4]

The Polykratean failure to respect the ties of gift exchange (both one's
own and those of others), paired with the giving of debased currency,
strikes a familiar chord: this story sequence in fact literalizes and histori-
cizes the pattern we observed in Theognis (see above, Chapter 1). There,
the *kakoi* and *deiloi*, the base outside the aristocratic *hetaireia*, are repeatedly characterized by two significant traits: they have no *charis* (i.e., they
do not understand or respect the proper workings of gift exchange) and
they have a *kibdēlon ēthos*, a deceitful and counterfeit nature.[5] Given
the parallelism between this Theognidean paradigm and its Herodotean
literalization in narrative, it should come as no surprise that historians
have almost universally identified Herodotus's sources as Samian aristocrats descended from the noble opponents of Polykrates. The reasons for
this identification are largely pragmatic: Herodotus shows an intimate
familiarity with Samos, its artists, its monuments, and its internal politics.

---

of this "primal scene" of transgressive exchange for the ensuing Samian narratives. Cf.
Polyainos's gloss on this Herodotean characterization, which heads his entry on Polykrates
(*Strat.* 1.23): Πολυκράτει Σαμίῳ, καταθέοντι τὴν Ἑλληνικὴν θάλατταν, ἔδοξεν εἶναι
στρατηγικόν, εἰ κατάγοι καὶ τὰ τῶν φίλων, ὡς, εἰ ἀπαιτούμενα λαμβάνοιεν, φιλτέρους
ἕξοι· οὐδὲν δὲ λαβών, οὐκ ἂν οὐδ' ἀποδοῦναι δύνασθαι ("To Polykrates the Samian,
when he was ravaging the Hellenic sea, it seemed to be strategically advantageous to carry
off also the possessions of friends, so that, if they should get the things they requested
back, he would have them as [even] better friends. But if he were to take nothing, he
wouldn't have the power to return [anything].")

[4] I am not concerned here with the chronological problems posed by these thefts and
interventions, which have much vexed historians. Instead, I am concerned only with the
representational structure and coherence of the Samian narratives, in which these acts of
piracy are assimilated to Polykrates' general policy of "sacking everyone without distinction." I do not have time to consider the story of Periander's extraordinary cargo to Sardis
and the actions and reactions that lead to it; I would simply note that the embedded story
of Periander and his son Lykophron (Hdt. 3.48-53) continues and elaborates the obsessive
pattern of violated and ruptured exchange relations, here transposed from state and interstate
relations to those of the tyrant's family. For discussions of this story embedded in the first
Samian narrative, see Immerwahr 1956–57; Schmitt-Pantel 1979; Gould 1991: 51–53;
Sourvinou-Inwood 1991: 244–84.

[5] For these two traits, see Thgn. 105, 854, 955-56, 1038b, 1263-64 (*kakoi* and *deiloi*
have no *charis*); 117–24, 963–66 (*kakoi* and *deiloi* have a *kibdēlon ēthos*).

Furthermore, he shows marked sympathy throughout toward the Samians, and the presumption is that he had friends and contacts on the island
of his own (aristocratic) rank.[6] As B. M. Mitchell succinctly characterizes
Herodotus's Samian informants, "It is likely that his friends were of
similar rank and shared his attitude to tyranny. . . . [T]hey were opposed
both to tyranny and to medism."[7] Yet I think the identification of Herodotus's sources as aristocratic could be pressed further, to account not only
for the narrative of events offered, but also for the informing ideology.
For what governs and shapes Herodotus's Samian stories throughout is
an obsessive concern with the proprieties of gift exchange and their
violation. The prominence of this theme in the *Histories* in general and
in the Samian stories in particular has recently been emphasized by
John Gould:

> These two examples [the hostility of Athens and Aigina and the Samian
> stories] bring home to us how pervasive, how enduring and how compelling
> are the obligations of the gift in Herodotus' understanding of human behav-
> iour. They are only two examples of what is by far and away the most
> pervasive pattern of historical causation in Herodotus' narrative. For Herod-
> otus sees no implausibility, nothing for surprise, in the notion that the
> obligations of reciprocity, both positive and negative, alone and of them-
> selves explain major actions on the part of the most powerful actors in the
> world of his narrative, actions which had long-lasting consequences in the
> experience not only of previous generations but also of his own.[8]

Gould is right to underscore the structuring power of the gift in Herodotus's narrative; my only divergence from his eloquent and forceful argument is that the almost hysterical repetition of the theme of exchange
and its violation in certain passages—like the Samian stories—suggests
that the ideology of gift exchange is neither uncontested nor unproblematic. That is to say, it is an ideology constructed within the narratives
Herodotus tells us *in opposition to* another ideological position. And
what exposes the outlines of this opposing position, inverted as in a
photographic negative, is the seemingly inconsequential detail of Polykrates' minting of counterfeit coin. The issuing of local currency (note
epichōrion 3.56) asserts the autonomy and authority of the public
sphere—of the polis as an entity separate from and superior to individual
aristocrats and their private bonds of *hetaireia* and *xenia*. But in this
aristocratic narrative, the only coinage Polykrates is credited with issuing

---

[6] Mitchell 1975: 75–76, citing the evidence of the Suda entry on Herodotus. Mitchell is
followed by Cartledge 1982: 246; Shipley 1987: 75–76, 90–94.
[7] Mitchell 1975: 76–77.
[8] Gould 1991: 18; cf. Gould 1989: 82–85 and Cartledge 1982.

is debased—just as there is only counterfeit coinage in the figurative world of Theognis.[9] In opposition to what it represents as the corrupted sphere of money, the aristocratic ideology that informs these narratives valorizes gift exchange as the bedrock of human interaction, which is also a cosmic principle (for this is the point of the story of Polykrates' ring, as we shall see). By this constituted opposition between gift exchange and coinage, aristocratic ideology attempts to wrest back from the polis control of the long-term transactional order, construing money not as a competing, autonomous system of value, but as a threat to the existing "proper" social and cosmic order.

It is the onus of this ideological narrative to demonstrate the chaos that ensues when the system of gift exchange is violated. Thus the original statement of Polykrates' ruthless policy, "he used to sack and loot all, distinguishing no one" (3.39), not only registers the violation, but also points to its sequel—a complete breakdown of distinctions or discriminations (διακρίνων οὐδένα). In Polykrates' world it is impossible to tell friends from enemies, what is one's own from what is another's. In response Amasis's letter of advice is all about reestablishing distinctions— between the divine and human sphere, between good and bad fortune. Urging him to throw away what he holds most dear in order to secure a balanced alternation of fortunes, Amasis observes, "And somehow I wish, both for myself and for those I care about, to be fortunate in some matters and to trip up in others, and thus to pass one's life faring alternately rather than being fortunate in all respects (καὶ οὕτω διαφέρειν τὸν αἰῶνα ἐναλλὰξ πρήσσων ἢ εὐτυχέειν τὰ πάντα, 3.40.2–3). The phrase ἐναλλὰξ πρήσσων neatly conjures the reinstatement of distinctions, reinforced by διαφέρειν τὸν αἰῶνα. Though a common verb for "pass one's life," διαφέρειν is used only here in Herodotus with αἰῶνα, and it evokes living as a process of discrimination (picking up and restoring the δια- of διακρίνων, 3.39). In the end, though, Amasis comes to realize that Polykrates' fortune is irredeemable, so he imposes the only kind of discrimination possible—between himself and Polykrates: "Having sent a herald to Samos, he said that their xeiniē was dissolved" (διαλύεσθαι ἔφη τὴν ξεινίην, 3.43.2).

To make the point as strongly as possible, the narrative naturalizes gift exchange as a cosmic principle; this, more than anything else, accounts for the "fairytale" narrative of Polykrates' ring (3.40–43). Historians have

---

[9] It is worth noting that, in spite of Herodotus's skepticism, there are preserved electrum-coated lead slips from Samos; see Barron 1964: 216, 1966: 17–18. Aly 1921: 79 and Barron 1966: 17 accept Herodotus's story at face value, but other scholars have professed uncertainty about the real conditions and reasons for the minting of the gilded lead issues: cf. Kraay 1976: 29–30 and see below.

tended to despair of this episode, remarking with some embarrassment on Herodotus's lapse into the supernatural or the realm of folktale.[10] The exception is B. M. Mitchell, who attempts to offer a rationale for the anecdote within the logic of Herodotus's Samian aristocratic sources. Yet her account also founders on this episode, unable to produce a convincing explanation for Herodotus's apparent lapse into fantasy. Like many other historians, Mitchell acknowledges that the break between Amasis and Polykrates was most likely the initiative of the Samian tyrant, eager to ally himself with Persia once Kambyses controlled the Phoenician navy.[11] Why then should Herodotus's Samian sources, equally hostile to tyranny and medism, have suppressed this "historical fact," whitewashing Polykrates' behavior with the wildly "unhistorical" tale of the letter, the fish, and the ring? According to Mitchell, "The stylising and formalising of Polykrates' rise and fall was a suitably tragic theme. It conveniently camouflaged his swing to the Persian alliance and allowed Samians of the mid-fifth century to combine admiration for the thalassocracy and the public works of Polykrates' upward career with disapproval of the tyranny and medism which accompanied his success and helped to bring about his fall."[12] But in fact this "explanation" really explains nothing, since Herodotus's Samian aristocratic sources could just as well have registered their approval for the thalassocracy while admitting that Polykrates took the initiative in medizing. (Indeed, such an account

---

[10] Thus de Ste. Croix 1977: 145: "Herodotus often jumps from the natural level of explanation to the supernatural, and vice versa. It is true that he sometimes fails to provide a satisfactory human explanation, because he has his ready-made supernatural one, that something was 'bound to happen,' 'fated to happen.' But I can only think of one single occasion on which his obsession with the supernatural actually makes him distort the narrative of events. This is his account of the breaking off of the alliance between Polycrates, the tyrant of Samos, and Amasis, king of Egypt." Thus also Aly 1921: 90–92; Cartledge 1982: 246.

[11] Mitchell 1975: 79–80; cf. Andrewes 1956: 121; de Ste. Croix 1977: 145; Cartledge 1982: 246; Shipley 1987: 91, 96–97; Wallinga 1991.

[12] Mitchell 1975: 79–80. Other scholars, too, see Herodotus's purpose as the shaping of a "tragic" narrative: thus Fornara 1971b: 36 with n. 14; Versnel 1977. Van der Veen 1993: 448n. 39, 452–56 rightly critiques such a notion of the "tragic," which entails only the irresistible workings of fate or nemesis against an entirely innocent individual. As a second explanatory factor, Mitchell invokes Samian patriotism: "An aristocratic but patriotic Samian source would either condemn the tyranny as the Corinthians did (v 92), or, for patriotic reasons, might condone or conceal its more disreputable actions" (Mitchell 1975: 78). Again, I cannot quite see the logic of this: if they can be "patriotic" by doing the former, why should they do the latter? Yet another way to account for the story of Polykrates' ring is to categorize it as Herodotus's (more or less) simple moralizing (thus, e.g., Gernet 1981a: 123; Murray 1987: 106). But what this interpretation fails to acknowledge is the partisan, political nature of this moralizing impulse (cf. discussion of Gould in text).

would locate the blame for his fall more unequivocally in his own act of betrayal.)

To account for the story of Polykrates' ring, we need to acknowledge that the whole narrative serves pressing ideological needs beyond the purely pragmatic. As the climax to a sequence about transgressions of gift exchange, Amasis advises Polykrates to right a cosmic imbalance by throwing away "what he most values." To do so, as Louis Gernet has noted, is to send it to another world, to make a kind of offering to a nameless divinity.[13] To ward off misfortune, Polykrates must give back to the gods some part of his wealth (a gift-exchange practice for which we can find parallels in modern anthropology as well as ancient Greek texts).[14] But the object Polykrates chooses is his seal ring (σφρηγίς), "of emerald set in gold, the work of Theodoros son of Telekles" (3.41.1), and this choice complicates matters. As the creation of "gift of god," son of "far famed," the seal is the perfect choice—an *agalma* given by the gods is rendered back to them in a very public display.[15] But insofar as the carved stone is *also* Polykrates' seal, it is far more than a precious object: as Elena Cassin has argued from the Mesopotamian evidence, the seal is the owner's double, the symbol of his biological and social identity, and (in the case of royal seals) the hereditary talisman of his legitimate authority.[16] So, what does it mean for Polykrates to throw away his seal, symbol of his identity and his power?

But before we have even begun to grapple with this question, the narrative presents us with another: what does it mean for the Samian tyrant to reacquire his seal, as he does almost immediately, in the belly of a splendid fish? This dénouement suggests multiple, even conflicting interpretations. At one level (and I suspect this shaped the story at its invention), Polykrates' miraculous reacquisition of his seal serves as a

[13] Gernet 1981a: 127–31; cf. Versnel 1977: 25–45.

[14] Cf. Aesch. *Ag.* 933–34, 1008–14, 1574–76, and further parallels cited by Versnel 1977; for parallels in the modern anthropological literature, see Mauss 1967: 12–16; Sahlins 1972: 149–83; Taussig 1980; Parry 1986.

[15] For the significance of the name Theodoros, cf. Ogden 1997: 120. It may be objected that I should not etymologize the name of a real artist (whose activities we know from independent sources; cf. Plato *Ion* 533b; Vitruvius 7, *praef.*; Pliny *HN* 7.198; 34.83; 35.146, 152; 36.95; D. S. 1.98; Paus. 3.12.10, 9.41.1; Athenagoras *Legatio* 17). But the fact that Herodotus (and his sources) chose to preserve the artist's name and patronymic at this precise point in the story suggests that they did so for their surplus of signifying value— i.e., this is an issue not of "reality," but of narrative selection. For a strikingly similar collocation of a "gift of Zeus" and *kleos* associated with a ring cast into the sea, see Bacch. 17.74–80.

[16] Cassin 1960, following Gernet 1981a: 124–25; cf. Versnel 1977: 33–37; Seaford 1994: 231; Steiner 1994: 160–62; Ogden 1997: 120–21.

divine endorsement of his aspiration to thalassocracy. To receive back
the symbol of his authority in the belly of a fish should mean that the
god approves his rule of the sea, and this interpretation is confirmed by
a striking parallel in a Bacchylidean choral ode. In Poem 17 Bacchylides
tells the story of an aquatic ordeal, a contest that takes place at sea
between the Cretan King Minos and the youthful Theseus, on his way
to Crete to face the Minotaur. In a duel over their divine ancestries,
Minos prays for a sign (σᾶμ', 57) from his father, Zeus, and challenges
Theseus to recover his [Minos's] gold ring from the sea as proof of the
Athenian hero's claimed paternity from Poseidon (Bacch. 17.50–66).[17]
Zeus heeds Minos's prayer, sending a bolt of lightning, and Theseus
promptly leaps into the waves to retrieve Minos's ring (Bacch. 17.67–90).
Theseus returns miraculously from his visit to the underwater house of
Poseidon—but *without* the ring. In its stead Theseus bears other magical
agalmata, gifts of Amphitrite—a purple robe and the crown Aphrodite
had given Amphitrite for her wedding. As Gernet noted, the ring of Minos
is completely dispensable in this narrative (indeed, it is never mentioned
again once Theseus makes his leap), and precisely because of that, its
presence in this version of the myth is highly significant.[18] But, whereas
Gernet sees the losing of the ring in the sea as emblem and presage of
thalassocracy, I would suggest that it represents just the opposite.[19] Had
Theseus recovered Minos's ring, that would have confirmed the latter's
rule of the sea (and for this reason, his challenge to Theseus to do so is
described as a "new act of *mētis*," Bacch. 17.51–52). Instead, Minos's
ring remains at the bottom of the sea and Theseus returns with talismans
that are uniquely his own.[20] In the substitution of cloak and crown for
the ring, this mythic narrative marks the passing of Minos's thalassocracy,
its destruction at the hands of the Athenian hero Theseus.[21] Conversely,
the fact that Polykrates' seal ring comes back to him in a fish should

[17] That it is Minos's *seal* ring we are told by Pausanias, describing the wall painting by
Mikon in the sanctuary of Theseus (Paus. 1.17.3).

[18] Gernet 1981a: 124.

[19] Ibid: 125–27. Though Gernet recognizes this narrative as a "competition in royalty"
(125), he does not acknowledge that Theseus's magical tokens replace Minos's ring in
Bacchylides' narrative (and that that replacement prefigures a shift in supremacy).

[20] On the significance of these talismans and their substitution for Minos's ring, cf. Jebb
1905: 227; Segal 1979: 30–37; Scodel 1984: 140–42; Burnett 1985: 26–36. *Pace* Segal
and Scodel, who assimilate the cloak to the crown as a talisman of erotic allure, I would
emphasize the royal symbolism of the garment (cf. the cloak of Syloson, discussed below
in text). For a different reading of its significance, in the context of Athenian naval power
and ephebic symbolism, cf. Barron 1980; Francis 1990: 53–64; on the talismanic properties
of the crown in particular, see Burnett 1985: 165nn.16, 17; Kurke 1993.

[21] Cf. Segal 1979: 36–37 and Scodel 1984: 140–42 for similar interpretations.

confirm his thalassocracy. It is no accident, in light of this narrative, that Herodotus explicitly compares Polykrates' rule of the sea with that of the legendary Minos (Hdt. 3.122.2).

Yet everything in Herodotus's narrative works to discourage such an interpretation; instead, this story of talismanic authority has been inserted into a larger framework of gift-exchange relations gone awry. Indeed, in the narrative as we have it, the crisis of gift exchange operates on at least two levels. On an obvious level, as I have noted, the precious object made by Theodoros is offered back to the gods, but rejected by them. This imbalance in the workings of cosmic reciprocity is then rightly read by Amasis as a sign that Polykrates is doomed: "Amasis, reading the letter that came from Polykrates, concluded that it was impossible for one man to convey another to safety from what was going to happen, and that Polykrates was bound to end badly, being fortunate in all respects, who found even the things he threw away" (3.43.1).[22]

But these lines, which form the solemn coda to the story of Polykrates' ring, do not exhaust the tangled intricacies of its exchanges. For the narrative is in fact much more preoccupied with another act of gift exchange—one that at first sight seems extremely trivial:

> On the fifth or sixth day [after Polykrates threw away his ring] this happened to him. A fisherman who caught a great and beautiful fish deemed it worthy to be given as a gift to Polykrates; so, bearing it to his door, he said he wanted to come into Polykrates' sight, and when this one came, he gave him the fish and said, "O King, having caught this, I didn't deem it right to bear it to the agora, though I live by the work of my hands, but it seemed to me to be worthy of you and your rule (οὐκ ἐδικαίωσα φέρειν ἐς ἀγορήν, καίπερ γε ἐὼν ἀποχειροβίοτος, ἀλλά μοι ἐδόκεε σεῦ τε εἶναι ἄξιος καὶ τῆς σῆς ἀρχῆς). So, bringing it, I give it to you." And the other, delighted at these words, responds: "You have done very well, and my gratitude is double, both for the words and the gift (χάρις διπλή τῶν τε λόγων καὶ τοῦ δώρου). And we invite you to dinner." The fisherman, then, went away home, making a big deal of this, while [Polykrates'] servants, as they're cutting open the fish, find in its belly Polykrates' seal. (Hdt. 3.42.1–3)

We might read this surprisingly leisurely rendition of Polykrates' encounter with the fisherman as simply an instance of Herodotus's love of narrative elaboration, were it not for the fact that this represents the

---

[22] We should note what a different Amasis this narrative constructs from the demotic tyrant of Book 2: I would put this disparity down to the different sources that make use of him as the paradigm of the wise ruler. Here, in an aristocratic narrative, he has been completely coopted to support the ideology of gift exchange.

only occasion on which Polykrates behaves properly in a gift-exchange relation.[23] And that he does so in this slightly ludicrous encounter with a humble fisherman is itself suggestive. For normally, the bonds and exchanges of gift-giving are enacted between those who are more or less social equals.[24] That is to say, to exchange with a man who emphatically calls himself *apocheirobiotos*, "making a living by the work of his hands," assimilates Polykrates to his status. This wry twist, understated as it is, tips the narrative's hand (as it were), exposing the disdain of Herodotus's aristocratic sources for the *apocheirobiotos* tyrant and pirate. But there is still more to be said about this exchange. For insofar as the "great and beautiful fish" contains Polykrates' seal, the fisherman is in the anomalous position of restoring to Polykrates his identity and his "royal" authority. From this perspective, Polykrates is not even the fisherman's equal, but his inferior, incalculably in his debt for a gift he can never repay.[25]

Thus a narrative that seems originally to have been a mythological charter for Polykratean thalassocracy has been appropriated for an aristocratic morality play. Gernet, in discussing the mythic elements of the story, observes with some disdain, "In the form it takes in Herodotus (3.40–43), it has of course been adapted in the interests of a moralizing piety of the kind often to be found in that author."[26] "Moralizing piety" there is indeed, in the service of an aristocratic model of exchange

---

[23] We are, of course, told of the bond of *xeinie* which existed between Polykrates and Amasis; but we only ever see it being repudiated. Indeed, Polykrates' reception of the fisherman is the *only* time in Herodotus that he is given direct speech in a face-to-face encounter (even his letter in response to Amasis is reported in indirect speech). On the significance of the occurrence or suppression of direct speech in Herodotus's narrative, see the exemplary readings of Gould 1989: 50–54; for the generally negative valuation of mediated or indirect communication in Greek culture, see Bassi 1998: 43–98.

[24] For the relative equality of exchange partners, see Finley 1977: 64–67; Morris 1986a; Herman 1987.

[25] It is tempting to connect this episode of a Samian fisherman strangely bestowing sovereignty with an odd fragment of Anakreon preserved in the Homer scholia (ad *Od.* 21.71, 2.698 Di). Commenting on the peculiar use of *muthos* for *stasis*, the scholiast reports, "From where also Anakreon says of the fishermen who were rebels on Samos, 'And the rebels, o Megistes, throughout the island control the holy city' " (Anakr. fr. 8/353 *PMG*). This scholiast's report, together with brief mention in the *Etymologicum Genuinum* and the *Etymologicum Magnum*, is the only evidence we have for Samian fishermen as *stasiastai*, "rebels," while the language of Anakreon's fragment suggests that these rebels at some point had the upper hand (for διέπουσι, cf. Pindar O. 6.93; N. 10.53). We have no idea what the context of Anakreon's fragment was, but Herodotus's account looks strangely like the mythologization of some such political conflict. Cf. Ogden 1997: 119 for a similar connection. On these "fisherman" rebels, see the different interpretations of Bowra 1961: 274; Page 1966; Nafissi 1983: 430–37; Shipley 1987: 92.

[26] Gernet 1981a: 123.

relations; but not everything "in" Herodotus should necessarily be taken to be the histor's own moral or ideological position. For, as we shall see below, the final set of Samian stories offers us a counter-ideology that valorizes the public sphere and exposes the cost of gift exchange in civic violence.[27] But first we must read Herodotus's aristocratic morality play to its end and consider the punishment of Polykrates.

II. COSMIC RECIPROCITY (Hdt. 3.120–25)

I have insisted on the narrative coherence of violated gift exchange and debased currency because it is precisely these two that together conspire to destroy Polykrates, in a punishment that perfectly reciprocates his failures of reciprocity. The scene is set when Herodotus returns to Samos at 3.120, after the account of the Persian tribute and Darius's first act, the execution of Intaphrenes:

> I suppose it must have been at the time of Kambyses' illness that these following things happened. Oroites, a Persian, was the satrap of Sardis, having been appointed by Kyros. This one desired an unholy action: for neither having suffered anything nor having heard an insulting word from Polykrates the Samian nor even having seen him before, he desired to take him and destroy him (οὔτε γάρ τι παθὼν οὔτε ἀκούσας μάταιον ἔπος πρὸς Πολυκράτεος τοῦ Σαμίου οὐδὲ ἰδὼν πρότερον ἐπεθύμεε λαβὼν αὐτὸν ἀπολέσαι), as the majority say, on account of some such cause as the following: [they say that] when Oroites was sitting at the gates of the king with another Persian named Mitrobates, satrap of the province at Daskyleion, that these two fell from words into quarrels. And as they were vying over excellence (κρινομένων δὲ περὶ ἀρετῆς), Mitrobates said reproaching Oroites, "O sure, you belong in the roll of real men, who have not been able to acquire for the king the island of Samos, though it lies right next to your province and though it is so easily taken that one of the locals, having mounted a rebellion with fifteen hoplites, got it and now rules it." Some say that, when he heard this and grieved at the reproach, he desired not so much to punish the one who said these things, as utterly to destroy Polykrates, on whose account he had a bad reputation (οἱ μὲν δή μίν φασι τοῦτο ἀκούσαντα καὶ ἀλγήσαντα τῷ ὀνείδεϊ ἐπιθυμῆσαι οὐκ οὕτω τὸν εἴπαντα ταῦτα τείσασθαι ὡς Πολυκράτεα πάντως ἀπολέσαι, δι᾽ ὅντινα κακῶς ἤκουσε).

---

[27] Cf. the remarks of Gould 1989: 58–62, 81–82, 127–29, on the effects of competing *gnōmai* and stories in Herodotus. See also Flory 1987: 154–58; Flory recognizes the same phenomenon but then feels that he must decide between competing narratives and attribute that decision to Herodotus.

But the minority say that Oroites sent a herald to Samos in order to ask for
something or other (for this, at any rate, is not said), and that Polykrates
happened to be reclining in the *andreōn*, and that Anakreon the Teian was
also there. And somehow, whether he intentionally despised the affairs of
Oroites, or it was simply an accident—for [they say] that the herald of
Oroites, coming in, spoke and that Polykrates (for he happened to be reclining facing the wall) neither turned around nor gave any answer. (τόν τε
γὰρ κήρυκα τὸν Ὀροίτεω παρελθόντα διαλέγεσθαι καὶ τὸν Πολυκράτεα
(τυχεῖν γὰρ ἀπεστραμμένον πρὸς τὸν τοῖχον) οὔτε [τι] μεταστραφῆναι
οὔτε τι ὑποκρίνασθαι). (Hdt. 3.120–21)

This narrative offers us a dizzying proliferation of breakdowns in communication and randomly directed acts of violence. As such, it represents
the culmination of the crisis of distinctions Polykrates himself had engen-
dered by his own random aggression. In a world where there is no
distinction between friends and enemies, one's own and another's, no
one is safe. Thus the entire narrative is set under the sign of a triple
negation of any prior contact between Oroites and Polykrates: οὔτε γὰρ
τι παθὼν οὔτε ἀκούσας . . . οὐδὲ ἰδών. We can compare this emphatic
sequence with the almost hysterical list of negations in Alkaios fr. 69 V:

Ζεῦ πάτερ, Λύδοι μὲν ἐπα[σχάλαντες
συμφόραισι δισχελίοις στά[τηρας
ἄμμ’ ἔδωκαν, αἴ κε δυνάμεθ’ ἴρ[αν
ἐς πόλιν ἔλθην,

οὐ πάθοντες οὐδάμα πῶσλον οὐ[δ’ ἔ]ν
οὐδὲ γινώσκοντες· ὁ δ’ ὡς ἀλώπα[ξ
ποικ[ι]λόφρων εὐμάρεα προλέξα[ις
ἤλπ[ε]το λάσην.

Zeus Father, the Lydians, distressed by our misfortunes, have given us two
thousand staters, if we can go to the holy city, not having experienced
anything, not even one noble thing, nor knowing us at all. But that one,
like a crafty-minded fox, hoped to escape notice predicting an easy outcome.

To register the complete lack of prior gift-exchange relations, the poet
stutters through four negatives in a line and a half. Alkaios has in mind
positive contact (οὐ πάθοντες οὐδάμα πῶσλον), Herodotus negative
(μάταιον ἔπος); but the baseline of aristocratic reciprocity is the same
for both.[28] According to the logic of this narrative, the proper object of
Oroites' vengeful lust should be Mitrobates, who *has* directed a *mataion
epos* against him (this is implied as self-evident by the narrator's *sotto*

---

[28] On Alkaios fr. 69 V, cf. Kurke 1991: 252–53.

voce οὕτω). But instead Oroites directs his wrath at an unsuspecting third party, with whom he has no relations but whom he regards as the ultimate cause of his bad reputation.

The second, less popular, version of the story (3.121) is still under the sign of the triple negative. It too emphasizes lack of communication, though the noncontact of Polykrates and Oroites is in this instance more "direct," mediated only through a herald.[29] And here too, Herodotus is at pains to suggest the obscurity of motive and the predominance of randomness. Oroites has sent a messanger to ask for something, but we don't know what; Polykrates *happens* to be facing the wall; and he snubs the messenger either deliberately, or, perhaps, just by accident. Once the channels of proper reciprocity break down, we find ourselves in a murky world where *tuchē* rules and human motivations are utterly opaque. All we know for sure is that there is no contact: the double οὔτε of the last line (οὔτε [τι] μεταστραφῆναι οὔτε τι ὑποκρίνασθαι) picks up and completes the estrangement of the initial triple negation.

Indeed, the narrator himself seems to succumb to the uncertainty and randomness of this twilight world. Herodotus concludes, "These are the two causes told of the death of Polykrates; but it is present to believe whichever of them one wishes" (3.122.1). Is this because the two accounts of the disintegration of reciprocity are simply equivalent? Perhaps. It almost feels as if the reciprocal contract of narrator and listener itself begins to waver—Herodotus throws up his hands and invites us to choose for ourselves.[30]

Thus the original motivation of Oroites' nefarious scheme is set in the context of a pervasive crisis of proper gift-exchange relations. But once his resolve is taken, Oroites baits his trap by an act of counterfeiting that perfectly reciprocates Polykrates' counterfeit coinage. Learning that Polykrates aspires to thalassocracy but is short of cash, Oroites sends him a message (which appropriately echoes the language and formulae of Amasis's letter), offering Polykrates money for assisting the satrap's flight from Kambyses. He adds, "Thanks to this money you will rule all Hellas. But if you disbelieve me about the money, send whoever happens to be most trustworthy for you and I will show it to him" (3.122.4). Polykrates, delighted, sends his secretary Maiandrios, son of Maiandrios, "to inspect" (κατοψόμενον, 3.123.1). Oroites, then, prepares for the inspection,

---

[29] For another example of the homology between gift exchange and proper linguistic reciprocity in Herodotus, cf. Gould 1991: 8–9.

[30] Notice also the repetition of the indefinite κως (even in the time reckoning that links this story to the preceding!) and the odd anacolouthon at 3.121.2, which seems the narrative equivalent or enactment of the breakdown of proper dialogue between the herald and Polykrates.

Having filled eight chests with stones except for a very little bit around the lips, he cast gold upon the surface of the stones, and having bound the chests held them ready. But Maiandrios, having come and having viewed them, reported back to Polykrates. And he [Polykrates] was setting out to go, though his seers were strongly forbidding him, and his friends also, and in addition though his daughter saw such a vision in her sleep: it seemed to her that her father, aloft in the air, was washed by Zeus and anointed by Helios. When she saw this vision, she did everything she could to prevent Polykrates from going away to the court of Oroites . . . (Hdt. 3.123.2–124.2)

Polykrates goes to Oroites (now in Magnesia) and meets an ignominious end:

Oroites, having killed him in a way not worthy of narration, crucified him. . . . And Polykrates, crucified, fulfilled the entire vision of his daughter; for he was washed by Zeus when it rained, and anointed by the sun when he himself gave off the moisture of his body. Thus the many good fortunes of Polykrates ended in this, in the way that Amasis the king of Egypt had foretold for him.[31] (Hdt. 3.125.3, 125.4)

Within the perfect narrative arc of this story, which ends so satisfyingly with the reminiscence of Amasis, Oroites' act of "counterfeiting" forms a crucial link. It is instrumental in luring Polykrates to his death, but more importantly, it precisely corresponds to Polykrates' own act of bribing the invading Spartans with false currency.[32] Just as Polykrates coated lead with gold (μολύβδου καταχρυσώσαντα, 3.56.2), Oroites casts a thin layer of gold over stones (ἐπιπολῆς τῶν λίθων χρυσὸν ἐπέβαλε, 3.123.2), each to deceive an enemy. Within the terms of this tale, Polykrates makes a grave mistake when he imagines that he can be a "real" or legitimate ruler while issuing false coinage. The money he produces bearing his symbol, like his seal, is an extension of himself, his "emanation" in Cassin's terms.[33] Thus, to issue lead coated with gold is to declare himself false and illegitimate and to invite destruction. Furthermore, the dissemination of a false *sēma* seems permanently to alienate him, not only from rule, but also from control of signification. We see this latter in his repeated failure to understand or fathom doubled or ambiguous messages—the evidence of his secretary and the prophetic dream of his daughter. Like a counterfeit coin, her vision offers a gilded message that conceals a base end, but her father is unable to "read" it

---

[31] I follow Immerwahr 1956–57: 318 in accepting this last clause as genuine.

[32] For this narrative pattern of reciprocating "counterfeits," cf. Steiner 1994: 160–61; von Reden 1997: 171. Given their readings, neither Steiner nor von Reden can account for Herodotus's expressed skepticism about Polykrates' "counterfeit" coinage.

[33] Cassin 1960: 744.

aright.[34] Throughout the *Histories*, part of the dynastic survival kit is the ability to interpret ambiguous signifying systems (both objects and spoken/written messages);[35] by his combined violations of gift exchange and counterfeiting, Polykrates seems permanently to have abdicated this skill.

We should pause for a moment to consider the strange conception of coinage this narrative bespeaks. To our way of thinking, if Polykrates issues coinage, it cannot be counterfeit: it is simply the legal tender of Samos. Thus Colin Kraay accounts for the electrum-coated lead coins that have been identified as Samian issues:

> Such leaden pieces, no doubt originally covered with electrum foil, may well have given rise to the story incredulously reported by Herodotus that Polycrates induced the Spartans to raise the siege of Samos in 525/524 by bribing them with leaden coins plated with gold (III, 56, 2); we may agree with Herodotus' doubts about its authenticity, for the Spartans can hardly have been as gullible as that. Polycrates held out only with difficulty against his enemies and, cut off from mainland supplies of bullion, may have been compelled to resort to some kind of token coinage for internal use, as Athens was to do more than a century later.[36]

This rational, modern view of coinage feels no discomfort with its symbolic or token aspects, and assumes that under conditions of scarcity of precious metal, the coinage circulating within the city could be debased. But, as we have seen in Chapters 1 and 2, the symbolic function of coinage rarely figured in ancient discourses, which preferred to emphasize essence over function. Where the symbolic or token value was acknowledged, it was linked to the deceit of the *kapēlos*, the illegitimacy of the tyrant, or the specter of arbitrary change (as in Aristotle).[37]

---

[34] Cf. Herodotus's use of the phrase "counterfeit oracle" (on which, see Ch. 4 below). We see a very similar pattern (a gilded prophecy that conceals a bad outcome) in the tradition of the Pythia's response to Polykrates' question whether he should call the games he organized on Delos "Delian" or "Pythian": the Pythia responded "Both Delian and Pythian for you" (ταῦτά σοι καὶ Δήλια καὶ Πύθια, *Paroem. Gr.* I.165–66, II.629; Apostolius 15.9; Suda p. 3128, τ 174). This response, which Polykrates took positively (and celebrated the games as "Delian and Pythian") became proverbial for "You've had it" ("for she was signaling that he would die immediately," ἐσήμαινε γὰρ ὅτι εὐθέως ἀποθανεῖται). According to the suggestion of Dobree 1831: 607, the "lead" meaning within the gilded oracle is revealed by an etymological pun on δηλεῖσθαι and πύθειν (i.e., "You will perish and rot," though it should be noted that δηλέομαι is normally deponent—passive in form, but with an active meaning "to harm, kill").

[35] Cf. Dewald 1985, 1993; Lavelle 1991; McGlew 1993: 29; Christ 1994.

[36] Kraay 1976: 30.

[37] We should emphasize that, if Polykrates experimented with token coinage for whatever purpose (as the numismatic evidence suggests he did), this was one of the earliest instances of a very rare phenomenon in the Greek world. There is numismatic evidence for base silver staters circulating on Lesbos in the first half of the sixth century (Kraay 1976: 38–39);

So here too, the aristocratic sources of Herodotus's story occlude the communal symbolic function of money, engaging in a kind of doubled essentialism: coinage is seen first as the metal of which it is made, and simultaneously, as the emanation of the issuer's essence. Thus the coin, like the seal, is the personal token of the issuer, not a political symbol— the magical doublet of his identity.[38] As such, the base metal of which the coin is made bodies forth Polykrates' own baseness and corruption, assimilating this narrative structure even more closely to the Theognidean figure of the "counterfeit self." Given this conception, it is insane for Polykrates to imagine that he can issue money that is false and base without betraying and destroying himself; and this is the message of the reciprocating counterfeits that structure the narrative.

In light of this odd perspective on coinage, we can see more clearly how counterfeiting complements violations of gift exchange; how they form the two halves of a single transgression. For the latter (violations of gift exchange) represents and precipitates a crisis of distinctions—a world in which no distinctions are made—while Polykrates' counterfeiting assumes that too much of a distinction is possible between the issuer and the coin. In other terms (to use the vocabulary of *oikeion/allotrion* that figures prominently throughout Book 3), Polykrates' violations of gift exchange treat everything as his own, recognizing no boundaries of self and propriety, while his debased currency represents the setting of

---

the next known instance of token currency (as Kraay acknowledges) is that issued in Athens at the end of the Peloponnesian War. Finally, the Pseudo-Aristotelian *Oikonomika* tells of a token currency issued by the Athenian general Timotheos in an expedition against Olynthos (363–359 B.C.E.; [Arist.] *Oik.* 2.2.23.1). For the general, long-standing Greek resistance to debased or token currency, see Kraay 1976: 11; Howgego 1995: 113. It may be that the "mythic" narrative of reciprocating counterfeits that accreted around Polykrates represents in part a phobic response to his early experiment with token coinage.

[38] On the parallel between coin and seal, see Seaford 1994: 224–26; Steiner 1994: 159–63. For a very suggestive discussion of coinage-as-sign vs. an older form of talismanic value, see Gernet 1981a: 145–46: "The invention of money certainly makes possible the deployment of an abstract conception of value. With the new state of affairs there comes the use of an instrumental agent whose substance (in the philosophical sense; whose material composition) might seem of little interest or importance: it was left to Plato and Aristotle, neither of them friends of the mercantile economy, to construct a theory of money-as-sign and money-as-convention. That was a logical theory, since of course these philosophers were interested only in the aspect of exchange and circulation. ... And there can be no doubt that the instrumental agent once invented was admirably fitted to circulate. Circulate it did in Greece, both early and widely. But in the historical milieu in which money-as-sign first appeared, the religious, aristocratic and agonistic symbols stamped on its first specimens were attestations of origin: a mythical way of thinking endured right to the very moment at which the invention of coinage became possible. By which I mean to say that there is, in 'value' and so in the very token that represents it, a core which cannot be reduced to what they call rational thought."

the boundaries of self too narrowly, not reckoning with the coin as the extension of the self. Others have noted that this inability to negotiate the boundary of self and other, *oikeion* and *allotrion*, is the tyrannic problem par excellence in Greek thought.[39] I would suggest that this representation serves an important ideological function, since it is at least partly written over the tyrant's *redefinition* of the boundaries of self and other in the process of inventing the public space. That is to say, the opposition *oikeion/allotrion* functions in aristocratic discourse to mask the real opposition *idion/koinon*, which, in an ongoing negotiation, reconfigures the boundaries of self to accommodate the demands of the public sphere. In the case of coinage in particular, the tyrant is represented as fatally misconstruing the boundaries of the self, for coinage is read as the quintessential inalienable possession in the logic of the gift. But this is precisely the logic that coinage as a communally legislated and conventionally accepted token is intended to explode. Instead of the essentialism of precious metal and the noble self as index and standard of value, coinage institutes the value regime of the civic community. Thus, the tyrant as violator of the gift conceals from view the tyrant as "inventor" of a new regime of value.[40]

Yet, given the remarkable correspondences between the two episodes —Polykrates' counterfeiting and Oroites' entrapment of Polykrates— Herodotus's rejection of the original story as a *mataioteros logos* becomes all the more puzzling. Why does Herodotus dismiss the tale of Polykrates gilding lead and bribing the Spartans when, in a sense, the logic of the entire narrative hinges on this one fateful action? Here, at least, we can pinpoint a gap between Herodotus's own view and the version he got from his Samian aristocratic sources (for whom, I have argued, the story's perfect reciprocities are its *point*). But what accounts for Herodotus's resistance? Modern scholars have offered various explanations for his skepticism. Colin Kraay, in the passage quoted above (p. 115), assumes as self-evident a practical rationale: "we may agree with Herodotus' doubts about [the story's] authenticity, for the Spartans can hardly have been as gullible as that." I find myself not completely comfortable with the easy assumption that we are dealing with economic rationality and savvy, especially in the case of the Spartans, who, lacking a precious metal currency of their own, were notoriously susceptible to the gleam of gold in Greek tradition.[41] In any case Herodotus certainly does not

---

[39] Farenga 1981; Vernant 1988: 135–40; McGlew 1993: 29–34; Seaford 1994: 232–34; von Reden 1997: 171–72.

[40] Cf. Farenga 1985 on the "numismatic strategies" of the Greek tyrants: i.e., the tyrant is redefining the categories of *oikeion/allotrion* (or rather, of public and private—*idion/koinon*).

[41] On the Spartan susceptibility to bribery, see Finley 1985b: 150–51; Noethlichs 1987.

say (as he could have), "because the Spartans would not have been *that* gullible." Another tack would be to say that Herodotus is here combining different sources—that he had competing accounts from the Samian aristocrats and his Spartan informant Archias, whom he mentions by name in chapter 55. According to this interpretation, the Spartans (of course) deny the charge of accepting bribes, and the histor sides with them, rejecting the story as silly in the interests of Spartan reputation. There are two problems here. First, Herodotus does not offer two contrasting accounts, as he frequently does: he does not say, "The Samians say this, but the Spartans deny it."[42] It may be suggested that he simply rejects the story to spare the Spartans' reputation, out of partiality toward his *xenos* Archias. But this claim too runs afoul of the evidence, for in the story in which he first introduces the elder Archias, he says quite bluntly what he thinks of the Spartans: "Now if those of the Lakedaimonians who were present had been like Archias and Lykopes on this day, Samos would have been taken" (εἰ μέν νυν οἱ παρεόντες Λακεδαιμονίων ὅμοιοι ἐγίνοντο ταύτην τὴν ἡμέρην Ἀρχίῃ τε καὶ Λυκώπῃ, αἱρέθη ἂν Σάμος, 3.55.1). It is not simply that Herodotus questions their courage and fighting skill: by using only the designation Λακεδαιμόνιοι and insisting that the rest were not ὅμοιοι of the two who died, Herodotus denies the bases of Spartiate self-representation.[43] He implicitly challenges the Spartiates' right to call themselves *Homoioi*, and as we have seen in the sympotic diction of Theognis, this is the equivalent of labeling them "base" and "counterfeit." This can hardly be regarded as sparing the Spartans' feelings or reputation.

How then to account for Herodotus's rejection of the story of counterfeiting and bribing as a *mataioteros logos*? I would suggest that it is precisely to disturb the narrative's perfect symmetry on this point that he denies it. That is to say that, though he reproduces the story of Polykrates' ring, he does not completely accede to an aristocratic construction of the world that subsumes coinage to gift exchange for its model of cosmic reciprocity. Lest this interpretation seem hopelessly farfetched,[44] I would point to Herodotus's other clear divergence from his sources and the terms in which it is couched. In narrating the death of Polykrates, the histor reveals a sneaking admiration for the tyrant:

---

[42] For precisely this kind of account involving the Samians and the Spartans, cf. the complex of competing claims transcribed at Hdt. 1.70.

[43] For the pun involved in Herodotus's use of *homoioi* here, see Shimron 1979. For the importance of the distinction between "Spartiate" and "Lakedaimonian," see Lippold 1929: 1280–83, 1291–92; Cartledge 1982: 255–56.

[44] It should be pointed out that Herodotus gives us no specific grounds for his skepticism, nor is it clear precisely what he disbelieves—(1) that Polykrates minted debased currency in the first place, or (2) that he used it to bribe the Spartans.

ἀπικόμενος δὲ ἐς τὴν Μαγνησίην ὁ Πολυκράτης διεφθάρη κακῶς, οὔτε
ἑωυτοῦ ἀξίως οὔτε τῶν ἑωυτοῦ φρονημάτων· ὅτι γὰρ μὴ οἱ Συρηκοσίων
γενόμενοι τύραννοι, οὐδὲ εἷς τῶν ἄλλων Ἑλληνικῶν τυράννων ἄξιός ἐστι
Πολυκράτεϊ μεγαλοπρεπείην συμβληθῆναι. ἀποκτείνας δέ μιν οὐκ ἀξίως
ἀπηγήσιος Ὀροίτης ἀνεσταύρωσε· (Hdt. 3.125.2–3)

Having come to Magnesia, Polykrates perished badly, in a way worthy
neither of himself nor of his ambitions; for, excepting those who became
tyrants of the Syracusans, no one of the other Greek tyrants is worthy to
be compared to Polykrates in *megaloprepeia*. And Oroites, when he had
killed him in a way not worthy of narration, crucified him.

This is surely not what Herodotus's Samian aristocratic sources thought
of Polykrates. For a moment, we glimpse a figure very different from the
ruthless pirate portrayed in the earlier narrative. And the one quality
Herodotus singles out to justify his praise in this brief eulogy (this is the
force of γάρ) is Polykrates' *megaloprepeia*. *Megaloprepeia*, or lavish public expenditure, was perhaps an invention of the tyrants of the seventh and
sixth centuries, as a way of appropriating the protocols and ideological
investments of aristocratic gift exchange and transferring them to the
public sphere.[45] Insofar as it directs the same energies and "investments"
elsewhere, *megaloprepeia* represents a threat to the established parapolitical order of gift exchange. Thus *megaloprepeia*, like coinage, heralds a
new regime of civic value, often mediated by tyrants throughout the
archaic Greek world.

Herodotus's praise of Polykrates' *megaloprepeia* is unexpected, for we
have had no hint of it before—or perhaps we should say, only one very
broad hint, if we follow the theory of B. M. Mitchell. She suggests that
the three grandiose Samian building projects invoked by Herodotus in
3.60 to justify his Samian "digression" were the ἔργα Πολυκράτεια
referred to by Aristotle (*Pol.* 1313b24). Mitchell argues persuasively
that Herodotus's elite Samian sources deliberately suppressed Polykrates'
responsibility for these monuments (thus, no one is given credit for them
at 3.60). If this is so, Herodotus's brief eulogy of Polykrates represents
the narrative return of the repressed (as it were), since his mention of
Polykrates' *megaloprepeia* receives no other corroboration in the text.[46]

In his unqualified praise for Polykrates' *megaloprepeia*, Herodotus

---

[45] On *megaloprepeia* in general, see Kurke 1991: 163–256; on the agency of the tyrants
as "inventors" of *megaloprepeia*, see Farenga 1985; Shipley 1987: 92–94; Kurke 1991:
180–82 with n. 37.

[46] Mitchell 1975: 82–84, followed by Shipley 1987: 75–80, 92–94. For independent
testimony of Polykrates' *megaloprepeia*, we should note the assertion of Alexis of Samos
(*FGrH* 539 F 2, preserved in Athen. *Deipn.* 12.540d–e) that "Samos was adorned by
Polykrates (κοσμηθῆναι τὴν Σάμον), who imported Molossian and Lakonian hounds, goats

briefly disengages himself from the driving narrative logic of aristocratic gift exchange and positions himself somewhere else. Rather than representing Polykrates' relation to value and valuables simply as a series of transgressions of cosmic and human gift exchange, *megaloprepeia* frames those same activities positively, as a contribution to and adornment of the public sphere.[47] Thus I suggest that we must connect these two moments of divergence or resistance in the narrative. For the first (3.56) refuses to read coinage simply as a personal token, a talisman inalienable from its issuer's essence, while the second (3.125) likewise refuses to construe the tyrant's public works simply as the pillaging of the aristocratic domain. In both instances, a space is briefly and incongruously carved out for the public domain—for a civic regime of value—within a narrative whose purpose is precisely to foreclose that possibility.

Indeed, the key issue is "value." What is striking about Herodotus's brief narrative commemoration of Polykrates is its obsessive emphasis on "value" or "worth": forms of ἄξιος (as adjective and adverb) are repeated three times in as many sentences. Polykrates dies in a manner not worthy (ἀξίως) of himself or his ambitions; no other tyrant is worthy (ἄξιος) to be compared with Polykrates; Oroites kills him in a way not worthy (ἀξίως) of narration. This triple repetition of *axios* takes us back to the beginning of Polykrates' story. There, Amasis had advised his Samian *xenos* to pick out the possession that was "worth most" to him (ἐόν τοι πλείστου ἄξιον) and throw it away (3.40.4), while the fisherman "deemed his great and beautiful fish worthy to be given as a gift to Polykrates" (ἠξίου μιν Πολυκρατέϊ δῶρον δοθῆναι, 3.42.1). Finally, in a phrase that foreshadows most closely the histor's own eulogy, the fisherman explains to the tyrant that the fish seemed to him to be "worthy of you and of your rule" (σεῦ τε εἶναι ἄξιος καὶ τῆς σῆς ἀρχῆς, 3.42.2).[48] In this opening narrative of the ring and the fish, the issue of worth or value is completely imbricated in the problematic relations of gift exchange

---

from Skyros and Naxos, sheep from Miletos and Attica, and who, he says, encouraged the immigration of skilled craftsmen with the highest wages."

[47] Cf. the remarks of Shipley 1987: 93–94: "The purpose of the public works was not, as Aristotle thought, to keep the people poor and too busy to think, but to keep them prosperous and loyal while depriving aristocrats of their traditional base of support in kinship-groups and preventing them getting richer and winning power. . . . Grand projects were a means of acquiring popularity and prestige, the only safeguards of Polycrates' power."

[48] Van der Veen 1993: 450 notes the significant repetition of forms of *axios*, but draws a different conclusion. Two more occurrences of *axios* and its compounds bracket the narrative: 3.47.3 (the corselet dedicated by Amasis at the temple of Athena Lindos is θωμάσαι ἄξιον); 3.123.1 (the furnishings from Polykrates' *andreōn* dedicated by Maiandrios are ἀξιοθέητον).

Polykrates engenders.[49] By the end of his story, this same language of value has shifted to a positive depiction of the tyrant and his relation to the public sphere. In this obsessive repetition of the language of value, we can perhaps read the tension between the histor and his Samian aristocratic sources. The triple occurrences of forms of *axios* bracketing the story insistently raise the questions: What constitutes value? What are Polykrates and his rule worth? To judge from the narrative's final gesture, the histor situates himself in a somewhat different place from his aristocratic informants, for in the end "not worthily of himself and his ambitions" collapses with "not worthily of narration," so that the narrator seems to align himself with and speak from the site of tyrannic imagination and aspiration (φρονημάτων).

III. GIFT EXCHANGE AS CIVIC VIOLENCE (Hdt. 3.139–49)

The narrator's ambivalent relation to his aristocratic informants leads us finally to the last sequence of Samian stories, near the close of Book 3. For these stories too seem obsessed with the issues of gift exchange, tyrannic rule, and value, but from a very different perspective. This sequence begins with the tale of Polykrates' one surviving brother, Syloson, in Egypt at the time of Kambyses' invasion (Hdt. 3.139). Syloson is strolling through the marketplace of Memphis, wearing a red mantle (χλανίδα ... πυρρήν), when Darius, who we are told is only a lowly spearbearer of Kambyses, happens by and is very taken with the garment: "And Syloson, seeing Darius greatly desiring the mantle (μεγάλως ἐπιθυμέοντα τῆς χλανίδος), experiencing some divine fortune says, 'I'll sell this to you for no amount of money, but I give it to you for nothing, since thus it is necessary that it be entirely yours.' Darius, praising these things, takes the garment, while Syloson believed that this was lost to him through simplemindedness" (δι᾽ εὐηθίην, 3.139.3). The sequel, of course, is that when Darius becomes king, Syloson turns up at his court claiming to be the king's benefactor. Admitted to his presence, Syloson reminds Darius of the gift of the cloak, thereby provoking a suitably royal response:

"O most noble of men (γενναιότατε ἀνδρῶν), you are that one who gave to me, though I had no power yet, even if small things, still the gratitude is likewise equal (ἴση γε ἡ χάρις ὁμοίως) as if I should get something great

---

[49] These earlier occurrences are closer to the conventional use of *axios* as a buzzword for "noble" character; cf. Aesch. *Eum.* 435; Eur. *Ion* 735 and see LSJ, s.v. ἄξιος II. Notice, though, how in the course of the Polykrates narrative, Herodotus transvalues *axios*.

from somewhere now. In exchange for these things I give you endless gold and silver, so that you never regret treating Darius the son of Hystaspes well." (Hdt. 3.140.4)

We seem to have landed in the same numinous gift-exchange world that Polykrates unwittingly inhabited. But Syloson is the opposite of his brother: where Polykrates took indiscriminately from *philoi*, Syloson gives to strangers. And, as in the earlier sequence, objects are charged with otherworldly or talismanic value: the red mantle that Syloson senses "must belong" to Darius (δεῖ γενέσθαι πάντως τοι) is clearly the presage and symbol of his royal election. Thus we have, to all appearances, a simple story of virtue rewarded. The impulse that Syloson attributes to simplemindedness (εὐηθίη) turns out to be an act of true "good nature," and Syloson's gift of a red mantle symbolizing sovereignty is neatly reciprocated with the gift of sovereignty in Samos.[50]

Yet the sequel—the Persian conquest of Samos—is anything but neat. For Syloson's story is strangely intercalated with that of another set of three brothers: Maiandrios (who tries very hard not to be like Polykrates) and his brothers, Lykaretos and Charileos. We are told that Maiandrios, who now held power in Samos as Polykrates' steward,

> wanted to be the most just of men, but it turned out to be impossible for him to do so (τῷ δικαιοτάτῳ ἀνδρῶν βουλομένῳ γενέσθαι οὐκ ἐξεγένετο). For when the death of Polykrates was announced, he did the following things: first, he established an altar of Zeus Eleutherios and measured out around it the precinct which now exists in the suburb. But afterward, when this had been done, he called an assembly of all the citizens and said, "To me, as you also know, the scepter and all the power of Polykrates have been entrusted, and it is available for me now to rule over you. But the things that I disapprove of in my neighbor, I shall not do myself, as far as it is in my power: for neither Polykrates was pleasing to me when he lorded it over men who were like him (οὔτε γάρ μοι Πολυκράτης ἤρεσκε δεσπόζων ἀνδρῶν ὁμοίων ἑωυτῷ) nor any other who does such things. Polykrates now has fulfilled his fate, but I, putting the rule in the middle, proclaim *isonomia* for you (ἐγὼ δὲ ἐς μέσον τὴν ἀρχὴν τιθεὶς ἰσονομίην ὑμῖν προαγορεύω). So many privileges, though, I deem it right to have—six talents picked out from the property of Polykrates, and in addition to these things, I choose the priesthood of Zeus Eleutherios for myself and my descendants

---

[50] Thus Strabo tells the story: "And Syloson was left a private citizen by his brother. And he gratified Darius the son of Hystaspes with a garment, which that one desired when he saw [Syloson] wearing it. And Darius was not yet king at that time, but when he became king, [Syloson] got his tyranny as a gift in return" (Strabo 14.1.17/638).

in perpetuity, since I myself founded the shrine and I crown you with freedom" (τὴν ἐλευθερίην ὑμῖν περιτίθημι). (Hdt. 3.142.1–4)

The tone of this passage and the way in which it is introduced by the narrative voice suggest that it represents a very different perspective from the two earlier Samian sequences. If those narratives of the rise and fall of Polykrates formulated the view of tyranny "from above," from the elitist aristocratic position, this story of the hapless Maiandrios, in contrast, seems to sketch a portrait of tyranny "from below," from the middling, egalitarian point of view.[51] Thus, Maiandrios aspires to be the most just of men by putting power *es meson*, making it common to all the citizens in the form of *isonomia*.[52] And whereas Polykrates was represented as ruinously failing to make proper distinctions on the basis of *philia*, Maiandrios is positively portrayed in his attempt to efface all distinctions of power and status within the citizen body (thus his assertion that they are all *homoioi*).[53]

That an egalitarian perspective informs this narrative is confirmed by the immediate sequel:

ὁ μὲν δὴ ταῦτα τοῖσι Σαμίοισι ἐπαγγέλλετο, τῶν δέ τις ἐξαναστὰς εἶπε· Ἀλλ' οὐδ' ἄξιος εἶς σύ γε ἡμέων ἄρχειν, γεγονώς τε κακῶς καὶ ἐὼν ὄλεθρος, ἀλλὰ μᾶλλον ὅκως λόγον δώσεις τῶν μετεχείρισας χρημάτων. ταῦτα εἶπε ἐὼν ἐν τοῖσι ἀστοῖσι δόκιμος, τῷ οὔνομα ἦν Τελέσαρχος. (Hdt. 3.142.5– 143.1)

[Maiandrios] indeed announced these things to the Samians, but one of them stood up and said, "But you are not even worthy to rule us, being baseborn and a pest, but rather [see to it] that you give an account of

---

[51] Indeed, this is one of the passages cited by Morris (1996: 36–37) to support his claim that egalitarian representations of rule placed *es meson* proliferate in the years around 520. Mitchell 1975: 86, followed by Shipley 1987: 103–5, contends that Herodotus's sources for this episode remain Samian aristocrats. But such an attribution does not adequately account for (1) the offer of *isonomia* (which Mitchell asserts, but gives no evidence to prove, is "consistent with aristocratic control"; against this, cf. Ostwald 1969: 107–13; Robinson 1997: 118–20), and (2) the histor's interventions attributing "justice" to Maiandrios and Kleomenes (Hdt. 3.142, 148.2). For a critique of this position, cf. McGlew 1993: 128–29. For different interpretations of Maiandrios's assembly and its implications, see Flory 1987: 144–46; McGlew 1993: 124–34, Steiner 1994: 173–74.

[52] On the significance of the phrase *es meson*, see Vernant 1982: 46–48, 52–68; Detienne 1996: 91–102; Morris 1996: 36–37.

[53] Of course, some are more equal than others: on the nomothete's "wolflike" desire to get more than his share, see Detienne and Svenbro 1989. I am less persuaded by McGlew's argument that Maiandrios's actions and demands make his offer "a spurious form of freedom" (1993: 126–30, quote from p. 129). Again, this seems to ignore the histor's clear statement that "he wanted to be the most just of men," while it requires a strained

the money you've been managing." The one who said these things was a
distinguished man among the citizens, whose name was Telesarchos.

We should not be deceived by the procedure this outraged citizen demands, which bears an uncanny resemblance to the *euthunai* magistrates
were required to undergo in democratic Athens: he is, nonetheless, no
democrat. As Herodotus makes clear in his identification (deliberately
delayed for climactic effect), this recalcitrant Samian is a nobleman and
proud of it, as the histor's use of *dokimos* and the name Telesarchos
reveal.[54] Indeed, everything in his response to Maiandrios is about reestablishing hierarchical distinctions of class and status between citizens. He
tells Maiandrios that he is baseborn and an *olethros*, a term of contempt
with clear class connotations.[55] And, revealingly, he reintroduces the
language of differential worth into Maiandrios's idealized vision of a
group of *homoioi* sharing power *es meson*: he insists that Maiandrios is
not worthy (ἄξιος) to rule, though this is not at all what Maiandrios
had proposed.[56]

Maiandrios understands only too well the oligarchic implications of
Telesarchos's sniping: "grasping that, if he will let go the rule, some other
will establish a tyranny instead of him, he decided indeed not to let
it go" (Hdt. 3.143.1). Instead he lures the citizens (i.e., the *dokimoi*?)
individually to the acropolis on the pretext of giving an account of the
money, then arrests and imprisons them. At this point Maiandrios conveniently falls sick and his overambitious brother Lykaretos executes all the
prisoners. In this brief set of civic confrontations, the story of Maiandrios
enacts and comments on the Persian debate on the constitutions. The
unwilling tyrant attempts to institute *isonomia*, only to be foiled by
the competitive jockeying of the few. In the terms of Darius's critique
of oligarchy:[57]

---

interpretation of Herodotus's wry observation that the Samians apparently "didn't want
to be free" (Hdt. 3.143.2).

[54] Steiner 1994: 173–74 identifies Telesarchos simply as a townsman, but the narrative
cues make this interpretation unlikely. Detienne and Svenbro 1989: 152 also make this
mistake ("this industrious private citizen"): they are too influenced by the ass in Aesop's
fable. McGlew 1993: 125–29; Van der Veen 1995: 130, 142–44; Robinson 1997: 119
rightly identify him as an aristocrat.

[55] Cf. Demosthenes' usage of *olethros* to vilify Aeschines as "a miserable secretary"
(*grammateus*) and a dishonest cheat (Dem. 18.127, 21.209).

[56] Notice σύ γε, which implies that someone else *is* ἄξιος . . . ἄρχειν.

[57] Cf. Flory 1987: 145 for the application of Darius's critique of oligarchy to the Samian
situation. Lateiner 1984, 1989: 163–86 sees the constitutional debate as an important
structuring pattern in the *Histories* but focuses almost entirely on its application to problems
of monarchic/tyrannic rule.

But in oligarchy, with many men cultivating excellence in public, strong private hatreds tend to arise. Since each man wishes to be the leader and to prevail with his opinions, they [all] come to great hatreds of each other, and from these arise [acts of] civil strife, and from civil strife [comes] murder, and from murder it ends up in monarchy . . . (Hdt. 3.82.3)

Herodotus concludes ironically, "For indeed, as it appears, they didn't want to be free men" (3.143.2).

It is in this markedly anti-aristocratic context that we must set the story of royal gift exchange gone terribly awry. Given its outcome, we cannot read the account of Syloson's exchange with the Great King as a simple narrative of virtue rewarded.[58] As Syloson's story comes to intersect more narrowly with that of Maiandrios and his brothers, conflicting codes of aristocratic behavior conspire to destroy the Samian demos (in a kind of oligarchic competition gone mad). First, Maiandrios's "half insane" (ὑπομαργότερος, 3.145.1) brother Charileos appeals to the rights of family and the proprieties of aristocratic vengeance. Imprisoned for "some wrongdoing," as Herodotus tells us, he abuses Maiandrios when he sees from his prison "those of the Persians who were worth the most setting up seats and sitting facing the acropolis" (3.144) to receive the peaceful surrender of the city:

"Me, o basest of men, being your own brother, and having done no wrong worthy of bonds, you have bound and deemed worthy of prison (ἐμὲ μέν, ὦ κάκιστε ἀνδρῶν, ἐόντα σεωυτοῦ ἀδελφεὸν καὶ ἀδικήσαντα οὐδὲν ἄξιον δεσμοῦ δήσας γοργύρης ἠξίωσας), but seeing the Persians casting you out and making you homeless, you don't dare to take vengeance on them, being indeed so easy to capture; but if you are afraid of them, give me the mercenaries and I will punish them for coming here. And you yourself I am prepared to send off the island." Charileos said these things. And Maiandrios adopted the suggestion, as I think, not having come to such a point of folly that he imagined that his power could best that of the king, but rather begrudging it to Syloson if he was without toil going to take back the city unharmed (ἀλλὰ φθονήσας μᾶλλον Συλοσῶντι εἰ ἀπονητὶ ἔμελλε ἀπολάμψεσθαι ἀκέραιον τὴν πόλιν). (Hdt. 3.145.2–146.2)

Charileos first opposes the common good (which presumably lies behind his imprisonment) with the bonds of family, censuring Maiandrios as the "basest of men" because he has seen fit to imprison his own brother.

---

[58] Cf. Van der Veen 1995, who emphasizes the pattern of give-and-take in these chapters and the ruinous effects of Darius's and Syloson's gift exchange. In contrast to the political interpretation offered here, Van der Veen sees the point of this narrative of ruinous exchange as a universal one, confirming Solon's admonitions about the uncertainty of human fortune.

The aristocratic cast of his discourse is reinforced by his insistence on the language of differential worth: like the *dokimos* Telesarchos, he calibrates value with forms of *axios*. He then appeals to the proper aristocratic impulses to punish and to take revenge—on the proper object, "those of the Persians who were worth most" (τῶν Περσέων οἱ πλείστου ἄξιοι, 3.144). Charileos's madness reinscribes a hierarchy of value and status within the city and in its relations with others. Maiandrios, still perhaps trying to be the most just of men, suddenly snaps into oligarchic spite (φθονήσας): in the competition of the *dokimoi*, he would rather see the city devastated than safely in the hands of another. He turns his crazy brother loose to massacre the Persian nobles, while he flees the island (3.146–47).

Otanes, the Persian commander, reacts with predictable violence (he too is bound by an aristocratic code of vengeance):

> Otanes the commander, when he saw the great suffering the Persians suffered, though he remembered, forgot the commands with which Darius dispatched him—not to kill or enslave any one of the Samians and to render the island back to Syloson untouched by evils (ἀπαθέα τε κακῶν ἀποδοῦναι τὴν νῆσον Συλοσῶντι). [Instead] he commanded the army to kill indiscriminately everyone they caught, adult and child alike (ὁ δὲ παρήγγειλε τῇ στρατιῇ πάντα τὸν ἂν λάβωσι, καὶ ἄνδρα καὶ παῖδα, ὁμοίως κτείνειν). At that point part of the force was besieging the acropolis, while the rest were killing everyone who crossed their path, likewise in the temple precinct and outside it (ὁμοίως ἔν τε ἱρῷ καὶ ἔξω ἱροῦ). (Hdt. 3.147.1–2)

In a bitter historical irony, Otanes, who had spoken for *isonomia* in the Persian debate on the constitutions, horribly reinstates Maiandrios's vision of all the Samians as *homoioi*. For in revenge for the killing of the "most worthy" of the Persians, Otanes finally makes all the Samians "like"—only in death (notice the twice repeated ὁμοίως). Herodotus concludes, "The Persians, when they had dragnetted the island, turned it over to Syloson empty of men. Still, at a later time, the commander Otanes also helped populate it, [motivated] by a dream vision and a disease that happened to afflict him in the genitals" (3.149).

This, the third Samian narrative, consistently limns the evils of gift exchange and aristocratic ideology for the civic good: the *charis* between Syloson and Darius turns into a kind of potlatch of citizens, while the arrogance and ambition of the *dokimos* Telesarchos transform Maiandrios from well-meaning democrat to vindictive oligarch. And in the narrative's final gesture, the civic good, repeatedly sacrificed for aristocratic ambition and retribution, is aligned with the cosmic good of the long-term transactional order. Some greater-than-human force afflicts Otanes with a disease of the genitals in cosmic retribution for the destruction he visited on Samos; he understands the logic of his punishment and so enables the recreation of Samian civic order.

We might note in conclusion that this anti-aristocratic, anti-gift-exchange message is reinforced by two elements of the story. First, in a final intercalation of stories (embedded between Otanes' order to kill the Samians indiscriminately and Herodotus's description of the Persians' work as "dragnetting"), we get our last view of Maiandrios. He has fled to Sparta with some valuables, which he deploys to effect his return:

> Whenever he would put out his gold and silver cups and the servants were polishing them, at this same time he would be in conversation with Kleomenes son of Anaxandrides, king of Sparta, and he would bring him home. And when Kleomenes would see the cups, he would marvel at them and be amazed, and Maiandrios would bid him carry away home however many of these he wished. And when Maiandrios had said this two or three times, Kleomenes became the most just of men, who did not deem it right to take things given, and understanding that giving to others of the citizens he would find vengeance (ὁ Κλεομένης δικαιότατος ἀνδρῶν γίνεται, ὃς λαβεῖν μὲν διδόμενα οὐκ ἐδικαίου, μαθὼν δὲ ὡς ἄλλοισι διδοὺς τῶν ἀστῶν εὑρήσεται τιμωρίην), he went to the Ephors and said it was better for Sparta that the Samian stranger depart from the Peloponnese, in order that he not persuade either himself or some other of the Spartiates to be base. And they acceded and ordered Maiandrios out of the country. (Hdt. 3.148.1–2)

In case we had missed the point of the civic threat represented by gift exchange, this tale repeats it for us in a different venue. Kleomenes recognizes the danger for Sparta and her citizens (here significantly called Spartiates)[59] of Maiandrios's top-rank giftgiving in quest of aristocratic vengeance. And for his own abstention from the gift-exchange circuit and clear-sighted recognition that other citizens are at risk, Kleomenes earns the designation "most just of men," in a phrase that harks back to Maiandrios's failed attempt to institute *isonomia* on Samos.[60] The narrative voice that regards both *isonomia* and the rejection of gift exchange as "most just" is consistent throughout this sequence, but completely at odds with the ideology informing the earlier Samian stories.

The second element that confirms the anti-aristocratic, anti-gift-exchange slant of this narrative is Herodotus's punning deployment of the name of Syloson. Historians have suggested that this name derives from σύλη (plunder, booty) and reflects the family's inherited right of privateering. That is to say, the family of Polykrates may traditionally

---

[59] On the rarity of the use of "Spartiate," see Lippold 1929: 1291–92; Cartledge 1982: 255–56 (and see note 43 above).

[60] Van der Veen 1995: 139–40 also notes the verbal echo.

have been pirates licensed by the Samian state to seize foreign merchant-men.[61] I would suggest that Herodotus is conscious of this connection and that he reetymologizes the name to expose the piratical violence Syloson wreaks against his own community by his implication in the circuit of interstate gift exchange. For, on two occasions in this narrative, Herodotus seems consciously to be punning on Syloson's name, specifically in relation to the condition of his city. First, speculating on Maiandrios's motives in acceding to the wishes of his crazed brother Charileos, Herodotus suggests that "he begrudged Syloson if without toil he would take the city back unharmed" (ἀλλὰ φθονήσας μᾶλλον Συλοσῶντι εἰ ἀπονητὶ ἔμελλε ἀπολάμψεσθαι ἀκέραιον τὴν πόλιν, 3.146.2). In the second instance, Herodotus recalls Darius's commands to Otanes (at the moment Otanes willfully forgets them): "not to kill or enslave any one of the Samians and to render the island back to Syloson untouched by evils" (ἀπαθέα τε κακῶν ἀποδοῦναι τὴν νῆσον Συλοσῶντι, 3.147.1). In both cases, Herodotus carefully gives us the name of Syloson in the dative (the recipient of a gift), his city or island in the accusative (the gift itself), and a predicate adjective describing the condition of the city—ἀκέραιον and ἀπαθέα ... κακῶν, both synonyms for ἄσυλον, "untouched, inviolate."[62] In both cases, too, these expressions describe the integrity of the city at the moment a character in the narrative plans or effects its devastation. At the intersection of the competitive oligarchic pursuit of *arete* and the workings of interstate gift exchange, the city is subject to terrible violence. The *charis* of aristocratic gift exchange is inscribed in the *bie* it enacts on the city, and the significant name of Syloson ("the looter") exposes this fearful collapse of categories.[63]

---

[61] Cf. Barron 1964: 214n.4: "We may recall here the Samian practice of issuing Letters of Marque (σῦλαι), apparently in the name of Hera, to judge by the dedicatory inscription of Aiakes ος τηι Ηρηι την συλην επρησεν κατα την επιστασιν (S.I.G.³ 10 . . .). Aiakes was evidently a relative of the tyrants who dedicated a tithe of the proceeds of his duties as ἐπιστάτης σύλων. The office may have been hereditary in the family, hence the recurrent name Συλοσῶν." See also Barron 1964: 218–19; Andrewes 1956: 119; Shipley 1987: 71. If Polykrates' family did indeed enjoy hereditary rights of *sule*, we might again see *to koinon* peeking out behind the aristocratic representation of Polykrates as pirate and looter of *philoi*.

[62] ἀπαθής is used only here in Herodotus for a country rather than a person. Notice also the collocation of the two verbs, ἀπολάμψεσθαι and ἀποδοῦναι, which suggests the equivalence of giving and (violent) taking.

[63] It may be that this same pun on the name of Syloson is at work in Strabo's version, in the proverb he reports—ἕκητι Συλοσῶντος εὐρυχωρίη, "plenty of room thanks to Syloson" (Strabo 14.1.17/638). Still, we should note that gift exchange is not directly the culprit in Strabo's version as it is in Herodotus's: in Strabo, the Persian conquest apparently goes without a hitch ("he got his tyranny as a gift in return from the king," βασιλεύσαντος ἀντέλαβε δῶρον τὴν τυραννίδα); it is instead the harshness of Syloson's rule that makes for *euruchorie*.

Thus this third Samian narrative presents us with an account significantly at odds with the earlier Samian stories in the models it valorizes and condemns. In contrast to those sequences, which staked and supported the human gift-exchange order on the certainty of cosmic retribution, this last set of Samian stories reveals the civic violence that works through the gift, while it endorses *isonomia* and the perpetuation of polis order with its own brand of cosmic punishment (3.149). As in the stories around Darius and Amasis, we can see a contest of paradigms being fought out, this time inscribed in the "history" and interpretation of events of this single island. The histor enables us to see the conflicts and oppositions clearly by his respectful transmission of what must be different traditions. But, though he may be evenhanded, he is not disinterested, so that we see also the traces of his resistance (the *mataioteros logos*), his allegiances (to *isonomia*), and his qualified approval (of Polykrates' *megaloprepeia*).

CHAPTER 4

Kroisos and the Oracular Economy

WITH THE SAMIAN STORIES, the motif of counterfeiting led us to the complexities of gift exchange—a system multiply contested at the levels of cosmos and community. The same contest of paradigms over the validity of cosmic and human gift exchange informs the narratives around one of the most familiar figures in Herodotus's *Histories*: Kroisos, tyrant of Lydia. Gregory Nagy has recently focused on Kroisos, arguing that he is a traditional figure, with a coherent signification, within the forms of Greek *ainos* (subsuming thereby both epinikion and Herodotus's prose account).[1] It will be my contention (and the purpose of this chapter) to argue that Greek texts offer us, in fact, many different traditions of Kroisos, conditioned at least partly by their implication in a politically interested struggle over regimes of value. That is to say, rather than seeing Kroisos as a single figure whose ambiguities (positive and negative) correspond to the doubled message of *ainos*, I would like to read the Lydian dynast instead as an emblem for gift-exchange relations, appropriated differently by different ideological positions within the Greek city.[2] As with the Samian stories, the different representations of cosmos and community will turn out to be connected; we shall find that divergent patterns of community and political power entail and are predicated on competing cosmic models.

For the purposes of the argument, it is necessary to read the epinikian Kroisos and the Herodotean version separately, to appreciate their different inflections of the theme of generosity. Thus, rather than using one tradition to supplement the other, to supply its "implicit meaning," as Nagy does, I will consider first the epinikian uses of Kroisos and then turn to Herodotus's account to observe the changes he rings on this stock praise figure.[3]

---

[1] Nagy 1990b: 215–313.

[2] For a comparable divergence from Nagy 1990b, cf. Kurke 1992.

[3] For examples of Nagy's use of epinikion and Herodotus to "read" each other, see Nagy 1990b: 278–79. Other treatments of Kroisos in Bacchylides and Herodotus emphasize the contrasts between the two accounts: see Segal 1971, Crane 1996. Segal 1971 articulates the contrast within the framework of a humanistic reading: "The two treatments of the Croesus story exemplify basic differences between archaic and classical art. The archaic poet concentrates on externals. . . . Herodotus brings out the inner dimension of the action. . . . Bacchylides' narrative is god-centered; Herodotus focuses on man" (Segal 1971: 49). My

I. KROISOS IN EPINIKION

It is commonly acknowledged that Kroisos's main association in classical Greek literature is with the generosity of the gift. As Nagy observes, "The generosity of Croesus is a traditional theme of epinician song, worthy of direct comparison with the generosity of the given patron who has commissioned the given epinician poem and who is destined to be praised in that poem."[4] The notion of Kroisos as a stock figure for gift exchange is an important one, but it must be read within the larger political and ideological functions of epinikian poetry. For Nagy is right to assert that the generosity of Kroisos is a traditional theme of epinikion, but we should note that this theme is demographically circumscribed within the corpus. Kroisos serves as comparandum only within two poems composed for Hieron, tyrant of Syracuse. As I have argued elsewhere, the rhetoric of epinikion diverges significantly in the odes to tyrants from what we might call its "ideological baseline" in the celebration of private citizens. In the odes for tyrants, hyperbolic praise of the patron's power and wealth are not constrained by the need to allay citizen *phthonos*, "envy."[5] This observation requires further unpacking and contextualization, since for both Pindar and Bacchylides, their only tyrannic patrons are Sicilian—the Deinomenid tyrants of Gela, Syracuse, and Aitna and the Emmenid dynasty of Akragas. What is it precisely in Deinomenid and Emmenid ideology that evokes such hyperbolic praise? In the case of the Deinomenids (the brothers Gelon, Hieron, and Polyzelos), this is at least partly because they emerged from the local aristocracy "as a bulwark of the old order against the demos." In contrast to the archaic tyrants of mainland Greece, the Sicilian despots did not rise to power as champions of the people.[6] Gelon and Hieron traced their ancestry back to one of the original colonists of Gela and held the hereditary priesthood of the infernal gods in that city, so they were certainly members of the local aristocracy. Gelon gained possession of Syracuse after an inauspicious and chaotic attempt

---

interpretation will build on Segal's insights, but attempt to inflect them ideologically and politically. My reading also has much in common with Crane 1996, who sees a conflict of paradigms played out between Bacchylides and Herodotus, though he does not focus on gift exchange and the conflict of exchange systems, nor on the political struggle these exchanges betoken within the city.

[4] Nagy 1990b: 276.

[5] Kurke 1991: 195–224; in contrast, Nagy 1990b: 175–98 does not distinguish between the rhetoric of praise for private citizens and that for tyrants.

[6] On the Sicilian tyrants, see How and Wells 1928: II.195 (*ad* Hdt. 7.156), 338–39; Andrewes 1956: 128–42 (quote taken from p. 135). Of course, the archaic tyrants of mainland Greece were, to all appearances, also aristocrats, but in general, they seem to have supported civic and egalitarian interests against the traditional aristocracy; cf. How and Wells 1928: II.338–47; Andrewes 1956: 7–116; McGlew 1993.

at democracy and consistently aligned himself with the *Gamoroi*, the Syracusan landowning class. Gelon's aristocratic outlook and sympathies are nowhere clearer than in Herodotus's account of his treatment of the rebellious subject-city of Megara Hyblaea:

> The rich [lit., the fat] among them who had organized the war and were expecting to perish on account of this, he led off to Syracuse and made citizens; the demos of the Megarians, on the other hand, not being responsible for this war and [so] not expecting to suffer anything bad, these too he led to Syracuse and sold for export [as slaves] from Sicily. And he did this same thing to Euboia in Sicily, having divided up the population. And he did these things to both these groups believing that the people are a thing most unpleasant to live with (νομίσας δῆμον εἶναι συνοίκημα ἀχαριτώτατον). (Hdt. 7.156.2–3)

It has been suggested that Herodotus's striking phrase συνοίκημα ἀχαριτώτατον ("a thing most unpleasant to live with") represents Gelon's own words.[7] However that may be, the phrase conjures up the image of aristocratic power so absolute that it can eclipse or negate the polis order: the measure of value is aristocratic *charis*; the implicit comparandum the noble *oikos*. And yet how can a city exist without a demos or an aristocracy without a city?

It is precisely the extremity of this position that reveals the paradox of Deinomenid power. The notion of the common people as *sunoikēma acharitōtaton* seems an eminently aristocratic one, but one no Greek aristocrat could or would put in action as Gelon did, wiping a Greek city off the map.[8] For the Deinomenids exercised power on an unprecedented scale: both Gelon and Hieron uprooted whole populations, transplanted cities, founded new ones, and sought heroic honors.[9] As Moses Finley observes, "There was something self-consciously archaic, even 'heroic' about them, and more than a touch of megalomania."[10]

That is to say, the Deinomenids' extraordinary deployment of power can be read as the logical extrapolation of heroic aristocratic ideology, but one that thereby rendered the model from which it emerged utterly inadequate. The Syracusan tyrants seemed both of the aristocracy and qualitatively different—better, more heroic, even godlike. And what was true in the domain of power also applied in the sphere of wealth and its display. The wealth of Syracuse was proverbial. Thus the story preserved

---

[7] Andrewes 1956: 135.

[8] Contrast Gelon's policies with the statements of Theognis, who can say that "the *deiloi* have no *charis*" (Thgn. 854) but does not for that reason advocate liquidating the city as such.

[9] For these extraordinary activities of the Deinomenids, see Hdt. 7.156, D.S. 11.49, 66, Strabo 6.2.3/268.

[10] Finley 1979: 55.

in Strabo (6.2.4/269) that the Delphic oracle offered the city's founder Archias a choice of "health or wealth"—when he chose "wealth," the Pythia alloted Syracuse to him. After 480, this native prosperity was enhanced by the huge indemnity exacted from the Carthaginians after the Battle of Himera, a Sicilian victory Pindar pregnantly termed πλούτου στέφανωμ' ἀγέρωχον ("a lordly crown of wealth," P. 1.50).[11] And we know that the Deinomenids made very visible use of their vast wealth— thus Herodotus's acknowledgment that they exceeded even Polykrates in *megaloprepeia* (Hdt. 3.125.2).

But while the Deinomenids surpassed the Greek world in the scale and scope of their wealth and power, they still aspired to acceptance by the larger Hellenic community—expecially by the Hellenic aristocracy. Moses Finley notes the reluctance of the Deinomenids to give themselves an official title on their coins and dedicatory inscriptions, and offers the following explanation: "This touch of reticence was one facet of a larger concern to be accepted and to have their greatness acknowledged through-out the Greek world, and that at a time when tyranny had effectively disappeared in Greece proper and the once neutral word 'tyrant' had become, in many quarters, strictly pejorative, a synonym for 'despot.' The one entrée the Sicilians had was through their wealth, with their victorious chariots and their very rich gifts and dedications to the major shrines."[12] The pursuit of *hippotrophia* and the lavish dedications at Panhellenic shrines imply a particular audience—the rich and powerful interpolis elite who gathered at Olympia and Delphi to network and engage in their zero-sum contests of prestige.[13]

In this policy of winning the approval of the Panhellenic aristocracy, Gelon seems to have succeeded much better than did his brother Hieron. Thus Diodorus Siculus tells us that Gelon was remembered for his fair and humane treatment of those he conquered, and the "gentleness" of his rule (D.S. 11.67.2–3). Hieron, in contrast, seems to have lost the vote of history, which stigmatized him in the harshest terms. Again according to Diodorus Siculus, "He was greedy and violent and, in general, com-pletely the opposite of [noble] simplicity and gentlemanly quality" (ἦν γὰρ καὶ φιλάργυρος καὶ βίαιος καὶ καθόλου τῆς ἁπλότητος καὶ καλο-κἀγαθίας ἀλλοτριώτατος, D. S. 11.67.4). The terms of this denunciation reveal by their negation the status and legitimacy Hieron sought, for they expose him as a failed aristocrat in the language of metals. Tellingly, he

[11] Gildersleeve 1890: 246 notes the literal force of this phrase: "The booty gained at Himera was immense." For the enormous indemnity paid by the Carthaginians (including a crown made of 100 talents of gold), cf. D.S. 11.26.2–3.

[12] Finley 1979: 56.

[13] See Kurke 1991: 85–159.

is greedy for money (φιλάργυρος), while he lacks the qualities of "purity" (ἁπλότητος) and "sameness" (ἀλλοτριώτατος) that constitute true *kalokagathia*. Thus, within the terms of this representational struggle, Hieron seems to have had all the more need to project an image of aristocratic "purity" and generosity on the stage of the Panhellenic elite.[14]

It was precisely the task of epinikion to counter the negative portrait of Hieron and inscribe him into the tradition as a paragon of aristocratic virtue. I suggest that the epinikian poets responded to this challenge—and to the paradox of Deinomenid power and aspiration—by invoking the figure of Kroisos.[15] On the one hand, Kroisos stood outside the Greek world, as an Eastern potentate who exercised extraordinary power and effortlessly culled incalculable weath from the gold-bearing Paktolus. On the other hand, though non-Greek, Kroisos eagerly participated in the circuit of aristocratic gift exchange: forming a *xenia* alliance with the Spartans, gifting the Athenian Alkmeon, and making fabulous dedications at Greek religious centers. This participation, so punctiliously documented by Herodotus, seems early on to have made Kroisos a kind of "honorary Greek," as well as a hero of the Hellenic aristocracy with his own mythology.[16] It is perhaps no accident that the reign of Kroisos fell right in the middle of the Greek aristocratic craze for a lifestyle of Eastern—specifically Lydian—luxury.[17] As I have argued elsewhere, this "cult of *habrosunē*" was a lifestyle with clear political and social implications, whereby some members of the Greek aristocracy aligned themselves with the East in order to distinguish themselves from other elements in the polis. In a sense Kroisos figured every archaic aristocrat's wish-fulfillment fantasy: fabulous wealth and power unconstrained by civic order.

Thus we might read Kroisos in epinikion as a mediating figure, revived together with the "cult of *habrosunē*" to accommodate the peculiar needs

---

[14] Hieron's campaign to assert his "aristocratic" virtues included massive expenditure on horseracing, as well as dedications, special coin issues, and epinikia to commemorate his victories. In all, he won three Olympic and three Pythian crowns for equine events and commissioned seven major epinikia from Pindar and Bacchylides. He also, according to Theopompos (*ap.* Athen. *Deipn.* 6.232b), dedicated a tripod and a Nike of refined gold at Delphi. For Hieron's multimedia victory displays, see Dougherty 1993: 83–102.

[15] Cf. Burnett 1985: 66–69; Crane 1996: 65–66.

[16] For Kroisos as an honorary Greek, see Hdt. 1.54.2; for traces of a Kroisos "mythology," cf. the famous Myson amphora representing Kroisos on the pyre (dated ca. 500 B.C.E.; now in the Louvre, G 197; ARV² 238, 1638).

[17] The traditional dates for Kroisos's reign are 560–546 B.C.E. (see Hdt. 1.86.1), situating him squarely between the celebrations of Lydian luxury found in Alkman, Sappho, and Alkaios and those preserved in the sympotic fragments of Anakreon, Simonides, and on the "Anakreontic" vases of Attic red-figure (on all this material, see Kurke 1992). It is worth noting that both Bacchylides and Herodotus associate Kroisos with *habro*-compounds (Bacch. 3.48; Hdt. 1.55.2; cf. Nagy 1990b: 263, 282).

of the Deinomenid tyrants. On the one hand, only a non-Greek potentate from the Eastern edge of the Greek world could adequately parallel the outlandish authority the Western tyrants wielded. On the other hand, Kroisos had already shown the way for the reintegration of such extraordinary wealth and power into Greek elitist ideology.

With that preamble, let us turn to consider the specific uses of Kroisos in epinikion. Kroisos appears briefly in the last triad of Pindar's *Pythian* 1, in the context of the poet's extended exhortation to Hieron to continue his lavish expenditure:

εὐανθεῖ δ' ἐν ὀργᾷ παρμένων,
εἴπερ τι φιλεῖς ἀκοὰν ἁδεῖαν αἰεὶ κλύειν, μὴ κάμνε λίαν δαπάναις·

. . . .

ὀπιθόμβροτον αὔχημα δόξας
οἷον ἀποιχομένων ἀνδρῶν δίαιταν μανύει
καὶ λογίοις καὶ ἀοιδοῖς. οὐ φθίνει Κροί-
σου φιλόφρων ἀρετά.
τὸν δὲ ταύρῳ χαλκέῳ καυτῆρα νηλέα νόον
ἐχθρὰ Φάλαριν κατέχει παντᾷ φάτις· (Pindar P.1.89–90, 92–96)

But remaining in that blooming temper, if indeed you love always to be sweetly spoken of, do not toil too much over expenditures. . . . Only the acclaim of men to come, consisting of glory, reveals the way of life of men who have passed away, by means both of chroniclers and poets. The kindly generosity of Kroisos does not waste away, but everywhere a hateful report holds down Phalaris, the one who cooked with the bronze bull, pitiless in mind. . .

Pindar is, as often, elliptical about the precise nature of the expenditures he exhorts; but there can be no doubt about the point of comparison with Kroisos. As Gildersleeve observed succinctly, "ἀρετά: 'Generosity,' as often."[18] In these lines, the generosity of Kroisos contrasts favorably with the savagery of the sixth-century Sicilian tyrant Phalaris. While Kroisos is associated with the openhanded giving of gold to the god (as we shall see in Bacchylides), Phalaris has bronze fashioned into a hollow bull as an instrument of torture. It is then not just a contrast of generosity and savagery that the two enact, for all the violent illegitimacy of tyranny is displaced onto Phalaris, while Kroisos attracts to himself all the charisma of legitimate kingship. In the language of metals, Kroisos is associated with the pure gold of just sovereignty; Phalaris with the violent acts of *hubris* that characterize Hesiod's race of bronze.

Bacchylides 3 offers a more extended comparison of Hieron with

---

[18] Gildersleeve 1890: 252.

Kroisos. After the victory announcement (1–4), the poem launches into hyperbolic praise of Hieron, described as ὄλβιος in line 8:

θρόησε δὲ λ[αὸς
"ἆ τρισευδαίμ[ων ἀνήρ,
ὃς παρὰ Ζηνὸς λαχὼν
πλείσταρχον Ἑλλάνων γέρας
οἶδε πυργωθέντα πλοῦτον μὴ μελαμ-
φαρέϊ κρύπτειν σκότῳ.
βρύει μὲν ἱερὰ βουθύτοις ἑορταῖς,
βρύουσι φιλοξενίας ἀγυιαί· (Bacch. 3.9–16)

And the crowd shouted . . . , "Ah, thrice-fortunate man, who has been allotted from Zeus the honor of ruling the most people of the Greeks, and who knows not to hide his towered wealth in black-cloaked darkness. The shrines teem with ox-sacrificing festivals, the streets teem with hospitality to strangers. . . .

These lines themselves make plain the paradox of Deinomenid authority, for they point to the Sicilian tyrant's incomparable power and wealth, but do so in the form of the public acclamation of a Greek crowd at Olympia.[19] The remarkable assertion, "Zeus has granted [him] the honor of ruling the most people of the Greeks," unparalleled in epinikion, sets Hieron apart from all other Greek rulers, while the reference to his "towered wealth" evokes the monumental building projects of Eastern despots.[20] It is revealing of the poem's purpose that we are given no explicit marker of where the quotation ends: the natural place is immediately after σκότῳ (14), but the idea of "not hiding his wealth" is then picked up with μέν (15) and elaborated for another eight lines, which themselves lead into the poem's myth. That is to say, the poem allows us to hear its entire length as the admiring shout of a Greek crowd, thereby enacting the Hellenic approval it works to forge for Hieron.[21]

---

[19] Maehler (1982, vol. 2.43) punctuates with a period at the end of line 9, insisting that lines 10ff. cannot be a direct quote. He offers two reasons: (1) the praise concerns Hieron's power in Syracuse, not his athletic victory at Olympia; and (2) there is no marker for the end of direct quotation. I want to follow the traditon of Jebb 1905: 254–55, Wilamowitz 1922: 315, Burnett 1985: 67–68 in reading lines 10ff. as the quoted exclamation of the *laos* in line 9, and I regard both of Maehler's objections (1) and (2) as symptomatic of the ideological work the poem is doing, rather than as fatal arguments against the possibility of direct quotation. For the appropriateness of lines 10–14 as part of the traditional *makarismos* of the athletic victor, see Fränkel 1973: 431n.12; Burnett 1985: 67–68, and cf. Pindar N. 11.11–16; Hdt. 1.31.3.

[20] Cf. Deiokes (Hdt. 1.96–99); Alyattes (1.93); Cheops and the Great Pyramid (2.126); in Bacchylides, cf. the language used for Kroisos's palace and pyre (Bacch. 3.32, 49).

[21] This is a remarkable instance of the phenomenon I have termed "scripted spontaneity" in epinikion: cf. Kurke 1991: 122–25 for discussion of other, more local examples.

It is significant too that the uses of wealth singled out for praise (and linked by the doubled βρύει ... βρύουσι) are the lavish expenditure on festivals of the gods and human *xenia*. This pairing, repeated throughout the poem, represents Hieron's praiseworthy use of wealth as private aristocratic gift exchange, rather than the public works of a city's ruler.[22] Then, in an almost imperceptible shift, we move from the streets of Syracuse (15–16) to gold tripods glittering before the temple at Delphi (17–21):

λάμπει δ' ὑπὸ μαρμαρυγαῖς ὁ χρυσός,
ὑψιδαιδάλτων τριπόδων σταθέντων
πάροιθε ναοῦ, τόθι μέγι[στ]ον ἄλσος
Φοίβου παρὰ Κασταλίας [ῥ]εέθροις
Δελφοὶ διέπουσι. (Bacch. 3.17–21)

And gold shines with glimmerings, from the high-ornamented tripods set up before the temple, where the Delphians manage the greatest grove of Phoibos beside the streams of Kastalia.

Like the earlier unclosed quotation, this geographic elision collapses Syracuse into the Panhellenic shrines of mainland Greece, even as it acknowledges the extraordinary wealth of the Western city.[23] Again the paradox: Syracuse is both part of Greece and incalculably other, just as its ruler both practices aristocratic gift exchange and unbalances the circuit of *charis* by giving on a scale no other Greek can match. The stage is set for Kroisos as comparandum: he alone can hold the two halves of the paradox in suspension, as the other who is also the most revered model for Greek elitist ideology.

Through the mediation of Kroisos and Apollo, the poem as a whole plays out its praise of the two forms of gift-giving encapsulated in lines 15–16: human-divine gift exchange and the "horizontal" gifting of *xenia* and festivity. The two are linked by the concept of *charis* and the image of gold. First, picking up line 15, the poet offers a general injunction: θεὸν θ[εό]ν τις ἀγλαϊζέθω γὰρ ἄριστος [ὄ]λβων ("Let a man glorify the god, for this is the best of prosperities," 22).[24] This leads into the "myth" of Kroisos, whom we are told immediately "gold-sworded Apollo

---

[22] Contrast the places where Kroisos is *not* invoked as a comparandum, where we find explicit praise of Hieron's public works and civic expenditures: e.g., Pindar *O.* 1.12; *O.* 6.95–96 (festival of Demeter and Kore); *P.* 1.35–40; *P.* 1.70; *P.* 2.56–58; *P.* 3.70–72.

[23] The geographic indeterminacy of these lines is noted by Burnett 1985: 68; Crane 1996: 67.

[24] I follow Jebb 1905: 256–57 and Burnett 1985: 69 in the interpretation of ὁ ... ἄριστος [ὄ]λβων. For a different interpretation ("He [the god] is the best of prosperities"), see Nagy 1990b: 276; Crane 1996: 67. Burnett 1985: 67–76 likewise emphasizes the thematic importance of gold in Bacch. 3.

guarded" at the fated fall of Sardis. This brief version is then elaborated
(in typical epinikian fashion). Kroisos responds to the fall of his city by
constructing a pyre on which to immolate himself, first challenging the
gods in direct speech:

"ὑπέρβιε δαῖμον,
πο]ῦ θεῶν ἐστι[ν] χάρις;
πο]ῦ δὲ Λατοίδ[ας] ἄναξ;" (Bacch. 3.37–39)

"O mighty divinity, where is the grace of the gods? And where is the lord,
son of Leto?"

The divine response to this challenge is immediate—Zeus sends rain to
quench the pyre and Apollo whisks Kroisos off to the enchanted land of
the Hyperboreans. The reason for this prompt solicitous concern and
remarkable translation to bliss? "Because of his piety, because of mortals
he sent the greatest things to holy Pytho" (61–62). The reciprocal relations
of man and god are unproblematic and unmediated. The giving of lavish
gifts incurs a debt of gratitude (*charis*) from the gods and their motivations
and actions are transparent—precisely those of good *xenoi* toward their
human exchange partners.

It is worth noting in this context that, although it is specified that
Kroisos's gifts were sent to Pytho (62), throughout the myth Apollo has
no Delphic epithets. He is χρυσά[ορος (28), Λατοίδ[ας] ἄναξ (39), and
at the climactic moment of his translation of Kroisos to the Hyperboreans,
Δαλογενή[ς (58). While the god's Delian connection may be appropriate
for his association with the Hyperboreans, there is a slight asymmetry
built into the reciprocal relations.[25] That is to say, Kroisos offers lavish
gifts to *Delphic* Apollo, but it is the lord of *Delos* who reciprocates by
snatching him from harm and translating him to bliss. I suggest that this
asymmetry results from Bacchylides' careful avoidance of the topic of
Apollo's oracular exchanges with Kroisos, which, if explored as they are
in Herodotus, would seriously problematize the poet's radiant model of
human-divine gift exchange.[26] For in the world of oracular utterance, as
we shall see, the *charis* of the gods is ambiguous, their messages riddling,
their motives inscrutable, and thus the ideology of the oracle does not
sort well with the model of perfect human-divine *xenia* the elitist tradition constructs.

---

[25] On the connections of the Delian cult of Apollo with the Hyperboreans, see Jebb 1905:
261 and cf. Hdt. 4.32–35. For a similar cultic asymmetry (though for a different reason)
in Pindar *I.* 1, see Kurke 1991: 150–51.
[26] Cf. Burnett 1985: 180n. 8: "Bacchylides suppresses all suggestion of the motif of the
misleading oracles that is so important to Herodotus: the poet's Apollo is a receiver of
gifts, a giver of salvation and victory, but not an oracle-speaker."

Only when the poet has made the transition back from Kroisos to Hieron does he designate Apollo by the most riddling of his Delphic epithets:

ὅσο[ι] <γε> μὲν Ἑλλάδ' ἔχουσιν, [ο]ὔτι[ς,
ὦ μεγαίνητε Ἱέρων, θελήσει
φάμ]εν σέο πλείονα χρυσὸν
Λοξί]α πέμψαι βροτῶν. (Bacch. 3.63–66)

And however many hold Greece, at least, no one of mortals will wish to claim that he has sent more gold than you to Loxias, o greatly praised [or, much-advised] Hieron.

Loxias, traditionally etymologized by the Greeks as derived from λοξός, "crooked," is the epithet consistently used for Apollo in contexts that highlight his opaque oracular persona.[27] The built-in ambiguity of "Loxias" is enhanced in these lines, as Nagy has observed, by the double meaning of μεγαίνητος—"he who is greatly praised," but also "he who receives great *ainos*."[28] Hieron's future is not yet secured: μεγαίνητος suggests he must take to heart the exemplum of Kroisos and continue in what Pindar calls his φιλόφρων ἀρετά.

Beyond this parainetic warning, even the aristocratic model of perfect human-divine *charis* must allow for the possibility of inexplicable misfortune and contingency.[29] Yet this shadow—this trace of uncertainty conjured by the name of Loxias—is quickly subsumed into aristocratic ideology by another incarnation of Apollo in Bacchylides' evocation of the Admetos Song. The Admetos Song seems to have been one particular instantiation of a genre of mythological *hypothēkai* traditionally performed in the context of the elite symposium.[30] Bacchylides uses the allusion to prescribe the proper aristocratic response to life's uncertainties. As Apollo advises Admetos,

---

[27] See Jebb 1905: 262 and cf. Aesch. *Ag.* 1208, 1211, *Ch.* 269, 558, 900, 954, 1030, 1039, *Eum.* 19, 61, 235, 241, 465, *Seven* 618, *Prom.* 669; Pindar *P.* 11.5; Soph., *OT* 853, 994; Eur. *Bacchae* 1336; *El.* 399, 1266, *Herakl.* 1028, *Ion* 67, 243, 728, 774, 781, 974, 1218, *IT* 1013, 1084, 1438, *Or.* 165, 285, 1666, *Pho.* 409, 1703, *Suppl.* 7; Hdt. 1.91.2, 4, 5, 4.163.

[28] Nagy 1990b: 277–78. Nagy reads an implicit warning in the *ainos* of *megainētos*.

[29] Cf. Crane 1996.

[30] Scodel 1979: 51–54, 62; Kurke 1990: 104–7; Wohl 1998: 149–50. The elitist slant of the "Admetos Song" is clear from its opening lines, quoted by Aristophanes (*Wasps* 1238) and supplemented by the scholia *ad loc.*: Ἀδμήτου λόγον ὦ ἑταῖρε μαθὼν τοὺς ἀγαθοὺς φίλει, / τῶν δειλῶν δ' ἀπέχου γνοὺς ὅτι δειλῶν ὀλίγα χάρις ("Having learned the saying of Admetos, o companion, love good men and keep away from the base, knowing that the gratitude of base men is slight," Praxilla 3/749 *PMG* = *Carm. conv.* 14/897 *PMG*). For the similarity of the sentiments expressed here with those found in the Theognidea, see Scodel 1979: 51–54.

ὁ δ' ἄναξ ['Απόλλων
. . . . .]. 'λος εἶπε Φέρη[τος υἷι·
"θνατὸν εὖντα χρὴ διδύμους ἀέξειν
γνώμας, ὅτι τ' αὔριον ὄψεαι
μοῦνον ἀλίου φάος,
χὤτι πεντήκοντ' ἔτεα
ζωὰν βαθύπλουτον τελεῖς.
ὅσια δρῶν εὔφραινε θυμόν· τοῦτο γὰρ
κερδέων ὑπέρτατον." (Bacch. 3.76–84)

And the lord Apollo [the herdsman?] said to the son of Pheres, "Since you
are mortal, you ought to cultivate twin notions, both that you will see only
tomorrow's light of the sun, and that you will accomplish a life of fifty years
deep in wealth. Doing holy things rejoice your spirit; for this is the highest
of profits."

Apollo's recommendation to "cultivate twin notions" picks up and elaborates a topos of sympotic poetry, in which the addressee is urged to turn
from contemplation of unhappiness or mortality to enjoyment of present
festivity.[31] Though one scholar reads this vignette as a democratizing
gesture—"a form of piety open to the very poor and the very rich as
well"—I would emphasize the elite sympotic context in which this carpe
diem sentiment regularly occurs.[32] Faced with the uncertainty of the future, it dictates the proper style of enjoyment and conduct.

But even this universal acknowledgment of uncertainty is reframed
within a specific sheltering structure of human-divine gift exchange, for
Admetos, according to tradition, was lavishly rewarded for his generous
xenia of Apollo by the god's intercession with the Moirai to delay his fated
death.[33] According to Euripides' version, Apollo, angered over Zeus's
execution of Asklepios, killed the Kyklopes who forged Zeus's lightning-
bolts. As punishment, Zeus compelled Apollo to serve a mortal man, and
so he worked as herdsman for the pious Admetos (Eur. Alk. 1–9). As
Apollo succinctly summarizes the story in the prologue to Euripides' play:

ὁσίου γὰρ ἀνδρὸς ὅσιος ὢν ἐτύγχανον
παιδὸς Φέρητος, ὃν θανεῖν ἐρρυσάμην,

[31] Cf. Alkaios frr. 38A, 335, 338, 346 V; Thgn. 567–70, 719–28, 757–68, 789–92,
877–84, 973–78, 1007–12, 1047–48, 1063–68, 1069–70b. Maehler 1982: 2.54–55 notes
how rare the idea of "twin thoughts" is (citing Epicharmos fr. 267 Kaibel as a parallel).
At the same time, Maehler acknowledges a close parallel for εὔφραινε θυμόν in Mimnermos
fr. 7 W (= Thgn. 795), σὴν αὐτοῦ φρένα τέρπε.
[32] Burnett 1985: 73–74 (quote taken from p. 74).
[33] Different elements of the myth are referred to or narrated in Hes. Eoiai fr. 54–57
Merkelbach-West; Aesch. Eum. 723–28; Eur. Alk.; Plato Symp. 179b; Callimachos Hymn

Μοίρας δολώσας· ἤνεσαν δέ μοι θεαὶ
Ἄδμητον ᾅδην τὸν παραυτίχ᾽ ἐκφυγεῖν,
ἄλλον διαλλάξαντα τοῖς κάτω νεκρόν.
(Eur. *Alk.* 10–14)

Being holy myself, I happened upon a holy man, the son of Pheres, whom
I saved from dying by tricking the Fates; for the goddesses consented for
me that Admetos could escape immediate death by substituting another
corpse for those below.

As in Bacchylides' version, the emphasis falls on character or conduct
that is *hosios* ("holy" or "pious"), thereby winning extraordinary divine
recompense. If Kenyon's supplement ὁ βουκόλος ("the herdsman") at
Bacchylides 3.77 is correct, the poem explicitly reminds us of the bond
of *xenia* in the context of Apollo's teaching, revealing the pattern of
human-divine gift exchange working behind the arbitrary phenomena
of mortality.[34]
Furthermore, the vignette of Apollo and Admetos allows the poet to
shift from the vertical to the horizontal axis—from lavish dedications
and festival celebrations (15) to φιλοξενίαι (16). And this shift in turn
enables the thematic focus on human gift exchange which informs the
poem's closing sequence. As Anne Carson has argued, the poem pivots
to this theme in the course of the priamel in lines 85–92:

φρονέοντι συνετὰ γαρύω· βαθὺς μέν
αἰθὴρ ἀμίαντος· ὕδωρ δὲ πόντου
οὐ σάπεται· εὐφροσύνα δ᾽ ὁ χρυσός·
ἀνδρὶ δ᾽ οὐ θέμις, πολιὸν π[αρ]έντα
γῆρας, θάλ[εια]ν αὖτις ἀγκομίσσαι
ἥβαν. ἀρετᾶ[ς γε μ]ὲν οὐ μινύθει
βροτῶν ἅμα σ[ώμ]ατι φέγγος, ἀλλὰ
Μοῦσά νιν τρ[έφει.] (Bacch. 3.85–92)

I sing things understandable to the thoughtful man: the deep air is unpolluted,
and the water of the sea does not rot, and gold is festivity. And it is not
allowed for a man, when he has passed by grey old age, to convey back
blooming youth. Still, the light of achievement does not diminish together
with the body of mortals, but the Muse nurtures it.

φρονέοντι συνετὰ γαρύω signals the riddling quality of the priamel,
which, according to Carson's reading, depends on the double inscription
of "gold" as a pure, untaintable natural element—like air and seawater—

---

to Apollo 47–54; Apoll. *Bibl.* 1.9.15, 3.10.3–4. Wohl 1998: 134–35, 162–70 emphasizes
the importance of human-human and human-divine *xenia* in Euripides' *Alkestis*.

[34] Jebb 1905: 263–64 favors Kenyon's supplement; Maehler 1982: 2.54 is less enthusiastic.

and as aristocratic expenditure for festivity (εὐφροσύνα).[35] I would simply add to her interpretation the suggestion that in both of these forms, "gold" figures as an allegory for the proper aristocratic self: first, in its personal integrity, then in its implication in the circuit of top-rank gift-giving at banquet and symposium. In both these aspects, the poet's depiction of Hieron's "golden" nature belies what was to become the judgment of history (cf. D.S. 11.67.4, cited above): the Deinomenid tyrant partakes of the ἁπλότης of pure gold, while avoiding avaricious stinginess (φιλαρ-γυρία) in his lavish expenditures on εὐφροσύνα. Carson's doubled reading of χρυσός in the priamel suggests that the ἀρετά that forms the conceptual counterpart to gold at line 90 is also double. It evokes both Hieron's extraordinary athletic achievement and his noble generosity (what Pindar terms the φιλόφρων ἀρετά of Kroisos). This double ἀρετά then leads into the poem's final lines, which construct a relation of perfect gift-exchange reciprocity between patron and poet. For Hieron's athletic victory and his generous *xenia* of the poet engender in response the poem of praise, significantly designated "the grace of the Kean nightingale" in the poem's last words (χάριν Κηΐας ἀηδόνος, 97–98).[36]

The parallelism of divine and human *charis* is quite exact: as Apollo's "favor" preserves Kroisos among the Hyperboreans, so the poet's "grace" immortalizes Hieron in memory.[37] This perfect intercalation of divine and human *charis* may remind us (incongruously) of Gelon's quip about the demos of Megara Hyblaea as συνοίκημα ἀχαριτώτατον. I say "incongruously" since, although poem and bon mot participate in the same aristocratic value system, everything in the poet's presentation is intended to naturalize and thereby efface the politics implicated in this circuit of *charis*. In the sack of Sardis (as in that of Megara Hyblaea), Apollo responds to Kroisos's indignant question, "Where is the *charis* of the gods?" by the same process of "skimming off the fat," while the poet, unsurprisingly, makes no mention of the fate of the "demos" of Lydia's capital.

II. GIFT EXCHANGE, THE GROTESQUE BODY, AND THE CIVIC NORM

Thus epinikion deploys Kroisos programmatically to endorse the structures of aristocratic gift exchange, precisely where the wealth and power of the epinikion patron have carried that system to almost unimaginable

---

[35] Carson 1984; cf. Burnett 1985: 75. On the opening words of line 85 as signaling a riddle, cf. Hes. *W&D* 202–12; Pindar O. 2.85, *I*. 2.12–13 and see Maehler 1982: 2.58, Morris 1996: 39 (though Morris reads the *ainos* message differently).

[36] Interpreting this phrase with Fränkel 1973: 467; Maehler 1982: 2.60–61; Burnett 1985: 76, 183–84n.29; Crane 1996: 69. Differently Jebb 1905: 266–67; Wilamowitz 1922: 316; Woodbury 1969.

[37] For the parallelism of divine and human *charis*, cf. Crane 1996: 69–70.

extremes. The fashioning of this signification of Kroisos both entails and requires a whole "metaphysics of gift exchange" in which the gods respond reliably and unhesitatingly to the summons of their mortal exchange partner. If we turn from epinikion to Herodotus's portrait of Kroisos, we find this signifier for gift exchange riven with ideological tensions and contradictions, multiply problematized and destabilized in the histor's shifting narrative. On occasion, Herodotus seems to offer us the unproblematic gift-exchange figure of the praise tradition: thus we get the extended rendition of his fabulous dedications at Delphi, the Amphiareion, Ephesus, and Miletus (Hdt. 1.50–52, 1.92),[38] and his pious and generous gift of gold to the Spartans for a cult image of Apollo (1.69.4). These narratives (as long as we don't attend too closely to the narrator's ironic juxtapositions) offer us an approximation of the epinikian Kroisos, the "patron saint" of gift exchange. But with the Lydian potentate's two most famous encounters, we bump up against the same civic hostility to gift exchange that we saw so forcefully embodied in the third Samian narrative. With these two tales—the stories of Alkmeon's and Solon's strange encounters in Sardis—we travel from the ridiculous to the sublime, from the grotesque body to cosmic principles.[39]

First, in the story of how the Athenian Alkmeonids originally became κάρτα λαμπροί ("very distinguished," 6.125.1), Herodotus maps the effects of Eastern gift exchange on the male citizen body. Kroisos, learning that Alkmeon the son of Megakles had been a "helper" (συμπρήκτωρ) to his emissaries sent to consult the oracle at Delphi, summons the Athenian to his court in Sardis. When he arrives,

> Kroisos presents to him as much gold as he can carry out on his body in a single trip. And Alkmeon, with respect to this gift being such, presented himself when he had made the following preparations: he put on a great tunic (κιθῶνα μέγαν) and left the fold of the tunic deep, and he put on the widest *kothornoi* he could find and went into the treasure-house to which they led him. And falling into a heap of golddust, first he crammed beside his calves as much gold as the *kothornoi* would hold, then he filled the entire fold [of the tunic] with gold and smeared the gold dust into the hair on his head and took other [gold dust] in his mouth. [Thus] he came out

[38] Though even in these passages, there are odd inconcinnities that destabilize the picture of perfect generosity: at 1.51.5, the dedication of the three-cubit gold statue of his "breadbaker" (on which see duBois 1988: 110–16; Garrett and Kurke 1994: 80–83, and see below on prostitutes and courtesans); at 1.92, the description of his execution of an enemy on the "carding comb" (on which see below).

[39] It is worth noting that both these encounters are anachronistic: both Alkmeon and Solon belonged to the generation before Kroisos, but Greek tradition has paired them with the most famous Lydian monarch (on Solon, see How and Wells 1928: I.66–67; on Alkmeon, How and Wells 1928: II.116, Thomas 1989: 267n.79).

from the treasure-house, dragging his *kothornoi* with difficulty, looking like anything more than a person (παντὶ δέ τεῳ οἰκὼς μᾶλλον ἢ ἀνθρώπῳ). And his mouth had been plugged up and all [the parts of his body] swollen out. And laughter overcame Kroisos when he saw him, and he gives him all that and in addition presents him with another set no less than that. Thus this house became extremely wealthy, and this Alkmeon thus began keeping four-horse chariots and won the Olympic games. (Hdt. 6.125.2–5)

Rosalind Thomas has recently reconsidered this story in light of the long-held scholarly belief that Herodotus 6.121–31 represents "Alkmeonid family tradition." Thomas forcefully refutes this view, pointing out that this narrative of Alkmeon's encounter with Kroisos, as well as the story of his betrothal to the Sikyonian Agariste, which follows immediately (6.126–30), cast the family's eponymous founder in a very unflattering light indeed. Following Hermann Strasburger, Thomas suggests that, in fact, Herodotus' account of Alkmeonid early history (6.125–31) is intended to ironize and undercut the family's apologia as *misoturannoi*, presented in chapters 121–24.[40] She concludes that the story of Alkmeon in Kroisos's treasury is likely to have "a popular provenance":

> But we can be more precise about the nature and origin of the story. A common type of tale explains a person's wealth by some sudden stroke of luck, one sudden find, rather than by any long-term explanation. It is particularly common in some peasant societies. It has been explained by the difficulty of accumulating wealth simply through hard work in a subsistence economy. . . . So wealth has to be attributed to something external, a sudden find of treasure or a windfall. . . . The popular milieu of this kind of tale confirms that the Croesus story was not the family's own version of the origin of its riches, though the family might have known it.[41]

I find Thomas's argument for the story's "popular provenance" completely convincing, and I would take it a step further. What I would like to emphasize in this fantastic tradition is the popular deployment of the grotesque body against the system of elite gift exchange. For the gift is exposed in this instance as the basest form of profit, obscenely inscribed

[40] Thomas 1989: 265–72 (citing Strasburger 1965: 598). On 6.125 in particular, Thomas observes: "The tale reflects badly on the family's wealth. It also undercuts their 'defence' against medism and favouring tyranny. For we now read that the eponymous ancestor gained the family's wealth from a Lydian king, both a barbarian and in some sense a tyrant. We are even told explicitly that Alcmaeon was an 'assistant' (συμπρήκτωρ) to Croesus at Delphi, which prompted the reward in the first place (VI 125.2)." (Thomas 1989: 267)

[41] Thomas 1989: 266–67. It should be noted, however, that Tzetzes ascribes the narrative of this tale to "some poem of Pindar" (*Chiliades* 1.8). One would dearly like to have Pindar's version of this story.

on Alkmeon's body: he drags his feet, his form is swollen and distended, and his mouth stopped with golddust. His greed temporarily assimilates him to Alkaios's scathing portrait of Pittakos—all distended belly and dragging feet.[42] But here, in contrast, the figure of the grotesque body serves as the representational weapon of popular tradition against aristocratic mores and ideology. Kroisos's gift makes Alkmeon "like to anything more than a person."

Furthermore, this exchange is represented as multiply problematic. Though commentators and scholars have recognized that this portrait of Alkmeon is unflattering, they still tend to idealize Kroisos as a very positive figure in the tale. Thus How and Wells, with apparent approval: "Mahaffy . . . contrasts the under-bred sharpness of the Greek and the courteous generosity of the Oriental."[43] Likewise Rosalind Thomas: "Here, while the vanity of wealth may remain in the background for Herodotus and his audience, the laugh is against Alcmaeon, and Croesus is the fabulously rich but generous Lydian king able to rise above greed. In this story (in its Herodotean form at least) the credit goes to Croesus rather than Alcmaeon."[44] These scholarly assessments imply that it is simply Alkmeon's behavior that is being spoofed, while the Lydian dynast and his generous gift-giving remain wholly positive features. Yet, a closer look at the elements in the story suggests that the exchange as a whole may be more ambiguous and Kroisos's laughter more sinister than has generally been acknowledged.

To my knowledge, no commentator has remarked on the significance of Alkmeon's costume in context, though J. E. Powell notes in his entry for κιθών that it is almost universally in Herodotus the garb of women and Easterners (the only exceptions are Histiaios at Susa, 5.106 and Alkmeon, 6.125). Powell concludes, "Thus, effeminate and non-Greek."[45] In fact, Herodotus himself offers us a precise parallel for the costume of tunic (κιθών) and *kothornoi*, along with a telling commentary on its significance. After his capture of Sardis, Kyros is dismayed by the insurrection of the Lydians led by Paktyes and asks Kroisos whether he had not

---

[42] Cf. Alkaios frr. 129, 429 V and see discussion in Kurke 1994. Cf. Stallybrass and White's characterization of the grotesque body: "Grotesque realism images the human body as multiple, bulging, over- or under-sized, protuberant and incomplete. The openings and orifices of this carnival body are emphasized, not its closure and finish" (Stallybrass and White 1986: 9).

[43] How and Wells 1928: II.116 (*ad* 6.125); cf. Erbse 1992: 30: "Dem goldgierigen, pfiffigen Griechen steht der großzügige Gastgeber gegenüber, der über den kindlichen Eifer Alkmaions lacht und ihn mit der Geste des Grandseigneurs noch reichlicher beschenkt."

[44] Thomas 1989: 267.

[45] Powell 1938: 195 (s.v. κιθών).

better enslave them all (1.154–155.2). Kroisos urges him to punish the leader of the rebellion, while imposing behavior modification on the Lydians:

> Pardon the Lydians and give them the following commands, in order that they neither revolt nor be fearsome [in future]. Send to them and forbid them to wear martial equipment, and [instead] bid them wear tunics underneath their garments and *kothornoi*, and order them to educate their children in playing the kithara and plucking the lyre and practicing retail trade. And soon, o King, you will see them become women instead of men, so that there will be no fear that they revolt. (Hdt. 1.155.4)

This parallel suggests that the male citizen body is made not only grotesque but also effeminate by gift exchange with the Lydian dynast, and that Kroisos himself is quite conscious of the implications of Alkmeon's garb. It is not simply that Kroisos is "able to rise above greed," but that he actively participates in an exchange that rewards Alkmeon for his debased behavior and feminizing costume. This exchange, ostensibly so "noble," assimilates Alkmeon to the debilitating luxury of the East, while it makes him a thrall to a foreign potentate. Thus I would argue that it is not simply Alkmeon's bad or inappropriate behavior that compromises an otherwise unproblematic exchange: instead, popular imagination uses the grotesque body and effeminate Eastern garb to stigmatize extra-polis aristocratic gift-giving *tout court*.[46]

All this is relevant to the more familiar encounter of Kroisos and Solon (1.30–35), which scholars have often paired with that of Kroisos and Alkmeon.[47] Usually this comparison is limited to Solon's restraint versus Alkmeon's discreditable behavior when faced with Kroisos's treasure-house, but again I would like to expand the view to take in the ideology of gift exchange that informs both stories alike. For the later account (with Alkmeon) suggests very strongly that 1.30–33 represents an aborted gift exchange: we are told that Kroisos "hosted" Solon (ἐξεινίζετο, 1.30.1) and bid his servants "lead him around the treasure chambers and show him everything being great and blessed" (περιῆγον κατὰ τοὺς θησαυρούς, 1.30.1; cf. τὸν θησαυρὸν ἐς τόν οἱ κατηγέοντο, 6.125.3). Surely this tour is the prelude to the offering of a guest gift, which, as in Homer, the host presents to the guest on his departure. Yet here the exchange never takes place because Solon refuses to fulfill his end of the bargain: when asked "who of all men he has seen is most blessed," Solon "refuses

---

[46] Thus, as in the case of Mitchell's identification of Samian aristocrats as Herodotus' sources, I want to extend Thomas's argument for "popular provenance" to the realm of ideology: this story is not just anti-Alkmeonid but anti-gift-exchange.

[47] E.g., Strasburger 1965: 598–99; Thomas 1989: 267.

to flatter" Kroisos (Σόλων δὲ οὐδὲν ὑποθωπεύσας, 1.30.3). This matter-of-fact parenthesis reveals that the scene is, in fact, predicated on an *exchange*, whereby Solon is expected to flatter the Eastern potentate to receive a gift in return.

But Solon short-circuits this exchange by interposing the city. That is, he replaces the network of aristocratic gift exchange with the polis as arbiter of value and bestower of society's most precious gifts. Thus Tellos is most blessed because he "died most nobly in battle" and received burial "at public expense" and "great honor" from the Athenians (1.30.5).[48] Thus also, Kleobis and Biton, when they have been given the gift of death by the god, receive a signal honor from their fellow citizens: "And the Argives had images made of them and dedicated them at Delphi, on the grounds that they had become the best men" (ὡς ἀνδρῶν ἀρίστων γενομένων, 1.31.5). This last phrase is particularly striking, since, as Nicole Loraux has argued, "to become a good man" is a fixed formula in democratic Athenian discourse for those who have died in battle fighting for their city and been rewarded with civic commemoration.[49] This locution assimilates Kleobis and Biton's extraordinary feat of strength to the ultimate civic service, death in battle, here reciprocated (as in the case of Tellos) by civic monuments of eternal commemoration.

But it is important to note that the verbal exchange of Solon and Kroisos is not only a contest of paradigms for human life and how it should be lived; each speaker predicates his *paradeigmata* on a different model of the divine, its nature, and its relation to humanity. Kroisos equates material riches with "blessedness" (ὀλβίη, εὐδαιμονίη), in what Gregory Crane has recently noted is a tendentious distortion of aristocratic ideology. For in epinikion, the "prosperity" of tyrants is consistently hedged round with acknowledgments of human mutability: "Herodotus assigns to Kroisos, his archetypal rich potentate, a simplistic attitude toward *olbos* that has no parallel in the picture that Pindar and Bacchylides sketch for any of their patrons. The Herodotean Kroisos is a 'straw man,' who endorses an unsophisticated and unacceptable view of *olbos* that the poetic representations of tyranny methodically eschew."[50] I would

---

[48] For the possibility that Herodotus implies hero-cult honors for Tellos, see Regenbogen 1965: 382; Nagy 1990b: 244 with n. 125; Kurke 1993: 154. If this is the case, Solon is pointing to a kind of "transport to the blessed" that is bestowed by the civic community.

[49] Loraux 1986: 3, 100–101, 104–6, 168; cf. Gould 1989: 61–62. It is worth comparing the perfect nude bodies of the sculpted Kleobis and Biton (discovered by French excavators at Delphi) with Alkmeon in Hdt. 6.125—dressed in effeminate Eastern garb, body misshapen and distended for profit. With Kleobis and Biton we see the other side of the egalitarian deployment of the grotesque body in the civic appropriation of the "classical norm."

[50] Crane 1996: 81 and cf. the discussion above of the acknowledgment of contingency in Bacch. 3.

simply add that the distortion that makes Kroisos a "straw man" is precisely the extension to human-divine relations of the predictable and unproblematic patterns of human gift exchange. Herodotus's Kroisos assumes that his extraordinary wealth is proof of divine favor, favor he can maintain as long as he offers lavish gifts to the gods in return.[51] Solon, in contrast, offers a vision of the divine as inscrutable, unpredictable, and arbitrary. Thus he observes "that he knows the divine to be entirely jealous and a source of disorder in human affairs" (τὸ θεῖον πᾶν ἐὸν φθονερόν τε καὶ ταραχῶδες . . . ἀνθρωπηίων πρηγμάτων πέρι, 1.32.2), while "a human being is entirely accident" (πᾶν ἐστι ἄνθρωπος συμ-φορή, 1.32.4).

It is a common trope of Herodotean criticism to disembed Solon's observations on the mutability of fortune and read them as programmatic for Herodotus's own view of history, thereby saddling the historian with the lawgiver's moralizing stance.[52] I would like, instead, to point out the ways in which Solon's model of cosmic inscrutability endorses and subtends the egalitarian ideology of the city. It is telling that Solon's final analogy in his lengthy exposition to Kroisos (largely ignored in moralizing readings of the encounter) is the comparison of the individual human being to a χώρη, "land" or "country":

> It is impossible, being mortal, to get all things at one time, just as no land is sufficient furnishing all things to itself, but it has one thing and lacks another. But the one that has the most, this is best. And thus also one body of a human being is not at all self-sufficient (αὐταρκες); for it has one thing, but another it lacks. But whoever passes his life having the most and then ends his life pleasantly (εὐχαρίστως), this one is deserving (δίκαιος) to win this name [of blessed] from me, o King. But one must consider the end of each thing, how it comes out. For indeed, the god, once having given a peek of blessedness to many, has wiped them out root and branch. (Hdt. 1.32.8–9)

In this instance, the claim about the uncertainty of divine favor, coupled with the failure of environmental and individual *autarkeia*, limns the first steps of an argument, very familiar from Aristotle, for the logical and

---

[51] This is not stated directly in his interview with Solon, but enacted in Book 1 by the repeated narratives of gifts to gods—cf. 1.50–52, 1.69, 1.92, with discussion above.

[52] See, for example, Regenbogen 1965: 391–95; Erbse 1992: 13–14; Van der Veen 1995. While the narrator does on occasion articulate in his own voice the mutability of human affairs (e.g., 1.5.4), it is worth noting that the notion that "the divine is envious" is always put into the mouth of a character in the *Histories* and never said directly by the histor himself (Solon at 1.32.1; Amasis at 3.40.2; Artabanus at 7.46.4). I would contend that it is worth respecting this gap between the histor and his characters, just as we would not automatically assume that a character in Greek tragedy expresses the unmediated sentiments of the author. Cf. Stambler 1982: 218–20; Lang 1984: 62; Gould 1989: 79–82.

natural priority of *civic* order. Thus at the opening of the *Politics*, Aristotle asserts:

> The partnership arising from [the union of] several villages that is complete is the city. It reaches a level of full self-sufficiency, so to speak; and while coming into being for the sake of living, it exists for the sake of living well. Every city, therefore, exists by nature, if such also are the first partnerships. For the city is their end, and nature is an end: what each thing is—for example, a human being, a horse, or a household—when its coming into being is complete is, we assert, the nature of that thing. Again, that for the sake of which [a thing exists], or the end, is what is best; and self-sufficiency is an end and what is best.

> That the city is both by nature and prior to each individual, then, is clear. For if the individual when separated [from it] is not self-sufficient, he will be in a condition similar to that of the other parts in relation to the whole. One who is incapable of participating or who is in need of nothing through being self-sufficient is no part of a city, and so is either a beast or a god. (Arist. *Pol.* 1252b27–1253a1; 1253a25–29, trans. C. Lord 1984)

I suggest that Solon's last analogy partakes of this same argument for the city as intermediary between the complete but inscrutable power of divinity and the vulnerability and lack of the individual human body. But, lest I be accused of anachronism in reading Herodotus through Aristotle, I would offer another parallel for the argument, a poetic comparandum much closer to Herodotus, which shows us explicitly what is at stake in Solon's discourse. Consider Simonides' challenge to Pittakos, a poetic disquisition on what it means to be good:

> Truly to become a good man is hard, built foursquare with hands and feet and mind without censure. . . . (τετράγωνον ἄνευ ψόγου τετυγμένον)

> And the saying of Pittakos is not held harmoniously for me, though spoken from a wise man: he said that it is hard to be noble. The god alone would have this honor, but it is not possible for a man not to be bad, whomever impossible misfortune overtakes (ὂν ἀμήχανος συμφορὰ καθέλῃ). For when he fares well, every man is good, but bad when he fares badly. . . .

> Therefore, never shall I cast empty hope into an unaccomplished lot in life, seeking what cannot exist, a man entirely blameless, however many of us win the fruit of the broad-seated earth. But if I find one, I will report back to you. But I praise and love all, whoever willingly does nothing shameful: not even the gods fight with necessity. . . .

> [I am not a lover of censure, since he is pleasing to me, at any rate, whoever is not base] nor too resourceless, who at least knows city-benefiting justice,

he [is] a healthy man (μηδ᾽ ἄγαν ἀπάλαμνος εἰδώς γ᾽ ὀνησίπολιν δίκαν, ὑγιὴς ἀνήρ). I will not blame him, for the race of fools is boundless. All things, to be sure, are noble, with which shameful things are not mixed. (Simon. fr. 37/542 PMG)

Simonides' poem is an argument that leads irrevocably to the conclusion of the primacy of civic order by the progressive redefinition of what a "good man" is. The stages of the argument are articulated by the imagery of concentric squares, built structures that define and delimit the human condition. Because of his vulnerability to συμφορά, it is nearly impossible for a mortal to be "built foursquare" on his own (3)—to be perfectly autarkic, in the terms of Herodotus's Solon. In contrast to the perfection of divinity (14), Simonides locates his "unaccommodated man" alone in the boundless square of the "broad-seated earth": εὐρυεδέος ὅσοι καρπὸν αἰνύμεθα χθονός (24–25). The phrase reveals, in turn, the source of man's vulnerability in Hesiodic form: because we must eat to live, the platform of the earth leaves us needy and exposed. The solution for Simonides is a built structure intermediate between the foursquare individual and the boundless earth; for in the last lines we have, the poet introduces the city, which provides the standard of justice (ὀνησίπολιν δίκαν) and a workable definition of human "health."[53]

It is no accident that Solon's analogy of mortal to χώρη corresponds very closely to Simonides' implicit argument, for both, I would suggest, lead to the same conclusion. Humanity contrives its defense against the uncertainty and inscrutability of the divine by the institution of the civic community. Though Herodotus's Solon does not draw this conclusion explicitly, it is revealing that he first deploys the language of justice here in the phrase "he is deserving to win this name" (τὸ οὔνομα τοῦτο . . . δίκαιός ἐστι φέρεσθαι). Thus, for the first time in Solon's speech, δίκαιός ἐστι (1.32.9) replaces ἄξιός ἐστι (1.32.7), just as δίκαν first occurs at the third stage of Simonides' argument, tellingly coupled with the epithet ὀνησίπολιν. The introduction of dikē into Solon's discourse conjures up the framework of the city, which is both premise and end of his argument. The notion that the divine is φθονερόν τε καὶ ταραχῶδες must be understood as part of this syllogism, by which Solon reinvents the relations of the cosmos and vests the long-term transactional order in the civic community.

Read thus, Herodotus's portrait of Solon's encounter with Kroisos and the contest of paradigms in which they engage corresponds closely to Morris's analysis of the two opposing poetic traditions:

---

[53] For Simonides as a proponent of "middling" or civic values, questioning the validity of aristocratic essentialism, see Gentili 1988: 63–71; Detienne 1996: 107–16; Morris 1996:

There was no way to transcend the polis in the middling tradition. . . . . The differences between the two poetic traditions came down to a single point: the elitists legitimated their special role from sources outside the polis; the middling poets rejected such claims. The former blurred distinctions between male and female, present and past, mortal and divine, Greek and Lydian, to reinforce a distinction between aristocrat and commoner; the latter did the opposite.[54]

We might add that gift exchange is one important means of establishing a privileged connection between "present and past, mortal and divine, Greek and Lydian" within the elitist paradigm, and for this reason, it is negatively represented in Solon's encounter with Kroisos. As I have suggested, the stage is set for an exchange of gifts between dynast and sage: but because Solon refuses to cooperate but instead interposes the city as final instance, all exchange breaks down. Herodotus ends his narrative of the encounter:

ταῦτα λέγων τῷ Κροίσῳ οὔ κως οὔτε ἐχαρίζετο, οὔτε λόγου μιν ποιησάμενος οὐδενὸς ἀποπέμπεται, κάρτα δόξας ἀμαθέα εἶναι, ὃς τὰ παρεόντα ἀγαθὰ μετεὶς τὴν τελευτὴν παντὸς χρήματος ὁρᾶν ἐκέλευε. (Hdt. 1.33)

Saying these things, he was somehow not gratifying Kroisos, and considering him of no account, he [Kroisos] sends him away, thinking that he is very foolish, who neglects present goods and bids him look to the end of everything.

Strikingly, once the relationship of *charis* fails (οὔ κως οὔτε ἐχαρίζετο), the syntax itself mirrors the breakdown of exchange in the abrupt and unmarked change of subjects. How and Wells grudgingly acknowledge the problem, but offer no solution: "The change of subject from Solon (ἐχαρίζετο) to Croesus (ἀποπέμπεται) is harsh (though not without parallel; cf. 31.1), and so is the non-correspondence of οὔτε, οὔτε."[55] Herodotus registers the alienation between paradigms and exchange systems in his very syntax: Solon and Kroisos each isolated within his clause, uncomfortably joined only by the asymmetrical negative.

38–39. Different interpretations of this fragment are offered by Svenbro 1976: 141–72; Carson 1992.

[54] Morris 1996: 35–36.

[55] How and Wells 1928: I.70 (*ad* 1.33). Notice that their parallel passage also comes from the Solon-Kroisos encounter, when Solon cites Tellos as a paradigm of "blessedness," and (with an unmarked change of subject) Kroisos asks whom he would rank second. Here again, the abrupt shift in syntax is iconic for the two characters' incompatible conceptual models.

III. COMPETING ECONOMIES, COMPETING EPIPHANIES

If the encounter of Kroisos and Solon poses gift exchange and the city as competing frames for the long-term transactional order, the story of Kroisos's offerings and consultation of the oracles plays out this contest of paradigms in action. For Kroisos presumes an unproblematic gift exchange between his dedicatory offerings to Apollo at Delphi and the god's oracular responses, only to discover too late that the two represent discrete and incommensurable "economies." And, whereas the god to whom dedications are made will show his *charis* to Kroisos on the pyre, the oracular divinity proves himself the inscrutable force of Solon's admonition. That is to say, the "economy of oracles" turns out to have more in common with the civic economy than the model of gift exchange Kroisos thinks to impose on it. This association of oracular and civic economies is underscored, in turn, by a surprising but persistent strand of coinage imagery. Thus, I would like to consider the extended narrative of Kroisos's testing and consultation of the oracles, his war on the Persians, and his own fall and near destruction as it enacts the same problematization of gift exchange we have traced in the Alkmeon and Solon stories.

Kroisos famously tests the oracles and finds Delphi and the Amphiareion alone to be true (Hdt. 1.46–49). As a result, he makes extraordinarily lavish offerings at Delphi and the Amphiareion: Herodotus's narrative account fills three chapters (1.50–52). Finally, in chapter 53, Herodotus informs us that the Lydians who brought the gifts to Delphi were assigned also to consult the oracle on Kroisos's behalf, as they say in their own words, "Kroisos, king of the Lydians and other nations, in the conviction that these are the only [true] oracles among men, has both given you gifts worthy of the things found out and now asks you if he should make an expedition against the Persians and if he should acquire any force of men as his ally" (Hdt. 1.53.2). The τε ... καί structure of the question assumes continuity and reciprocity between Kroisos's past benefactions and the present oracular information requested: the emissaries hold out the promise of even more lavish offerings if the oracle will "cooperate." And in the phrase "gifts worthy of the things found out" (ἄξια δῶρα ... τῶν ἐξευρημάτων), they reveal an easy assumption of equivalence between the material and oracular economies. What, after all, is oracular truth "worth"? Can it be calibrated on a scale of gold and silver? To be sure, Kroisos, overjoyed with the oracle's response, reciprocates with precious metal, gifting each Delphic citizen with two staters of gold (1.54.1). And so, for the moment, reciprocity seems to obtain.

The first warning that something is amiss in his calculation of symmetrical exchange comes to Kroisos in the embedded narrative of the current status of Athens and Sparta. (The oracle had bidden him find out which was the "most powerful" state in Greece and make it his ally; the result of Kroisos's researches, the summary history of Athens and Sparta to the mid-sixth century, fills chapters 56 through 68 of Book 1.) In this story within a story, Sparta engages in a pair of problematic exchanges with the Delphic oracle. First, Herodotus tells us, they consult the oracle "about all the land of the Arkadians":

> And the Pythia prophesies these following things:
>
>> You ask me for Arkadia? You ask a great deal; I will not give it.
>> Many are the acorn-eating men of Arkadia,
>> who will prevent you. But I do not entirely begrudge you.
>> I will give you foot-tapping Tegea to dance on
>> and the beautiful plain to measure out with a rope.
>
> When the Lakedaimonians heard these things reported back, they held back from the rest of the Arkadians, but bearing shackles they were making an expedition against the Tegeates, trusting to a counterfeit oracle (χρησμῷ κιβδήλῳ πίσυνοι), [in the belief] that they would enslave the Tegeates. But, worsted in battle, however many of them were captured alive, wearing the shackles that they themselves had borne and measuring [it] out with a rope they were working the plain of the Tegeates. And these shackles in which they were bound still even to my time were preserved in Tegea, hung around the temple of Athena Alea. (Hdt. 1.66.2–4)

This narrative (which Kroisos hears but does not heed) is programmatic for the mismatch between human interpretation and divine inscrutability. Though the oracle emphatically speaks the language of gift exchange (οὔ τοι δώσω, οὔτι μεγαίρω, δώσω τοι), for its human recipients it turns out to be a "counterfeit," with a surface meaning of gold and a subtext of lead. As in Theognis (121–24, 963–66), the imagery inherent in this use of *kibdēlos* seems to require that we understand it as "counterfeit [coin]" rather than simply consistently debased "metal alloy," since it marks a sharp contrast between a positive surface meaning and a base or negative "core" that is hidden.[56]

The breakdown of human-divine reciprocal understanding is thus figured as a conflict of exchange systems—the Spartans assuming the "good-faith economy" of gift exchange, the oracle in fact intruding like a counterfeit coin to violate the "trust" of the Homoioi.[57] Strikingly in this instance, the riddling oracle aligns itself metaphorically with the civic economy of coin, even as its deceptive message assures Tegeate autonomy against Spartan aggression. And finally, in its conclusion, Herodotus's narrative

[56] For the semantics of *kibdēlos*, see Chapter 1 above.
[57] For the language of "trust" in contexts of *homoioi*, cf. Thgn. 65–82, 415–18, 1164e–h.

reverts unexpectedly to a dedicatory economy—not the dedications the victorious Spartans might have offered in thanks at Delphi, but the shackles, whose signification shifts as ambiguously as the oracle's, dedicated by the Tegeates to their own Athena.

There follows immediately a second Spartan oracular narrative, which replays and to some extent redresses the trickery of the first. Herodotus tells us:

> When they were being worsted in battle by the Tegeates, having sent emissaries to Delphi, they were asking whom of the gods they should propitiate to be superior to the Tegeates in war. And the Pythia prophesied to them that, when they had brought over the bones of Orestes the son of Agamemnon, [they would be superior.] But when they were unable to discover the tomb of Orestes, they were sending again to the god to ask the place in which Orestes lay. And to the emissaries asking these things the Pythia says the following:
>
> > There is a certain Tegea in the level land of Arkadia,
> > where two winds blow by mighty necessity,
> > and there is stroke and counterstroke, and grief is laid upon grief.
> > There the grain-giving earth holds Agamemnon's son:
> > When you have conveyed him safely home, you will be lord of Tegea.
> >
> > (Hdt. 1.67.2–4)

This episode shows us that the Spartans have learned from their "counterfeit oracle": first, their question is framed in terms of pious propitiation; second, they think to ask again when their first oracular behest is too obscure. But here again, the oracle seems to align itself with *civic* structures: the Spartans ask whom of the gods (τίνα ... θεῶν) they should propitiate; the Pythia in response substitutes the local, civic institution of hero cult for the worship of divinity.[58]

Furthermore, the terms of this oracle systematically invert those of the first Tegeate oracle, operating by the same riddling language to achieve the opposite effect. Where the first Tegeate oracle spoke of gifts, this one speaks only of necessity; where the first promised dancing, this one offers only grief and toil (πῆμα). Where the first pictured the Arkadians feeding on the uncultivated fruits of oak trees (βαλανηφάγοι), this one evokes agricultural cultivation in the formulaic phrase φυσίζοος αἶα. Indeed, in its resolution, this Tegeate oracle locates the Spartans firmly in the Iron Age, whereas the first had tantalized them with a delusory golden age of bliss. For, as Lichas the Spartan *agathoergos* discovers, the oracle indexes

---

[58] For the civic quality of hero cult in general, see Nagy 1979: 69–210; Burkert 1985: 204–8; Seaford 1994: 109–20; de Polignac 1995: 128–49; for the local, civic aspects of the cult of Orestes in Sparta, see Boedeker 1993.

a smithy where iron is forged. Herodotus explains that in a period of peace and free interaction between Tegea and Sparta:

> [Lichas] having gone to a smithy was observing iron being drawn out and was amazed seeing the thing done. And the smith perceiving him marvelling stopped his work and said, "To be sure, O Lakonian stranger, if you had seen the very thing I have, you would be very amazed, since now you happen to consider the working of iron such a wonder. For I wanted to make a well in the courtyard, and, in digging, happened upon a coffin of seven cubits. And out of disbelief that people were ever larger than those now, I opened it and saw a corpse equal in length to the coffin. And when I had measured it, I buried it again." And he was telling him the things he had seen, but the other, comprehending the things said, put together that this was Orestes according to the oracle, putting it together in this way: seeing the smith's two bellows, he discovered them to be the "winds," and the anvil and hammer the "stroke and counterstroke," and the iron drawn out the "grief laid upon grief," likening it according to some such thing, that iron was discovered on terms of evil for men. (Hdt. 1.68.1–4)

In his series of equations concluding with worked iron as "grief laid upon grief," Lichas interprets the oracle (correctly) within the frame of the Hesiodic Iron Age. As opposed to the first oracle's idyllic festivity (ὀρχή-σασθαι) and "automatic" natural sustenance (βαλανηφάγοι), the third oracle associates iron with the griefs of the human condition in Hesiod's last age—implicitly the iron plow and the iron sword. Yet Hesiod's Iron Age, with its distant and hoarding gods necessitating human cooperation and industry, is precisely the model that subtends civic ideology, as we have seen in the formulations of Herodotus's Solon and Simonides. Thus, this oracle again aligns itself firmly with a civic economy of value, which in this instance favors the Spartans over the Tegeates. If the first oracle was "counterfeit" gold, this response, for all its seeming iron, is transmuted into "gold" by a proper, civic reading.

Still, this paradigm of failed, then proper, oracular consultation and response is lost on Kroisos. He unquestioningly "puts his trust in" the oracle that if he crosses the river Halys, he will destroy a great empire (τῷ χρηστηρίῳ πίσυνος, 1.73.1), just like the Spartans, misguidedly assuming that Delphic Apollo is his *pistos hetairos*. Indeed, Herodotus deliberately echoes the narrative of the first Tegeate oracle to the Spartans in his preface to Kroisos's campaign proper, suggesting the parallelism of the two stories:

> Kroisos, blaming Kyros for these things, was both sending if he should make an expedition against the Persians, and especially, when the counterfeit oracle came (ἀπικομένου χρησμοῦ κιβδήλου), expecting that the oracle was

on his side, was making an expedition against the allotment of the Persians.
(Hdt 1.75.2)

Again, as in the case of the Spartans, the "counterfeit oracle" (χρησμὸς
κίβδηλος) is not false; it is simply duplicitous, with a surface meaning
of gold and a core (or "soul") of lead. Kroisos, convinced that the oracle
is "on his side" (πρὸς ἑωυτοῦ), is content to accept it at face value rather
than plumb its depths, and so he makes his disastrous expedition against
the Persians.[59]

The dénouement of this extended oracular narrative—the fall of Sardis
and the final fate of Kroisos—draws together Solon's civic paradigm with
the incommensurability of dedicatory and oracular economies, revealing
the imbrication of Delphic inscrutability and civic truth. First, in the
midst of the account of the city's fall, the Pythia's last oracle to Kroisos
in power (strategically delayed in the narrative) reminds us vividly of
Solon's language and admonitions. In the time of his good fortune, Herodotus tells us, Kroisos consulted the oracle about his surviving son, who
was mute, and got the following response:

Λυδὲ γένος, πολλῶν βασιλεῦ, μέγα νήπιε Κροῖσε,
μὴ βούλευ πολύευκτον ἰὴν ἀνὰ δώματ' ἀκούειν
παιδὸς φθεγγομένου. τὸ δέ σοι πολὺ λώιον ἀμφὶς
ἔμμεναι· αὐδήσει γὰρ ἐν ἤματι πρῶτον ἀνόλβῳ. (Hdt. 1.85.2)

Lydian in race, king of many, great fool Kroisos,
Do not wish to hear throughout the house the much-prayed-for voice
of your child speaking. But it is much better for you for it to
be apart; for you will hear it first on a luckless day.

And so indeed, the son first finds his voice to yell at an oncoming Persian,
"O man, do not kill Kroisos."[60] But aside from its dramatic fulfillment,
the oracle functions as a kind of précis or recapitulation in miniature of
Solon's advice. For this oracle, again, registers Kroisos's complete lack
of understanding of the workings of the divine as they create paradoxes
and slippages in human fortune. Thus even the oracle's first verse can be
read as a one-line gloss on Solon's message: you can be king of many
and still a great fool. Solon's version had been more tactful and less
abrupt, though it pointed to the same disparity between the material
accoutrements of wealth and power and the reality of *olbos*:

οὕτω ὦν, ὦ Κροῖσε, πᾶν ἐστι ἄνθρωπος συμφορή. ἐμοὶ δὲ σὺ καὶ πλουτέειν
μέγα φαίνεαι καὶ βασιλεὺς πολλῶν εἶναι ἀνθρώπων. . . . πολλοὶ μὲν γὰρ

---

[59] Cf. Immerwahr 1966: 159, who notes the incommensurability between Kroisos's golden
offerings and the "deceptive or spurious" oracles he receives.
[60] Cf. Sebeok and Brady 1979 on the thematics of communication in this narrative.

ζάπλουτοι ἀνθρώπων ἄνολβοί εἰσι, πολλοὶ δὲ μετρίως ἔχοντες βίου εὐτυ-
χέες. (Hdt. 1.32.4–5)

Thus, o Kroisos, a human being is entirely accident. And you seem to me
to be both very wealthy and king of many men. . . . But many extremely
wealthy men are unhappy, and many who have a moderate livelihood are fortunate.

The echoes of βασιλεὺς πολλῶν and ἄνολβος (which occurs only in these
two passages in Herodotus) conjure up Solon at this crucial point in the
narrative, linked to the cosmic inscrutability that is both message and
medium of the Delphic oracle.

Solon's phantom presence is appropriate, for he will play an active
role in the salvation of Kroisos from the pyre. In the very next chapter,
in what seems like a grim parody of Kroisos's lavish holocaust offering
to Delphic Apollo (Hdt 1.50.1), Kyros mounts Kroisos himself in chains
on a great pyre. The story is familiar to us from Bacchylides' epinikian
treatment, but Herodotus's account offers two significant divergences.
First, Kroisos on the pyre provides the culmination of an elaborate *oracular* narrative (which is elided in Bacchylides' version). Second, Herodotus
doubles Bacchylides' epiphany, offering us an initial civic "epiphany" of
Solon, and then, only as an ancillary intervention, the saving grace of
Delphic Apollo. It is my contention that these two divergences are crucially
linked to each other—that the oracular narrative demands and finds its
telos in the Solonic epiphany—and that the doubled epiphanies correspond to the competing, incommensurable economies of oracles and dedications.

But first, let me demonstrate how carefully and systematically Herodotus has constructed Kroisos's reminiscence of Solon as an epiphanic moment. We have just been told by the narrator that Kyros may have put
Kroisos on the pyre because he "wanted to know if anyone of the gods
(τίς . . . δαιμόνων) would save him from being burnt alive" (1.86.2),
when the narrative shifts to indirect discourse:

[They say that Kyros] did these things, but for Kroisos standing upon the
pyre there came to him (ἐσελθεῖν), although he was in such great evil, the
thought of Solon, that it had been said with a god for him, that no one of
the living is blessed. And when this [thought] stood beside him (ὡς δὲ ἄρα
μιν προσστῆναι τοῦτο), [they say that] having come to himself and groaned
from much peace he called the name "Solon" three times. And Kyros, when
he heard, bid the interpreters ask Kroisos who was this he invoked (τίνα
τοῦτον ἐπικαλέοιτο), and they approached him and asked. And Kroisos for
a time held silent being asked, but afterwards, when he was compelled, he
said, "The one whom I would have preferred to much money to come to

words for all tyrants" (τὸν ἂν ἐγὼ πᾶσι τυράννοισι προετίμησα μεγάλων χρημάτων ἐς λόγους ἐλθεῖν). But since he was declaring things unintelligible to them (ὡς δέ σφι ἄσημα ἔφραζε), they were asking him again the things said. And when they persisted and furnished a disturbance, he was saying indeed that when Solon came originally and saw all his prosperity, he had made light of it (having said the sorts of things he said) and that all things had turned out for him exactly as that one had said, though he spoke no more to himself than to the entire human condition, and most of all to those among them who thought themselves blessed. [They say that] Kroisos described these things, but that [meanwhile] the edges [of the pyre] were burning since the fire had already been kindled. And [they say that] Kyros, having heard from the interpreters what things Kroisos said, changed his mind and reflected that he himself, also a human being, was giving live to the fire another human being, who had been no less fortunate than himself. And, in addition to these things, fearing some vengeance and reflecting that no condition among mortals holds steadfast, he bid [them] quench the burning fire as quickly as possible and bring down Kroisos and those with him. And [they say that] the men trying could no longer overcome the fire. And, at this point, it is said by the Lydians that Kroisos, understanding Kyros's change of mind, since he saw every man trying to quench the fire but no longer able to control it, shouted out invoking Apollo, if any pleasing thing had been given by himself, to stand beside him and save him from the present evil (ἐπιβώσασθαι τὸν Ἀπόλλωνα ἐπικαλεόμενον, εἴ τί οἱ κεχαρισμένον ἐξ αὐτοῦ ἐδωρήθη, παραστῆναι καὶ ῥύσασθαί μιν ἐκ τοῦ παρεόντος κακοῦ). And [they say that] he, weeping, invoked the god, but that from a clear and windless sky, clouds suddenly ran together and a storm erupted and it rained violently, and the fire was quenched. And thus indeed Kyros came to understand that Kroisos was both beloved of the gods and a good man (καὶ θεοφιλὴς καὶ ἀνὴρ ἀγαθός), and he brought him down from the pyre and asked him. . . . (Hdt. 1.86.3–87.2)

Into a narrative that Herodotus has meticulously set up to anticipate divine intervention sneaks "the thought of Solon" (τὸ τοῦ Σόλωνος), "coming over" Kroisos just as pity or laughter or the suspicion of divinity overtake other Herodotean actors.[61] Indeed, we might be tempted to read Kroisos's realization that Solon's admonition was "said with a god" (σὺν θεῷ εἰρημένον) as a typically Herodotean rationalization of divine epiphany, were it not that the epiphanic language and structure now become even more dense and concrete. The thought of Solon "stands beside" Kroisos: προσστῆναι is used only here (metaphorically) of a

---

[61] Cf. Herodotus's other uses of ἐσέρχομαι: for emotions: 1.116.1, 2.93.1, 6.125.5, 7.46.2; particularly associated with prodigies or divine interventions: 3.42.4, 8.137.3.

thought; it is otherwise in Herodotus always used literally of people. Other compounds of ἵστημι, comparable in semantic force to προσστῆναι, frequently occur in Herodotus's text for dream visions or divine epiphanies: thus at 1.87, Kroisos calls on Apollo to "stand beside him and save him" (παραστῆναι καὶ ῥύσασθαι), while the vision of a great and beautiful being "stands over" Xerxes at 7.12 (ἐπιστάντα). Kroisos reacts with the incantatory, almost magical naming of Solon "three times," and perhaps most remarkably, Kyros has his interpreters ask Kroisos who he is "invoking" (ἐπικαλέοιτο). ἐπικαλέω is the normal Herodotean verb for invoking a divinity, occurring thirteen times (active and middle) in this meaning. In the very next chapter, middle forms of the verb are used twice for Kroisos invoking Apollo's aid (τὸν Ἀπόλλωνα ἐπικαλεόμενον; ἐπικαλέεσθαι τὸν θεόν). And indeed, Kroisos's "invocation" of Solon is efficacious: his name and the narrative to which it is linked succeed in converting Kyros to pity and mercy. Though Kyros's intention has changed, the fire cannot be put out, so that the miraculous intervention of Apollo is relegated to the mere mechanical function of quenching the blaze.[62]

The parallelism between the epiphany of Solon in 1.86 and the epiphany of Apollo in 1.87 could hardly be more exact. But, while structurally exactly analogous, the two epiphanies correspond to two different paradigms of order and resolve different threads of the Kroisos narrative. In Herodotus as in Bacchylides, the ground of Apollo's saving intervention is *charis*, divine grace that reciprocates Kroisos's abundant dedications at Delphi (cf. especially εἴ τί οἱ κεχαρισμένον ἐξ αὐτοῦ ἐδωρήθη). The Apollo who intervenes is the reliable *xenos* duty-bound to assist his gift-exchange partner Kroisos in his moment of need. In contrast, Solon (like the oracle) represents a cosmos of inscrutable gods and unstable fortune, whose only defense is the mediating rationality of civic order. We might say it is the ultimate presumption of the civic appropriation of the long-term transactional order to replace the saving divinity with the saving lawgiver, whose wisdom structures and makes sense of an unintelligible cosmos. The civic epiphany of Solon preempts that of Apollo, just as the city constitutes itself, on the unstable ground of oracular inscrutability, as the final instance.

It is worth noting further that these two epiphanies are articulated with the two competing economies we have been tracing. This is obvious enough in the case of Apollo's intervention, which is figured in Herodotus as in Bacchylides as a unique bond of *charis* linking the god with the giver of lavish dedications. What is more striking (because more apparently

---

[62] For the importance of Solon and the subsidiary intervention of Apollo, cf. Segal 1971: 49, Crane 1996: 77.

gratuitous) is Kroisos's emphatic association of Solon's wisdom with a
money economy and all it implies. Recall his exact words in answer to
the Persian interpreters: "[I invoke] the man whom I would have preferred
to much money to come to words for all tyrants" (τὸν ἂν ἐγὼ πᾶσι
τυράννοισι προετίμησα μεγάλων χρημάτων ἐς λόγους ἐλθεῖν). Kroisos
in effect uses money as a universal equivalent, a standard against which
to measure the value of Solon's discourse, and by so doing, he puts Solon's
wisdom in the marketplace. In addition, his emphasis on the *generic*
appropriateness of Solon's teaching, as a desirable commodity "for all
tyrants," transfers the interchangeability and equivalency of money to
this economy of civic wisdom (in marked contrast to the uniqueness of
the bond that links Apollo to Kroisos as gift-exchange partners). And
indeed, in the emphatic use of τυράννοισι, the same civic discourse that
subtends the free circulation of money and logoi seems to leak into
Kroisos's self-characterization: it is only from the perspective of the Greek
city that all Eastern monarchs are tyrants.[63]

Intriguingly, Kroisos' image of wisdom on the open market baffles his
interlocutors, who find his words, like a riddling oracle, unintelligible
(ἄσημα). Inverting tenor and vehicle from the twice-repeated image of
the "counterfeit oracle," here talk of a money economy and the free
circulation of words conjures the image of oracular consultation, with
the interpreters "persisting" until they get a more normative response.
Still, whichever way the image goes, money and prophecy are strongly
linked, so that coinage, oracles, and the lawgiver's civic wisdom all converge in the knot of Solonic epiphany.

This dialectic of divergent economies at work in the two epiphanies
is confirmed in Kroisos's final exchange with the Delphic oracle (Hdt.
1.90–91). Having given Kyros good advice on the regulation of resources
in the sack of Sardis, Kroisos requests a reciprocating boon of the Persian king:

> He said, "O master, you will gratify me most by allowing me to question
> the god of the Greeks, whom I honored most of the gods, having sent these
> shackles along, if it is his custom to deceive his benefactors" (εἰ ἐξαπατᾶν
> τοὺς εὖ ποιεῦντας νόμος ἐστί οἱ). And Kyros asked him what he was
> referring to in making this request. And Kroisos repeated for him his entire
> plan and the answers of the oracles and most of all his dedications and how,
> encouraged by the oracular response, he made an expedition against the
> Persians. And saying these things he ended by asking again for permission
> to reproach the god with this. (Hdt. 1.90.2–3)

---

[63] For Herodotus's systematic differentiation of the terms *basileus, turannos,* and *mounarchos,* see Ferrill 1978. Kroisos's usage here strikingly contravenes Ferrill's observation that

Kyros laughs indulgently and authorizes one last offering and consultation:

> [Kroisos] sending [some] of the Lydians to Delphi bid them put the shackles on the floor of the temple and ask if he is not at all ashamed at having encouraged Kroisos with oracles to make an expedition against the Persians, on the promise of ending the power of Kyros, from which such victory offerings resulted (showing the shackles). [And he bid them] ask both these things and if it is customary for the Greek gods to be without *charis*. (εἰ ἀχαρίστοισι νόμος εἶναι τοῖσι Ἑλληνικοῖσι θεοῖσι). (Hdt. 1.90.4)

In spite of his momentary illumination on the pyre, Kroisos here reverts to his unquestioned assumption of gift-exchange relations with Delphic Apollo, reproaching him, like a bad *xenos* or *hetairos*, with deceit (ἐξαπατᾶν) and failure of *charis* (ἀχαρίστοισι).[64] For Kroisos persists in equating "the answers of the oracles and most of all his dedications" in a single paratactic list: he regards them as commensurable objects and systems of exchange. And thus he seeks to reproach and insult the god with a final demeaning dedication "worthy" of his oracular practice: the shackles with which he was bound on the pyre. The Pythia's response to Kroisos reinscribes the distinction he elides between Apollo as recipient of dedications and as mantic divinity:

> But to the Lydians coming and saying the things ordered, it is said that the Pythia said the following: "It is impossible even for the god to escape the allotted share. And Kroisos filled out the wrongdoing (ἁμαρτάδα) of his fifth ancestor, who, being a spearbearer of the Herakleidai, following womanly wiles, killed his master and got the honor of that one, though it didn't belong to him at all. And, though Loxias was eager that the suffering of Sardis occur in the time of Kroisos's children and not in his own time, he was not able to deflect the Moirai. But as much as they granted, [so much] he accomplished and gratified him (ὅσον δὲ ἐνέδωκαν αὗται, ἤνυσέ τε καὶ ἐχαρίσατό οἱ): for he delayed the sack of Sardis for three years, and let Kroisos know this—that he was taken three years later than was fated. And

---

tyrants never refer to themselves as such in Herodotus's text (1978: 396), suggesting that a Greek civic perspective has somehow leaked into the Eastern dynast's discourse.

[64] For both of these motifs, see Thgn. 237–54, 851–54. For ἀχάριστος in the context of another "counterfeit oracle," cf. Hdt. 5.91.2: the Spartans complain to their allies that, "encouraged by counterfeit oracles, we drove out men who were most our *xenoi*" and handed Athens over to the "ungrateful demos" (δήμῳ ἀχαρίστῳ, cf. 5.90.1). Here "counterfeit" has a different meaning, for the Spartans contend that the Pythia was suborned with Alkmeonid money to give false oracles (cf. Hdt. 5.62.3–63.2). Still, it is noteworthy that in this context as well Herodotus represents the same antagonism between different exchange systems: the top-rank *xenia* of the Spartans with the Peisistratidai vs. the economy of oracles and money that supports the civic autonomy of Athens.

second, he came to his aid when he was being burnt. But, as for the oracular response, not rightly does Kroisos blame what happened (κατὰ δὲ τὸ μαντήιον τὸ γενόμενον οὐκ ὀρθῶς Κροῖσος μέμφεται). For Loxias foretold for him, if he made an expedition against the Persians, he would destroy a great empire. But he, if he was going to plan well in regard to these things, ought to have sent and asked whether he [Apollo] meant his own empire or Kyros's. But, since he neither comprehended the thing said nor asked again, let him declare himself responsible. And to him consulting the oracle for the last time Loxias spoke concerning the mule, but not even this did he comprehend. For Kyros himself was the mule, for he was born from two parents unlike in race, from a better mother and an inferior father. For she was a Mede and daughter of Astyages, king of the Medes, but he was a Persian and ruled by those, and, though inferior to them all, he lived with his own mistress. These things the Pythia answered to the Lydians, and they went back to Sardis and announced them to Kroisos. And he, when he had heard, recognized that the fault was his and not the god's. (ὁ δὲ ἀκούσας συνέγνω ἑωυτοῦ εἶναι τὴν ἁμαρτάδα καὶ οὐ τοῦ θεοῦ). (Hdt. 1.91)

In response to Kroisos's accusations, the Pythia outlines two distinct economies, which correspond to the two epiphanies to Kroisos on the pyre. First, she details the gift economy whereby Apollo favors Kroisos (implicitly for his dedications) by delaying his fated fall for three years and by putting out the fire. Here, the language of gifting, gratification, and service predominates (ἐνέδωκαν; ἐχαρίσατο; ἐπήρκεσε).[65] But with a marked contrastive δέ (κατὰ δὲ τὸ μαντήιον), the Pythia articulates in the second half of her answer a completely distinct economy of interpretation that governs oracular questioning and response. In this context, what counts is not gift and countergift but intellectual perspicuity, comprehension, and repeated questioning. The language of recognition, understanding, and misunderstanding replaces that of reciprocal gratification (οὐ συλλαβών; ἀποφαινέτω; οὐδὲ . . . συνέλαβε; συνέγνω). This is the cosmos of opaque and inscrutable forces that Solon had outlined and the oracle enacted—forces that demand the labor of interpretation but promise nothing to fallible mortal intelligence.[66]

The emblem of this world of contingency, in Herodotus as in Bacchyl-

---

[65] This sphere of human-divine gift exchange, in which Apollo wants to "deflect the Moirai" but is unable to do so, strongly recalls the Apollo-Admetos story, with its dynamic of aristocratic virtue rewarded.

[66] Cf. Christ 1994: 189–93, who notes that Kroisos's "error" in the oracular narrative is not moral wrongdoing but intellectual failure. This contrast is, in fact, mapped in the contrasting meanings of ἁμαρτάς in 1.91.1 and 1.91.6: in the world of aristocratic xenoi, Gyges' usurpation is a moral "error," while, in the domain of oracular consultation, Kroisos' "fault" is a failure of understanding.

ides 3, is the name Loxias, which occurs here first in the *Histories* (and indeed, appears in 1.91 three of its total four occurrences in Herodotus[67]). The narrative builds up to this moment by its coy references to "the god of the Greeks" (1.87.3; 1.90.2; cf. 1.90.4), making the Pythia's thrice-repeated use of Apollo's oracular epithet "Loxias" all the more striking. Still, there is a final irony here: twice, the Pythia names Loxias in the context of his "counterfeit" oracles to Kroisos (1.91.4, 5); but the first time, she uses the name within the "other" economy—the "reliable" movement of human-divine gift and countergift (1.91.2). There are two ways of accounting for this apparent discrepancy. The more superficial interpretation would point out that all of 1.91 is itself an oracular response, so that even the gift economy of dedications is filtered through the language and ideology of riddling oracles. Yet, we might be tempted to go further still and imagine that the strategic use of Loxias here suggests that even the economy of gift and countergift is mired in contingency: how, after all, do we know a divine gift when we see one? It may be a burst of rain out of a clear sky, or it may be three extra years of uneventful time.[68] How, also, do we know that the forces we oblige to us with gifts are the only or even the most powerful forces at work in the cosmos? Kroisos has won Apollo as *xenos* and *philos*, but he cannot overcome the Fates. At some level the human and divine spheres are simply incommensurable. Even within the gift economy, contingency is reinscribed, casting us back on the Solonic construction of the city as mediating force and final instance.

Herodotus then concludes the sequential narrative of Kroisos with a final chapter detailing his dedications at various shrines (1.92; a common form of Herodotean closure). This dedicatory catalogue provides him the opportunity for one last disturbing anecdote, the note on which the account of Lydian history closes:

> Kroisos's dedications at Branchidai of the Milesians, as I learn, are equal in weight and similar to those at Delphi. And the things now that he dedicated at Delphi and at the Amphiareion were his own property and the first-fruits from his ancestral property, but the other dedications were from the property of an enemy, who before [Kroisos] became king, was a political opponent very eager for Pantaleon to get the rule of the Lydians. And Pantaleon was the child of Alyattes and the brother of Kroisos from a different mother;

---

[67] The fourth occurrence is at 4.163, also in a riddling, oracular context.

[68] Furthermore, think about the chronology: at 1.46 Herodotus says that Kroisos mourned his son for two years, then started investigating oracles. Does this mean that, if Apollo had not intervened, Sardis would have fallen before the death of Kroisos's son? If so, might things have been different? If this is not simply irrelevant speculation, it suggests that the gifts of the gods are at best ambiguous for mortals.

for Kroisos was born to Alyattes from a Kaeirian woman, but Pantaleon from an Ionian woman. But when, with his father giving it, Kroisos won the rule, he killed this man his opponent (τὸν ἀντιπρήσσοντα) by dragging him over the comb, but his property which he had even before vowed, then he dedicated in the way I've said to the amount stated. And concerning the dedications let so much be said. (Hdt. 1.92.2–4)

If the extended narrative of Kroisos on the pyre confronts the aristocratic ideology of human-divine gift exchange with the specter of contingency, this closing paragraph puts in question the morality of Kroisos's brand of reciprocity. For here Herodotus reenacts the dedicatory narrative of 1.50–52, doubling the dedications at Delphi and simultaneously exposing the ominous dialectic between generous gift-giving and savage punishment. We should notice first how Herodotus's casual participial phrase ἔτι πρότερον κατιρώσας ("having vowed the dedication still before [he gained power]") conjures up a nefarious bargain with the god who is the recipient of this treasure. It is as if Kroisos makes a deal with the god: treasure devoted in exchange for acquiring the rule of the Lydians—a deal predicated on the horrific violence done to the nameless opponent. And the climactic term Herodotus uses to designate Kroisos's antagonist, τὸν ἀντιπρήσσοντα, sets the episode squarely within the frame of reciprocity, standing as a nice counterpoint to the histor's use of συμπρήκτωρ to characterize Alkmeon's assistance to Kroisos at Delphi (6.125.2). That is, ἀντιπρήσσων reminds us that this kind of unconstrained aristocratic reciprocity has its negative as well as its positive side.[69] Indeed, given the dedicatory context, we are forced to see positive and negative as inextricably interconnected: Kroisos's gift to the god depends on his ruthless reciprocating violence.

Finally, we might imagine that the reason Herodotus closes his account of Kroisos here is that the flayed body of his unfortunate opponent is not just particular but also emblematic of another kind of violence on which his dedicatory generosity depends.[70] For, with the account of Kroi-

---

[69] Cf. Gould 1989: 82–85; 1991: 15–18.

[70] Already in antiquity, [Plutarch] On the Malice of Herodotus felt and objected to the undermining force of this closing anecdote, which, he observed, transformed Kroisos's "one noble trait"—"honoring the gods with many and lavish dedications"—into the "worst act of irreverence" (ἀσεβέστατον . . . ἔργον, [Plut.] Mor. 858e–f). Modern commentators have been likewise discomfited. How and Wells, for example, are troubled both by this narrative itself *and* by its placement: "H. here winds up his Lydian history. This chapter shows Croesus in a new light, as a cruel Oriental prince. . . . It clearly comes from another source. As it is not likely to be a later addition, it is probably a fragment of H.'s original material, which he has not worked into harmony with his narrative" (How and Wells 1928: I.100). Cf. Immerwahr 1966: 159n.27, who notes the "unfavorable" portrait of Kroisos's wealth at 1.92.

sos's rivalry with his half-brother Pantaleon in which the unnamed enemy participates, Herodotus reintroduces the issues of race and domination that first occasioned the Kroisos narrative. At 1.5–6, Herodotus famously starts his account with "the man who, to my knowledge, first made a beginning of unjust acts against the Greeks" (1.5.3):

> Kroisos was Lydian in race, child of Alyattes, and tyrant of the races within the River Halys, which, flowing from the south between the Syrians and the Paphlagonians, drains into the sea called the Euxine toward the North Wind. This Kroisos first of barbarians whom we know subdued some of the Greeks to the paying of tribute, and made others his friends. The ones he subdued were the Ionians and Aeolians and Dorians (those in Asia), and the ones he made his friends were the Lakedaimonians. (Hdt. 1.6.1–2)

As Gregory Crane has astutely observed, this first characterization resonates significantly behind Herodotus's narratives of Kroisos's dedications, since the tribute levied on the conquered Greek cities of Asia Minor constituted one source of Kroisos's fabulous wealth.[71] This also applies to the narrative of 1.92, perhaps with even greater force. Are we entitled to wonder what the fate of the Ionian cities would have been had Pantaleon, the son of an Ionian woman, succeeded to the throne instead of Kroisos? If so, we might read the horrific fate of Pantaleon's advocate at Kroisos's hands as an emblem of the violent subjection of the Greek cities of Asia Minor.[72] If we allow this resonance behind Herodotus's seemingly unprepossessing narrative, the story of Kroisos ends where it began, thereby exposing the civic violence underlying and supporting the luminous circuit of human-divine gift exchange.

IV. LYDIANS AND LUDOPATHEIS: THE GAP BETWEEN HISTORY AND ETHNOGRAPHY

I would like to return briefly to Herodotus's scene of doubled epiphany to consider one more detail. At 1.87, the histor prefaces the tale of Apollo's divine intervention with his only explicit source acknowledgment: ἐνθαῦτα λέγεται ὑπὸ Λυδῶν ("thereupon, it is said by the

---

[71] Crane 1996: 79–84.

[72] For the significant return of the theme of Kroisos's relation to the Greeks at 1.92, see Immerwahr 1966: 20n.12. This reading is supported by the fact that there was an alternative account of Kroisos's victim's wrongdoing: according to Nikolaos of Damaskos (*FGrH* 90 F 65), this man offended Kroisos by refusing him a loan when he was crown prince (cf. How and Wells 1928: I.101). Notice that Nikolaos of Damaskos's account, then, does not raise the issue of Ionians vs. their barbarian conquerors, nor does it locate Kroisos's revenge within a circuit of gift exchange.

Lydians that . . ." 1.87.1). ἐνθαῦτα signals that *only* what follows is the
report of the Lydians, though the histor had distanced himself from the
narrative by the use of indirect discourse already at 1.86.3 (at the moment
of Solon's "epiphany"). Why does Herodotus mark off just this part as
the Lydians' version? And what are the implications of this attribution?
Who, then, is Herodotus's source for the rationalized account whereby
Kroisos saves himself by recalling the advice of the wise lawgiver? Are
we to assume that the default category for the implied λέγουσι at 1.86.3
is "the Greeks"? If so, we have an almost too-neat dichotomy: "the
Greeks" explain Kroisos's survival by the civic epiphany of Solon, while
"the Lydians" link it to the circuit of human-divine *charis* and supernatural intervention.[73]

However that may be, the precise specification of Apollo's intervention
as the Lydian version suggests that "Lydian" here is code for an elitist
aristocratic position that needs to affirm the reality of human-divine
reciprocity. In this respect, this subsection of the narrative is very comparable to Bacchylides' third ode, in its audience, its ideology, and its
deployment of *habrosunē* and gift exchange. Herodotus's strangely focused source attribution leads to the general question, What does the
designation "Lydian" signify in the text of the *Histories*?

I would suggest that Herodotus's text in fact incorporates two contradictory representations of the Lydians, uncomfortably—and anachronistically—juxtaposed. We might regard the characterization that emerges
from the historical account, centered around Kroisos, as the aristocratic,
pro-*habrosunē* valorization of the Lydian monarch and the Lydian people.
But this model seems to coexist very uneasily with the Lydian ethnographic account the histor offers at 1.93-94, which portrays the Lydians
in very different terms. And, while this latter model is distanced from
Kroisos by the atemporality of ethnography, the inconcinnities between
the two accounts call into question the elitist portrait of the noble, luxurious, and warlike Lydians.

So let us consider the two versions of the Lydians in order. In the
historical account, what is characteristic of the Lydians emerges first
through implicit contrast to their enemies the Persians. Thus, as Kroisos
is preparing his campaign against Kyros, he receives the following advice
from the wise Lydian Sandanis:

> "O King, you prepare to make an expedition against such men who wear
> leather trousers and the rest of their garments are leather, and who eat not
> as much as they wish but as much as they have, since they have a harsh

---

[73] In this context, it is worth noting the suggestion of Fehling 1989: 249: "The Lydian
data . . . where they are not merely conjectural, probably come from the Greek poets" (cf.
Fehling 1989: 153).

land. And, in addition, they do not use wine, but they drink water, nor do they have figs to eat, nor any other good thing. On the one hand then, if you win, what will you take from them who have nothing? On the other hand, if you are defeated, learn how many good things you will cast away. For once having tasted of our goods, they will cling to them, nor will they be thrust away. And I now have gratitude for the gods, that they do not put it in the Persians' mind to make an expedition against the Lydians." Saying these things, he was not persuading Kroisos. [Though he was right,] since for the Persians before they overthrew the Lydians, there was nothing either luxurious nor good. (. . .ἦν οὔτε ἀβρὸν οὔτε ἀγαθὸν οὐδέν). (Hdt. 1.71.2–4)

What most characterizes the Lydians in this oppositional structure is their enjoyment of ἀβρόν and ἀγαθόν—the good things that make for a luxurious lifestyle. We assume from Sandanis's portrait of the Persians that these "goods" include fine wool garments (vs. leather) and an abundance of food and wine. But having strongly associated the Lydians with the lifestyle of *habrosunē*, Herodotus is at pains in the historical account to assure us (against fifth-century Greek expectation) that the Lydians of Kroisos's time were not ennervated or unmanned thereby. Thus the histor narrates Kroisos's battle preparations when Kyros unexpectedly leads the entire Persian army against Sardis, knowing full well that Kroisos has demobilized his force for the winter months:

> At that point Kroisos, having come to great resourcelessness, since things went contrary to what he himself had expected, still led the Lydians out to battle. (And at this time there was no nation in Asia more manly or courageous than the Lydian. But they used to fight from horses and carried great spears and they were themselves good horsemen.) (Hdt. 1.79.2–3)

Herodotus's parenthetic assertion of the manliness and courage of the old-time Lydians is necessary to counter the prevailing (egalitarian) association of *habrosunē* with debilitating Eastern luxury.[74] Thus he offers us, in the Lydians of Kroisos's day, the elitist ideal: an Eastern people, ruled by the fabulously wealthy and generous Kroisos, who are distinguished simultaneously for their luxurious lifestyle and their martial valor. Unsurprisingly, this vignette of the Lydians corresponds closely (as How and Wells note) to the evocations of Bacchylides' epinikian portrait: at the moment he introduces Kroisos, the poet characterizes him as δαμασίππου

---

[74] Cf. How and Wells 1928: I.95: "H. adds this, because the Lydians of his own day were a proverb for effeminacy." On this association of Eastern barbarians with effeminacy, see Hall 1989: 126–33, 206–10; on the egalitarian politics that animated this representation, see Kurke 1992.

Λυδίας ἀρχαγέταν ("leader of the horse-breaking Lydians," Bacch. 3.23–24).[75]

And yet, having established the courage and heroism of the old-time Lydians, it seems that Herodotus feels the need to reconcile this portrait with their current degenerate state. Thus he offers us a historical narrative for how the Lydians became Λυδοπαθεῖς—a byword in the egalitarian discourse of the Greek city for Eastern luxury and the effeminacy it entails.[76] Recall Kroisos's advice to Kyros on how to tame his rebellious subjects (quoted above in relation to his encounter with Alkmeon):

> Pardon the Lydians and give them the following commands, in order that they neither revolt nor be fearsome [in future]. Send to them and forbid them to wear martial equipment, and [instead] bid them wear tunics underneath their garments and *kothornoi*, and order them to educate their children in playing the kithara and plucking the lyre and practicing retail trade. And soon, o King, you will see them become women instead of men, so that there will be no fear that they revolt. (Hdt. 1.155.4)

Kroisos recommends all the attributes of a luxurious lifestyle—fine clothes, comfortable shoes, training in lyre and kithara—conjoined with *kapēleia* to remove the Lydians from the stage of history. His advice is effective: thus the histor informs us in his own voice, "From this command, the Lydians changed their entire lifestyle" (Hdt. 1.157.2). It is egalitarian ideology that seems to inform this anecdote, constructing proper "manly" (read Greek civic) behavior between the poles of *habrosunē* and *kapēleia*, devaluing the former as an elitist lifestyle that excludes the city and the latter as a disembedded activity that misuses civic space. The conjunction of these apparent opposites is intriguing, for it suggests that in the discourse of the city, *habrosunē* is assimilated to *kapēleia* as the antitype to the embedded money economy of the polis. Thus this anecdote at least partly undercuts the elitist idealization of the luxurious, warlike Lydians, even as it establishes a precise historical cause for their decline.

Yet even here, the reign of Kroisos is discursively protected as an elitist golden age, in which aristocratic luxury comfortably coexisted with "manliness" and military prowess (recall οὔτε ἀνδρηιότερον οὔτε ἀλκιμώτερον, 1.79.3). But I would suggest that even this positive representation of the "old-time" Lydians is incongruously juxtaposed with a very different portrait in Herodotus's ethnographic account. After the closure of the sequential narrative of Kroisos's reign at 1.92, Herodotus

---

[75] How and Wells 1928: I.95.

[76] Λυδοπαθεῖς is a one-word fragment of Anakreon (fr. 136/481 *PMG*), preserved in a scholion to Aeschylus's *Persians*; for discussion, see Kurke 1992: 93–94.

pauses for a brief ethnography of the Lydians, surveying the usual topics in the usual order—θώματα, ἔργα, and customs of the people:[77]

> The Lydian land does not have much in the way of marvels, compared to other lands at any rate, outside of the gold dust carried down from [Mt.] Tmolus. But it furnishes much the greatest monument (ἔργον) outside of the Egyptian and Babylonian works (ἔργα): there is in this place the tomb of Alyattes, father of Kroisos, whose foundation is of great stones, but the rest of the tomb is of heaped earth. And it was built by the tradespeople and the handiworkers and the whores who plied their trade in the land (ἐξεργάσαντο δέ μιν οἱ ἀγοραῖοι ἄνθρωποι καὶ οἱ χειρώνακτες καὶ αἱ ἐνεργαζόμεναι παιδίσκαι). And still even to my time there were five boundary-stones set up above upon the tomb, and letters had been inscribed on them what each group had contributed to the building. And when it was all measured, the work of the whores appeared to be the greatest. For the daughters of the demos of the Lydians are prostituted—all of them, collecting dowries for themselves [and] doing this until they settle down in marriage. And they give themselves away [i.e., choose their own husbands]. And the perimeter of the tomb is six stades plus two plethra, and its width is thirteen plethra. And there is a great lake hard by the tomb, which the Lydians claim is ever-flowing: and it is called the Gygean Lake. Such then is this.
>
> And the Lydians use customs very similar to the Greeks, apart from the fact that they prostitute their female children (χωρὶς ἢ ὅτι τὰ θήλεα τέκνα καταπορνεύουσι). And first of men whom we know they minted and used gold and silver coinage, and they were also the first retail traders (κάπηλοι). And the Lydians themselves say that also the games which are now established for themselves and the Greeks were their invention. And they say that at the same time as these were invented among them, they also settled Tyrsenia. . . . (Hdt. 1.93–94.2)

With 1.93, we are already in very strange territory. The tomb of Alyattes, Kroisos' father, is paid for by the most disembedded mercantile elements in the state—tradespeople, craftsmen, and whores. This great monument to royal prestige—the apex of the long-term transactional order in a monarchical system—is causally linked to the lowest elements of the short-term transactional order.[78] And while this vertiginous affiliation is still distanced from Kroisos, its existence in his father's time strikes a discordant note. We may be inclined to believe that the martial, luxurious Lydians coexist with tradespeople, craftsmen, and whores as

---

[77] On this order, cf. Immerwahr 1966: 318–19.

[78] For this collapse of transactional orders, by which Herodotus associates the monumental tombs of Eastern dynasts with prostitution, see Steiner 1994: 137–38, 164; von Reden 1997: 169–73.

two distinct classes or statuses (after all, Herodotus tells us parenthetically that it is the daughters of the Lydian demos who are prostituted), but the information added in 1.94 makes this assumption harder. Herodotus says simply, "The Lydians use customs very similar to the Greeks, apart from the fact that they prostitute their female children." Our instinct is to reconcile this offhand remark with the mention of the demos at 1.93 (and with our own assumptions). Witness the reaction of How and Wells: "No doubt the custom in Lydia was mainly confined to the lower classes, who may have been of a different race."[79] But Herodotus articulates no such restriction here, though he does so in other ethnographic contexts (cf. 1.196.5). On the contrary, this statement is as universal as it could be, apparently applying to all the Lydians and in an eternal ethnographic present that implies that these things have always been thus. Does this mean that the courageous, luxury-loving Lydians of Kroisos's day prostituted their daughters? How do we reconcile these two accounts?

We confront the same dilemma again with the mention of *kapēleia* in 1.94. In context, *kapēleia* is associated with the invention of coinage, of games, and the settlement of Tyrsenia. The association with games might suggest to the Greeks a development of great antiquity: after all, wouldn't the Lydian "invention" have to precede Nausikaä's ballplaying in the *Odyssey*?[80] This cluster of cultural contributions, then, raises the questions, When precisely were money and *kapēleia* first invented? And by whom? 1.94 gives us no answer, resolutely adhering to the atemporality of ethnography. Herodotus sedulously avoids linking these two innovations to Kroisos at this point (though numismatists have been quick to do so). But even so, for *kapēleia*, the association with Kroisos is made explicit at 1.155.4 (quoted above). Readers and commentators on Herodotus have taken this collocation of passages for granted, not recognizing that it opens Herodotus's text to another anachronistic paradox. For 1.93 informs us that the Lydians were already tradesmen and shopkeepers at the time of Alyattes, while 1.155 implies that it was Kyros, on the advice of Kroisos, who first transformed them into *kapēloi*.[81]

Either way we read, we are confronted by paradox: if we take 1.94 to refer to some primordial Lydian invention of *kapēleia*, it cannot be reconciled with 1.155; if, on the other hand, we harmonize 1.94 and 1.155, 1.93 and 1.94 seem to controvert each other. I would suggest

[79] How and Wells 1928: I.102.

[80] Cf. Athenaios *Deipn.* 1.19 for an ancient expression of puzzlement at this "anachronism."

[81] N. Smith 1989 implicitly acknowledges this paradox; it is partly because of the anachronism between 1.93 and 1.94 that Smith would like to give to *kapēlos* a unique meaning in Herodotus. For discussion of Smith's position (and arguments against it), see above, Ch. 2, note 16.

that the paradox is precisely the point: that Herodotus has deliberately juxtaposed two irreconcilable representations of the Lydians. The historical narrative conforms to an elitist idealization of the Lydians as models of noble *habrosune*, while the ethnographic account offers us a scathing egalitarian portrait of them as a nation of shopkeepers who prostitute their daughters.[82] It is not possible to reconcile the two modes: the ethnographic account suggests that they have *always* been like this. By his deadpan collocation, by appending this strange ethnographic coda to the story of Kroisos, Herodotus seems to undermine the aristocratic ideology that informs parts of his narrative. For elitist ideology depends on the constitution of the lifestyle of *habrosune* as central to the long-term transactional order, while this other portrait of the Lydians equates luxury with the worst vices of a disembedded economy—prostitution and retail trade. Thus for *habrosune* as for gift exchange, Herodotus' narrative of Kroisos and the Lydians seems to play different representations off against each other to unsettle any comfortable adherence to elitist ideology.

---

[82] We know this latter portrait from other ancient sources; cf. the proverb Λυδὸς καπηλεύει (*Paroem. Gr.* II.510).

Part Two

PRACTICES

CHAPTER 5

The *Hetaira* and the *Pornē*

I SUGGESTED in the last section that Herodotus's ethnographic account of the Lydians deliberately forces a rift within the Greek imaginary of this Eastern people, just as his historical narrative of Kroisos undermines any wholeheartedly positive valuation of gift exchange. At this point I want to consider in more detail one system or register through which Herodotus accomplishes this problematization of the luxury-loving Lydians, as it is represented by the remarkable claim that "the Lydians use customs very similar to those of the Greeks, except that they prostitute their female children" (1.94). As commentators have long acknowledged, there is no historical evidence for this practice among the Lydians,[1] so we may wonder what motivates Herodotus's ethnographic fancy. In more general terms, how does the histor use the economy and exchange of women within the discursive struggles we have been charting? Much excellent structuralist work has analyzed in detail the signifying permutations of Herodotus' characterization of different peoples by their sexual and marital mores.[2] Michèle Rosellini and Suzanne Saïd, for example, observe how Herodotus uses promiscuous relations, polygamy, and other marriage customs regarded as aberrant by the Greeks systematically to constitute a spectrum of "others": from the bestial (those who have sex "at random outside like animals") to the civilized and hypercivilized (those who, like the Greeks, practice monogamy). What has been much less explored by such studies is Herodotus's ethnographic fascination with prostitution, and that is what I would like to focus on in Chapters 5 and 6.

For Herodotus *is* fascinated with strange and diverse forms of prostitution in his narratives of exotic "others." In addition to his offhand observation that universal prostitution of their own daughters is what differentiates Lydians from Greeks, Herodotus takes the opportunity to tell us

---

[1] How and Wells (1928: I.101–2) displace it onto "the lower classes, who may have been of a different race"; Pembroke (1967: 4–5) notes that even Strabo balked at Herodotus's claim for universal prostitution of Lydian girls (Strabo 11.14.16/533) and attributes it to Herodotus's desire to represent the "Oriental subjection of women"; S. West (1985: 295–96) puts Herodotus's claim that the prostitutes paid for the largest share of Alyattes' tomb down to "that sturdy determination not to be overawed by the pomp and circumstance of an Oriental monarchy which meets us, in a rather more elevated form, in the story of Solon and Croesus."

[2] See, e.g., Pembroke 1967; Tourraix 1976; Rosellini and Saïd 1978; Redfield 1985.

about bride auctions in the villages of Babylon (1.196); temple prostitution in Babylon itself (1.199); various Egyptian pharaohs' prostitution of their own daughters (2.121, 2.126); and even the scandals and successes of the courtesan Rhodopis in Egypt (2.134–35). How are we to understand these passages, in which economics and the exchange of women oddly and insistently intersect, safely projected onto exotic places and peoples?

Of all these passages, I would like to bracket for the moment Herodotus's two discussions of Babylonian practices (1.196, 1.199), which form a complementary pair and need to be read together. Instead, I start from the Lydians' prostitution of their own daughters and Herodotus's aside about Rhodopis, for these two passages provide the terms of a significant cultural opposition—the *pornē* vs. the *hetaira*. As we have seen, Herodotus's brief ethnography of the Lydians (1.93–94) informs us,

> For the daughters of the demos of the Lydians are all prostituted (πορνεύον-ται), collecting dowries for themselves, until, doing this, they cohabit [with a husband]. And they give themselves away. (Hdt. 1.93.4)

and "The Lydians use customs very similar to those of the Greeks, except that they prostitute their female children" (τὰ θήλεα τέκνα καταπορνεύ-ουσι, 1.94.1). Aside from one other occurrence of καταπορνεύω in the account of Babylon (1.196.5), forms of the verb (compound or simplex) appear only here in the text of the *Histories*. The noun *pornē* never occurs.

In Book 2, Herodotus's narrative of the monuments of Egypt leads him to a brief excursus about the famous courtesan Rhodopis:

> And this man [Mykerinos] left behind a pyramid much smaller than his father's, each side of three plethra short twenty feet, quadrangular, and up to half of Ethiopian stone. Various of the Greeks indeed say that it [the pyramid] belongs to the *hetaira* Rhodopis (Ῥοδώπιος ἑταίρης γυναικὸς εἶναι), not speaking correctly. These then appear to me to speak not even knowing who Rhodopis was (for [otherwise] they would not have attributed it to her to make such a pyramid, the sort on which thousands of talents, without number so to speak, were spent), and besides [not knowing] that Rhodopis flourished in the kingship of Amasis, but not in the kingship of this one [Mykerinos]. For Rhodopis existed very many years later than these kings who left behind these pyramids: she was from Thrace in origin, and slave of Iadmon, a Samian man of Hephaistopolis, and she was fellow-slave of Aesop, the fable-maker (Αἰσώπου τοῦ λογοποιοῦ). And in fact, this one [the owner of Aesop] *was* Iadmon, as he showed not least in this way: for when, with the Delphians summoning many times from an oracular command, whoever wished to accept recompense for the life of Aesop, no other appeared, but [only] another Iadmon, grandson of Iadmon, accepted it—thus [it's clear that] Aesop also belonged to Iadmon.

But Rhodopis came to Egypt when Xanthos the Samian conveyed her, but having come for business (ϰατ' ἐϱγασίην), she was freed for a lot of money by a Mytilenean man, Charaxos, son of Skamandronymos and brother of Sappho the melic poet (Σαπφοῦς τῆς μουσοποιοῦ). Thus indeed Rhodopis was freed and remained in Egypt and, being very attractive, acquired a great deal of money (as far as being a Rhodopis is concerned, but not so as to come to such a pyramid, at any rate). For it is possible still, even to this day, for everyone who wants to, to view a tenth of her property, so that there is no need to attribute great property to her. For Rhodopis desired to leave behind a monument of herself in Greece, having made as her object this, the sort of thing which does not happen to have been discovered and dedicated by any other in a temple—to dedicate this as her memorial at Delphi. So then, having converted a tenth of her property into many spits for oxen, made of iron, as many as a tenth contained for her, she was sending them away to Delphi. And they even now still are heaped behind the altar which the Chians dedicated, opposite the temple itself.

And somehow, the courtesans (ἑταῖϱαι) in Naukratis tend to be very attractive: for in the first place, this woman, concerning whom this story is told, became so glorious (ϰλεινή) indeed that even all the Greeks learned the name of Rhodopis, and in the second place, later than this one, the one whose name was Archedike became celebrated in song (ἀοίδιμος) throughout Greece (though less talked about than the former [ἧσσον δὲ τῆς ἑτέϱης πεϱιλεσχήνευτος]). But when Charaxos, having released Rhodopis, returned to Mytilene, Sappho abused him very much in lyric (ἐν μέλεϊ Σαπφὼ πολλὰ ϰατεϰεϱτόμησέ μιν). And now, concerning Rhodopis I make an end. (Hdt. 2.134–35)

This extraordinary passage reads like an ancient "Lives of the Rich and Famous," providing us with Herodotus's only mentions of Sappho, her brother Charaxos, Aesop, and his master Iadmon. This titillating quality of the narrative has led scholars to read it very much at face value, and yet, it is precisely the uncritical circulation of stories around celebrities that Herodotus is here debunking. Once we allow ourselves to acknowledge the strangeness of these chapters, questions proliferate: Why does Rhodopis dedicate iron spits at Delphi, and what is the relation of her "monument" to the Egyptian pyramids? Why Herodotus's sudden interest in the attractiveness and fame of the courtesans of Naukratis? And why end on the note of Sappho's "abuse" of her wayward brother?

I hope to be able to engage these questions, but by a circuitous route. For in addition to the unique dazzle of celebrities gracing these anecdotes, this passage also represents Herodotus's only use of the term *hetaira*, "high-class prostitute" or "courtesan" (twice—at 2.134.1 and 2.135.5). In fact Herodotus's text provides us here with the earliest attested use of

this term (as adjective and noun) in Greek literature. In order to understand Herodotus's strange ethnographic engagement with prostitution,
we must first analyze the cultural construction and functioning of the
binary *hetaira* vs. *pornē* in the archaic period. Thus, this chapter explores
the terms of the opposition, while the next applies this background to a
reading of Herodotus's various invocations of exotic practices: Lydian
prostitution, courtesans in Egypt, Babylonian temple prostitution, and
bride auction.

I. INVENTING THE *HETAIRA*

According to the traditional scholarly account, the opposition of *hetaira*
and *pornē* is one of status. The *hetaira* is a "courtesan" or "mistress,"
often supported by one or two men alone, serving as their companion
at symposia and revels, as well as servicing their sexual desires. The
pornē, in contrast, is the common streetwalker or occupant of brothels,
providing sex for payment to a large and anonymous clientele. The terms
of this opposition are confirmed by Xenophon's portrait of the courtesan
Theodote, interviewed by a wry Socrates in the *Memorabilia* (3.11).
Theodote, expensively apparelled and attended by an entourage of her
mother and well-groomed maids, explains that she supports herself by
the kindness of "friends" (φίλοι) who are willing to give her gifts in
return for "gratification" (χαρίζεσθαι, 3.11.4-14). Xenophon's language
very deliberately locates Theodote's sexual "favors" within an economy
of aristocratic gift exchange, in which *philoi* who are "wealthy and lovers
of beauty" (τοὺς φιλοκάλους καὶ πλουσίους) exchange gifts and gratify
one another. The *pornē*, in contrast, who derives her name from the verb
πέρνημι, "to sell (especially slaves)," represents the commodification of
sex for pay.[3]
   And yet, as is well known, there is frequent slippage between the two
terms in ancient sources, and it is often difficult to maintain the distinction
in status. For both the *hetaira* and the *pornē* can be slave or free, both
can have a "pimp" or "pander" or be "self-employed." And there is,
finally, a large grey area of women of uncertain status—the flute-girls,

---

[3] On the opposition, see Hauschild 1933: 7–9; Herter 1957: 1154, 1181–82, 1960: 83;
Peschel 1987: 19–20; Harvey 1988: 249; Calame 1989: 103–4; Dover 1989: 20–21. Thus
Harvey 1988: 249: "The word *hetaira*, 'companion,' was a euphemism for a woman with
whom a man of the leisured classes maintained a fairly long-term sexual relationship, based
on 'gift-giving' (cf. Xen. *Mem.* 3.11), whereas a *pornē* is a woman from whom any man
might buy a single session on a purely commercial basis." On the special association of
the verb *pernēmi* with the sale of slaves, see Benveniste 1973: 112; on the etymology of
pornē, see Chantraine 1968-80: 888.

acrobats, and dancers who provide the largely unremarked backdrop to the symposium. When they provided sexual services as well (as they apparently often did), were they *hetairai* or *pornai*?[4] This slippage and confusion of terms have led certain scholars to question the stability and reality of the *hetaira-pornē* distinction in antiquity. Thus, for example, Sir Kenneth Dover contends,

> . . . the dividing line between the two categories could not be sharp; how, for instance, should one classify a woman who had intercourse with four different men in a week, hoped on each occasion to establish a lasting and exclusive relationship, and succeeded in doing so with the fourth man? Moreover, whether one applied the term *pornē* or the term 'hetaira' to a woman depended on the emotional attitude towards her which one wished to express or to engender in one's hearers. Anaxilas fr. 21 draws a distinction in terms of loyalty and affection, but fr. 22, an indignant vilification of the greed and deceitfulness of women who sell themselves, begins and ends (lines 1, 31) by calling them hetairai but in the middle (line 22) calls them *pornai*.[5]

James Davidson takes this argument one step further, suggesting that we must "view such representations not as reflections of discrete realities, but as discursive strategies, attempting to create distinctions in precisely those areas where difference is most awkward and problematic."[6] According to Davidson, this discursive opposition is constituted along the axis of gift- vs. commodity-exchange, identified with the *hetaira* and the *pornē* respectively:

> . . .it is possible to distinguish two main dynamics, two distinct tendencies in the language used to describe expenditure on women in antiquity especially in Greece. One group of statements, associated with the idea of the *hetaira* deals with specific women, often named and individually characterised, and emphasises the control they exercise over men and their appetites. It is fundamentally a phobic discourse, which we can associate with the discourse of gift-exchange and seduction, a never-ending cycle of *involvement, founded on dissimulation and avoidance of definition.* Another strategy, associated

---

[4] On this class of women and their sexual services, cf. Aristoph. *Wasps* 1341–70; Xen. *Symp.* 2.1, 2.7–22, 3.1, 9.2–7; Plato *Symp.* 176e7-8, 212d6; and see the discussions of Herter 1960: 97–98; Peschel 1987: 21–25.

[5] Dover 1989: 21; cf. Hauschild 1933: 8–9, Lesky 1976: 107–8, and Vernant 1980: 58–61 on the fluidity of different female statuses. In effect, the same position is espoused by Licht 1932: 330 (if in somewhat more old-fashioned terms): "The Greeks, if they wished to avoid the ugly name 'whores' (πόρναι), delicately called girls who sold themselves for money by the name of ἑταῖραι, properly 'comrades,' 'companions.' "

[6] Davidson n.d. p. 4 (cf. Davidson 1994: 139–42). On the fluidity of such discursive categories, cf. Henry 1986: 147: "The difference between wife and harlot is not absolute, but rather resides in men's ability to define and maintain the borders between the two."

with the idea of the *pornē*, attempts to depersonalise, reify and commodify women, their bodies, their time and their services, constantly defining and separating them into discrete units. It is primarily a discourse of contempt. In terms of expenditure, this discourse focusses on waste and loss, and ephemeral pleasures.[7]

I consider Davidson's notion of "discursive strategies" an essential analytic tool for understanding the *hetaira-pornē* binary, though I would not wholeheartedly endorse his characterization of the discourses under discussion, for two reasons. First, Davidson's analysis is based almost entirely on fourth-century Athenian sources, primarily Attic law speeches, which both temporally and generically represent the unequivocal triumph of egalitarian ideology.[8] That is to say, his characterization of these two discourses presents only half the picture, once democratic ideology has "cleared the field," as it were. In contrast, I would like to recover the discursive conflict over these terms that was still an active *process* in the archaic period by drawing as much as possible on contemporary sources

---

[7] Davidson 1994: 115–211 (quotation taken from 141–42; italics in original); cf. Davidson 1997: 109–36. We might compare Davidson's analysis of this discursive opposition with the general model of Kopytoff 1986. According to Kopytoff, all cultures constitute a spectrum along which objects (and often people) move, from one pole of complete commoditization to another, of complete "singularization" or "individuation": "To be saleable for money or to be exchangeable for a wide array of other things is to have something in common with a large number of exchangeable things that, taken together, partake of a single universe of comparable values. To use an appropriately loaded, even if archaic term, to be saleable or widely exchangeable is to be 'common'—the opposite of being uncommon, incomparable, unique, singular, and therefore not exchangeable for anything else. The perfect commodity would be one that is exchangeable with anything and everything else, as the perfectly commoditized world would be one in which everything is exchangeable or for sale. By the same token, the perfectly decommoditized world would be one in which everything is singular, unique, and unexchangeable" (Kopytoff 1986: 69). In Kopytoff's terms the *pornē* is the "perfect commodity," the *hetaira* the ultimate "singular."

[8] On the complex workings of democratic ideology in the speeches of the Attic orators, cf. Ober 1989. Davidson also relies on the evidence of fragments of Middle Comedy. For the purposes of this discussion, I wish to avoid consideration of prostitutes (both *hetairai* and *pornai*) in Old, Middle, and New Comedy, because the permutations of the system are immensely complicated and, I believe, dependent on the archaic model I attempt to sketch out here. Thus, comedy seems to have available for its use both sides of the archaic system: it can appropriate the aristocratic valorization of the *hetaira* (especially as applied to an ἀστή, a citizen girl, as in Antiphanes fr. 210 K.-A.) or it can choose to celebrate the democratic availability of *pornai* (as in Philemon fr. 3 K.-A., Euboulos fr. 67 K.-A., Xenarchos fr. 4 K.-A.). Given this complexity, I have tried to avoid basing any arguments on comic evidence; yet, given the extreme scarcity of material, especially for the early period, I have on occasion drawn on comedy for support of an argument based on other materials (e.g., Anaxilas fr. 21 K.-A.; Antiphanes fr. 210 K.-A.; Euboulos fr. 41 K.-A.). For extended discussion of prostitutes in the comic tradition, see Hauschild 1933; Fantham 1975; Anderson 1984; Henry 1985, 1986; Konstan 1987a; Wiles 1989; Brown 1990, 1993.

(both literary and visual). Second, Davidson focuses on "expenditure" and economics generally as devoid of politics. Yet I take it as axiomatic (especially for the earlier period) that a conflict over economic systems is also, inextricably, a political conflict. Thus, if the *hetaira* and the *pornē* figure the opposition of gift and commodity through the circulation of women, the motives behind the forging of this opposition must be political as well as economic. Finally, I would diverge from Davidson in seeing a mutually reinforcing system of discourse and practice at work. For, while the *hetaira-pornē* binary is a discursive opposition within our texts, it is one that was simultaneously instituted at the level of practice in Greek culture more broadly. As far as the Greeks were concerned, there were *hetairai* and *pornai*, participating in and helping to constitute by their presence distinct spheres of social life. And the tensions and conflicts generated by the practice of their participation produced in turn the slippages and instabilities observable in the discourses of our texts.

According to Carola Reinsberg, the existence of the *hetaira* as a particular form of prostitution only emerged in the early sixth century B.C.E. To be sure, there is no evidence of such a category in the Homeric or Hesiodic poems, and the earliest reference to a *hetaira* is to Rhodopis, a contemporary of Sappho. Reinsberg attributes the appearance of this particular form of prostitution to an increase in long-distance trade, which produced a whole class of itinerant traders with surplus wealth to spend.[9] And yet Reinsberg's purely materialist aetiology does not really account for the peculiarities of *Hetärentum* as a unique form of prostitution; that is to say, it does not account for the *hetaira* as a discursive and ideological construct. After all, why should an increase in long-distance trade produce a completely new conceptual category of prostitution, rather than simply increasing the numbers of *pornai* at work in burgeoning mercantile centers? What needs generated this new category? And what conceptual "work" was the opposition *hetaira-pornē* doing in Greek culture in the period of its inception?

I would suggest that it is no accident that the category of the *hetaira* appears roughly contemporaneously with the adoption of coinage by the Greek cities and with the first appearance of the "language of metals" in Greek poetry. For the *hetaira* (like the language of metals) is an invention of the symposium; as her name implies, this is her proper sphere.[10] Within the "anti-city" of the elite symposium, the institutional and discursive category of the *hetaira* participates in the complete exclusion of the

---

[9] Reinsberg 1989: 161. On the dating and aetiology, Schneider 1913: 1332 offers very much the same account.

[10] On the close connection of *hetairai* to the symposium, see Herter 1960: 95–97; Brendel 1970: 19, 29–36; Peschel 1987; Calame 1989: 103–8; Reinsberg 1989: 91–120.

public sphere, especially the city's monetarized economy. Instead, the impulse to mystify economic relations for sex generates the category of the *hetaira* within the framework of gift exchange. As the fourth-century comic poet Anaxilas observed, the *hetaira* gratified her patron πρὸς χάριν, "as a favor."[11] And while the *hetaira* affirms and embodies the circulation of *charis* within a privileged elite, the *porne* in aristocratic discourse figures the debased and promiscuous exchanges of the agora. Thus I would concur with Davidson's mapping of the *hetaira-porne* binary along the axis of gift- vs. commodity-exchange, though I would suggest a different moral inflection for this discursive opposition in the archaic period.

If we are seeking contemporary evidence for this opposition and the purposes it served, we must turn to archaic poetry. The *porne* had been a staple of blame poetry since Archilochos. Thus later commentators report that Archilochos used the term μισητή, "lewd" or "lascivious" for "a woman who is common and easy" (τὴν κοινὴν καὶ ῥᾳδίαν), in a one-liner that became proverbial, "A woman with thick ankles is a whore" (περὶ σφυρὸν παχεῖα, μισητὴ γυνή, fr. 206 W). The same sources preserve a whole string of other abusive designations Archilochos coined for the *porne* (frr. 207-209 W): δῆμος ("because she is common to the demos"), ἐργάτις ("working girl"), and μυσάχνη ("froth of defilement," "on the analogy of Homeric 'sea-foam' ").[12] These terms, even without their context, suggest the negative associations of the *porne*—lewdness, pollution, the humiliating necessity of working for pay, and excessive commonality in the public sphere.

The discourse of the *hetaira* in archaic poetry stands in radical opposition to that of the *porne*. In contrast to the shockingly coarse and explicit

---

[11] Anaxilas fr. 21 K.-A.:

ἐὰν δέ τις μέτρια † καὶ λέγουσα
τοῖς δεομένοις τινῶν ὑπουργῇ πρὸς χάριν,
ἐκ τῆς ἑταιρείας ἑταίρα τοὔνομα
προσηγορεύθη, καὶ σὺ νῦν οὐχ ὡς λέγεις
πόρνης, ἑταίρας δ' εἰς ἔρωτα τυγχάνεις
ἐληλυθὼς ἄρ' ὡς ἀληθῶς· ἔστι γοῦν
ἁπλῆ τις. (Β.) ἀστεία μὲν οὖν, νὴ τὸν Δία

And if someone [even speaking measured things?] does service to those in need of something as a favor, from her companionship she has been called a *hetaira*—and you now happen to have fallen in love, not with a *porne* (as you say), but with a *hetaira* then truly. She is someone honest then. (B.) Yes, by Zeus, and refined.

[12] Eustathios *Comm. Hom.* p. 1329.33; 4.836.2-3 Valk, p. 1651.1; Hesychios s.v. ἐργάτις (all cited by West as testimonia to fr. 206). For other references to *pornai* in archaic poetry, see Archilochos *dub.* fr. 302 W, *spur.* fr. 328 W; Hipponax frr. 135, 135a, 135b W; Alkaios fr. 117b V. For a speculative reconstruction of what prostitution signified in Archilochos's poetic system, see Burnett 1983: 78–97.

language of blame, the presentation of the *hetaira* is delicate and indirect, indeed so indirect that we need some ingenuity in locating the *hetaira* in Greek verse. For, as a recent student of Greek prostitution has observed, those aristocratic sources well-disposed to the institution never use the term *hetaira*, preferring polite periphrases. (Xenophon, for example, introduces Theodote coyly as "the sort of woman who would keep company with any man who persuaded her," *Mem.* 3.11.1.)[13] This suggests that *hetaira* is a term of derision, applied by those outside the aristocratic symposium to mock the sympotic equality of prostitute and elite participant (*hetairos*). In any case, then, we cannot expect to find the term itself in archaic sympotic poetry. Still, several fragments of Anakreon (together with the guidance provided by the later authors who quote him) bear out the ideologically loaded opposition of *hetaira* and *pornē*. Anakreon, the quintessential sympotic poet, provides a surprising number of references to both types of prostitute in his meager corpus, and though he is generally read simply as the hedonistic celebrator of wine and love, I would suggest that these references form part of a specific political agenda.

One of Anakreon's most familiar fragments, fr. 78 Gentili (= 417 *PMG*, the address to the "Thracian filly") may be directed to a *hetaira*, at least to judge from the introduction of the first-century C.E. commentator Herakleitos who quotes it:

καὶ μὴν ὁ Τήιος Ἀνακρέων ἑταιρικὸν φρόνημα καὶ σοβαρᾶς γυναικὸς
ὑπερηφανίαν ὀνειδίζων τὸν ἐν αὐτῇ σκιρτῶντα νοῦν ὡς ἵππον
ἠλλογόρησεν οὕτω λέγων·

πῶλε Θρηκίη, τί δή με λοξὸν ὄμμασι βλέπουσα
νηλεῶς φεύγεις, δοκεῖς δέ μ' οὐδὲν εἰδέναι σοφόν;
ἴσθι τοι, καλῶς μὲν ἄν τοι τὸν χαλινὸν ἐμβάλοιμι,
ἡνίας δ' ἔχων στρέφοιμί σ' ἀμφὶ τέρματα δρόμου·
νῦν δὲ λειμῶνάς τε βόσκεαι κοῦφά τε σκιρτῶσα παίζεις,
δεξιὸν γὰρ ἱπποπείρην οὐκ ἔχεις ἐπεμβάτην.

(Herakleitos *Quaest. Hom.* 5)

And indeed Anakreon the Teian, reproaching the meretricious [lit. "hetairic"] attitude and disdain of a haughty woman, allegorized her skittering mind as a horse, speaking thus,

O Thracian filly, why, looking askance at me with your eyes, do you flee pitilessly, and think that I know nothing skillful? Know that I would mount the bridle well upon you, and holding the reins, I would turn you about the limits of the track. But now [as it is], you feed in

---

[13] D. Christodoulou, private correspondence. Cf. Davidson 1997: 106, who notes that it was extremely rare for the women involved to call themselves *hetairai*.

meadows, and lightly frisking, you play, for you do not have a skillful
rider experienced of horses.

Two elements in the poem tend to confirm the later commentator's identification of its addressee as a *hetaira*. First, her address in the opening
words as "Thracian filly" suggests a foreign origin; recall Herodotus's
mention that Rhodopis was originally from Thrace (2.134).[14] Second, the
characterization of her current activity in line 5 of the poem: "But now
you feed in meadows, and lightly frisking, you play." As Bruno Gentili
has observed, the image of a horse ranging free in a meadow—as opposed
to safely locked in its stall—suggests a woman who is sexually free and
promiscuous.[15] And yet the poem evokes no moral disapproval of the
woman's "loose" behavior, instead playfully suggesting that the speaker
could offer her a more skillful "ride." There is no hint of economic
negotiation for favors, for the Thracian filly, like Xenophon's Theodote,
must be *persuaded* to turn her attention elsewhere. The poem as a whole
conjures up the privileged space of the symposium, where the speaker
(whose self-representation as a skillful "rider" marks him as an aristocrat)
banters cheerfully with a female symposiast.

Anakreon fr. 93 Gentili (= 373 *PMG*) produces very much the same
effect:

ἠρίστησα μὲν ἰτρίου λεπτοῦ μικρὸν ἀποκλάς,
οἴνου δ' ἐξέπιον κάδον· νῦν δ' ἁβρῶς ἐρόεσσαν
ψάλλω πηκτίδα τῇ φίλῃ κωμάζων †παιδὶ ἁβρῇ†.[16]

I breakfasted, having broken off a little bit of slender honey-cake, and I
drained my vessel of wine; and now I delicately pluck the lovely Lydian
lyre, celebrating the *kōmos* with a dear and dainty girl.

[14] Cf. also the use of πῶλος, which, according to Hesychius, was a term for *hetairai* in
Euboulos (Hesychios s.v. πῶλος). Cf. Gentili 1958: 193n.3.

[15] Gentili 1958: 186–94. To the parallels collected by Gentili one might add the metaphorical use of φορβάς in Pindar fr. 122.19 SM; Sophocles fr. 720 Radt; Pollux *Onom.* 7.203.
Claude Calame suggests to me that the language of Anakreon's poem is, in fact, deliberately
ambiguous: a large part of its wit (and seductiveness) inheres in the rhetorical techniques
of praising a *hetaira* by assimilating her to a virgin. Thus, much of the poem's diction
would be equally appropriate to a virgin girl as yet "unyoked." For the same assimilation
of a *hetaira*'s appearance and behavior to that of a "modest virgin," cf. Xen. *Mem.* 3.11.14,
and see the passages cited below, p. 214.

[16] παιδὶ ἁβρῇ is marked corrupt for metrical reasons; but notice that, among the emendations Gentili prints in his *apparatus criticus* (to his fr. 93) are πάϊδ' ἁβρῇ and παϊδὶ ἁβρῇ,
which heal the meter with very minor changes. Alternatively, Wilamowitz suggested that
a proper name was concealed by this corruption (1884: 317n. 27; 1913: 103n.1). Thus I
assume that "delicate girl" or something very like it stood in this spot; but even if the line

Wine, the pektis (or Lydian lyre), and the *kōmos* establish the sympotic setting of this brief fragment, while the twice-repeated ἁβρῶς, ἁβρῇ evokes a context of aristocratic luxury. As I have argued, the espousal or rejection of *habrosunē* represents a political and ideological choice in archaic Greek poetry. Here as elsewhere, Anakreon's wholehearted embrace of the "cult of *habrosunē*" signals his allegiance to an aristocratic elite with close links with the East.[17] And central to the lifestyle of *habrosunē* in this sympotic fragment is the company of a "girl" who is φίλη, "dear"—in this context, almost certainly a *hetaira*. Again, there is no talk of wage or payment, only the language of pleasure and aristocratic friendship. The relationship of symposiast and *hetaira* is completely mystified as one of mutually comfortable and willing companionship.[18]

Thus the fragments of Anakreon suggest a very specific context for the "invention of the *hetaira*": she is a product of the sympotic space where the lifestyle of *habrosunē* was actively espoused as a form of self-definition and distinction by an aristocratic elite throughout the sixth century. Within the world of the symposium, the conceptual category of the *hetaira* served at least three functions. First, the constitution of this category within the framework of aristocratic gift exchange enabled the complete occlusion of the explicit, monetarized economics of the public sphere. In this respect, the *hetaira-pornē* binary functioned just like the opposition of metals and money, to define and differentiate the sympotic world from the public space of the agora in elitist discourse.[19] Second, the presence

---

ended with a proper name, that would not much affect my argument, since the gender and status of this mysterious figure are still determined by τῇ φίλῃ earlier in the line.

[17] On the political implications of *habrosunē*, see Mazzarino 1947; Arthur 1984: 37–49; Kurke 1992; Morris 1996; on this fragment in particular, Kurke 1992: 93–94.

[18] Other fragments of Anakreon that refer to women in sympotic settings (and hence, probably to *hetairai*): fr. 82/427 *PMG* (on which, see Section III below); fr. 110/455 *PMG*.

[19] Indeed, it may be that the association of the *hetaira* with gold (for which we have evidence in Middle Comedy) is an inheritance from the sympotic language of metals. Thus Chrysis ("Goldie") is a common *hetaira*-name attested from the fourth century on (Timokles fr. 27 K.-A., Menander *Samia*, Lucian *Dialogues of Courtesans* 8); while the fourth-century comic poet Antiphanes offers what might be read as an extended gloss on the name:

> οὗτος δ' ὃν λέγω
> ἐν γειτόνων αὐτῷ κατοικούσης τινὸς
> ἰδὼν ἑταίρας εἰς ἔρωτ' ἀφίκετο,
> ἀστῆς, ἐρήμου δ' ἐπιτρόπου καὶ συγγενῶν,
> ἦθός τι χρυσοῦν πρὸς ἀρετὴν κεκτημένης
> ὄντως ἑταίρας· αἱ μὲν ἄλλαι τοὔνομα
> βλάπτουσι τοῖς τρόποις γὰρ ὄντως ὂν καλόν. (fr. 210 K.-A.)

This one of whom I speak caught sight of a *hetaira* living at his neighbor's house and fell in love with her, a citizen girl, but bereft of guardian and relatives,

of sexually available women infused the sympotic space with a generalized eroticism which was an important element in the lifestyle of *habrosunē* (at least as Sappho and Anakreon celebrated it).[20] As such, the women functioned as so much sympotic furniture, like the couches and pillows— objects to serve the needs of the male symposiasts and create a certain atmosphere. (Thus, Anakreon's Thracian filly may have a choice of mounts, but it is never in question that she is the horse and the male the rider.[21]) Finally, in tension with their erotic objectification, the category of the *hetaira* seems at times to entail a deliberate mystification of status, an effort to play down distinctions between the symposiasts and their female companions.[22] That is to say, as Ian Morris has observed of elitist ideology in general, status boundaries of male and female are minimized, while the single distinction—aristocratic elites vs. others—becomes paramount.[23] The deliberately obscure standing of the *hetaira*[24] assists the constitution of this inviolable barrier between the sympotic space and all those outside it (hence the derisive use of the term itself to characterize what, from the outside, must have seemed the bizarrely egalitarian dynamics of the elite symposium).

One might say that the relative discursive primacy of these two latter functions depends on whether one focuses on the internal workings of the symposium or on its oppositional relation to the public sphere: if the former, emphasis falls on the hierarchy of male symposiasts and female attendants; if the latter, on the companionship and identity of *hetairoi*

---

possessed of a golden nature when it came to virtue, truly a "companion." For the rest of those women harm the name that is truly fair with their ways.

The notion that possessing a "golden nature" (ἦθός τι χρυσοῦν) makes her a "true *hetaira*" recalls Theognis's obsessive wish to find a *pistos hetairos* just like himself, "refined gold when rubbed on a touchstone" (Thgn. 415–18, 449–52). The similarity of language and theme suggests that the "hooker with a heart of gold," who becomes a staple of New Comedy, is an adaptation of an older aristocratic ideal.

[20] Cf. Murray 1990b: 7. Richard Neer has suggested to me that part of the point of this erotic element is to counter the association of *habrosunē* with effeminacy by those hostile to this aristocratic lifestyle. On representational links between *habrosunē* and effeminacy, see Kurke 1992: 98–106.

[21] Contrast her position to that of the boy in Anakreon fr. 15 Gentili (= 360 PMG), who is the "charioteer" of the speaker's soul. This erotic objectification of women as part of the sympotic entertainment is clearly reflected in Carm. conv. 904 PMG: ἁ ὗς τὰν βάλανον τὰν μὲν ἔχει, τὰν δ' ἔραται λαβεῖν·/ κἀγὼ παῖδα καλὴν τὴν μὲν ἔχω, τὴν δ' ἔραμαι λαβεῖν. ("The sow has one acorn, but longs to take another; and I have one beautiful girl, but long to take another.")

[22] This is perhaps partly the necessary result of constituting the relation as one of gift exchange, which requires approximate equality of partners.

[23] Morris 1996: 36.

[24] Recall the terms of Davidson's analysis of the discourse of the *hetaira*: "a never-ending cycle of involvement, founded on dissimulation and avoidance of definition."

and *hetairai*. The dialectic between these two positions is precarious and difficult to maintain, and it is perhaps for this reason that scholars have tended to latch onto one function to the complete exclusion of the other.[25] Even in archaic representations, the balance is occasionally lost, and the discourse flip-flops precipitously from one pole to the other.

II. THE *PORNĒ* AND THE PUBLIC SPHERE

But before we can explore the faultlines within the ideology of the *hetaira*, we must complete the opposition; several other fragments of Anakreon suggest the terms of the portrait of the *pornē* as the *hetaira*'s opposite number. The sole appearance of the stem πορν- in the corpus of Anakreon occurs in fr. 82 Gentili (= 388 *PMG*), a stunningly savage lampoon of a certain Artemon:[26]

πρὶν μὲν ἔχων βερβέριον, καλύμματ' ἐσφηκωμένα,
καὶ ξυλίνους ἀστραγάλους ἐν ὠσὶ καὶ ψιλὸν περὶ
πλευρῇσι <δέρριον> βοός,

νήπλυτον εἴλυμα κακῆς ἀσπίδος, ἀρτοπώλισιν
κἀθελοπόρνοισιν ὁμιλέων ὁ πονηρὸς Ἀρτέμων,
κίβδηλον εὑρίσκων βίον,

πολλὰ μὲν ἐν δουρὶ τιθεὶς αὐχένα, πολλὰ δ' ἐν τροχῷ,
πολλὰ δὲ νῶτον σκυτίνῃ μάστιγι θωμιχθείς, κόμην
πώγωνά τ' ἐκτετιλμένος·

νῦν δ' ἐπιβαίνει σατινέων χρύσεα φορέων καθέρματα
πάϊς Κύκης καὶ σκιαδίσκην ἐλεφαντίνην φορέει
γυναιξὶν αὔτως

Formerly having a turban, wasp-like headcoverings, and wooden knuckle-bones in his ears and a worn oxhide around his ribs, unwashed covering of a lousy shield, keeping company with breadwomen and willing whores, wicked Artemon made his living by crime, many times putting his neck in the stocks, many times on the wheel, and many times having his back scourged with a leather lash, and his hair and beard plucked out; but now he mounts carriages, wearing golden earrings, the child of Kyke, and bears a little ivory parasol—just like women.

---

[25] Thus, for example, Keuls 1985: 160–86 registers only the erotic subjugation of the *hetaira*, while Calame 1989 and Reinsberg 1989 mainly emphasize the elements of equality and companionship in her status.
[26] Text after Gentili.

A single sentence of twelve lines, this poem (complete or not) represents our most substantial fragment of Anakreon. It has traditionally been read as abuse of a social climber, and Christopher Brown has recently confirmed that reading by offering a compelling word-by-word analysis in which he demonstrates the movement of its subject Artemon from the lowest rungs of society (1–9) to sudden *arriviste* wealth and luxury (10–12).[27] Thus, Brown suggests that the βεϱβέϱιον, some kind of tight "wasplike" headcovering, is intended to contrast with the long, flowing hair of aristocratic fashion, while "wooden knucklebones" for earrings represent a poor man's version of outlandish Eastern ornament. He cites parallels in Theognis and Aristophanes for the rustic and low-class garb of worn hide, and notes that "breadwomen" and "willing whores" suggest coarse lowlife companions.[28] He interprets χίβδηλον εὑϱίσχων βίον as "he made his living by crime," and points out that the next stanza continues the theme of Artemon's criminality: "Pollux (10.177) records that dishonest traders were put on the rack (δόϱυ) and whipped. From Aristophanes we learn that adulterers suffered depilation."[29]

Brown notes in conclusion,

In the first section of the poem Anacreon depicts Artemon as socially low, criminal, and sexually loose. When we next see him, he is miraculously changed, no longer crass and inelegant, but outfitted in golden jewellery, carrying a parasol, and riding on σατίναι. If it were not for the last line, we might suppose that Anacreon is merely describing Artemon dressed as an Ionian aristocrat, but the phrase γυναιξὶν αὕτως makes the reference to effeminacy explicit. What we have of the poem does not allow us to say with any precision in what way Artemon is effeminate, but it is undeniable that something about his new life-style is woman-like. His effeminacy is

---

[27] Brown 1983 convincingly refutes the revisionist reading of Slater 1978, who claims that the fragment represents two different incarnations of ritual transvestism. Cf. also M. Davies 1981 for an attack on Slater 1978.

[28] Brown 1983: 12–13. As Brown notes, we cannot determine whether ἐθελόποϱνοι is intended to refer to male or female prostitutes, since it is a compound adjective of two terminations. The association of breadsellers and prostitutes is common in Greek literature: Brown cites Aristoph. *Frogs* 112; cf. also Pollux's mention that Hermippus referred to a prostitute as a "rotten whore" and a "sow" in a play called *The Breadwomen* (Ἑϱμιππος . . . ἐν Ἀϱτοπώλισι φησὶν, ὡς σαπϱὰ πόϱνη, καὶ κάπϱαινα, Pollux *Onom.* 7.202). For the association, cf. also Herter 1960: 74–75; for "breadbaker" as slang for prostitute or courtesan, see duBois 1988: 110–16; Garrett and Kurke 1994: 80–83.

[29] Brown 1983: 13–14. Specifically Pollux says, "When Kratinos says in the *Nemesis*, 'having his neck in the pillory,' it must be understood that this was a certain kind of market-regulatory equipment, in which the one who does wrong concerning the market must put his neck and be whipped" (Pollux, *Onom.* 10.177). In the same context, Pollux notes that "Deinolochos in the *Amazons* spoke of the [harness] of the retailer's yoke" (καπηλικοῦ ζυγοῦ).

underlined by the appellation παῖς Κύκης (11). It has been suggested that this phrase indicates that Artemon is of illegitimate birth, which would be appropriate to his low origins. This is plausible, but it is more relevant to note the basic ambiguity of the word παῖς, which can be use of either sex, and here its collocation with the name of the mother suggests a female child.[30]

I find Brown's detailed analysis completely persuasive and would suggest that, following his reading, we must take this abuse as the flipside of the fragments already considered. For if they constitute the privileged sympotic world of *habrosunē*, this fragment reaffirms that lifestyle by programmatic opposition. And indeed, in the fragment's first three stanzas at least, the contrast crucially depends on locating Artemon in the agora, a public space characterized by debased and illicit mercantile and sexual exchanges. His designation as ὁ πονηρὸς Ἀρτέμων and παῖς Κύκης make his low-class origin and status explicit,[31] while his garb of worn oxhide delivers the same message more obliquely, to judge from a Theognidean parallel:

> Kyrnos, this city is still a city, but the people are different. Those who before knew neither judgments nor laws but used to wear out goatskins about their ribs and pasture outside of the city like deer—they are now the "good," son of Polypaos, while those who were formerly noble are now base. Who could endure seeing these things? And they deceive each other, laughing at each other, knowing the wisdom neither of the base nor of the good. (Thgn. 53–60)

Brown cites Theognis line 55 to demonstrate the association of leather garments with low-class rustics, but in context I would suggest that it conjures up another group as well. As I have argued, the characterization "they deceive each other, laughing at each other" in line 59 represents an aristocratic sneer at the practice of retail trade (*kapēleia*), so that we may read Theognis's boorish rustics garbed in goatskin also as *kapēloi*.[32] Given the parallel, the association with *kapēleia* may also be the implication of Artemon's secondhand skins in Anakreon's lampoon.

However that may be, lines 4–9 of Anakreon's poem consistently associate Artemon with petty traders in the agora, first with "breadwomen" (4) and then with merchants punished for dishonest dealing on the rack (7–8). It is noteworthy that, in each case, trade is closely paired with some form of morally debased sexual activity: Artemon keeps company with "breadwomen and willing whores" in stanza two, while he suffers

---

[30] Brown 1983: 14.

[31] Though Gerber (1970: 234) and Brown (1983: 14) prefer to read a suggestion of effeminacy into παῖς Κύκης, Young (1973: 413) takes it as an intimation of illegitimacy.

[32] Kurke 1989 and see discussion above, Chapter 2.

the punishments for commercial deceit and adultery in stanza three. I would contend that this coupling is deliberate, for each debased activity, mercantile and sexual, figures the other. To be a petty retailer is to be a "willing whore," and a thieving merchant an adulterer (and vice versa): in elitist terms, the disembedded economics of the agora taints all it touches. The exact center of the fragment, line 6, adds the final element to this picture—κίβδηλον εὑρίσκων βίον. Brown is right to emphasize its metaphorical usage; as he notes, in Aristophanes κιβδηλία means "dishonesty." Nonetheless, as we have seen, κίβδηλος is the *vox propria* for adulterated metal or counterfeit coin, so that here it continues the theme of deceit by conjuring up the specter of coinage.[33] Thus the first nine lines of Anakreon's poem read like a phobic aristocratic gloss on Herodotus 1.94: all the elements of prostitution, coinage, *kapēloi*, even games (recall the knucklebones of line 2!) are here, grotesquely transmogrified as the obscenities of the public sphere. And where Herodotus's deadpan ethnography seems to be an indictment of Lydian *habrosunē*, Anakreon marshals this array against an interloper, branding him as low-class and thereby reaffirming "true" aristocratic luxury by his exclusion. The discursive weapon of disembedded economics can be deployed by either side against the other: in each case, at its center stands the figure of the *pornē*.

The one other appearance of Artemon in the extant fragments of Anakreon may participate in the same denunciation of the public sphere. Athenaios cites the two-line fragment, whose second line had become proverbial:

ξανθῇ δ' Εὐρυπύλῃ μέλει
ὁ περιφόρητος Ἀρτέμων. (fr. 8 Gentili = 372 *PMG*)

The notorious Artemon is a concern to blonde Eurypyle.

Though Athenaios explains περιφόρητος literally as "being carried around on a couch on account of luxurious living,"[34] Artemon's epithet seems actually to mean "carried around [in the mouths of all]," hence "notorious" or "infamous." The term may even indicate sexual looseness and availability, for, as Brown notes, an Aristophanic scholiast refers the proverb ὁ περιφόρητος Ἀρτέμων "to a boy who is fair and snatched by

---

[33] Brown 1983: 13, citing Aristoph. *Birds* 158. For κίβδος and κίβδηλος signifying a base alloy, see van Groningen 1966: 50–51 (*ad* Thgn. 117, 119); Hangard 1963: 62–66, 94; LSJ, s.v. κιβδηλεία, κίβδος. On the other hand, κίβδηλος is used to designate generically various kinds of counterfeit coin: see Stroud 1974: 171–72 and Caccamo Caltabiano and Radici Colace 1983: 442–43. On the imagery of counterfeiting in Anakreon's poem, cf. Levine 1984: 133–35.

[34] Cf. Plut. *Per.* 27 (= Gentili fr. 8, *test.* iii).

all" (ἐπὶ καλοῦ καὶ ἁρπαζομένου πρὸς πάντων παιδός, Schol. Ar. *Ach.* 850 = Gentili fr. 8, *test.* ii).[35] In either case, whether he is "borne around" in mouths or hands, the epithet refers disparagingly to Artemon's excessive circulation in the public domain. And it may be that this public promiscuity is associated with prostitution, since Artemon's companion in the fragment bears the suggestive name Eurypyle, "wide gate." Though later ancient writers speculated that Eurypyle was one of Anakreon's lovers, her name is most apt for a prostitute (again with emphasis on her promiscuity or public availability).[36]

Another more substantial fragment that may chronicle the career of a prostitute is fr. 60 Gentili (= 346 *PMG*), first published from papyrus in 1954:[37]

οὐδε . . . [.] ς . φ . . α . .[. . .] . .[
φοβερὰς δ᾽ ἔχεις πρὸς ἄλλῳ
φρένας, ὦ καλλιπρό[σ]ωπε παίδ[ων.

καί σε δοκέει μὲν ἐ[ν δό]μοισι
πυκινῶς ἔχουσα [μήτηρ
ἀτιτάλλειν· σ[ὺ δὲ – ◡ βόσκεαι

τὰς ὑακιν[θίνας ἀρ]ούρας,
ἵ]να Κύπρις ἐκ λεπάδνων
ἐρο]έσσα[ς κ]ατέδησεν ἵππους.

. . . . .]δ᾽ ἐν μέσῳ κατῆ<ι>ξας
ὁμάδ]ῳ, δι᾽ ἄσσα πολλοί
πολ]ιητέων φρένας ἐπτόεαται,

λεωφ]όρε, λεωφόρ᾽ Ἡρο[τ]ίμη,

Nor . . . , and in addition you have fearful wits, o lovely-faced of children. And your mother imagines that, holding you at home, she fosters you assiduously, but you graze [instead?] in the hyacinth fields where Kypris bound down lovely mares [freed] from the yoke. And you leapt into the

[35] Brown 1983: 14 with n. 79. Cf. Slater 1978: 186n. 8 for the negative connotations of περι- compounds; thus Theognis 581–82: ἐχθαίρω δὲ γυναῖκα περίδρομον ἄνδρά τε μάργον,/ ὃς τὴν ἀλλοτρίαν βούλετ᾽ ἄρουραν ἀροῦν ("I hate the woman who runs around and the greedy man who wants to plow another's field.") and Pollux *Onom.* 7.203, who lists περίπολις as a term for a *pornē*.

[36] Cf. Brown 1983: 7. For ancient sources who cite Eurypyle as a lover of Anakreon, see Dioskourides *AP* 7.31.10, Antipater Sidonios *AP* 7.27.5; for modern scholars who follow their lead, see Smyth 1963: 290, Gerber 1970: 233; for opposition, Brown 1983: 7. For the obscene use of πύλη, see Aristoph. *Lysistrata* 250, 265, 423, 1163 and especially fr. adesp. 805 Kock, in which δημίαισι πύλαις is glossed as "common whores" by Hesychios (s.v.) and cf. Henderson 1991: 137.

[37] Text after Gentili's edition.

middle of the throng, through which many of the citizens are fluttered in
wits, O much-trafficked, much-trafficked Herotime. . . .

Significantly, the epithet the poem's subject Herotime bears in the fragment's last legible line—λεωφόρος—had been preserved independently
from antiquity as a term Anakreon used to designate a *pornē* (Suda 3.429
Adler; Eustathios *Comm. Hom.* p. 1329.34; 4.835.36 Valk = fr. 163
Gentili, 446 *PMG*). Hence, there is at least some evidence in the ancient
lexicographical tradition that this fragment concerns a common prostitute, though its damaged and partial state makes it difficult to reconstruct
with any certainty.

For the most part, I follow the interpretation of Gregorio Serrao,
who reads the fragment as a sequence of diverse moments in the life of
Herotime, chronicling her development from innocent young girl to public
prostitute.[38] Thus the opening lines describe her as a timid child (1–3),
whose mother imagines that she is safely immured and supervised within
the house (3–6). But with a strong syntactic break in line 6 (and probably
a δέ answering the μέν in line 4),[39] the lovely-faced child is revealed
grazing "in hyacinth fields where Kypris binds down lovely mares [freed]
from the yoke." As Gentili has forcefully argued, horses in the hyacinth
fields of Kypris represent those who have abandoned themselves to sensuality; the hyacinth is sacred to Aphrodite, and horses ranging free (like
Anakreon's Thracian filly) suggest women who are promiscuous and
readily available.[40] Finally, according to this interpretation, the last four
lines complete the picture, setting Herotime in public among a throng of
admirers. As Serrao concludes, the fragment represents "the normal *cur-
sus honorum* of a high-class courtesan."[41]

As opposed to other interpretations, which make the καλλιπρόσωπε
παίδων of line 3 a boy, or insist that the contrast is one of simultaneous,
contradictory attitudes in a lascivious girl who pretends to be "nice,"
Serrao's reading has the virtue of making coherent sense of the lines
preserved.[42] Yet perhaps because of a certain delicacy in Italian scholar-

---

[38] Serrao 1968, with the refinements added by Cavallini 1990. Serrao offers a comprehensive summary of other interpretations of the fragment to date.
[39] Posited first by Gallavotti 1955: 48.
[40] Gentili 1958: 182–90.
[41] Serrao 1968: 51.
[42] For the former interpretation see Latte 1955: 496; Merkelbach 1956: 96–97; West
1994: 102; for the latter, Gentili 1958: 194. Gerber (1976: 121) objects to Serrao's reading,
arguing that all the verbs are present-tense, whereas we should expect a shift from past-
to present-tense forms if the poem does in fact chronicle the career of a single figure over
time. This criticism has some force, but given the fragmentary state of the poem, it is hard
to be sure. Thus, we do not really know what "you have fearful wits" (2–3) refers to,
while the rest of the fragment can be understood as a single moment viewed from three

ship, which tends to characterize all Anakreon's female subjects as *hetairai*, this reading has not taken account of all the shifts and developments within the fragment.[43] For, while Gentili and Serrao acknowledge the contrast of the protected, enclosed space of the mother's house and the open meadows of Aphrodite, they do not recognize the abrupt and shocking shift in tone between the third and fourth stanzas of the poem (which precisely corresponds to the representational shift from *hetaira* to *pornē*). That is to say, lines 7–9 may figure a sexually available woman but do so in lyrical and allusive terms, constructing an idyllic "other" space of sexuality (hence their similarity to the landscape of the "Thracian filly"). In contrast (marked by δέ in line 10), the last stanza locates Herotime very explicitly in the real space of the city center and culminates in the degrading refrain λεωφόρε, λεωφόρ' Ἡροτίμη. The contrast has the effect of exploding any illusions that might remain about Herotime's status and, with a surprise twist, demoting her definitively from "high-class courtesan" to common whore.[44]

It is striking that the moment of her exposure corresponds exactly to the mention of citizens (πολιητέων) and her location ἐν μέσῳ (which we might read as a brutal Anakreontic joke on the catchphrase of egalitarian ideology). This collocation suggests that what Serrao terms the fragment's "malicious irony" (1968: 50) is directed not simply at the hapless Herotime, but also, through her, at the public sphere of citizen activity. As in the scathing lampoon of Artemon, the public domain of the agora is depicted as obscene and debased through the location and circulation of the *pornē* within it.

On this reading, the movement and strategy of this fragment seem to be the opposite of fr. 82 Gentili (though for the same thematic point). Where the Artemon poem moves through a meticulous comic blazon of Artemon's corrupt activities in the public sphere to a final brief description of his incompetent aping of the lifestyle of *habrosunē*, the Herotime poem lingers over the mystified beauties of innocent girlhood and adult sensuality before gleefully exploding them with a final vision of the "much-trafficked" Herotime leaping into the midst of the *hoi polloi*. Indeed, the poem's use of Homeric echoes (much commented on by

---

perspectives: (1) the mother, who believes Herotime is safely immured within the house; (2) the speaker who describes Herotime as a *hetaira*; and (3) the speaker who describes Herotime as a *pornē*. If my reading is correct, this movement is calculated to shock and surprise the listener.

[43] Thus Gentili, Serrao, and Cavallini consistently refer to Herotime as "etera" rather than *pornē*, the category the ancient lexicographical tradition supports.

[44] For consideration of possible contexts for such a representational shift, see Section III below. For a similar interpretation (though without the political dimension), see Gallavotti 1955: 50.

scholars) confirms this movement. As Serrao notes, lines 6–9 of the fragment echo the language and imagery of *Iliad* 15.263–68, a simile describing Hektor's renewed vigor for battle:[45]

> As when some stalled horse, corn-fed at the manger, has broken his bond and run, striking his hooves over the plain, accustomed to wash in a well-flowing river, glorying in his strength. And his head holds high, and his mane flows about his shoulders. And he trusts to his splendor and his knees bear him lightly to the haunts and pasturage of horses.

Even if we take the application of this image to the domain of erotics as "mock-epic" or tongue-in-cheek, the echo identifies Herotime fleetingly with a Homeric hero and, by association, endows her with a certain stature. But, as has also been noted, λεωφόρος itself is a Homeric word, appearing once in an Iliadic simile:

ὡς δ᾽ ὅτ᾽ ἀνὴρ ἵπποισι κελητίζειν ἐῢ εἰδώς,
ὅς τ᾽ ἐπεὶ ἐκ πολέων πίσυρας συναείρεται ἵππους,
σεύας ἐκ πεδίοιο μέγα προτὶ ἄστυ δίηται
λαοφόρον καθ᾽ ὁδόν· πολέες τέ ἑ θηήσαντο
ἀνέρες ἠδὲ γυναῖκες· ὁ δ᾽ ἔμπεδον ἀσφαλὲς αἰεὶ
θρῴσκων ἄλλοτ᾽ ἐπ᾽ ἄλλον ἀμείβεται, οἱ δὲ πέτονται· (*Iliad* 15.679–84)

> And as when a man skilled in riding horses, when he yokes together four horses from many, driving them from the plain he speeds toward a great city along a highway (lit., a people-bearing road). And many men and women marvel at him, but he keeps leaping and shifting continuously from horse to horse, and they fly along.

Gentili cites this passage to parallel the crowd of admiring citizens in lines 10–12 and to justify the reading κατη<ι>ξας as *variatio* for the Homeric θρῴσκων, but he does not seem to register the precise context of λαοφόρος as an epithet of ὁδός.[46] Given the allusion, Anakreon's climactic use of λεωφόρος represents a brutal and sudden demotion, as it were: in Homeric terms, Herotime has been abruptly transformed from a horse (9) or a rider (10) to a public thoroughfare.[47]

---

[45] Serrao 1968: 44–46. The same simile is used at *Iliad* 6.506–14 for Paris entering battle.

[46] Gentili 1958: 191–92.

[47] The same shocking inconcinnity is, in fact, embodied in the combination of epithet and name, λεωφόρ᾽ Ἡροτίμη. The name Herotime, "honored by the hero," or "honor of the hero," seems very aristocratic and evocative of the noblest Homeric characters, while the epithet λεωφόρος explodes the name's aristocratic pretensions. (The significance of the name Herotime was suggested to me independently by Deborah Boedeker and Kate Gilhuly.) In modern Greek, λεωφορεῖον is the regular word for "bus"; Taillardat 1967: 124, in his

By my reading, λεωφόρος gives the game away: it registers aristocratic loathing for the commonality or universal availability of resources in the public sphere. It is significant, then, that the same implication of too-great accessibility characterizes a whole string of abusive epithets for *pornai* attributed to Anakreon by later commentators and lexicographers. Thus, in addition to λεωφόρος, the Suda offers the terms πανδοσία and μανιόκηπος, while Eustathios adds πολύυμνος to the list (fr. 163 Gentili = 446 *PMG*). μανιόκηπος signifies the mad (and therefore indiscriminate) lust of the *pornē*, since κῆπος, "garden" or "orchard," figures the female genitalia. πανδοσία and πολύυμνος share the same ironic compound structure: their second elements, "giving" and "hymning," normally positive in aristocratic terms, are negated by their first elements, which signify the universal scope of the activities. She who "gives herself to everyone" is not participating in gift exchange, but in the common traffic of the marketplace; she who is "hymned by many" incurs not praise but blame.[48]

The proliferation of references to *pornai* in the corpus of Anakreon is itself intriguing. Other scholars have recently noted the diversity of Anakreon's poetic output even in its fragmentary state. Thus both Christopher Brown and Patricia Rosenmeyer have emphasized the existence of blame poetry as another facet of Anakreon's rich poetic talent, opposing it to the light, witty sympotic verse of the traditional conception.[49] Yet I would suggest that behind this apparent diversity of forms—praise and blame, sympotic celebration and abuse—there is a coherent political agenda. While the sympotic fragments constitute an ideal world of aristocratic *habrosunē*, much of Anakreon's abuse vilifies the tenets of egalitarian ideology and the civic center that is their symbolic site. The poet is not simply lampooning contemporary individuals who have crossed his path (like Artemon and Herotime), but the nonelite "other" through these representatives. And the frequency of his abusive references to whores, I would suggest, is an index of the level of aristocratic anxiety at the emergence of the public sphere.

In a sense, the argument for the *political* significance of the ready availability of the *pornē* has already been made for a later period by David Halperin. Halperin brilliantly analyzes what we might call the somatics of Athenian democratic ideology: the bodily integrity of the male citizen (first instituted by Solon's abolition of debt-bondage) and

---

commentary on the ancient term, notes that in modern French such a woman is "un vrai boulevard."

[48] Other possible references to *pornai* in Anakreon: fr. 94/439 *PMG*; fr. 135/480 *PMG* καταπτύστην, "execrable" (feminine; cf. Anaxilas fr. 22.6 K.-A., describing prostitutes as τοῦ καταπτύστου γένους, "of that execrable race"); and especially fr. 2/347 *PMG*, line 12 τὴν ἀρίγνωτον γυναῖκα (perhaps the second line of a new poem? see fr. 72 Gentili).

[49] Brown 1983; Rosenmeyer 1992: 37–49; cf. Fränkel 1973: 300–301.

his "democratic right" to penetrate others. Based on these two pillars of democratic ideology, Halperin argues that we must understand as a paired structural system the heavy political sanctions against male citizen prostitution and the institution of cheap, state-subsidized brothels where *pornai* are available for all.[50] To allow oneself to be penetrated indiscriminately for pay is to feminize oneself and prove oneself unworthy of citizen rights (hence the punishment of *atimia* for a citizen male who has prostituted himself in the past and then wants to act in the public sphere). On the other hand, in Halperin's account, to be a citizen means always having a place to put your penis; thus there is a tradition that Solon himself, who first constituted citizen bodily integrity, also founded a series of state-subsidized brothels, so that any citizen, no matter how poor, could enjoy a *pornē*.[51] Few scholars would accept the ancient tradition crediting this founding act of benevolence to Solon, but, as Halperin notes, the authenticity of the tradition matters less than its existence, since it shows "that some people in classical Athens evidently considered prostitution an intrinsic constituent of democracy."[52] This position takes the association of the *pornē* with the indiscriminate availability of resources in the public sphere, which we have charted in Anakreon, and valorizes it as an index of democracy. As in the stories around Amasis, the same discursive system has been turned on its head in the service of egalitarian ideology. Thus the fourth-century comic poet Philemon offers us an enthusiastic paean to Solon's wise innovation:

σὺ δ᾽ εἰς ἅπαντας εὗρες ἀνθρώπους νόμον·
σὲ γὰρ λέγουσιν τοῦτ᾽ ἰδεῖν πρῶτον, Σόλων,
δημοτικόν, ὦ Ζεῦ, πρᾶγμα καὶ σωτήριον,
(καί μοι λέγειν τοῦτ᾽ ἐστὶν ἁρμοστόν, Σόλων)
μεστὴν ὁρῶντα τὴν πόλιν νεωτέρων
τούτους τ᾽ ἔχοντας τὴν ἀναγκαίαν φύσιν
ἁμαρτάνοντάς τ᾽ εἰς ὃ μὴ προσῆκον ἦν,
στῆσαι πριάμενόν τοι γυναῖκας κατὰ τόπους
κοινὰς ἅπασι καὶ κατεσκευασμένας.
ἑστᾶσι γυμναί, μὴ ᾽ξαπατηθῇς· πάνθ᾽ ὅρα.
οὐκ εὖ σεαυτοῦ τυγχάνεις ἔχων, ἔχεις

---

[50] Halperin 1990: 88–104.

[51] Sources (assembled in Athen. *Deipn.* 13.569d) are Philemon fr. 3 K.-A. (4th c. B.C.E.) and Nikander of Kolophon *FGrH* 271/2 F 9. As Halperin (1990: 186n.89) notes, these may not be independent traditions; Nikander could be cribbing from Philemon.

[52] Halperin 1990: 100–101; quote taken from 187n.89. Surprisingly, Herter 1960: 73 defends the Solonian provenance of Athenian brothel-foundation. For the fourth-century idealization of Solon as "founding father" of the democratic regime, see Mossé 1979; Hansen 1989.

<ἐρωτικῶς> πως. ἡ θύρα 'στ' ἀνεωγμένη.
εἰς ὀβολός· εἰσπήδησον. οὐκ ἔστ' οὐδὲ εἷς
ἀκκισμός, οὐδὲ λῆρος, οὐδ' ὑφήρπασεν,
ἀλλ' εὐθὺς ἦν βούλει σὺ χῶν βούλει τρόπον.
ἐξῆλθες· οἰμώζειν λέγ, ἀλλοτρία 'στί σοι.[53] (Philemon fr. 3 K.-A.)

But you invented a law for all mankind; for they say that you, Solon, first envisioned a matter democratic and saving, by Zeus, (and it's appropriate for me to say this, o Solon). Seeing the city crammed with young men, and seeing them having their necessary nature and going wrong in the direction of what didn't belong to them, you set women you'd bought in [public] places, arrayed for action and common to all. They stand there naked, lest you be deceived: look everything over. Say you're not doing well, you're feeling erotic. The door's open. [Price] one obol: jump right in. There's no coyness, no nonsense, she doesn't snatch [herself] away, but straightaway whichever one you want and in whatever position you want. Then out you go: tell her to go hang, she's nothing to you.

Even if this speech is tongue-in-cheek (and Kock suggested long ago that it was spoken by a pimp[54]), it parrots the catchphrases of democratic discourse: Solon's invention serves "all mankind" (1), it is "democratic" (3), and provides women who are "common to all" (9). And, the speech suggests, Solon's innovation achieves this effect of political democracy by completely disembedding the women from any social networks. Thus prostitution prevents young men from "going wrong in the direction of what doesn't belong to them" (7)—a roundabout reference to adultery with citizen wives or daughters.[55] In contrast, Solon's prostitutes are available to everyone because they *belong* to no one. The last line blithely asserts, "she's nothing to you" (literally ἀλλοτρία, "she's not your property, of your household"). But if the prostitutes of this speech are constituted in opposition to citizen wives and daughters enmeshed in the networks of household and family, they are also defined in oppositon to *hetairai*. In contrast to the elaborate games of ornamentation and self-presentation Xenophon's Theodote describes, these brothel-inmates are "stripped for action," completely naked. What they offer, in contrast to the seduction and romance of the *hetaira*, is demystified sex; rather than a connection of *charis*, they provide a physical act with a stranger (ἀλλοτρία, 16).

[53] I follow the text of Kassel-Austin, except for transposing νόμον (2) and Σόλων (1) with Kock 1880–88, and reading <ἐρωτικῶς> πως (12) with Edmonds 1961.
[54] Kock 1880–88, vol. 2.479 (*ad* fr. 4.4). In fact, this line seems to me to suggest rather a young citizen male who has himself enjoyed the benefits of Solon's system.
[55] The contrast of the ready availability of prostitutes with the dangers of adultery is a comic topos; cf. Euboulos, fr. 67 K.-A.; Xenarchos fr. 4 K.-A.

Indeed, in their perfect interchangeability and alienability, the prostitutes in this speech approximate the circulation of coinage in the public
sphere. Like coinage, the success of the system is predicated on their
symbolic sameness (one girl is much like another) and ability to circulate
(once you're done with her, she's ἀλλοτρία).[56] Like coinage (according
to this tradition) they represent a civic intervention into the circulation
of goods and services to equalize the status of all citizens. For, as coinage
breaks down the aristocratic monopoly on precious metals and top-rank
goods and provides a standard against which all labor can be measured,
these state-subsidized prostitutes (at least in the Athenian imaginary)
endow all citizens with an equal phallic power. If *hetairai* function like
metals in the fantasy of the aristocratic symposium, the *pornē* circulates
like money in the agora. James Davidson notes that, at the extreme of
the commodifying discourse that characterizes the *pornē*, the woman is
represented as bearing the name of the coin that is her wage: thus in a
brothel scene on a cup by the Ambrosios Painter (late sixth-century B.C.E.),
one of the inmates is labeled "Obole."[57]

It is precisely the equalizing power of the universal availability of
resources that aristocratic discourse abhors, and, I have argued, allego-

[56] Henry 1992: 261 emphasizes the commodification of the women in Philemon fr. 3
K.-A. Cf. the remarks of Simmel (1978: 376–77) on the conceptual connections between
money and prostitution: "Since in prostitution the relationship between the sexes is quite
specifically confined to the sexual act, it is reduced to its purely generic content. It consists
of what any member of the species can perform and experience. It is a relationship in which
the most contrasting personalities are equal and individual differences are eliminated. Thus,
the economic counterpart of this kind of relationship is money, which also, transcending
all individual distinctions, stands for the species-type of economic values, the representation
of which is common to all individual values. Conversely, we experience in the nature of
money itself something of the essence of prostitution. The indifference as to its use, the
lack of attachment to any individual because it is unrelated to any of them, the objectivity
inherent in money as a mere means which excludes any emotional relationship—all this
produces an ominous analogy between money and prostitution."

[57] Davidson 1994: 156, 163–164, 1997: 88, 118–19; on the cup (which is currently in
a private collection in Munich), see Zanker 1975 (with pl. 33, no. 148) and discussion in
Williams 1993: 96–97 (though Immerwahr 1984.11 expresses some doubt that the name
should be interpreted as "Obole"). For another identification of *pornai* with money/coins,
cf. Euboulos fr. 82 K.-A and see Davidson 1994: 143–73.

All this suggests that Halperin's structural opposition [forbidden male citizen prostitution :
subsidized female prostitution] represents only the democratic half of a four-way opposition.
If we add the domain of the aristocratic symposium to his model, we get:

> *hetaira* : *pornē*
> good (sympotic) eromenos : male whore,

both of which oppositions can be figured as

> metals : money (or gold : silver).

Within this system, each term can signify in opposition to any and all others, depending
on the discursive needs of the context.

rizes through the figure of the *pornē*. As a final piece of evidence for the aristocratic position, I would like to juxtapose Philemon's celebration of Solon's "democratic" reform with an anonymous two-line drinking song preserved by Athenaios:

πόρνη καὶ βαλανεὺς τωὐτὸν ἔχουσ' ἐμπεδέως ἔθος·
ἐν ταὐτᾷ πυέλῳ τόν τ' ἀγαθὸν τόν τε κακὸν λόει
(Athen. *Deipn.* 15.695e = Carm. conv. 905 *PMG*)

The whore and the bathman have the same nature consistently; [each] washes good and bad alike in the same trough.

This couplet, perhaps itself the product of the archaic symposium,[58] functions like Anakreon's ironic compounds πανδοσία and πολύυμνος. For the first line offers what looks like anomalous praise of the whore and the bathman: in aristocratic terms, "to have the same nature consistently" is the highest desideratum.[59] The second line then springs the trap: what whore and bathman do consistently is equalize noble and base by immersing them in the same common filth. One could hardly wish for a more graphic image to express aristocratic revulsion at the indiscriminate exchanges of the public sphere.[60]

III. IDEOLOGICAL FAULTLINES

Let us return to the *hetaira* and the ideological ambiguities that surround her, considering first another domain of evidence—visual representations.[61] The iconography of Attic vase painting tends to corroborate the dating and context for the construction of the *hetaira* gleaned from the literary sources. Vases painted in the first half of the sixth century (600–550) represent sympotic scenes without any female participants; as Reinsberg notes, though *pornai* are mentioned as early as Archilochos, they do not participate in aristocratic banquets or at least are not considered

---

[58] Reitzenstein 1893: 13–17 argues that Athenaios's compilation of twenty-five skolia (or drinking songs) is based on a collection that was already constituted by the mid-fifth century, with many of the individual poems dating back to the archaic period.

[59] Cf. Thgn. 315–18, 319–20, 1083–84 and Chapter 1 above.

[60] For explicit association of baths and *pornai*, cf. Aristoph. *Clouds* 991–97, *Knights* 1397–1401. In the former, the Δίκαιος Λόγος, spokesman for the old aristocratic education, insists that a well-brought-up young man will shun the agora, baths, and *pornai*. In the latter, the Paphlagonian is punished by being relegated to the gates of the city, where he will "sell sausages. . . , be abused for getting drunk with *pornai*, and drink the dirty water from the baths."

[61] For this entire discussion of the visual evidence, I owe thanks to Richard Neer for his insights and conversation, which helped me formulate issues and arguments.

worthy of representation.[62] Then slowly, starting in the mid sixth century, individual female participants appear in scenes of symposia and *kōmoi* (first on black-figure, then on red-figure vases). Finally, in the last quarter of the sixth century, scenes of symposia with several *hetairai*, with the participants ranging from fully clothed to undressed, and scenes of explicit sex become popular for approximately fifty years (525–475 B.C.E.).[63] The shapes of the vessels make it certain that these representations were painted for use at symposia: indeed, 79 percent of all such images occur on drinking cups.[64] Some scholars want to attribute this phase of explicit sex scenes to a "popularization" of the aristocratic symposium and the spread of the custom to newly wealthy traders, as if "real" aristocrats could not have been capable of such coarse pleasures.[65] There is no internal evidence for such a shift in clientele; indeed, just the opposite, since the period of the production of these vases is almost exactly contemporary with the so-called Anakreontic vases, and in two cases, both elements of representation occur on the same vessels.[66] The Anakreontic vases (so called for the figure of Anakreon labelled on three of them) represent male symposiasts reveling in extravagant Eastern garb—long, flowing robes, turbans and headbands, earrings, and even parasols.[67] As

[62] Reinsberg 1989: 108.

[63] Brendel 1970: 19–36; Sutton 1981: 74–113 and 117, Table L.1; Peschel 1987; Reinsberg 1989: 104–12; Stewart 1997: 156–67.

[64] See Sutton 1981: 75 and 117, Table L.2; Sutton 1981: 75 reckons that 88 percent of all such representations occur on vases specially designed for sympotic use (the other 12 percent are imaginable in that context, but not limited to it). See also Brendel (1970: 30), who emphasizes the shift in venues of erotic representations from the archaic to the classical period; in the former, the bulk of such scenes occur on drinking cups; in the latter period, they shift to other types of vases and objects like mirror cases, which would have been used in private.

[65] Reinsberg 1989: 108; cf. Brendel 1970: 26. Reinsberg uses as evidence the naming of the pot-painter Smikros on one such vase, but it is a mistake to "read" such moments of self-portraiture as literal fact rather than fantasy: see Robertson 1992: 26, Neer 1998. Another scholarly strategy for avoiding the implications of these images and exculpating Greek aristocrats is to claim that these scenes were painted purely for the export market, for Etruscans who liked that sort of thing (cf. Reinsberg 1989: 105–8). For a cautious rejection of taking these sex scenes as painted for the Etruscan market, see Sutton 1981: 109–12; for an authoritative dismantling of the theory of production for the Etruscan market in general, see Arafat and Morgan 1994.

[66] For the connection of lovemaking scenes and Anakreontic vases, see Sutton 1981: 98; Stewart 1997: 167. The two vessels are (1) Berlin inv. no. 3251 by the Thalia painter, dated ca. 510 B.C.E. (discussed below), in which several of the male participants sport *sakkos* (snood) and earrings; and (2) Athens, Vlastou-Serpieri 74 MVF, dinos frgs. by the Pan Painter, dated 470–460 B.C.E., in which both male participants wear earrings.

[67] On these representations and their significance, see De Vries 1973; Snyder 1974; Kurtz and Boardman 1986; Frontisi-Ducroux and Lissarrague 1990; Miller 1992, 1997: 153–87, 192–98.

I have argued elsewhere, these images represent the visual equivalent of the literary "cult of *habrosunē*" embraced in elitist sympotic poetry. Thus these representations flourish in the last quarter of the sixth century (when perhaps, with the rise of middling ideology and mercantile wealth, the aristocratic elite had to work most strenuously to distinguish itself), and disappear abruptly in the democratic climate of the post-Persian War period.[68] I would suggest that the explosion of representations of female participants at symposia forms part of the same phenomenon; one element of the carefully crafted lifestyle of *habrosunē* was refined sensuality, figured on the vases by the presence of accommodating female partners. As Reinsberg recognizes, we cannot necessarily conclude from the visual evidence that women only entered the world of the symposium in the last third of the sixth century—only that, at this point, they became "worthy of representation,"[69] not for themselves but for the ways in which their presence served and affirmed the ideology of *habrosunē*. It is this shift in representational practices (both literary and visual) that I have termed "the invention of the *hetaira*."

But the visual evidence also confirms the shifts and indeterminacy in the status of the *hetaira* I suggested for the literary sources. On the one hand, the constitution of an impermeable boundary between the symposium and the outside inspires a mystification of the *hetaira*'s standing and the identification of *hetaira* and *hetairos*. On the other hand, as if in compensation for this strange sympotic equality, other images accentuate the relations of domination between male symposiast and female attendant. Though some scholars have attempted to construct a developmental narrative out of these two classes of images, they are almost contemporary and so suggest rather the simultaneous, contradictory possibilities for the representation of the *hetaira*.[70]

The first category of image is exemplified by a kylix [cup] in Berlin, dated to ca. 510 B.C.E. (the name-piece of the Thalia Painter; Figures 1 and 2).[71] The outside of the vessel depicts eight men (six unbearded, all with erections) and nine women, all of them naked and engaged in an orgiastic *kōmos*. The remains of five lampstands indicate that it is evening or night, while the cups and cooling-jars some of the participants still

---

[68] See Kurke 1992: 97–104.

[69] Reinsberg 1989: 108–14.

[70] Thus Peschel 1987: 197–209 wants to trace a development toward greater intimacy and emotional connection in representations of the period 500-475 B.C.E., while Reinsberg 1989: 114–20 suggests that an increase in scenes of sympotic violence correlates with the rise of democratic ideology after ca. 500 B.C.E.

[71] Berlin inv. no. 3251; *ARV*[2] 113, 7, *Para.*[2] 332, *Add.*[2] 173. On this cup see Brendel 1970: 22–25; Peschel 1987: 50–55. (On all the vases discussed in this section, I have drawn much from the careful descriptions of Peschel 1987.)

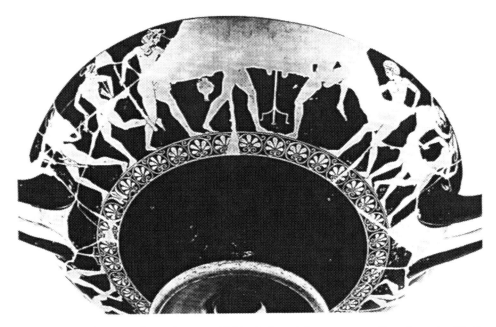

Figure 1. Antikensammlung, inv. no. 3251. Attic red-figure cup attributed to the Thalia Painter, ca. 510 B.C.E. Photo courtesy of Antikensammlung, Staatliche Museen zu Berlin—Preussischer Kulturbesitz.

carry suggest the late stages of sympotic celebration. The figures range from a couple engaged in wild dance, to a *hetaira* leading a young man off by his penis, to a bearded man pursuing a running *hetaira* with an aulos-case suspended from his erect penis, to a couple standing in the far corner copulating. If we had any doubts about the status of these women, several of them are labeled with names that confirm that they are *hetairai*: [Aphr]os ("Foamy," linking her to the foam-born Aphrodite); Korone ("Crow"); Thalia ("Blooming," or "Festivity," as an adjective a traditional epithet of banquet and symposium); Smikra ("Little one" or "La petite," whose name appears on several *hetaira* scenes at the turn of the century).[72]

Several elements of iconography visually assimilate the male and female participants in the *kōmos*: all the women and several of the men wear earrings and elaborate snoods or headcoverings (*sakkoi*), the only difference being that the women have ponytails that emerge from the back. Because most of the men are represented as unbearded youths, their profiles are almost identical to those of the *hetairai*, except for slight

---

[72] On these and other *hetaira*-names on vases, see Peschel 1987: 74–79, 183–84.

Figure 2. Reverse of Figure 1. Photo courtesy of Antikensammlung, Staatliche Museen zu Berlin—Preussischer Kulturbesitz.

shading that indicates the first growth of beard along their jawlines. Indeed, as one scholar has noted in the case of the dancing couple, "The treatment of bodies, head, and extremities is nearly identical."[73] Furthermore, as has also been noted, the women seem to take a very active role in the sex depicted.[74] Thus at one end of the frieze, a *hetaira* leads a man off by his penis, turning to look back at him, while at the other end, the female of the copulating pair raises her leg and grasps her partner enthusiastically. Perhaps most remarkably, the woman next to this couple raises her left leg high in dance while a young man reclining in front of her seems to be about to initiate cunnilingus. If this is indeed what the vase depicts (and there is some dispute on the matter), it is the only representation of cunnilingus in all of Greek art. For the protocols of Greek culture regarded oral sex as particularly demeaning for the partner who gave it, so that, while scenes of women fellating men are fairly common, depictions of cunnilingus are almost nonexistent.[75] Thus,

[73] Ibid: 53.
[74] Ibid: 51.
[75] On the possibility of cunnilingus, see Brendel 1970: 23; Sutton 1981: 91; Peschel 1987: 50–55; Kilmer 1993: 71; for a different interpretation of the figures, see *CVA* Berlin 2,

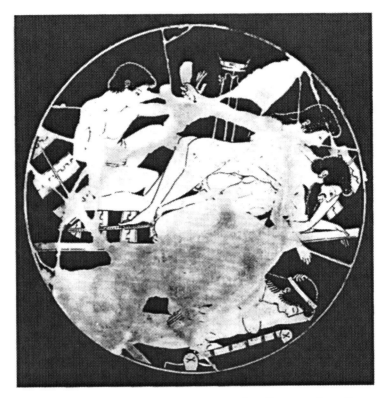

Figure 3. Tondo of Figure 1. Photo courtesy of Antikensammlung, Staatliche Museen zu Berlin—Preussischer Kulturbesitz.

this extraordinary frieze seems to unsettle the hierarchical relations of
sex usually encountered in Greek representations: it is not at all clear
who is servicing and pleasuring whom in this sympotic fantasy.

The same elements of assimilation of male and female partners and
the female's taking an active role in sex are evident in the cup's tondo,
which depicts the complex intertwining of four bodies in what appears
to be another stage of the evening's entertainment (Figure 3). A lamp,
klinē, several pillows, and a stool mark this as a symposium scene. A
bearded man is copulating with a young woman, who threatens him with
a sandal raised in her right hand. Behind them sits a young man, watching
the activity and masturbating. The male partner of the couple gazes
downward, apparently watching a young woman who lies beneath or in

---

p. 14; Dover 1989: 101–2; for the relative status of partners in oral sex, see Dover 1989:
100–2, 182–84.

front of the couch, who seems also to be masturbating.[76] The composition connects the three figures on the couch, since their legs overlap and the young man stretches out his left hand behind the raised sandal in the *hetaira*'s right. All three figures face right, gazing in profile so that their heads form an arc. The female figure below is isolated by her closed eyes and the strong horizontal demarcation of the couch separating her from the other figures, but their combined gazes lead us to her supine form at the bottom of the tondo. All four figures have nearly the same elaborate hairdo, treated the same way, and it is difficult to untangle and identify the various limbs of the couple in the center.

The effect of the tondo, as Peschel notes, is to fuse the entire sympotic group into a single organism, the alternating male and female bodies united by their intercalated limbs, their gaze, and their common sexual arousal.[77] The same can be said of the cup's outside frieze, in which the almost identical male and female bodies form a snakelike whole, moving in unison in an elaborately choreographed dance of desire. This fusion gives palpable form to the ideal of the aristocratic symposium, which unites its participants while excluding all others, and, I would contend, the sexual and iconographic identification of female and male participants serves the constitution of this ideal.

A similar identification (for a similar end) may explain a series of eight representations ranging from 520–480 B.C.E., which Peschel designates "*reine Hetärensymposia*," "*hetaira*-only drinking parties." On these vases, one, two, or more *hetairai* are represented at symposia, aping the dress and activities of male symposiasts: they recline at the head of the couch, drink, play *kottabos*, and sometimes even wear their clothes in male fashion (with just himation draped over the lower body).[78] Both Peschel and Reinsberg take these representations as proof that *hetairai* had their own symposia in this period (as a way of asserting their status), but these images are susceptible of another interpretation.[79] I would sug-

---

[76] For the possibility that this female figure, labeled Smikra, is masturbating, see Greifenhagen 1967: 25n.82; Brendel 1970: 24n.22; Sutton 1981: 92; Peschel 1987: 52; Kilmer 1993: 65. Other scholars insist that she is simply resting or asleep, but as Sutton observes, this interpretation does not account for the position of her right hand, nor for "the obvious interest of the man above in what she is doing."

[77] Peschel 1987: 54–55.

[78] See Peschel 1987: 70–74 and 110–12 for discussion of all known examples of the type.

[79] Peschel 1987: 73–74; Reinsberg 1989: 112–14 (see also Robertson 1992: 27). Both Peschel and Reinsberg contend that the labeling of the figures in various scenes of *hetaira*-symposia proves that the vase-painters wanted to represent "real people" at "real occasions," though as Peschel herself notes, most of the *hetaira*-names preserved on vases are clearly *redende Namen*, given to the women to signify their profession (Peschel 1987: 74–81). Cf. Csapo and Miller 1991: 380 and Goldhill 1992: 197 for skepticism about Reinsberg's assumption that representations of all-female symposia prove that they really happened.

gest instead that these vessels represent fantasies painted for the gaze of
male symposiasts, who enjoyed seeing their own activities mirrored in
those of sexually available female "companions" (often nude or semi-
nude). As evidence for male consumers of these images, I would cite a
hydria attributed to Phintias now in Munich (dated to ca. 510 B.C.E.).[80]
The principal representational field of the hydria depicts a music lesson,
in which a youth and a boy (labeled Euthymides and Smikythos respectively), accompanied by their paidagogos, receive instruction in the lyre
from a bearded teacher. On the shoulder of the hydria, immediately above
this scene, two *hetairai* are shown reclining on pillows, playing *kottabos*
and engaged in animated conversation (the pillows and drinking cups
signal the sympotic context). The two are dressed like typical male symposiasts: upper body completely bare, lower body covered by a loosely
draped himation. The thinner of the two, on the left, turns to her companion and speaks as she casts the lees of her wine; lettering between the
two gives us her words, "For you, beautiful Euthymides, [I cast] this"
(καλοι σοι τενδι Εὐθυμιδει).[81] The object of her desire is thus one of the
participants in the music lesson in the register below. In this case, it
seems, the *hetairai* on the hydria's shoulder are there to ventriloquize
male desire: male symposiasts can savor the fantasy of a gathering of
sexually active women sharing their longing for the beautiful Euthymides.[82] And through their shared desire, the represented *hetairai* can stand
metonymically for the eroticized sphere of the elite symposium generally.

A similar effect is produced by the *hetaira*-symposium represented on
a psykter (wine-cooler) in Leningrad, signed by Euphronios.[83] On this
vessel, four entirely naked *hetairai* (each labeled and occupying a quarter
of the visual field) engage in typical sympotic activities. Smikra plays

---

My reading of these vases is similar to that suggested by Csapo and Miller 1991: 380: "We
may freely doubt the existence of 'Hetärensymposien' in Archaic Athens. Did hetairai really
get together to drink and play kottabos? Or is this simply a humorous inversion of reality
(where prostitutes play for the favors of free youths), an erotic daydream, and the painter's
witty compliment to a παῖς καλός, a symposium joke for the symposium?"

[80] Munich inv. no. 2421; *ARV*[2] 23, 7, *Para.*[2] 323, *Add.*[2] 155.

[81] Or, according to a slightly different reading and interpretation recently proposed by
Csapo and Miller 1991: 373–80, the inscription represents a dialogue between two speakers:
one *hetaira* asks τοι τενδι ("For whom [shall I toss] this?"), while the second answers καλοι
Εὐθυμιδει ("For beautiful Euthymides").

[82] We may compare this triangulation of desire to the literary topos of praising a young
man's attractiveness by imagining his effect on female spectators: cf. Pindar *P.* 9.97–103,
P. 10.59 (vs. *O.* 10.100–105, where the gaze of homoerotic desire is expressed directly
through a comparison of the boy victor to Ganymede). One difference between these two
phenomena is that Pindar's choral poetry uses desiring women as a metonymy for the city
as a whole (hence, they are "maidens" and their mothers), while the vase representations
deploy these figures as metonymy for the sympotic group (hence, the women are *hetairai*).

[83] Hermitage B 644; *ARV*[2] 16, 15, *Para.*[2] 509, *Add.*[2] 153; dated to ca. 510 B.C.E.

kottabos, while to her right, Agape holds one skyphos and offers the other to Sekline, who plays the aulos. On Sekline's right, Palaisto holds a kylix in her left hand and a skyphos in her right, paying no attention to Smikra, who turns to tell her for whom she tosses her wine lees (lettering at her side reads, "I toss this for you, Leagros"). As if to confirm the interior, sympotic setting, all four recline on mattresses and pillows, and an aulos-case hangs suspended on the wall between Agape and Sekline.

Leagros, for whom Smikra casts her wine, was the subject of frequent "kalos" inscriptions on contemporary vases, suggesting that he too is the object of male homoerotic desire triangulated through a fantasized all-female symposium.[84] But what is truly remarkable about the vessel is the representation of Palaisto, who gazes directly out at the viewer as she drinks, her face masklike and half-concealed behind her raised cup (Figure 4). For frontality is quite rare in Attic red-figure vase painting and confined to certain well-defined contexts. One such context is symposium scenes, where drinkers are sometimes represented frontally, the bottoms of their faces concealed behind the skyphos as they drink. As Françoise Frontisi-Ducroux argues, this convention transforms them into masks—like Dionysus himself, who presides over drinking—and offers a mirror held up to the viewer who encounters the image as he himself puts the cup to his lips.[85] In these cases the painted image is the drinker's double and counterpart, inviting complete identification with the perfect sympotic world of the cup. Palaisto's frontal gaze, behind the skyphos that masks the bottom half of her face and makes her features indistinguishable from a male symposiast's, produces the same uncanny effect: her eyes seize the viewer and draw him in, even as the dedication of the *kottabos* throw to the beautiful boy Leagros suggests that the vessel was intended for a male audience.[86] The psykter, or wine-cooler, would have stood in the

---

[84] On the homoerotic and aristocratic context of kalos inscriptions, see Robinson and Fluck 1937; Shapiro 1983, 1987. Robinson and Fluck 1937 list 45 "Leagros Kalos" inscriptions on vases; Beazley *Add.*[2] 396–97 adds another half-dozen instances; Boardman 1992: 47–48 counts "about 80 occurrences" of the name, which he contends "were inscribed within a comparatively short period toward the end of the sixth century." (I owe these references to Richard Neer.)

[85] Frontisi-Ducroux 1989: 163 with fig. 228, 1996: 85–86. On the categories of figures represented frontally, cf. Korshak 1987, who notes that Euphronios's *hetaira* is probably the earliest representation of sympotic frontality (p. 11).

[86] Another element that may assimilate or identify the represented *hetairai* to male symposiasts is the figures' distinctly masculine physiognomy. Peschel (1987: 71) and Robertson (1992: 27) note this, apparently ascribing it to an early inability to represent female physiognomy successfully, but perhaps the physical similarity is deliberate. We might also note that three of the four *hetairai* hold two drinking cups each—are they meant to be proffering them to male viewers, inviting them into the scene?

Figure 4. Hermitage, inv. no. 6.1650. Attic red-figue psykter painted by
Euphronios, ca. 510 B.C.E. Photo courtesy of the Hermitage Museum.

center of the *andrōn*, where male symposiasts, reclining and engaging in
the same activities as the represented *hetairai*, could contemplate the
eroticized scene, both desiring and identifying with the painted participants in their luxurious pursuits.

   But if these vessels (and others like them) achieve the sexual and sympotic assimilation of *hetairoi* and *hetairai*, other contemporary vases take
pains to rearticulate the differences and hierarchy within the sympotic

Figure 5. Louvre, inv. no. G 13. Attic red-figure cup attributed to the Pedieus Painter, ca. 510 B.C.E. Photo by M. Chuzeville, courtesy of the Louvre.

world. On one kylix by the Pedieus Painter, housed in the Louvre (dated ca. 510 B.C.E.), repeated scenes of violence and sexual abuse of female participants contrast starkly with the jovial antics of the Thalia Painter's cup (Figures 5 and 6).[87] Like that vessel, the outer frieze of the kylix represents a continuous scene of an orgiastic *kōmos*, in which at least four women and eight men, all nude, participate.[88] Of the figures sufficiently preserved, all the men sport enormous erections, and, with one exception, are involved in sexual threesomes or foursomes. At one end of the frieze, a young man kneels on a cushion, holding a drinking-horn in his right hand (evidence of the symposium from which this *kōmos* has developed), while a *hetaira* squats on all fours in front of him, taking the head of his oversize penis in her mouth. Lines around her mouth signify the effort she must make to accommodate him, while his left arm is stretched over her back, evidently to force her should she pull away. On the other side of the handle, another *hetaira* is precariously perched on her side on a

---

[87] Louvre G 13; *ARV²* 86, α, *Add.²* 170. On this vase and others like it, see Brendel 1970: 27–30; Keuls 1985: 180–86; Peschel 1987: 57–70; Reinsberg 1989: 117–20; Stewart 1997: 165.

[88] The vase is broken, so that there may be other figures whose activities cannot be made out. Peschel 1987: 64–65 suggests that there is yet another pair of figures copulating in the damaged space next to one of the handles.

Figure 6. Reverse of Figure 5. Photo by M. Chuzeville, courtesy of the Louvre.

stool, with her back to the viewer. A young man on her left guides his
penis into her wide-open mouth with his left hand and holds her back
with his right. Another, bearded komast stoops slightly to enter her from
behind, supporting her right leg on his shoulder, with his left hand in
the small of her back. With his right hand, he holds a sandal extended
over her torso, with which to threaten her. Like the first *hetaira*, lines
around her mouth underscore the size of the penis she is fellating, while
lines drawn on her neck suggest the uncomfortable twist of her body.
She appears to be using her right arm to steady herself on the stool, while
her left hangs limp and useless in front of the young man's legs. To the
right of this group, another young man bends over a *hetaira* kneeling on
all fours in front of him and forces his penis into her mouth (his left arm
encircles her head to prevent any resistance). Though the vessel is broken
at this point, the remains of two feet behind hers, pointing in the same
direction, and a right hand stretched over her back make clear that
another komast takes advantage of her position to enter her from behind.
Finally, on the other side of the handle from this group, a *hetaira* squats
and offers herself obediently for a komast to enter from behind. Here
again, the vase is broken, but her partner's lower leg is preserved behind
her. In addition, there are remains of a bearded man striding behind her
right to left, apparently with his right arm raised. Peschel suggests that
he, like the other bearded komast, wields a sandal to threaten or excite

the copulating pair in front of him.[89] Another young man behind him strides toward the pair, apparently to provide more light, since he holds a lamp stretched out in his right hand (he has just removed it from a lampstand still clutched in his left hand). He, too, sports a huge erection and seems eager to join in the activity.[90]

As Peschel notes, everything in this vase serves to differentiate the male and female participants. The women are perforce objectified and passive in the sexual acts represented, while the men dominate and direct these activities (thus Peschel takes as emblematic the limp and useless left hand of the *hetaira* balanced on a stool). Furthermore, the men's heads consistently occupy the upper register of the visual field (even when they are stooping or kneeling); in contrast, all the women are portrayed in animal-like postures, squatting or on all fours, their heads well below those of their male partners. Finally, the painter has carefully differentiated the physiognomy of the male and female figures: all the male komasts have slim, elegant physiques, while the females have large, sagging bodies, in which the contours of breasts and buttocks are grotesquely exaggerated.[91] The result of these systematic contrasts is to unite the male komasts through the humiliation and objectification of the women. Here again, as Peschel notes, the threesome with the *hetaira* on a stool produces effects emblematic of those of the frieze as a whole: the two males form a unit, connected by the gaze of the bearded komast at his youthful counterpart, and by their hands just touching on the woman's back. The male sympotic group fuses around and through the violence done to the purely instrumental female subordinates.[92]

And yet, even here, hidden within the scenes of violent sexual domination that decorate the cup's exterior frieze, its tondo offers a remarkable image of sympotic companionability (Figure 7). The circle of the tondo frames two figures: in front a woman, elaborately dressed in a chiton

[89] Peschel 1987: 63.

[90] Richard Neer suggests to me that this youth's approach with a lamp may have a more sinister purpose, since lamps were used for depilation (cf. Aristoph. *Lys.* 823–28, *Thesmo.* 238–48, *Ekkl.* 13–14; Attic cup in the manner of Onesimos [*ARV*² 331, 20] and see discussion in Kilmer 1982).

[91] Peschel 1987: 62–66; cf. Reinsberg 1989: 117–18. Brendel 1970: 27 optimistically suggests that this vase "is intended as a vehicle of social criticism," but Sutton (1981: 107–8) and Peschel (1987: 387n.144) rightly dissent from this position.

[92] Cf. Peschel 1987: 63–64; Reinsberg 1989: 117–18; Stewart 1997: 163–65 on the "homosocial male bonding" achieved by these scenes. Stewart, following Reinsberg, attributes these scenes of explicit violence in sympotic settings to the pressure of democratic ideology to figure as clearly as possible the phallic power of the male citizen participant. But this interpretation collapses the opposition of symposium and public sphere and fails to account for the temporal and iconographic links with the Anakreontic vases and the abrupt disappearance of both types around 480-475 B.C.E.

Figure 7. Tondo of Figure 5. Photo by M. Chuzeville, courtesy of the Louvre.

and playing a large lyre, supporting it with her left hand and holding the plektron or pick in her right; behind her, a young man naked except for a himation draped over his shoulders and short boots (*kothornoi?*), with his right arm encircling the lyre player and his left hand extended out behind her, holding a kylix and supported by a walking stick. The female figure is drawn entirely in profile, while the young man behind her pivots—his right leg (the only one shown) is in profile, but his shoulders and head are presented frontally. As a result, his body surrounds and frames hers, and their faces seem to merge. Her mouth and his form one continuous line, their chins and noses touch, their hairlines meet, and their eyes are drawn identically. But for a slight asymmetry caused by the tilt of his head behind hers, their features form a single face. The drawing of their bodies effects the same merging of figures: the flat elaboration of drapery makes it hard to untangle her form from his, and there is a confusion of arms and hands. It almost appears to be the *woman's* left arm that extends with kylix and walking stick, except for the hand that peeks through and supports the strings of the lyre. The walking stick itself, that phallic object *par excellence*, is not actually held by the hand that supports the cup; it seems instead to hover strangely behind, properly attached to neither figure. All these visual details conjure a moment of perfect sympathy and identification between *hetairos* and *hetaira*. I have been describing two different classes of vases that represent the contradictory constructions of the *hetaira*, but in fact, the Pedieus Painter's cup captures in a single object the oscillation between identification and difference, companionability and humiliation. Both are available to the viewer in the dialectic of tondo and outer frieze: the drinker, draining his cup, could savor a private moment of idyllic refinement and sympathy, or flip the cup over for graphic scenes of group sex and sympotic domination.

On occasion, we can catch this same sudden shift from idealizing mystification of the *hetaira* to violence or abuse preserved in the literary remains. Thus in a fragment of Anakreon quoted by Athenaios because of the unusual term for a drinking cup the poet uses, we serendipitously catch a flash of sympotic abuse:[93]

μηδ' ὥστε κῦμα πόντιον
λάλαζε τῇ πολυκρότῃ
σὺν Γαστροδώρῃ καταχύδην
πίνουσα τὴν ἐπίστιον. (fr. 48 Gentili = 427 *PMG*)

Do not babble like the swell of the sea, drinking your cup down greedily together with noisy Gastrodore.

The speaker prescribes correct sympotic behavior to the addressee, holding up Gastrodore as a negative exemplar.[94] The use of the feminine participle πίνουσα makes clear that the addressee is a woman participating in the symposium (and therefore almost certainly, like Gastrodore herself, a *hetaira*). The speaker singles out two features of bad sympotic behavior—endless chatter (λάλαζε) and the greedy gulping of wine (καταχύδην πίνουσα)—and identifies them with the benighted Gastrodore.

To understand what is at stake in these prescriptions, we need to set Anakreon's brief fragment against later literary sources that contextualize somewhat more the discourse of the *hetaira*'s proper behavior at banquet

---

[93] Text after Gentili, who reads Γαστροδώρῃ for Γαστροδώρῳ in line 3.

[94] For the topos of advice on sympotic behavior, which is extremely common in archaic poetry, cf. Alkaios frr. 50, 58, 332, 335, 338, 346, 347a, 352, 369, 376, 401 V; Anakr. frr. 356, 383, 396, 410, 412 *PMG*; Thgn. 211–12, 413–14, 473–510, 627–28, 837–44, 873–84, 989–90, 1039–42, 1047–48; Xenoph. fr.B 1 DK. As Kate Gilhuly points out to me, though prescriptions to *hetairoi* on how to *drink* are frequent, only women are advised how to *eat*. This association of the woman with the *gastēr* is inevitably demeaning (cf. Just 1989: 163–64, 185–86).

and symposium. Thus, Athenaios tells us at one point, "Euboulos in *The Hunchback* introduces a decorous *hetaira* (κοσμίαν ἑταίραν) by saying,"

ὡς δ' ἐδείπνει κοσμίως,
οὐχ ὥσπερ ἄλλαι τῶν πράσων ποιούμεναι
τολύπας ἔσαττον τὰς γνάθους καὶ τῶν κρεῶν
ἀπέβρυκον αἰσχρῶς, ἀλλ' ἑκάστου μικρὸν ἂν
ἀπεγεύεθ' ὥσπερ παρθένος Μιλησία.
(Athen. *Deipn.* 13.571f–572a = Euboulos fr. 41 K.-A.)

How decorously she used to dine, not just like those other women who, making balls of leeks, were stuffing their jaws with them and were shamefully gobbling down meats, but she would just taste a little from each dish like a Milesian maid.

Nearly half a millennium later, Lucian puts a similar description into the mouth of a mother advising her daughter on how to become a classy *hetaira*, citing the example of another successful young woman:

Krobyle: In the first place, she adorns herself attractively and she's neat and beaming toward all the men, not to the point of laughing out loud easily, as you tend to, but smiling sweetly and attractively. Next, she's clever company and never cheats a visitor or an escort, and never throws herself at the men. And if ever she gets a wage for going to dinner, she doesn't get drunk—for that's ludicrous and men hate women like that—nor does she vulgarly stuff herself with dainties, but she picks at [the food] with her fingertips, [eating] in silence, and she doesn't stuff mouthfulls into both cheeks, and she drinks quietly, not greedily gulping, but taking breaks (πίνει δὲ ἠρέμα, οὐ χανδόν, ἀλλ' ἀναπαυομένη).
Korinna: Even if she happens to be thirsty, Mother?
Krobyle: Especially then, o Korinna. And she never speaks more than necessary, nor makes fun of any of the men present, and she has eyes only for the one who's hired her. And on account of this the men love her. And when it's time to bed down, she would never do anything loose or sloppy, but from everything she hunts this one thing, how she might lead him on and make that man her lover. And these are the things all men praise in her.   (Lucian, *Dialogues of Courtesans* 6.294)

This coincidence of passages suggests that ironic commentary on the *hetaira*'s eating and drinking habits was a literary topos (perhaps of Old and Middle Comedy) and that the Atticizing Lucian drew on this tradition for his mock-*hypothēkai* of mother to daughter.

In both cases, as Kate Gilhuly has observed, the prescriptions for the decorous behavior of a *hetaira* entail presenting herself as the perfect mirror of the *kalos k' agathos* who is her client, and, by her daintiness and delicacy, providing the simulacrum of a well-bred young lady (ὥσπερ παρθένος Μιλησία). Lucian in particular reveals that this mirroring of *kalokagathia* requires the denial on the part of the woman of all appetite or excess: she must dress neatly, smile but not laugh out loud, eat and drink daintily (even when she is thirsty), and not talk too much. Finally, in bed she must do nothing loose (ἀσελγές) or sloppy (ἀμελές)—that is, the woman must be nothing more than an attractive surface onto which the man can project his own desires without interference.[95]

In all three cases, the activities that are censured are those that shatter the mirror, as it were, by underscoring the *hetaira*'s difference, both of gender and of class. Thus both Euboulos and Lucian explicitly label the excessive consumption of food as low-class (Euboulos αἰσχρῶς; Lucian ἀπειροκάλως), while both strongly advise against behaviors that were for the Greeks stereotypically "feminine"—gluttony, bibulousness, and licentiousness.[96] Anakreon's four-line fragment, I would suggest, censures the same articulations of difference, for gulping down wine is proof of coarse origins, while the empty babble signified by λαλάζω is particularly associated with the female.[97] The fragment, by exposing Gastrodore's difference, ostracizes her from the sympotic group, and, in the process of representation, brands her by its rhetoric as a *pornē*. As several scholars have noted, "Gastrodore" is a joke name ("Gift of the belly" or "Piggy") that replicates on a stylistic level her declassé activities (we might compare this sobriquet to the visual representation of the grotesquely enlarged bodies of *hetairai* by the Pedieus Painter).[98] But what assimilates Gastrodore even more emphatically to the representation of the *pornē* is her epithet πολυκρότη, which I rendered above as "noisy." For, as Christopher Brown notes, "it seems more pointed to understand [the epithet] as meaning 'much-pounded' and referring to Gastrodore's promiscuity."[99] On this interpretation, the coarse adjective πολυκρότη takes us back to the domain of the *pornē* in Anakreon's abuse, recalling terms like πολύυμνος, πανδοσία, and λεωφόρος.

---

[95] I owe this interpretation of Lucian to Gilhuly 1999. Cf. Socrates' admonitions to Theodote on correct behavior with her *philoi* (Xen. *Mem.* 3.11.10–11, 14). For a parallel reading of the construction of the ideal wife in Xenophon's *Oikonomikos*, see Murnahan 1988.

[96] See the discussions of Dover 1974: 100–102 and Just 1989: 157–64, 184–93, both with ample citation of ancient sources. See also Henry 1992: 258–59 for the association of women with immoderate consumption of food and drink.

[97] On λαλάζω, see Carson 1994 and cf. Anaxilas fr. 22.23 K.-A., Horace *Odes* 1.22.10.

[98] Wilamowitz 1913: 155n.1; Brown 1983: 3. Wilamowitz even suggests that the victim's real name is Metrodore, which occurs frequently in inscriptions from Ionia.

[99] Brown 1983: 3; for the obscene sense of κροτέω (like English "bang"), cf. Henderson 1991: 171n.88.

This is not to say that we must imagine some real occasion on which a hapless *hetaira* misbehaved and thereby called down the wrath of the sympotic poet (though this may have happened); rather, the intrinsic indeterminacy of the category makes the *hetaira* available for various kinds of affirmation of the sympotic group. She can serve as its mirror, supporting the games of privilege and desire, or as its other, uniting the group by her instrumentality or exclusion. Thus, in this instance, the real impetus behind these prescriptions of proper behavior is less how women conduct themselves than how the true nobility of the male sympotic group shines through by contrast.[100]

In another instance, a different kind of violation of the norm provokes a vertiginous discursive shift from *hetaira* to *pornē*. Near the end of the first book of the Theognidea, we find these strange lines:

μή μ' ἀφελῶς παίζουσα φίλους δένναζε τοκῆας,
    Ἄργυρι· σοὶ μὲν γὰρ δούλιον ἦμαρ ἔπι,
ἡμῖν δ' ἄλλα μέν ἐστι, γύναι, κακὰ πόλλ', ἐπεὶ ἐκ γῆς
    φεύγομεν, ἀργαλέη δ' οὐκ ἔπι δουλοσύνη,
οὔθ' ἡμᾶς περνᾶσι· πόλις γε μέν ἐστι καὶ ἡμῖν
    καλή, Ληθαίῳ κεκλιμένη πεδίῳ. (Thgn. 1211–16)[101]

Do not, playing bluntly, abuse my dear parents, Arguris; for upon you is the day of slavery, but for me, although there are many other evils, o woman, since we are in exile from our land, nonetheless grievous slavery is not upon us, nor do they sell us. And there is also for us, at any rate, a beautiful city, resting on the Lethaian Plain.

These verses, especially the final couplet, have provoked an enormous amount of scholarly controversy. Some scholars understand the speaker's final riddle to refer to a city in mainland Greece or Ionia, others interpret it as a cryptic reference to the underworld, spoken by a dead man.[102] There is also dispute about the identity of the addressee: one critic takes the poem as a funerary epigram, addressed by a dead man to his widow, Arguris; another understands "arguris" as a type of silver bowl, and the whole poem as the imagined exchange between two funerary monu-

---

[100] Of course, these sympotic injunctions also imply agency for the *hetairai* addressed—an agency that is itself problematic within the complex power dynamics of the symposium. For extended discussion of the *hetaira*'s problematic agency and subjectivity within representation, see Goldhill 1998; Gilhuly 1999.

[101] I follow van Groningen (1966) and West (1992) for the division of poems, but van Groningen and Young (1971) for the reading Ἄργυρι (vs. West's Ἀργυρί).

[102] Young 1971 (apparatus criticus *ad loc*) takes the city to be Magnesia; Harrison 1902: 277, Carrière 1948: 133–34, McKay 1961a, and Nagy 1985: 77 understand the "Lethaian Plain" to signify the underworld.

ments.[103] But, as van Groningen notes, these fanciful interpretations have very little support in the text, and none of them accounts for the emphatic references to slavery.

I follow van Groningen in taking these lines instead as a moment of sympotic confrontation, in which the speaker lashes out at a *hetaira* who has presumed to mock his parentage.[104] In doing so, she has in a sense assimilated *hetairos* to *hetaira* too much (or in the wrong direction), attempting to make them equivalents on her level. This is also to disrupt the perfect, unobtrusive mirroring the *hetaira* should provide: recall that Lucian's mother-to-daughter advice includes a prohibition against "making fun of any of the men present" (οὔτε ἀποσκώπτει ἔς τινα τῶν παρόντων). The woman's attempt at appropriation combines with the male symposiast's own uncertain position (he is an exile, after all) to produce a violent negative reaction. As in Anakreon's Gastrodore fragment and the Pedieus Painter's cup, the differences in status must be fiercely rearticulated. Thus the speaker reminds Arguris in no uncertain terms that she is a woman (γύναι) and a slave, stripping away the mystifications of status that usually surround the *hetaira*. To do so is to transform her discursively into a *pornē*, as the emphatic use of the verb περνᾶσι indicates. The verb occurs only here in Theognis: suddenly, the buying and selling of the agora erupt into the pristine space of the symposium. In context, it is surely no accident that the object of this vilification bears the name Arguris, "Silvery." As we have seen, Chrysis ("Goldie") is a common *hetaira*-name (at least from the fourth century on),[105] bespeaking the aristocratic values the *hetaira* should properly reflect, but "Arguris" is attested nowhere else. Here the name signifies in two registers at once: within the sympotic language of metals, it encodes its bearer's *hubris* and presumption against the aristocratic "gold standard," while in the idiom of the agora, it evokes the image of money (*argurion*) and so confirms the woman's identification as a *pornē*.[106]

It is this radical rearticulation of distinctions, I suggest, that accounts for the speaker's final enigmatic lines. Whatever we take to be their

[103] For the former interpretation, see Carrière 1948: 133–34; for the latter, McKay 1961a, 1961b.

[104] van Groningen 1966: 438–39.

[105] Cf. Timokles fr. 27 K.-A.; Menander *Samia*; Lucian *Dialogues of Courtesans* 8; Schneider 1913: 1363–64 and see discussion above.

[106] Cf. Figueira 1985: 152: "Aithon [the name the speaker gives himself at Thgn. 1209] upholds his position against Arguris, who has experienced slavery, while the speaker, for all his other troubles, has not. Her name is an adaptation of the word for silver, **arguros**. The name is unattested otherwise, but compare Khrusis, the name of a courtesan (Lucian *Courtesan Dialogues* 299–301). Can Arguris be a generic figure who embodies the capacity for enslaving or for confounding social distinctions inherent in money?"

reference, we can make sense of the *impulse* to riddle within the poem's logical economy. For speaking and understanding riddles distinguishes the sympotic *sunetoi* from all others, in particular from the "simple, blunt playing" (ἀφελῶς παίζουσα) of the slave Arguris.[107] In addition, the riddle's content serves to remystify the symposiast's status, endowing him with an idealized homeland physically and conceptually inaccessible to his base interlocutor. Indeed, given the rhetorical effect of the riddle, we might go a step further and understand the "city on the Lethaian Plain" as a kenning for the symposium itself, playing on the usual association of wine and song with forgetfulness (λησμοσύνη).[108] In support of this interpretation, it might be suggested that κεκλιμένη in line 1216 is also a sympotic image: the city "reclines" on the Plain of Forgetfulness like a banqueter on his couch. Thus, having located Arguris squarely in the domain of the agora, the speaker constitutes his "homeland" as an inviolable sympotic paradise. The absolute distinction between them is reinforced by a final bit of wordplay: while the speaker enjoys the embrace of sympotic forgetfulness (λήθη), he consigns Arguris to "grievous slavery," transmuting her name by a pun from Arguris to ἀργαλέη.[109]

Thus, the discourses and practices of prostitution function as a lens through which we can bring into focus certain political and ideological conflicts, as well as the faultlines within those ideological formations.

[107] Cf. Nagy 1979; 1985; 1990b on *ainos* and the *sunetoi*, and for Theognis's articulation of this position, cf. Thgn. 681–82. Mark Griffith suggests to me that there might also be a pun on παίζουσα and παῖς meaning "slave," so that παίζουσα signifies essentially "slave talk" in contrast to the riddling discourse of the sympotic *sunetoi*. In this context we might note that the category of the *pais* (as eromenos) shares some of the ideological ambiguities of the *hetaira*. Thus, in most cases in the Theognidea, the *pais* is the object of the speaker's erotic interest, affection, and paternalistic advice, but, on occasion, the boy's bad behavior precipitates an articulation of his unequal status. Notice in particular the way in which Theognis concludes his famous reproach to Kyrnos at 237–54: αὐτὰρ ἐγὼν ὀλίγης παρὰ σεῦ οὐ τυγχάνω αἰδοῦς,/ ἀλλ᾿ ὥσπερ μικρὸν παῖδα λόγοις μ᾿ ἀπατᾷς (Thgn. 253–54, "But I don't happen upon [even] a little respect from you, but you deceive me with words just as if I were a little boy."). These lines unnervingly reveal the vulnerability of the *pais* and the asymmetrical relation that exists between erastes and eromenos. We might imagine that complications could arise from the tension between the erotic mystification of the boy's position and his unequal or uncertain status in the sympotic world of men. On the ideologically precarious position of the boy, see Foucault 1985: 187–214; Dover 1989: 39–109; on pederasty and the symposium, see Lewis 1985; Bremmer 1990.

[108] This solution to the riddle was suggested to me by Mark Griffith; for the association of wine and/or song with forgetfulness, cf. Hes. *Theog.* 55, 102; Alkaios fr. 70.9-10 V; Eur. *Bacchae* 279–85.

[109] For another literary text that enacts the same abrupt discursive shift from *hetaira* to *pornē* to ward off the anxieties of the male symposiasts, see Pindar fr. 122 SM (with discussion in Kurke 1996).

The opposition of *hetaira* and *pornē* operates within a complex network of economic, social, and political differentiation of middling and elitist traditions, whereby the aristocratic symposium invents the *hetaira* to shield itself from the public sphere, which it figures and traduces through the obscenity of the *pornē*. Egalitarian discourse, in contrast (at least by the fourth century) can embrace precisely what the aristocratic texts revile, celebrating the universal availability of *pornai* as an emblem and badge of democracy.[110] Yet even within the elitist construction, the representational category of the *hetaira* seems to involve its makers in an ideological double bind. Her sexual role at the symposium depends on difference and pulls against her complete assimilation to the male symposiasts. And if the category is created originally to constitute a pristine sympotic space, the pressures and anxieties of the male participants occasionally refashion her as a *pornē*, with all the disembedded economics attendant on that category. Of necessity, then, the trafficking of the agora infiltrates the symposium, as the celebrants struggle desperately to distinguish themselves from the women they have introduced, now become bearers of difference.

[110] I am referring here to the strand of democratic discourse represented by Philemon fr. 3 K.-A.; this is not to deny that there are other inflections of the system available within democratic ideology. Thus, for example, the pseudo-Demosthenic *Against Neaira* ([Dem.] 59) takes a different tack, systematically opposing the sacralized public space identified with the Basilinna to the foreign corruption of *hetaira* and *pornē* as interchangeable terms. We might see this system as an adaptation of the aristocratic model to democratic ends.

CHAPTER 6

Herodotus's Traffic in Women

The ideological indeterminacies that surround the category *hetaira*, at times even assimilating her to the *pornē*, form the context for understanding Herodotus's ethnographic manipulations of the *hetaira-pornē* binary. For if on occasion aristocratic poetry is forced into an inadvertent flip-flopping of terms, Herodotus seems to exploit the potential ambiguities of the system to destabilize this opposition entirely. Thus, at 1.94, the prostitution of the daughters of the Lydians goes appropriately with the invention of coinage and *kapēleia* to figure the extreme of a disembedded economy, but, as I have argued in Chapter 4, all these terms clash violently with the luxurious, war-loving Lydians of the historical account. The practice of prostitution challenges and exposes the pretensions of Lydian *habrosunē*, subverting this ideal of Greek elitist ideology.

A similar subversion of terms is at work in Herodotus's digression on Rhodopis. For if the Lydian ethnography works against the historical account by juxtaposing the lifestyle of *habrosunē* with the explicit economics of the *pornē*, Herodotus's narrative of Rhodopis systematically exposes the disembedded economics involved in the circulation of *hetairai* and thereby demystifies the aristocratic system of which the *hetaira* is a part. The fact that Herodotus uses the term *hetaira* (for the first time in Greek literature) suggests that he is unsympathetic to the institution, and that possibility is confirmed by the histor's ironic treatment of Rhodopis, her career, and the aristocrats who interact with her (for the sake of the discussion, I repeat here the relevant chapters):

> And this man [Mykerinos] left behind a pyramid much smaller than his father's, each side of three plethra short twenty feet, quadrangular, and up to half of Ethiopian stone. Various of the Greeks indeed say that it [the pyramid] belongs to the *hetaira* Rhodopis ('Ροδώπιος ἑταίρης γυναικὸς εἶναι), not speaking correctly. These then appear to me to speak not even knowing who Rhodopis was (for [otherwise] they would not have attributed it to her to make such a pyramid, the sort on which thousands of talents,

without number so to speak, were spent), and besides [not knowing] that Rhodopis flourished in the kingship of Amasis, but not in the kingship of this one [Mykerinos]. For Rhodopis existed very many years later than these kings who left behind these pyramids: she was from Thrace in origin, and slave of Iadmon, a Samian man of Hephaistopolis, and she was fellow-slave of Aesop, the fable-maker (Αἰσώπου τοῦ λογοποιοῦ). And in fact, this one [the owner of Aesop] *was* Iadmon, as he showed not least in this way: for when, with the Delphians summoning many times from an oracular command, whoever wished to accept recompense for the life of Aesop, no other appeared, but [only] another Iadmon, grandson of Iadmon, accepted it—thus [it's clear that] Aesop also belonged to Iadmon.

But Rhodopis came to Egypt when Xanthos the Samian conveyed her, but having come for business (κατ' ἐργασίην), she was freed for a lot of money by a Mytilenean man, Charaxos, son of Skamandronymos and brother of Sappho the melic poet (Σαπφοῦς τῆς μουσοποιοῦ). Thus indeed Rhodopis was freed and remained in Egypt and, being very attractive, acquired a great deal of money (as far as being a Rhodopis is concerned, but not so as to come to such a pyramid, at any rate). For it is possible still, even to this day, for everyone who wants to, to view a tenth of her property, so that there is no need to attribute great property to her. For Rhodopis desired to leave behind a monument of herself in Greece, having made as her object this, the sort of thing which does not happen to have been discovered and dedicated by any other in a temple—to dedicate this as her memorial at Delphi. So then, having converted a tenth of her property into many spits for oxen, made of iron, as many as a tenth contained for her, she was sending them away to Delphi. And they even now still are heaped behind the altar which the Chians dedicated, opposite the temple itself.

And somehow, the courtesans (ἑταῖραι) in Naukratis tend to be very attractive: for in the first place, this woman, concerning whom this story is told, became so glorious (κλεινή) indeed that even all the Greeks learned the name of Rhodopis, and in the second place, later than this one, the one whose name was Archedike became celebrated in song (ἀοίδιμος) throughout Greece (though less talked about than the former [ἧσσον δὲ τῆς ἑτέρης περιλεσχήνευτος]). But when Charaxos, having released Rhodopis, returned to Mytilene, Sappho abused him very much in lyric (ἐν μέλεϊ Σαπφὼ πολλὰ κατεκερτόμησέ μιν). And now, concerning Rhodopis I make an end. (Hdt. 2.134–135)

Herodotus first comes to the topic of Rhodopis because "certain Greeks" attribute to her (incorrectly) the pyramid of Mykerinos. This is in a sense to aggrandize the courtesan of Naukratis, equating her with Egyptian

kings and crediting her with a permanent memorial in this strange landscape.[1] Herodotus debunks this tradition with two very practical objections: the chronology is wrong and the scale of expenditure would have
been prohibitive for a woman of her profession. This latter issue particularly engages Herodotus's interest (as his discussion of her dedication at
Delphi makes clear), with the result that, within this narrative, the only
thing Rhodopis's monument signifies or could signify is how much money
she made at her trade.

Thus Herodotus completely undermines the meaning of the monument,
reducing it from foreign grandeur to a symbol of income and arithmetic.
In this respect, he assimilates the fantasy of Rhodopis's pyramid to a
story he has already told, of the pharaoh Cheops, builder of the great
pyramid, and his fundraising efforts:

> And [they say that] Cheops came to this point of baseness that, being in
> need of money he set his own daughter in a house [i.e., a brothel] and
> ordered her to charge however much money it was (for this wasn't said),
> and [they say] that she exacted the things ordered by her father, but that
> also she got the idea of leaving behind a monument for herself alone, and
> [so] she asked of each one who went in to her that he give her one stone.
> And from these stones they said was built the pyramid standing in the middle
> of the three, in front of the great pyramid, of which each side measures one-
> and-one-half plethra. (Hdt. 2.126)

As in the case of Alyattes' tomb in Lydia (1.93), this narrative of barbarian
monumentality seems to short-circuit the proper relations of long- and
short-term transactional orders. The monumental tomb of the king, because of its excessive scale, requires the prostitution of the king's own
daughter, thus collapsing what should be the apex of the long-term transactional order into the basest necessities of the short-term cycle. As part
and parcel of this terrible topsy-turvy system, the daughter's pyramid
stands as a monumental accounting-sheet, commemorating and quantify-
ing her forced prostitution.[2] In the process the king is exposed as a tyrant,
and his monumental ambitions as the extreme of depravity (notice how
Herodotus introduces the story: ἐς τοῦτο δὲ ἐλθεῖν Χέοπα κακότη-
τος . . .). Fewer than ten chapters later, when we encounter the legend
of Rhodopis's pyramid, it is nearly impossible not to think of the monu-

---

[1] We might see this as the beginning of the trend, begun in antiquity and continuing in
modern scholarship, to weave romantic fantasies around the "great courtesans." Cf. Reinsberg 1989: 80–86, Henry 1995 for critique of this tendency; I would simply note that such
romanticization serves the interests of elitist ideology.

[2] Cf. Steiner 1994: 138, von Reden 1997: 172–73 for discussion of this episode. Fehling
1989: 199 notes the repetition of the same motif in nearby stories.

ment of Cheops's daughter, and Herodotus helps us along by insisting on the issues of cost and quantification.

Having effectively demystified Rhodopis's legendary monument, Herodotus proceeds to undercut every element in the elitist construction of the *hetaira* through his deadpan narrative of who Rhodopis actually was. The histor tells us she was a Thracian and a slave, "the fellow-slave of Aesop the fable-maker," thus underscoring her foreignness and low-class origins. Indeed, in the fact that she was the fellow-slave of Aesop, we might see her low-class status figured also in terms of literary genre: the humble fables of Aesop stand very low in the hierarchy of genres, in contrast to the high art of "Sappho the melic poet" (Herodotus's language deliberately contrasts Aesop ὁ λογοποιός with Sappho ἡ μουσοποιός). The interconnection of literary forms and issues of social and economic status runs through Herodotus's portrait of Rhodopis and other courtesans—unsurprisingly, since melic poetry (along with visual representations) was the main vehicle for the propagation and dissemination of the mystified construct of the *hetaira*.

Herodotus's narrative continues in a relentlessly materialist vein: we are told that Rhodopis came to Egypt "for work" (κατ' ἐργασίην), that she was freed by Charaxos "for a great deal of money" (χρημάτων μεγάλων), and that she proceeded to make a lot of money (μεγάλα ... χρήματα) because she was very attractive. In context, the expression κατ' ἐργασίην is very deceptive: it has the appearance of a euphemism, but it is a euphemism almost universally used elsewhere for *pornai* (a *pornē* is *ergatis*, "a working girl," according to Archilochos, and a brothel *ergastērion*, "a workshop," in Attic slang).[3] Behind its apparent delicacy, this expression exposes the economic reality of the *hetaira*'s profession as "work" rather than pleasure and thereby erases the distinction between *hetaira* and *pornē*.

This materialist narrative then subsumes the account of Rhodopis's actual monument, the iron spits she dedicated at Delphi. Our narrator asserts that it was Rhodopis's ambition to dedicate "what no other had found and dedicated," and we might imagine that the motivation was also to insert her gift completely into a sacral economy of sacrifice. For Rhodopis seems actually to have made such an offering: archaeologists have found what they believe to be the base that supported the spits at Delphi. In context, a dedication of iron spits seems an attempt to demonetarize income, converting money earned in the short-term transactional order (by prostitution) into the long-term order of sacrifice and

[3] Arch. fr. 208 W; for *ergastērion*, cf. [Dem.] 59.67, Alkiphron fr. 5.1 and see Davidson 1997: 84, 87.

dedication.[4] If that was Rhodopis's intention, she is defeated by Herodotus's narrative, which resolutely *remonetarizes* her offering, dragging it back from the symbolic domain of sacrifice to real money. For the histor's only interest in the spits is that one can calculate from them a tithe of Rhodopis's net worth.

At this point, astonishingly, Herodotus digresses from his digression to observe that "the courtesans of Naukratis tend somehow to be very attractive" (2.135.5). Given the apparent irony of his presentation of Rhodopis, this seems a surprising narrative turn, but I would suggest that we must read this coda itself as tongue-in-cheek, as signaled by the emphatically repeated (and derogatory) denomination *hetairai*. Herodotus's irony here centers on the terms he chooses to characterize the courtesans' celebrity: Rhodopis became κλεινή, "glorious," while another courtesan, Archedike, was ἀοίδιμος, "sung of in song." Both of these are high poetic words, drawn from epic and lyric poetry, and extremely rare in prose.[5] The inconcinnity of Herodotus's use of them after his determinedly practical account of Rhodopis suggests parody, both of the mystifying rhetoric of the *hetaira* and of the aristocratic lyric poetry that purveyed it.[6] Thus κλεινός occurs only once more in Herodotus's text,

[4] For archaeological evidence of Rhodopis's dedication, see Mastrocostas 1954: 133, 444; Cook and Boardman 1954: 158; Robert and Robert 1955: 229. In spite of Herodotus's assertion that Rhodopis was inventing something new, there is evidence for several dedications of spits at Greek sanctuaries; see Jeffery 1990: 122–24; A. B. Lloyd 1988: 87 (*ad* Hdt. 2.135). For the circumscribed, elite context for the dedication of spits, see Strøm 1992; von Reden 1997: 173–74: "There is also some indication that [spits] referred to an archaic high-class social context connected, perhaps, with the near Eastern banquet tradition" (quote from p. 173).

[5] κλεινός does not occur in epic, but frequently in lyric poetry: cf. Alkman fr. 13d.4 *PMG*; Stes. fr. 184 *PMG*; Pindar O. 3.2, O. 6.6, O. 7.81, O. 9.14, P. 1.31, P. 4.280, P. 5.20, P. 8.23, P. 9.15, 112, N. 1.2, I. 2.19, I. 9.1, fr. 76.2; Bacch. 5.14, 8.32, 9.22, 11.78, etc. LSJ (s.v. κλεινός) notes that the adjective is "rare in prose," in the fifth century occurring only in this passage of Herodotus and twice in Plato (*Laws* 721c, *Soph.* 243a). ἀοίδιμος occurs once in Homer (*Iliad* 6.358) and occasionally in subsequent poetry: cf. Pindar O. 14.3, P. 8.59, N. 3.79, Paian 6.6, fr. 76.1; Arist. fr. 1/842 *PMG*, line 17. Herodotus uses this adjective in one other passage (2.79), to indicate that the Linus-Song is "sung" (ἀοίδιμος) in Phoenicia. Steiner 1994: 139, following Benardete 1969: 56, notes the importance of these terms, which she reads as opposing barbarian inscribed monuments with the living oral tradition of Greeks: "This is true public commemoration, the kind that lives on the lips of men and can give the lie to words inscribed in stone." While Steiner is right to emphasize these adjectives, I think she misses the irony of Herodotus's use of such high poetic terms for the celebrity of prostitutes. Cf. von Reden (1997: 174), who also reads Herodotus's remark positively, but apparently misapplies the adjective *epaphroditoi*, transferring it from the "attractive" courtesans of Naukratis to the "charm" of Rhodopis's dedication.

[6] Thus we might say that Herodotus's terms recall (and parody) Anakreon's mock-epic use of terms like πολύυμνος and ἀρίγνωτος to denounce *pornai*.

embedded in Simonides' epigram for the seer Megistias, who fell at Thermopylae: μνῆμα τόδε κλεινοῖο Μεγιστία . . . ("This is the monument of glorious Megistias," Hdt. 7.228.3).[7] Its use in a real, honorific funeral monument only underscores the incongruity of Rhodopis's "glory and fame throughout Greece," since she was famous, after all, as a prostitute. ἀοίδιμος, the term Herodotus applies to the aristocratically named Archedike, has a significant poetic pedigree: it occurs only once in Homer, when Helen in the *Iliad* asserts to Hektor that "Zeus put an evil doom upon us, so that we might be ἀοίδιμοι for men to come" (*Iliad* 6.357–58). The parallel is at once apt and absurd, since Helen is in some sense the prototype of every courtesan, but the weight of her claim for the Trojan War dwarfs and ridicules Herodotus's use of ἀοίδιμος for a prostitute's reputation.[8]

The suggestion of parody is confirmed by the last adjective in the sequence: "[Rhodopis] became so famous (κλεινή) that even all the Greeks learned her name, and second, later than this one, the woman named Archedike was sung of (ἀοίδιμος) throughout Greece, though less talked of in the men's clubs (περιλεσχήνευτος) than the former." After κλεινή and ἀοίδιμος, the abrupt shift in style to the pedestrian περιλεσχήνευτος can only be described as bathetic. This last term pulls us up short, exposing the absurd pretensions to poetic glory to which the other adjectives lay claim. More than that—Herodotus appropriates the περι- prefix of compounds like Anakreon's περιφόρητος, Theognis's περίδρομος, and περίπολις (preserved in Hesychios) and applies it incongruously to the reputation of *hetairai*. For the adjectives on which the term is modeled all bespeak the excessive circulation of the *pornē* in the public sphere, but Herodotus has transferred that derogatory sense to the circulation of *hetairai* in the men's clubs (λέσχαι). That is to say, he has deployed the discursive weapons of aristocratic poetry against its own pretensions, yet once more demystifying the privileged status and occluded exchanges of the *hetaira*.

On this reading, it is less surprising that Herodotus returns in the final lines of the chapter to Sappho and Charaxos, because, in a sense, lyric poetry has been his subject (along with *hetairai*) since 2.135.5, through the adjectives κλεινή and ἀοίδιμος. What is unusual, though unremarked by commentators, is the collocation ἐν μέλεϊ . . . κατεκερτόμησε, which is in terms of Greek poetic decorum nearly an oxymoron. κατακερτομέω

---

[7] In fact, κλεινός occurs once more as a variant reading in a hexameter oracle at Hdt. 5.92ε, though Hude in the OCT text prefers the reading κλειτοῖο.

[8] This reading of the poetic resonance of *aoidimos* is confirmed by its occurrence in the newly published Plataia Elegy of Simonides, where it designates the sacked city of Troy at the moment of the Greeks' departure (Simon. fr. 11.13 W²).

is a strong word, glossed by LSJ as "rail violently" and, in its one other occurrence in Herodotus, used to describe the defector Harpagos's mockery of the newly deposed Astyages (1.129). Its coupling with ἐν μέλεϊ suggests generic crisis, for such violent abuse might find a home in iambic poetry, or even on occasion in elegy, but should under no circumstances violate the domain of lyric.[9] By his mention of Sappho's lyric abuse, Herodotus puts light pressure on the ideological ambiguities we explored in the last section of Chapter 5. Presumably, Sappho abused her brother for the folly and expenditure of freeing the slave Rhodopis and in the process, we might imagine, used against her the rhetoric and topoi of the *pornē*.[10] But to do so, as we have seen in Anakreon and Theognis, is to allow the trafficking of the agora into the symposium, paradoxically opening that privileged space to all the concept of the *hetaira* was meant to shield it from. Even worse: to turn on women who attend the symposium and ridicule them as low-class threatens the stability of the terms. If they are low-class, why are they there in the first place? And isn't the poet who uses coarse terms to abuse them also demeaned and debased by that stylistic lapse? Sappho rails (like a breadwoman?) and is perhaps no better than the object of her vilification. Abuse taints all it touches. Herodotus exploits the unstable dance of identification and difference between *hetaira* and aristocrat to undermine the category of the *hetaira*, the pristine aristocratic symposium it helps to conjure, and the lyric poetry that is its preferred medium of expression.[11]

He then, finally, concludes: "Concerning Rhodopis, I make an end

---

[9] On the protocols and decorum of different metrical and generic forms in Greek poetry, see West 1974: 22–34; Kurke 1994.

[10] We may actually have a snippet of such lyric abuse preserved in *P. Oxy.* 1788, fr. 4.24–39, which runs in part: "What one gives to a whore (πόρναι) is the same as cast into the swell of the grey sea. . . . If a man keeps company with whores (π[όρν]αισιν), these things happen to him: after the business itself, he must inevitably [suffer] shame and much ruinous evil." This fragment is generally attributed to Alkaios on grounds of meter and style (= Alk. fr. 117b V, lines 21–40), but already in his review of Lobel's edition of Sappho, Fränkel 1928: 275 suggested that this might be a poem of Sappho's about her brother Charaxos and his unfortunate dalliance with the courtesan Rhodopis.

[11] Here, it may be that Herodotus's ironic identification of *hetaira* and aristocrat/poet is facilitated by Sappho's gender, both because she and Rhodopis are more alike to start with, and because in Greek terms the female is more readily associated with low-class, shrill abuse (Greek breadwomen, like our fishwives, are proverbial in this regard). Cf. the later tradition that makes Sappho herself (or a woman of the same name) into a *hetaira* (Aelian *VH* 12.19; Athen. *Deipn.* 13.596e; Seneca *Epist.* 88.37). Paul Cartledge suggests to me that Herodotus may have a more specific implicit target in this debunking of the *hetaira* and her aristocratic milieu—Perikles' paramour Aspasia and the discourses that surrounded her. While I think this quite probable, I would not want to limit Herodotus's critique to one particular individual, rather than the institutions and discourses that constituted the *hetaira* in general.

(πέπαυμαι)." In contrast to Greek aristocrats, who simply cannot stop talking—and singing—about *hetairai* (ἀοίδιμος, περιλεσχήνευτος), Herodotus demonstrates admirable restraint. In fact, with the absurdities and pretensions of the elitist system thoroughly unmasked, there is nothing more to say.

II. HERODOTEAN ALTERNATIVES: REIMAGINING THE PUBLIC SPHERE (Hdt. 1.196, 1.199)

In the opposition of *hetaira* and *pornē*, we have seen women functioning as bearers of meaning within a discourse that is essentially political. In particular, I have argued that the *pornē* serves as an emblem for the circulation of goods in the public sphere, while the *hetaira* is meant to shield and distinguish the aristocratic symposium from the traffic of the marketplace. A modern theorist has observed that the category "woman" is so available as a signifier that woman is a metaphorical "equivalent more universal than money,"[12] and this is nowhere more true than in ancient Greece. Indeed, I have tried to suggest in Chapter 5 that many of the conflicts and anxieties around coinage, competing exchange systems, and the political order of the city are displaced onto "woman" within the constructed opposition of *hetaira* and *pornē*. By charting the circulation of this "equivalent" in Greek texts, we can access indirectly ancient anxieties and discursive struggles over the functions and movements of that other signifying token, coinage. And if we expand the circle of our reading beyond the *hetaira-pornē* binary to other, stranger, forms of the traffic in women in Herodotus's ethnographies, we may find through them other figurations of the polis and the public sphere. For while Herodotus debunks and deconstructs the *hetaira-pornē* opposition, he simultaneously makes use of women and their circulation "allegorically" to imagine a positive alternative to the standoff of symposium and agora.

Thus I should like to read Herodotus's narrative of two different types of circulation of women in his account of the customs of Babylon as his alternative to the discredited opposition of courtesan and whore. As W. Martin Bloomer has noted, the two customs form a characteristically Herodotean pair, singled out as contrasting superlatives: the "most beautiful" and "most shameful" *nomoi*, as the histor editorializes them.[13] Herodotus first offers a detailed account of what he regards as the Babylonians' noblest usage:

---

[12] de Lauretis 1987: 45, quoting Lea Melandri.
[13] Bloomer 1993: 43 on "superlative *nomoi*."

And this following is their wisest [custom] (ὁ μὲν σοφώτατος ὅδε) in our opinion, which I learn that the Enetai of the Illyrians also use. In each of the villages (κατὰ κώμας ἑκάστας) they used to do these following things once each year. Whenever the young women were ripe for marriage, whenever they would lead all these together, they used to collect them and lead them to a single place (ἐς ἓν χωρίον), and a throng of men stood around them. And setting them up, each of them, one by one, a herald would sell them (πωλέεσκε), first the most attractive one of all, but afterwards, whenever she was sold, having fetched a great sum of money (εὑροῦσα πολλὸν χρυσίον πρηθείη), he would auction another—she who was the most attractive after that one. But they were selling them for marriage [lit. for cohabitation; not for concubinage]. And however many wealthy Babylonians (ὅσοι μὲν δὴ ... εὐδαίμονες) were looking to marry, striving to outdo each other they were buying up the pretty girls; but however many men of the people (ὅσοι δὲ τοῦ δήμου) were looking to marry, these had no need of an attractive appearance, but they would take the uglier girls together with cash (χρήματά τε καὶ αἰσχίονας παρθένους ἐλάμβανον). For when indeed the herald had gone through selling the most attractive girls, then he would set up the ugliest girl—or if one of them was crippled—and he would auction her off, until he attached her to the man who demanded the least—[that is,] whoever was willing to marry her when he had gotten the least amount of money (ἐλάχιστον χρυσίον λαβών). But the money would come from the attractive girls, and thus the pretty ones gave away [i.e., dowered] the ugly and crippled girls. And no man was allowed to give his daughter in marriage to whomever he wished, nor was the one who bought the girl allowed to lead her away without surety, but he was required to establish a surety that he would marry her, and [only] on these terms could he lead her away. But if they should not get along, the custom was established to return the money [with the girl]. And it was also permitted for a man to come from another village to buy, if he so wished. This then was their noblest custom (ὁ μὲν νυν κάλλιστος νόμος), though it has not still continued in existence now, but they have recently invented some other thing. For since, having been conquered in war, they were ruined and their homes were destroyed, every one of the demos, lacking the means of livelihood, prostitutes his female children (πᾶς τις τοῦ δήμου βίου σπανίζων καταπορνεύει τὰ θήλεα τέκνα). (Hdt. 1.196)

From this extended narrative, Herodotus moves to the "second wisest custom" of the Babylonians (to which we shall return) and then concludes his brief ethnography with what he calls their basest practice:

And this following is the most shameful of the customs the Babylonians have (ὁ δὲ δὴ αἴσχιστος τῶν νόμων ἐστὶ τοῖσι Βαβυλωνίοισι ὅδε). Every local woman must sit in the temple of Aphrodite once in her life and have sex with a stranger. And many women not deeming it right to mix with the rest, since they are proud on account of wealth (πολλαὶ δὲ καὶ οὐκ ἀξιεύμεναι ἀναμίσγεσθαι τῇσι ἄλλῃσι οἷα πλούτῳ ὑπερφρονέουσαι), having driven to the temple upon chariots take up their position in covered carts, and a great train of servants follows behind them. But the majority do it thus: many women sit in the precinct of Aphrodite wearing a crown of string around their heads. For as some leave, others arrive. And straight lanes just like roads lead through the women, through which strangers, going through, pick out [women]. Whenever a woman sits there, she does not depart home until some stranger has cast money on her knees and had sex with her outside the temple (ἢ τίς οἱ ξείνων ἀργύριον ἐμβαλὼν ἐς τὰ γούνατα μειχθῇ ἔξω τοῦ ἱροῦ). But as he casts it, he must say this: "I invoke the goddess Mylitta." And Mylitta is what the Assyrians call Aphrodite. And the money (τὸ ἀργύριον) is however much it is in amount, for it will not be refused; since it is not lawful. For this money is holy (γίνεται γὰρ ἱρὸν τοῦτο τὸ ἀργύριον). And she follows the first one who casts [money at her] and she does not refuse anyone (οὐδὲ ἀποδοκιμᾷ οὐδένα). And whenever she has had sex, having discharged her sacred duty to the goddess, she departs home, and from this time on, there is no amount you can give her big enough to take her. And however many are possessed of form and size, they depart quickly; but however many are ugly, they wait a long time, unable to fulfill the law. For in fact, some of them wait three or four years time. And in some parts also of Kypros there is a custom very similar to this. (Hdt. 1.199)

These remarkable narratives clearly belong together. Beyond being labeled "best" and "worst" custom, both concern the exchange of women for money, and in both Herodotus goes to great lengths to differentiate the experiences of rich and poor, attractive and ugly. What is it precisely then that makes them polar opposites? Why does the histor endorse one system of circulation and find the other abhorrent? What finally is the purpose of the entire account, with its programmatic oppositions projected onto the customs of Babylon?

For there can be little doubt that these narratives are projections. Scholars of Babylonian history and culture find no native evidence for bride auctions, while temple prostitution was practiced—if it was practiced at all—only by a particular group of women (not, as Herodotus claims, universally).[14] What function did these fantasized Eastern customs

---

[14] On both customs, see How and Wells 1928: I.150–51; Baumgartner 1950: 79–83; Pembroke 1967: 4–5 (quoted in text); MacGinnis 1986: 76–78; on bride auction alone, see McNeal 1988: Beard and Henderson 1997 challenge the critical orthodoxy on sacred prostitution, questioning whether the practice ever existed anywhere in the ancient Near East. They suggest that scholars have simply been duped into finding evidence to support what is essentially a fantasy of ancient Greek ethnography. The main debate about the

play within the Greek imaginary? And more particularly, why is it the Babylonians to whom bride auction and universal temple prostitution are attributed, rather than (say) the Lydians or Persians? In answer to these questions, Simon Pembroke has suggested that these anecdotes form part of a larger system through which Herodotus represents the "Oriental subjection of women":

> For Herodotus there are three continents—Europe, Asia and Libya. . . . Asia stands for slavery, Darius and Xerxes for the attempt to extend it into Europe. Something of these categories can be felt in the background when Herodotus comes to describe the treatment of women in Persia and Babylon. For the tendency of these descriptions, which can to some extent be isolated from their factual content, for which there is independent evidence, is to represent the highest condition to which a woman can aspire as inferior to that of a free woman in Greece. . . . The same tendency can be seen in his statement that at least once in a lifetime, every woman in Babylon—not just a particular class of them, though this is what the Babylonian texts indicate— has to undergo prostitution in a temple; or again, more clearly still, when he says that the Babylonians sell their daughters—as wives, not concubines . . . —by annual public auction. . . . Herodotus' account of marriage in Asia, then, shows a consistent tendency to exaggerate the subjection of women.[15]

While this interpretation has the advantage of acknowledging that it is Greek fantasy we must account for, Pembroke does not really engage the particularities of Herodotus's ethnography. "Oriental subjection" covers a host of different customs (including Persian polygamy and Lydian prostitution), without really explaining the distinctiveness of Babylon. More problematic still, Pembroke treats all Herodotus's descriptions as equally demeaning and oppressive to women, but that ignores the histor's contrasting evaluations of temple prostitution and bride auctions, as well as his pointed contrast between then (public auctions) and now (individual prostitution; Hdt. 1.196).[16]

Babylonian logos seems to be whether or not Herodotus actually visited Babylon himself; pro: How and Wells 1928: I.135–36; Ravn 1942; Baumgartner 1950; MacGinnis 1986; Pritchett 1993: 235–42; contra: Sayce 1883: xxviii–xix, 104; Fehling 1989: 243; Rollinger 1993: This debate is irrelevant to my discussion here, since even Herodotus's staunchest supporters (like Baumgartner, MacGinnis, and Pritchett) are forced to acknowledge that his account of Babylonian history and customs is dubious at best. This suggests that, whether Herodotus's account was based on autopsy, cribbed from an earlier description (e.g. Hekataios), or simply invented, his narrative is informed by—and revelatory of— Greek interests and obsessions.

[15] Pembroke 1967: 4–5.

[16] Cf. Redfield 1985: 109–10; Steiner 1994: 165: "The all-pervasive role of money, and its power to transform a man or woman into a commodity or sign, takes its place alongside other distinctions between Herodotus's worlds of East and West. On several occasions the narrator refers to the foreign practice of selling women, whether to accumulate money for

I suggest that, in a sense, Pembroke's mistake is in taking these narratives at face value and imagining that they are actually "about" women, their status, and their circulation. Instead, I would contend, we must understand Herodotus's women as signifiers and the three different forms of exchange described (bride auctions, private prostitution, and temple prostitution) as figurations of different economies or systems of circulation. Thus, we must look elsewhere for the motor that generates these narratives. The comparison of Herodotus's account with that of Strabo, writing in the first century B.C.E., confirms the "allegorical" reading I propose, for the later ethnographer's précis underscores by contrast the issues that obsess the fifth-century chronicler. Strabo appears to derive his account of the customs of Babylon from Herodotus, but his compressions and elisions reveal the gap between the two historians, four hundred years apart.[17] Thus in Strabo's account of the bride auctions, the Babylonians "appoint three men who are wise as rulers of each tribe (φυλῆς), who lead together the marriageable girls and auction them off to bridegrooms, always [selling] the more highly prized first" (ἀεὶ τὰς ἐντιμοτέρας πρώτας; Strabo 16.1.20/745). Strabo has preserved nothing of what Herodotus seems to find particularly appealing about this custom: the complex system whereby the pretty girls dower the ugly ones by an elaborate calculus of communal exchange. Strabo furthermore describes this custom in the present tense, as still existing, while Herodotus adumbrates a whole narrative of change and decline through the shift from public bride auction to private prostitution.[18] A little later in his account, when Strabo offers his version of temple prostitution, the narrative changes are equally telling:

> For all the Babylonian women it is a custom according to some oracle to have sex with a stranger, when they have come to some temple of Aphrodite with a great mob of attendants (ἀφικομέναις μετὰ πολλῆς θεραπείας καὶ

---

their dowries, or as a means of disposing of the less attractive brides in a community (1.93.4, 1.196.2–5)." Steiner rightly emphasizes the issues of money and commodification, but again, like Pembroke, she offers a single sweeping account of "Eastern practices" that explains neither the particularity of Babylonian customs nor Herodotus's enthusiasm for the system of bride auction.

[17] For Strabo's dependence on Herodotus, I follow How and Wells 1928: I.150; MacGinnis 1986: 83; Fehling 1989: 146n. 6. Other scholars have argued that Herodotus and Strabo are both drawing on a common source, which is probably Hekataios (thus Baumgartner 1950: 71, 80). As with the issue of Herodotus's autopsy of Babylon (to which this issue is related), I would contend that it does not affect my argument which reconstruction of sources is correct. For even if Herodotus and Strabo are drawing on Hekataios, the fact that they choose to pick out and emphasize very different elements suggests that each account is symptomatic of its own historical and cultural context. Furthermore, as a matter of methodology, it seems to me more productive to read and analyze the details of the text we have (Herodotus), rather than attempting to reconstruct the text we do not have (Hekataios).

[18] Cf. Beard and Henderson 1997: 488, 491–93.

ὄχλου). And each is crowned with string. But a man, approaching and having deposited on her knees however much money is acceptable (ὅσον καλῶς ἔχει ἀργύριον), has sex with her, leading her away from the precinct. And the money is considered sacred to Aphrodite. (Strabo 16.1.20/745)

Strabo has generalized one characteristic of Herodotus's "wealthy" (a large crowd of attendants) to all the women who must submit to temple prostitution, while he elides the earlier account's elaborate four-way distinction of women as wealthy or demotic, attractive or ugly. Along with this, he has changed Herodotus's random amount of money ("However much the men offer, it will not be refused") to "however much is acceptable," almost implying a standard price. These changes combine to make Herodotus's narrative more palatable, for part of its disturbing effect inheres in the painfully inequitable distribution of resources (both money and looks) on the women's side, *and* the lack of correlation between the indiscriminate amount of money and the qualities of the woman it buys.

In each case, the contrast between the two accounts shows Herodotus actively thinking about and thinking through the circulation of goods in civic space, within a context of unequal distribution of property and status. Unsurprisingly, what fascinates the fifth-century chronicler, but has become irrelevant to his first-century imitator, is the imagination of resources set *es meson*, circulating in the public sphere. Thus the best and worst Babylonian *nomoi*—bride auction and temple prostitution— must be understood as programmatic positive and negative figurations of that distinctively Greek space, τὸ μέσον.

In this respect, an interpretation of these two *nomoi* must be set within the larger context of Herodotus's whole account of Babylon, for in these chapters he figures Babylon obsessively as the antitype of the Greek city—a sprawling metropolis with no communal center. I begin with Herodotus's narrative of how Kyros first captured Babylon. Kyros gains access to the city by diverting the course of the Euphrates and sending his troops in the river gates. They catch the Babylonians unawares, and proceed to wreak havoc:

> And now the Persians were present for them unexpectedly. And because of the size of the city, as is said by its inhabitants, when those around the edges of the city had been captured, those of the Babylonians living in the center did not know that they were taken (τῶν περὶ τὰ ἔσχατα τῆς πόλιος ἑαλωκότων τοὺς τὸ μέσον οἰκέοντας τῶν Βαβυλωνίων οὐ μανθάνειν ἑαλωκότας), but (since they happened to be having a festival) they were dancing and enjoying themselves at this time, until they found out with a vengeance. And thus Babylon was taken then for the first time. (Hdt. 1.191.6)

The problem with Babylon is that it is simply too big—those at the center have no idea what's happened at the periphery. They continue to celebrate, ignorant that their city has already fallen. Thus Babylon's mammoth size negates its civic identity. In this detail, Aristotle follows and amplifies Herodotus, making explicit the political concerns that animate the historian's account. For the philosopher cites Babylon as the paradigm case of an overlarge city—in Greek terms, a nation (*ethnos*) masquerading as a polis:

> And similarly in the case of human beings inhabiting the same location, [if one asks] when the city should be considered one. For it is surely not by the fact of its walls—it would be possible to build a single wall around the Peloponnese. Babylon is perhaps a city of this sort, or any which has the dimensions of a nation rather than a city; at any rate, they say that its capture was not noticed in a certain part of the city for three days. (Arist. *Pol.* 1276a24–30, trans. C. Lord 1984)

Aristotle's "three days" looks like an elaboration of Herodotus's report of the fall of Babylon. But notice that both historian and philosopher use Babylon in the same way, as a figure for vast urbanization devoid of civic coherence.

It is this fantasy of an *ethnos* masquerading as a polis that accounts for Herodotus's extraordinary figures for the length and height of the walls of Babylon. The histor first introduces Babylon with enormous emphasis on its size, informing us that the city constituted a square, surrounded by a wall of 480 stades in length (= 56 miles, Hdt. 1.178.2). He goes on to describe in detail the city's massive fortifications and tells us that the height of the wall is 200 royal cubits (= 335 ft., Hdt. 1.178.3). Modern excavations, unsurprisingly, have revealed that Herodotus's figures are vastly exaggerated: the outer wall of Babylon had a circuit of perhaps 10 miles, while it is not physically possible that it stood more than 70–75 feet in height.[19] Nonetheless, this fantasy of Babylon as megalopolis endured tenaciously, for, as John MacGinnis notes, the entire tradition of Greek history and ethnography followed Herodotus. Thus Strabo, Ktesias, Kleitarchos, and Quintus Curtius all give us similarly exaggerated figures for the length of the walls of Babylon (though none is as large as Herodotus's estimates).[20]

But it is not just Babylon's extraordinary size that plays obsessively

---

[19] For the inaccuracy of Herodotus's measurements, see Sayce 1883: 102; Ravn 1942: 37–38, 93–94; Baumgartner 1950: 74; MacGinnis 1986: 68–69.

[20] MacGinnis 1986: 69; cf. Sayce 1883: 102. That Herodotus's out-of-scale vision of "Oriental" magnificence made an impression already in the fifth century is suggested by Aristophanes' extended parody of Herodotus's narrative in his description of the building of the walls of Cloudcuckooland (*Birds* 1124–63; produced in 414 B.C.E.); for the allusion, cf. Fornara 1971a.28–29. In a sense, Aristophanes' parody makes explicit where Herodotus's Babylon stands—constructed in the never-neverland of Greek fantasy.

through Herodotus's Babylonian logos. I would return for a moment to Herodotus's narrative of Kyros's capture of the city to focus on the histor's use of the phrase *to meson*. Here the mention of *to meson* controverts our expectations; instead of uniting the citizens, the constitution of center and periphery divides them. Those in the center (who, in Greek terms, should know most what is going on) celebrate, ignorant that their city has already fallen. I would suggest that this paradoxical mention of *to meson* is emblematic of the concerns of the Babylonian logos as a whole. These chapters provide the histor a way of thinking by contrast about the meaning of civic community and the setting of goods and power *es meson*. Again and again, the narrator seems to play on our expectations to be told what occupies the city's "center." Thus, we learn first that the enormous walled city is split by the River Euphrates, so that, as Herodotus puts it, "the river divides the middle of it" (τὸ γὰρ μέσον αὐτῆς ποταμὸς διέργει, Hdt. 1.180.1).

Then, for each side, we are told what is ἐν μέσῳ ("in the middle"):

> And in each part of the city had been built in the middle (ἐν μέσῳ), on the one side, the royal palace with a great and strong ring wall, and on the other side, the bronze-gated precinct of Zeus Baal, which still existed even to my time, being a square of two stades on each side. And in the middle of the precinct (ἐν μέσῳ δὲ τοῦ ἱροῦ) is built a solid tower, one stade in length and breadth, and upon this tower another tower stands, and another on top of this, up to eight towers. And an ascent to these has been made holding from the outside in a circle around all the towers. But for a person in the middle of the ascent (μεσοῦντι δέ κου τῆς ἀναβάσιος) there is a landing and benches to rest on, on which those ascending can sit and take a break. And in the last tower there is a great temple; and in the temple is set a great couch, well appointed, and a golden table is set beside it. And no image is housed there, nor does anyone of mortals pass the night there except a single woman of the locals, whichever one the god chooses from all, as the Chaldaians say, who are priests of this god. And these same men say (saying things not believable to me) that the god himself comes to the temple and sleeps upon the couch, just as in Egyptian Thebes in the same way, as the Egyptians say (for in fact there also a woman sleeps in the temple of Theban Zeus, and both women are said to go to the company of no men). . . (Hdt. 1.181.2–182.2)

In Herodotus's narrative, each half of Babylon resembles an elaborate set of Chinese boxes, structure within structure, and we search in vain for an agora or communal space constituted *es meson*. Herodotus's topographical description has long troubled scholars looking for the "real" Babylon, since that city is known to have had at least three major palaces (two on the same side as what seems to be Herodotus's Ziggurat) and two major temple complexes (one on each side of the river).[21] And yet, we can see the appeal of Herodotus's highly schematic rendering, which fills the middle of each half of the city with a different form of absolute authority (royal and divine), emblematized by the towering structures that occupy what would have been the level space of the agora in a Greek city.[22]

We can even perhaps go a step further in this programmatic contrast with Greek civic space, for scholars of Babylonian religion have concluded that a Sacred Marriage between a god and a mortal woman has no parallel in native religious practice.[23] This rite, which Herodotus locates in the temple at the center of the tower, at the center of the precinct, at the center of one-half of Babylon, has much more in common with *Greek* religious practice. Thus it resembles nothing so much as the Athenian *hieros gamos* in which the Basilinna, the wife of the Archon Basileus, was united with the god Dionysus during the festival of the Anthesteria.[24] In Athens this ritual union took place in the Boukoleion, near the Prytaneion in the Agora.[25] But if it is modeled on something like the Athenian *hieros gamos*, Herodotus's account of the Babylonian rite also offers significant contrasts. In Athens the woman is the wife of a city magistrate chosen by lot, who owes her office to her husband's civic position; in Babylon, according to what Herodotus tells us, the god himself "chooses" a local woman (no mention of father, brother, or husband). In Athens the Sacred Marriage forms part of an elaborate three-day civic festival, in which the Basilinna's activities can be taken as the ultimate emblem of Athenian-ness;[26] in Babylon we are offered no context whatsoever for the union, though it seems to occur in secret. Finally, the Athenian ritual

[21] On the topography of Babylon and the problems of Herodotus's account, see Sayce 1883: 103; How and Wells 1928: I.140–41; Baumgartner 1950: 75–76; MacGinnis 1986: 70–74.

[22] For evidence that the Greeks thought in terms of such symbolic topography, cf. Aristotle's remarks on the geographic features suitable for different regimes: "With regard to fortified places, what is advantageous is not the same for all regimes. For example, a fortified height is characteristic of oligarchy and monarchy; levelness is characteristic of democracy; neither of these is characteristic of aristocracy, but rather a number of strong places." (*Pol.* 1330b17–21; trans. C. Lord 1984).

[23] MacGinnis 1986: 72–73 notes three different possibilities for Sacred Marriage rites: (1) between a god and a goddess; (2) between a goddess and the king; (3) between a god and a priestess. Babylonian rituals generally either unite two gods or a goddess and a mortal man (the king); but, according to MacGinnis, there is no parallel for the union of a god and a mortal woman in Neo-Babylonian times.

[24] Sources: [Arist.] *Ath. Pol.* 3.5; [Dem.] 59.73, 76; Hesychios s.v. Διονύσου γάμος. For modern discussions of the *hieros gamos* within the context of the Anthesteria, see Deubner 1966: 100–110; Parke 1977: 110–13; Burkert 1983: 232–38; 1985: 239–41.

[25] [Arist.] *Ath. Pol.* 3.5.

[26] As they are treated by [Dem.] 59.72–111.

takes place not on the Acropolis, but in a humble building in the Agora, a topographical feature that Walter Burkert takes to have social and political significance:

> The role of "king" and "queen" is doubtless very ancient, even if not directly rooted in the Mycenaean kingship; in the Linear B texts the *basileus* is not in fact the king but a master of a guild, especially the head of the smiths. So too the Anthesteria festival has nothing to do with the Acropolis, nothing to do with Erechtheus; it is more likely that it always belonged to the peasants and craftsmen.[27]

In marked contrast, the Babylonian union takes place in private, in the topmost chamber of the towering Ziggurat that occupies the city's center. Thus, in both spatial and ritual terms, religious practice seems to displace and replace communal interests, opposing Greek civic religion with Eastern theocracy.

Herodotus continues to play on our expectations when he informs us that, among her major building projects, Queen Nitokris engineered a great bridge joining the two halves of the city:

> Then, where it was somehow most in the middle of the city (κατὰ μέσην κου μάλιστα τὴν πόλιν), she built a bridge with the stones which she had dug up, binding them with iron and lead. And she used to stretch upon it, whenever it was day, quadrangular boards of wood, upon which the Babylonians made the crossing. But at nights they used to take these boards away on account of this—in order that they not go to and fro and steal from each other (ἵνα μὴ διαφοιτέοντες κλέπτοιεν παρ᾽ ἀλλήλων). . . . And thus the ditch becoming a marsh seemed to exist opportunely and a bridge was prepared for the citizens (καὶ τοῖσι πολιήτῃσι γέφυρα ἦν κατεσκευασμένη). (Hdt. 1.186.2–4)

Herodotus's narrative here playfully gives with one hand and takes away with the other. We are first asked to imagine a bridge as the midmost point of the city, a communal space joining the two halves and enabling them to function as a single polis. But almost as soon as this image has been conjured up, the narrative whisks it away: the bridge is made impassable at night, its common space removed to prevent those on either side from crossing over and "stealing from each other."[28] No commonality of civic trust exists between the two halves; instead, they must be fortified

---

[27] Burkert 1985: 241.

[28] Excavators have found Herodotus's bridge: see Ravn 1942: 74–76; Baumgartner 1950: 75; MacGinnis 1986: 75. MacGinnis notes, "If there is any truth in the story of the flooring being taken up at night, it is . . . to allow the passage of ships," while Baumgartner indulgently terms Herodotus's account of the motivation for removing the flooring "reichlich naiv."

against each other like separate principalities, and the bridge that links them by day divides them by night. Herodotus perhaps underscores the irony by his one and only reference to the Babylonians as "citizens" in his concluding sentence: "And thus . . . a bridge was prepared for the citizens."

It is in this context of Babylon as anti-city that we can understand Herodotus's description of temple prostitution and his aversion to it. For at first glance, it almost looks like the setting of goods (here women) *es meson*, but through a strange distorting mirror. Thus, it is a universal requirement that the women make themselves publicly available, and they sit in orderly fashion, disposed geometrically like the streets of a democratic polis.[29] In fact, this custom functions as a grotesque parody of the public sphere of a Greek city, for here divine law displaces and even controverts civic integrity. The city's interest is the reproduction of the citizen body through lawful marriage and the strict regulation of citizen wives; here, divine ordinance (θέμις) requires the random sexual congress of citizen wives with "strangers" who can be of any quality and any rank. Indeed, part of the strange, anti-civic quality of this scene is the complete elision of the patriarchal household from Herodotus's description: there is no mention of fathers, husbands, or brothers of the women in the temple of Aphrodite, and in contrast to normal Greek practice, the women handle the money and transactions themselves, without the intervention of male *kurioi*. Finally, of course, they do this in the service of the goddess Mylitta, so that we might say that the inversion of theocracy is figured and underscored by gender inversion.[30]

To signify the civic damage done by such aleatory mixing of citizen wives and "strangers," Herodotus uses the verb ἀποδοκιμάω (the woman can "refuse no man"), which, in its more common form ἀποδοκιμάζω, is the technical term in Athenian legal parlance for rejecting as unfit a candidate for office.[31] The use of this pregnant term here underscores the ways in which divine law eclipses civic sanctions: in the temple of Aphrodite, there is no possibility for public adjudication, nor for civic intervention to regulate the worth of members of the community. We have already seen this displacement of civic by divine authority figured in Herodotus's elaborate description of the Temple of Zeus Baal, occupying the center

---

[29] For democratic street plans, cf. Hippodamos of Miletus (as described by Arist. *Pol.* 1267b22–33, 1330b21–24); Lengauer 1989; Lévêque and Vidal-Naquet 1996: 81–85.

[30] It is worth noting in this context that, although Herodotus promises us a full discussion of the kings of Babylon in his "Assyrian logos," in what we have, he only describes the reigns and works of two *queens*. Is this another figuration of the strangeness of Babylon through gender inversion?

[31] For the technical use of *apodokimazein*, see Lysias 13.10, Din. 2.10, Dem. 25.30; Herodotus uses the same verb at 6.130 to refer to Kleisthenes of Sikyon's rejection of all but one of the suitors of his daughter Agariste.

of one-half of the great city (1.181.2–5). It is as if the description of
temple prostitution allows Herodotus to play out in horrific detail the
implications of the anti-civic theocracy the Ziggurat of Zeus Baal represents in spatial terms.[32]

We might say that Herodotus's depiction of temple prostitution attempts to envision a long-term transactional order utterly antithetical to
the Greek civic ideal. For if, as we have suggested, the sixth and fifth
centuries saw the city's attempt to displace the divine as the apex of the
long-term transactional order, and this forms the context for the invention
of coinage, Herodotus imagines Babylon as the terrifying inverse of the
Greek system. Here, instead, the circulation of goods in what looks like
a common space negates community. The arbitrary and random exchange
of women and money as universal equivalents produces atomization and
alienation instead of the commonality their circulation is intended to forge
in Greek civic space. Thus the possibility of *universal* temple prostitution
(where the circulation of women and money figure each other) affords
Herodotus the context for fantasizing the workings of money without a
civic framework, playing out all the worst features of a disembedded
money economy. In this scenario the amount of money is irrelevant;
money has become a pure sign, yet the civic community cannot regulate
its value.[33] Worse than that, universal circulation exacerbates preexisting
divisions within the community, as each group serves its own private
interests (and this process particularly engages the histor's attention). At
the same time, this custom also alienates groups with different *natural*
gifts, liberating the attractive women quickly, while the ugly ones must
wait in isolation to fulfill the divine ordinance.[34]

This nightmare vision, in turn, accounts for Herodotus's highly positive
valuation of the custom of bride auction, for this *nomos* functions as the
programmatic opposite of the grotesque disembedded economy of temple

---

[32] Notice the parallels between the two descriptions: (1) Zeus, like the *xeinoi* of 1.199,
"chooses a girl from the locals" (the only two occurrences of ἐπιχώριος in the Babylonian
logos); (2) in both cases, the woman is completely disembedded from her proper place
within the patriarchal household—that is, both descriptions suppress any mention of the
chosen woman's father, husband, or brothers. Both can be read as forms of temple prostitution or sacred marriage (for this interpretation of the rite at 1.199, see Stern 1989: 18).
For the notion that the description of temple prostitution signifies theocracy, cf. Benardete
1969: 26: "The most beautiful law levels as it preserves the natural differences in beauty,
the ugliest law, *which is a sacred law*, heightens as it destroys the same natural differences."
(my emphasis)

[33] Cf. Steiner 1994: 165; Beard and Henderson 1997: 499n.33: "*Precisely* what mattered
was that the value of the coin did *not* matter."

[34] Cf. Saxonhouse 1996: 43: "There is no attempt by the law to erase natural inequalities
in beauty. Instead, custom works to perpetuate those inequalities and is thus judged the
ugliest of customs."

prostitution. Notice first that the bride auctions took place (when they took place) not in the city of Babylon, but in the outlying villages (κατὰ κώμας ἑκάστας): Herodotus here contrasts the inhuman size of Babylon itself with the more manageable (that is to say, more Greek) scale of the village communities. In contrast to temple prostitution, this practice does not enact random, anonymous sex with strangers but promotes legitimate marriage (Herodotus is very emphatic that no one can lead a girl away without providing surety that he will marry her). And where temple prostitution atomizes the different groups of women—rich, poor, attractive, and ugly—the village practice brings together the women and the whole community through their circulation (notice that, according to the histor, no man is allowed to give his daughter away privately). As one last element in this programmatic contrast, we might note that while the word Herodotus uses for "specie" or "money" in the context of temple prostitution is *argurion* (three times), in the context of bride auction, the histor consistently uses *chrusion* (four times). We can offer a practical explanation for this divergence: the purchase of a woman for life is understandably more expensive than the outlay for a single act of sex. And yet I am unwilling to limit the reading to pragmatics; in the language of metals, Herodotus's contrast of gold and silver signals unequivocally the histor's evaluation—the justice of the one custom and the *hubris* of the other.

In light of this evaluative coding of metals, we might go even further and read bride auction as the depiction of a *competing* long-term transactional order. If temple prostitution figures Eastern theocracy, the village circulation of women constitutes the civic community and its interests as paramount. Thus Simon Pembroke observes that this custom is almost certainly Herodotus's fantasy, and that it requires a peculiarly Greek institution to function:

> In this case there is a mass of evidence from Babylon to prove that they did nothing of the kind; but it can almost be shown from the text of Herodotus himself. When Cyrus received a message from the Spartans ordering him not to interfere with any Greek city, he expressed his contempt for them by saying "I have never yet been afraid of any men who have a set place in the middle of their city where they come together to cheat each other and forswear themselves"; and Herodotus, having put the words into his mouth, goes on to explain that unlike the Greeks, who buy and sell in market-places, the Persians do not conduct business in this way and in fact do not have such things as market-places at all. A century of excavations has shown that this is perfectly true, for Persia and Babylon alike. . . . Yet marriage in Babylon, as Herodotus describes it, does seem to require a market-place. Even so, he cannot bring himself to set the scene in one; he has the girls rather

vaguely "collected together in one place" instead. On his own showing, the institutions needed to make the practice feasible were Greek.[35]

Pembroke here limits the category of the Greek agora, to which he refers, to its economic, market functions, but in fact what makes Herodotus's narrative here so distinctive is his imagination of this phantom agora primarily as a *political* space. For, by this account, it is not simply that the marriageable girls are collected together "in one place" and sold (as Strabo has it), but that there is a communal regulation of the circulation of goods and of value so as to distribute resources equitably. The men who are rich contribute lavishly from their private fortunes in order to secure wives whose attractiveness befits their standing; in exchange, the poor get financial assistance from the community as well as partners whose appearance is commensurate with their lowly position. We can almost read this narrative as a schematic model of the Greek liturgy system: the city exploits the rich and their competition for prestige in the service of the whole community. If women and money figure each other, as I have claimed in the case of temple prostitution, this village practice represents a money economy properly embedded in civic structures: the rich gladly render their money to the city in order to acquire attractive wives as badges of honor, and these women function in future as "visible wealth," to mark out the elite within the city.[36]

Lest the reader be skeptical that civic order can be represented entirely through the circulation of women, we should note a striking parallel for Herodotus' account in an obscure plan for constituting the ideal city, critiqued by Aristotle in the *Politics*:

> There are certain other regimes as well, some of private individuals, others of philosophers and political [rulers]. . . . For some of them hold that a fine arrangement concerning property is the greatest thing: it is about this, they assert, that all factional conflicts arise. The first to introduce this was Phaleas of Chalcedon, who asserts that the possessions of the citizens should be equal. He supposed this would not be difficult to do in [cities] just being settled; in those already settled he supposed it would be troublesome, but that a leveling could be quickly brought about by having the wealthy give dowries but not receive them, and the poor receive but not give them. (Arist. *Pol.* 1266a31–1266b5; trans. C. Lord 1984)

---

[35] Pembroke 1967: 5.

[36] For the political element in Herodotus's model, cf. McNeal 1988, Saxonhouse 1996: 40–41. McNeal reads 1.196 as Herodotus's misunderstanding of some current *Greek* marital practice, though he acknowledges that we have no evidence for any real Greek practice that corresponds to Herodotus's account (1988: 69).

We know nothing else about Phaleas of Chalcedon, not even when he lived and wrote, but it is tempting to imagine him as senior or contemporary to Herodotus, so that the historian might have known his work.[37] For his plan of equalizing property through the selective give-and-take of dowries bears an uncanny resemblance to Herodotus's fantasized system of bride auction, though there are a couple of significant differences. In Herodotus's system, property is not necessarily equalized, since gradations have been introduced into the give-and-take: the price of the most attractive girls is driven up by auction, while the bidding for the ugly ones requires that the man who is willing to take the *least* money get the girl. In addition, Phaleas's system does not necessarily require civic regulation of the allotment of brides; presumably, marriages could still be contracted privately, as long as only the rich give dowries and the poor only take them. Herodotus's system thus imposes another level of civic control in the ranking and distribution of women by their attractiveness or ugliness. In these divergences, I suggest, Herodotus may actually be refining Phaleas's scheme for constituting the perfect civic order, for Herodotus's system essentially solves the problems Aristotle detects in Phaleas's model. In his usual matter-of-fact tone, the philosopher points out the limitations in Phaleas's scheme for the equalization of property:

Yet even if one were to arrange a moderate level of property for all, it would not help. For one ought to level desires sooner than property; but this is impossible for those not adequately educated by the laws. . . . Further, factional conflict occurs not only because of inequality of possessions, but also because of inequality of honors, though in an opposite way in each case; for the many [engage in factional conflict] because possessions are unequal, but the refined do so if honors are equal (οἱ μὲν γὰρ πολλοὶ διὰ τὸ περὶ τὰς κτήσεις ἄνισον, οἱ δὲ χαρίεντες περὶ τῶν τιμῶν, ἐὰν ἴσαι)—hence the verse "in single honor whether vile or worthy." Nor do human beings commit injustice only because of the necessary things—for which Phaleas considers equality of property a remedy, so that no one will steal through

<hr>

[37] McNeal 1988: 65 also cites Phaleas's scheme as a parallel for Hdt. 1.196, suggesting that Herodotus and Phaleas were independently influenced by some current Greek social practice. Scholars offer different dates for Phaleas: Guthrie 1969: 152 locates him "about the end of the fifth century"; Nestle 1938: 1658 at the beginning of the fourth. These suggested dates seem to be based largely on the parallelism of Phaleas's scheme for the redistribution of property with Aristophanes' *Ekklesiazousai*, but the parallel between Phaleas and Herodotus might suggest an earlier date for this pioneer of political theory. In any case I have no wish to insist on his being a contemporary or influence on Herodotus; the main point is that Herodotus, Phaleas and, of course, Aristotle are all engaged in the same debate—on the nature of the ideal city and the circulation of goods and honors within it—ranging through the fifth century and into the fourth.

being cold or hungry; they also do it for enjoyment and the satisfaction of desire. (Arist. *Pol.* 1266b28–1267a5; trans. C. Lord 1984)

Herodotus's model, by contrast, does not equalize property; it simply adjusts its distribution somewhat. More importantly, his system is predicated on *proportional* honors and satisfaction of desires. For if we understand the attractive women as tokens of honor and status, as I have suggested, the rich (Herodotus's εὐδαίμονες; Aristotle's χαρίεντες) spend their money and submit to civic regulation for the sake of distinctive prestige and enjoyment within the polis community. Thus money and property are not the end, as Aristotle objects they are in Phaleas's scheme, but merely the means to constituting a civic order mutually satisfactory to the haves and have-nots.

Finally, we should note that Herodotus's account shares one other feature with fourth-century theorizing about the ideal form of the city: it possesses the homeostasis of a closed system. Although men are allowed to go to other villages to bid, the balance between pretty girls and ugly girls, income and outlay, seems to be perfectly calibrated. Herodotus does not say, "If there is extra money, they . . ." or "If there isn't enough money, they . . .". Instead, the implication is that the pool of girls is exactly the right size and proportion to marry them all off appropriately.[38] In this respect, Herodotus's narrative conjures up an image of perfect civic self-sufficiency, which, according to Aristotle, is the main criterion in determining the proper size of a polis:

> Similarly with the city as well, the one that is made up of too few persons is not self-sufficient, though the city is a self-sufficient thing, while the one that is made up of too many persons is with respect to the necessary things self-sufficient like a nation, but is not a city; for it is not easy for a regime to be present. Who will be general of an overly excessive number, or who will be herald, unless he has the voice of Stentor? Hence the first city must necessarily be that made up of a multitude so large as to be the first multitude that is self-sufficient with a view to living well in the context of the political partnership (ὃ πρῶτον πλῆθος αὔταρκες πρὸς τὸ εὖ ζῆν ἐστι κατὰ τὴν πολιτικὴν κοινωνίαν). (Arist. *Pol.* 1326b2–9; trans. C. Lord 1984)

Herodotus's village, like Aristotle's ideal polis, appears to be "the first multitude that is self-sufficient with a view to living well in the context of the political partnership"—as is signified in the histor's account by the proper circulation and distribution of brides.

---

[38] On Herodotus's images of homeostasis in general (with no particular political emphasis), see Redfield 1985: 103. As parallels for this homeostatic system, we might note the construction of the walls of Babylon (Hdt. 1.179), and the reciprocal bearing of ships and donkeys, downstream and up, respectively (Hdt. 1.194).

It may be worthwhile in this context to quote Aristotle a little further, for the philosopher's thinking moves almost automatically from size of city to type of regime, setting up an opposition that has much in common with Herodotus's contrasting customs:

> It is possible for [a city] that exceeds this on the basis of number to be a greater city, but this is not possible, as we said, indefinitely. As to what the defining principle of the excess is, it is easy to see from the facts. The actions of the city belong on the one hand to the rulers, on the other to the ruled. The task of a ruler is command and judgment. With a view to judgment concerning the just things and with a view to distributing offices on the basis of merit, the citizens must necessarily be familiar with one another's qualities; where this does not happen to be the case, what is connected with the offices and with judging must necessarily be carried on poorly. For in connection with both it is not just to improvise—the very thing that manifestly happens in an overly populous city. Further, [in such cities] it is easy for aliens and foreigners to assume a part in the regime (ἔτι δὲ ξένοις καὶ μετοίκοις ῥᾴδιον μεταλαμβάνειν τῆς πολιτείας): it is not difficult for them to escape notice on account of the excess of number. It is clear, therefore, that the best defining principle for a city is this: the greatest excess of number with a view to self-sufficiency of life that is readily surveyable. (Arist. *Pol.* 1326b9–24; trans. C. Lord 1984)

The parallels between Aristotle's theorization and Herodotus's accounts of temple prostitution and bride auction are striking, especially if we try the experiment of reading the women as allegories of civic offices to be allotted (πρὸς τὸ τὰς ἀρχὰς διανέμειν, *Pol.* 1326b15). On this reading, temple prostitution represents a certain "improvisatory" quality to the distribution, with "aliens and foreigners" easily intruding and getting a share of civic authority because of the vast scale of Babylon. Temple prostitution thus figures democracy out of control, an overlarge system where anyone can attain one-time office by the random process of sortition. Bride auction, by contrast, ensures the distribution of offices (here women) "according to worth" (κατ᾽ ἀξίαν) and according to the citizens' accurate "knowledge of each other's quality" (γνωρίζειν ἀλλήλους, ποῖοί τινές εἰσι, τοὺς πολίτας, *Pol.* 1326b16). In this respect, Herodotus's villages verge on an oligarchic or timocratic system, where offices are held permanently by "the best people."[39] Readers may resist this imposition of

---

[39] Mark Griffith suggests to me that there might be a more specific set of parallels between Herodotus's portrait of Babylon and the cities of contemporary Greece: the overlarge, sprawling city where sortition is out of control may suggest imperial Athens, while the timocracy of bride auction may evoke Sparta, which was known as a city of separate κῶμαι (cf. Thuc. 1.10; Arist. *Poetics* 1448a36). On the other hand, certain elements—like the freedom to handle money and property notoriously allowed to Dorian women—point in

yet another level of allegorization, and I have no wish to insist on this reading. I offer it tentatively, simply to highlight the similarities between these two seemingly disparate discourses. What I want to suggest is that Herodotus is thinking through the same issues that occupy Aristotle and other Greek theorists—the proper constitution of the city and its public sphere—though his medium is ethnographic fantasy rather than philosophic speculation.[40]

Many of the same aspects of civic functioning are figured again in what Herodotus deems the Babylonians' "second wisest custom," the exposure of the sick:

> They have this other custom which is second in wisdom [to bride auction]. They bear the sick out to the agora (ἐς τὴν ἀγορήν); for they do not use doctors. Those going by the sick man then offer advice concerning his illness, if anyone either himself has suffered the sort of thing that the sick man has or has seen another suffering [it]. Passersby advise and recommend these things, whatever [each one] has done to escape a similar disease or has seen another escape [by doing]. But to pass by in silence is not permissible for them, until they enquire what disease the man has. (Hdt. 1.197)

Here we should note that the "marketplace" implicit in the system of bride auctions has become explicit; Herodotus cannot resist locating the exposure of the sick in the nonexistent Babylonian agora. Again, as in the case of the two other customs considered, Assyriologists are skeptical of Herodotus's report, since there is substantial evidence for doctors and medical expertise in Babylonian texts of all periods.[41] Still, it is easy to see the complementary function this *nomos* fulfills within the economy of Herodotus's narrative: if bride auctions ensure the proper distribution of wealth and honors to individuals within the community, the exposure of the sick requires from each citizen a reciprocating service in the public sharing of knowledge. Hence, we might say that the exchange of information Herodotus describes is another figure for the proper functioning of an autonomous civic community. Indeed, it is not just civic, but democratic: in its valorization of amateur experience over professional expertise, this *nomos* evokes the tenets of democratic ideology, perhaps most

---

the other direction, suggesting parallels between Herodotus's depiction of temple prostitution and Spartan customs. The multiform oppositions of Sparta and Athens might most usefully be thought of as a floating grid that colors Herodotus's thinking about civic space without completely dictating it.

[40] This same point is well made by Saxonhouse 1996: 31–57.

[41] Wiseman 1985: 106: "There is no evidence that the Babylonians were treated in public." MacGinnis's apologia for Herodotus—"it may well be that our sources do not reflect the treatment available to the common man"—smacks of special pleading (1986: 76–77). See also Ravn 1942: 89–90; G. E. R. Lloyd 1987: 56; Pritchett 1993: 236–37.

clearly represented in the *Histories* by Herodotus's account of Themistokles' refutation of the professional oracle-readers before the Battle of Salamis (Hdt. 7.144).[42]

Yet if the customs Herodotus singles out as "wisest" and "best" enable the fantasy constitution of autonomous civic communities in the villages of Babylon, his brief mention of current conditions signals the degradation and collapse of this system under the oppression of foreign rule. Thus at the end of 1.196, as we have seen, the histor concludes:

> This then was their noblest custom (ὁ μέν νυν κάλλιστος νόμος), though it has not still continued in existence now, but they have recently invented some other thing. For since, having been conquered in war, they were ruined and their homes were destroyed, every one of the demos, lacking the means of livelihood, prostitutes his female children (πᾶς τις τοῦ δήμου βίου σπανίζων καταπορνεύει τὰ θήλεα τέκνα).

The Persian domination of Babylon has undermined the material preconditions for community, destroying houses (οἰκοφθορήθησαν) and reducing the members of the demos to abject poverty (ἐκακώθησαν). As a result, the carefully calibrated autonomy of communities is obliterated. The poor are forced to abandon the system of setting their daughters *es meson*, and instead, they prostitute them privately for economic survival. In the opposition of bride auction and temple prostitution, Herodotus figures two competing long-term transactional orders, civic and sacral, through two different systems of the exchange of women. In the brief mention here of private prostitution, both systems are eclipsed by the sheer necessities of the short-term cycle. As in the case of the Lydians' prostitution of their own daughters (described in identical terms at 1.94), the degrading act of καταπορνεύειν signifies in the sexual register a vacuum where there should be civic structure. And in this case, that absence is made more poignant by the contrast of then and now, of utopian possibility and oppression.

Herodotus's ethnography of Babylon offers complex and eclectic models of civic structure thought through the multiple allegories of the traffic in women. Thus, I have suggested reading the opposing customs of temple prostitution and bride auction as emblematic of all that circulates or can be alloted within the city: money, property, honors, and offices. Within this multiple allegorization, the different signifieds pull in somewhat different directions. If we read the circulation of women in terms of money

---

[42] For the egalitarianism of this Babylonian custom, see Saxonhouse 1996: 41–42; for Hdt. 7.144 as a paradigm of democratic decision-making, see Vernant 1991: 311–15; Maurizio 1997.

and property, temple prostitution figures extremes of inequity with no communal regulation—a condition I have suggested represents the threat of theocracy for a Greek audience. In contrast, bride auction represents the equitable distribution of money and property under communal oversight, a reassuring model of economy embedded in civic structure. But if we read these same customs in terms of honors and offices, temple prostitution figures somewhat differently an excessive equity or availability of offices by lot, strangely merging features of extreme democracy with theocracy; while bride auction represents the proportional distribution of honors and the permanent assignment of offices characteristic of an oligarchic regime. I would contend that we cannot extract a single consistent constitutional preference from Herodotus's utopian fantasies, perhaps partly because of the density of allegorization.

What we can be sure of instead is that Herodotus exploits and plays with elements of the *hetaira-porne* binary to debunk existing alternatives, and then, within the play-space of extended ethnography, imagines a system using the same symbolic code (the exchange of women) but at a skew line to current oppositions. Archaic poetry had used the *hetaira* to constitute the privileged space of the symposium, infused with eroticism and protected from the explicit economics of the agora, while it employed the *porne* to figure the degraded exchanges of the public sphere. Herodotus turns both categories against the elite to expose the disembedded economics of the aristocratic system. Thus he deliberately associates Lydian *habrosune* with *kapeleia* and the prostitution of one's own daughters and insists relentlessly on the material economy behind the circulation of *hetairai*. Herodotus replaces this system with the Babylonian circulation of women, offering a positive as well as a negative figuration of the public sphere by reimagining it as a political space. As we have seen in other instances, Herodotus stands poised between a poetic past and a philosophic future, using the implicit or figural idiom of archaic poetry for the conceptualization of philosophic issues; using a discourse of otherness where Aristotle will explicitly confront the same—for the theorization of the Greek city.

CHAPTER 7

Games People Play

WE HAVE SEEN how different forms of prostitution help constitute the domains of symposium and public sphere, with the *hetaira* and the *pornē* aligned with the competing symbolic economies of gift and coin. At this point I would like to add another set of terms to these oppositions, with the consideration of ancient Greek games (again taking my lead from the collocations of Herodotus's Lydian ethnography). Like coins, games represent a symbolic signifying system; like prostitution, they may enable us to see ideology as it is forged through everyday practice.

Games may seem an absurdly trivial domain for scholarly investigation, but I would contend that it is precisely their lowly, unexamined status that endows games with extraordinary power to inculcate values within culture. Thus Pierre Bourdieu has taught us to see the informing power of quotidian bodily practices to shape the *habitus*, the enduring disposition, of social actors in conformity with their social status, roles, and expectations.[1] As Bourdieu puts it, we must attend to all that "goes without saying because it comes without saying," to all that is on the near side of language, the "diffuse education which moves directly from practice to practice without passing through discourse."[2] Games would seem to be a paradigm case for such sociological analysis, since continuously and from an early age, children participate in these symbolic, rule-bound structures that teach them how to behave in "real life."

At another level the apparent triviality of games makes them an ideal object for our inquiry. For games, unlike coins, are purely symbolic and culturally "gratuitous," and as such they are not subject to the kind of narrowly economistic explanations to which coinage and other phenomena (like prostitution) are susceptible. That is to say, we cannot claim that the Greeks invented certain games at certain times "for profit," or to facilitate trade, or as a result of increased mercantile activity. If, then, we can demonstrate a parallel pattern in the sphere of games as in these other areas, that alignment itself will tend to confirm the kinds of ideological claims I have made for those other domains as well. And as we shall see, sixth-century Greece witnessed the emergence not just of coinage

---

[1] See Bourdieu 1977: 72–158, 1984: 466–84, 1990: 52–111.
[2] Quotes taken from Bourdieu 1977: 167, 1990: 103.

and the category of the *hetaira*, but also of a whole array of games—
board games like *pente grammai* and *polis*, the institutionalization of the
palaistra and its games, and symposium games like *kottabos*. In this
proliferation of new pastimes, I will argue, we can make out again the
lineaments of a symbolic opposition between the symposium and the
public sphere, constituted and reinforced in their competing ideologies
by the games played. An analysis of games will furthermore add to the
picture of competing paradigms that is emerging from this study, for
games seem to give the Greeks a way of thinking concretely about self
and other, embodiment and disembodiment, and the relation of the body
to symbolic order.

But with the notion of "thinking" through games, I must acknowledge
a limitation on the investigation. With games, as with prostitution, though
my concern is with practice, it is practice already at one remove, refracted
and mediated through literary and visual representations. We do not have
the luxury of anthropologists, to observe games as they are played "in
the field," but only in the scanty and haphazard references that survive
in the remains of Greek cultural production. Thus, though it is my contention that games do their cultural work as practice, prior to verbalization
and theory, we can catch them only on the other side of that divide, fixed
in texts and images like insects in amber.

I. GAMES AND OTHER SYMBOLIC SYSTEMS

Let us return to Herodotus's strange ethnography of the Lydians at 1.94.
At this point we have considered the imaginary function of practically
all the elements of Herodotus's list—prostitution, coinage, retail trade—
with the single exception of games. Recall that Herodotus's list of Lydian
inventions culminates with an elaborate aetiology of the invention of
games:

> And the Lydians use customs very similar to the Greeks, apart from the fact
> that they prostitute their female children. And first of men whom we know
> they minted and used gold and silver coinage, and they were also the first retail
> traders. And the Lydians themselves say that also the games which are now
> established for themselves and the Greeks were their invention. And they say
> that at the same time as these were invented among them, they also settled
> Tyrsenia, speaking thus concerning these things: in the kingship of Atys the
> son of Manes, an intense famine occurred throughout all Lydia. And [they say
> that] for a time the Lydians persevered living [with it], but that afterwards,
> when it didn't stop, they sought remedies, different people contriving different
> strategies against it. [They say that] there were invented then the forms of dice

and knucklebones and of ball and of all the other games except draughts; for
the invention of these the Lydians do not claim as their own (ἐξευρεθῆναι δὴ
ὦν τότε καὶ τῶν κύβων καὶ τῶν ἀστραγάλων καὶ τῆς σφαίρης καὶ τῶν ἀλλέων
πασέων παιγνιέων τὰ εἴδεα, πλὴν πεσσῶν· τούτων γὰρ ὦν τὴν ἐξεύρεσιν
οὐκ οἰκηιοῦνται Λυδοί). But they did thus with respect to the famine when
they had invented them: one day, they played the entire day, in order not to
seek food, and the other day they stopped playing and ate. In such a way they
lived for eighteen years. But when the evil did not abate, but raged still more
violently, their king, thus having divided two shares of all the Lydians allotted
one group for staying and another for emigration from the land, and over the
one group allotted to stay there the king himself was in command, and over
the one departing his own child, whose name was Tyrsenos. And those who
had been allotted to go out from the land went down to Smyrna and contrived
a sailing, putting into the ships all, however much moveable property was
useful to them, and sailed away in search of livelihood and land, until, having
passed many nations, they came to the Ombrikoi, where they established cities
and where they live up to this time. And instead of Lydians, they changed their
name after the son of the king who led them; making themselves eponymous
after this one, they were called Tyrsenians. (Hdt. 1.94.1–7)

Already in antiquity, Herodotus was criticized for this claim: thus Athenaios observed that Homer had already represented ballgames and knucklebones as elements of the heroic age, long predating the reign of the Lydian
king Atys.[3] Given that this report has no secure basis in fact (or even in
Greek cultural fantasy), it provokes the following questions concerning
Herodotus's account of the Lydian claim: In what way do games form
a natural class with prostitution, coined money, and kapēleia? Why do
the Lydians in Herodotus's account claim credit for the invention of
games? And why their peculiar insistence that they invented all the games
except pessoi?

One way of approaching these questions is to set Herodotus's list in
the context of other such inventories, which seem to have enjoyed a
peculiar popularity in the fifth and fourth centuries. Though no other
source corroborates Herodotus's attribution of all these inventions to the
Lydians, several fifth- and fourth-century writers offer analogous lists of
εὑρήματα, crediting them variously to Palamedes, Prometheus, or other,
foreign, culture heroes.[4] Thus Gorgias, in his set-speech in defense of

---

[3] Athen. Deipn. 1.19a: "Herodotus is wrong in saying that games were invented in the
reign of Atys when there was a famine; for the heroic age antedated his time."

[4] On the motif of the πρῶτος εὑρετής, see Kleingünther 1933; Kleingünther regards the
topos as post-Homeric, a development of sixth- and fifth-century rationalism and historical
research. Xenophanes somewhere attributed the invention of coinage to the Lydians (fr. 4
W = Pollux Onom. 9.83), but we have no way of knowing if this was part of a list of

Palamedes (falsely accused of treason against the Greek host at Troy by Odysseus), has his beleaguered hero claim to be a "great benefactor of the Greeks and all mankind" because of his many inventions:

τίς γὰρ ἂν ἐποίησε τὸν ἀνθρώπειον βίον πόριμον ἐξ ἀπόρου καὶ κεκοσμημένον ἐξ ἀκόσμου, τάξεις τε πολεμικὰς εὑρὼν μέγιστον εἰς πλεονεκτήματα, νόμους τε γραπτοὺς φύλακας [τε] τοῦ δικαίου, γράμματά τε μνήμης ὄργανον, μέτρα τε καὶ σταθμὰ συναλλαγῶν εὐπόρους διαλλαγάς, ἀριθμόν τε χρημάτων φύλακα, πυρσούς τε κρατίστους καὶ ταχίστους ἀγγέλους, πεσσούς τε σχολῆς ἄλυπον διατριβήν; (Gorgias fr. B 11a.30 DK)

For who [else] could have made human life resourceful from resourceless and ornamented from unadorned, by inventing military tactics as the greatest [defense] against acts of overreaching, and written laws as guardians of justice, and writing as an instrument of memory, and weights and measures as reconciliations of commercial exchanges, and number as the guardian of property, and fire signals as the strongest and swiftest messengers, and *pessoi* as a painless pastime for leisure?

Indeed, the false accusation, trial, and condemnation of Palamedes represented a favorite topic of Attic tragedy: Aeschylus, Sophocles, and Euripides (along with Astydamas the Younger) are each known to have composed a *Palamedes*, while we know of four separate tragedies that staged the revenge of Palamedes' father Nauplios.[5] A staple of these plays appears to have been Palamedes' (or Nauplios's) cataloging of his (or his son's) beneficial inventions (probably, as in Gorgias, as part of his self-defense). Thus a fragment of Aeschylus's *Palamedes* credits the title character with the invention of military tactics and three meals a day (fr. 182 R), while a fragment from Sophocles' *Nauplios* attributes to Palamedes the invention of the Greek defense wall, of number, weights and measures, military tactics, and the "measure and courses of the stars" (Soph. fr. 432 R). Most similar to Herodotus's account of the Lydian invention of games as a distraction from famine is another Sophoclean list of Palamedes' benefactions:

οὐ λιμὸν οὗτος τῶνδ' ἔπαυσε, σὺν θεῷ
εἰπεῖν, χρόνου τε διατριβὰς σοφωτάτας
ἐφηῦρε φλοίσβου μετὰ κόπον καθημένοις,
πεσσοὺς κύβους τε, τερπνὸν ἀργίας ἄκος;[6] (Soph. fr. 479 R)

---

inventions like Herodotus's. Prometheus, of course, also figures in such lists (e.g., Aesch. *Prom.* 446–506), but he is nowhere credited with the invention of games.

[5] See Goossens 1952: 150.

[6] Though, as Goossens notes, Sophocles does not necessarily make the invention of games a palliative against famine in this fragment; instead, "releasing from famine" and the invention of *pessoi* and *kuboi* are separate elements in a list of benefactions, linked simply

Did this one not stop the famine from those [men], so to speak with god's grace, and did he [not] invent the cleverest pastimes for those sitting at ease after the stroke of battle—*pessoi* and *kuboi* as a pleasant cure of idleness?

By the fourth century, the anonymous author of Alkidamas's *Odysseus* had expanded this list to include μουσική and νόμισμα along with military tactics, writing, number, weights and measures, *pessoi*, *kuboi*, and fire signals (Alk. *Ody.* 22), while, by the time of Philostratos's *Heroikos* (second century C.E.), Palamedes had assumed the lineaments of a universal culture hero, responsible for inventing the seasons, the cycle of the months, the year, and coinage, as well as the traditional weights and measures, number, *pessoi*, and writing (*Her.* 33.1–3).

Finally, Plato has Socrates attribute a very similar list of inventions (including games) to the Egyptian god Theuth, in a famous passage from the *Phaedrus*. According to Socrates, Theuth "invented number and reckoning and geometry and astronomy, and in addition *petteia* and *kubeia*, and especially writing" (*Phdr.* 274c5–d2). Scholars have traditionally compared these lists to question the particular inventors, positing competing local traditions; or to trace the direction of influence in their constitution.[7] I am less interested in the specifics of individual lists than in the phenomenon in general: what accounts for the Greek fascination with such lists of inventions, and what is the common thread that unites their elements? Specifically, why do games figure so frequently in these inventories of culturally significant contributions? If we return for a moment to Gorgias's list, as the single most complete of those closest in time to Herodotus's, we can observe two features that seem to characterize all its elements. First, each invention represents a symbolic signifying system that imposes itself as a kind of second-order organizing principle: military tactics organize fighting men; written laws structure the customary usages of the city; weights, measures, and number regulate material property; fire signals transform and communicate messages over long distances. Second, as Gorgias's rhetoric makes particularly clear, all these inventions are said to have a positive moral value in their service to the community. That is to say, there seems to be an intimate connection between each of these symbolic systems and the order of the Greek polis.[8]

---

by τε in the second line. According to Eustathios (*Comm. Hom.* p. 228.1; 1.346.17 Valk; cf. p. 1397.10), they used to show the stone at Troy on which the Greeks played *pessoi*. Other fifth-century representations of Palamedes as the inventor of games: Eur. *IA* 195, Polygnotos, Nekuia in Lesche of the Knidians at Delphi (Paus. 10.31.1).

[7] Thus Lamer 1927: 1906–8; Kleingünther 1933: 28–29; Wüst 1942: 2505–10 (on Palamedes); Goossens 1952.

[8] This argument, which has traditionally been made for writing and the Greek city, has recently been challenged by Steiner 1994; she argues that several of the symbolic inventions on these lists—including writing, coinage, and fire signals—were strongly associated with

This is expressed not only by the moralizing characterization Palamedes attaches to each element in his list, but also by the defense he proceeds to mount based on the catalogue:

> Clearly, I devote my attention to such things, making a sign (σημεῖον) that I keep away from wicked and shameful deeds. For it is impossible that one who devotes his attention to *those* things attend to such things. And I deserve, if I do you no wrong, not to be wronged by you.

> And in fact, not even for my other pursuits do I deserve to be badly treated, either by the younger men or by the elders. For I cause no pain to the elders and I am not without use to the younger men, not envious of those who prosper, pitying those who do badly; neither despising poverty nor privileging wealth over virtue but virtue over wealth; neither useless in councils nor idle in battles, doing that which is ordered, obedient to those in power (οὔτε ἐν βουλαῖς ἄχρηστος οὔτε ἐν μάχαις ἀργός, ποιῶν τὸ τασσόμενον, πειθόμενος τοῖς ἄρχουσιν). (Gorgias fr. B 11a.31–32 DK)

Palamedes' defense, especially in its final stages, has a distinctly civic, even democratic ring. The proof that he participates properly in the symbolic activities of war and councils, and submits to the symbolic authority of "those in power" emerges logically from his commitment to symbolic inventions. In this sense his discoveries are doubly σημεῖον (as Gorgias playfully signals): they are "signifying systems" in themselves, and they signify the proper moral and political commitment to the community.

This same association of Palamedes' symbolic inventions with the proper virtues of the polis informs by opposition the anonymous setpiece composed as Odysseus's denunciation of Palamedes, preserved under the name of the orator Alkidamas. This mythological exercise, which reads like a response to Gorgias's showpiece, first offers a comprehensive list of all Palamedes claims to have invented: τάξεις . . . πολεμικάς, γράμματα, ἀριθμούς, μέτρα, σταθμούς, πεττούς, κύβους, μουσικήν, νόμισμα, πυρσούς ("military tactics, writing, numbers, measures, weights, *pessoi, kuboi*, musical art, coinage, fire signals," Alk. *Ody.* 22). The speaker then deploys two strategies to discredit Palamedes' claim; first, he argues that several of his "inventions" (tactics, writing, *mousikē*, number, and coinage) had already been developed by others. For those inventions that remain, the speaker discredits them by representing them as sources of

---

Eastern despotism by sixth- and fifth-century Greeks. While Steiner's argument is a valuable corrective to the too-easy modern association of writing, written law, and democracy, the passages considered here suggest that, at least by Gorgias's time, the identification of these symbolic systems with the order of the polis was an available one for a Greek audience.

damage to the community, pointedly contrasted to his articulation of proper civic virtue:

μέτρα δὲ καὶ σταθμὰ ἐξηῦρε καπήλοις καὶ ἀγοραίοις ἀνθρώποις ἀπάτας καὶ ἐπιορκίας, πεττούς γε μὴν τοῖς ἀργοῖς τῶν ἀνδρῶν ἔριδας καὶ λοιδορίας. καὶ κύβους αὖ μέγιστον κακὸν κατέδειξε, τοῖς μὲν ἡττηθεῖσι λύπας καὶ ζημίας, τοῖς δὲ νενικηκόσι καταγέλωτα καὶ ὄνειδος· τὰ γὰρ ἀπὸ τῶν κύβων προσγιγνόμενα ἀνόνητα γίγνεται, τὰ δὲ πλεῖστα καταναλίσκεται παραχρῆμα. πυρσοὺς αὖ ἐσοφίσατο, ἀλλ᾽ ἐπὶ τῷ ἡμετέρῳ κακῷ, ὃ διενοεῖτο ποιεῖν, χρήσιμον δὲ τοῖς πολεμίοις.

ἀρετὴ δέ ἐστιν ἀνδρὸς τοῖς ἡγεμόσι προσέχειν καὶ τὸ προσταττόμενον ποιεῖν καὶ τῷ πλήθει ἀρέσκειν παντί, αὐτόν τε παρέχειν ἄνδρα πανταχοῦ ἀγαθόν, τούς τε φίλους εὖ ποιοῦντα καὶ τοὺς ἐχθροὺς κακῶς. ὧν τἀναντία πάντων οὗτος ἐπίσταται, τοὺς μὲν ἐχθροὺς ὠφελεῖν, τοὺς δὲ φίλους κακῶς ποιεῖν. (Alk. Ody. 27–28)

Measures and weights he invented as means of deceit and forsworn oaths for petty traders and marketmen; *pessoi* [he invented] as quarrels and abuses for idlers. And *kuboi*, in turn, he revealed as the greatest evil, for the losers a source of grief and damage, for the winners a mockery and a reproach. For the gains that accrue from *kuboi* turn out to be useless, and most of them are squandered immediately. And fire signals again he contrived, but on terms of evil for us, which he intended to make, but useful for our enemies.

But a man's virtue is to heed those in command and to do what's ordered and to please the entire people, to furnish himself as a good man in every respect, helping his friends and hurting his enemies. The opposite of all these things is what this man knows—to help the enemy, but to hurt his friends.

In his assertion of what man's *aretē* ought to be, the speaker echoes almost exactly the language of Gorgias's Palamedes, exposing thereby the effort required to disengage this string of semiotic inventions from the symbolic order of the polis.

This association of systems of symbolic logic with civic structure makes the final term in Gorgias's list all the more intriguing. I have thus far deliberately excluded the game of *pessoi* from my discussion of Palamedes' inventions and avoided offering any modern equivalent as translation, in order not to prejudge what precisely the game is and how it fits in this context. To modern sensibilities, the games that adorn these lists (*pessoi* or *pessoi* and *kuboi*) represent the odd men out, the strange intermingling of trivial with profound, and yet somehow their inclusion has a logic for Greek writers and audiences. How are we to understand the functioning of games in these inventories? Games are, after all, symbolic systems *par excellence*, and their collocation with military tactics, number, written laws, and coinage suggests that the Greeks themselves regarded them as such.

Finally, what are we to make of Herodotus's list of Lydian inventions in the context of these other catalogues of εὑρήματα? What emerges most forcefully from the comparison is the oddness of Herodotus's set—coinage coupled with prostitution and *kapēleia* rather than military tactics and written laws, and, as Herodotus emphasizes, the Lydian claim to have invented all the games except *pessoi*. Are the anomalies of this list conditioned by Herodotus's notion of the oddness of the Lydians, and, if so, what is the symbolic significance of the games the histor specifies here? In order to answer these questions, we must examine in detail the precise nature and associative connections of Herodotus's games—*kuboi* and *astragaloi*, *sphairē* and *pessoi*.

II. *PESSOI*: THE MEDIATION OF THE GAME BOARD

The reconstruction of ancient Greek games (especially board games) is extremely difficult and inconclusive, based as it is on brief allusions in literary texts from Homer onward and more extended accounts in much later commentators and lexicographers (Pollux, Hesychios, Suidas, Eustathios; some or all of which depend on a lost treatise of Suetonius, *On Greek Games*). These latter antiquarians write long after many of the games they attempt to identify have become obsolete, and in contexts where they are exposed to the very different system of Roman games—both facts that can distort the information they transmit. As one scholar observes, "Some of the difficulties may be realized by trying to reconstruct a game of Ombre entirely from Pope's *Rape of the Lock*, or a game of cricket from Dickens' account of All Muggleton vs. Dingley Dell. . ."[9] Nonetheless, certain facts can be established with some probability. *Pessoi* and *petteia* function in our sources as generic terms, designating "board games" in general.[10] *Pessoi* are specifically the pieces moved on the board, also called λίθοι and ψῆφοι. Certain board games, at least in the post-Homeric era, entailed the use of dice (*kuboi*) as well as pieces on a board (*pessoi*), so that on occasion we find the terms *pessoi* and *kuboi* conjoined.

The term *pessoi* occurs once in all of Homer—in the *Odyssey*, where it characterizes the activity of the suitors of Penelope. It is worth tracing out the theme of games in the *Odyssey* in some detail, for it will establish the framework within which later symbolic references to *pessoi* also

---

[9] The material in this paragraph represents a summary of Lamer 1927 and especially Austin 1940: 257–61. Quotation from Austin 1940: 257.

[10] Austin 1940: 260; Cilley 1986: 33–34.

operate. In schematic terms the suitors' activity of game-playing is consistently linked with their violations of *xenia*, their unscrupulous and one-sided consumption of another man's household. That is to say, the playing of board games marks the suitors as bad aristocrats, engaged in disembodied activity that is itself equivalent to the vicarious enjoyment and expropriation of another's property. It is thus characteristic of the suitors that they not only "play *pessoi*" but stage a boxing match of beggars for their own amusement (Book 18) and imagine that Penelope is to be won in the contest of the bow (Book 21). Odysseus, in contrast, proves his nobility and asserts his proprietary and regal prerogatives by *re-embodying* the symbolic contest of the bow, forcing the suitors from game to real warfare and there destroying them.

In our very first view of the suitors (through the eyes of Athena disguised as Mentes), we catch them playing *pessoi*:

εὗρε δ' ἄρα μνηστῆρας ἀγήνορας. οἱ μὲν ἔπειτα
πεσσοῖσι προπάροιθε θυράων θυμὸν ἔτερπον,
ἥμενοι ἐν ῥινοῖσι βοῶν, οὓς ἔκτανον αὐτοί.
κήρυκες δ' αὐτοῖσι καὶ ὀτρηροὶ θεράποντες
οἱ μὲν ἄρ' οἶνον ἔμισγον ἐνὶ κρητῆρσι καὶ ὕδωρ,
οἱ δ' αὖτε σπόγγοισι πολυτρήτοισι τραπέζας
νίζον καὶ πρότιθεν, τοὶ δὲ κρέα πολλὰ δατεῦντο. (*Od.* 1.106–12)

And then she found the lordly suitors. They were then rejoicing their spirit with *pessoi* in front of the doors, sitting on the skins of cattle, which they themselves had killed. And their heralds and nimble servants—some were mixing wine and water in kraters, others in turn were cleaning the tables with sponges full-of-holes and setting them out, still others were dividing up many pieces of meat.

Here the suitors' disembodied pastime is significantly associated with their vicarious appropriation of another man's household: they lounge on the skins of Odysseus's cattle they have themselves killed, drink his wine, and prepare to eat his meat. This first view is emblematic, marking through their activities the suitors' transgression of the norm of embodied exchange in *xenia*. At the same time, their unproductive symbolic activity is accentuated by contrast with the bustle of servants in attendance, preparing a banquet for their idle masters.

The precise nature of the game they played was apparently the source of some speculation in antiquity, as we learn from Athenaios:

Apion of Alexandria says that he actually heard Kteson of Ithaca tell what sort of game the suitors played. "The suitors," he says, "numbered one hundred and eight, and divided the counters (ψήφους) between opposing sides, each side equal in number according to the number of players themselves, so that there were fifty-four on a side. A small space was left between them, and in this middle space they set one counter which they called Penelope; this they made the mark to be thrown at with another counter. They then drew lots, and the one who drew the first took aim. If a player succeeded in pushing Penelope forward, he moved his piece to the position occupied by her before being hit and thrust out, then again setting up Penelope he would try to hit her with his own piece from the second position which he occupied. If he hit her without touching any other player's piece, he won the game and had high hopes of marrying her. Eurymachos had won the greatest number of victories in this game, and looked forward to his marriage with confidence." In this way, because of their easy life, the suitors' arms were so flabby that they could not even begin to stretch the bow (οὕτω δὲ διὰ τὴν τρυφὴν τὰς χεῖρας οἱ μνηστῆρες ἔχουσιν ἁπαλὰς ὡς μηδὲ τὸ τόξον ἐντεῖναι δύνασθαι). (Athen. *Deipn.* 1.16f–17b, trans. C. B. Gulick).

Though this elaborate rendition of what is essentially a game of marbles may strike the modern reader as absurd, the ancient scholar has in fact picked up and expanded on the broader significance of this fleeting Homeric reference to the suitors' playing *pessoi*. For what Kteson describes is ultimately a system of symbolic or vicarious wooing, whereby the suitors compete for the hand of Penelope not directly, but through the interaction of tokens.[11] "Penelope" here unites in a single token all the property and prestige of Odysseus for which the suitors vie. Furthermore, the ancient commentator captures the essence of an Odyssean opposition in his final rationalizing note that the suitors' constant pitching of marbles enfeebled their arms so that they could not string the bow. This slightly comic touch highlights the antipathy between the disembodied or symbolic games favored by the suitors and proper aristocratic contests of strength.

---

[11] The suitors' game as imagined here bears a certain resemblance to a Kabyle game described by Bourdieu 1990: 293–94n.10: "Thus in the game of *qochra*, which the children play in early spring. . . . The cork ball (the *qochra*) which is fought for, passed and defended, is the practical equivalent of woman. In the course of the game the players must both defend themselves against it and, once possessing it, defend it against those trying to take it away. At the start of the match, the leader of the game repeatedly asks, 'Whose daughter is she?' but no one will volunteer to be her father and protect her; a daughter is always a liability for men. And so lots have to be drawn for her, and the unlucky player who gets her must accept his fate. He now has to protect the ball against the attacks of all the others, while at the same time trying to pass it on to another player; but he can only do so in an honourable, approved way. A player whom the 'father' manages to touch with his stick, telling him 'She's your daughter now', has to acknowledge defeat, like a man temporarily obliged to a socially inferior family from whom he has taken a wife. For the suitors the temptation is to take the prestigious course of abduction, whereas the father wants a marriage that will free him from guardianship and allow him to re-enter the game. The loser of the game is excluded from the world of men; the ball is tied under his shirt so that he looks like a girl who has been got pregnant."

The second stage of the suitors' "gaming" is the boxing match they mount between the competing beggars, the disguised Odysseus and "Iros." The poet's introduction of Iros at the beginning of Book 18 already casts him in the role of an intermediary, living at the behest of others, for we are told that his given name was Arnaios, but he was called Iros "because he was always carrying messages, whenever anyone should bid him" (*Od.* 18.5–7). When Iros and the disguised Odysseus come into conflict over begging territory, the suitors seize the opportunity for entertainment: Antinoös stages a match, offering as prize goats' bellies that emblematize the combatants' own enforced and degraded bodiliness (*Od.* 18.43–49).[12] Indeed, as the suitors are inappropriately disembodied, vicariously enjoying the dangers of competition as spectators, the two combatants become excessively bodily. Odysseus laments that his "evil-working belly" (γαστήρ . . . κακοεργός, *Od.* 18.53–54) compels him to suffer blows, and then the poet provides us with an elaborate description of his mighty thews once his rags are cast off (*Od.* 18.67–70). When Iros quails, Antinoös threatens him with grotesque bodily mutilation at the hands of King Echetos on the mainland (thus even physical punishment is to be enacted through an intermediary). Finally, the stricken Iros falls bellowing like a mortally wounded animal from Odysseus's blow.[13]

The poet then stages the suitors' reaction in a remarkable line:

> ἀτὰρ μνηστῆρες ἀγαυοὶ
> χεῖρας ἀνασχόμενοι γέλῳ ἔκθανον. (*Od.* 18.99–100)

But the proud suitors, holding up their hands, died laughing.

The suitors "holding up their hands" exactly mimic the gesture of the combatants (described as χεῖρας ἀνέσχον at 89 and ἀνασχομένω at 95). The gestural echo points the contrast, since the young men raise their hands only to laugh. More remarkable still is the poet's bold metaphor γέλῳ ἔκθανον ("they died laughing"). Metaphors are extremely rare in Homer compared to similes; here the metaphoric usage offers the stylistic equivalent of the the suitors' logic of substitution, underscoring their disembodied relation to the life-or-death struggle. And, of course, as

---

[12] As Russo notes (in Russo, Fernández-Galiano, and Heubeck 1992: 49–50) the *gastēr* as prize picks up and literalizes Odysseus's repeated laments about the compulsions of the belly (cf. *Od.* 7.216–21, 15.344–45, 17.286–89, 470–74). Cf. Svenbro 1976: 50–59 and Rose 1992: 108–10 on the centrality of the motif of the belly in the *Odyssey*. Notice that for the suitors, even the prize offered is *allotrios*, since it is the belly of one of Odysseus's goats sacrificed for their midday meal.

[13] As Levine (1982: 201) notes, the half-line describing his collapse, κὰδ δ' ἔπεσ' ἐν κονίῃσι μακών ("And he fell in the dust bellowing," *Od.* 18.98) is always used elsewhere in Homer for animals mortally wounded. Cf. Antinoös's address to Iros as βουγάϊε (which seems to mean something like "you dumb ox") at *Od.* 18.79.

Odysseus's actions in the bow contest make the game real, so also he will literalize the poet's metaphor.

The combination of laughter and bold linguistic usage links this fleeting image in Book 18 with the uncanny hilarity of the suitors at the end of Book 20. There Athena sends upon them grotesque laughter as they consume blood-flecked meat and drip tears:

οἱ δ' ἤδη γναθμοῖσι γελώων ἀλλοτρίοισιν,
αἱμοφόρυκτα δὲ δὴ κρέα ἤσθιον· ὄσσε δ' ἄρα σφέων
δακρυόφιν πίμπλαντο, γόον δ' ὠίετο θυμός. (Od. 20.347–49)

And they were laughing with jaws not their own, and they were eating meat flecked with blood; and their eyes were filled with tears, and their spirit was intent on lamentation.

We can attempt to explain ἀλλοτρίοισιν by saying that the suitors are "possessed" by Athena, but that doesn't adequately account for the strangeness of "jaws not their own."[14] It is instead an act of justice, both poetic and divine, that reciprocates their expropriation of Odysseus's property and status. For the term *allotrios* functions as a leitmotif in the *Odyssey* to mark the suitors' improper consumption of Odysseus's household.[15] Here, remarkably, the suitors become alienated from themselves and, as the seer Theoklymenos recognizes, this turnabout signals their impending destruction.

The final act in this drama of games and gamesmanship is, of course, the contest of the bow in Book 21. The suitors engage in what they imagine is a purely symbolic contest of strength and skill, even as they offer a series of escalating threats of violence to their social inferiors (in this respect, the contest appears to conform closely to the pattern of the boxing match in Book 18). Thus Antinoös responds to the beggar Odysseus's request to try the bow with renewed threats of grievous bodily mutilation, first implicitly by likening the drunken beggar to the centaur Eurytion, then explicitly threatening to ship him off to the fearsome King Echetos (Od. 21.295–310). This apparent contrast between the symbolic activity in which they are engaged and the prospect of real bodily harm climaxes with the dueling threats the suitors and Telemachos make to the swineherd Eumaios as he finally conveys the bow into the hands of the "beggar." The suitors abuse him with the prospect of his own dogs consuming him if he gives the bow to Odysseus, while Telemachos counters with the threat that he will himself stone the old man if he fails in his errand (Od. 21.362–65, 369–75).

---

[14] Russo 1992: 124 offers the explanation of divine possession.
[15] Cf. Od. 1.160, 17.452, 456, 18.18, 280, 20.171, 221.

And yet, finally, it is the suitors who become the victims, as Odysseus literalizes the game and makes them his targets. The moment at which the game pivots into real violence is marked by the same kind of verbal echo that articulated the levels of combatants and spectators in Book 18. As Odysseus puts the first arrow in the now-strung bow and prepares to shoot through the axeheads, the poet describes the quiver full of arrows "of which the Achaians were soon going to make trial" (τῶν τάχ᾽ ἔμελλον Ἀχαιοὶ πειρήσεσθαι, Od. 21.418). The verb "to make trial" (πειρήσεσθαι) significantly echoes Odysseus' own "testing" of the bow some twenty lines earlier (πάντῃ ἀναστρωφῶν, πειρώμενος ἔνθα καὶ ἔνθα, "turning it in every direction, making trial of it here and there," Od. 21.394), with the crucial difference that Odysseus tests the bow as marksman, while the suitors will test the arrows as targets, now fully incorporated in the game.

Finally, after the shot that wins the symbolic contest, the "beggar" grimly calls for dinner:

νῦν δ᾽ ὥρη καὶ δόρπον Ἀχαιοῖσιν τετυκέσθαι
ἐν φάει, αὐτὰρ ἔπειτα καὶ ἄλλως ἑψιάασθαι
μολπῇ καὶ φόρμιγγι· τὰ γάρ τ᾽ ἀναθήματα δαιτός. (Od. 21.428–30)

Now it is time to make dinner for the Achaians in the light, and then afterward also to play with song and lyre: for these are the ornaments of the feast.

Odysseus engages in a last disturbing bit of metaphor, likening the slaughter of the suitors (which follows immediately) to the perennial uninvited feasts they have enjoyed, while he transforms them from banqueters to dinner.[16] In this context, his use of the verb ἑψιάασθαι is striking; though here it is associated with the "play" or "entertainment" of "song and lyre," its one other occurrence in the poem describes the suitors playing games "while seated at the doors or in the house itself."[17] Thus Odysseus's brutally ironic words here on the verge of slaughter carry us all the way back to our first view of the suitors, idly playing *pessoi* as they consume another man's household.

The *Odyssey*'s pattern of game and real violence constitutes an ideology of embodiment: noble men themselves make contact with *xeinoi*, participate in war or in the elegant athleticism of the Phaiakians. The suitors,

[16] Stanford (1971: 2.370) notes the way in which the mention of dinner here recalls the poet's own ominous reference to the "unlovely feast" prepared for the suitors by "a god and a mighty man" at Od. 20.392–94.
[17] Od. 17.530–38, where again the suitors' play is associated with their inappropriate consumption of the household goods. Apollonius Rhodius uses ἑψιάομαι to describe Eros and Ganymede playing *astragaloi* at *Argonautica* 3.118.

in contrast, reveal their inadequacy in this system by their predilection for substitution. Their co-option of Odysseus's house and property has nothing to do with *xenia*, since they barely reciprocate from the "body" of their own houses. All their behavior within Odysseus's house is shaped by the same logic of symbolic substitution: they are perennially waited on by others; they enjoy the sexual services of the maidservants as a substitute for those of the mistress; and they use Odysseus' servants and beggars as "pawns" in their sadistic entertainments. This whole array of inappropriate disembodied activity is communicated in shorthand the first time we see the suitors, by the significant detail that they are "playing *pessoi*." The use of symbolic counters or tokens and the mediation of the symbolic space of the gameboard stand in direct opposition to the embodied ideals of Greek manhood.[18] This conflict between an ideology of embodiment and symbolic activity represented by the gameboard endured in Greek literature, though, strikingly in the archaic and classical periods, we can trace a strand of thought that valorized the game in opposition to the bodily ideal of the elite.

Among the innovations of the archaic period, two distinct forms of *pessoi* (neither identifiable as the suitors' game) appear to have their origin.[19] The first is a game which, according to Pollux, is called *polis*:

ἡ δὲ διὰ πολλῶν ψήφων παιδιὰ πλινθίον ἐστί, χώρας ἐν γραμμαῖς ἔχον διακειμένας· καὶ τὸ μὲν πλίνθιον καλεῖται πόλις· τῶν δὲ ψήφων ἑκάστη, κύων· διῃρημένων δὲ εἰς δύο τῶν ψήφων κατὰ τὰς χρόας, ἡ τέχνη τῆς παιδιᾶς ἔστι περιλήψει τῶν δύο ψήφων ὁμοχρόων τὴν ἑτερόχρουν ἀναιρεῖν·[20] (Pollux *Onom.* 9.98)

---

[18] This is not to say that the *Odyssey* represents or endorses *only* what I have termed an "ideology of embodiment"; Odysseus and the text in which he figures are much more complex. Thus, for example, Odysseus as a bowman (especially one who uses poisoned arrows) himself controverts or problematizes an ideal of embodied warfare, or, in other terms, we might note how embodiment characterizes both those at the top and at the very bottom of the social scale (Odysseus as king and as beggar). For an insightful discussion of the ideological tensions and complexities of the poem, see Rose 1992: 92–140.

[19] In the following summary, I rely mainly on the arguments and conclusions of Austin 1940, who emphasizes the need for great caution and exactitude in differentiating the various games played on a board. *Contra* Lamer 1927: 1937–39, I do not find any good fifth-century evidence (as opposed to much later evidence) for the claim that the terms *pessoi, psēphoi, kuboi,* and *astragaloi* were used interchangeably in the sources.

[20] Cf. Eustathios *Comm. Hom.* p. 1397.44–45 (ad *Od.* 1.107ff): "There is another form of game 'polis,' in which the taking of pieces occurs back and forth when many pieces have been disposed on spaces divided by lines. And they used to call the lined spaces 'poleis' quite wittily, and the pieces opposed to each other 'dogs,' on account (I suppose) of their shamelessness."

The game played through many pieces is a board that has spaces disposed between lines; and the board is called "polis" and each of the pieces a "dog." The pieces are divided in two by color and the art of the game is to capture the other-colored piece by surrounding it with two of the same color.

As described by Pollux, this game functions within a general typology of board games as a "battle game": played with many pieces (Photios tells us there were thirty on each side), as a game of skill without dice. Within the game, all the pieces appear to have been equal in status; that is to say, it is more like modern checkers than chess.[21] As R. G. Austin reconstructs it: "The tactics consisted in preventing the enemy from maintaining his massed formation, and by breaking through it to manoeuvre until his force was gradually scattered and so taken. An isolated man brought danger to himself and to his side."[22] It is probably *polis* to which Plato and Polybius refer as a game of strategy requiring great tactical skill. Philostratos too may have this particular game in mind when he characterizes *petteia* as "no idle game, but one full of wisdom and needing great attention" (οὐ ῥάθυμον παιδιὰν ἀλλ' ἀγχίνουν τε καὶ εἴσω σπουδῆς, *Heroikos* 33.4).[23] We know that the game existed at least as early as the second half of the fifth century, since Pollux quotes a passage from Kratinos to illustrate the use of the terms *polis* and *kuōn* (Pollux *Onom.* 9.99 = Kratinos fr. 61 K.-A.).

A second game, called *pente grammai*, remains much more obscure. As Pollux describes it:

πέντε δὲ ἑκάτερος εἶχε τῶν παιζόντων ἐπὶ πέντε γραμμῶν, εἰκότως εἴρηται Σοφοκλεῖ, 'καὶ πεσσὰ πεντέγραμμα καὶ κύβων βολαί.' τῶν δὲ πέντε τῶν ἑκατέρωθεν γραμμῶν μέση τις ἦν ἱερὰ καλουμένη γραμμή· καὶ ὁ τὸν ἐκεῖθεν κινῶν πεττὸν παροιμίαν ἐποίει, κίνει τὸν ἀφ' ἱερᾶς. (Pollux *Onom.* 9.97–98)

[21] For the typology of board games, see Austin 1940: 259: "The simplest board-games of most countries are based on three primitive activities of man—the battle, the race, and the hunt—modern types of which are chess, backgammon, and fox-and-geese. Such types one would expect to find among the Greek games. . . . The object of the battle-game is to hem in one's opponents and drive them off the board; no specified number of men or size of board is needed, and in the earliest forms of the game there is no differentiation of pieces; no dice are used. In the race-game, the aim is to bring one's men to an appointed terminus and so be first off the board; again there is no differentiation, but the number of men is fixed, usually 15 on each side; dice are used to control moves. In the hunt, a single piece tries to escape from an opposing pack; no Greek or Roman game seems to have been of this type, which was common, however, in Scandinavia and among the early Celts."
On non-differentiation or equality of pieces as a characteristic feature of G (as opposed to their Roman counterparts), see Lamer 1927: 1927.
[22] Austin 1940: 264.
[23] Cf. Plato *Rep.* 487b, Polybius 1.84 (all three references are dra'
1940: 261–66).

Each of those playing had five [*pessoi* or *psēphoi*] upon five lines, so that it is suitably said in Sophocles, "five-lined boards and the throws of the dice."[24] And of the five lines from [on?] either side there was a middle one called the "holy line"; the one who moved the piece from there made the saying, "Move from the holy line."

Eustathios adds that the "move from the holy line" was the last resort for a player who was being beaten, "whence the proverb . . . for people who are desperate and in need of final aid" (ὅθεν καὶ παροιμία . . . ἐπὶ τῶν ἐν ἀπογνώσει δεομένων βοηθείας ἐσχάτης, Eustathios *Comm. Hom.* p. 633.57–59; 2.277.15–17 Valk). Unfortunately, these accounts do not provide enough detail to reconstruct the game with any certainty, and modern scholars debate the exact layout of the board and structure of play.[25] Thus, for example, it is unclear whether this game involved dice as well as pieces moved on a board; the combination of dice and board would make it typologically a "race-game" like backgammon. There is some evidence to suggest the use of dice in *pente grammai*, and we have ancient references to an unnamed game that combined the throwing of three dice (*kuboi*) with pieces moved on a board.[26] If these passages do *not* refer to *pente grammai*, they refer to a third distinct form of *petteia* whose name is unknown to us. R. G. Austin summarizes the murky state of the evidence:

> We are bound to accept the conclusion that this "sacred line" is not only in itself an insoluble problem without further evidence, but also precludes identification of the Greek game with any other until its nature can be satisfactorily established. S. G. Owen assumed . . . that the game was a race-game, played with dice, like the Roman XII *scripta*; the idea of γραμμαί might support this (although "five lines" was not necessarily the name of the game), and the evidence of the scholiast to Plato . . . might also be

[24] For the interpretation of this line, I follow Lamer 1927: 1914; Austin 1940: 268n.10.

[25] For proposed reconstructions, see Becq de Fouquières 1873: 396–405; Murray 1952: 28–29. Lamer 1927: 1973 and Austin 1940: 267–71 refuse even to attempt a reconstruction (Austin observing grimly, "The obscurity of all this evidence is impenetrable" [268]). More recently, Cilley 1986: 41–55 has offered a new reconstruction, based largely on the study of twenty lined boards preserved in the archaeological record (ibid: 48–51, building on and expanding the catalogue offered by Pritchett 1968: 189–96).

[26] Cf. Aesch. *Ag.* 32–33 (with notes of Fraenkel 1950: 19–22); Aristoph. *Frogs* 1400; a small painted clay model of a gaming board from Athens, now in Copenhagen (dated to the second quarter of the sixth century; see Breitenstein 1941, pl. 19, no. 171, reproduced in Pritchett 1968 as plate 7.1); and the Exekias amphora in the Vatican, on which Achilles and Ajax are clearly moving pieces on a board, but the words *tria* and *tesara* are inscribed coming out of their mouths (hence dice throws? for discussion of this image, see below). Soph. fr. 429 R (cited by Pollux *Onom.* 9.97) may also support the use of dice in *pente grammai*, but only if we assume that the two halves of the line refer to a single game.

quoted; but the apparent shape of the board, so far as it can be inferred, is against this interpretation, while the age of the game, going back as it does to Alcaeus at least, would seem not to be in favour of a game of hazard; also, the "sacred line" and its function is no more clear in this type of game than it would be in the battle-type.[27]

In one detail I would diverge from Austin's cautious and sensible account. One reference to the game of *pente grammai* in the scholia to Theokritos asserts that the piece moved from the holy line was called "the king" (βασιλεύς, Schol. *ad* Theokr. 6.18.19a). Most modern scholars (Austin among them) discount this bit of information, because it occurs in a context in which the scholiast asserts that the game referred to is ζατρίκιον ("chess"), suggesting that the commentator is conflating an obsolete board game with a later game he knew.[28] And yet, I believe there is early evidence that at least one form of *pessoi* involved a piece called the king. In a famously obscure fragment, Herakleitos characterizes time (αἰών) as a "boy playing *pessoi*": αἰὼν παῖς ἐστι παίζων, πεσσεύων· παιδὸς ἡ βασιληίη ("Time is a boy playing, playing *pessoi*; kingship belongs to the boy," fr. B 52 DK). Though this fragment has generally been taken to refer to the arbitrary or random nature of events in time, Charles Kahn offers a different interpretation:

> My own solution to this most enigmatic of Heraclitean riddles is indicated by the translation of *pesseuōn* as "moving pieces in a game," where this is understood as an echo of 'things transposed' (*metapesonta*) in [fr. B 88 DK]. What was there said to be moved back and forth was "living and dead, and the waking and the sleeping, and young and old." Such reversals constitute the very principle of cosmic order. More specifically, these three pairs define the structure of human experience as an alternating pattern of being kindled and going out. On my view the fundamental thought is not the childlike and random movements of the game (as some interpreters have supposed) but the fact that these moves follow a definite rule, so that after one side plays it is the other's turn, and after the victory is reached the play must start over from the beginning. The rules of the *pessoi*-game thus imitate the alternating measures of cosmic fire.

My interpretation assumes a continuity of thought and imagery between [fr. 88] and [fr. 52]. This continuity would be guaranteed if we could be sure that the game of *pessoi* envisaged in [fr. 52] involved the use of dice, like modern *tavli* or backgammon. . . . For the verb *metape*

---

[27] Austin 1940: 270–71.

[28] Cf. Gow 1952: 2.122–23; Gow is inclined to credit the scholiast's clai acknowledges the difficulties.

transpositions in [fr. 88] has the literal sense "fall out otherwise" and could immediately suggest the fall of a die.[29]

Kahn's notion that Herakleitos's game should combine throws of dice with pieces moved on a board may connect it with *pente grammai*, as we have seen. Given this suggestive context, Herakleitos's mention of "kingship" is striking. In his interpretation Kahn abruptly shifts at this point from ludic vehicle to cosmic tenor: "It is obvious why the player possesses 'kingship', since the game is a cosmic one, and the player must be lord of the universe."[30] And yet we might imagine that Herakleitos expresses this cosmic dominion *while maintaining* the image of *pessoi*; it may be that, in terms of the metaphor, "kingship belongs to the boy" because he controls the "king-piece."[31]

This possibility may find confirmation in a brief fragment of Alkaios quoted by Eustathios to illustrate the proverb, "he moves from the holy line:"

νῦν δ' οὗτος ἐπικρέτει
κινήσαις τὸν ἀπ' ἴρας †πυκινὸν† λίθον (Alk. fr. 351 V)

But now this one rules, having moved the piece from the holy line.

If we assume that this passage refers to the rule of Pittakos as elected tyrant or *aisymnētēs*, again the notion of a king-piece on the board suits Alkaios's metaphoric usage. The poet bitterly and dismissively characterizes his opponent as (merely) a pretend king in a board game. Indeed, the evocation of a *basileus*-piece may have particular resonance if, as some scholars argue, the early tyrants used *basileus* as their title.[32]

Even given the limited amount we can reconstruct about these games, their names and forms of play are suggestive. The regulated, rule-bound movement of pieces on a board appealed to the Greeks as an image of various forms of symbolic order. Thus Plato on one occasion, perhaps following Herakleitos, figures the creator of the cosmos as a *pessoi*-player (πεττευτής) who disposes "parts for the sake of the whole" as he places

[29] Kahn 1979: 227, citing Marcovich 1967: 494 for the suggestion that this game of *pessoi* involves dice.

[30] Kahn 1979: 228.

[31] Admittedly, the combination of the use of dice with a king-piece in a single game would contravene Austin's typological model (see above, n. 21), but it may be (as I argue below) that this combination has a particular appeal in a Greek cultural and political context.

[32] For archaic tyrants using *basileus* as their title, see Pleket 1969: 21; Oost 1972; Ogden 1997: 148–51; for Pittakos in particular, this suggestion is supported by the language of a Lesbian grinding song preserved by Plutarch (= Carm. pop. 23/869 PMG): ἄλει μύλα ἄλει / καὶ γὰρ Πιττακὸς ἄλει / μεγάλας Μυτιλήνας βασιλεύων ("Grind, mill, grind; for even Pittakos grinds, he who is king in great Mytilene").

different souls in different bodies (*Laws* 903c5–e1).[33] According to Timaios, *petteia* "was also sometimes called 'geometry' " (γεωμετρίαν), and we are told that Klearchos likened the five pieces in *pente grammai* to the five planets.[34] In other contexts, *petteia* serves Plato as a favorite image for the process of dialectic (e.g., *Gorg.* 461d1–3, *Rep.* 487b1–c3).

But of all the things the game board and pieces can signify, I would like to focus on the civic symbolism inherent already in the names and structure of these games. For the game called *polis*, this is clear; somehow the board is like the city whose framing structure endows its citizens with identity and equal status. In the case of *pente grammai* (bracketing for the moment the possibility of a "king-piece"), the "holy line" as the midmost of five lines may evoke the temples and sanctuaries that tend to occupy the acropolis at the center of the city, so that the game board mimes civic geography.[35] And whether it was *pente grammai* or some other board game that involved the use of dice, the combination of pure chance and movement on a board elegantly figures the mediation of the polis, which interposes itself as a screen between individual citizens and the devastating force of *tuchē*.[36]

If we are willing to accept the existence of a king-piece in the game of *pente grammai*, we can carry the game-city analogy even a step further; we may say that *polis* analogizes the democratic city, while *pente grammai* mimes the form of oligarchy. Thus the former is played with many pieces, all of equal status, on an undifferentiated gameboard; the latter with few pieces in competition for supreme status, on a board whose space is itself differentiated and hierarchized. We might recall Aristotle's remarks on the ideal geography for different regimes:

> With regard to fortified places, what is advantageous is not the same for all regimes. For example, a fortified height (ἀκρόπολις) is characteristic of oligarchy and monarchy; levelness is characteristic of democracy; neither of these is characteristic of aristocracy, but rather a number of strong places. (Arist. *Pol.* 1330b17–21, trans. C. Lord 1984)

We may catch a glimpse of this differential civic symbolism of the two forms of *pessoi* in an exchange from Euripides' *Suppliant Women*. A messenger from Thebes enters and asks Theseus, "Who is sole ruler

---

[33] Kahn 1979: 328n.302 suggests that the Platonic passage is "haunted with Heraclitean reminiscences."

[34] For Timaios and Klearchos, see Taillardat 1967: 150, 154.

[35] For a particular Greek city designed to have five sectors, see Svenbro 1982 on Megara Hyblaea.

[36] Plato on one occasion uses the image of a game combining dice and pieces on a board to allegorize the proper relation of chance and reason in human life: *Rep.* 604c5–d2; cf. Plut. *Mor.* 467a–b.

of this land?" (τίς γῆς τύραννος; *Suppl.* 399). His question sparks a spontaneous debate on the relative virtues of different constitutions:

Θη· πρῶτον μὲν ἤρξω τοῦ λόγου ψευδῶς, ξένε,
   ζητῶν τύραννον ἐνθάδ'· οὐ γὰρ ἄρχεται
   ἑνὸς πρὸς ἀνδρός, ἀλλ᾽ ἐλευθέρα πόλις.
   δῆμος δ᾽ ἀνάσσει διαδοχαῖσιν ἐν μέρει
   ἐνιαυσίαισιν, οὐχὶ τῷ πλούτῳ διδοὺς
   τὸ πλεῖστον, ἀλλὰ χὠ πένης ἔχων ἴσον.
Αγ· ἓν μὲν τόδ᾽ ἡμῖν ὥσπερ ἐν πεσσοῖς δίδως
   κρεῖσσον· πόλις γὰρ ἧς ἐγὼ πάρειμ᾽ ἄπο
   ἑνὸς πρὸς ἀνδρός, οὐκ ὄχλῳ κρατύνεται.
                                    (Eur. *Suppl.* 403–11)

> *Theseus:* First, you have begun your speech falsely, stranger, seeking a tyrant
>   here; for it is not ruled by a single man, but it is a free city. But the demos
>   rules by yearly exchanges of power in turn, not giving the greatest share
>   to the rich man, but the poor man also has an equal share.
> *Herald:* This one thing you concede to us is better, just as in *pessoi*. For
>   the polis from which I am present is [ruled] by a single man, not dominated
>   by a mob.

The Theban herald's use of the simile of *pessoi* in the midst of this debate confirms the political resonances of board games, but it almost seems that Theseus and his interlocutor are modeling according to two different games within the same generic rubric. Theseus imagines Athens on the model of the game of *polis*, in which all the pieces have equal standing. The Theban, in contrast, seems to be envisioning a different game, in which Theseus's assertion that there is no single ruler on his side is the greatest concession he can make to his opponent. Thus the collision of regimes is also a clash of game structures.

But, as this passage from the *Suppliants* proves, the analogy between game and city works both ways. If the board game is somehow like the city for the archaic inventors and players of *pessoi*, the converse is also true: being a citizen in a city is a symbolic activity like a game. It is this half of the analogy that radically unsettles the elite "ideology of embodiment" we traced in the *Odyssey*. We can see the beginnings of this disorientation already in Alkaios, who conjures the image of the game board to belittle and dismiss his opponent Pittakos (fr. 351 V, quoted above). Like many other Alkaian fragments, this bit of political invective works by the torque of oxymoron; the verb ἐπικρέτει strains against the following line, not just because of the implication that Pittakos has snatched victory from the jaws of defeat (the point of the proverb), but also because of the juxtaposition of real power with the make-believe of the game. And yet the tool of the belittling image seems to turn in the poet's hand; in this respect, Alkaios's lines almost invite their own subversion, in a way reminiscent of fr. 348 V:

τὸν κακοπατρίδα<ν>
Φίττακον πόλιος τὰς ἀχόλω καὶ βαρυδαίμονος
ἐστάσαντο τύραννον, μέγ' ἐπαίνεντες ἀόλλεες

They set up the baseborn Pittakos as sole ruler of the gutless and ill-fated city, acclaiming him greatly *en masse*.

Here the torsion is too great and the oxymoron snaps. The purpose of these lines is to expose Pittakos as "baseborn" and the people as "gutless and ill-fated," and yet the poet cannot quite obscure the act of demotic courage and consensus by which the commonality elected Pittakos their ruler (notice how μέγ' ἐπαίνεντες ἀόλλεες unbalances the invective). This act of public acclaim is in fact very relevant to the image in fr. 351 V, for election within the polis endows Pittakos with the symbolic standing of the king-piece in a game, but it is not less real and efficacious for being symbolic.

It may be that Pittakos, at least as he is represented in the tradition, understood and embraced the reality of symbolic political activity. Thus, where Alkaios asserts "wine is the window into a man" (οἶνος γὰρ ἀνθρώπω δίοπτρον, fr. 333 V), Pittakos is said to have quipped, "Office shows the man" (ἀρχὴ ἄνδρα δείκνυσιν, D.L. 1.77). While the poet affirms the essentializing value of the aristocratic symposium to reveal the true nature of its participants, Pittakos, the perfect functionalist, prefers the symbolic activities of the public sphere.[37]

In opposition to Alkaios's elitist hostility, an anecdote involving the philosopher Herakleitos may reflect a positive appreciation for the game-like quality of civic action.[38] According to Diogenes Laertius:

Being asked to make laws [by the Ephesians], he disdained to do so, on account of the city's already being ruled by a wicked constitution. And [instead] he withdrew to the temple of Artemis and played knucklebones with the boys (μετὰ τῶν παίδων ἠστραγάλιζε). And when the Ephesians

---

[37] For a more extended reading of Alkaian political invective along these lines, see Kurke 1994. For independent evidence of Pittakos's appreciation of the wisdom of games, see Diogenes Laertius 1.80: when a man asked Pittakos if he should marry above his station, Pittakos directed him to follow the advice of boys spinning tops, who admonish each other, "Keep to your own [sphere]" (τὴν κατὰ σαυτὸν ἔλα). Finally, we should note that, according to Pollux (*Onom.* 7.204), φύσγων (the term with which Alkaios abuses Pittakos in fr. 129 V) was one of the names for a lucky throw of dice.

[38] For Herakleitos's positive valuation of the city and its laws, see Schottlaender 1965; Vlastos 1970: 70–73; Kahn 1979: 178–81; Seaford 1994: 221–28.

gathered around him, he said, "Why do you marvel, o worst of men? Is it
not better to do this than to participate in the city with you?" (ἢ οὐ κρεῖττον
τοῦτο ποιεῖν ἢ μεθ' ὑμῶν πολιτεύεσθαι;) (D.L. 9.2–3)

Like many Herakleitean sayings and anecdotes, this one draws its point
from paradox, from the speaker's incongruous preference for children's
games over the deadly serious activity of lawmaking. And yet, in a sense,
the paradox is doubled: children's games are deadly serious to them (and
this may be especially true of *astragaloi*, as we shall see below), while
"making laws" (νόμους θεῖναι) is itself a symbolic activity like playing
a board game. It may be that Herakleitos is not opposing a game (ἠστραγάλιζε) to "real life" (πολιτεύεσθαι), but one kind of game to another,
in an effort to teach his fellow citizens an object lesson. (Thus, perhaps
πολιτεύεσθαι has a secondary meaning: "to play *polis*," like πεσσεύειν,
"to play *pessoi*.") By his performance, the philosopher may imply that
being a citizen in a polis means playing a game—engaging in symbolic
activity—in deadly earnest.[39]

Indeed, we may find the culmination of this paradoxical structure,
again invoking *pessoi* to characterize the symbolic activity of the polis,
in a famous passage of Aristotle (which, in its complexity, needs to be
quoted at length):

> From these things it is evident, then, that the city belongs among the things
> that exist by nature, and that man is by nature a political animal. He who
> is without a city through nature rather than chance is either a mean sort or
> superior to man; he is "without clan, without law, without hearth," like
> the person reproved by Homer; for the one who is such by nature has by
> this fact a desire for war, insofar as he is isolated, like a piece in a game of
> *pessoi* (ἅμα γὰρ φύσει τοιοῦτος καὶ πολέμου ἐπιθυμητής, ἅτε περ ἄζυξ
> ὢν ὥσπερ ἐν πεττοῖς). That man is much more a political animal than any
> kind of bee or any herd animal is clear. For, as we assert, nature does nothing
> in vain; and man alone among the animals has speech. The voice indeed
> indicates the painful or pleasant, and hence is present in other animals as
> well; for their nature has come this far, that they have a perception of the

---

[39] The same analogy of civic governance and game may inform another anecdote preserved
in Diogenes Laertius, as well as a fragment of Herakleitos's own writing: (1) When the
Ephesians banished Herakleitos's friend Hermodoros, the philosopher said, "The Ephesians
deserve to die, every grown man of them, and leave the city to the beardless boys" (D.L.
9.2); (2) Iamblichos tells us "how much better [than some other theorist] did Herakleitos
judge in considering the opinions of men to be boys' games?" (πόσῳ δὴ οὖν βέλτιον Ἡ.
παίδων ἀθύρματα νενόμικεν εἶναι τὰ ἀνθρώπινα δοξάσματα; fr. B 70 DK). We might
also recall the tradition that Herakleitos abdicated hereditary kingship in Ephesus in favor
of his brother (D.L. 9.6)—is this the "wicked constitution" to which our anecdote refers?
On Herakleitean performances, see Battegazzore 1979: 9–25; Steiner 1994: 22–23, and cf.
Martin 1993 on the analogous performances of the Seven Sages.

painful and pleasant and indicate these things to each other. But speec.
serves to reveal the advantageous and the harmful, and hence also the just
and the unjust. For it is peculiar to man as compared to the other animals
that he alone has a perception of good and bad and just and unjust and
other things [of this sort]; and partnership in these things is what makes a
household and a city. (Arist. *Pol.* 1253a1–18; trans. C. Lord 1984, with
slight modifications)

As Austin observes, Aristotle's comparison of the *apolis* man to an "isolated piece in *pessoi*" almost certainly refers to the battle-game of *polis*,
in which a piece "has become cut off from the main force and so is in
danger itself and a danger to others."[40] The man who is *apolis* has lost
his place within the symbolic structure that gives him identity and endows
his activities with sense; the polis, like the board, is the mediating structure
that gives meaning to its citizens.[41]

While the narrow context of Aristotle's comparison is military (it explains why "one who is such by nature" is a "desirer of war"), it is worth
teasing out the broader implications of the image of *pessoi* for this passage.
We can understand the whole paragraph as an elaborate, repeated unpacking or gloss on its opening paradoxical claim, that "man is by nature
a political animal" (in which Aristotle summarily reconciles the claims
of *nomos* and *phusis*). The sentence that contains the image of *pessoi*
reenacts the same paradox in its comparison of "one who is such *by
nature*" (φύσει) to a piece in a game: how can something in nature be
like a symbolic counter in a game? Aristotle proceeds to justify both
paradoxes ("political by nature," "game by nature") by the argument
that man alone of all the animals possesses *logos* and therefore the ability
to articulate abstract concepts like good and bad, just and unjust. Thus
the paragraph as a whole makes three claims: man is by nature a political
animal; man is by nature a game-playing animal; and man is by nature
a signifying animal. The implicit logic of the passage asserts the isomor-
phism of these three claims: to be one of these things is to be *necessarily*
each of the others. We may read this as a recasting in terms of *nomos*
and *phusis* of Herakleitos's paradox—polis is a game we play in
deadly earnest.[42]

We should note how far we have come from the *Odyssey*. There,
"playing *pessoi*" is almost an unnatural act, opposed to the naturalized
physical activity and embodiment of the good aristocrat. Four centuries

[40] Austin 1940: 265; on the meaning of ἄζυξ, see also Tréheux 1958.
[41] Cf. Vernant 1988: 136 and 437n.123 for a similar interpretation of the Aristotelian
passage.
[42] For other examples of *pessoi* used as an image in political contexts, cf. Aesch. *Suppl.*
11–15; Aristoph. *Ekkl.* 985–88; Plato *Rep.* 374c2–d6. We find an intriguing turn on the
image in Euripides fr. 360 N², Plato *Rep.* 422e, in which civic ideology constitutes its own

later, Aristotle, the great theorist and apologist of the polis, can unself-consciously justify the naturalness of civic order by invoking the symbolic activities of game-playing and *logos*. In light of this double analogy— the board game is like a city, the city is like a game—it is easier to understand the recurrence of *pessoi* in the lists of symbolic inventions with which we began. If we return to Gorgias's list, we recall that the links we found among its terms (excluding *pessoi*) were that all the inventions represented second-order signifying systems and all were claimed to serve the common good. We can see now that these same features, according to Greek thinking, characterized board games: for (some) Greeks of the archaic and classical periods, playing *pessoi* taught the player how to be a citizen in the polis. For the game called *polis*, this was true in at least two senses. Narrowly understood, the rules and strategy of this battle-game impressed on its players the importance of maintaining their place in the hoplite battle line rather than becoming ἄζυξ, "isolated" (and thus *pessoi* goes appropriately with military tactics, the first item on Gorgias's list). More broadly construed, the player learned what it meant to submit himself to the rules and symbolic order of the city that constituted him as a citizen equal in status to all other citizens.[43]

It is perhaps in light of these symbolic associations that we should read the iconographic type of the board-game-playing heroes, which enjoyed extraordinary popularity from the middle of the sixth century through the first quarter of the fifth. The representation of two armed heroes playing a game on a plinth set between them occurs as early as the mid sixth century on carved seals and shieldstraps found in Aigina, Olympia, and near Tarentum in Italy. But the bulk of these scenes occur on Attic vases from approximately 540 through 480 B.C.E. (a recent inventory numbers 152 black-figure and 16 red-figure versions of the scene).[44] Perhaps the most famous of these images is that on a black-figure belly amphora by Exekias, very close to the beginning of the series (ca. 540–530 B.C.E.), currently housed in the Vatican (Figure 8).[45] On it, two warriors,

---

essentialism. In these passages, *pessoi* serve as an image of bad—because diverse and arbitrary—polis structures.

[43] In this context, cf. what Thucydides has the Corinthians say of the Athenians (as the extreme of democratic, imperial citizen character): according to Thucydides' speaker, the Athenians "treat their bodies as if they were most someone else's on behalf of the city" (ἔτι δὲ τοῖς μὲν σώμασιν ἀλλοτριωτάτοις ὑπὲρ τῆς πόλεως χρῶνται, Thuc. 1.70.6)—like pieces played in the city's games of conquest?

[44] The information in this paragraph is drawn from Buchholz's catalogue of "brettspielen-den Helden" in Laser 1987: 126–84; see p. 184, Table 60 for statistics, and cf. the catalogue of Woodford 1982: 181–84.

[45] Inv. no. 16757 (344); *ABV* 145, 13.

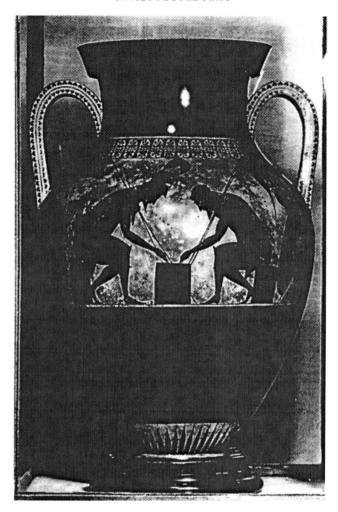

Figure 8. Vatican Museum, inv. no. 344. Attic black-figure
belly amphora painted by Exekias, ca. 540–530 B.C.E. Photo:
Hirmer Fotoarchiv, Munich.

identified by inscriptions as Ajax and Achilles, sit fully armed on low
blocks, intently moving pieces on a board set between them. It is impossible to determine what game they are playing, though the words *tesara*
(four) and *tria* (three) inscribed next to their mouths suggest that the
game involves the throw of dice as well as pieces moved on a board.[46]

---

[46] On the indeterminacy of the game they are playing, see Lamer 1927: 1995; Woodford
1982: 184–85. Nonetheless, it is clear that the figures are moving pieces on a board, and

Archaeologists have speculated that the image might have a literary source in an episode from one of the lost cyclic epics, but I think this highly unlikely.[47] Instead, I would suggest that the scene was invented in the sixth century as part of a civic appropriation of the Trojan War story—an attempt to translate the heroes of epic into the context of the polis. This civic appropriation (which has much in common with the practices of tragedy) would account for the extraordinary popularity of this type in the late sixth and early fifth centuries, as well as for the fact that Athena begins to appear in Attic versions of the scene once the iconography is established (according to Buchholz's catalogue, the goddess figures in 89 of the total 168 known representations).[48] Finally, we should note that a marble statue group representing the same scene may have been dedicated on the Athenian Acropolis (as we know from remains of it found in the *Perserschutt*).[49] It may be that this same impulse to appropriate the Trojan War saga for the world of the city informs the lists of Palamedes' inventions with which we began this chapter. As military tactics, written laws, weights and measures, coinage, and *pessoi* progressively accrue to the Greek culture hero, the Plain of Troy comes to look more and more like a Greek city.

To return to the specifics of Exekias's image, I would suggest that this translation to the world of the polis is implied not just by the fact that the heroes wear hoplite armor and wield hoplite shields (which lean behind them in this scene), but also by the fact that they are represented *playing a board game*. Or rather, a game that combines dice and pieces moved on a board. The throw of the dice we can understand, with Jeffrey Hurwit, as an ominous sign of the fate that awaits the doomed heroes:

> [I]t is not too much to suggest that the game of chance—the focus of the scene, on which all compositional lines (the spears, which themselves pick up the diagonal thrust of the handles, the fixed gaze of the eyes, even the oblique words *tesara* and *tria*) converge—is also a metaphor for fate. No Greek could have failed to observe that both heroes would die at Troy, that

---

this fact by itself makes impossible the interpretation of Boardman 1978, who connects this image with Herodotus's narrative of how the Athenian rebels at Pallene were defeated when caught unawares by Peisistratos's army as they were "playing *kuboi*" (Hdt. 1.63). Whatever Ajax and Achilles are playing, it *cannot* be *kuboi*. For other critiques of Boardman, see Hurwit 1985: 260; Buchholz in Laser 1987: 183–84.

[47] Cf. Lamer 1927: 1994; D. L. Thompson 1976; Woodford 1982: 178–80 for skepticism about an epic source for the image.

[48] Buchholz in Laser 1987: 184, Table 60.

[49] See Schrader and Langlotz 1939: figs. 142, 160, and 168; Payne and Mackworth-Young 1950: figs. 121, 4 and 6; 124, 3 and 6. Schrader and Langlotz date the remains to ca. 500 B.C.E.; for the argument that the two figures must be playing a board game on a plinth, see Deonna 1930; D. L. Thompson 1976.

Akhilleus, the victim of Paris' arrow, would be carried from the field by Ajax himself (Exekias painted the subject several times), and that Ajax would fall on his own sword.[50]

But what Hurwit's analysis ignores is that the heroes play not just a game of chance, but also a game of order: if the throw of the dice portends the doom beyond their control, the mediation of the game board rein-scribes their individual fates within the structure and meaning of the larger civic order. In the familiar euphemism of the Greek city, to die in battle fighting for the polis is "to become a good man."[51]

But, in order to be efficacious, this recuperating civic structure requires the complete identification of the individual warrior with the piece on the game board. It is finally this identification that Exekias's extraordinary image achieves. I quote Hurwit's masterful description of the composition:

> In a panel framed by lustrous black glaze Exekias drew a symmetrical and deceptively tranquil scene of Homeric heroes at play. Akhilleus and Ajax . . . bend over a table, call out the roll of the dice (the scores are written by their lips—*tesara*, four, for Akhilleus, *tria*, three, for Ajax), and move their pieces on the board. The silhouettes are like cutouts pasted over the undis-guised red wall of the vase. And although the spears of Akhilleus disappear behind the table and those of Ajax cross in front, the scene is flat and seemingly backlit. The light ground is not read as air or space but as a neutral void pushing the figures forward to the surface: luminous, it shows through the incisions within the forms. It is as if the red ground were not considered part of the image. Moreover, the eye naturally equates the black pictorial forms with the glaze outside the panel, and so they seem as tightly surface-bound as the vase's ornamental black skin. The planarity of the image is complemented by clarity of contour and precision of line, and anyone who doubts the incising tool's capacity for lavish meticulousness need only study the heroes' hair, cloaks (the patterns are doily-like), and armor.[52]

In Hurwit's description, the image invites us to see the flat cutout figures as pieces, the red ground as the surface of the gameboard. Indeed, we can take this reading even a step further, once we note that, in Attica at least, *pessoi* were often made of ornamented bits of old pottery smoothed into circular shapes (Figure 9).[53] Thus the highly patterned forms of the

---

[50] Hurwit 1985: 260–61; cf. Vermeule 1979: 81–82; Buchholz 1987: 183–84; S. P. Morris 1997: 68–70; S. P. Morris and Papadopoulos forthcoming.

[51] For the expression, see Loraux 1986: 3, 100–101, 104–6, 168, Gould 1989: 61–62 and cf. Hdt. 1.95.2, 1.169.1, 5.2.1, 6.14.1, 6.114, 7.224.1, 7.226.1–2, 9.71.3, 9.75.

[52] Hurwit 1985: 260.

[53] For game pieces made of pottery, see Lamer 1927: 1901, 1997–98; Laser 1987: 126 and plate IIIc.

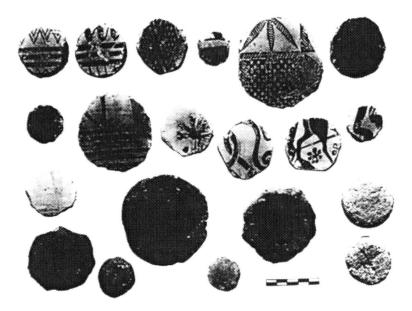

Figure 9. Athens, Agora Museum, inv. no. P 538, P 1793–1795, P 471, P 1796–99, P 537, P 1800. Game pieces (*pessoi*) fashioned from geometric pottery fragments, found on the northern slope of the Athenian Areopagos. Photo courtesy of the American School of Classical Studies at Athens: Agora Excavations.

heroes' hair, armor, and especially their cloaks, articulating the shape of their bodies, are the *very stuff* of game pieces, to which the artist draws our attention by his elaborate incising technique. In content and in style, the image affirms that the heroes are played in the game of civic warfare even as they play on the board between them.[54]

[54] S. P. Morris and Papadopoulos (forthcoming) follow Vermeule (1979: 77–82) in seeing the iconographic type of the board-game-playing heroes as an Egyptian import to Greece, whose main symbolic significance is eschatological. Thus the type of two figures playing a board game (in one instance with a female figure standing behind) occurs in Egyptian tombs from the Eleventh Dynasty (2000–1780 B.C.E.) on, while the moves of the Egyptian game of *snt* (or *senet*) were explicitly linked to the passage of the soul through the underworld on Egyptian game boards and in Egyptian texts (Vermeule 1979: 78–80; Cilley 1986: 5–9; Buchholz 1987: 182–83). All this endows the image of Ajax and Achilles (or two unnamed warriors) gaming with fateful resonances. I do not regard these two readings as mutually exclusive: the interpretation offered here is meant to supplement the eschatological reading, suggesting that Exekias's image is complex and multivalent. Thus the iconography both acknowledges the heroes' vulnerability to fate or chance *and* recuperates their fated death within the ordering framework of the polis (just as the game combines the randomizing effect of dice with the strategic order of pieces moved on a board). I would note that the

III. ARISTOCRATIC GAMES: EMBODIMENT, CHANCE, AND ORDEAL

If the archaic period saw the invention and currency of board games closely associated with civic order, it was also the period in which aristocratic games—the games of palaistra and symposium—emerged and assumed their distinctive form.[55] Games that appear to have had an elite association within the culture fall into two main types: games of embodiment (athletic games, ball games) and games of chance (*kottabos, astragaloi*). Games of embodiment perpetuated the essentializing valorization of the body that we traced in the *Odyssey*. We might find the elite association with games of chance a little puzzling, but we can understand it if we recall Ian Morris's schema of middling and elitist ideologies; the latter predicates its claims to authority on special links with the gods, the heroes, and the East.[56] On this model, elite games were either contests of physical strength and skill or trials of divine will and favor[57]; without the mediation of the game board, which figured that of the polis, the individual confronted the workings of fate directly. And indeed, a certain fateful or numinous quality particularly imbued this latter set of aristocratic pastimes. Thus, for example, both *kottabos* and *astragaloi* functioned as forms of *mantikē*, enabling direct access to divine will.[58] Nor was it the

---

theory of cultural borrowing alone cannot account for (1) the sudden reappearance of the iconography, as well as real game boards in Greek burials, in the early archaic period for the first time since the Bronze Age (Vermeule 1979: 80–82; S. P. Morris and Papadopoulos forthcoming: 8); (2) the transformation of the standing female servant of the Egyptian image into Athena; (3) the fact that with only three exceptions, all Greek representations of game-players are hoplites (cf. Woodford 1982: 177, who notes that the iconography in no way requires this specialization). All three phenomena (which differentiate the Greek images from their Egyptian prototypes) seem to me explicable as the civic inflection of an eschatological theme. Thus we might see the process of cultural influence or borrowing as the superimposition of a distinctively Greek set of connotations on a preexisting Egyptian model.

[55] In Athens at least, the emergence of the palaistra as a separate and defined space was a phenomenon of the sixth century; thus Hölscher 1991: 363: "This was the time when the aristocracy built its sports grounds outside the city, which are the scene of many late archaic vase paintings: at least the Academy, maybe the Lykeion as well, seems to have been established by the tyrants already in the sixth century. Thus the living spaces of the social classes must partially have become separated."

[56] Morris 1996: 19–20, 31–36.

[57] Indeed, as the rhetoric of Pindar's epinikia makes clear, these two categories are not really separable: every physical contest is also an ordeal (in the technical sense). The same applies to aristocratic games besides athletics—by and large, they combine elements of individual skill and style with tests of divine favor.

[58] Evidence for prophetic uses: for *kottabos*, see *Et. Mag.* 533.20; Schol. *ad* Aristoph. *Peace* 343; Schol. *ad* Lucian *Lexiphanes* 3 (fr. 195 R); Sartori 1893: 57–61; for *astragaloi*, see Schol. *ad* Pindar *P.* 4.337; Paus. 7.25.10; Kaibel 1876; Reiss 1896: 1793; Halliday 1913: 212–15; Hampe 1951: 20–21, 36–37nn. 56, 57; Amandry 1984a: 377–78; Simon 1986: 386–87; Gilmour 1997: 172–73.

case that all games of chance served as proper aristocratic pursuits, enjoying this numinous quality. For, as we shall see, there was a marked discursive opposition between *kuboi* (dice) and *astragaloi* (knucklebones).[59] In this section, I would like to consider each of these elite pastimes in turn—first ball games and *kottabos*, then the systematic oppositions between dice and knucklebones.

Ball and Kottabos

Ball games, of course, already figure in the *Odyssey*. Among the Phaiakians, Nausikaä plays ball with her attendants (*Od.* 6.99–101), and the young nobles Halios and Laodamas put on a display of combined dancing and ball-playing (*Od.* 8.370–80). In both cases, the beauty and grace of the princely players inspire awe and comparison with divinity; thus, the poet immediately segues from the description of Nausikaä playing ball to an extended comparison with Artemis (*Od.* 6.102–9), while Odysseus himself likens her to a beautiful date-palm sapling growing beside the altar of Apollo at Delos (*Od.* 6.161–69). Indeed, in both cases, Odysseus uses the same half-line to describe his reaction to the unearthly beauty of Nausikaä and the two Phaiakian youths engaged in their athletic displays: σέβας μ' ἔχει εἰσορόωντα ("awe holds me as I look upon [them]," *Od.* 6.162 = 8.384). These associations with the heroic age and with divine beauty and grace precisely suit the claims to preeminence of the elite, and they appear to endure in connection with ball-playing, at least to judge from a fragment of the fourth-century comic playwright Damoxenos preserved by Athenaios:

νεανίας τις ἐσφαίριζεν εἰς
ἐτῶν ἴσως . . . . . ἑπτακαίδεκα,
Κῷος· θεοὺς γὰρ φαίνεθ' ἡ νῆσος φέρειν.
ὃς ἐπεί ποτ' ἐμβλέψειε τοῖς καθημένοις,
ἢ λαμβάνων τὴν σφαῖραν ἢ διδούς, ἅμα
πάντες ἐβοῶμεν· " . . . .
ἡ δ' εὐρυθμία, τὸ δ' ἦθος, ἡ τάξις δ' ὅση
ἐν τῷ τι πράττειν ἢ λέγειν ἐφαίνετο.
πέρας ἐστὶ κάλλους, ἄνδρες. οὔτ' ἀκήκοα

---

[59] For evidence of a native system of categorization along the lines I am suggesting, cf. Pollux's chapter heading at *Onom.* 9.94: περὶ τῶν ἐν συμποσίοις παιδιῶν, περὶ κύβων, περὶ πεττῶν καὶ τοῦ κινήσω τὸν ἀφ' ἱερᾶς καὶ τῶν ἑξῆς ("Concerning the games [played] at symposia, *kuboi, pettoi* and the 'I will move from the holy [line],' etc."), where each use of περί marks a domain that was felt to be distinct.

ἔμπροσθεν οὔθ' ἑόρακα τοιαύτην χάριν.
κακὸν ἄν τι μεῖζον ἔλαβον, εἰ πλείω χρόνον
ἔμεινα· καὶ νῦν δ' οὐχ ὑγιαίνειν μοι δοκῶ. (Damoxenos fr. 3 K.-A.)

There was a young man playing ball, perhaps . . . seventeen years old, from
Kos—for that island appears to bear gods. And whenever he looked over
at us seated there, when he was catching or throwing the ball, we all shouted,
" . . . " What rhythm, what style, what form, whenever he did or said
anything! He is the limit of beauty, gentlemen. Never before have I heard
of or seen such grace. Something much worse would have happened to me,
if I had stayed there longer; as it is, I don't feel quite well.

Damoxenos's speaker makes explicit the undercurrent of eroticism already present in Odysseus's encounter with Nausikaä, inspired by the
aristocratic attributes of beauty (κάλλος), grace (χάρις), and rhythm
(εὐρυθμία) in the youthful ball-player. In contrast to skill at *pessoi*, which
requires "wisdom" and strategy, this aristocratic pursuit celebrates style
as the highest virtue.

We find the visual equivalent of Damoxenos's paean to aristocratic
form on the ball-player relief that once stood in the Athenian Kerameikos,
where it served as the base for a funerary kouros. The shallow relief of
six young men playing ball, dated to ca. 510 B.C.E., offers us a comprehensive study of the ideal male nude, each player providing a different view.[60]
Together with the kouros the base once supported (now lost), this representation of ephebic play celebrated for all eternity the bodily nobility
of its entombed aristocrat.[61]

All these resonances contribute to the aristocratic delicacy of Anakreon's fantasized ball game with Eros:

σφαίρῃ δηὖτέ με πορφυρέῃ
βάλλων χρυσοκόμης Ἔρως
νήνι ποικιλοσαμβάλῳ
     συμπαίζειν προκαλεῖται.
ἡ δ', ἔστιν γὰρ ἀπ' εὐκτίτου
Λέσβου, τὴν μὲν ἐμὴν κόμην,
λευκὴ γάρ, καταμέμφεται,
     πρὸς δ' ἄλλην τινὰ χάσκει. (fr. 13 Gentili = 358 PMG)

---

[60] Athens NM 3476; on its stylistic features, see Hurwit 1985: 301: "The relief is a
manual for the rendering of the body in action, a visual handbook of possible poses."

[61] For the link between the kouros and aristocratic bodily ideals, see Stewart 1986; Mack
1996. For this connection it is also worth noting the two other representations on the base:
(1) two wrestlers poised between a runner or jumper and a javelin-thrower; (2) youths
seated and standing, who are setting two animals to fight (see Robertson 1975: 226–27).

Golden-haired Eros, striking me again with a purple ball, calls me out to play with a girl with embroidered sandals. But she, since she is from well-built Lesbos, blames my hair, because it is white, but she's [really] gaping at another [feminine].

Here Anakreon exploits the erotic associations of ball-playing, while he links it to aristocratic luxury (the flash of purple, gold, and the embroidered sandal), the East (the girl is from Lesbos), and the gods. But ball-playing, as Eustathios informs us, is particularly for the young (the word he uses is ἐφηβική).[62] The eternally youthful god of love calls him out for a ball game, but the poet is getting too old for the sport; that is part of the irony—and self-irony—of the piece.

Yet, the mystified aura of Eastern luxury, eroticism, and grace that surrounded the ball game should not obscure the fact that the game also taught its young players how to rule. For, as we are told by a scholiast to Plato, "Of those playing these things [ball games], they used to call the winners 'kings' (βασιλεῖς) and whatever they would command to the rest, they used to obey, but the losers [they used to call] 'asses' (ὄνους)."[63] Those who committed errors or mistakes in play, whose form wasn't perfect, were reproved and humiliated by identification with the most ungainly and graceless of animals; but those who mastered the physical demands of the game were rewarded with rule over others (temporary though it might have been).

A second aristocratic game, which clearly had its origin in the archaic period, was *kottabos*, a game played at the symposium, in which the player flicked the wine lees from his cup at a target (either a small disk balanced on top of a stand, or little cruets floating in water in a larger vessel).[64] Thus *kottabos*, first referred to in the fragments of Alkaios and Anakreon, partook of both games of skill and games of chance. Many of our sources emphasize the element of physical embodiment, prescribing

---

[62] Eustathios *Comm. Hom.* p. 1601.35, cited in Taillardat 1967: 68. Notice how frequently Anakreon associates Eros with various aristocratic sports and games: Eros plays ball (fr. 13 Gentili); Eros boxes (fr. 38 Gentili); Eros wears the crown of an athletic victor (fr. 37 Gentili); and Eros plays knucklebones (fr. 111 Gentili).

[63] Schol. *ad* Plato *Theaet.* 146a (cited after Taillardat 1967: 69; cf. Eustathios *Comm. Hom.* p. 1601.41–46); the scholiast offers an explanatory gloss on a passage in which Socrates tries to draw boys into philosophical discussion by analogizing it to ball-playing: "And who of us would speak first? The one who is wrong, and whoever is wrong on each occasion, he will sit down as an ass (as boys say when they play ball). But whoever maintains himself without an error, he will be our king and he will command whatever he wishes [us] to answer" (*Theaet.* 146a1–5).

[64] For the two forms of *kottabos, kottabos kataktos* and *kottabos di' oxubaphōn*, see Athenaios *Deipn.* 15.666e–668a; Sartori 1893: 18–47; Hayley 1894. Athenaios is our most important single source for *kottabos*, to which he devotes nearly half of Book 15, as well as various *obiter dicta*.

just the right style for holding the wrist. For example, the fourth-century comic poet Antiphanes stages a scene of one character tutoring another in the fine points of *kottabos*-play:

Β. ᾧ δεῖ λαβὼν τὸ ποτήριον δεῖξον νόμῳ.
Α. αὐλητικῶς δεῖ καρκινοῦν τοὺς δακτύλους
οἶνόν τε μικρὸν ἐγχέαι καὶ μὴ πολύν·
ἔπειτ᾿ ἀφήσεις. Β. τίνα τρόπον; Α. δεῦρο βλέπε·
τοιοῦτον. Β. <ὦ> Πόσειδον, ὡς ὑψοῦ σφόδρα.
Α. οὕτω ποιήσεις. Β. ἀλλ᾿ ἐγὼ μὲν σφενδόνῃ
οὐκ ἂν ἐφικοίμην αὐτόσ᾿. Α. ἀλλὰ μάνθανε.
(Antiphanes fr. 57 K.-A., 14–20)

B: Taking hold of the cup, show me how it should be done.
A: You have to curve your fingers like an aulos-player, pour in a little bit of wine—not too much—then let it go. *B:* How? *A:* Look here. Like this.
B: O Poseidon, how very high [you threw it]! *A:* That's how you've gotta do it. *B:* But I couldn't reach that with a slingshot. *A:* Well, learn!

Athenaios, who preserves this fragment, elaborates on the speaker's instructions for how to hold the hand: "For one has to bend the wrist very gracefully (σφόδρα ... εὐρύθμως) in throwing *kottabos*, as Dikaiarchos says, and also Plato in the *Zeus Outraged*. There, someone bids Herakles not to hold his hand stiff (μὴ σκληρὰν ἔχειν τὴν χεῖρα) when he is going to toss" (*Deipn.* 15.667b). The analogy to playing a musical instrument (αὐλητικῶς) is suggestive, linking the sympotic game with another form of elite expertise. Like ball-playing, *kottabos* required εὐρυθμία, the effortlessly graceful physical style that marked the true aristocrat. On another occasion, Athenaios quotes an anonymous trochaic verse that sums up this emphasis on physical style and skill: καί τις ἦν ἀκριβὴς εὐχέρεια τῆς βολῆς ("And there should be a certain accurate dexterity of the throw," *Deipn.* 15.667e).

Again like ball-playing, *kottabos* had strong erotic associations. According to Athenaios, "In the old days, toasts of the participants did not occur, as Theophrastos says in his treatise *On Drunkenness*. Instead, in the beginning, the libation was rendered to the gods, and the *kottabos* to beloveds" (ἀλλ᾿ ἦν ἀπ᾿ ἀρχῆς τὸ μὲν σπένδειν ἀποδεδομένον τοῖς θεοῖς, ὁ δὲ κότταβος τοῖς ἐρωμένοις, *Deipn.* 10.427d). What does it mean for *kottabos* to be "dedicated" or "rendered" to the beloved? On another occasion Athenaios quotes two lines from a satyr play (= Achaios 20 fr. 26 *TrGF*) and explains the usage:

ῥιπτοῦντες, ἐκβάλλοντες, ἀγνύντες, τί μ᾿ οὐ
λέγοντες; "ὦ κάλλιστον Ἡρακλεῖ λάταξ."

τοῦτο δὲ "λέγοντες" παρ' ὅσον των ἐρωμένων ἐμέμνηντο ἀφιέντες ἐπ' αὐτοῖς τοὺς λεγομένους κοσσάβους.[65] (Athen. *Deipn.* 15.668a–b)

> Throwing, tossing, shattering—what do they not say of me? "Most beautifully, now, o wine-drop, for Herakles."

And this [phrase] "say of me" insofar as they made mention of their beloveds as they let go the so-called *kossaboi* for them.

ἐπ' αὐτοῖς is again ambiguous: does it mean "for them" as "dedicated to them," or "to win them"? Scholars have proposed different explanations: was it a way of honoring the beloved in what amounts to a form of flirtation; a predictor of erotic success (like "she loves me, she loves me not"); or the setting of a prize for a successful toss?[66] In support of this last possibility, we should note that kisses were sometimes offered as the prize for the winner in *kottabos*.[67] I am not sure, however, that we can or should necessarily choose one of these options to the exclusion of the others; the play space of the symposium presumably promoted a whole set of erotic possibilities. For our purposes, what is worth noting is the close association of the grace and good form of the successful *kottabos* toss with the fulfillment of erotic desire, whatever the precise mechanics might have been.

Finally, *kottabos*, like ball-playing, in spite of its luxurious and erotic associations (or, perhaps better, through them) worked to imprint a social hierarchy. For as we know from Antiphanes, at least one version of *kottabos* (*kottabos kataktos*) involved a piece called the manes, which was said to break the fall of the disk struck by wine lees. The manes was thus almost certainly the large central disk that surrounded the *kottabos* shaft (clearly visible in many vase representations of the game).[68] But Manes was also a generic name for foreign, especially Phrygian, slaves; indeed, Athenaios preserves a fragment of Antiphanes that plays on this very homonymy (drawn from the same scene of one character tutoring another in the game):

---

[65] For the text of Achaios's fragment, I follow Nauck rather than Snell (*TrGF*), who emends unnecessarily.

[66] For different interpretations of how exactly *kottabos* functioned in erotic contexts, see Sartori 1893: 57–64; Schneider 1922: 1538; Mingazzini 1950–51; Sparkes 1960: 207; Lissarrague 1990: 83–86; Csapo and Miller 1991.

[67] For kisses as prize, see Euboulos fr. 2 K.-A.; Plato Comicus fr. 46 K.-A., 5; Kallimachos fr. 2 Pfeiffer. For other contexts in which the erotic associations of *kottabos* are suggested, see Soph. fr. 537 R (= Athen. *Deipn.* 11.487d), Aristoph. *Clouds* 1071–73.

[68] Thus Sparkes 1960: 205–6 vs. Sartori 1893: 22–39, 114, who took manes to refer to the small statuettes that supported the top disk on some *kottabos* stands found in Etruria.

A. ἐγὼ διδάξω· καθ᾽ ὅσον ἂν τὸν κότταβον
ἀφεὶς ἐπὶ τὴν πλάστιγγα ποιήσῃ πεσεῖν—
B. πλάστιγγα; ποίαν; A. τοῦτο τοὐπικείμενον
ἄνω τὸ μικρόν B. τὸ πινακίσκιον λέγεις;
A. τοῦτ᾽ ἔστι πλάστιγξ—οὗτος ὁ κρατῶν γίγνεται.
B. πῶς δ᾽ εἴσεταί τις τοῦτ᾽; A. ἐὰν θίγῃ μόνον
αὐτῆς, ἐπὶ τὸν μάνην πεσεῖται καὶ ψόφος
ἔσται πάνυ πολύς. B. πρὸς θεῶν, τῷ κοττάβῳ
πρόσεστι καὶ Μάνης τις ὥσπερ οἰκέτης;
(Antiphanes fr. 57 K.-A., 5–13)

A: I will teach you. According to whatever extent [a man] releasing his
   kottabos upon the disk, makes it fall—
B: Disk? What disk?
A: This little one placed on it above.
B: You mean the little tiny disklette?
A: Yes, that's the disk—this one's the winner.
B: But how will anyone know this? A: If he only grazes it, it will fall on
   the manes and there'll be a great noise. B: By the gods, does the *kottabos*
   have some Manes of its own, just like a house slave?

The ignorant student exclaims in amazement that the *kottabos* has its
own "house slave," but in fact, the principle of the game is that the entire
symposium can recognize the winner (ὁ κρατῶν) as the one who makes
the manes ring. As one scholar explains the comic playwright's image:
"The comparison of the manes with the house slave in Antiphanes' comedy comes not from their physical similarity but from the 'very loud
noise' they both make when struck!"[69] Thus each game of *kottabos* was
a lesson in proper social hierarchy, in which the physical relations of up
and down, striking and struck, encode the domination of West over East,
Greek over barbarian, and master over slave.[70]

That the Greeks themselves appreciated the implications of the game
as a model for social domination is suggested by a fragment of Aeschylus
and an anecdote in Aristotle. The former (again preserved by Athenaios)
comes from Aeschylus' satyr-play *Ostologoi* (*The Bone Collectors*), presumably spoken by Odysseus:

Εὐρύμαχος †οὐκ ἄλλος† οὐδὲν ἧσσον<->
ὕβριζ᾽ ὑβρισμοὺς οὐκ ἐναισίους ἐμοί.
ἦν μὲν γὰρ αὐτῷ σκοπὸς ἀεὶ τοὐμὸν κάρα,

---

[69] Sparkes 1960: 206.

[70] And, of course, the ability to assert one's mastery in various states of intoxication is
the ultimate proof of noble quality; cf. Lissarrague 1990: 68–86.

τοῦ δ' ἀγκυλητοὺς κοσσάβους ἐπίσκοπος
†ἐκτεμὼν† ἡβῶσα χεὶρ ἐφίετο. (Aesch. fr. 179 R)⁷¹

Eurymachos—[no other?]—did [no less?] unseasonable acts of *hubris* against me. For my head was always his target, and his youthful and accurate hand used to let fly bended *kottaboi* at it.

Here the playwright replaces the suitors' Odyssean weapons—the footstool and the cowhoof—with the *kottabos* toss deftly aimed at the beggar's head. The splatter of wine lees, though much less dangerous than the traditional weapons, clearly articulates the relative social status of shooter and target; thus Eurymachos asserts his aristocratic preeminence and reduces the disguised Odysseus to the status of slave. Because it *is* Odysseus (and because the scene has shifted from Iron Age Ithaca to the stage in the democratic city), Eurymachos's party game is an act of *hubris*—the arrogant violation of another man's standing, or, as Demosthenes was to define it, "treating free men as if they were slaves."⁷²

An anecdote from Aristotle's *Rhetoric* extends the scope of domination analogized by the game from the personal to the civic. Aristotle, cataloguing various justifications for wrongdoing, tells the story of Ainesidamos, tyrant of Leontini, who once signaled his grudging admiration for Gelon, tyrant of Syracuse, by sending him a significant gift:

> And those [injustices] that are going to be done by others, if we don't do them ourselves, since it is no longer possible to deliberate, just as Ainesidamos is said to have sent *kottabos*-prizes to Gelon when he had enslaved [some city], because he had anticipated him, when he himself was intending to do it. (Arist. *Rhet.* 1373a21–24)

Gelon anticipates Ainesidamos in the conquest of a neighboring city both tyrants coveted, and Ainesidamos acknowledges his success with the gift of *kottabia* (eggs, cakes, and fruit traditionally given as the prizes for *kottabos*). It is wholly in keeping with the style of the Sicilian tyrants, who, as we saw in Chapter 4, aspired to the status of super-aristocrats, to figure the reduction and enslavement of an entire city as a winning *kottabos* toss. Indeed, the *kottabos* analogy is doubly significant, for it

---

⁷¹ The text of this fragment is very corrupt, though the general idea is clear (Eurymachos seems to be aiming *kottabos* throws at the head of Odysseus, an act which Odysseus regards as *hubris*). I have therefore incorporated into the text *exempli gratia* the emendations of Dobree in line 3 (σκοπὸς ἀεί) and Wecklein in line 4 (ἀγκυλητοὺς κοσσάβους ἐπίσκοπος), simply in order to be able to translate. For a much more cautious text and full *apparatus criticus*, see Radt.

⁷² Dem. 21.180, cf. 21.185; on *hubris*, see Fisher 1976, 1979, 1992.

acknowledges not only that Gelon is the conqueror (ὁ κρατῶν), but that he has a perfect sense of timing, an appreciation of *kairos* essential to aristocratic style.[73]

Kuboi vs. Astragaloi

To our minds, dice and knucklebones should form a natural set—both thrown in games of chance with the score reckoned from the exposed sides. *Kuboi*, like conventional modern dice, had six sides, each marked with dots from one to six, disposed on a cube in such a way that the sum of opposite sides was always seven. *Astragaloi*, (sheep or goat) knucklebones, since they could not land upright on their two narrow ends, had only four relevant sides, each recognizable by its natural contour.[74] Aside from these differences of four vs. six sides, and natural form vs. conventional marking, *astragaloi* and *kuboi* would seem to be identical in function and method of play. Indeed, in a single instance, in Aeschines' speech *Against Timarchos*, both are identified together as tools of the trade of a slave who runs a gaming establishment (Aeschines 1.59). And yet, with very few exceptions, the representational contexts in which the two games figure were rigorously distinguished throughout Greek antiquity. Given the practicalities of play, this opposition emerges as largely discursive and ideological, much like the opposition of *hetaira* and *porne*. Thus the relation of *astragaloi* to economic realities was generally mystified, as they were positively linked to aristocratic luxury and fateful style. *Kuboi*, in contrast, bore the onus of negative associations, consistently identified with pure risk and with the damaging, disembedded economic activity of gambling.[75]

Let us survey the semantic sphere or set of discursive associations of each game in turn. Whether or not they existed at the time of epic composition, *kuboi* are never mentioned in the Homeric poems. According to Pausanias, Palamedes, when he had invented dice, dedicated them in what the Periegete took to be "the oldest shrine to *Tuchē*," in the Argolid (Paus. 2.20.3). This association of *kuboi* with random fortune is emblematic and enduring; thus the fourth-century comic poet Alexis

---

[73] Cf. the commentary of Cope and Sandys 1877: 1.242: "Ainesidamos sends a ⌐ to Gelo of eggs, cakes, and sweetmeats, the ordinary prize of the game of · ' prize, in acknowledgement of his superior foresight, quickness and de⸱ 'anticipation' of himself."

[74] See Arist. *Hist. An.* 2.499b.

[75] It is worth recording Lamer's observation that, while there are tions of *astragalizontes/ -ousai* preserved from antiquity, we do n⸢ dice players (Lamer 1927: 2020–21).

uses dice as a conventional figure for the uncertainty and changeability of mortal existence (in a passage that is no less revealing for being utterly banal):

τοιοῦτο τὸ ζῆν ἐστιν ὥσπερ οἱ κύβοι·
οὐ ταῦτ' ἀεὶ πίπτουσιν, οὐδὲ τῷ βίῳ
ταὐτὸν διαμένει σχῆμα, μεταβολὰς δ' ἔχει.[76] (Alexis fr. 35 K.-A.)

Life is just like a game of dice: they don't always fall the same way, and life doesn't keep the same pattern, but it has ups and downs.

Perhaps because of the association with random fortune, dice served as a kind of shorthand for all the vices of a disembedded economy. Recall the extraordinary animus expressed by the author of Alkidamas's *Odysseus* against *kuboi*; the worst he can find to say about *pessoi* is that they promote quarrels among idlers, while dicing inspires a veritable jeremiad: "And *kuboi*, in turn, he revealed as the greatest evil, for the losers a source of grief and damage, for the winners a mockery and a reproach. For the gains that accrue from *kuboi* turn out to be useless, and most of them are squandered immediately." *Kuboi* are the "greatest evil" not simply because they produce financial loss and damage sooner or later, but because they encourage the perverse privileging of the short-term transactional order—the quick fix of personal profit—over the morally anchored systems of family and state. As the emblem of personal expenditure and pleasure unmoored from any system, dicing was excoriated within both egalitarian and elite traditions. Thus for the Attic orators, speaking to persuade popular juries, "dicing away" one's patrimony was a staple accusation of a profligate opponent (cf. Lysias 14.27.4, κατακυβεύσας), while a speaker defending himself in the context of public scrutiny for office (*dokimasia*) could make much of the fact that he *didn't* play *kuboi*:

And thus I have administered my private affairs; but as for public affairs, I consider the greatest proof of my respectability to be that, however many of the young men happen to make dicing or drinking or such licentious activities their pastimes (ὅσοι περὶ κύβους ἢ πότους ἢ τὰς τοιαύτας ἀκολασίας τυγχάνουσι τὰς διατριβὰς ποιούμενοι), you will see that all of them are at odds with me, and that these men most of all make up stories and lies about me. (Lysias 16.11)

It is striking that nonparticipation in dicing is not included among the speaker's rendition of his exemplary personal habits, but rather as the

---

[76] For the explicit association of *kuboi* with τύχη, cf. Soph. fr. 947 R; Plato *Rep.* 604c5–d2; ·. *Mor.* 467a–b.

greatest proof of his suitability for office in the public domain. By a logic of contraries, his rejection of dicing and all the other forms of "licentiousness" (ἀκολασίας) proves his commitment to the long-term transactional order of the city and its well-being.

Dicing plays a similar role in Isocrates' extended account of the decadent state of Athenian youth in the *Antidosis*:

καὶ γάρ τοι πεποιήκατε τοὺς μὲν ἐπιεικεστάτους αὐτῶν ἐν πότοις καὶ συνουσίαις καὶ ῥᾳθυμίαις καὶ παιδιαῖς τὴν ἡλικίαν διάγειν, ἀμελήσαντας τοῦ σπουδάζειν ὅπως ἔσονται βελτίους, τοὺς δὲ χείρω τὴν φύσιν ἔχοντας ἐν τοιαύταις ἀκολασίαις ἡμερεύειν, ἐν αἷς πρότερον οὐδ' ἂν οἰκέτης ἐπιεικὴς οὐδεὶς ἐτόλμησεν· οἱ μὲν γὰρ αὐτῶν ἐπὶ τῆς Ἐννεακρούνου ψύχουσιν οἶνον, οἱ δ' ἐν τοῖς καπηλείοις πίνουσιν, ἕτεροι δ' ἐν τοῖς σκιραφείοις κυβεύουσι, πολλοὶ δ' ἐν τοῖς τῶν αὐλητρίδων διδασκαλείοις διατρίβουσι. (Isoc. *Antid*. 286–87)

> For in fact, you have caused the most reputable [of the young men] to spend their youth in drinking bouts and hanging out and relaxation and games, neglecting to be serious about how they will become better men, while those who have a worse nature spend their days in such acts of licentiousness in which not even a self-respecting house slave would have dared spend his time in the old days. For some of them cool their wine in the Nine Springs, others drink in taverns, still others play dice in the gambling houses, and many of them spend their time idling around the schools for flutegirls.

Here, Isocrates offers us two grades of debauchery; the "better sort" of young men spend their time in drinking, hanging out, idleness, and games, while the completely irredeemable engage in activities that a self-respecting house slave would not have dared in former days. It is worth noting that the activities of these young men beyond the pale consistently represent a kind of mercantilization or monetarization of the first-order decadence: thus the better sort of young men drink, the worse sort drink in taverns; the better sort play games, the worse sort play dice; the better sort hang out, the worse sort hang out around the schools for hired flutegirls. In each case their activities are worse because they have come to involve the domination of money disembedded from its proper social networks, a process marked by the turning-inside-out of civic space. For the other thing that characterizes the second-order debauchery as opposed to the first- in this passage is that activities that should pr' private—sympotic drinking and game-playing—have invad' over the public domain (hence the geographic specificit list in contrast to the first). And all these pursuits cons nightmare vision to transform the city from political place of private pleasures. Under the circumstances comparison of the worse sort of young men to the "self-respecting house slave" is not fortuitous: Isocrates implies that in their addiction to the pleasures of drinking, dicing, and ogling girls, these youths have relinquished the self-control and autonomy that make them free men.[77]

This same trope of dicing as a form of submission to the rule of pure chance, money, opportunism, and pleasure recurs in the writings of elitist authors, where it stands in opposition to the nobleman's proper cultivation of his household. Thus Xenophon has Socrates argue that rich men who know how to improve their estates but fail to do so are like slaves dominated by "deceitful mistresses dressed up as pleasures—dicing and useless associations of men . . . which rule them and keep them from productive activities" (Xen. *Oik.* 1.19–20). In other contexts, dicing figures within the aristocratic tradition as the obscene triumph of the short-term transactional order, in a public space that was always imagined as merely a marketplace. So Aristotle classes the dice-player (κυβευτής) with the pimp, the usurer, the footpad, and the pirate as examples of the vice of αἰσχροκέρδεια, the acquisition of (small) profits by shameful means (Arist. *NE* 1121b31–1122a8). Theophrastos goes his teacher one better in his remarkable portrait of the "insane man" (ὁ ἀπονενοημένος), who is in fact the incarnation of disembedded economic shamelessness. Theophrastos introduces this character as "by disposition a marketman (ἀγοραῖος), obscene, and willing to do anything" (*Char.* 6.2), then proceeds to a full list of his capabilities:

δεινὸς δὲ καὶ πανδοκεῦσαι καὶ πορνοβοσκῆσαι καὶ τελωνῆσαι καὶ μηδεμίαν αἰσχρὰν ἐργασίαν ἀποδοκιμάσαι, ἀλλὰ κηρύττειν, μαγειρεύειν, κυβεύειν· τὴν μητέρα μὴ τρέφειν, ἀπάγεσθαι κλοπῆς, τὸ δεσμωτήριον πλείω χρόνον οἰκεῖν ἢ τὴν αὑτοῦ οἰκίαν. (Theophr. *Char.* 6.5–6)

He's terribly good at innkeeping and pimping and tax-farming and not refusing any shameful business, but [he'll] act as herald, he'll cook, and play dice; he won't support his mother, he'll be led away on a charge of theft, and he'll spend more time in jail than in his own home.

This is a portrait of the short-term transactional order run rampant, unchecked by any sense of obligation to parents or household, the highest aristocratic goods. It is noteworthy (if unsurprising) that *kuboi* and *pornai* tend to occur together in such contexts, since both figure the depraved triumph of monetary exchanges in the public space of the agora.

---

[77] For this same trope of enslavement to decadent pleasures (including dicing), see Aeschines 1.42: "But he did these things enslaved to the most shameful pleasures, dainty living and expensive meals and flutegirls and *hetairai* and *kuboi* and the rest, by none of which ʼble and free man should be dominated."

But the identification of dice with the reign of *tuchē* engenders another set of associations completely separate from these portraits of monetary dystopia: dicing becomes an enduring symbol for the risks and uncertainties of warfare. As Aeschylus' Eteokles describes the nature of combat with characteristic curtness, "Ares decides the action in a game of dice" (ἔργον δ᾽ ἐν κύβοις Ἄρης κρινεῖ, *Seven against Thebes* 414).[78] Euripides uses the image on several occasions; thus Dolon in the *Rhesus*, asked by Hektor what he wants to infiltrate the Greek camp, replies,

ἵππους Ἀχιλλέως· χρὴ δ᾽ ἐπ᾽ ἀξίοις πονεῖν
ψυχὴν προβάλλοντ᾽ ἐν κύβοισι δαίμονος.[79] (Eur. *Rhesus* 182–83)

The horses of Achilles—for a man ought to toil for worthy rewards when he wagers his life in the god's dice game.

Xenophon nicely elucidates this association of dicing and combat in an anecdote he tells about Socrates in the *Memorabilia*:

And Socrates used to pray to the gods simply to give good things, on the grounds that the gods knew best what sorts of things *were* good. But he considered that those who prayed for gold or silver or tyranny or any other such thing prayed for nothing different than if they would pray regarding dicing or battle or any other of the things that are patently unclear how they might turn out. (ἢ εἰ κυβείαν ἢ μάχην ἢ ἄλλο τι εὔχοιντο τῶν φανερῶς ἀδήλων ὅπως ἀποβήσοιτο). (Xen. *Mem.* 1.3.2)

This anecdote depends for its point on its being commonly acknowledged that dice-playing and battle stand under the aegis of random fortune— unlike the popular conception of the acquisition of wealth and tyranny.[80]

In marked contrast to *kuboi*, knucklebones (*astragaloi*) seem to have had largely positive associations. This is perhaps because, where *kuboi* were

---

[78] It may be that the image has special relevance here, since the line occurs in Eteokles' posting of the first Theban champion against the boastful Tydeus. In context, Eteokles' strong assertion of the chance element in warfare refutes the notion that Tydeus's shield device is prophetic of his victory.

[79] Cf. Eur. *Rhesus* 444–46; *Suppl.* 328–31.

[80] Plutarch seems to have been particularly fond of the image of the dice-game of battle, since he uses variations of it in the *Lives of Pyrrhus* (26), *Fabius Maximus* (14), *Coriolanus* (3), and, of course, famously, *Julius Caesar* (32), where the biographer describes Caesar's crossing the Rubicon thus: "And in the end with some spirit, just as if casting himself forth from calculation to what was going to happen, he uttered the prelude common to those who mount on chances without resources and acts of boldness—'Let the die be cast'—and he set out on the crossing." The only instance I have found of *astragaloi* replacing *kuboi* in this image is Plut. *Aratus* 29, where it is perhaps significant that the metaphor occurs

an artificial construction, *astragaloi* were strongly identified with the virtues of embodiment: they came from the bodies of animals, and their different sides were naturally differentiated, so that they required no markings to be read when thrown. The four relevant sides of the knuckle-bone were commonly known as ὕπτιον (concave, worth three), πρανές (convex, worth four), χῖον (s-shaped, worth one), and κῷον (flattish, worth six).[81] Since it was convention that endowed the different sides with numerical value, *astragaloi* did, of course, operate symbolically; nonetheless, their physical form allowed that symbolic order to be natural-ized as preexistent.[82]

Together with their alignment with embodiment, *astragaloi* were stron-gly associated with the long-term transactional order—with those ele-ments perceived to be unchanging and constitutive of social and cosmic order. Thus knucklebones were almost never discursively associated with gambling for money and the other disembedded economic activities atten-dant on gambling; instead, *astragaloi* seem to have been identified with sacrifice, with the gods and fate, with the dead, and with the innocent games of children. The association with sacrifice is understandable in a culture in which the consumption of meat took place only in the context of sacrificial ritual and in which knucklebones normally derived from two of the three most prevalent sacrificial animals, sheep and goats.[83] The association of knucklebones with the gods and fate is most clearly seen in the practices of *astragalomanteia*, reported to us mainly by late sources. According to Pausanias, there was a small shrine to Herakles in a grotto in Achaia in which "it was possible to get prophecies by means of a tablet and *astragaloi*. For the one consulting the god prays in front of the image, and after the prayer he takes up four *astragaloi*—for they lie beside Herakles in abundance—and lets them go upon the table. And for every fall of the knucklebone, things inscribed on the tablet have a suitable exegesis of that schema" (Paus. 7.25.10). A scholiast to Pindar reports a similar practice "in shrines," while excavations in Pamphylia in the last century unearthed a tablet exactly like the one Pausanias

---

in the context of a general exhorting his own troops; does he use *astragaloi* to suggest the fatefulness and inevitability of the outcome instead of his army's vulnerability to chance?

[81] For the names of the different sides of the *astragalos*, see Arist. *Hist. An.* 2.499b; for their respective worth, see Mau 1896: 1794; Lamer 1927: 1934–35; Laser 1987: 120–21.

[82] It should be noted that *astragaloi* were frequently worked in antiquity, their sides planed to make them fall more evenly, or weighted with lead to make them heavier; cf. Amandry 1984a: 356–70, Gilmour 1997: 171.

[83] For archaeological evidence of *astragaloi* in sacrificial contexts, see Foster 1984; Simon 1986: 387 notes "the astragal might commemorate the sacrifice and would therefore be a suitable offering" (suggesting that this applies particularly to finds of astragals at the Theban Kabirion and in a sixth-century foundation deposit in Samothrace).

describes, offering different general predictions for each possible combination of knucklebones thrown.[84] The archaeological record seems to confirm these reports of mantic use at a much earlier date, for *astragaloi* are found in shrines and temples all over Greece from as early as the Geometric and archaic periods on.[85] In these practices the throw of *astragaloi* offered a fateful or numinous connection with the invisible world of the divine; the game of chance became an ordeal, revealing to the consultant his own special lot. Where *kuboi* figured the reign of *tuchē*, random chance, *astragaloi* opened up the prospect to *moira* or *klēros*, each man's particular fated allotment.[86]

In addition, we have evidence for the association of knucklebones with the dead from a very early period, for astragals are found in burial sites dating back to the Bronze Age and continuing through the archaic and classical periods.[87] As Donna Kurtz and John Boardman note:

> Astragals—knuckle-bones—are far more commonly found. They could be thrown like dice, played like our 'jacks', strung as necklaces or made up into whips. . . . They are not uncommon in Greek graves but the remarkable feature is the number found with single burials—far more than required for any of the purposes named. There is an extreme example at Locri where hundreds are strewn over the lid of the sarcophagus of an old woman, with more inside as well as a mirror and *alabastron*. They seem appropriate for men, women and especially children.[88]

---

[84] Schol. *ad* Pindar *P.* 4.337; for the Pamphylian inscription (dated to the second or third century C.E.), see Kaibel 1876 and Kaibel 1878 no. 1038; cf. also Suetonius, *Life of Tiberius* 14, Artem. *Oneir.* 2.69. For modern discussions of *astragalomanteia*, see Halliday 1913: 212–15; Hampe 1951: 20–21, 36–37nn. 56, 57; Amandry 1984a: 377–78, 1984b: 411; Simon 1986: 386–87; Gilmour 1997: 172–73.

[85] For a catalogue of known finds of astragals in temples and shrines, see Simon 1986: 379–83; Simon (ibid: 387) rightly emphasizes that not all astragals in temples would have served oracular purposes. For detailed discussion of one spectacular find (from the Korykeion Cave above Delphi on Parnassos) with abundant comparative material, see Amandry 1984a. Amandry records the excavation of 22,771 astragals dating from the period when the cave was sacred to Pan and the Nymphs, between the sixth and third centuries B.C.E. He offers two possible explanations for this extraordinary accumulation of knucklebones: (1) dedication by the young of both sexes to the Nymphs, symbolic of their passage from childhood to adulthood (and marriage?); (2) divinatory practice through the casting of knucklebones. To support this latter possibility, Amandry suggests that we should perhaps connect the Nymphs of the cave with the prophetic Thriai mentioned at the end of the *Homeric Hymn to Hermes* (lines 552–66, Amandry 1984a: 377–78, 1984b: 411).

[86] According to Kaibel (1876: 193n.1), knucklebones are specifically called κλῆροι in late Greek.

[87] See references collected by Hampe 1951: 15–16, 34–35nn. 28–36; Simon 1986: 382; Laser 1987: 117n.579.

[88] Kurtz and Boardman 1971: 208. It is this association of knucklebones with the dead that gives special point to a pair of witty Hellenistic epigrams that imagine funeral stelai

In the fifth century, Polygnotos depicted the daughters of Pandareos, carried off young and unmarried by the Harpies, playing knucklebones in the Underworld (Paus. 10.30.2).

Artemidoros, in his second-century C.E. dreambook, confirms the special connection of *astragaloi* with both allotment and the dead:

παιδίον δὲ παῖζον ἰδεῖν κύβοις ἢ ἀστραγάλοις ἢ ψήφοις οὐ πονηρόν· ἔθος γὰρ τοῖς παιδίοις ἀεὶ παίζειν· ἀνδρὶ δὲ τελείῳ καὶ γυναικὶ πονηρὸν τὸ ἀστραγάλοις δοκεῖν παίζειν, εἰ μὴ ἄρα κληρονομῆσαί τινα ἐλπίζων ἴδοι τις τὸ ὄναρ τοῦτο· ἐκ νεκρῶν γὰρ σωμάτων γεγόνασιν οἱ ἀστράγαλοι. διὸ κινδύνους τοῖς λοιποῖς προαγορεύουσιν. (Artem. *Oneir.* 3.1)

To see a child playing with *kuboi* or *astragaloi* or *psēphoi* [*pessoi*?] is not bad; for it is characteristic for children to play all the time. But for a grown man or woman it is bad to seem to play with *astragaloi*, unless someone should see this dream when he is expecting some inheritance. For *astragaloi* come into being from dead bodies; wherefore they presage dangers for the rest.

Notice that the one exception to the ominous import of a dream of playing *astragaloi* is for those expecting an inheritance—literally "an allotment" (κληρονομῆσαι). For all the rest, the dream predicts dangers, since *astragaloi* "come from dead bodies." In both cases, it seems to be knucklebones' connection to bodies and embodiment that endows them with fateful power.[89]

Finally, Artemidoros confirms the association of *astragaloi* with the innocent game-playing of children. Though in his rendition several games are equally identified with children, *astragaloi* often seem to have a privileged connection with childhood, while they retain their associations with social and cosmic order. We recall that when Herakleitos refuses to "play polis" with his Ephesian fellow-citizens, he withdraws to the temple to "play *astragaloi* with boys." In the pseudo-Platonic dialogue *Alcibiades* (I), the title character claims that long before he entered the public domain, he had an intuitive sense of justice and injustice from playing *astragaloi* as a boy (*Alc.* I.110b). And in an anecdote Plutarch tells repeatedly, the Spartan general Lysander is said to have quipped that " 'One must deceive children with *astragaloi*, and men with oaths,' thus imitating Polykrates of Samos." The biographer proceeds to editorialize that "it was not proper for a general to imitate a tyrant, nor was it Lakonian to treat the

---

with no distinguishing marks except knucklebones carved in various throws: cf. Leonidas, *AP* 7.422 and Antipater, *AP* 7.427 (both with commentary by Gow and Page 1965). On the complexities of interpretation in these epigrams, see Goldhill 1994: 199–210.

[89] In contrast, notice that according to Artemidoros, to dream of "playing *kuboi* signifies quarreling with somebody over money" (*Oneir.* 3.1.1).

gods as enemies" (Plut. *Lys.* 8.3–4).[90] I would suggest that this editorializing applies to both *astragaloi* and oaths, for the two share a numinous quality, backed by divine authority. It is almost as if "boys playing *astragaloi*" emblematize a natural sense of justice or intuitive instinct to right. Hence it is appropriate that Polykrates of Samos, that arch-violator of gift exchange, serve as Lysander's model in these parallel assaults on cosmic justice.[91]

It may be objected that most of the evidence for these associations comes from late sources, but, in fact, many of these resonances are already present in the earliest mention of a game of *astragaloi* in a literary text. In the single reference to the game in the Homeric poems, the shade of the dead Patroklos reminds Achilles of their childhood connection:

μὴ ἐμὰ σῶν ἀπάνευθε τιθήμεναι ὀστέ᾽, Ἀχιλλεῦ,
ἀλλ᾽ ὁμοῦ, ὡς τράφομέν περ ἐν ὑμετέροισι δόμοισιν,
εὖτέ με τυτθὸν ἐόντα Μενοίτιος ἐξ Ὀπόεντος
ἤγαγεν ὑμέτερόνδ᾽ ἀνδροκτασίης ὕπο λυγρῆς,
ἤματι τῷ ὅτε παῖδα κατέκτανον Ἀμφιδάμαντος,
νήπιος, οὐκ ἐθέλων, ἀμφ᾽ ἀστραγάλοισι χολωθείς·
ἔνθα με δεξάμενος ἐν δώμασιν ἱππότα Πηλεὺς
ἔτραφέ τ᾽ ἐνδυκέως καὶ σὸν θεράποντ᾽ ὀνόμηνεν·
ὣς δὲ καὶ ὀστέα νῶϊν ὁμὴ σορὸς ἀμφικαλύπτοι
χρύσεος ἀμφιφορεύς, τόν τοι πόρε πότνια μήτηρ. (*Iliad* 23.83–92)

Do not put my bones apart from yours, Achilles, but together, just as we were raised in your house, when Menoitios led me, still little, from Opus

---

[90] This anecdote (which is variously attributed to Lysander, the tyrant Dionysios, and Philip of Macedon) is repeated at Plut. *Mor.* 229b, 330f, 741c; D. S. 10.9.1; Dio Chrys. *Or.* 74 (399 R, 640 M); and Aelian *VH* 7.12.

[91] See Chapter 3 above. A similar tyrannic confounding of long- and short-term transactional orders may account for a strange episode in Rhodian history, as narrated by Theopompos: "They [the oligarchic rulers led by Hegesilochos] violated many well-born women and wives of the foremost men, and corrupted not a few boys and young lads; they went so far in their licentiousness that they even presumed to gamble (κυβεύειν) with one another for the possession of free-born women, and stipulated among themselves which one of the women of the city was to be brought to the winner for his enjoyment by those whose throw with the dice (τοῖς ἀστραγάλοις) was the less. . . . Some of the other Rhodians also played at this kind of dicing (ταύτην τὴν κυβείαν), but the one who played at it most conspicuously and most often was Hegesilochos himself, who presumed to rule over the state" (Theopompos *FGrH* 115 F 121 = Athen. *Deipn.* 10.444e–445a, trans. C. B. Gulick 1930). Lamer (1927: 1937–39) cites this passage as proof that the terms *kuboi* and *astragaloi* were used interchangeably already in the classical period, but I would contend that everything about this passage marks the oligarchs' activities as transgressive. Thus they not only debauch noble wives and freeborn boys, but they signify their violation of these properly sacrosanct categories by dicing *with knucklebones*.

to your house under [the ban of] grievous manslaughter, on that day when
I killed the son of Amphidamas, foolishly, unwillingly, angered over a game
of *astragaloi*; there receiving me in his house, the horseman Peleus raised
me carefully and named me your henchman. Therefore let the same golden
two-handled vessel cover both our bones—the vessel your mistress mother
once gave you.

Here, as in the later references, playing *astragaloi* is peculiarly associated
with childhood, but this passage is also haunted by a kind of fateful
embodiment. Patroklos kills "foolishly, unwillingly," because he is unable
to keep play competition from verging into real violence, as the players
come to embody the game. More disturbing still is the way in which the
mention of this childhood game of knucklebones is ringed by Patroklos's
wish that his bones be mingled with those of Achilles. The double mention
of ὀστέα endows Patroklos's game of *astragaloi* with an uncanny resonance, as if the play with those bones leads inexorably to the mingled
bones on the battlefield. Finally, lurking behind Patroklos's mournful
request is the hint of another kind of embodiment: the identification of
bones with bones, suggesting the ghostly image of the heroes themselves
dying in combat as [knuckle]bones played by the gods.[92]

This remarkable Homeric passage offers a kind of template for an elite
ideology of embodiment that stands in direct contrast to the symbolic
logic of board games in the archaic and classical periods. Because of their
alignment with the gods, fate, the dead, and children's untutored bodily
impulses to justice, *astragaloi* would seem perfectly suited to the aristocratic tradition, and indeed, there is evidence to suggest that the elite
worked to appropriate this nexus of associations through significant representations of knucklebones. Pausanias, for example, describes a statue
group of the three Graces sharing a statue base with Eros, in which "one
[Grace] holds a rose, the middle one an astragal, and the third a small
branch of myrtle" (Paus. 6.24.6–7). The Periegete suggests that the astragal signifies the association of grace with youth, since the knucklebone
is the plaything of young men and women, but we need not limit ourselves
to his speculation (explicitly marked as such). Grace (χάρις) was the
highest virtue of aristocratic style, denoting the perfection of bodily form
and movement, the numinous value bestowed on *agalmata*, the radiant
circuit of gift exchange, and the pleasures of festivity.[93] In addition, the
German excavation at Olympia in the last century unearthed a statue

---

[92] For this association, we should note that *astragalos* occurs three more times in the
Homeric poems, as the normal word for a human vertebra, always in contexts of a hero
sustaining a mortal injury (*Iliad* 14.466, *Od.* 10.560, 11.65).

[93] On the aristocratic value of *charis*, see Kurke 1991: 103–7, 111–12, 116, 120–21,
137–46, 154–59.

base carved in the form of an astragal near the entrance to the racetrack, where Pausanias tells us there stood altars to Hermes Agonios and Kairos (Paus. 5.14.9). Although the attribution is much disputed, one plausible reconstruction takes the knucklebone to be the base for a Polykleitan or Lysippan statue of Kairos.[94] If this reconstruction is correct, the statue group associated the astragal, represented in its luckiest throw, the χῷον, with that other cardinal virtue of aristocratic embodiment—kairos, the opportune moment and the instinct to seize it in a contest. As we know from Pindar's epinikia, the knowledge of *kairos* was crucial to athletic victory; hence the significant placement of the altar of Kairos near the racetrack at Olympia.[95] Together, we might say, *charis* and *kairos* represented social and cosmic justice embodied as aristocratic style, and these two monuments linked these noble virtues with the astragal.

In addition, *astragaloi* were typically played in the palaistra and symposium, and, like ball and *kottabos*, had clear erotic associations.[96] Thus the best throw of the conventional four knucklebones (a 1-3-4-6 combination) was called "Aphrodite," while the general categories of names used suggest an elite, sympotic ambience. According to a scholiast to Plato,

εἰσὶ δὲ αἱ σύμπασαι τῶν ἀστραγάλων πτώσεις ὁμοῦ τεσσάρων παραλαμβανομένων πέντε καὶ τριάκοντα. τούτων δὲ αἱ μὲν θεῶν εἰσιν ἐπώνυμοι, αἱ δὲ ἡρώων, αἱ δὲ βασιλέων, αἱ δὲ ἐνδόξων ἀνδρῶν, αἱ δὲ ἑταιρίδων. (Schol. *ad* Plato *Lysis* 206e; Greene 1938: 456 = Eustathios *Comm. Hom.* p. 1289.55; 4.690–691.18–20 Valk)

There are in all thirty-five throws of four *astragaloi* taken together, and of these some are named for gods, others for heroes, others for kings, still others for eminent men, and others for *hetairai*.

The first two categories here, gods and heroes, echo the traditional first two libations at the symposium, while the whole list reads like an aristocratic honor roll.[97] Only the last category—*hetairai*—seems strangely out

---

[94] Publication of the astragal statue base: Treu 1897: 212–14. For the reconstruction, see Benndorf 1885. Benndorf argues for a Polykleitan statue of Kairos based on the report of Pliny the Elder (*HN* 34.55, *nudum talo incessentem*) and notes that the modeling of the astragal makes it a representation of the best throw, the χῷον. Though Benndorf's thesis is challenged by Treu and Guarducci 1966: 291–92, a modified version (a Lysippan Kairos) is tentatively accepted by Stewart 1978: 163n.2. Even if the astragal statue-base cannot be securely linked to an image of Kairos, its existence near the racetrack at Olympia tends to support the elite, fateful, and embodied associations we have observed.

[95] On *kairos*, cf. Pindar O. 13.48, P. 4.286, P. 8.7, P. 9.78, N. 8.4, I. 2.22 and see Fränkel 1973: 447–48; Bundy 1986: 18.

[96] For *astragaloi* in the palaistra, see Plato *Lysis* 206e3–9.

[97] For the sequence of libations at the symposium—first to Zeus Olympios, second to the heroes, third to Zeus Soter—see Schol. *ad* Pindar *I.* 6.10a, citing Aesch. fr. 55 R. We

of place with the other terms: in contrast to gods, heroes, kings, and eminent men, it conjures up the playful eroticism of the symposium. Where *kuboi* were identified with the disembedded economics of *pornai* in the elite tradition, knucklebones seem to have been aligned with the mystified status of *hetairai*.

Anakreon captures all these associations in one brief characterization of Eros:

ἀστραγάλαι δ' Ἔρωτός εἰσιν
μανίαι τε καὶ κυδοιμοί. (fr. 111 Gentili = 398 *PMG*)

The knucklebones of Eros are madnesses and the dins of battle.

The lightness and grace of the lilting verses suit a sympotic paean to love, but the enduring associations of knucklebones with the gods, fate, and embodiment weight Anakreon's lines with greater significance. Like the Homeric gods, Eros "the limb-loosener" (λυσιμελής) plays on and through the bones of men, with no more thought for them than a child with his toys.[98]

Still, precisely because of their manifold associations with the long-term transactional order—with models of social and cosmic justice—the aristocratic appropriation of *astragaloi* seems not to have gone completely unchallenged in the archaic period. Two bits of archaeological evidence suggest that the city attempted to mobilize the material symbology of astragals for itself. First, standard weights made of metal in the form of knucklebones have been found in use from Miletus to Gela. Indeed, the knucklebone was one of only five standard types of Attic weights, conventionally representing the top of the weight scale, the "heavy mina" of 873 grams.[99] Given the astragal's alignment with fateful embodiment, sacrifice, and natural justice, it was the ideal form to guarantee true and accurate weight untainted by the sharp practices of the the market. It is

---

find confirmation for the scholiast's list of categories in the archaeological record; thus Amandry reports that 31 of the astragals found in the Korykeion Cave had names inscribed on them, among which Herakles, Thetis, Achilles, Ajax, Nyx, and Nika were clearly legible. Amandry compares astragals from other sites with names inscribed: ΕΡΩΣ and ΑΙΑΣ on the same knucklebone from Taman; Nike, Achilles, and Hektor on astragals from Gordion; ΕΡΩΣ, ΝΙΚ and ΙΕΥΣ on astragals from Delos; and ΕΟΡΤΗ on an astragal from Myrina (Amandry 1984a: 370–75).

[98] For Eros λυσιμελής, see Archilochos fr. 196 W, Sappho fr. 130 V, Hes. *Theog.* 911. Apollonius Rhodius exploits this erotic association at *Argonautica* 3.114–126, where Eros himself plays with Ganymede using knucklebones of gold. For other erotic associations of knucklebones in Greek texts and visual representations, see Hampe 1951: 21–30.

[99] On astragal weights, see Michon in Daremberg and Saglio, s.v. "Pondus" (1877: 5.550); Hampe 1951: 12–13, 31n. 8; Laser 1987: 117. The other four Attic types are the amphora, the tortoise, the dolphin, and the crescent.

perhaps the same associations that account for the appearance of the knucklebone on one of the earliest coins issued in Athens, one of the so-called *Wappenmünzen* that preceded the establishment of the standard Athena/owl type. This series of fourteen different types has been dated by numismatists to the reign of Peisistratos, starting perhaps around the mid-sixth century and ending with the introduction of the standard owl type in the last quarter of the century.[100] It has been noted that many of these coin types have special associations with Athena and the Panathenaic Festival, and this connection has been used to account for the occurrence of the astragal. The linkage of knucklebones with the city goddess is certainly attested,[101] but I would suggest it is only part of the nexus of associations this coin type exploited. Insofar as coinage operated as one means to wrest control of the long-term transactional order from the dominant elite, the astragal was a remarkably canny device: on a symbolic token, it asserted embodiment; on a conventional currency, it laid claim to the prestige of nature. The astragal type was an icon that denied its own iconicity, naturalizing coinage by linking it to the eternal order of the gods, the dead, and the body.

IV. HERODOTEAN GAMES

Let us now finally return to Herodotus 1.94—to the Lydians' invention of games. We have noted that Herodotus's list looks anomalous in light of other such catalogues of inventions; we are now in a position to appreciate the significance of the particular games Herodotus conjoins. In terms of their associations, we have argued that knucklebones and ballgames are elite pastimes, while dice epitomize the short-term transactional order of gambling and personal pleasure. Yet the histor offers these three specifically as the Lydians' inventions, producing an unsettling fusion of long- and short-term transactional orders, of marketplace with palaistra and symposium. I would contend that this vertiginous conjunction of transactional orders that should properly be separate is characteristic of the Lydian ethnography as a whole—we have noted it already in the narrator's assertion that the tomb of Alyattes was financed by merchants, craftsmen, and whores (1.93.2–3). From Herodotus's perspective, what should be the mediating term and conversion mechanism between the

---

[100] On the *Wappenmünzen*, see Kraay 1956, 1976: 56–60; Hopper 1968; Cahn 1975; von Reden 1995: 179–81. The astragal was in fact an extremely common coin-type in cities throughout the Greek world: see the catalogue of Hampe 1951: 36n. 55.

[101] For the close association of *Wappenmünzen* types with Athena and the Panathenaia, see Yalouris 1950: 52–54, Cahn 1975.

extremes of short- and long-term transactional orders, disembedded and embedded economic structures, is the polis, which the Lydians conspicuously lack. And this lack is registered here by the exclusion of *pessoi*: the Lydians do not invent *pessoi* because they cannot conceptualize the symbolic order of the city. Hence the difference between Herodotus's list of Lydian inventions and the profusion of inventories with which we began this chapter. Those lists, as we suggested, have as their object the equation of polis structure with a whole inventory of second-order symbolic systems; Herodotus's catalogue, by contrast, intends just the opposite, exposing the schizophrenic conjunction of luxury and economic degradation when the informing principle of the polis is lacking. Thus Kroisos's Lydians are emblems of *habrosunē* who prostitute their own daughters; recipients of a river full of gold who become the first minters of coins and the first retail traders.

In case we missed the point, Herodotus underscores it with his strange aetiology of Lydian games. We might say that, without the polis, the Lydians do not and cannot invent games of order (*pessoi*), only games of chance (dice, knucklebones) and games of embodiment (ball). Thus the narrative of the invention of games is a story of the Lydians' submission to random fortune and physical deprivation for eighteen years. Finally, after eighteen years of bad luck, the Lydian king essentially invents *pessoi* through the bodies of his people. In the elaborately rehearsed division of the populace in two by lot, the king seems unwittingly to have devised a game of *polis* played with and on his subjects. And it is strikingly only at this point in the narrative that Herodotus finally attributes to the Lydians (now turned Etruscans) the "founding of cities" (ἐνιδρύσασθαι πόλιας, 1.94.6).

Thus in 1.94, at least, games function as part of a material symbology through which Herodotus thinks political and economic structures and their interaction. Can we find other occasions in which games figure significantly in Herodotus's narrative? Earlier in Book 1, Herodotus offers us a paradigm for competing game structures as a model for different styles of warfare. In his brief account of the history of Athens in the sixth century, the histor describes Peisistratos's third and final capture of power:

> But the Athenians from the city, as long as Peisistratos was collecting money, and in turn, when he took Marathon, paid no attention (λόγον οὐδένα εἶχον), but when they found out that he was advancing from Marathon against the city, then indeed they ran to aid against him. And these men went with their entire force against the returned exiles, and those about Peisistratos, when, setting out from Marathon, they were heading for the city, converging on the same place they met at the shrine of Athena Pallenis

and they ranged their arms opposite each other. At that point, with divine guidance, there stands beside Peisistratos Amphilytos the Akarnanian, a soothsayer, who, approaching, prophesies these following things in hexameter verse:

> The cast has been thrown and the net is spread out,
> and the tunny-fish will swarm through the moonlit night.

And he, being inspired, prophesies these things, but Peisistratos comprehending the oracle and saying that he accepted the thing prophesied, led out his army. But the Athenians from the city had at that point just turned to lunch, and after lunch, some of them [turned] to *kuboi*, others to sleep. But those about Peisistratos, falling on the Athenians, rout them. And when these men were fleeing, Peisistratos at that point contrives his wisest plan, so that the Athenians not still remain massed, but be scattered. Mounting his children on horses, he sent them forth, and they caught up with the men in flight and said the things ordered by Peisistratos, bidding them to take heart and each to go about his own business. And when the Athenians obeyed, thus indeed Peisistratos, having got hold of Athens for the third time, properly rooted his tyranny. . . . (Hdt. 1.62.2–64.1)

I would contend that the fact that Peisistratos's Athenian opponents are characterized as playing *kuboi* at a crucial point in this episode is more than a bit of local color. At the most obvious level, of course, it signifies their breaking ranks after lunch, thereby making themselves vulnerable to Peisistratos's attack. Beyond that literal level, playing dice bespeaks the Athenians' inadequate commitment to civic and tactical order: it suggests that they simply submit themselves to random fortune in war rather than deploying symbolic logic to maintain their polis structure. Thus men who play dice are also men who show no forethought or planning to deal with Peisistratos's machinations in advance—literally, men who "had no logos" (λόγον οὐδένα εἶχον, 1.62.2). Peisistratos, in contrast, plays an astute game of strategy—he keeps his men in order, comprehends and swiftly acts on Amphilytos's inspired prophecy, and knows how to follow up his victory to good effect. Indeed, the text suggests that while his opponents play dice, Peisistratos "plays polis," keeping his troops massed, isolating the enemy, and sending them off individually to their homes. It is this last strategic maneuver (rather than the battle itself) that Herodotus singles out for praise; just as in a game of *pessoi*, Peisistratos knows how to make the enemy men ἄζυγες ("isolated" but also literally "unyoked" from their hoplite arms and ranks). Given the tyrant's strategic gamesmanship, it is no surprise that he wins the day against his ineffectual opponents, and so firmly roots his rule in the city.

Thus in Herodotean narrative and ethnography, as in Aristotle's seemingly unreflective simile and in the profusion of vase paintings of game-playing warriors, we catch reflexes of a cultural pattern I would contend preexists and informs these representations. The emergence in the archaic period of competing systems of games—games of order, games of chance, and games of embodiment—seems to go hand in hand with the emergence of new political, social, and economic structures, as well as with the conflict of competing models of social and cosmic order. This is not to claim that a particular Greek individual or set of individuals consciously invented the game of *polis*, say, or *kottabos*, in order to reflect and reproduce the egalitarian order of the city or the hierarchical relations of the elite symposium; that would be to replicate the Greeks' own mythopoeic obsession with the *prōtos heuretēs*, the "first inventor," as well as to succumb to an inappropriate language of intentionalism. Instead, I would suggest that by a kind of social alchemy impossible to reconstruct in retrospect, cultural formations produce the practical apparatus through which they perpetuate themselves. Games are one such form of practice, doing their work more effectively because they are unassuming, trivial, and pervasive. Thus a ball game might teach an elite Greek boy to be a "king" instead of an "ass"; the throwing of knucklebones might infuse him with a sense of the numinous power of embodiment; and playing the board game *polis* might help form him as a citizen of the city.

CHAPTER 8

Minting Citizens

> Solon used to say that those who had influence
> with tyrants were like counting pebbles employed
> in reckoning (ταῖς ψήφοις ταῖς ἐπὶ τῶν λογισμῶν).
> For as each of the counting pebbles signified (ση-
> μαίνειν) sometimes more and sometimes less, so
> tyrants would treat each man sometimes as great
> and famous, and sometimes as of no account
> (ἄτιμον).
>
> (Diogenes Laertius 1.59)

THIS ANECDOTE about Solon, though recorded in a very late source, offers us a bridge back from the purely symbolic system of *pessoi* to the more ambiguous sphere of coinage. For this image, which we might take to be a fabrication of later democratic Athens once Solon became its "patron saint,"[1] hovers between the figure of game pieces on a board (ψῆφοι) and that of men under a tyranny as another kind of signifying token— as coins. The gap between each of these systems and the details of "Solon's" image precisely articulates the monstrosity of the tyrant in the imaginary of the democratic city. Unlike a game, the tyrant's "abacus" of men functions on no commonly agreed upon mediating board—that is, as we have seen in the terms of *pessoi*, the city itself and its *nomoi*, "the rules of the game."[2] On the other hand, unlike the system of Greek coins, counting pebbles are pure symbols with no intrinsic worth—that is, there is no allowance made in the tyrant's manipulations for individual *phusis*, for the inherent quality of different men. In other terms, we might say that the democratic city figures the tyrant as an extreme functionalist with a consensual community of one. The problem with the tyrant is not that he treats men as signifying tokens, but that he does so arbitrarily, not respecting the guidelines of *nomos* and *phusis*. The polis sets itself in contrast to this phantasmatic despot by its proper valuation and use of citizens, figured by the double valence of civic coin.

---

[1] For the fourth-century democratic idealization of Solon as "first inventor" of the Athenian democratic constitution, see Mossé 1979; Hansen 1989: 77–99.

[2] Additionally, the use of *psēphoi* in this image may conjure up by contrast the citizen's normal right to vote and thereby legislate *nomoi* for himself.

For the implicit contrast with the tyrant's arbitrary valuations of those who serve him reminds us what a strange sort of thing a Greek coin is—both material and symbol, both matter and trope. This is true to some extent of all coinage, but we should remember that the Greeks never invented paper money and only very reluctantly and occasionally resorted to the expedient of fiduciary coinage.[3] That is to say, in classical Greece the dominant idea of coinage is the merging of precious metal and civic stamp. We have been exploring the "meanings of money" in ancient Greece by considering the company coinage keeps—prostitutes, tyrants, and retail traders in elitist representations; games, writing, and other symbolic systems in the imaginary of the city. But we have not come to terms with the fundamental doubleness of coinage, as it merges essentialist and functionalist ideologies in a single token.

Thus far, we have been content to follow the dispassionate analytic division of Aristotle and the highly tendentious disarticulation of precious metal and counterfeit token in archaic elitist texts. It is now time to bring the two sides of coinage back together, in a consideration of how coinage functions within civic practice and discourse of the classical period. This will entail first an exploration of the ideological investments around coinage itself, then a consideration of the use of coinage as an image for the citizen in relation to the overarching order of the polis. In a sense, this discussion follows upon and completes that of Chapters 1 and 2. There, we mapped out the social, topological, somatic, and psychic oppositions through which archaic elitist discourse opposed noble to base, symposium to agora, and golden *hetairoi* to counterfeit others. I want now, in conclusion, to trace further down in time and into different genres the democratic permutations of the metals-coinage opposition for selves. In another sense, though, it has been necessary to travel the entire arc of the argument, through the variegated material symbology by which symposium and public sphere constitute themselves as opposing sites. For only by the consideration of counterfeiting, gift exchange, oracular and dedicatory economies, prostitution, and games, have we been able to analyze in detail the bricolage of civic ideology, which, in all these domains, opposes what is valorized by the elitist tradition but, on occasion, can also appropriate it. This complex dialectic of opposition and appropriation will serve as a useful model for reading the figure of coinage

---

[3] By "fiduciary coinage" I mean only the use of token currency for large denominations, since the Greeks did, of course, eventually mint bronze coins as small change (in Athens, for values below the obol). On the Greeks' lack of fiduciary coinage for large denominations, see Howgego 1995: 20, 90. Examples of debasing the currency to create a fiduciary coinage are, with a single exception (Hdt. 3.56.2), all late fifth century or later (and, even then, very infrequent): cf. the instances recorded in [Arist.] *Oikonomika* 2.2.16–23 (1348b24–1350a30), Polyainos *Strat.* 3.10.14, 4.10.2 (as cited in Melville Jones 1993, nos. 536–41).

in fifth- and fourth-century texts. Of necessity, this concluding discussion focuses on Athens, since virtually all the relevant texts and traditions derive from there.

I. THE TWO SIDES OF THE COIN: MATERIALITY AS IDEOLOGY

Athens is the Greek city about whose coinage practices we are best informed, from numismatic, inscriptional, and documentary evidence. Before turning to coinage as a figure in literary texts, then, I would like to consider the practice and representation of coining in the fifth century and later, in an attempt to think about how ideology informs the materiality of practices.[4] Recent scholarship on Greek coinage has tended to polarize into what we might call symbolist and materialist readings of the phenomenon. Thus the former category (mainly literary scholars and some historians) see coinage only as a symbolic token, while the latter group (mainly ancient historians and numismatists) focus on the matter of coinage, framed almost exclusively in a positivist, economistic account of cause and effect. It is my contention that we cannot properly understand Greek coinage until we can see these two sides together, and the dialectic of symbol and matter that takes place between them.

Thus a common topos of the first strand of scholarship aligns Athenian coinage with "seeming" as opposed to "being," and credits it with a part in the development of symbolic or propositional logic. Jesper Svenbro, for example, argues that the different receptions accorded Aristagoras of Miletus with his bronze map of the world in Sparta and Athens around 500 B.C.E. (as recorded in Hdt. 5.49–51, 97) reflect the gap between Sparta's still concrete thought and Athenian citizens' ability to abstract. As Herodotus tells the story, Aristagoras, in search of allies for his revolt against the Persian king, displays to both King Kleomenes of Sparta and the Athenian assembly a schematized map of the world fashioned on a bronze tablet:

> What appeared to Cleomenes as a deceitful and malevolent object was evidently a reasonable representation in the eyes of the Athenians, already capable, as I think, of mastering propositional operations. It remains to explain how a society like the city engendered a mentality that aroused the suspicion of a Cleomenes, himself remaining at a level of concrete operations. What is the mechanism that permits us to think what is unthinkable to others? I limit myself here to sketching an explanation that departs from

---

[4] I do not consider here the question of exactly when coinage began in Athens and why; on the topic in general, see above, Introduction; on Athens in particular, see Kraay 1976: 55–77, Howgego 1995: 18–21, 44–45, 111–13, von Reden 1995: 171–217, Kroll 1998.

some reflections on the propositional *practices* of the city: monetary practice
and the practice of democratic decision-making. For that which concerns
the first, it turns out that it manifests its propositional character already
on the level of vocabulary: to the expression *khrēmata dokima* (literally
"merchandise of agreed-upon value," that is, "legal tender") of the Eretrian
laws of the sixth century, corresponds the inverse expression *to nomisma
adokimon poiein* ("to render the currency *adokimon*," that is, "to annul
the agreed-upon value of coins"—in order to buy them at their real value)
in the *Oeconomica* of Pseudo-Aristotle. In monetary practice, one acts *as
if* the agreed-upon value were the real value of the minted piece: already
the first minters had paid for unstruck gold with minted pieces whose real
value did not at all correspond to the "agreed-upon" value. "Installed as
true"—"truth" imposed by the state—the agreed-upon value was employed
in commercial operations.[5]

Deborah Steiner, following Svenbro, applies the same dichotomy to a
reading of the shield of Amphiaraos in Aeschylus' *Seven against Thebes*:

> Amphiaraos's blank shield also presents a coin without a stamp. Rejecting
> the realm of mere semblance, τὸ δοκεῖν, he refuses the convention that
> makes a surface mark represent the coin's actual value. The language of
> coinage draws on the same terms of seeming and semblance, implicitly
> exposing the symbolic or conventional order on which currency depends. . . .
> It is stamps that consign the metal pieces to the world of appearances and
> replace an actual weight and value with a relative one. By choosing a shield
> without a blazon, Amphiaraos has distanced himself from the sphere of
> conventional representations and has reclaimed objects back from their
> codes.[6]

Both Svenbro and Steiner make a valuable point about the link between
coinage and symbolic thought (a point supported, I would contend, by
the association of coinage with games we traced in Chapter 7). Still,
their simple alignment of coin with semblance as opposed to essence
elides the materiality of Athenian coinage, reducing it to a symbol and
missing the significant doubleness of Greek currency. For the history
of Athenian coinage, as we shall see, is precisely a history of resistance
to merely symbolic or conventional value. For two hundred years or
more (?550–350), the Athenians minted only silver coinage that was
famously pure and reliable. Athenian owls were so pure, and their silver

---

[5] Svenbro 1976: 97, my translation, with original emphasis.
[6] Steiner 1994: 56–57, though Steiner acknowledges that *dokimos* derives not from *dokein*
(to seem) as Svenbro implies, but from *dechomai* (to accept); for the association of coin
with seeming or convention, cf. Seaford 1994: 202, 216–17.

content so close to their face value that they circulated all over the Mediterranean.[7]

At the same time, there is a certain trend in numismatic scholarship to deny that the materiality of Greek coinage has anything but the most pragmatic motivations. Thus John Kroll has recently suggested that silver bullion operated as money in Athens long before the first minting of coins, and that the motivation to shift from bullion to coinage was simply one of profit; he estimates a gap of approximately 5 percent between the real value of the silver and the face value of coinage, skimmed off by the state in the minting process.[8] Such an argument denies any significance to the symbolic dimension of coinage championed by scholars like Svenbro, Steiner, and von Reden, but it also occludes the fact that the very matter of ancient coinage is enmeshed in ideology. Why, after all, did Greek coinage have to be *silver*? Kroll's explanation is again a practical one— because the Athenians had the Laureion silver mines. But another numismatist, Christopher Howgego, offers a salutary corrective to the self-evidence of this account:

It is also worth asking why civic gold and electrum coinage is so rare. There were some sizeable issues which extended over a reasonable period. The electrum of Cyzicus, Mytilene, and Phocaea has already been mentioned, and one might add the gold of Lampsacus and Syracuse in the fourth century, and of Ephesos and Rhodes in the late hellenistic period. Most other issues were exceptional, and may often be associated with emergencies. . . . It remains unclear why there were not more regular gold coinages. Prudence (i.e. saving for emergencies), alternative uses (cult objects etc.), and the high value of gold (making inconveniently high-value coins) may have played a part. Access to mines clearly lay behind most of the major series, but gold was surely available more widely than is implied by the production of coinage. Was there some taboo that gold should not be generally used for coinage unless absolutely necessary?[9]

---

[7] For the purity of Athenian silver coinage, see Buttrey 1981: 82–83; for its wide circulation throughout the Mediterranean, see Kraay 1964: 80–82, 1976: 60–63, 67. Cf. also the remarkable assertion of Xenophon (*Poroi* 3.2) that Athenian silver coinage made a good export because it could be sold "everywhere abroad" at *more* than its face value (cited by Kraay 1976: 76).

[8] Kroll 1998; cf. Wallace 1987 for an analogous argument about the early electrum issues of Asia Minor.

[9] Howgego 1995: 8–9. Elsewhere Howgego notes that some Greek cities that minted only silver and started minting quite early did not have access to mines but had to import: thus studies of metallic make-up reveal that in the archaic period, Aigina got its silver from Siphnos, while Corinthian silver derives from Athens' Laureion mines(!). The fact that these cities chose to mint *only* silver when they had no direct access to the raw material supports Howgego's point that the choice is anything but self-explanatory (Howgego 1995: 24–25).

Howgego's formulation suggests that, even when it comes to the stuff of coinage, causality might be overdetermined—that is, there might be a combination of practical and (what we might call) irrational or ideological motives for the avoidance of gold. Howgego's notion of some kind of taboo against gold is intriguing in light of the language of metals mapped out in Chapters 1 and 2. For, as we saw there, gold in the traditional elite system is strongly associated with the gods (from the time of Homer on), with kingship or sovereignty, with the East (where rivers flow with gold), and with Eastern despots like Midas, Gyges, and Kroisos. I would contend, further, that sympotic poetry of the archaic period identified the Greek elite with the gods, sovereignty, and the East by figuring the proper aristocratic self as gold within a ranked hierarchy of metals. All that the elitist strand valorized, and the middling poets of the archaic period rejected, is neatly summed up by Archilochos's lines spoken in the persona of Charon the carpenter:[10]

οὔ μοι τὰ Γύγεω τοῦ πολυχρύσου μέλει,
    οὐδ' εἷλέ πώ με ζῆλος, οὐδ' ἀγαίομαι
θεῶν ἔργα, μεγάλης δ' οὐκ ἐρέω τυραννίδος·
    ἀπόπροθεν γάρ ἐστιν ὀφθαλμῶν ἐμῶν. (Arch. fr. 19 W)

I do not care for the property of Gyges rich in gold, nor yet has envy taken me, nor am I jealous of the works of the gods, and I don't lust after great tyranny. For [these things] are far from my eyes.

Tyranny, the East, the gods, conjoined with the significant epithet *poluchrusos* (rich in gold): though they predate the beginnings of Greek mainland coinage by a century or more, Archilochos's verses might be read in hindsight as a manifesto for silver coinage within civic ideology. Thus, I suggest, at least part of the reason silver became *the* metal for Greek civic coinage was symbolic opposition to the elitist identification with gold.[11]

If silver was aligned with *hubris* in the archaic language of metals (recall Herodotus's story of Darius and Aryandes, or Theognis's use of the name "Arguris" for an uppity *hetaira*), the city transvalued silver as

---

[10] Cf. Morris 1996: 34, who refers to this fragment as the rejection of "a virtual checklist of elitism."

[11] There is, of course, a chicken-and-egg problem. Which came first—elitist identification with gold, or the choice of silver for civic coinage? It is impossible to know, and perhaps best to treat it as a dialectic rather than the result of simple, unidirectional cause and effect. In the post-Persian War period, this opposition is reinforced by the contrast of Greek silver with Persian gold (cf. Aesch. *Pers.* 237–38), but even before that, the massive gold dedications of Gyges and Kroisos at various Panhellenic centers must have been familiar to many Greeks (Hdt. 1.14, 50–52, 92). The strong association of gold with the East in Greek thought is emphasized by Caccamo Caltabiano and Radici Colace 1985, 1989: 216–17; Hall 1989: 127–28; Lewis 1989: 234.

the "middling" metal—not so high as gold, but still precious metal in contrast to base bronze. For the other striking (and strikingly "irrational") feature of Greek coinage practices in general, and those of Athens in particular, is the long-term resistance to the use of bronze. Recent numismatic work has demonstrated that very small denominations of silver were minted already in the archaic period, very possibly in large quantities, by cities such as Athens, Corinth, and Aigina.[12] The smallest Athenian silver coin that has been found to date is a sixteenth of an obol, weighing an infinitesmal .044 grams.[13] Numismatists frequently remark on the extreme inconvenience of using such tiny coins and the difficulty of distinguishing among them (thus Kraay notes that there were six other fractional units, minutely different in weight, between the eighth-obol and the obol in fourth-century Athens).[14] Yet in spite of the practical difficulties, Athens resisted the regular use of much larger bronze coins for small denominations until the second half of the fourth century, long after bronze token coinage had been adopted in Sicily and South Italy (in the second half of the fifth century), and throughout much of central Greece by ca. 350 B.C.E.[15] How to account for this resistance to bimetallism for two centuries, when the minting of only silver apparently had no practical advantages and, in fact, imposed severe impediments on the easy circulation of coin? Here again, matter seems inextricably imbricated in ideology. In the symbolism of the democratic city, all coins, like all citizens, were made of the same stuff, and all were pure and precious matter. The silver-only coinage of Athens thus stands in opposition both to the elitist hierarchy of values and exchange spheres (gold-silver-bronze) and to the impure mixture of base metal (bronze is an alloy of copper and tin).[16] The avoidance of bronze is furthermore the avoidance of token coinage—by the time Athens adopted bronze currency in the mid-fourth century, there was no connection between the weight of bronze and the face value of the coin, so that the long-term Athenian resistance to bronze must also be read as a reluctance to make coinage merely conventional.

[12] Howgego 1995: 6–7, citing Kim 1994, vs. Kraay 1964.

[13] Pászthory 1979: 4–6, cited by Howgego 1995: 7.

[14] Kraay 1976: 75; on the impracticality of very small silver fractions, see also Price 1968: 92–93; Kraay 1976: 69–70; Howgego 1995: 7.

[15] On the chronology, distribution, and spread of early bronze coinage, see Price 1968, 1979; Kraay 1976: 75, 230–31; on the dating of Athenian bronze coinage in particular, see Kroll 1979. We should note here the existence from the fifth century of bronze *kolluboi*, bronze tokens mentioned in Old Comedy (Aristoph. *Peace* 1198, Eupolis fr. 247 K.-A.) and found in quantity in Attica (some from the Agora). These *kolluboi* are generally regarded by numismatists as privately issued merchants' tokens; thus Robinson 1960: 6–8; Kraay 1976: 69; Price 1979: 356, 362–63.

[16] Cf. Morris's description of middling ideology as opposing both excessive wealth and display and abject poverty in the standing of the *metrios* citizen (Morris 1996: 22).

In Athens, of course, there was another factor at work as well. Silver was not only the "middling" metal, but also a native product of the Attic soil. As Athenian texts proudly proclaim, in language that resonates with formulations of citizen worth, their silver is autochthonous. Thus Aeschylus has his Persian chorus explain the source of Athenian wealth to the bewildered Persian queen: "They have some spring of silver, a treasurehouse of the earth" (ἀργύρου πηγή τις αὐτοῖς ἐστι, θησαυρὸς χθονός, *Pers.* 238). And thus, even more explicitly, Xenophon numbers among the natural bounties of Attica its "hidden riches," bestowed by divine dispensation:

καὶ μὴν ὑπάργυρός ἐστι σαφῶς θείᾳ μοίρᾳ· πολλῶν γοῦν πόλεων παροικουσῶν καὶ κατὰ γῆν καὶ κατὰ θάλατταν εἰς οὐδεμίαν τούτων οὐδὲ μικρὰ φλὲψ ἀργυρίτιδος διήκει. (Xen. *Poroi* 1.5)

And again, there is [land] that has silver beneath it, clearly by divine allotment: for, though many cities are our neighbors, both by land and sea, not even a single small vein of silver ore goes through into any of them.

Just as, in Athenian ideology, Attica alone of Greek mainland states maintained her pristine autochthonous population, so also Athens alone enjoyed the divine gift of silver coursing through her soil.[17] That there was symbolic (as well as practical) value attached to silver coinage in Athens is confirmed by two remarkable exceptions to the silver-only code that occurred toward the end of the Peloponnesian War. In 413 B.C.E. the Spartans occupied the fort of Decelea in Attica, in the process cutting off the Athenians' access to the Laureion silver mines (Thuc. 6.91, 7.27). Massive state expenditure on the Sicilian Expedition, conjoined with the growing unwillingness of the allies to pay their tribute, led to a severe shortage of silver within Athens, until finally, in the last years of the war, the Athenians resorted to two unparalleled expedients. In 407/6, gold coinage was issued in place of the usual silver, minted from fourteen talents of gold melted down from seven Nikai (Victory statues) dedicated on the Acropolis. The next year the Athenians resorted to a different strategy, issuing a bronze token coinage in place of silver.[18] Both these issues have left traces of anxiety in the literary record, and both were unique experiments, never repeated in the history of Athenian coinage.

In Thucydides' *History*, Perikles at the beginning of the Peloponnesian

---

[17] On the ideology of Athenian citizen autochthony, see Loraux 1993; Dougherty 1996: 254–62. For parallel language in the context of citizen autochthony, cf. Plato *Menexenus* 237b2–238b1.

[18] For both gold and bronze issues, see Aristoph. *Frogs* 720–33 with scholia *ad loc.* (citing Hellanikos and Philochoros); for exact details of these issues, see Robinson 1960: 8–15; Thompson 1970; Kraay 1976: 69–70; Howgego 1995: 111–12.

War had already anticipated the possibility that gold from the chryselephantine statue of Athena might have to be removed and melted down for the war effort (Thuc. 2.13.3–5). But even Thucydides' hyper-rational Perikles registers some discomfort at the prospect of making use of this sacred gold: he mentions it as the absolutely final resort, after private and public dedications, the sacred equipment used in processions and games, and the booty captured from the Persians, and sternly warns that, "if they borrow [this gold] for their salvation, they must restore at least as much again" (Thuc. 2.13.5).[19] Other ancient texts are even more explicit about the anxiety that hedged round the conversion of sacred gold into civic coin. Thus Demetrios, in his late Hellenistic treatise *On Style*, recounts a telling anecdote illustrating the value of euphemism in oratory:

τάχα δὲ καὶ ὁ εὐφημισμὸς καλούμενος μετέχοι τῆς δεινότητος, καὶ ὁ τὰ δύσφημα εὔφημα ποιῶν, καὶ τὰ ἀσεβήματα εὐσεβήματα, οἷον ὡς ὁ τὰς Νίκας τὰς χρυσᾶς χωνεύειν κελεύων καὶ καταχρῆσθαι τοῖς χρήμασιν εἰς τὸν πόλεμον οὐχ οὕτως εἶπεν προχείρως, ὅτι κατακόψωμεν τὰς Νίκας εἰς τὸν πόλεμον. δύσφημον γὰρ ἂν οὕτως καὶ λοιδοροῦντι ἐοικὸς ἦν τὰς θεάς, ἀλλ᾽ εὐφημότερον, ὅτι συγχρησόμεθα ταῖς Νίκαις εἰς τὸν πόλεμον. οὐ γὰρ κατακόπτοντι τὰς Νίκας ἔοικεν οὕτως ῥηθέν, ἀλλὰ συμμάχους μεταποιοῦντι. (Demetr. *On Style* 5.281)

And what is called euphemism may partake of skill in speaking, the one making ill-omened words auspicious and [making] blasphemies into pieties. For example, the one who proposed melting down the golden Victories and using the money for the war, didn't say thus straight out, "Let's cut up the Victories for the war." For this would have been ill-omened, and would have seemed like someone abusing the goddesses, but he said it more auspiciously, "Let us make joint use of the Victories for the war." For thus it was said not like someone cutting up the Victories, but transforming them into allies.[20]

---

[19] Cf. Diodorus Siculus 12.40.1–3, who interestingly uses the same image of "borrowing from the gods" (χρησαμένους παρὰ τῶν θεῶν).

[20] The same story is repeated by Quintilian (*IO* 9.2.92): *Confinia sunt his celebrata apud Graecos schemata, per quae res asperas mollius significant. Nam Themistocles suasisse existimatur Atheniensibus, ut urbem apud deos deponerent, quia durum erat dicere, ut relinquerent. Et qui Victorias aureas in usum belli conflari volebat, ita declinavit, victoriis utendum esse* (Similar to these things are the schemata popular among the Greeks, through which they signify harsh things in softer terms. For Themistocles is believed to have urged the Athenians "to put their city in the hands of the gods," because it was [too] harsh to say "to abandon it." And the man who wanted the golden Victories to be melted down for use in war thus turned it aside, that they "must make use of the Victories.") Quintilian's pairing of the story with that of Themistocles is intriguing, for both turn on the issue of the city's relation to its gods.

In this instance, the anecdote and the blasphemy are particularly pointed because these are statues of Victory and because the verb κατακόπτω means both "cut up for coinage" and "kill" or "destroy" (thus the gauche orator would seem to propose "destroying the Victories for the war"). But I would contend that this is only part of the *frisson* of this anecdote; there is a more general dread felt at taking the gold that forms the very body of divine images and transforming it into the common currency of the city. This transgression of the symbolic opposition of gold and silver produces anxiety that ripples through centuries, still palpable several hundred years later. Indeed, the numinous quality of this gold issue and all that pertained to it is confirmed by the treatment of the dies, anvils, and hammers from which it was struck; sometime after this single minting of gold, all this equipment was dedicated in the treasury of Athena, where it still shows up in temple inventory inscriptions more than eighty years later.[21]

Similar anxieties seem to haunt the token bronze issue of 406/5. Thus Athenaios, writing in the second or third century C.E., still preserves the memory of an Attic orator Dionysios who "was called *Chalkous* because he advised the Athenians to use bronze coinage" (*Deipn.* 15.669d). Given the date of the orator Dionysios, we might plausibly link his eponym to the emergency bronze issue at the end of the Peloponnesian War.[22] However that may be, we know from a reference in Aristophanes' *Ekklesiazousai* that this token bronze was demonetized some time before 393/2 B.C.E. and never again attempted.[23] For when Athens finally resorted to bronze token coinage nearly forty years later, it was adopted only for small denominations (fractions below the obol) and never in place of the traditional silver tetradrachms.[24]

---

[21] *IG* II², 1388; 1408; 1409; 1469, lines 107–9; 1471, lines 56–57 (these last two inventories dating to 320 and 318 B.C.E. respectively); for discussion, see Robert 1962: 22–24. The pragmatic explanation for this dedication of equipment is that storage in a god's temple is the easiest way of guaranteeing safekeeping, in case they want to reuse the dies for another gold issue at some later point. Given that the Athenians never did mint another gold issue, we may be inclined to think that the dedication was not a completely practical measure. Perhaps the dies, like the gold they minted, were felt to be the gods' property and thus, like dedications, could not simply be destroyed.

[22] According to Plutarch (*Nik.* 5), a Dionysios took part in the foundation of Thurii in 443 B.C.E.; cf. Robinson 1960: 6, Howgego 1995: 7; otherwise Price 1968 (who connects Dionysios with the early issuing of bronze token coinage in Thurii in the last quarter of the fifth century).

[23] Aristoph. *Ekkl.* 815–22 (cf. Pollux *Onom.* 9.63). It is worth noting the exact wording of the decree as Aristophanes reports it: "Let no one accept bronze in future, for we use silver."

[24] See Robinson 1960; Kraay 1976: 75; Howgego 1995: 111.

This fitful history of stops and starts and anxious anecdotes preserved for centuries cannot be adequately explained by a purely rational or pragmatic account. Instead, Athenian coinage seems to have carried a powerful symbolic valence for those who minted and used it—as a civic token that wedded *nomos* and *phusis*, pure and valuable essence imprinted with a civic stamp. Indeed, I would contend that the facts we have rehearsed only make sense if we read the substance and circulation of coinage as analogous to the community of citizens and assume that that analogy imposes symbolic constraints on its production and material. This is one way in which ideology informs matter, but the analogy operates in the other direction as well (as we saw already in the case of games): if coins are like citizens, citizens are like coins. How, after all, does ideology become reality? W. R. Connor has recently articulated the need to look beyond constitutional structure to the realm of civil society to understand how democracy establishes and maintains itself. I would go a step further and say we need to look beyond civil society to cultural practice, and to the nodes where all three notionally distinct spheres converge. Once Athenian silver coinage is established as practice, its ongoing production and circulation not only reflect, but in some measure constitute, the community of citizens. Thus, in what we might call the micro-mechanics of ideology, material practices contribute to the civic imaginary, as pure silver coinage helps constitute the "imaginary community" of citizens who use it.[25] As opposed to bronze token coinage, it asserts that civic order is more than just conventional; as opposed to bronze used at its full value or to debase the silver issue, it constitutes all citizens as the same noble substance. In contrast to gold, it rejects the elitist hierarchy of essence within the citizen body, while it imposes a firm boundary between the human, civic community and the domain of the gods. Finally, of course, its stamp implies that all citizens take shape from and submit to the civic authority that forms them.

That there was an analogy operative between citizens and coins in the civic imaginary is confirmed by the Athenian legal practice of the *dokimasia* (and, as we shall see in the next section, by the representations of coinage in literary texts). The *dokimasia* was a procedure by which the democratic city proofed its citizens, testing the quality of their birth and behavior. According to our literary sources, there were four occasions

[25] Cf. Connor 1996, esp. 222–23: "Benedict Anderson's *Imagined Communities* implicitly challenges classicists to think more closely about the role of social imagination in the constitution of ancient societies. It is especially important to examine more closely how such imagination works. It does little good to think of it in abstract terms. Rather it is a highly metaphorical activity, in which specific practices from one realm are envisioned as operating in another realm." Cf. Ober 1989: 40–41; Anderson 1991: 12.

for *dokimasiai*: annually, when young men became ephebes (at the point of first being enrolled in the citizen body), and for all officials chosen by election or lot, before they took up office; exceptionally, for new citizens and for rhetors who addressed the assembly.[26] We are best informed about the procedure for the archons-elect (which was presumably similar to that for other officials), for here the Aristotelian *Athenaiōn Politeia* gives us a detailed account. Each archon-elect underwent *dokimasia* first in the Boule, then in the lawcourt; on each occasion, he was asked

> "Who is your father and from what deme, and who is your father's father, and who is your mother, and who is your father's mother and from what deme?" And after this [they ask] if he has [a cult of] Apollo Patroös and Zeus Herkeios and where these shrines are, then if he has family tombs and where these are, then if he treats his parents well, and pays his taxes, and [ask him] his campaigns if he has served on campaign. And when [the questioner] has asked these things, he says, "Call witnesses of these things." ([Arist.] *Ath. Pol.* 55.3–4)

After witnesses were called, anyone who wished had the opportunity to lay accusations against the archon-elect, and he had the right to defend himself. Through these questions, the *dokimasia* proofed both the nature and the obedience to law of the individual examined. Thus, the queries about father's and mother's families, shrines, and family tombs served to check that he was descended from Athenian citizens on both sides, while the questions about treatment of parents, taxes, and army service scrutinized not just behavior or character but specifically proper submission to the laws of the city. For legislation traditionally said to date back to Solon required the support of fathers in old age, while the pair of questions about paying taxes and serving in the army checked that the archon-elect had willingly expended "from his property and from his body" for the city which was felt to be the real owner of both.[27]

But *dokimasia* and the verb δοκιμάζω, from which the noun is derived, were also technical terms for examining and approving coinage as legal tender (*dokimos*). Thus, in a lengthy inscription set up in the Athenian agora, dated 375/4 B.C.E., we are given a detailed description of the proper activities of the public *dokimastēs*:

---

[26] For *dokimasia* of ephebes, see Aristoph. *Wasps* 578; Lysias 32.9; Isoc. 7.37, 12.28; Dem. 21.157, 27.5, 36, 30.6; of officials, Lysias 16, 25, 26, 31; Xen. *Mem.* 2.2.13; Dem. 57.66; Aeschines 3.15, 29; [Arist.] *Ath. Pol.* 55; Pollux *Onom.* 8.85–86; of new citizens, [Dem.] 59.105; of rhetors, Aeschines 1.2, 28–32, 186; Harpokr. s. v. δοκιμασθείς; Pollux *Onom.* 8.43, 45. On the various types of *dokimasiai* and their procedures, see Hansen 1991: 218–20, 258–59.

[27] For thorough discussion of the content and purpose of the *dokimasia*, see Koch 1903: 1268–73; Rhodes 1981: 617–19; Adeleye 1983. For the pair "property" and "body" offered by the citizen in service to the city, see Dem. 21.145.

τὸ ἀργύριον δέχεσθαι τὸ Ἀττικὸν ὅτ[αν δεικνύητ]-
αι ἀργυρõγ καὶ ἔχηι τὸν δημόσιογ χα[ρακτῆρα. ὁ δὲ]
δοκιμαστὴς ὁ δημόσιος καθήμενος με[ταξὺ τῶν τρ]-　　　　5
απεζῶν δοκιμαζέτω κατὰ ταῦτα ὅσαι ἡ[μέραι πλὴν]
ὅταν ἦ[ι] χρημάτωγ καταβολή, τότε δὲ ἐ[ν τῶι βολευτ]-
ηρίωι. ἐὰν δέ τις προσενέγκηι ξ[ε]ν[ικὸν ἀργύριον]
ἔχον τὸν αὐτὸγ χαρακτῆρα τῶι Ἀττι[κῶ]ι, ἐ[ὰν καλόν,]
ἀποδιδότω τῶι προσενεγκόντι. ἐὰν δὲ ὑπ[όχαλκον]　　10
ἢ ὑπομόλυβδον ἢ κίβδηλον, διακοπτέτω πα[ραυτίκ]-
α καὶ ἔστω ἱερὸν τῆς Μητρὸς [τ]ῶν θεῶγ καὶ κ[αταβαλ]-
λέτω ἐς τὴμ βολήν. . . .

. . . ἐὰν δέ τις μὴ δέχηται τὸ ἀ[ρ]γ[ύρ]ιον ὅ τ[ι ἂν ὁ δοκι]-　　16
μαστὴς δοκιμάσηι, στερέσθω ὧν ἂμ [π]ωλῆτ[αι ἐκείν]-
ηι τῆι ἡμέραι. . . .

To accept Attic silver currency when [it is shown to be] silver and has the
public stamp. Let the public *dokimastēs* sit among [the] tables and evaluate
[sc. coin] in accordance with these provisions every [day except] whenever
there is a cash payment; at that time let him evaluate in [the bouleuterion.]
If anyone proffers [foreign silver currency] having the same stamp as the
Attic, [if it is good,] let him return it to the one who proffered it; but if it
is [bronze at the core,] or lead at the core, or counterfeit, let him cut it
across [immediately] and let it be sacred to the Mother of the Gods and let
him [deposit] it with the Council. . . . And if anyone does not accept silver
currency the *dokimastēs* has approved, let him be deprived of all the things
he has for sale on that day. . .[28]

The original editor, R. S. Stroud, argued that the position of public
dokimastēs must have preexisted this particular law, going back to 398/
7 B.C.E. at least.[29] More recently, T. V. Buttrey has suggested that the
innovation of the law of 375/4 was to have the *dokimastēs*, who normally
worked in the bouleuterion evaluating incoming payments to the state,
divide his time and carry on his activity also in the agora (lines 5–8).
Buttrey has argued further that the law of 375/4 B.C.E. was essentially a
"legal tender act," requiring the acceptance of Athenian silver coinage,

---

[28] Text and translation follow the original edition of Stroud 1974, with some modifications
suggested by Buttrey 1979, 1981. In one respect I diverge from Buttrey's interpretation:
he insists that δοκιμάζω (because it is etymologically derived from *dokimos*, which is in
turn derived from *dechomai*) cannot mean "test, evaluate, assay," but only "approve."
Here Buttrey succumbs to the etymological fallacy; whatever the etymology of δοκιμάζω
might be, it is clear that within the synchronic system of fourth-century usage, the verb
regularly means "test, evaluate" in the present tense, while it tends to mean "approve" in
the aorist (as Buttrey 1981: 94 himself acknowledges in an addendum, citing M. H. Hansen).
[29] Stroud 1974: 166, 176–77; cf. Buttrey 1981: 74–75.

once approved by the *dokimastēs*, for all transactions within the state. He recognizes the occasion for the law in a massive influx of Egyptian-minted imitations of Attic tetradrachms in the fourth century B.C.E., which threatened to dilute the pure Athenian coinage, and presumably led to merchants' uncertainty about the provenance of coins in circulation.[30] Thus the *dokimastēs* is instructed to approve Attic coinage "when it is shown to be of silver and has the public stamp" (lines 3–4, 6); but simply to return to the one who proffers it "foreign coin having the same stamp as the Attic" (lines 8–10), and finally to confiscate all coins that are base or counterfeit, thus withdrawing them from circulation (lines 10–11). As Buttrey observes, the *dokimastēs* must always have had the tasks of examining and approving Attic coinage and of withdrawing base and counterfeit coins from circulation: what is new in the 375/4 law is the need to differentiate Attic silver coins from foreign coins that looked nearly identical to them.[31]

Still, leaving aside the particular developments of the 375/4 ordinance, we should note the striking parallels between the testing of coin and the *dokimasia* of citizens. Just as the *dokimastēs* approves coinage as *dokimos* (legal tender) based on the dual requirements of purity of silver and civic stamp, the evaluating body approves candidates-elect as *dokimoi* (respected/acceptable) based on the purity of citizen birth and the proper formation by and acquiescence to civic law.[32] Indeed, in one instance, in a speech written for a civic *dokimasia*, the speaker's language seems to register the parallelism between citizen and coin and the procedures used to proof them. Lysias 31 is a speech of accusation, written to be delivered at the *dokimasia* of one Philon, who has been selected by lot for a seat on the Boule. Among Philon's transgressions of proper civic norms, the speaker alleges that he chose to live as a metic in Oropus during the period of the rule of the Thirty and the struggle to overthrow them (404/3 B.C.E.). The speaker construes this choice as a betrayal of Athens, Philon's desertion of his city in its hour of need. He concludes that he could make many more charges, but even without them he trusts the members of the Boule to make the right decision:

οὐ γὰρ ἄλλοις τισὶν ὑμᾶς δεῖ περὶ τῶν ἀξίων ὄντων βουλεύειν τεκμηρίοις χρῆσθαι ἢ ὑμῖν αὐτοῖς, ὁποῖοί τινες ὄντες αὐτοὶ περὶ τὴν πόλιν

---

[30] Buttrey 1979 and especially 1981.

[31] Buttrey 1981.

[32] The use of the adjective *dokimos* for people already suggests the evaluative authority of the city; as opposed to absolute terms like *agathos*, *esthlos*, or *aristos*, *dokimos* connotes the approval of an individual by the community of which he is a part. We should note that *dokimos* is one of Herodotus's favorite adjectives for persons, occurring thirty-seven times in this usage. Is the application of the term to persons itself inspired by the expression

ἐδοκιμάσθητε. ἔστι γὰρ τὰ τούτου ἐπιτηδεύματα καινὰ παραδείγματα καὶ πάσης δημοκρατίας ἀλλότρια. (Lysias 31.34)

For you ought not to use any other proofs concerning those who are worthy to be members of the Boule than yourselves, what sort you have been approved to be in regard to the city. For the habits of this man are patterns that are new and foreign to the whole idea of democracy.

What is intriguing here is the speaker's transformation of both judges and the man being judged into signifying tokens—the current bouleutai become their own best τεκμήρια of proper worth (notice ἀξίων), while the habits of the corrupt Philon offer "patterns" or paradigms that are "new and foreign to the whole idea of democracy." The juxtaposition of native and foreign signifying tokens corresponds exactly to Aristotle's glancing description of how men test and approve coinage: "just as each group of men test and approve coinage with reference to that which is best known to themselves . . ." (ὥσπερ γὰρ τὰ νομίσματα πρὸς τὸ αὐτοῖς ἕκαστοι γνωριμώτατον δοκιμάζουσιν, *Hist. An.* 491a20–22). The philosopher's analogy suggests the image implicit in the concluding exhortation of Philon's accuser: the current bouleutai are to be both judges and their own "best known" coinage, while Philon's behavior and character, set against the known civic standard, will be revealed to be base and foreign. Indeed, the speaker's use of ἀλλότρια within the analogy of coin is particularly apt, for it signifies in general terms Philon's violation of the proprieties of good citizenship, but it also evokes the specific fact that he preferred to be a metic in Oropus rather than a citizen at home. In the concluding words of the accusation, Philon is exposed as foreign coin instead of "legal tender."[33]

Given the analogy of citizens and coins instantiated in the *dokimasia*, it is worth juxtaposing this procedure with another civic, legal procedure—the *basanos*. In the language of the Athenian lawcourts, *basanos* was judicial torture, which was required for slaves if they were to give evidence in a court case. In contrast to the bodies of slaves, who had to be tortured to give evidence, the bodies of free citizens were all but inviolable in classical Athens. As Page duBois argues, the institution of judicial torture thus serves to articulate and maintain a clear boundary

---

chrēmata dokima (which, as Svenbro [1976: 97] notes, already figures in a sixth-century inscription from Eretria)?

[33] For the relevance of the citizen-coin analogy to another form of *dokimasia*, cf. the expression κόμμα καινόν ("a new striking"), preserved in Hesychios with the gloss, "Not just for coinage, but also for new citizens." It may be that Hesychios derives the phrase from a literary text (say, e.g., Old Comedy), but the image (whatever its source) may be inspired partly by the fact that new citizens were required to undergo a *dokimasia*.

between slave and free.[34] But this use of *basanos*, the technical term
for judicial torture, is derived by way of the meaning "test" from the
touchstone, so dear to archaic elitist poetry as an image for proofing the
pistos hetairos.[35] By this procedure, the democratic city transfers the
unalloyed essentialism of elitist ideology to the body of the slave, which
becomes in torture, as Page duBois observes, "pure materiality."[36] Thus
the opposition *dokimasia-basanos* radically reconfigures the metals-
money dichotomy of archaic elitist texts. Citizens, like coins, undergo a
symbolic proofing of their *phusis* and *nomos*; slaves, as mere matter
unformed by the imprint of civic law, must submit to the relentless
material examination of the torture.[37]

This network of association and analogy between Athenian silver coinage and the good citizen may finally help us understand some strange
provisions included in the archons' oath as reported by Aristotle. Immediately after its detailed description of the questions and procedures of the
archons' *dokimasia*, the *Ath. Pol.* relates,

> when they have been approved in this way (δοκιμασθέν<τες> δὲ τοῦτον
> τὸν τρόπον), [the archons] go to the stone on which are parts of the sacrificial
> victim . . . and mounting upon this, they swear to administer their office
> justly and according to the laws, and not to take bribes (δῶρα) for the sake
> of their office, and if they do take anything to dedicate a golden statue
> (ἀνδριάντα ἀναθήσειν χρυσοῦν).[38] ([Arist.] *Ath. Pol.* 55.5)

References to the archons' oath in Plato and Plutarch provide additional
information about these gold statues—they were to be life-size images

---

[34] duBois 1991: 39–68; cf. Hunter 1994: 173–76.

[35] For the development in meaning of *basanos*, see duBois 1991: 9–62; for its association
with testing the *pistos hetairos*, see Chapter 1 above.

[36] duBois 1991: 39.

[37] Cf. ibid: 52, observing suggestively in a slightly different context, "Slaves are bodies;
citizens possess *logos*, reason." We might also note in this connection the intriguing theory
of Glotz 1908, that the number of blows of the whip legislated in punishment for a slave
corresponded to the number of drachmas assessed as a fine for a free man who committed
the same offense. Glotz's argument is summarized and critiqued by Hunter 1994: 155–62:
though the correspondence Glotz detected does not always hold, it does seem to represent
a tendency in Athenian law, and a telling one. In this system, coins serve as symbolic
substitutes for the body of the citizen, while slaves have no such recourse.

[38] For a simpler version of the archons' oath, cf. *Ath. Pol.* 7.1, where Solon is said to
have written and set up new laws and to have required the nine archons to swear "that
they would dedicate a golden statue, if they transgressed any of the laws." Rhodes 1981:
135, 621 thinks that the more detailed version of the oath given at 55.5 (which links the
golden statue specifically with bribe-taking) is more likely to be correct. The association
of a golden statue with *dōrodokia* is confirmed by Plato *Phdr.* 235d8–e1 and Pollux
Onom. 8.86.

of the dedicator, set up at Delphi.[39] The dedication of life-size gold statues is a bizarre form of punishment for corrupt officials, and its presence in the oath has long stymied commentators. To be sure, such a dedication would require enormous expenditure and that is part of the point, but if that were all the statues achieved, it could as easily be accomplished (with more profit to the state) by levying a fine on the offending archon.[40] Clearly, the requirement of a gold statue carries powerful symbolic resonances, but how are we to understand them? The parallel often cited by scholars to make this practice more comprehensible is the exaction at Olympia of bronze statues of Zeus from athletes who gave or took bribes (Paus. 5.21.2–18).[41] And while this parallel serves to illustrate the potent commemorative effects of such public dedications—Pausanias describes eighteen such "Zanes" set up at Olympia, each with its tale of corruption attached—it does nothing to account for the two strangest elements in the archons' punishment. For unlike the punitive statues of Zeus at Olympia, the archon's statue is meant to be *gold* (not bronze) and a lifesize portrait of *himself* (not the deity whose precinct the statue adorns). In this latter respect, the city's punishment oddly approximates the highest honor to which individual aristocrats aspired, for the right of setting up a life-size image of oneself was reserved for victors at the Panhellenic Games.[42]

I would contend that this strange provision of a gold statue can only be understood within the symbolic field of metals and money we have been tracing. In going through the *dokimasia*, the archon-elect is affirmed as good civic coin, autochthonous silver formed by and property of the city and its laws. Emerging from that civic proofing, he swears to respect the city's laws (*nomoi*) and not to debase his office by accepting gifts (*dōra*). The opposition of law and gift stages the tension between the values of the civic community and that of the system of inter-polis elite gift exchange. If the archon privileges the latter, the city symbolically extrudes him, exiling his image in perpetuity to the "other" space of

[39] Cf. Plato *Phdr.* 235d8–e1 and Plut. *Solon* 25.3.

[40] Thus Sandys (1912: 25, ad *Ath. Pol.* 7.1) records the ingenious suggestion of Bergk 1858.448–52, that the requirement that the statue be ἰσομέτρητον (mentioned in both Plato and Plutarch) means not "life-size" but "equal in weight" to the bribe, thereby levying the usual tenfold fine for bribery, given a gold:silver ratio of 10:1. Bergk's notion is open to two objections: (1: the positivist objection) numismatic evidence suggests that the gold:silver ratio in ancient Greece fluctuated between 11:1 and 13:1 (so that this would represent something more than a tenfold fine); (2; the semiotic objection) Bergk's solution still does not explain why the bribe-taker would be required to set up a statue of *himself* at *Delphi*.

[41] See, e. g., Harvey 1985: 95, who incorrectly describes the statues of Zeus at Olympia as "golden," though Pausanias specifically says they were bronze (Paus. 5.21.2).

[42] For the Panhellenic victor's right to set up a life-size statue, see Paus. 5.21.1, 6.1.1; for discussion of the function of such statues, see Kurke 1993: 141–55.

Delphi. And, in that movement, the offending official reverts from the civic economy of coin to the elitist hierarchy of metal, transmuted from silver to gold, and from interchangeable coin to singular *agalma*. The life-size gold statue is an extraordinary form of punishment, for it aligns the individual represented with images of the gods (especially Apollo, at Delphi) and of Eastern potentates.[43] The city thus takes the highest goods of elitist ideology—the gods, gold, the East—and radically revalues them as tokens of the greatest crime against the civic community. There is no evidence that any archon ever paid this extravagant penalty; nonetheless, the city needed this phantasmatic exaction, ritually reinvoked each year in the archons' oath, to mark out its imaginary boundaries.

Thus coinage seems to operate in a variety of contexts, symbolically and discursively, as a boundary phenomenon, articulating the border between the citizen community and its others. Insofar as a citizen is like a coin, he is not a slave, a metic, a barbarian, or the victim of a tyrant; nor is he overwealthy or divine. Implicated in these various systems of difference, the coin's reassuring materiality reifies and guarantees a category defined by its exclusions. We know what citizens are made of— what they are—partly because of the analogy with coin. And the power of that guarantee derives in large measure from the naturalizing symbolism of precious metal ("our autochthonous silver") imprinted with the civic stamp.

II. COINS ARE GOOD TO THINK WITH

We have suggested that coinage offers ways of thinking the relation of the city to its citizens, both through the coin's own material symbolism

---

[43] Pausanias mentions seventeen gold or gilded images of gods or heroes throughout Greece, including a solid gold statue of Apollo in the *aduton* of the temple at Delphi (Paus. 1.29.16; 1.42.4; 2.1.8; 2.2.6; 2.9.6; 5.2.3; 5.10.4; 6.24.6; 6.25.4; 7.20.7; 8.22.7; 8.53.7; 9.4.1; 9.35.6; 10.5.12; 10.15.4; 10.24.5); for Eastern potentates, recall Herodotus's account of the gold statues Kroisos set up at Delphi: (1) A solid gold lion, which I argued represents Kroisos himself (Chapter 1, above); (2) A gold statue of the woman who baked his bread, measuring three cubits (Hdt. 1.50.3–51.5). Gold or gilded statues of human beings (as opposed to gods or heroes) seem to have been very rare in Greece in the classical period. Thus Herodotus tells us that Alexander I of Macedon had a gold statue at Delphi (Hdt. 8.121), while the only gilded statues of mortals Pausanias reports having seen at Delphi were life-size images of the courtesan Mnesarete, set up by her lover Praxiteles, and of the famous sophist Gorgias of Leontini (Paus. 10.15.1; 10.18.7; it is interesting to note that both these figures were, in a sense, marginal to the Athenian polis, itinerant, and strongly associated with lucrative gifts and wages). Finally, inscriptional evidence may give us one more example; according to a supplement, *SIG*[3] 126 decrees the erection of a [gilded] bronze statue of Konon by the people of Erythrai in 394 B.C.E.

and through legal procedures such as the *dokimasia*. It is time now to consider the way in which coinage functions as a trope or token in literary texts, to see if it carries any of the same symbolic freight when it operates as a figure. I will begin with two fourth-century texts which are essentially contemporary with the civic practices under discussion and which are explicitly political in their focus. They will provide us with a rich network of associations that will be helpful in considering the more elliptical fifth-century uses of the image of coinage.[44]

In his speech against Timokrates, charged on a *graphē paranomōn*, Demosthenes constructs an elaborate analogy between coinage and civic law:

> I want then to narrate to you that also, which they say Solon once said when he was prosecuting someone who had proposed an unsuitable law (νόμον . . . οὐκ ἐπιτήδειον). For it is said that he said to the jurors, when he had presented the rest of his prosecution, that the law exists for virtually all cities, if anyone debases the currency, that the penalty be death. And having asked if the law appeared to them also to be just and good, when the jurors assented, he said that he himself considered silver coinage (ἀργύριον μὲν νόμισμα) to have been invented by private individuals for the sake of private exchanges, while he considered laws to be the currency of the city (νόμισμα τῆς πόλεως). And indeed it was much more necessary for the jurors to hate and punish any man who debased the currency of the city and introduced counterfeit [currency] than if someone [did that] to the currency of private individuals. And he added as proof that the wrongdoing of the one who debases the laws is much greater than that of the one who debases the silver currency (τὸ ἀργύριον), the fact that many cities, though they openly use silver currency mixed with bronze or lead, are safe and suffer no harm from this, but men who use wicked laws (νόμοις δὲ πονηροῖς) or allow the existing laws to be debased have never yet survived. (Dem. 24.212–14)

Demosthenes does not offer this argument in his own name but attributes it anachronistically to Solon, whose lawmaking activities probably pre-dated the beginnings of coinage in Athens by half a century. As such, it makes an interesting counterweight to the anecdote about Solon with which we began this chapter: in contrast to the tyrant, whose valuation of the men he uses is arbitrary and shifting, civic law should be a fixed

---

[44] My treatment of coinage as a literary trope will not be exhaustive but selective. This is partly because the literary material is fairly well known, but also because coinage is a complex and multivalent symbol—in texts as in life. For other discussions of coinage imagery, see Körte 1929; F. Will 1960; duBois 1991; Steiner 1994.55, 105–6; von Reden 1995: 149–64; Kurke 1998: 159–64; Wohl 1998: 59–99.

and known quantity founded on a "silver standard." For Demosthenes' "Solon" constructs an a fortiori argument that grudgingly admits that literal coinage can be debased with no lasting damage to the state, but that, implicitly, civic *nomos* must remain pure silver.[45] The analogy to coinage thus conjures an effect of naturalization, implying that proper civic law, like good silver coinage, is backed by an absolute standard of natural law or equity. Specifically, this naturalization effect works through and exploits the opaque evaluative terms ἐπιτήδειον and πονηροί, for Demosthenes never says what makes a law "suitable" or "wicked" but by his language coopts the jury's consent that these terms have an unambiguous and universally recognized meaning. Attached to the materiality of silver, the evaluation of "law" becomes unproblematic.

We find a very similar image of silver coinage and counterfeiting used in Aristotle's *Rhetoric*, in a passage that reveals much more specifically what is at stake in Demosthenes' analogy. Among the "non-technical means of persuasion," Aristotle numbers "law" and proceeds to describe how a defense would be mounted if one's case clearly violates the written law:

> For it is clear that if the written law is opposed to our case, we must use the universal [law] and what is equitable as more just. And [we must say] that [the juror's oath] "by my best judgment" is this, not to use the written law entirely. And [we must say] that the principle of equity (τὸ μὲν ἐπιεικές) remains always and never changes, nor does the universal [law change] (for it is according to nature), but the written laws change often, whence are said the things in Sophocles' *Antigone*; for she defends herself that she buried contrary to the law of Kreon, but not contrary to the unwritten law,
>
> > For not just something now or of the other day [they are] but always, . . .
> > And I was not going to, [fearing] these things from any man. . . .
>
> And [we must say] that justice is that which is true and advantageous, but not the [mere] seeming, so that written law is not [really] law; for it does not do the proper work of law. And [we must say] that the juror is like a tester of silver, to distinguish counterfeit from true justice (καὶ ὅτι ὥσπερ ἀργυρογνώμων ὁ κριτής ἐστιν, ὅπως διακρίνῃ τὸ κίβδηλον δίκαιον καὶ τὸ ἀληθές). And [we must say] that it is characteristic of a better man to use and abide by unwritten rather than written laws. (Arist. *Rhet.* 1375a27–b8)

It is worth pausing for a moment to appreciate precisely how odd this alignment of terms is: Aristotle equates good silver coinage with

---

[45] This speech, delivered in ca. 353 B.C.E., is in fact exactly contemporary with Athens's late and reluctant adoption of bronze token coinage for small denominations, and perhaps also looks back to the coinage crises at the end of the Peloponnesian War.

unwritten law, the unchanging and eternal principle of equity, nature, and authenticity, while he aligns counterfeit coin with particular, written law, with change, mere convention, and semblance.[46] This is precisely where, in the terms of the archaic elitist language of metals considered in Chapter 1, we would expect an opposition of gold and silver (or gold and bronze). Indeed, even in his own brief statement of why some disapprove of coinage in the *Politics* (which I suggested derives from the phobic elitist tradition), Aristotle had invoked just the opposite set of associations for coin:

> But sometimes coinage seems to be nonsense and entirely convention, but nothing by nature, since if those using it change, it is worth nothing nor useful toward [the purchase of] any of the necessaries. . . (*Pol.* 1257b10–14)

As we have seen, this tendentious identification of coinage with (mere) convention has even been taken up by modern scholars like Svenbro and Steiner, to argue for coinage as a form of symbolic logic. But Aristotle's brief, offhand simile in the *Rhetoric* reveals a significantly different nexus of associations for coinage, which must also have been current. Within this system, coinage is linked to nature and authenticity, and even to universality, by virtue of the pure silver, the stuff of which it is made. By means of a remarkable mystification, the Athenians (and, under their influence, Aristotle) have projected coinage from the level of the particular (for, in a sense, nothing is more *idion* to a community than its coinage) to the level of the universal. This was perhaps easy to do when Athens's silver coinage circulated and set the standard all over the known world; no wonder the Athenians were so reluctant to mint bronze.[47] Aristotle's analogy exposes for us the city's need to re-essentialize and naturalize its ideology, to transmute civic *nomos* into universal law.

But to leave it at that would be to overemphasize just one aspect of coinage—its material *phusis*. In urging the juror in the civic lawcourt to act as *argurognōmōn*, empowered to discriminate good from counterfeit justice, Aristotle reconciles the domains of particular and universal law precisely through the image of coin. The good silver coin that will circulate throughout the city once it has been approved by the tester figures the proper balance of *idion* and *koinon*, the reliance of *nomos* on *phusis* that subtends the practices of civic life. As with his simile of *pessoi* at the

---

[46] That the ἀργυρογνώμων is specifically the tester of silver *coinage* is confirmed by its use in the Pseudo-Platonic *De Virtute* (378d7–e1).

[47] Cf. the proud assertion of Xenophon *Poroi* 3.2, that Athenian silver coinage alone would fetch more than its face value "anywhere else in the world"; and recall the recent discovery of Buttrey (1981), that Egypt in the fourth century was minting millions of silver tetradrachms made to look identical to Attic owls. For other coinage in imitation of Attic, see Kraay 1976: 76; Price 1993: 31–35.

beginning of the *Politics*, Aristotle's offhand image here uses coin to think the peculiar knot of *nomos* and *phusis* that constitutes the city and its relation to its citizens.

What then of the fifth-century uses of the image of coin? Here we turn from Aristotle's and Demosthenes' explicit political discussions of law to the glancing and apparently arbitrary imagery of coin in other texts. Do these images conjure the same doubleness of *nomos* and *phusis* for their respective contexts? And does the image of coin in literary texts do the same work of articulating status boundaries, which we saw the practice and representation of real coinage serving? Consider first the term *charaktēr*, which designates both the upper stamp or die that strikes the hot flan in minting and the impression that it leaves on the coin.[48] In perhaps the earliest metaphorical occurrence of the word, Aeschylus has Pelasgos describe the appearance of the suppliant Danaids:

> ἄπιστα μυθεῖσθ', ὦ ξέναι, κλύειν ἐμοί,
> ὅπως τόδ' ὑμῖν ἐστιν Ἀργεῖον γένος.
> Λιβυστικαῖς γὰρ μᾶλλον ἐμφερέστεραι
> γυναιξίν ἐστε κοὐδαμῶς ἐγχωρίαις·
> καὶ Νεῖλος ἂν θρέψειε τοιοῦτον φυτόν·
> Κύπριος χαρακτὴρ τ' ἐν γυναικείοις τύποις
> εἰκὼς πέπληκται τεκτόνων πρὸς ἀρσένων· (Aesch. *Suppl.* 277–83)

O strangers, you say things unbelievable for me to hear, that this Argive race is yours. For you look more like Libyan women and not at all like locals. And the Nile would nurture such a creature, and a Kyprian stamp is like to have been struck on female shapes by male craftsmen.

The image of the chorus as coins "struck with Kyprian stamp" suggests several things simultaneously: first, perhaps, the interchangeability of the choreuts, whom Aeschylus likes to designate by mass nouns like "band" (ὅμιλος) or "swarm" (ἑσμός). The image of "female shapes struck by male craftsmen" may also contain a distant echo of male violence against women, even as it suggests that women should properly circulate, like coin, among the men who form and use them. But its most obvious meaning is that of civic or ethnic identity—Pelasgos inspects the women's outward appearance, as a *dokimastēs* inspects coin, to differentiate native coin from foreign currency.[49] Yet even this articulation of the semiotics of outward appearance through the figure of coin is not without a significant connection to inner quality, for what inspires Pelasgos's simile is the chorus's claim that they are "Argive in race" (Ἀργεῖαι γένος, 274, cf.

---

[48] Cf. LSJ and Körte 1929 on the semantic development of *charaktēr*.
[49] Cf. Steiner 1994: 106.

278). Pelasgos struggles to gauge inner nature from the outward signs, significantly evoking their *phusis* immediately before using the image of the *charaktēr* by describing them as τοιοῦτον φυτόν ("such a creature," 281).

Indeed, to understand Pelasgos' image of coin, we need to set it against his first speech on encountering the Danaids, itself an extraordinarily dense articulation of competing semiotic systems that anticipates the simile of the *charaktēr*. The king's first words on entering raise the question of the women's provenance and how to read it:

ποδαπὸν ὅμιλον τόνδ' ἀνελληνόστολον
πέπλοισι βαρβάροισι κἀμπυκώμασιν
χλίοντα προσφωνοῦμεν· οὐ γὰρ Ἀργολὶς
ἐσθὴς γυναικῶν, οὐδ' ἀφ' Ἑλλάδος τόπων.

. . . .

κλάδοι γε μὲν δὴ κατὰ νόμους ἀφικτόρων
κεῖνται παρ' ὑμῖν πρὸς θεοῖς ἀγωνίοις·
μόνον τόδ' Ἑλλὰς χθὼν συνοίσεται στόχῳ.
καὶ τἄλλα, πόλλ' ἔτ' εἰκάσαι δίκαιον ἦν,
εἰ μὴ παρόντι φθόγγος ἦν ὁ σημανῶν. (Aesch. *Suppl.* 234–37, 241–45)

What sort of band is this we address, garbed in no Greek fashion, luxuriating in barbarian garments and headbands? For [this] is not Argive women's dress, nor even from Greek places. . . . But still, [these] suppliant branches are laid beside you, before the assembled gods, according to the rules of suppliants; in this respect alone, [the idea] "Greek land" will agree with my guess. And, as for the rest, it would be just to conjecture many things still, if there were not someone present with a voice to indicate.[50]

Pelasgos starts out very confident that this band of women cannot be Greek, based on the reading of their outlandish garb (ἀνελληνόστολον, 234). But their use of "suppliant branches" (κλάδοι, 241) gives him pause, for it is done "according to the rules" and agrees with the theory of Greek origin. Finally, the king raises the possibility of the spoken word as signifier (φθόγγος . . . ὁ σημανῶν, 245). In essence, Pelasgos's first speech posits three different outward signs from which to judge the women's *phusis*: their dress, their suppliant branches, and their "signifying voice." In his response to their claim to be "Argive in race," Pelasgos first attempts to confine the meaningful *sēma*, the *charaktēr*, to their dress. But in the event, it is their suppliant status and their spoken narrative of descent from Io that prove the true tokens of their *phusis* and compel

---

[50] Greek text and translation are mainly dependent on those of Friis Johansen and Whittle 1980 (I.89–90, II.189–98).

their acceptance by the community. Implicitly the women are found to be legal tender of Argos because they combine native *phusis* (descent from Io) with common *nomos* (supplication and narrative).

We find *nomos* and *phusis* similarly impacted in Herodotus's sole use of the metaphor of the *charaktēr*. In his narrative of the recognition of the boy Kyros by his grandfather Astyages, king of the Medes (who had plotted his death in infancy), Herodotus tells us that Astyages recognized him because "the cast of his features (χαρακτὴρ τοῦ προσώπου) seemed to resemble his own" (Hdt. 1.116). In context, the image is particularly apt (if anachronistic), for the Eastern coinages with which fifth-century Greeks would have been familiar usually bore the image of the Great King as their stamp.[51] Hence the "stamp" of Kyros's face would be the authentic impress of his grandfather's features, like a well-minted coin. But this image needs to be set in context, for it occurs as the climax of an extended narrative that plays insistently on the issues of the constitution of community and differential status. Thus Herodotus relates the circumstances of Kyros's recognition:

And when the boy was ten years old, the following event occurring to him revealed him. He was playing in the same village where his father kept the cows, and he was playing with other boys of his age in the road. And the boys playing chose this one to be their king—the so-called son of the herdsman. And he ordered some of them to build houses, others to be spearbearers, one of them (I suppose) to be the King's Eye, and to another he gave the honor of bearing in messages, as assigning his task to each. But one of the boys participating in the game, who was the son of Artembares, a prominent man among the Medes (ἀνδρὸς δοκίμου ἐν Μήδοισι), did not do what was ordered by Kyros, so Kyros bid the other boys to take hold of him, and, when they obeyed, he treated the boy very harshly, beating him with a whip. And the boy, as soon as they let him go, was even more incensed about it, since he felt that he had suffered things unworthy of himself (ἀνάξια ἑωυτοῦ), and when he went down to the city to the presence of his father, he complained loudly about the treatment he had met with at Kyros's hands, saying not "Kyros" (for this was not yet his name), but "at the hands of the son of Astyages' herdsman." And Artembares, going in a rage, just as he was, to the court of Astyages and leading with him his son, said that he had suffered unsuitable things (ἀνάρσια πρήγματα), saying "O King, we have been thus outrageously insulted (περιυβρίσμεθα) by your slave, the son of the herdsman," as he showed his boy's shoulders. And Astyages, when he had heard and seen, wishing to avenge the boy for the sake of Artembares'

---

[51] For the image of the Great King on Persian darics and sigloi, see Kraay 1976: 32–33; Carradice and Price 1988: 34–35; Root 1989.

honor, sent for the herdsman and his son. And when they were both present, Astyages, looking at Kyros, said, "Did you, being the son of one who is such, dare to inflict such injury upon the son of this man who is first at my court?" And Kyros answered thus, "O Master, with justice I did these things to this one. For the boys of the village, of whom this one was one, playing, set me up as their king, since I seemed to them to be the most suitable for this [office] (ἐπιτηδεότατος). And all the rest of the boys were executing my commands, but this one refused to heed and considered them of no account, until he got justice. If, then, I deserve some evil on account of this, here I am present." And as the boy was saying these things, recognition of him came over Astyages, [because] the cast of his features seemed to him to resemble his own, and his reply seemed to be too free [for a slave], and the time of the exposure seemed to correspond to the age of the boy. (Hdt. 1.114–116.1)

In this account, Herodotus seems to have incorporated many of the same associations of coin we detected in Athenian practice and discourse, but to have transposed them to a fantasy world of Medes and Persians. For here as there, the image of coin functions as a boundary marker, articulating the moment at which Kyros passes from slave to free status. Thus as the story begins, Kyros is nominally the son of a slave, the king's herdsman, but he is chosen king in a game by the boys of his village. In that capacity Kyros constitutes the Median community in miniature, precisely recreating the founding acts and institutions of Deiokes, the first king of the Medes (1.114.2; cf. 1.98–100). And as "king," he whips the son of a Median nobleman who refuses to do his bidding, thereby precipitating the confrontation with Astyages that leads to his eventual recognition.

This part of the story turns on the apparent misfit between game and reality, in which a freeborn, noble boy is whipped and manhandled by the son of a slave (to Artembares, as to a fifth-century Athenian, this is an act of *hubris*; cf. περιυβρίσμεθα, 1.114.5). Here the language of the tale is permeated with words for worth, value, and suitability, as Artembares and Astyages struggle to correct the status inversions the game seems to have imposed on reality. But the narrative of recognition is precisely the revelation that there is no gap between game and reality; the boys choose Kyros as their king because of his innate royal quality, and his conduct in the game is further proof of his nature.[52] The collusion

---

[52] Herodotus's narrative evokes the ancient Greek game of *basilinda*, which, according to Eustathios (*Comm. Hom.* p. 1425.41) was "a game appointing some boys kings." Significantly, according to Pollux (*Onom.* 10.110), in the Greek version of the game, different boys became "kings" and "servants" by lot. Thus Herodotus's Median version of the game differs from its Greek analogue in that Kyros is *chosen* king because of his natural suitability, rather than being selected by lot.

of *nomos* and *phusis*, the perfect merging of game and reality, inevitably brings Kyros to light.

What the narrative figures first through the workings of the game is then recapitulated in the image of coin. Astyages recognizes his grandson because of a combination of *phusis* and *nomos*, nature and behavior: the "cast of his features" and his answer that is "too free" to be that of a slave.[53] This combination thus legitimates Kyros as the authentic royal issue, his authenticity and legitimacy troped as coin. Finally, in Astyages' reaction to his realization, Herodotus returns to the theme of differential status, of slave and free, one more time. For if Kyros is the genuine regal issue (as χαρακτήρ implies), his nominal father, the herdsman, is mere metal to be "put to the test." Herodotus tells us that Astyages quickly dismissed Artembares and sent Kyros off with servants, so that he could question the herdsman (the verb used is βασανίζω, 1.116.2). Kyros's newfound status as coin is partly articulated and differentiated by the contrast with the vulnerable matter of his supposititious father.

Thus Aeschylus and Herodotus use the image of coin to express the same fusion of *nomos* and *phusis* that Demosthenes and Aristotle articulate in the domain of civic law. In contrast to the fourth-century uses, however, both Aeschylus and Herodotus seem to displace the *charaktēr* from Greek coinage to foreign issues, using the image to figure the appearance of outlandish others. And yet, as we have seen, it is precisely the doubleness of coinage (embodying both *nomos* and *phusis*) that allows it to function in these texts as a boundary marker, articulating the moment at which the excluded other becomes a full-status member of the community (whether it be the city of Argos or the Median royal family).[54]

It is in the context of this precise tropological system that I would like to set one of the most familiar and extended uses of the imagery

---

[53] Parodoxically here, it is the *charaktēr* that represents *phusis* in this opposition, while Kyros's "too free" manner instantiates *nomos*. This inversion of the Greek terms intensifies the "Alice through the looking-glass" quality of Herodotus's narrative of Eastern events.

[54] I will not consider here Euripides' uses of the image of coin, because the complexity and elaboration of this issue would require a separate chapter. Thus Euripides uses the image of the *charaktēr* six times in all (more than any other fifth-century author): *El.* 569, 572; *Hecuba* 379; *HF* 659; *Medea* 519; fr. 329 N². Euripides also frequently invokes the image of counterfeiting in the context of human nature or character (e.g. *El.* 550–551; *Hipp.* 616; *Medea* 516). I would contend that many of Euripides' uses of the image of coin also serve to articulate a boundary, but in this case it is the boundary between the opaque and arbitrary workings of the divine and the human community (with its own criteria for evaluation; cf. esp. *El.* 367–79; *HF* 655–700). For discussion of Euripides' use of the imagery of coinage, see Körte 1929: 74–77; F. Will 1960; Padel 1992: 14; Steiner 1994: 106; Zeitlin 1996: 239–61.

of coin in any ancient Greek text—Aristophanes' elaborate conceit in the Parabasis of the *Frogs*. With the *Frogs*, we shift back from the imagery of coinage used for "others" to the analogy of citizens and coins, while at the same time, Aristophanes' extraordinary elaboration of the image confirms many of the associations we have noted in other texts. In the middle of the *Frogs*, following the convention of Old Comedy, the chorus steps out of character and addresses the audience directly:

> It is just for this holy chorus to join in advising and to teach useful things for the city. First then, it seems best to us to make the citizens equal (ἐξισῶσαι) and to take away their fears. And if anyone went wrong, tripped up in some way by the wrestling [holds] of Phrynichos, I say that it ought to be permissible for those who slipped then, having cast away the blame, to undo their former mistakes. Next, I say that no one should be deprived of citizen rights (ἄτιμον) in the city. For it is shameful that those who fought a single naval battle with us are straightway "Plataians" and masters instead of slaves. And I certainly wouldn't want to claim that this was not well done, but I praise it; for these are the only things you've done that have any sense. But in addition, for those who, themselves and their fathers, have fought many naval battles with you and are related to you in race—it is suitable for you to pardon this single misfortune when they ask. But, having let go of your anger, O you who are cleverest by nature (ὦ σοφώτατοι φύσει), let us willingly possess all men as kindred and enfranchised and citizens, whoever fights a naval battle together with us. (Aristoph. *Frogs* 686–702)

Produced in 405 B.C.E., the *Frogs* refers here to the disenfranchisement of those citizens involved in Phrynichos's oligarchic coup of 411 and the extraordinary granting of citizen rights to those slaves who fought at the Battle of Arginousai in 406 B.C.E.[55] Aristophanes' advice to the demos once again makes for an interesting comparison with "Solon's" parable of the tyrant preserved in Diogenes Laertius. As opposed to the tyrant's arbitrary valuation of men, the city is urged to "make its citizens equal" and not to leave anyone in the city "deprived of citizen rights" (ἄτιμον; notice Diogenes Laertius's use of the same term in a nontechnical sense). The criterion espoused for equality and enfranchisement—what should put all citizens on the same level—is common participation in war (here, the naval battles of the Pentacontaetia and the Peloponnesian War). But *phusis* also plays a complicated and ambiguous part in this calibration of citizen worth. For the demos is exhorted first to forgive

---

[55] On the events of 411, see Thuc. 8.45–98; on the service and reward of slaves in 406, see Xen. *Hell.* 1.6.24; Hellanikos *FGrH* 323a F 25.

its former (now disfranchised) citizens by the argument that they are "related in race" (προσήκουσιν γένει, 698),[56] while just a few lines later, the chorus inverts the priority of terms, urging that "we should possess as kindred (συγγενεῖς)" all those who "fight in the navy together with us" (701–2).

As in Aristotle's *Rhetoric*, this complex knot of *nomos* and *phusis* (here in the constitution of citizens) precipitates the image of coin—but with an extraordinary twist:

πολλάκις γ᾽ ἡμῖν ἔδοξεν ἡ πόλις πεπονθέναι
ταὐτὸν εἴς τε τῶν πολιτῶν τοὺς καλούς τε κἀγαθοὺς
εἴς τε τἀρχαῖον νόμισμα καὶ τὸ καινὸν χρυσίον.
οὔτε γὰρ τούτοισιν οὖσιν οὐ κεκιβδηλευμένοις,
ἀλλὰ καλλίστοις ἁπάντων, ὡς δοκεῖ, νομισμάτων
καὶ μόνοις ὀρθῶς κοπεῖσι καὶ κεκωδωνισμένοις
ἔν τε τοῖς Ἕλλησι καὶ τοῖς βαρβάροισι πανταχοῦ
χρώμεθ᾽ οὐδέν, ἀλλὰ τούτοις τοῖς πονηροῖς χαλκίοις
χθές τε καὶ πρώην κοπεῖσι τῷ κακίστῳ κόμματι.
τῶν πολιτῶν θ᾽ οὓς μὲν ἴσμεν εὐγενεῖς καὶ σώφρονας
ἄνδρας ὄντας καὶ δικαίους καὶ καλούς τε κἀγαθοὺς
καὶ τραφέντας ἐν παλαίστραις καὶ χοροῖς καὶ μουσικῇ
προυσελοῦμεν, τοῖς δὲ χαλκοῖς καὶ ξένοις καὶ πυρρίαις
καὶ πονηροῖς κἀκ πονηρῶν εἰς ἅπαντα χρώμεθα
ὑστάτοις ἀφιγμένοισιν, οἷσιν ἡ πόλις πρὸ τοῦ
οὐδὲ φαρμακοῖσιν εἰκῇ ῥᾳδίως ἐχρήσατ᾽ ἄν.
ἀλλὰ καὶ νῦν, ὠνόητοι, μεταβαλόντες τοὺς τρόπους
χρῆσθε τοῖς χρηστοῖσιν αὖθις· (Aristoph. *Frogs* 718–35)

We've often thought that the city suffered the same thing with regard to her good and noble citizens as [she suffered] with regard to the old currency and the new gold coinage. For, although these are not counterfeit, but the best of all currencies, as it seems, and the only ones rightly struck and sounded both among the Greeks and the barbarians everywhere, we don't use them at all, but we use these wicked little bronzes struck yesterday or the day before in the worst minting. And those of the citizens who are men we know to be noble and self-restrained, and just and gentlemen and raised in the palaistrai and amidst choruses and musical training, we treat outrageously, but those bronze and foreign and red-headed, and wicked sons of wicked fathers, we use for everything—the most recent arrivals, whom the city would not easily have used before at random even for scapegoats. But now, you fools, change your ways and use the good again.

---

[56] As Dover notes (1993: 279), this phrase conjures up the ideology of common, autochthonous origin.

This highly elaborated conceit reads like a palimpsest of the two discursive systems we have been tracing. The extraordinary gold and bronze coin issues of the two years preceding the production of the *Frogs* offer the poet a unique opportunity to fuse the ideology of civic currency with the elitist language of metals. Thus insofar as all citizens, old and new, are useful to the city by their service in war, they are all interchangeable common currency. But within that domain of conventional equality, some are more equal than others. The city's functionalism is never pure, and here it is alloyed with a generous mix of essentialism. For Aristophanes appropriates for the old-time citizens all the signifying values of the elitist hierarchy of metals. They are the *kaloi k' agathoi* (719, 728), analogous to the good old silver and the new gold (in contrast to the "wicked little bronzes," 720, 725). They are pure, not counterfeit (721); they ring true (723); they were formed in the genteel pursuits of elite education (729); and they have always been here, in contrast to the *arriviste* ex-slaves (732).[57] In a final flourish, Aristophanes adds to the high-low oppositions he has constructed the ultimate figure for the abjected, grotesque body: these former slaves, "wicked sons of wicked fathers," whom the poet has affirmed it was right to enfranchise (695–96), would not even have served in the old days as public scapegoats, *pharmakoi* to be beaten and excised from the civic body. At this point the torque of Aristophanes' comic logic is almost unsustainable—we have moved from the inclusive rallying-cry "make all the citizens equal" to the phantasmatic incorporation of the most degraded other. Here, abruptly, the Parabasis ends.

In the years that followed, the paradoxes and pressures of differential citizen quality appear to have been as unsustainable in public practice as in the poet's rhetoric. After the catastrophe of Aigospotamoi, the *atimoi* of 410 were re-enfranchised by the decree of Patrokleides, while some time before 393/2, as we have already seen, the city, with an almost audible sigh of relief, returned to its silver-only coinage, demonetizing the bronze issues.[58] For another forty years, the Athenian democracy would maintain its pure silver-only currency, at least in part to do the ideological work of representing and constituting the community of citizen equals.

---

[57] We might note an intriguing parallel for Aristophanes' elaborate coinage metaphor in nineteenth-century Australian slang for different classes of citizens: according to Hughes 1986: 354–55, "The term for these native-born 'Currency lads' and 'Currency lasses' came from monetary slang—'currency' meaning coins or notes that were only good in the colony, makeshift stuff, implying raffishness or worse, unlike the solid virtues of the 'Sterling,' the free English immigrants." (I owe this reference to Kathleen McCarthy.)

[58] For the text of the decree of Patrokleides (which also re-enfranchised state debtors), see Andokides 1.77–79; for the demonetization of the emergency bronze coinage, see Aristoph. *Ekkl.* 815–22 (quoted above, note 23).

III. CHANGING THE CURRENCY

We have seen how coinage operated as a signifier within the civic imaginary to analogize both the noble substance and the proper symbolic
formation of citizens. In contrast to the archaic sympotic language of
metals, which figured noble selves as pure gold and others as coinage
that was always and only counterfeit, the discourses and practices of
Athenian democracy opposed autochthonous silver to foreign gold, while
they exploited the materiality of coinage to transubstantiate civic custom
into universal law.

In conclusion I want to consider two anecdotes that articulate a shift
from the world of the classical city to a new era through the image of
coin. The first is the story, recounted by Diogenes Laertius in the opening
chapters of his biography of Diogenes the Cynic, that he was driven
out of his home city of Sinope for "falsifying (or changing) the currency"
(παραχαράξαι τὸ νόμισμα, D.L. 6.20–21). According to the biographical
tradition, this criminal act made Diogenes an exile and a philosopher
(6.49), but it also provided him with a potent image for his activities
as a Cynic.[59] For, as the formula is glossed later in Diogenes Laertius's
Life, "such things he used to say and he clearly acted accordingly, truly
changing the currency, since he gave no such [authority] to convention
as to natural law" (ὄντως νόμισμα παραχαράττων, μηδὲν οὕτω τοῖς
κατὰ νόμον ὡς τοῖς κατὰ φύσιν διδούς, 6.71).[60] Diogenes privileged
the claims and needs of rational nature as the way to live well, imitating
the mouse in his minimalist existence (6.22). Thus it is said that he
would "use any place for anything" (6.22), famously answering the call
of nature by eating and masturbating in the agora (6.46, 58, 61, 69).
But this life according to nature also led him to challenge established
custom and usage that seemed to him irrational or inconsistent; as A. A.
Long has argued, we can understand much of Diogenes' "lifestyle and
discourse [as] defacing the currency, that is, trying to put bad money

---

[59] For the early dating of the material in Diogenes Laertius, cf. Long 1996: 30: "Fortu-
nately, Diogenes Laertius wrote a life of the Cynic Diogenes rich in material that has a
good chance of being authentic or at least true to the spirit of Diogenes' discourse. . .";
for this tradition in particular, Long (ibid: 34) observes: "We shall probably never know
whether Diogenes or his father actually defaced the currency of Sinope, as the biographical
tradition maintains (D.L. 6.20–21). It does seem certain, however, that the story was in
circulation during his residence at Athens and that, so far from denying it, he supported
its diffusion." On the possible numismatic reality behind these traditions, see Seltman 1938
and (more cautiously) Bannert 1979.

[60] Cf. D.L. 6.38: "He used to say that he opposed courage to chance, nature to convention,
and reason to passion."

out of circulation."[61] Thus the original Cynic was concerned to expose
the hypocrisies of custom, and the ways in which it made men themselves
counterfeit: masters and kings who were really slaves to their desires
(6.43, 44, 55, 63, 66), "leaders of the people" who were really "flunkies
of the mob" (6.24, 41), temple officials who were really "great thieves"
(6.45). As he asks an attractive young man who "babbles inappropriately," "Aren't you ashamed to draw a lead dagger from an ivory
scabbard?" (6.65).[62]

But at least one ancient author offers an alternative reading of the
richly suggestive metaphor of "changing the currency." Plutarch, in a
treatise *On the Fortune and Virtue of Alexander the Great*, recounts the
famous story that Alexander went to visit Diogenes in his jar and was
inspired by the meeting to remark, "If I were not Alexander, I would be
Diogenes" (*Mor.* 331f; cf. *Alex.* 14). Plutarch then feels the need to gloss
this apophthegm at great length, replacing it with a fantasized monologue
in which Alexander explains his conquest of the world as the civilizing
power of Greek philosophy in action (*Mor.* 332a–c). As the climax to
this fantasized monologue, "Alexander" asserts, "I too have to restrike
the currency and impose the stamp of Greek government on the barbarian
world" (δεῖ κἀμὲ νόμισμα παρακόψαι καὶ παραχαράξαι τὸ βαρβαρικὸν
Ἑλληνικῇ πολιτείᾳ, *Mor.* 332c). What precisely is implied by the imposition of Greek custom Plutarch had already specified earlier in the treatise,
describing Alexander's efforts to educate the conquered peoples of the
East:

> He taught the Hyrcanians to marry and the Arachosians to farm, and per-
> suaded the Sogdians to support their fathers, not to kill them, and persuaded
> the Persians to revere their mothers, not to marry them. O wondrous

---

[61] Long 1996: 34; cf. Branham 1996: 90n.30.

[62] Long usefully considers these passages and others under the related rubrics of attacking
the hypocrisy and inconsistency of convention and that of language: "His defacing of the
currency included an attempt to stimulate reflection by reforming the language. In rejecting
the standard denotations of certain terms and in renaming certain things, he indicated the
gulf between current ethical discourse and what he took to be the natural meaning of
terms." (Long 1996: 34–36, quotation from p. 36)
    It is worth noting that in the contemporary city of corrupted *nomoi*, Diogenes himself
symbolically occupied the position of the counterfeit coin, for Diogenes Laertius tells us
that he lived in a jar (*pithos*) in the Metroön (6.23). As we know from the coinage decree
of 375/4 (cited above, p. 311), counterfeit coins were first "cut across," then dedicated *in
the Metroön*, while Roman-era inscriptions from Rhodes provide evidence for the storage
of counterfeit coins in jars (*stamnoi*), dedicated in temples (for the former, see Stroud 1974:
177–78; for the latter, see Robert 1951: 144–78; for a different interpretation of the
significance of the Metroön as Diogenes' residence, see Martin 1996: 155).

philosophy, through which the Indians worship Greek gods and the Scythians
bury their dead instead of eating them! (Plut. *Mor.* 328c)

Summing all this up, Plutarch declares proudly that Alexander "founded
more than seventy cities among the barbarian nations and sowed all
Asia with Greek magistracies, and thus overcame their uncivilized and
savage way of life" (τῆς ἀνημέρου καὶ θηριώδους ἐκράτησε διαίτης,
Mor. 328e). Plutarch's catalogue draws on many of the topoi of Herodotean ethnography in order to point a very un-Herodotean moral. Where
Herodotus had affirmed that the burial practices of Indians and Greeks
were equally legitimate within their contexts because "*nomos* is king
of all" (Hdt. 3.38), Plutarch deploys this parade of lurid ethnographic
commonplaces to justify Greek conquest. Always more heavily essential-
ized in the Greek imagination, the barbarian is here rescued from a
vicious state of nature by the pattern and paradigm of Greek *nomos*
and philosophy.

I wish to end with these two complementary interpretations of "changing the currency" because they reveal both significant continuities and
epochal changes from the classical polis to the Hellenistic world. Our
inquiry has focused almost entirely on the period from ca. 600 B.C.E.
down to the time of Aristotle, but these two emblematic anecdotes open
up a prospect to subsequent centuries. In one sense, the metaphor of
"changing the currency" participates in and continues the imagistic system
we have detected within the ideology of classical Athenian democracy:
both Diogenes and "Alexander" use *nomisma* as a mastertrope for the
order of the Greek polis, with the particular balance of *nomos* and *phusis*
on which it depends. Within this system, Diogenes' point is the radical
division or deviation of the conventional order imposed by the city from
the proper laws of nature. Hence the original Cynic and his followers
want to recalibrate *nomisma* in the direction of *phusis*. "Alexander's"
point, conversely, is the need to impose Greek form and *nomos* on raw,
barbarian matter; hence his use of the image valorizes *nomos* over *phusis*.
Still in both cases, as in the earlier occurrences, the image of coin maintains
the dialectic of *nomos* and *phusis*, implying their ideal balance in proper
civic order.

At the same time, the image of "changing the currency" is, in itself,
also an explicit formulation of the epochal shift perceived to have occurred
in the status of the Greek polis in the Hellenistic period. In these terms
the image of "reminting" or "changing the stamp" represents the radical
reconfiguring of the precarious balance of *nomos* and *phusis*, the relation
of city to citizen, that is symbolized by civic coin. For Diogenes, and for
much of Hellenistic philosophy in his wake, life "in accordance with
nature" essentially liberates the individual from his dependence on civic

order. It is no longer the city that protects the individual from the randomness of fortune and guarantees his "worth" within a social order of value, but his own reason and self-mastery.[63] And for the centuries-long Orientalist fantasy of Alexander as world civilizer, the unique fusion of Greek "form" and barbarian "matter" justifies a new kind of polis that would proliferate and fill the known world.[64]

[63] Recall again D.L. 6.38, where Diogenes opposes his own (individual) "courage to chance" and "reason to passion." I do not mean to imply that the Greek (democratic) polis disappeared in the Hellenistic and Roman periods; on the contrary, it is clear that the polis system endured tenaciously. I want simply to highlight a development within Hellenistic philosophy that differentiates it from the thought of Plato and Aristotle.

[64] We may see the prototype for such justification of empire already in the fifth-century Athenian Coinage Decree, which required all subject cities to use only Athenian weights, measures, and silver coinage. Whether or not the terms of the Decree were enforced (or even enforceable), they functioned symbolically to assert that only Athenians were full citizens, while the population of the subject cities became mere matter regulated by Athenian *nomos* and *nomisma*. On the Athenian Coinage Decree in general, see Meiggs 1972: 167–73. On its symbolic significance, see also E. Will 1988; Howgego 1995: 39–46, 60: "The extraordinary attempt by Athens to impose its own civic coinage on its allies is indeed suggestive of how Athenians may have come to conceive of their empire as a *polis* writ large, with themselves holding a monopoly of political and judicial power, and of prestige." (quote taken from Howgego 1995: 60)

Ideology, Objects, and Subjects

I BEGAN from the strange fact that mention of coinage (*nomisma*) barely occurs in Greek literary texts for a century or more after its invention. Indeed, nowhere do we find any kind of explicit statement of the rationale behind the original minting of coin until we get to Aristotle. And yet the term *nomisma* itself, whether etymologically "result of lawful distribution" or "conventional standard, customary usage," bespeaks the city's control over hierarchies of value and their constitution. Its name implies that, to Greek thinking, coinage participated in the sphere of *nomos* legislated by the city. This possibility has been corroborated by Maria Caccamo Caltabiano and Paola Radici Colace, who have analyzed the lexicon of coinage terms preserved in the second-century C.E. *Onomastikon* of Pollux; they observe that the Greek terms for "good" and "counterfeit" coin tend to emphasize issues of legality and authorization by the community (rather than purity of metal or weight).[1] In the gap between explicit discussions of coinage and the concept of civic authority encoded in many of the terms themselves, we confront the shape of an absence, but it is perhaps a shape whose lineaments we recognize. Among ancient historians, it is a well-known paradox that Athens never produced any genuine democratic theory composed by those sympathetic to democracy. As A.H.M. Jones observes: "It is curious that in the abundant literature produced in the greatest democracy of Greece there survives no statement of democratic political theory. All the Athenian political philosophers and publicists whose work we possess were in various degrees oligarchic in sympathy."[2] Thus we confront the paradox that egalitarian ideology and democracy emerge in Greece, but almost all the written sources that take up the issue explicitly are hostile toward these developments. The phenomenon of coinage in its relation to the literary sources might be thought of as a subset of this same paradox: the cities of Greece invent

---

[1] Caccamo Caltabiano and Radici Colace 1983, 1985, 1989; the last article in particular contrasts Greek coinage terms, with their emphasis on isonomic distribution and legality, to the known terms for Eastern coinages, which emphasize purity of metal.

[2] Jones 1957: 41; for the paradox, cf. Loraux 1986: 173–80, 204–6. Jones's solution is to attempt to reconstruct what democratic political theory would have looked like; for a critique of this procedure and discussion of the problem, see Finley 1983: 124–25 with n. 7, 1985: 48–49; Ober 1989: 38–40.

coinage as a civic standard, but our earliest and most substantial references to coin are hostile to it, representing it as "mere convention," changeable, arbitrary, inevitably counterfeit, and linked to the debased mercantile practices of a disembedded economy.

But perhaps with coinage, as with democratic "theory" itself, we perceive only absence because we've been looking in the wrong places. Perhaps we need to look at the "embodied" discourses of imagery and anecdote, and at lived practices.[3] Once we adjust our sights, Herodotus comes into his own as a source. A.H.M. Jones, continuing from the passage I've just quoted, reviews all the extant fifth- and fourth-century prose writers and comes finally to Herodotus: "Only Herodotus is a democrat, but his views have not carried much weight, partly because of his reputation for naïveté . . ."[4] It is my contention that what has traditionally been construed as Herodotus's "naïveté"—his penchant for anecdotes that to us seem silly and improbable, and his wildly unrealistic ethnographies—in fact represents a concrete form of political thinking that we must learn how to read.[5] In a sense Herodotus is a particularly valuable, even unique source, because of his roots in oral culture. This is not only because oral culture tends to think through embodied discourses and practices,[6] but also because Herodotus appears to preserve competing, sometimes even contradictory logoi from oral informants across a whole spectrum of socioeconomic and ideological positions. I have suggested that we should think of Herodotus's text as an open agora of logoi, jostling one another, with the histor as our sly tour guide among them.

Thus, taking my lead from several passages in the Histories (especially Herodotus's Lydian ethnography), I have traced out a network of mutually reinforcing discourses and signifying practices that emerge in the sixth century and seem to pattern meaningfully in archaic poetry. The establishment of the central space of the agora (around 600 B.C.E. in Athens), the emergence of tyrants and stories about tyrants in different cities throughout Greece, the invention of coinage, and the appearance of new board-games cluster in opposition to the foundation of palaistrai where Greek elites cultivated bodily perfection, the "cult of habrosunē," the sympotic language of metals, the invention of the hetaira and of symposium games like kottabos. I have argued throughout that this is not just a random collection of phenomena; that all these elements are

---

[3] This solution is akin to that of Ober 1989 for the constitution and analysis of democratic ideology.

[4] Jones 1957: 41.

[5] For exemplary efforts to read Herodotus's concrete political thinking, see Raaflaub 1987; Saxonhouse 1996: 31–57.

[6] Cf. Loraux 1986: 177–79 on democratic distrust of writing in a still largely oral culture. Loraux's insights are elaborated by Steiner 1994: 186–241.

related as parts of a struggle over what constitutes legitimate culture, indeed what constitutes the proper framework of social and cosmic order. One position constructs the polis as a central mediating term, which imposes order and identity on its citizens and screens them from cosmic forces that are arbitrary and inscrutable. The other position, resisting these implicit claims for the ultimate authority of the city, defines itself as elite through the cultivation of luxury, sympotic culture, and privileged links to the gods, the heroes, and the East.

It is my contention that this is not just a struggle played out within the elite—or within elite texts—since it involves also lowly and pervasive practices like the circulation of coin and the playing of games. Even if we cannot say exactly who the agents of such activities were (or whether they were always the same people), given the poor state of our evidence, this interaction of practices and representations suggests the existence of a broader non- or anti-elitist ideology forged through practice. This non- (or anti-) elitist logic of practice opposes functionalism to essentialism; the *pornē* to the *hetaira*; coin to gift; and the symbolic mediation of the polis to direct access to the divine through chance and ordeal. And yet, as we have traced this ideological strand through its variegated material symbology, we have found that the city often gets to have it both ways: it can appropriate the charged "bodyliness" of the astragal for its weights and coins, while coins themselves figure both symbolic function and noble essence (*nomos* and *phusis*) in the civic imaginary. This messiness should not surprise us; with Pierre Bourdieu and Michel de Certeau, we need to recognize that the logic of practice is complex and elaborated even if it defies the laws of theory.[7] Indeed, it is the messiness of practice that gives it such power and endurance. For such discursive contest and negotiation are not just phenomena of the sixth century but continue in practices, representations, and texts of the fifth century and later, deploying the same symbolic resources we have unearthed for the archaic period. The interaction and dialectic of these two positions in the fifth century and later—in the texts of Herodotus, Plato, and Attic tragedy, for example— produce some of the peculiar density and strangeness of canonical Greek literary texts.

Furthermore, precisely because many of the elements of this struggle are coded and concretized through the body, it profoundly affects identity formation—the prevalent societal notions of body and self. It is not my claim that the invention of coinage itself enables or catalyzes a new model of self as doubled or counterfeit; such an argument would be historically

---

[7] Cf. Bourdieu 1977, 1990; de Certeau 1984. The work of both serves as a healthy corrective to the assertion of M. I. Finley that there was no "articulated democratic theory" in Athens, only "notions, maxims, generalities" (Finley 1985a: 49).

naïve. Instead, I have suggested that classical Greek thinking about the self is implicated in—perhaps even constituted by—the conflict of exchange systems and transactional orders we have been considering. If, as I assume, in any given period, the available models of self are multiple, fluid, even contradictory, it is worth considering what strategic use is made of different models by different ideologically interested positions, and what instabilities might be found within these discourses. This is to subject to a materialist critique the work of Bruno Snell, who fifty years ago proposed a teleological reading of Greek literature as the slow emergence into light—the "discovery"—of the unified *Geist*.[8] While many scholars assume that Snell's portrait of "Homeric man" and of the "lyric discovery of the 'I' " are now completely discredited, I would contend that his seductive periodization still wields enormous influence, often implicit, both inside and outside the field.[9] Simply because there has been more explicit critique of Snell's account for earlier periods and genres, it is perhaps easiest to track this influence in the periodization of fifth-century Athens as high "classical" and tragedy as the apical development of Greek literature.

For nowhere is a materialist analysis more urgently needed than where the Greek "discovery of the self" seems most powerful and triumphant—that is, in Attic tragedy.[10] The extended narratives, complex characterization, direct speech, and animated bodies of tragedy most of all seduce us into a belief in authentic and pre-existent subjectivity ("like our own"), but it is precisely here that we must recognize the culture's most compelling ideological effects. We should perhaps instead see tragedy as a privileged site for competing, multiple constitutions of subjectivity through practice.[11] Thus, to take one example: Snell's account relies heavily on

---

[8] Snell 1948 (English translation 1953).

[9] Explicit critiques of Snell: (Homeric) Lloyd-Jones 1983, Williams 1993; (Lyric) Dover 1964, Most 1982, Nagy 1979, 1990b. Nonetheless, what might be called a modified Snellian model of the Homeric individual endures in such accounts as Fränkel 1973: 75–85, Redfield 1975: 20–23. Furthermore, Snell is still very much a live presence outside the field of classics: see, for example, Taylor 1989: 118–20.

[10] I have throughout consistently avoided detailed discussion of the texts of Attic tragedy, but a study of the interlinked domains of Greek discourse and material practices, such as that attempted here, raises pressing questions for the reading of tragedy. Too often scholars of Greek tragedy read only tragedy, or only tragedy and other Athenian material, or only tragedy and Homer. This study suggests that tragedy needs to be read against a broader and deeper cultural background, that goes back to the archaic period and outside of Athens for the reconstruction of the discursive conflicts and cultural symbolism played out on the Attic stage.

[11] The same, of course, might be said of all selves; cf. the remarks of Adorno (in a section of *Minima Moralia* entitled "Gold Assay"): "What presents itself as an original entity, a monad, is only the result of a social division of the social process. Precisely as an absolute, the individual is a mere reflection of property relations. In him the fictitious claim is made

images of depth and division of self, especially in tragedy.[12] Set within the context of the material and discursive systems traced here, we might see an ongoing struggle in tragedy between a model of selves as a ranked hierarchy of metals, qualitatively different since some are pure gold and others counterfeit coin, and a model in which all selves are the same civic coin, but, as such, all potentially divided or counterfeit. Such a shift in focus would challenge us to see the particular forms and images of identity formation as culturally contingent—as epiphenomena of a struggle taking place somewhere else.[13] This would be to conceive the Greek tragic self not as our origin and kin, but as alienated and different, intimately related to the materiality of practices.[14]

---

that what is biologically one must logically precede the social whole, from which it is only isolated by force, and its contingency is held up as a standard of truth. Not only is the self entwined in society; it owes society its existence in the most literal sense. All its content comes from society, or at any rate from its relation to the object." (Adorno 1974: 153–54). For the application of Adorno's materialism to the mutually constituting dialectic of subject and object in a particular historical period, see de Grazia, Quilligan, and Stallybrass 1996.

[12] Snell 1953: 90–112. Thus the only passage of Greek tragedy quoted directly in Snell's entire discussion is the remarkable opening of Pelasgos's speech of deliberation from Aeschylus's *Suppliants* (407–9): "Surely there is need of deep, saving thought—for an eye that sees and is not drunk to go to the depths like a diver." This striking image—of deliberation as the process of diving into the depths of one's own "soul"—is absolutely formative for Snell's argument about tragedy's new exploration of consciousness. It is precisely the image of diving into depths that constitutes for Snell a compelling model of moral struggle, because it is *our* image of consciousness.

Nor is Snell's narrative of the triumphant emergence of the autonomous self as discredited as some scholars believe; it may sometimes inform even the best work in the field. For example, in a brilliant reading of Euripides' *Hippolytus*, Froma Zeitlin argues that the play forces Hippolytus to learn that he, like all mortals, is a divided or counterfeit self, but can offer no better reason for Aphrodite's imposition of this harsh lesson than that such a model of self has greater explanatory adequacy (Zeitlin 1996: 219–84). For the specific claim that this model of self is "more adequate," see p. 241: "Woman as body may be relegated in the eyes of society to the corporeal side of human existence. But men's view of her mysterious physical nature as marked by a private interior space already predisposes her to a self-consciousness that replaces the virginal quality of 'self-containment' with a deeper subjectivity, which is capable of furnishing a more adequate model of the self"; cf. p. 255: "In this play, the secret—the knowledge of adulterous desire—that Phaedra and Hippolytus now share and would both deny provides the route to articulating a language, and hence a consciousness, more adequate to the complex geography of the body and world than the shallow surfaces of the untested meadow and the unchallenged language of the self would allow." It is not clear in what sense this model of self is "more adequate": because it is more complicated, or because it is more like our own?

[13] For a similar (anthropologically informed) critique of Snell 1953, see Padel 1992.

[14] For examples of such readings of tragedy, which combine psychoanalytic approaches with sociological and materialist analyses of exchange systems, see Griffith 1995, 1998; Wohl 1998. For analogous treatment of a different domain of evidence, see Neer 1998 (on self-portraiture and the constitution of subjectivity in Attic red-figure vase-painting).

Bibliography

Adeleye, G. 1983. "The Purpose of *Dokimasia*." *GRBS* 24: 295–306.

Adorno, T. 1974. *Minima Moralia: Reflections from Damaged Life.* Trans. E.F.N. Jephcott. London.

Aloni, A. 1997. "The Proem of Simonides' Elegy on the Battle of Plataea (Sim. frr. 10–18 W²) and the Circumstances of Its Performance." In *Poet, Public, and Performance: Essays in Ancient Greek Literature and Literary Theory*, ed. L. Edmunds and R. W. Wallace. Baltimore. 8–28.

Althusser, L. 1971. "Ideology and Ideological State Apparatuses: Notes toward an Investigation." In *Lenin and Philosophy and Other Essays*. Trans. B. Brewster. New York. 127–86.

Aly, W. [1921] 1969. *Volksmärchen, Sage, und Novelle bei Herodot und seinen Zeitgenossen: Eine Untersuchung über die volkstümlichen Elemente der altgriechischen Prosaerzählung.* Göttingen. Rept., with corrections and afterword by L. Huber.

Amandry, P. 1984a. "Os et Coquilles." In *L'Antre corycien.* II. *BCH* Supplement 9: 347–80.

——— 1984b. "Le Culte des Nymphes et de Pan à L'Antre corycien." In *L'Antre corycien.* II. *BCH* Supplement 9: 395–425.

Anderson, B. 1991. *Imagined Communities: Reflections on the Origin and Spread of Nationalism.* Rev. ed. London.

Anderson, W. S. 1984. "Love Plots in Menander and the Roman Adapters." *Ramus* 13: 124–34.

Andrewes, A. 1956. *The Greek Tyrants.* London.

Arafat, K., and C. Morgan. 1994. "Athens, Etruria and the Heuneburg: Mutual Misconceptions in the Study of Greek-Barbarian Relations." In *Classical Greece: Ancient Histories and Modern Archaeologies*, ed. I. Morris. Cambridge. 108–34.

Arthur, M. 1984. "Early Greece: The Origins of the Western Attitude toward Women." In *Women in the Ancient World: The Arethusa Papers*, ed. J. Peradotto and J. P. Sullivan. Albany. 7–58.

Austin, M. M. 1970. *Greece and Egypt in the Archaic Age. PCPS* suppl. no. 2.

Austin, M. M., and P. Vidal-Naquet. 1977. *Economic and Social History of Ancient Greece: An Introduction.* Berkeley.

Austin, R. G. 1940. "Greek Board-Games." *Antiquity* 14: 257–71.

Aymard, A. 1967. "Hiérarchie du travail et autarcie individuelle dans la Grèce archaique." In *Etudes d'histoire ancienne.* Paris. 316–33.

Babcock, B. A., ed. 1978. *The Reversible World: Symbolic Inversion in Art and Society.* Ithaca.

Babelon, E. 1901. *Traité des monnaies grecques et romaines.* 3 vols. Paris.

Bakhtin, M. M. 1968. *Rabelais and His World.* Trans. H. Iswolsky. Bloomington, Ind.

Balibar, E., and P. Macherey. 1981. "On Literature as an Ideological Form." In *Untying the Knot*, ed. R. Young. London. 79–99.

Bammer, A. 1990. "A Peripteros of the Geometric Period in the Artemision of Ephesus." *Anatolian Studies* 40: 137–60.

——— 1991. "Les Sanctuaires des VIIIe et VIIe siècles à l'Artémision d'Éphèse." *Revue archéologique* 1991, 1: 63–84.

Bannert, H. 1979. "Numismatisches zu Biographie und Lehre des Hundes Diogenes." *Litterae numismaticae Vindobonensis* 1: 49–63.

Barker, F. 1984. *The Tremulous Private Body: Essays on Subjection*. London.

Barron, J. P. 1964. "The sixth-century tyranny at Samos." *CQ* 58 (n.s. 14): 210–29.

——— 1966. *The Silver Coins of Samos*. Oxford.

——— 1980. "Bakchylides, Theseus and a Woolly Cloak." *BICS* 27: 1–8.

Barth, H. 1965. "Das Verhalten des Themistokles gegenüber dem Gelde." *Klio* 43: 30–37.

Bassi, K. 1998. *Acting like Men: Gender, Drama, and Nostalgia in Ancient Greece*. Ann Arbor.

Battegazzore, A. M. 1979. *Gestualità e oracolarità in Eraclito*. Genoa.

Baumgartner, W. 1950. "Herodots babylonische und assyrische Nachrichten." *Archiv Orientální* 18, 1-2: 69–106.

Beard, M., and J. Henderson. 1997. "With This Body I Thee Worship: Sacred Prostitution in Antiquity." *Gender & History* 9: 480–503.

Becq de Fouquières, L. 1873. *Les Jeux des Anciens*. 2d ed. Paris.

Bell, J. M. 1978. "Κίμβιξ καὶ σοφός: Simonides in the Anecdotal Tradition." *QUCC* 25: 29–86.

Benardete, S. 1969. *Herodotean Inquiries*. The Hague.

Benndorf, O. 1885. "Über ein Werk des älteren Polyklet." In *Gesammelte Studien zur Kunstgeschichte, eine Festgabe zum 4. Mai 1885 für Anton Springer*. Leipzig. 255–66.

Benveniste, E. 1938. "Traditions indo-iraniennes sur les classes sociales." *Journal asiatique* 230: 529–37.

——— 1973. *Indo-European Language and Society*. Trans. E. Palmer. London.

Bergk, T. 1858. "Über den Amtseid der attischen Archonten." *RhM* 13: 441–56.

Bhabha, H. K. 1994. "The Other Question: Stereotype, Discrimination and the Discourse of Colonialism." In *The Location of Culture*. London. 66–84.

Bloomer, W. M. 1993. "The Superlative *Nomoi* of Herodotus's *Histories*." *CA* 12: 30–50.

Boardman, J. 1978. "Exekias." *AJA* 82: 18–24.

——— 1992. "Kaloi and Other Names on Euphronios' Vases." In *Euphronios: Atti del Seminario Internazionale di Studi (Arezzo 27–28 Maggio 1990)*, ed. M. Cygielman, M. Iozzo, F. Nicosia, and P. Zamarachi Grassi. Florence. 45–50.

Boedeker, D. 1988. "Protesilaos and the End of Herodotus' *Histories*." *CA* 7: 30–48.

——— 1993. "The Bones of Orestes." In Dougherty and Kurke 1993: 164–77.

——— 1995. "Simonides on Plataea: Narrative Elegy, Mythodic History." *ZPE* 107: 217–29.

Boehm, C. 1893. "De cottabo." Inaug. Diss., Bonn.

Bogaert, R. 1968. *Banques et banquiers dans les cités grecques*. Leiden.

―― 1976. "L' Essai des monnaies dans l'antiquité." *Revue belge de numismatique* 122: 5–34.

―― 1986. *Grundzüge des Bankwesens im alten Griechenland*. Xenia: Konstanzer Althistorische Vorträge und Forschungen, v. 18. Konstanz.

Bohannan, P. 1959. "The Impact of Money on an African Subsistence Economy." *The Journal of Economic History* 19: 491–503.

Bohannan, P., and G. Dalton, eds. 1962. "Introduction." In *Markets in Africa*. Chicago. 1–26.

Bourdieu, P. 1977. *Outline of a Theory of Practice*. Trans. R. Nice. Cambridge.

―― 1984. *Distinction: A Social Critique of the Judgement of Taste*. Trans. R. Nice. Cambridge, Mass.

―― 1990. *The Logic of Practice*. Trans. R. Nice. Stanford.

―― 1991. *Language and Symbolic Power*. Trans. G. Raymond and M. Adamson. Cambridge, Mass.

Bowie, E. L. 1986. "Early Greek Elegy, Symposium and Public Festival." *JHS* 106: 13–35.

―― 1990. "*Miles Ludens*? The Problem of Martial Exhortation in Early Greek Elegy." In Murray 1990a: 221–29.

Bowra, C. M. 1961. *Greek Lyric Poetry*. 2d ed. Oxford.

―― 1970. "Xenophanes and the Luxury of Colophon." In *On Greek Margins*. Oxford.

Branham, R. B. 1996. "Defacing the Currency: Diogenes' Rhetoric and the *Invention* of Cynicism." In Branham and Goulet-Cazé 1996: 81–104.

Branham, R. B., and M.-O. Goulet-Cazé, eds. 1996. *The Cynics: The Cynic Movement and Its Legacy*. Berkeley and Los Angeles.

Bravo, B. 1977. "Remarques sur les assises sociales, les formes d'organisation et la terminologie du commerce maritime à l'epoque archaïque." *Dialogues d'histoire ancienne* 3: 1–59.

Breglia, L. 1974. "Gli stateri di Alceo." In *Numismatica e Antichità classiche*, ed. E. Bernareggi. Lugano. 7–12.

Breitenstein, N. 1941. *Catalogue of Terracottas*. Copenhagen.

Bremmer, J. N. 1983. "Scapegoat Rituals in Ancient Greece." *HSCP* 87: 299–320.

―― 1990. "Adolescents, *Symposion*, and Pederasty." In Murray 1990a: 135–48.

Brendel, O. 1970. "The Scope and Temperament of Erotic Art in the Greco-Roman World." In *Studies in Erotic Art*, ed. T. Bowie and C. V. Christenson. New York. 3–69.

Briant, P. 1989. "Table du roi, tribut et redistribution chez les Achéménides." In Briant and Herrenschmidt 1989: 35–44.

Briant, P., and C. Herrenschmidt, eds. 1989. *Le Tribut dans l'empire Perse*. Actes de la Table ronde de Paris 12–13 Décembre 1986. Louvain, Paris.

Broadhead, H. D., ed. 1960. *The "Persae" of Aeschylus*. Cambridge.

Brown, C. 1983. "From Rags to Riches: Anacreon's Artemon." *Phoenix* 37: 1–15.

―― 1989. "Anactoria and the Χαρίτων ἀμαρύγματα: Sappho fr. 16, 18 Voigt." *QUCC* (n.s. 32): 7–15.

Brown, N. O. 1947. *Hermes the Thief: The Evolution of a Myth*. Madison, Wisc.

Brown, P. 1990. "Plots and Prostitutes in Greek New Comedy." *Papers of the Leeds International Seminar* 6: 241–66.

———— 1993. "Love and Marriage in Greek New Comedy." *CQ* 43: 184–205.

Brown, W. L. 1950. "Pheidon's Alleged Aeginetan Coinage." *NC* (ser. 6), 10: 177–204.

Buchholz, H.-G. 1987. "Brettspielende Helden." In Laser 1987: 126–84.

Bundy, E. L. 1986. *Studia Pindarica.* Berkeley (= *University of California Publications in Classical Philology* 18: [1962] 1–34 and 35–92).

Burkert, W. 1979. "Kynaithos, Polycrates, and the Homeric Hymn to Apollo." In *Arktouros: Hellenic Studies presented to Bernard M. W. Knox,* ed. G. W. Bowersock, W. Burkert, and M.C.J. Putnam. Berlin, New York. 53–62.

———— 1983. *Homo Necans: The Anthropology of Ancient Greek Sacrificial Ritual and Myth.* Trans. P. Bing. Berkeley and Los Angeles.

———— 1985. *Greek Religion.* Trans. J. Raffan. Cambridge, Mass.

———— 1990. "Herodot als Historiker fremder Religionen." In *Hérodote et les Peuples non Grecs.* Fondation Hardt pour l'étude de l'antiquité classique. Entretiens 35. Geneva. 1–32.

Burnett, A. P. 1983. *Three Archaic Poets: Archilochus, Alcaeus, Sappho.* Cambridge, Mass.

———— 1985. *The Art of Bacchylides.* Cambridge, Mass.

Buttrey, T. V. 1979. "The Athenian Currency Law of 375/4 B.C." In *Greek Numismatics and Archaeology: Essays in Honor of Margaret Thompson,* ed. O. Mørkholm and N. M. Waggoner. Belgium. 33–45.

———— 1981. "More on the Athenian Coinage Law of 375/4 B.C." *Numismatica e Antichità classiche* 10: 71–94.

Caccamo Caltabiano, M., and P. Radici Colace. 1983. "*Argurion dokimon . . . to d' enantion parasēmon* (Pollux 3, 86)." *ASNP* ser. 3, vol. 13: 421–47.

———— 1985. "*Argurion eudokimon* (Pollux 3, 87)." *ASNP,* ser. 3, vol. 15: 81–101.

———— 1986. "Il siglos: dalla fase premonetale a quella monetale." *ASNP,* ser. 3, vol. 16: 1–14.

———— 1987. "L'eponimia monetale dall' esperienza orientale a quella di età ellenistica." *Numismatica e Antichità classiche* 16: 29–46.

———— 1989. "Darico Persiano e Nomisma Greco: Differenze strutturali, ideologiche e funzionali alla luce del lessico greco." *REA* 91, 1-2: 213–26.

Cahn, H. A. 1975. "Dating the Early Coinages of Athens." *Kleine Schriften zur Münzkunde und Archäologie.* Basel. 81–97.

Calame, C. 1974. "Réflexions sur les genres litteraires en Grèce archaique," *QUCC* 17: 113–28.

———— 1977. *Les Choeurs de jeunes filles en Grèce archaïque.* 2 vols. Urbino.

———— 1989. "Entre rapports de parenté et relations civiques: Aphrodite l'hétaïre au banquet politique des hétairoi," In *Aux sources de la puissance: Sociabilité et parenté.* Rouen. 101–11.

———— 1997. *Choruses of Young Women in Ancient Greece: Their Morphology, Religious Role, and Social Functions.* Trans. D. Collins and J. Orion. Lanham, Boulder, New York, London. [= Eng. ed. of Calame 1977, vol. 1]

Calhoun, G. M. 1913. *Athenian Clubs in Politics and Litigation. Bulletin of the University of Texas*, no. 262. Austin.

Camerer, L. 1965. "Praktische Klugheit bei Herodot: Untersuchungen zu den Begriffen *mēchanē, technē, sophiē*," Diss. Tübingen.

Campbell, D. A., ed. 1982. *Greek Lyric. Volume I: Sappho and Alcaeus.* Cambridge, Mass.

Carradice, I., and M. J. Price, eds. 1988. *Coinage in the Greek World.* London.

Carrière, J., ed. 1948. *Théognis: Poèmes élégiaques.* Paris.

Carson, A. 1982. "Wedding at Noon in Pindar's Ninth Pythian." *GRBS* 23: 121–28.

——— 1984. "The Burners: A Reading of Bacchylides' Third Epinician Ode." *Phoenix* 38: 111–19.

——— 1989. "Syracuse and the Monies of Simonides." In *Syracuse, the Fairest Greek City: Ancient Art from the Museo Archeologico Regionale Paolo Orsi,* ed. B. D. Wescoat. Rome. 29–30.

——— 1992. "How Not to Read a Poem: Unmixing Simonides from *Protagoras.*" *CP* 87: 110–30.

——— 1993. "Your Money or Your Life." *Yale Journal of Criticism* 6: 75–92.

——— 1994. "The Gender of Sound." *Thamyris* 1.1: 10–31.

Cartledge, P. 1982. "Sparta and Samos: A Special Relationship?" *CQ* 32: 243–65.

——— 1983. " 'Trade and Politics' Revisited: Archaic Greece." In *Trade in the Ancient Economy,* ed. P. Garnsey, K. Hopkins, and C. R. Whittaker. Berkeley and Los Angeles. 1–15.

——— 1997. *The Greeks: A Portrait of Self and Others.* Rev. ed. Oxford.

Cassin, E. 1957. "Le 'pesant d'or,' " *Rivista degli Studi Orientali* 32: 3–11.

——— 1960. "Le Sceau: Un Fait de civilisation dans la Mésopotamie ancienne." *Annales ESC* 15: 742–51.

Castoriadis, C. 1987. *The Imaginary Institution of Society.* Trans. K. Blamey. Cambridge, Mass.

Cavallini, E. 1990. "Erotima e la madre (Anac. fr. 1 P. = 60 Gent.)." *Giornale Italiano di Filologia* 40: 213–15.

Chamberlain, D. 1997. "Herodotean Voices: Reading Characters in the *Histories.*" Unpublished Ph.D. dissertation, University of California, Berkeley.

Chantraine, P. 1966. "Trois noms grecs de l'artisan (δημιουργός, βάναυσος, χειρ-, ῶναξ)." In *Mélanges de philosophie grecque offerts a MGR Diès.* Paris. 41–47.

Chantraine, P. 1968–80. *Dictionnaire étymologique de la langue grecque.* 4 vols. Paris.

Christ, M. R. 1990. "Liturgy Avoidance and Antidosis in Classical Athens." *TAPA* 120: 147–69.

Christ, M. R. 1994. "Herodotean Kings and Historical Inquiry." *CA* 13: 167–202.

Christodoulou, D. 1997. "The Hetaira in the Ancient World." Unpublished Ph.D. dissertation, Cambridge University.

Cilley, R. C. 1986. "Ancient Greek Board Games." Unpublished M.A. The University of Texas at Austin.

Clark, T. J. 1984. *The Painting of Modern Life: Paris in the Art of Man/ His Followers.* Princeton.

Cobb-Stevens, V. 1985. "Opposites, Reversals, and Ambiguities: The Unsettled World of Theognis." In Figueira and Nagy 1985: 159–75.

Cobet, J. 1971. *Herodots Exkurse und die Frage der Einheit seines Werkes.* Historia Einzelschriften 17. Wiesbaden.

——— 1977. "Wann wurde Herodots Darstellung der Perserkriege publiziert?" *Hermes* 105: 2–27.

Connor, W. R. [1971] 1992. *The New Politicians of Fifth-Century Athens.* Princeton; Rept., Indianapolis, 1992.

——— 1977. "Tyrannis Polis." In *Ancient and Modern: Essays in Honor of Gerald F. Else,* ed. J. H. D'Arms. Ann Arbor. 95–109.

——— 1987a. "Tribes, Festivals and Processions: Civic Ceremonial and Political Manipulation in Archaic Greece." *JHS* 107: 40–50.

——— 1987b. "Commentary on the Conference." *Arethusa* 20: 255–63.

——— 1993. "The Histor in History." In Rosen and Farrell 1993: 3–15.

——— 1996. "Civil Society, Dionysiac Festival, and the Athenian Democracy." In Ober and Hedrick 1996: 217–26.

Cook, J. M. 1983. *The Persian Empire.* London.

Cook, J. M., and J. Boardman. 1954. "Archaeology in Greece, 1953." *JHS* 74: 142–69.

Cook, R. M., 1958. "Speculations on the Origin of Coinage." *Historia* 7: 257–62.

Cooper, F., and S. P. Morris. 1990. "Dining in Round Buildings." In Murray 1990a: 66–85.

Cope, E. M., and J. E. Sandys. 1877. *The Rhetoric of Aristotle.* 3 vols. Cambridge.

Crane, G. 1993. "Politics of Consumption and Generosity in the Carpet Scene of the *Agamemnon.*" *CP* 88: 117–36.

——— 1996. "The Prosperity of Tyrants: Bacchylides, Herodotus, and the Contest for Legitimacy." *Arethusa* 29: 57–85.

Crump, T. 1981. *The Phenomenon of Money.* London, Boston, and Henley.

Csapo, E., and M. C. Miller. 1991. "The 'Kottabos-Toast' and an Inscribed Red-figured Cup." *Hesperia* 60: 367–82.

Culler, J. 1981. *The Pursuit of Signs: Semiotics, Literature, Deconstruction.* Ithaca.

Curtin, P. D. 1984. *Cross-cultural Trade in World History.* Cambridge.

Darbo-Peschanski, C. 1985. "Les 'Logoi' des autres dans les 'Histoires' d'Hérodote." *Quaderni Storia* 22: 105–28.

Darbo-Peschanski, C. 1987. *Le Discours du particulier: Essai sur l'enquête hérodotéenne.* Paris.

Daremberg, C., and E. Saglio, eds. 1877–1919. *Dictionnaire des Antiquités Grecques et Romaines.* 5 vols. Paris.

Daumas, F. 1956. "La Valeur de l'or dans la pensée égyptienne." *Revue d'histoire des religions* 149: 1–17.

Davidson, J. N. 1994. "Consuming Passions: Appetite, Addiction and Spending in Classical Athens." Ph.D. dissertation, Trinity College, Oxford University.

——— 1997. *Courtesans and Fishcakes: The Consuming Passions of Classical Athens.* London.

——— n.d. "Love and Money: Prostitution and the Discourse of Commodification at Athens." Unpublished MS.

Davies, J. K. 1971. *Athenian Propertied Families 600–300 B.C.* Oxford.

——— 1981. *Wealth and the Power of Wealth in Classical Athens.* New York.

Davies, M. 1981. "Artemon Transvestitus? A Query." *Mnemosyne,* ser. 4, 34: 288–99.

——— 1984. Review of A. P. Burnett, *Three Archaic Poets: Archilochus, Alcaeus, Sappho. Classical Review* (n.s. 34): 169–73.

——— 1988. "Monody, Choral Lyric, and the Tyranny of the Hand-Book." *CQ* (n.s. 38): 52–64.

Debrunner, A. 1910. Review of E. Boisacq, *Dictionnaire étymologique de la langue grecque. Göttingische gelehrte Anzeigen* 1910: 1–18.

de Certeau, M. 1984. *The Practice of Everyday Life.* Trans. S. Rendall. Berkeley and Los Angeles.

Degani, E., ed. 1991. *Hipponactis Testimonia et Fragmenta.* Stuttgart and Leipzig.

de Grazia, M., M. Quilligan, and P. Stallybrass, eds. 1996. *Subject and Object in Renaissance Culture.* Cambridge.

de Lauretis, T. 1987. *Technologies of Gender: Essays on Theory, Film, and Fiction.* Bloomington and Indianapolis, Ind.

Denniston, J. D., and D. L. Page, eds. 1972. *Aeschylus "Agamemnon".* Oxford.

Deonna, W. 1930. "Astragalizontes? Groupe isolé ou fronton?" *REG* 43: 384–97.

de Polignac, F. 1995. *Cults, Territory, and the Origins of the Greek City-State.* Trans. J. Lloyd. Chicago.

Derrida, J. 1992. *Given Time: I. Counterfeit Money.* Trans. P. Kamuf. Chicago.

Descat, R. 1989. "Notes sur la politique tributaire de Darius Ier." In Briant and Herrenschmidt 1989: 77–93.

Detienne, M. 1996. *The Masters of Truth in Archaic Greece.* Trans. J. Lloyd. New York.

Detienne, M., and J. Svenbro. 1989. "The Feast of the Wolves, or the Impossible City." In Detienne and Vernant 1989: 148–63.

Detienne, M., and J.-P. Vernant. 1978. *Cunning Intelligence in Greek Culture and Society.* Trans. J. Lloyd. Sussex.

——— eds. 1989. *The Cuisine of Sacrifice among the Greeks.* Trans. P. Wissing. Chicago.

Deubner, L. 1966. *Attische Feste.* 2d ed. Hildesheim.

De Vries, K. 1973. "East Meets West at Dinner." *Expedition* 15: 32–39.

Dewald, C. 1981. "Women and Culture in Herodotus' Histories." In *Reflections of Women in Antiquity,* ed. H. P. Foley. New York, London, Paris. 91–125.

——— 1985. "Practical Knowledge and the Historian's Role in Herodotus and Thucydides." In *The Greek Historians: Literature and History: Papers Presented to A. E. Raubitschek.* Saratoga, Calif. 47–63.

——— 1987. "Narrative Surface and Authorial Voice in Herodotus' *Histories.*" *Arethusa* 20: 141–70.

——— 1993. "Reading the World: The Interpretation of Objects in Herodotus' *Histories,*" In Rosen and Farrell 1993: 55–70.

Dewald, C., and J. Marincola. 1987. "A Selective Introduction to Herodotean Studies." *Arethusa* 20: 9–40.

Dillery, J. 1992. "Darius and the Tomb of Nitocris (Hdt. 1.187)." *CP* 87: 30–38.

Dobree, P. P. 1831. *Adversaria.* Vol 1. Berlin.

Donlan, W. 1980. *The Aristocratic Ideal in Ancient Greece*. Lawrence, Kans.
———— 1985. "*Pistos Philos Hetairos.*" In Figueira and Nagy 1985: 223–44.
———— 1989. "The Unequal Exchange between Glaucus and Diomedes in Light of the Homeric Gift-Economy." *Phoenix* 53: 1–15.
Dougherty, C. 1993. *The Poetics of Colonization: From City to Text in Archaic Greece*. New York.
———— 1996. "Democratic Contradictions and the Synoptic Illusion of Euripides' *Ion*." In Ober and Hedrick 1996: 249–70.
———— forthcoming. *The Raft of Odysseus*. New York.
Dougherty, C., and L. Kurke, eds. [1993] 1998. *Cultural Poetics in Archaic Greece: Cult, Performance, Politics*. Cambridge. Rept., Oxford, 1998.
Dover, K. J. [1964] 1987. "The Poetry of Archilochos." In *Archiloque*. Fondation Hardt pour l'étude de l'antiquité classique. Entretiens 10. Geneva. 183–212. Rept. in *Greek and the Greeks: Collected Papers I*. Oxford. 97–121.
———— 1974. *Greek Popular Morality in the Time of Plato and Aristotle*. Berkeley and Los Angeles.
———— 1989. *Greek Homosexuality*. 2d ed. Cambridge, Mass.
———— ed. 1993. *Aristophanes "Frogs"*. Oxford.
duBois, P. 1984. "Sappho and Helen." In *Women in the Ancient World: The Arethusa Papers*, ed. J. Peradotto and J. P. Sullivan. Albany. 95–105.
———— 1988. *Sowing the Body: Psychoanalysis and Ancient Representations of Women*. Chicago.
———— 1991. *Torture and Truth*. New York.
Dudley, D. R. 1937. *A History of Cynicism from Diogenes to the 6th Century* A.D. London.
Dumézil, G. 1979. *Romans de Scythie et d'alentour*. Paris.
Edmonds, J. M. 1961. *The Fragments of Attic Comedy after Meinecke, Bergk, and Kock*. Vol. IIIA. Leiden.
Edmunds, L. 1985. "The Genre of Theognidean Poetry." In Figueira and Nagy 1985: 96–111.
———— 1988. "Foucault and Theognis." *Classical and Modern Literature* 8: 79–91.
Ehrenberg, V. 1940. "Isonomia." *RE* Suppl. 7.293–301.
———— 1956. "Das Harmodioslied." *Wiener Studien* 69: 57–69.
Eichholz, D. E., ed. 1965. *Theophrastus. De Lapidibus*. Oxford.
Erbse, H. 1956. "Der erste Satz im Werke Herodots." In *Festschrift Bruno Snell*, ed. H. Erbse. Munich. 209–22.
———— 1992. *Studien zum Verständnis Herodots*. Berlin, New York.
Eustathios. 1825. *Commentarii ad Homeri "Odysseam" ad Fidem Exempli Romani Editi*. 2 vols. Leipzig.
Evans, J.A.S. 1991. *Herodotus, Explorer of the Past: Three Essays*. Princeton.
Fantham, E. 1975. "Sex, Status, and Survival in Hellenistic Athens: A Study of Women in New Comedy." *Phoenix* 29: 44–74.
Farenga, V. 1981. "The Paradigmatic Tyrant: Greek Tyranny and the Ideology of the Proper." *Helios* 8: 1–31.

———— 1985. "La tirannide greca e la strategia numismatica." In *Mondo classico: Percorsi possibili.* Ravenna. 39–49.

Farnell, L. R., ed. 1930. *The Works of Pindar.* 3 vols. London.

Fehling, D. 1989. *Herodotus and His 'Sources': Citation, Invention and Narrative Art.* Arca: Classical and Medieval Texts, Papers and Monographs 21. Trans. J. G. Howie. Trowbridge, Wiltshire.

Ferrari, G.R.F. 1988. "Hesiod's Mimetic Muses and the Strategies of Deconstruction." In *Post-structuralist Classics,* ed. A. Benjamin. London. 45–78.

Ferrill, A. 1978. "Herodotus on Tyranny." *Historia* 27: 385–98.

Figueira, T. J. 1981. *Aegina: Society and Politics.* New York.

———— 1985. "The Theognidea and Megarian Society." In Figueira and Nagy 1985: 112–58.

Figueira, T. J., and G. Nagy, eds. 1985. *Theognis of Megara: Poetry and the Polis.* Baltimore.

Fileni, M. G. 1983. "Osservazioni sull' idea di tiranno nella cultura greca arcaica (Alc. frr. 70, 6–9; 129, 21–24 V.; Theogn. vv. 1179–1182)." *QUCC* (n.s. 14): 29–35.

Finley, M. I [as M. I. Finkelstein]. 1935. "Ἔμπορος, Ναύκληρος, and Κάπηλος: A Prolegomena to the Study of Athenian Trade." *CP* 30: 320–36.

Finley, M. I. 1970. "Aristotle and Economic Analysis." *Past & Present* 47: 3–25.

———— 1977. *The World of Odysseus.* Rev. ed. New York.

———— 1979. *Ancient Sicily to the Arab Conquest.* Rev. ed. London.

———— 1983. *Politics in the Ancient World.* Cambridge.

———— 1985a. *Democracy Ancient and Modern.* 2d ed. London.

———— 1985b. "Sparta." In *Problèmes de la Guerre en Grèce ancienne,* ed. J.-P. Vernant. Paris. 143–60.

Firth, R. 1965. *Primitive Polynesian Economy.* London.

Fisher, N.R.E. 1976. "*Hybris* and Dishonour: I." *G&R* 23: 177–93.

———— 1979. "*Hybris* and Dishonour: II." *G&R* 26: 32–47.

———— 1992. *Hybris: A Study in the Values of Honour and Shame in Ancient Greece.* Warminster.

Flory, S. 1987. *The Archaic Smile of Herodotus.* Detroit.

Forbes, R. J. 1950. *Metallurgy in Antiquity: A Notebook for Archaeologists and Technologists.* Leiden.

———— 1964. *Studies in Ancient Technology.* Volume 8. Leiden.

Fornara, C. W. 1971a. "Evidence for the date of Herodotus' Publication." *JHS* 91: 25–34.

———— 1971b. *Herodotus: An Interpretative Essay.* Oxford.

———— 1981. "Herodotus' Knowledge of the Archidamian War." *Hermes* 109: 149–56.

Foster, G. V. 1984. "The Bones from the Altar West of the Painted Stoa." *Hesperia* 53, 1: 73–82.

Foucault, M. 1970. *The Order of Things: An Archaeology of the Human Sciences.* New York.

———— 1985. *The History of Sexuality.* Vol. 2. *The Use of Pleasure.* New York.

Fraenkel, E., ed. 1950. *Aeschylus: "Agamemnon".* 3 vols. Oxford.

Fränkel, H. 1928. Review of E. Lobel, ed. Σαπφοῦς μέλη and Ἀλκαίου μέλη. *Göttingische gelehrte Anzeigen* 190: 258–78.

Fränkel, H. 1973. *Early Greek Poetry and Philosophy*. Trans. M. Hadas and J. Willis. New York.

Francis, E. D. 1990. *Image and Idea in Fifth-Century Greece: Art and Literature after the Persian Wars*. London.

Friedländer, P. 1913. "ΥΠΟΘΗΚΑΙ." *Hermes* 48: 558–616.

Friis Johansen, H., and E. W. Whittle, eds. 1980. *Aeschylus: "The Suppliants"*. 3 vols. Copenhagen.

Frisk, H. 1960–1972. *Griechisches etymologisches Wörterbuch*. 3 vols. Heidelberg.

Frontisi-Ducroux, F. 1989. "In the Mirror of the Mask." In *A City of Images: Iconography and Society in Ancient Greece*. Trans. D. Lyons. Princeton. 151–65.

——— 1996. "Eros, Desire, and the Gaze." In *Sexuality in Ancient Art: Near East, Egypt, Greece, and Italy*, ed. N. B. Kampen. Cambridge. 81–100.

Frontisi-Ducroux, F., and F. Lissarrague. 1990. "From Ambiguity to Ambivalence: A Dionysiac Excursion through the 'Anakreontic' Vases." In *Before Sexuality: The Construction of Erotic Experience in the Ancient Greek World*, ed. D. Halperin, J. J. Winkler, and F. I. Zeitlin. Princeton. 211–56.

Frost, F. 1985. "Toward a History of Pisistratid Athens." In *The Craft of the Ancient Historian*, ed. J. Ober. Baltimore. 57–78.

Frow, J. 1986. *Marxism and Literary History*. Cambridge, Mass.

Furley, D. J., and R. E. Allen, eds. 1970. *Studies in Presocratic Philosophy*. Vol. I: *The Beginnings of Philosophy*. London.

Gabrielsen, V. 1986. "Φανερά and ἀφανὴς οὐσία in Classical Athens." *Classica et Mediaevalia* 37: 99–114.

Gallavotti, C. 1955. "Un restauro d'Anacreonte." *PdP* 40: 47–50.

Gammie, J. G. 1986. "Herodotus on Kings and Tyrants: Objective Historiography or Conventional Portraiture?" *Journal of Near Eastern Studies* 45, no. 3: 171–95.

Garrett, A., and L. Kurke. 1994. "Pudenda Asiae Minoris." *HSCP* 96: 75–83.

Geddes, A. G. 1987. "Rags and Riches: The Costume of Athenian Men in the Fifth Century." *CQ* (n.s. 37): 307–31.

Gentili, B., ed. 1958. *Anacreon*. Rome.

——— 1988. *Poetry and Its Public in Ancient Greece from Homer to the Fifth Century*. Trans. A. T. Cole. Baltimore.

Gerber, D. E., ed. 1970. *Euterpe: An Anthology of Early Greek Lyric, Elegiac, and Iambic Poetry*. Amsterdam.

——— 1976. "Studies in Greek Lyric Poetry: 1967–1975." *Classical World* 70.2: 66–157.

Gernet, L. 1981a. " 'Value' in Greek Myth." In *Myth, Religion and Society*. Trans. R. L. Gordon. Cambridge. 111–46.

——— 1981b. *The Anthropology of Ancient Greece*. Trans. J. Hamilton and B. Nagy. Baltimore.

Gildersleeve, B. L. 1890. *Pindar: The Olympian and Pythian Odes*. New York.

Gilhuly, K. 1999. "Representations of the *Hetaira*." Unpublished Ph.D. dissertation, University of California, Berkeley.

Gilmour, G. H. 1997. "The Nature and Function of Astragalus Bones from Archaeological Contexts in the Levant and Eastern Mediterranean." *Oxford Journal of Archaeology* 16: 167–75.

Glotz, G. 1908. "Les Esclaves et la peine du fouet en droit grec." *Académie des inscriptions et belles lettres, comptes rendus*: 571–87.

Godelier, M. 1977. *Perspectives in Marxist Anthropology*. Cambridge.

Goldhill, S. 1987. "The Great Dionysia and Civic Ideology." *JHS* 107: 58–76.

——— 1992. Review of Reinsberg, *Ehe, Hetärentum und Knabenliebe im antiken Griechenland* and Winkler, *The Constraints of Desire*. *JHS* 112: 196–98.

——— 1994. "The Naive and Knowing Eye: Ecphrasis and the Culture of Viewing in the Hellenistic World." In Goldhill and Osborne 1994: 197–223.

——— 1998. "The Seductions of the Gaze: Socrates and His Girlfriends." In *KOSMOS: Essays in Order, Conflict and Community in Classical Athens*, ed. P. Cartledge, P. Millett, and S. von Reden. Cambridge. 105–24.

Goldhill, S., and R. Osborne, eds. 1994. *Art and Text in Ancient Greek Culture*. Cambridge.

Goossens, R. 1952. "L'Invention des jeux (Cratès fr. 24 Kock)." *Revue belge de philologie et d'histoire* 30: 146–56.

Gould, J. 1989. *Herodotus*. London.

——— 1991. *Give and Take in Herodotus*. The Fifteenth Annual J. L. Myres Memorial Lecture. Oxford.

Goux, J.-J. 1990. *Symbolic Economies: After Marx and Freud*. Trans. J. C. Gage. Ithaca.

Gow, A.S.F., ed. 1952. *Theocritus*. 2 vols. Cambridge.

Gow, A.S.F., and D. L. Page. 1965. *The Greek Anthology: Hellenistic Epigrams*. Cambridge.

Graf, J. 1903. "Münzverfälschungen im Altertum," *Numismatische Zeitschrift* 35: 1–130.

Greene, W. C., ed. 1938. *Scholia Platonica*. APA Philological Monographs, no. 8. Haverford, Pa.

Gregory, C. A. 1982. *Gifts and Commodities*. London.

Greifenhagen, A. 1967. "Smikros: Lieblingsinschrift und Malersignatur." *Jahrbuch der Berliner Museen* 9: 5–25.

Griffith, M. 1983. "Personality in Hesiod." *CA* 2: 37–65.

——— 1995. "Brilliant Dynasts: Power and Politics in the *Oresteia*." *CA* 14: 62–129.

——— 1998. "The King and Eye." *PCPS* 44: 20–84.

Guarducci, M. 1966. "Divinità fauste nell' antica Velia." *PdP* 108–10: 279–94.

——— 1971. "Da Olympios Kairòs al Principe degli Apostoli." *Archeologia classica* 23: 124–30.

Gundert, H. 1935. *Pindar und sein Dichterberuf*. Frankfurt.

Guthrie, W.K.C. 1969. *A History of Greek Philosophy*. Vol. III: The Fifth-Century Enlightenment. Cambridge.

Hall, E. 1989. *Inventing the Barbarian: Greek Self-Definition through Tragedy*. Oxford.

Halliday, W. R. 1913. *Greek Divination: A Study of Its Methods and Principles*. London.

Halperin, D. 1990. *One Hundred Years of Homosexuality and Other Essays on Greek Love*. New York, London.

Hampe, R. 1951. *Die Stele aus Pharsalos im Louvre*. Winkelmannsprogramm der Archäologischen Gesellschaft zu Berlin, 107. Berlin.

Hanfmann, G.M.A. 1983. *Sardis from Prehistoric to Roman Times*. Cambridge.

Hangard, J. 1963. *Monetaire en Daarmee Verwante Metaforen*. Groningen.

Hansen, M. H. 1989. "Solonian Democracy in Fourth-Century Athens." *Classica et Mediaevalia* 40: 71–99.

—— 1991. *The Athenian Democracy in the Age of Demosthenes*. Oxford and Cambridge, Mass.

Hanson, V. D. 1995. *The Other Greeks: The Family Farm and the Agrarian Roots of Western Civilization*. New York.

—— 1996. "Hoplites into Democrats: The Changing Ideology of Athenian Infantry." In Ober and Hedrick 1996: 289–312.

Harris, W. V. 1989. *Ancient Literacy*. Cambridge, Mass.

Harrison, E. 1902. *Studies in Theognis*. Cambridge.

Hart, K. 1986. "Heads or Tails? Two Sides of the Coin." *Man* (n.s. 21): 637–57.

Hartman, M. 1988. "The Hesiodic Roots of Plato's Myth of the Metals," *Helios* 15: 103–14.

Hartog, F. 1988. *The Mirror of Herodotus: The Representation of the Other in the Writing of History*. Trans. J. Lloyd. Berkeley and Los Angeles.

Harvey, D. 1988. "Painted Ladies: Fact, Fiction and Fantasy." In *Proceedings of the 3rd Symposium on Ancient Greek and Related Pottery* (Copenhagen, August 31–September 4, 1987), ed. J. Christiansen and T. Melander. 242–54.

Harvey, F. D. 1965. "Two Kinds of Equality." *Classica et Mediaevalia* 26: 101–46.

—— 1985. "Dona Ferentes: Some Aspects of Bribery in Greek Politics." In *Crux: Essays in Greek History Presented to G.E.M. de Ste. Croix on his 75th Birthday*, ed. P. A. Cartledge and F. D. Harvey. Exeter and London. 76–117.

Hasebroek, J. 1933. *Trade and Politics in Ancient Greece*. London.

Hauschild, H. 1933. *Die Gestalt der Hetäre in der griechischen Komödie*. Leipzig.

Havelock, E. A. 1952. "Why Was Socrates Tried?" In *Studies in Honour of Gilbert Norwood*, ed. M. E. White. Toronto. 95–109.

—— 1963. *Preface to Plato*. Cambridge, Mass.

—— 1982. *The Literate Revolution in Greece and its Cultural Consequences*. Princeton.

Hayley, H. W. 1894. "The κότταβος καταχτός in the Light of Recent Investigations." *HSCP* 5: 73–82.

Healy, J. F. 1978. *Mining and Metallurgy in the Greek and Roman World*. London.

Heath, M. 1988. "Receiving the κῶμος: The Context and Performance of Epinician." *AJP* 109: 180–95.

Henderson, J. 1991. *The Maculate Muse: Obscene Language in Attic Comedy*. 2d ed. New York.

Henry, M. M. 1985. *Menander's Courtesans and the Greek Comic Tradition*. Studien zur klassischen Philologie, vol. 20. Frankfurt am Main.

———— 1986. "*Ēthos, Mythos, Praxis*: Women in Menander's Comedy." *Helios* (n.s. 13.2): 141–50.

———— 1992. "The Edible Woman: Athenaeus's Concept of the Pornographic." In Richlin 1992: 250–68.

———— 1995. *Prisoner of History: Aspasia of Miletus and Her Biographical Tradition*. New York and Oxford.

Herington, J. 1985. *Poetry into Drama: Early Tragedy and the Greek Poetic Tradition*. Berkeley and Los Angeles.

Herman, G. 1987. *Ritualised Friendship and the Greek City*. Cambridge.

Herter, H. 1957. "Dirne." *Reallexikon für Antike und Christentum* 3.1149–1213.

———— 1960. "Die Soziologie der antiken Prostitution im Lichte des heidnischen und christlichen Schrifttums." *Jahrbuch für Antike und Christentum* 3: 70–111.

Hölscher, T. 1991. "The City of Athens: Space, Symbol, Structure." In *City States in Classical Antiquity and Medieval Italy*, ed. A. Molho, K. Raaflaub, and J. Emlen. Stuttgart. 355–80.

Hopper, R. J. 1968. "Observations on the *Wappenmünzen*." *Essays in Greek Coinage Presented to Stanley Robinson*, ed. C. M. Kraay and G. K. Jenkins. Oxford. 16–39.

———— 1979. *Trade and Industry in Classical Greece*. London.

How, W. W., and J. Wells. 1928. *A Commentary on Herodotus*. 2 vols. Oxford.

Howgego, C. J. 1990. "Why did Ancient States Strike Coins?" *NC* 150: 1–25.

———— 1995. *Ancient History from Coins*. London.

Hudson-Williams, T. 1910. *The Elegies of Theognis*. London.

Hughes, R. 1986. *The Fatal Shore: The Epic of Australia's Founding*. New York.

Humphreys, S. 1978. "Homo politicus and homo economicus." In *Anthropology and the Greeks*. London. 159–74.

———— 1987. "Law, Custom and Culture in Herodotus." *Arethusa* 20: 211–20.

Hunter, V. J. 1994. *Policing Athens: Social Control in the Attic Lawsuits, 420–320 B.C.* Princeton.

Hurwit, J. M. 1985. *The Art and Culture of Early Greece, 1100–480 B.C.* Ithaca.

Immerwahr, H. R. 1956–57. "The Samian Stories in Herodotus." *CJ* 52: 312–22.

———— 1966. *Form and Thought in Herodotus*. Cleveland.

———— 1984. "An Inscribed Cup by the Ambrosios Painter." *Antike Kunst* 27: 10–13.

Irigaray, L. 1985. *The Sex Which Is Not One*. Trans. C. Porter. Ithaca.

Jacoby, F. 1913. "Herodotos." *RE Supplementband* 2.205–520.

Jaeger, W. 1945. *Paideia: The Ideals of Greek Culture*. Vol. I. Oxford.

Jahn, O. 1867. "Kottabos auf Vasenbildern." *Philologus* 26: 201–40.

Jameson, F. 1981. *The Political Unconscious: Narrative as a Socially Symbolic Act*. Ithaca.

Jebb, R. C., ed. 1905. *Bacchylides: The Poems and Fragments*. Cambridge.

Jeffery, L. H. 1990. *The Local Scripts of Archaic Greece*. Rev. ed. Oxford.

Jenkins, G. K. 1990. *Ancient Greek Coins*. 2d rev. ed. London.

Jones, A. H. M. 1957. *Athenian Democracy*. Oxford.

Just, R. 1989. *Women in Athenian Law and Life*. London and New York.

Kagan, D. 1982. "The Dates of the Earliest Coins." *AJA* 86: 343–60.

Kahn, C. H. 1979. *The Art and Thought of Heraclitus: An Edition of the Fragments with Translation and Commentary*. Cambridge.

Kaibel, G. 1876. "Ein Würfelorakel." *Hermes* 10: 193–202.

——— ed. [1878] 1965. *Epigrammata Graeca ex Lapidibus Conlecta*. Berlin. Rept., Hildesheim: Georg Olms.

——— ed. 1899. *Comicorum Graecorum Fragmenta*. Berlin.

Karwiese, S. 1991. "The Artemisium Coin Hoard and the First Coins of Ephesus." *Revue belge de numismatique et de sigillographie* 137: 1–28.

Kassel, R., and C. Austin, eds. 1983–. *Poetae Comici Graeci*. Berlin.

Kemp-Lindemann, D. 1975. *Darstellungen des Achilleus in griechischer und römischer Kunst*. Frankfurt am Main.

Keuls, Eva. C. 1985. *The Reign of the Phallus: Sexual Politics in Ancient Athens*. New York. Repr. Berkeley/Los Angeles, 1993.

Kilmer, M. F. 1982. "Genital Phobia and Depilation." *JHS* 102: 104–12.

——— 1993. *Greek Erotica on Attic Red-Figure Vases*. London.

Kim, H. S. 1994. "Greek Fractional Silver Coinage: A Reassessment of the Inception, Development, Prevalence, and Functions of Small Change During the Late Archaic and Early Classical Periods." Unpublished M. Phil. Dissertation, University of Oxford.

Kim, H. S. forthcoming.a. "Archaic Coinage as Evidence for the Use of Money."

——— forthcoming.b. "Small Change and the Moneyed Economy."

Kindstrand, J. F. 1981. *Anacharsis: The Legend and the Apophthegmata*. Uppsala.

Kirkwood, G. M. 1974. *Early Greek Monody: The History of a Poetic Type*. Ithaca.

Kiyonaga, S. 1973. "The Date of the Beginning of Coinage in Asia Minor." *Schweizerische numismatische Rundschau* 52: 5–16.

Kleingünther, A. 1933. Πρῶτος Εὑρετής: *Untersuchungen zur Geschichte einer Fragestellung*. Philologus Supplementband 26, vol. 1. Leipzig.

Koch, T. 1903. "Δοκιμασία." *RE* vol. 5.1, coll. 1268–73.

Kock, T. 1880–1888. *Comicorum Atticorum Fragmenta*. 3 vols. Leipzig.

Köhnken, A. 1990. "Der listige Oibares: Dareios' Aufstieg zum Großkönig." *RhM* 133: 115–37.

Körte, A. 1929. "ΧΑΡΑΚΤΗΡ." *Hermes* 64: 69–86.

Konstan, D. 1983. "The Stories in Herodotus' *Histories*: Book I." *Helios* 10: 1–22.

——— 1987a. "Between Courtesan and Wife: Menander's *Perikeiromene*." *Phoenix* 41: 122–39.

——— 1987b. "Persians, Greeks, and Empire." *Arethusa* 20: 59–73.

——— 1990. "A City in the Air: Aristophanes' *Birds*." *Arethusa* 23: 183–207.

Kopytoff, I. 1986. "The Cultural Biography of Things: Commoditization as Process." In *The Social Life of Things: Commodities in Cultural Perspective*, ed. A. Appadurai. Cambridge. 64–91.

Korshak, Y. 1987. *Frontal Faces in Attic Vase Painting of the Archaic Period*. Chicago.

Kraay, C. M. 1956. "The Archaic Owls of Athens: Classification and Chronology." *NC* (ser. 6), 16: 43–68.

——— 1964. "Hoards, Small Change and the Origin of Coinage." *JHS* 84: 76–91.

——— 1976. *Archaic and Classical Greek Coins*. Berkeley and Los Angeles.

——— 1977. "Review Article. The Asyut Hoard: Some Comments on Chronology." *NC* 17: 189–98.

Kroll, J. H. 1979. "A Chronology of Early Athenian Bronze Coinage, ca. 350–250 B.C." In *Greek Numismatics and Archaeology: Essays in Honor of Margaret Thompson*, ed. O. Mørkholm and N. M. Waggoner. Belgium. 139–54.

——— 1981. "From Wappenmünzen to Gorgoneia to Owls." *American Numismatic Society Museum Notes* 26: 1–32.

——— 1998. "Silver in Solon's Laws." In *Studies in Greek Numismatics in Memory of Martin Jessop Price*, ed. R. Ashton and S. Hurter. London. 225–32.

Kroll, J. H., and N. M. Waggoner. 1984. "Dating the Earliest Coins of Athens, Corinth and Aegina." *AJA* 88: 325–40.

Kurke, L. 1989. "ΚΑΠΗΛΕΙΑ and Deceit: Theognis 59–60." *AJP* 110: 535–44.

——— 1990. "Pindar's Sixth *Pythian* and the Tradition of Advice Poetry." *TAPA* 120: 85–107.

——— 1991. *The Traffic in Praise: Pindar and the Poetics of Social Economy*. Ithaca.

——— 1992. "The Politics of ἁβροσύνη in Archaic Greece." *CA* 11: 90–121.

——— 1993. "The Economy of *Kudos*." In Dougherty and Kurke 1993: 131–63.

——— 1994. "Crisis and Decorum in Sixth-Century Lesbos: Reading Alkaios Otherwise." *QUCC* (n.s. 47), 2: 67–92.

——— 1995. "Herodotus and the Language of Metals." *Helios* 22: 36–64.

——— 1996. "Pindar and the Prostitutes, or Reading Ancient 'Pornography'." *Arion* (3d ser.), 4, 2: 49–75.

——— 1997. "Inventing the *Hetaira*: Sex, Politics, and Discursive Conflict in Archaic Greece." *CA* 16: 106–50.

——— 1998. "The Cultural Impact of (on) Democracy: Decentering Tragedy." In *Democracy 2500? Questions and Challenges*, ed. I. Morris and K. A. Raaflaub. Dubuque, Iowa. 155–69.

Kurtz, D. C. and J. Boardman. 1971. *Greek Burial Customs*. London.

——— 1986. "Booners" in *Greek Vases in the J. Paul Getty Museum*. Occasional Papers on Antiquities, 2. Vol. 3: 35–70.

Lamer, H. 1927. "Lusoria tabula." *RE* vol. 13.2, coll. 1900–2029.

Lang, M. L. 1984. *Herodotean Narrative and Discourse*. Cambridge, Mass.

Lanza, D. 1977. *Il Tiranno e il suo pubblico*. Turin.

Laroche, E. 1949. *Histoire de la racine nem- en grec ancien*. Paris.

Laser, S. 1987. *Sport und Spiel*. Archaeologia Homerica. Kapitel T. Göttingen.

Lateiner, D. 1984. "Herodotus' Historical Patterning: 'The Constitutional Debate.'" *Quaderni Storia* 20: 257–84.

——— 1989. *The Historical Method of Herodotus*. Toronto.

Latte, K. 1955. Review of *The Oxyrhynchus Papyri* part XXII. *Gnomon* 27: 491–99.

Lattimore, R. 1958. "The Composition of the 'History' of Herodotus." *CP* 53: 9–21.

Laum, B. 1924. *Heiliges Geld: Eine historische Untersuchung über den sakralen Ursprung des Geldes*. Tübingen.

Laum, B. 1951–52. "Über die soziale Funktion der Münze." *Finanzarchiv* 13: 120–43.

Lavelle, B. M. 1991. "The Compleat Angler: Observations on the Rise of Peisistratos in Herodotus (1.59–64)." *CQ* 41: 317–24.

Lengauer, W. 1989. "Das griechische Gleichheitsdenken zwischen Aristokratie und Demokratie." In *Demokratie und Architektur: Der hippodamische Städtebau und die Entstehung der Demokratie*, ed. W. Schuller, W. Hoepfner, and E. L. Schwandner. Munich. 17–24.

Lesky, A. 1976. *Vom Eros der Hellenen*. Göttingen.

Lévêque, P., and P. Vidal-Naquet. 1996. *Cleisthenes the Athenian: An Essay on the Representation of Space and Time in Greek Political Thought from the End of the Sixth Century to the Death of Plato*. Trans. D. A. Curtis. Atlantic Highlands, N.J.

Levine, D. B. 1982. "*Odyssey* 18: Iros as Paradigm for the Suitors." *CJ* 77: 200–204.

——— 1984. "Counterfeit Man." In *Classical Texts and Their Traditions: Studies in Honor of C. R. Trahman*, ed. D. F. Bright and E. S. Ramage. Chico, Calif. 125–37.

Lewis, D. M. 1989. "Persian Gold in Greek International Relations." *REA* 91, 1-2: 227–34.

Lewis, J. M. 1985. "Eros and the **Polis** in Theognis Book II." In Figueira and Nagy 1985: 197–222.

Licht, Hans [= Paul Brandt]. 1932. *Sexual Life in Ancient Greece*. London.

Lippold, G. 1929. "Sparta." *RE* vol. 3.2, coll. 1265–1528.

Lissarrague, F. 1990. *The Aesthetics of the Greek Banquet: Images of Wine and Ritual*. Trans. A. Szegedy-Maszak. Princeton.

Lloyd, A. B. 1975. *Herodotus: Book II. Introduction*. Leiden.

——— 1988. *Herodotus: Book II. Commentary 99–182*. Leiden.

——— 1990. "Herodotus on Egyptians and Libyans." In *Hérodote et les Peuples non Grecs*. Fondation Hardt pour l'étude de l'antiquité classique. Entretiens 35. Geneva. 215–44.

Lloyd, G. E. R. 1987. *The Revolutions of Wisdom: Studies in the Claims and Practice of Ancient Greek Science*. Berkeley and Los Angeles.

Lloyd-Jones, H. 1983. *The Justice of Zeus*. 2d ed. Berkeley and Los Angeles.

Lobel, E., and D. Page, eds. 1955. *Poetarum Lesbiorum Fragmenta*. Oxford.

Lombardo, M. 1989. "Oro lidio e oro persiano nelle Storie di Erodoto." *REA* 91, 1-2: 197–208.

——— 1990. "Erodoto storico dei Lidî." In *Hérodote et les Peuples non Grecs*. Fondation Hardt pour l'étude de l'antiquité classique. Entretiens 35. Geneva. 171–203.

Long, A. A. 1996. "The Socratic Tradition: Diogenes, Crates, and Hellenistic Ethics." In Branham and Goulet-Cazé 1996: 28–46.

Loraux, N. 1986. *The Invention of Athens: The Funeral Oration in the Classical City*. Trans. A. Sheridan. Cambridge, Mass.

——— 1993. *The Children of Athena: Athenian Ideas about Citizenship and the Division between the Sexes*. Trans. Caroline Levine. Princeton.

Lord, C., trans. 1984. *Aristotle, "The Politics."* Chicago and London.

Lord, L. E. 1937. "The Touchstone." *CJ* 32: 428–31.

Luke, J. 1994. "The Krater, *Kratos*, and the *Polis.*" *G&R* 41: 23–32.

MacGinnis, J. 1986. "Herodotus' Description of Babylon." *BICS* 33: 67–86.

Macherey, P. 1978. *A Theory of Literary Production.* London.

Mack, R. 1996. "Ordering the Body and Embodying Order: The Kouros in Archaic Greek Society." Ph.D. dissertation, University of California, Berkeley.

Maehler, H., ed. 1982. *Die Lieder des Bakchylides. Erster Teil: Die Siegeslieder.* Mnemosyne Supplement 62. 2 vols. Leiden.

Marcovich, M. 1967. *Heraclitus, editio maior.* Merida, Venezuela.

Marg, W. 1965. *Herodot: Eine Auswahl aus der neueren Forschung.* 2d ed. Munich.

Markoe, G. E. 1989. "The 'Lion Attack' in Archaic Greek Art." *CA* 8: 86–115.

Martin, R. P. 1984. "Hesiod, Odysseus, and the Instruction of Princes." *TAPA* 114: 29–48.

———— 1989. *The Language of Heroes: Speech and Performance in the* "*Iliad.*" Ithaca.

———— 1992. "Hesiod's Metanastic Poetics." *Ramus* 21.1: 11–33.

———— 1993. "The Seven Sages as Performers of Wisdom." In Dougherty and Kurke 1993: 108–28.

———— 1996. "The Scythian Accent: Anacharsis and the Cynics." In Branham and Goulet-Cazé 1996: 136–55.

Martin, Roland. 1951. *Recherches sur l'agora grecque.* Paris.

Martin, T. R. 1985. *Sovereignty and Coinage in Classical Greece.* Princeton.

———— 1996. "Why Did the Greek *Polis* Originally Need Coins?" *Historia* 45: 257–83.

Masson, O. 1962. *Les Fragments du poète Hipponax: Edition critique et commentée.* Etudes et Commentaires 43. Paris.

Mastrocostas, N. 1954. "Phocide." In "Chronique des Fouilles et Découvertes Archéologiques en Grèce en 1953." *BCH* 78: 95–224.

Mau, A. 1896. "Ἀστράγαλος." *RE* vol. 2.2, coll. 1793–95.

Maurizio, L. 1997. "Delphic Oracles as Oral Performances: Authenticity and Historical Evidence." *CA* 16: 308–34.

Mauss, M. 1967. *The Gift: Forms and Functions of Exchange in Archaic Societies.* Trans. I. Cunnison. New York.

Mazzarino, S. 1947. *Fra oriente e occidente: Ricerche di storia greca arcaica.* Florence.

McGlew, J. F. 1993. *Tyranny and Political Culture in Ancient Greece.* Ithaca.

McKay, K. J. 1961a. "Studies in *AITHON* II: Theognis 1209–1216." *Mnemosyne* 14.1: 16–22.

———— 1961b. "The Griphos: A Vindication." *CQ* (n.s. 11): 6–8.

McNeal, R. A. 1988. "The Brides of Babylon: Herodotus 1.196." *Historia* 37: 54–71.

Meiggs, R. 1972. *The Athenian Empire.* Oxford.

Meikle, S. 1979. "Aristotle and the Political Economy of the Polis." *JHS* 99: 57–73.

———— 1995. *Aristotle's Economic Thought.* Oxford.

Mele, A. 1979. *Il Commercio greco arcaico: Prexis ed Emporie.* Naples.

Melville Jones, J. R. 1993. *Testimonia Numaria: Greek and Latin Texts concerning Ancient Greek Coinage*. Vol. 1. London.

Mendner, S. 1956. *Das Ballspiel im Leben der Völker*. Münster.

Merkelbach, R. 1956. "Literarische Texte unter Ausschluss der Christlichen." *Archiv für Papyrusforschung* 16: 82–129.

Merkelbach, R., and M. L. West. 1967. *Fragmenta Hesiodea*. Oxford.

Michaels, W. B. 1987. *The Gold Standard and the Logic of Naturalism: American Literature at the Turn of the Century*. Berkeley and Los Angeles.

Michon, E. 1877. "Pondus." In *Dictionnaire des antiquités Grecques et Romaines*, ed. C. Daremberg and E. Saglio. Paris. Vol. 4, 1.548–59.

Miller, M. C. 1989. "The *Ependytes* in Classical Athens." *Hesperia* 58: 313–29.

——— 1992. "The Parasol: An Oriental Status-Symbol in Late Archaic and Classical Athens." *JHS* 112: 91–105.

——— 1997. *Athens and Persia in the Fifth Century BC: A Study in Cultural Receptivity*. Cambridge.

Millett, P. 1984. "Hesiod and his World." *PCPS* 210 (n.s. 30): 84–115.

——— 1991. *Lending and Borrowing in Ancient Athens*. Cambridge.

Mingazzini, P. 1950–51. "Sulla pretesa funzione oracolare del kottabos." *Archäologischer Anzeiger* 65-66: 35–47.

Miralles, C., and J. Pòrtulas. 1983. *Archilochus and the Iambic Poetry*. Rome.

Mitchell, B. M. 1975. "Herodotus and Samos." *JHS* 95: 75–91.

Momigliano, A. 1958. "The Place of Herodotus in the History of Historiography." *Historia* 43: 1–13. Rept. in *Secondo contributo alla storia degli studi classici* (Rome, 1960), 29–44.

——— 1971. *The Development of Greek Biography*. Cambridge, Mass.

——— 1975. *Alien Wisdom: The Limits of Hellenization*. Cambridge.

——— 1979. "Persian Empire and Greek Freedom." In *The Idea of Freedom: Essays in Honour of Isaiah Berlin*, ed. A. Ryan. Oxford.

Morris, I. 1986a. "Gift and Commodity in Archaic Greece." *Man* 21: 1–17.

——— 1986b. "The Use and Abuse of Homer." *CA* 5: 81–138.

——— 1987. *Burial and Ancient Society: The Rise of the Greek City-State*. Cambridge.

——— 1989. "Circulation, Deposition and the Formation of the Greek Iron Age." *Man* 24: 502–19.

——— 1993. Review of Millett, *Lending and Borrowing in Ancient Athens*. *CP* 88: 340–46.

——— 1996. "The Strong Principle of Equality and the Archaic Origins of Greek Democracy." In Ober and Hedrick 1996: 19–48.

——— 1998. "Archaeology and Archaic Greek History." In *Archaic Greece: New Evidence and New Approaches*, ed. N. Fisher and H. von Wees. London. 1–91.

Morris, S. P. 1997. "Greek and Near Eastern Art in the Age of Homer." In *New Light on a Dark Age: Exploring the Culture of Geometric Greece*, ed. S. Langdon. Columbia, Mo. 56–71.

Morris, S. P., and J. K. Papadopoulos. Forthcoming. "Of Granaries and Games: Egyptian Stowaways in an Athenian Chest." In *Festschrift for Sara A. Immerwahr*. Hesperia Supplement. Ed. A. Chapin.

Mossé, C. 1979. "Comment s'élabore un mythe politique: Solon, 'père fondateur' de la démocratie athénienne." *Annales ESC* 34: 425–37.

Most, G. W. 1982. "Greek Lyric Poets." In *Ancient Writers: Greece and Rome*, ed. T. J. Luce. New York. Vol. 1.75–98.

Mullen, W. 1982. *Choreia: Pindar and Dance*. Princeton.

Munson, R. V. 1991. "The Madness of Cambyses (Herodotus 3.16–38)." *Arethusa* 24: 43–63.

Murnaghan, S. 1988. "How a Woman Can Be More Like a Man: The Dialogue between Ischomachus and His Wife in Xenophon's *Oeconomicus*." *Helios* 15, 1: 9–22.

Murray, H.J.R. 1952. *A History of Board-Games Other Than Chess*. Oxford.

Murray, O. 1983. "The Greek Symposion in History." In *Tria Corda: Scritti in onore di Arnaldo Momigliano*, ed. E. Gabba. Como. 257–72.

———— 1987. "Herodotus and Oral History." In *Achaemenid History II: The Greek Sources*. Proceedings of the Groningen 1984 Achaemenid History Workshop, ed. H. Sancisi-Weerdenburg and A. Kuhrt. Leiden. 93–115.

———— ed. 1990a. *Sympotica: A Symposium on the Symposion*. Oxford.

———— 1990b. "Sympotic History." In Murray 1990a: 3–13.

———— 1991. "War and the Symposium." In Slater 1991: 83–103.

———— 1995. "Forms of Sociality." In Vernant 1995: 218–53.

Musti, D. 1983. "Eraclito e i *chremata* del fr. 90 D.-K." In Rossetti 1983: 231–40.

Nafissi, M. 1983. "Anakreonte, i Tonea e la corona di lyges." *PdP* 38: 417–39.

Nagy, G. 1979. *The Best of the Achaeans: Concepts of the Hero in Archaic Greek Poetry*. Baltimore.

———— 1985. "Theognis and Megara: A Poet's Vision of His City." In Figueira and Nagy 1985: 22–81.

———— 1990a. *Greek Mythology and Poetics*. Ithaca.

———— 1990b. *Pindar's Homer: The Lyric Possession of an Epic Past*. Baltimore.

Neer, R. T. 1998. "*PAMPOIKILOS*: Representation, Style, and Ideology in Attic Red-Figure." Unpublished Ph.D. dissertation, University of California, Berkeley.

Nestle, W. 1938. "Phaleas." *RE* vol. 19.2, coll. 1658–59.

Nimis, S. 1988. "Aristotle's Analogical Metaphor." *Arethusa* 21: 215–26.

Noethlichs, K. L. 1987. "Bestechung, Bestechlichkeit und die Rolle des Geldes im der spartanischen Aussen- und Innenpolitik vom 7.–2. Jh. v. Chr." *Historia* 36: 129–70.

Ober, J. 1989. *Mass and Elite in Democratic Athens: Rhetoric, Ideology, and the Power of the People*. Princeton.

———— 1993. "The Athenian Revolution of 508/7 B.C.E.: Violence, Authority, and the Origins of Democracy." In Dougherty and Kurke 1993: 215–32.

———— 1998. *Political Dissent in Democratic Athens: Intellectual Critics of Popular Rule*. Princeton.

Ober, J., and B. Strauss. 1990. "Drama, Political Rhetoric, and the Discourse of Athenian Democracy." In Winkler and Zeitlin 1990: 237–70.

Ober, J., and C. Hedrick, eds. 1996. *Dēmokratia: A Conversation on Democracies, Ancient and Modern*. Princeton.

Ogden, D. 1997. *The Crooked Kings of Ancient Greece*. London.

Oost, S. I. 1972. "Cypselus the Bacchiad." *CP* 67: 10–30.

Ostwald, M. 1969. *Nomos and the Beginnings of the Athenian Democracy*. Oxford.

Padel, R. 1992. *In and Out of the Mind: Greek Images of the Tragic Self*. Princeton.

Page, D. L. 1955. *Sappho and Alcaeus: An Introduction to the Study of Ancient Lesbian Poetry*. Oxford.

——— ed. 1962. *Poetae Melici Graeci*. Oxford.

——— 1966. "Anacreon and Megistes." *Wiener Studien* 79: 27–32.

Parise, N. 1970. "Note per una discussione sulle origini della moneta." *Studi miscellanei* 15: 5–12.

Parke, H. W. 1977. *Festivals of the Athenians*. Ithaca.

Parry, J. 1986. "*The Gift*, the Indian Gift and the 'Indian Gift,' " *Man* (n.s. 21): 453–73.

Parry, J., and M. Bloch, eds. 1989. *Money and the Morality of Exchange*. Cambridge.

Pászthory, E. 1979. "Zwei Kleinmünzen aus Athen." *Schweizer Münzblätter* 29: 1–7.

Pavese, C. O. 1995. "Elegia di Simonide agli Spartiati per Platea." *ZPE* 107: 1–26.

Payne, H., and G. Mackworth-Young. 1950. *Archaic Marble Sculpture from the Acropolis*. 2d ed. New York.

Pedley, G. 1968. *Sardis in the Age of Croesus*. Norman, Okla.

Pembroke, S. 1965. "Last of the Matriarchs: A Study in the Inscriptions of Lycia." *Journal of the Economic and Social History of the Orient*. Vol. 8, Pt. 3: 217–47.

——— 1967. "Women in Charge: The Function of Alternatives in Early Greek Tradition and the Ancient Idea of Matriarchy." *Journal of the Warburg and Courtauld Institutes* 30: 1–35.

Peppas-Delmousou, D. 1960–61. "Gli stateri falsi nelle iscrizioni attiche." *Annale dell' Istituto Italiano di Numismatica* 7-8: 25–34.

Peschel, I. 1987. *Die Hetäre bei Symposion und Komos in der attisch-rotfigurigen Vasenmalerei des 6.–4. Jahrhunderts vor Christus*. Frankfurt am Main.

Picard, C. 1929. "Les Antécédents des 'Astragalizontes' polyclétéens, et la consultation par les dés." *REG* 42: 121–36.

Picard, O. 1980. "Aristote et la monnaie." *Ktema* 5: 267–76.

Pleket, H. W. 1969. "The Archaic Tyrannis." *Talanta* 1: 19–61.

Polanyi, K. 1968. *Primitive, Archaic, and Modern Economies: Essays of Karl Polanyi*, ed. G. Dalton. Garden City, N.Y.

Polanyi, K., C. M. Arensberg, and H. W. Pearson, eds. 1957. *Trade and Market in the Early Empires*. Chicago.

Powell, J. E. 1938. *A Lexicon to Herodotus*. Cambridge.

Price, M., and N. Waggoner. 1975. *Archaic Greek Silver Coinage: The "Asyut" Hoard*. London.

Price, M. J. 1968. "Early Greek Bronze Coinage." In *Essays in Greek Coinage Presented to Stanley Robinson*, ed. C. M. Kraay and G. K. Jenkins. Oxford. 90–104.

—— 1979. "The Function of Early Greek Bronze Coinage." In *Le origini della monetazione di bronzo in Sicilia e in Magna Grecia*. Atti del VI Convegno del Centro Internazionale di Studi Numismatici (Napoli 17–22 Aprile 1977). Rome. 351–65.

—— 1983. "Thoughts on the Beginnings of Coinage." In *Studies in Numismatic Method Presented to Philip Grierson*, ed. C.N.L. Brooke, B.H.I.H. Stewart, J. G. Pollard, and T. R. Volk. Cambridge. 1–10.

—— 1993. "More from Memphis, and the Syria 1989 Hoard." In *Essays in Honour of Robert Carson and Kenneth Jenkins*, ed. M. J. Price, A. Burnett, and R. Bland. London. 31–35.

Pritchett, W. K. 1968. " 'Five Lines' and *IG* I², 324." *California Studies in Classical Antiquity* 1: 187–215.

—— 1993. *The Liar School of Herodotos*. Amsterdam.

Raaflaub, K. A. 1979. "*Polis Tyrannos*: Zur Entstehung einer historischen Metapher." In *Arktouros: Hellenic Studies presented to Bernard M. W. Knox*, ed. G. W. Bowersock, W. Burkert, and M. C. J. Putnam. Berlin and New York. 237–52.

—— 1987. "Herodotus, Political Thought, and the Meaning of History." *Arethusa* 20: 221–48.

Ramnoux, C. 1968. *Héraclite, ou l'homme entre les choses et les mots*. 2d ed. Paris.

Ravn, O. 1942. *Herodotus' Description of Babylon*. Trans. M. Tovborg-Jensen. Copenhagen.

Redfield, J. M. 1975. *Nature and Culture in the "Iliad"*. Chicago.

—— 1985. "Herodotus the Tourist." *CP* 80: 97–118.

—— 1987. "Commentary on Humphreys and Raaflaub." *Arethusa* 20: 249–53.

Regenbogen, O. 1965. "Die Geschichte von Solon und Krösus. Eine Studie zur Geistesgeschichte des 5. und 6. Jahrhunderts." In Marg 1965: 375–403.

Regling, K. 1931. "*Subaeratus*." *RE* 4.A.I, coll. 471–74.

Reinhardt, K. 1960. "Herodots Persergeschichten. Östliches und Westliches im Übergang von Sage zu Geschichte." In *Vermächtnis der Antike: Gesammelte Essays zur Philosophie und Geschichtsschreibung*. Göttingen. 133–74.

Reinsberg, C. 1989. *Ehe, Hetärentum und Knabenliebe im antiken Griechenland*. Munich.

Reiss, A. 1896. "*Astragalomanteia*." *RE* vol. 2.2., col. 1793.

Reitzenstein, R. 1893. *Epigramm und Skolion: Ein Beitrag zur Geschichte der alexandrinischen Dichtung*. Giessen.

Rhodes, P. J. 1981. *A Commentary on the Aristotelian "Athenaion Politeia"*. Oxford.

Richlin, A. ed. 1992. *Pornography and Representation in Greece and Rome*. Oxford.

Riverso, E. 1983. "Eraclito, fr. 90 D.-K." In Rossetti 1983: 213–30.

Robert, J., and L. Robert. 1955. "Bulletin Épigraphique." *REG* 68: 185–298.

Robert, L. 1951. *Études de numismatique grecque*. Paris.

Robert, L. 1962. "Monnaies dans les inscriptions grecques." *Revue numismatique* (ser. 6), vol. 4: 7–24.

Robertson, M. 1975. *A History of Greek Art*. Cambridge.

———— 1992. *The Art of Vase-Painting in Classical Athens*. Cambridge.

Robinson, D. M., and E. J. Fluck. 1937. *A Study of the Greek Love-Names Including a Discussion of Paederasty and A Prosopographia*. Johns Hopkins University Studies in Archaeology, no. 23. Baltimore.

Robinson, E.S.G. 1951. "The Coins from the Ephesian Artemision Reconsidered." *JHS* 71: 156–67.

———— 1956. "The Date of the Earliest Coins." *NC* (ser. 6) 16: 1–8.

———— 1960. "Some Problems in the Later Fifth Century Coinage of Athens." *American Numismatic Society Museum Notes* 9: 1–16.

Robinson, E. W. 1997. *The First Democracies: Early Popular Government outside Athens*. Historia Einzelschriften. Vol. 107. Stuttgart.

Rösler, W. 1980. *Dichter und Gruppe: Eine Untersuchung zu den Bedingungen und zur historischen Funktion früher griechischer Lyrik am Beispiel Alkaios*. Munich.

Rollinger, R. 1993. *Herodots babylonischer Logos: Eine kritische Untersuchung der Glaubwürdigkeitsdiskussion*. Innsbrucker Beiträge zur Kulturwissenschaft, Supplement 84. Innsbruck.

Romm, J. 1992. *The Edges of the Earth in Ancient Thought: Geography, Exploration, and Fiction*. Princeton.

———— 1996. "Dog Heads and Noble Savages: Cynicism before the Cynics?" In Branham and Goulet-Cazé 1996: 121–35.

Root, M. C. 1979. *The King and Kingship in Achaemenid Art: Essays on the Creation of an Iconography of Empire*. Acta Iranica 19. Leiden.

———— 1989. "The Persian Archer at Persepolis: Aspects of Chronology, Style and Symbolism." *REA* 91, 1-2: 33–50.

———— 1991. "From the Heart: Powerful Persianisms in the Art of the Western Empire." In *Achaemenid History VI. Asia Minor and Egypt: Old Cultures in a New Empire*. Proceedings of the Groningen 1988 Achaemenid History Workshop, ed. H. Sancisi-Weerdenburg and A. Kuhrt. 1–29.

Rose, P. W. 1992. *Sons of the Gods, Children of Earth: Ideology and Literary Form in Ancient Greece*. Ithaca.

Rosellini, M., and S. Saïd. 1978. "Usages de femmes et autres *nomoi* chez les 'sauvages' d'Hérodote: Essai de lecture structurale." *ASNP*, ser. 3, 8: 949–1005.

Rosen, R. M. 1989. "Euboulos' *Ankylion* and the Game of Kottabos." *CQ* 39: 355–59.

Rosen, R. M., and J. Farrell, eds. 1993. *Nomodeiktes: Greek Studies in Honor of Martin Ostwald*. Ann Arbor.

Rosenmeyer, P. A. 1992. *The Poetics of Imitation: Anacreon and the Anacreontic Tradition*. Cambridge.

Rossetti, L., ed. 1983. *Atti del Symposium Heracliteum 1981*. Rome.

Rossi, L. E. 1971. "I generi letterari e le loro leggi scritte e non scritte nelle letterature classiche." *BICS* 18: 69–94.

Rumpf, A. 1953. "Zu einer Vase der Sammlung Robinson." *Studies Presented to David Moore Robinson*, ed. G. E. Mylonas and D. Raymond. Vol. 2.84–89.

Russo, J., M. Fernández-Galiano, and A. Heubeck, eds. 1992. *A Commentary on Homer's Odyssey*. Vol. III. Books XVII–XXIV. Oxford.

Rutter, K. 1981. "Early Greek Coinage and the Influence of the Athenian State." In *Coinage and Society in Britain and Gaul: Some Current Problems*, ed. B. Cunliffe. London. 1–9.

Sahlins, M. 1972. *Stone Age Economics*. New York.

——— 1976. *Culture and Practical Reason*. Chicago.

Said, E. W. 1978. *Orientalism*. New York.

Ste. Croix, G.E.M. de. 1977. "Herodotus." *G&R* (n.s. 24): 130–48.

Ste. Croix, G.E.M. de. 1981. *The Class Struggle in the Ancient Greek World from the Archaic Age to the Arab Conquests*. Ithaca.

Sancisi-Weerdenburg, H. 1989. "Gifts in the Persian empire." In Briant and Herrenschmidt 1989: 129–46.

Sandys, J. E., ed. 1912. *Aristotle's "Constitution of Athens."* London.

Sartori, K. 1893. *Studien aus dem Gebiete der griechischen Privataltertümer*. I. *Das Kottabos-Spiel der alten Griechen*. Munich.

Saxonhouse, A. W. 1996. *Athenian Democracy: Modern Mythmakers and Ancient Theorists*. Notre Dame and London.

Sayce, A. H., ed. 1883. *The Ancient Empires of the East: Herodotos I–III*. London.

Schmitt-Pantel, P. 1979. "Histoire de tyran ou comment la cité grecque construit ses marges." In *Les Marginaux et les exclus dans l'histoire*. Paris. 217–31.

——— 1990. "Sacrificial Meal and *Symposion*: Two Models of Civic Institutions in the Archaic City?" In Murray 1990a: 14–33.

——— 1992. *La cité au banquet: Histoire des repas public dans les cités grecques*. Paris and Rome.

Schneider, K. 1913. "*Hetairai*." *RE* vol. 8.2, coll. 1331–72.

——— 1922. "*Kottabos*." *RE* vol. 11.2, coll. 1528–41.

Schottlaender, R. 1965. "Heraklits angeblicher Aristokratismus." *Klio* 43-45: 23–27.

Schrader, H., and E. Langlotz. 1939. *Die archaischen Marmorbildwerke der Akropolis*. 2 vols. Frankfurt am Main.

Scodel, R. 1979. "'Ἀδμήτου λόγος and the *Alcestis*." *HSCP* 83: 51–62.

——— 1984. "The Irony of Fate in Bacchylides 17." *Hermes* 112: 137–43.

Seaford, R. 1994. *Reciprocity and Ritual: Homer and Tragedy in the Developing City-State*. Oxford.

Sebeok, T., and E. Brady. 1979. "The Two Sons of Croesus: A Myth about Communication in Herodotus." *QUCC* 30: 7–22.

Segal, C. P. 1971. "Croesus on the Pyre: Herodotus and Bacchylides." *Wiener Studien* 84: 39–51.

——— 1976. "Bacchylides Reconsidered: Epithets and the Dynamics of Lyric Narrative." *QUCC* 22: 99–130.

——— 1979. "The Myth of Bacchylides 17." *Eranos* 77: 23–37.

Seltman, C. T. 1938. "Diogenes of Sinope, Son of the Banker Hikesias." In *Transactions of the International Numismatic Congress (1936)*, ed. J. Allan, H. Mattingly, and E. S. G. Robinson. London. 121.

Serrao, G. 1968. "L'ode di Erotima: Da timida fanciulla a donna pubblica (Anacr. fr. 346, 1 P. = 60 Gent.)." *QUCC* 6: 36–51.

Shapiro, H. A. 1981. "Courtship Scenes in Attic Vase Painting." *AJA* 85: 133–43.

——— 1983. "Epilykos Kalos." *Hesperia* 52: 305–10.

—— 1987. "Kalos-Inscriptions with Patronymic." *ZPE* 68: 107–18.

—— 1989. *Art and Cult under the Tyrants at Athens.* Mainz.

—— 1992. "Eros in Love: Pederasty and Pornography in Greece." In Richlin 1992: 53–72.

Shell, M. 1978. *The Economy of Literature.* Baltimore.

—— 1982. *Money, Language, and Thought: Literary and Philosophical Economies from the Medieval to the Modern Era.* Berkeley and Los Angeles.

Shimron, B. 1979. "Ein Wortspiel mit Homoioi bei Herodot." *RhM* 122: 131–33.

Shipley, G. 1987. *A History of Samos, 800–188 BC.* Oxford.

Simmel, G. 1978. *The Philosophy of Money.* Trans. T. Bottomore and D. Frisby. Boston, London.

Simon, C. G. 1986. "The Archaic Votive Offerings and Cults of Ionia." Ph.D. dissertation, University of California, Berkeley.

Sinos, R. H. 1993. "Divine Selection: Epiphany and Politics in Archaic Greece." In Dougherty and Kurke 1993: 73–91.

Slater, W. J. 1978. "Artemon and Anacreon: No Text without Context." *Phoenix* 32: 185–94.

—— 1984. "Nemean One: The Victor's Return in Poetry and Politics." In *Greek Poetry and Philosophy: Studies in Honour of Leonard Woodbury,* ed. D. E. Gerber. Chico, Calif. 241–64.

—— ed. 1991. *Dining in a Classical Context.* Ann Arbor.

Smith, N. 1989. "Intervention" to Lombardo 1989. *REA* 91, 1–2: 208–12.

Smyth, H. W. 1956. *Greek Grammar.* Rev. G. M. Messing. Cambridge, Mass.

—— 1963. *Greek Melic Poets.* New York.

Snell, B. 1948. *Die Entdeckung des Geistes.* Hamburg.

—— 1953. *The Discovery of the Mind.* Trans. T. G. Rosenmeyer. New York. Rept. New York, 1982.

Snell, B., and H. Maehler, eds. 1970. *Bacchylidis Carmina cum Fragmentis.* 10th ed. Leipzig.

—— 1975. *Pindarus. Pars II. Fragmenta. Indices.* 4th ed. Leipzig.

Snodgrass, A. 1980. *Archaic Greece: The Age of Experiment.* London.

Snyder, J. M. 1974. "Aristophanes' Agathon as Anacreon." *Hermes* 102: 244–46.

Sourvinou-Inwood, C. 1991. " 'Myth' and History: On Herodotus 3.48 and 3.50–53." In *"Reading" Greek Culture: Texts and Images, Rituals and Myths.* Oxford. 244–84.

Sparkes, B. A. 1960. "Kottabos: An Athenian After-Dinner Game." *Archaeology* 13: 202–7.

Stallybrass, P., and A. White. 1986. *The Politics and Poetics of Transgression.* Ithaca.

Stambler, S. 1982. "Herodotus." In *Ancient Writers: Greece and Rome,* ed. T. J. Luce. New York. Vol. 1.209–32.

Stanford, W. B., ed. 1971. *The "Odyssey" of Homer.* 2 vols. 2d ed. New York.

Starobinski, J. 1975. "The Inside and the Outside." *Hudson Review* 28: 333–51.

Starr, C. G. 1992. *The Aristocratic Temper of Greek Civilization.* Oxford.

Stehle, E. 1996. "Help Me to Sing, Muse, of Plataea." *Arethusa* 29, 2: 205–22.

—— 1997. *Peformance and Gender in Ancient Greece: Nondramatic Poetry in Its Setting.* Princeton.

Stein-Hölkeskamp, E. 1989. *Adelskultur und Polis-gesellschaft: Studien zum griechischen Adel in archaischer und klassischer Zeit.* Stuttgart.

Steiner, D. T. 1994. *The Tyrant's Writ: Myths and Images of Writing in Ancient Greece.* Princeton.

Stern, J. 1989. "Demythologization in Herodotus: 5.92.η." *Eranos* 87: 13–20.

Stewart, A. F. 1978. "Lysippan Studies 1: The Only Creator of Beauty." *AJA* 82: 163–71.

——— 1986. "When Is a Kouros Not an Apollo?: The Tenea 'Apollo' Revisited." In *Corinthiaca: Studies in Honor of Darrell A. Amyx,* ed. M. A. Del Chiaro. Columbia, Mo. 54–70.

——— 1997. *Art, Desire, and the Body in Ancient Greece.* Cambridge.

Strasburger, H. 1965. "Herodot und das perikleische Athen." In Marg 1965: 574–608.

Strøm, I. 1992. "Obeloi of Pre- or Proto-monetary Value in Greek Sanctuaries." In *Economics of Cult in the Ancient World,* ed. T. Linders and B. Alroth. Boreas 21. Uppsala. 41–51.

Stroud, R. S. 1974. "An Athenian Law on Silver Coinage," *Hesperia* 43: 157–88.

Sutton, R. F., Jr. 1981. "The Interaction between Men and Women Portrayed on Attic Red-figure Pottery." Ph.D. diss. UNC Chapel Hill. UMI.

Svenbro, J. 1976. *La Parole et le marbre: Aux origines de la poétique grecque.* Lund.

——— 1982. "A Mégara Hyblaea: Le Corps géomètre." *Annales ESC* 37, no. 5–6: 953–64.

Szegedy-Maszak, A. 1978. "Legends of the Greek Lawgivers." *GRBS* 19: 199–209.

Taillardat, J., ed. 1967. *Suétone. ΠΕΡΙ ΒΛΑΣΦΗΜΙΩΝ. ΠΕΡΙ ΠΑΙΔΙΩΝ.* Paris.

Talamo, C. 1961. "Per le origini dell' eteria arcaica." *PdP* 16: 297–303.

Taussig, M. 1980. *The Devil and Commodity Fetishism in South America.* Chapel Hill, N.C.

Taylor, C. 1989. *Sources of the Self: The Making of the Modern Identity.* Cambridge, Mass.

Tedeschi, G. 1982. "Solone e lo spazio della communicazione elegiaca." *QUCC* (n.s. 10): 33–46.

Thomas, R. 1989. *Oral Tradition and Written Record in Classical Athens.* Cambridge.

——— 1992. *Literacy and Orality in Ancient Greece.* Cambridge.

Thompson, D. L. 1976. "Exekias and the *Brettspieler.*" *Archeologia classica* 28: 30–39.

Thompson, N. 1996. *Herodotus and the Origins of Political Community: Arion's Leap.* New Haven, Conn.

Thompson, W. E. 1970. "The Golden Nikai and the Coinage of Athens." *NC* (ser. 7), vol. 10: 1–6.

Thomson, G. 1955. *Studies in Ancient Greek Society.* Vol. II: *The First Philosophers.* London.

Thür, G. 1977. *Beweisführung vor den Schwurgerichtshöfen Athens: Die Proklesis zur Basanos.* Österreichische Akademie der Wissenschaften, Phil.-Hist. Klasse, Sitzungsberichte, vol. 317. Vienna.

Tourraix, A. 1976. "La Femme et le pouvoir chez Hérodote." *Dialogues d'histoire ancienne* 1: 369–90.

Tréheux, J. 1958. "Le Sens des adjectifs ΠΕΡΙΖΥΞ et ΠΕΡΙΖΥΓΟΣ." *Revue de Philologie* 32: 84–91.

Treu, G. 1897. *Die Bildwerke von Olympia in Stein und Ton* (= *Olympia, Die Ergebnisse* etc. III) Berlin.

Trumpf, J. 1973. "Über das Trinken in der Poesie des Alkaios." *ZPE* 12: 139–60.

Tuplin, C. 1989. "The Coinage of Aryandes." *REA* 91, 1-2: 61–83.

Ure, P. 1962. *The Origin of Tyranny*. New York.

van der Valk, M., ed. 1971–1987. *Eustathii Commentarii ad Homeri "Iliadem" Pertinentes*. 4 vols. Leiden.

van der Veen, J. E. 1993. "The Lord of the Ring: Narrative Technique in Herodotus' Story of Polycrates' Ring." *Mnemosyne* 46, 4: 433–57.

———— 1995. "A Minute's Mirth: Syloson and His Cloak in Herodotus." *Menmosyne* 48, 2: 129–45.

van Groningen, B. A. 1966. *Theognis: Le Premier Livre*. Amsterdam.

Vansina, J. 1985. *Oral Tradition as History*. London and Nairobi.

Vermeule, E. 1979. *Aspects of Death in Early Greek Art and Poetry*. Berkeley and Los Angeles.

Vernant, J.-P. 1980. *Myth and Society in Ancient Greece*. Trans. J. Lloyd. Brighton, Sussex.

———— 1982. *The Origins of Greek Thought*. Ithaca.

———— 1983. *Myth and Thought among the Greeks*. London.

———— 1988. "Ambiguity and Reversal: On the Enigmatic Structure of Oedipus Rex." In Vernant and Vidal-Naquet 1988: 113–40, 427–39.

———— 1989. "Food in the Countries of the Sun." In Detienne and Vernant 1989: 164–69.

———— 1991. "Speech and Mute Signs." In *Mortals and Immortals: Collected Essays*, ed. F. I. Zeitlin. 303–17.

————. ed. 1995. *The Greeks*. Trans. C. Lambert and T. L. Fagan. Chicago.

Vernant, J.-P., and P. Vidal-Naquet. 1969. "Tensions and Ambiguities in Greek Tragedy." In *Interpretation: Theory and Practice*, ed. C. S. Singleton. Baltimore. 105–21.

Vernant, J.-P., and P. Vidal-Naquet. 1988. *Myth and Tragedy in Ancient Greece*. Trans. J. Lloyd. New York.

Versnel, H. S. 1977. "Polycrates and His Ring: Two Neglected Aspects." *Studi storico-religiosi* 1: 17–46.

Vetta, M., ed. 1980. *Theognis: Elegiarum Liber Secundus*. Rome.

Vickers, M. 1985. "Early Greek Coinage, a Reassessment." *NC* 145: 1–44.

Vidal-Naquet, P. 1986. "A Study in Ambiguity: Artisans in the Platonic City." In *The Black Hunter: Forms of Thought and Forms of Society in the Greek World*. Trans. A. Szegedy-Maszak. Baltimore. 224–45.

Vlastos, G. 1946. "Solonian Justice." *CP* 41: 65–83.

———— 1953. "Isonomia." *AJP* 74: 337–66.

———— [1947] 1970. "Equality and Justice in Early Greek Cosmologies." *CP* 42: 156–78. Rept., in Furley and Allen 1970: 56–91.

Voigt, E.-M., ed. 1971. *Sappho et Alcaeus Fragmenta*. Amsterdam.

Volkmann, H. 1939. "ΔΟΚΙΜΑ ΧΡΗΜΑΤΑ." *Hermes* 74: 99–102.

von Reden, S. 1995. *Exchange in Ancient Greece.* London.

—— 1997. "Money, Law and Exchange: Coinage in the Greek Polis." *JHS* 117: 154–76.

Wallace, R. W. 1987. "The Origin of Electrum Coinage," *AJA* 91: 385–97.

—— 1988. "WALWE. and .KALI." *JHS* 108: 203–7.

Wallinga, H. T. 1991. "Polycrates and Egypt: The Testimony of the Samaina." In *Achaemenid History VI. Asia Minor and Egypt: Old Cultures in a New Empire.* Proceedings of the Groningen 1988 Achaemenid History Workshop, ed. H. Sancisi-Weerdenburg and A. Kuhrt. Leiden. 179–97.

Waters, K. H. 1971. *Herodotos on Tyrants and Despots: A Study in Objectivity.* Historia Einzelschriften 15. Wiesbaden.

—— 1985. *Herodotos the Historian: His Problems, Methods and Originality.* Norman, Okla.

Weidauer, L. 1975. *Probleme der frühen Elektronprägung. Typos,* vol. 1. Fribourg.

Wells, J. 1923. "The Persian Friends of Herodotus." In *Studies in Herodotus.* Oxford. 95–112.

West, M. L. 1974. *Studies in Greek Elegy and Iambus.* Berlin, New York.

—— ed. 1978. *Hesiod Works and Days.* Oxford.

—— ed. 1989. *Iambi et Elegi Graeci.* Vol. 1. 2d ed. Oxford.

—— ed. 1992. *Iambi et Elegi Graeci.* Vol. 2. 2d ed. Oxford.

—— trans. 1994. *Greek Lyric Poetry.* Oxford.

West, S. 1985. "Herodotus' Epigraphical Interests." *CQ* (n.s. 35): 278–305.

Wilamowitz-Moellendorff, U. von. 1884. *Homerische Untersuchungen. Philologische Untersuchungen,* vol. 7. Berlin.

—— 1913. *Sappho und Simonides: Untersuchungen über griechische Lyriker.* Berlin.

—— 1922. *Pindaros.* Berlin.

Wiles, D. 1989. "Marriage and Prostitution in Classical New Comedy." In *Themes in Drama 11: Women in Theatre,* ed. J. Redmond. Cambridge. 31–48.

Will, E. 1954. "De l'aspect éthique des origines grecques de la monnaie." *Revue historique* 212: 209–31.

—— 1955a. *Korinthiaka: Recherches sur l'histoire et la civilisation de Corinthe des origines aux guerres médiques.* Paris.

—— 1955b. "Réflexions et hypothèses sur les origines de la monnaie." *Revue de numismatique* 17: 5–23.

—— 1975. "Fonctions de la monnaie dans les cités grecques de l'époque classique." In *Numismatique antique, problèmes et methodes.* Nancy and Louvain. 233–46.

—— 1988. "Review of Thomas R. Martin, *Sovereignty and Coinage in Classical Greece." Echos du monde classique/Classical Views* 32 (n.s. 7): 417–20.

Will, F. 1960. "The Concept of χαρακτήρ in Euripides." *Glotta* 39: 233–38.

Williams, B. 1993. *Shame and Necessity.* Berkeley and Los Angeles.

Williams, D. 1993. "Women on Athenian Vases: Problems of Interpretation." In *Images of Women in Antiquity,* ed. A. Cameron and A. Kuhrt. 2d ed. London. 92–106.

Williams, R. 1977. *Marxism and Literature*. Oxford.

Winkler, J. J. 1990. *The Constraints of Desire: The Anthropology of Sex and Gender in Ancient Greece*. New York.

Winkler, J. J., and F. I. Zeitlin, eds. 1990. *Nothing to Do with Dionysos? Athenian Drama in Its Social Context*. Princeton.

Winter, I. 1995. "Homer's Phoenicians: History, Ethnography, or Literary Trope? [A Perspective on Early Orientalism]." In *The Ages of Homer: A Tribute to Emily Townsend Vermeule*, ed. J. B. Carter and S. P. Morris. Austin. 247–71.

Wiseman, D. J. 1985. *Nebuchadrezzar and Babylon*. Oxford.

Wohl, V. 1998. *Intimate Commerce: Exchange, Gender and Subjectivity in Greek Tragedy*. Austin.

Woodbury, L. 1969. "Truth and the Song: Bacchylides 3.96–98." *Phoenix* 23: 331–35.

Woodford, S. 1982. "Ajax and Achilles Playing a Game on an Olpe in Oxford." *JHS* 102: 173–85.

Wüst, E. 1942. "Palamedes." *RE* vol. 18.2, coll. 2500–12.

Yalouris, N. 1950. "Athena als Herrin der Pferde." *Museum Helveticum* 7: 19–64.

Young, D. C., ed. 1971. *Theognis*. Leipzig.

Young, Douglas. 1973. Review of D. E. Gerber, *Euterpe: An Anthology of Early Greek Lyric, Elegiac, and Iambic Poetry*. *Phoenix* 27: 412–13.

Yunis, H. 1996. *Taming Democracy: Models of Political Rhetoric in Classical Athens*. Ithaca.

Zaccagnini, C. 1989. "Prehistory of the Achaemenid Tributary System." In Briant and Herrenschmidt 1989: 193–215.

Zanker, P. 1975. "Münzen und Medaillen AG," *Auktion* 51. Basel.

Zeitlin, F. I. 1996. *Playing the Other: Gender and Society in Classical Greek Literature*. Chicago.

Zelizer, V. A. 1994. *The Social Meaning of Money*. New York.

Ziebarth, E. 1913. "Ἑταιρία." *RE* vol. 8.2, coll. 1373–74.

Index Locorum

General Index

habrosunē (cont.)
  parody, 59; of Lydians, 166–67 and
    n.74
Halperin, D., 195–96, 198n.57
Hartog, F., 66–67, 97n.71
Harvey, D., 178n.3
Hekataios, 231n.17
Herakleitos: on gold, 58n.36; relates civic
  action to games, 267–68 and n.39; —
  life to *pessoi*, 263–64. *See also Index
  Locorum*
Herakleitos, (first-century commentator),
  183
hero cult, 154 and n.58
Herodotus: and archaic poetry, 31–32 and
  n.83, 60–61, 69–72; on coins, 98–99,
  102, 104–5, 114–15, 116–17 and n.
  38, 322; concrete political theory in, xi,
  66–68 and n.4, 232–33, 332–33; cultural relativity in, 29, 87–89 and n.53,
  330; dating of, 4–5n.6; ethnography in,
  3–4, 36, 61–64, 168–71, 229–30n.14,
  245–46, 298, 300; oral sources of, 28–
  30 and nn. 73, 75, 103–4, 118; performance of, xii, 5n.6, 28n.73; politics of,
  28–31 and nn. 78, 82, 66–68, 96–
  98,117–18, 167–68, 181; quotes
  Pindar, 86–87, 87–88 and n.50; on
  tyrannic power, chs. 2–4. *See also*
  games; histor; *other individual topics;
  Index Locorum*
Hesiod: influence on Herodotus, 60–63,
  69, 70; myth of the races, 49–53, 69,
  155; metallurgy in, 48–49; silence on
  kibdēlos/basanos, 47–48 and n.18. *See
  also Index Locorum*
Hesychios, 44n.10, 254. *See also Index
  Locorum*
hetaira: in archaic poetry, 182–86, 223;
  associated with gold, 185–86n.19; compared with *pornē*, 178 and n.3, 219,
  220–27, 247; elitist associations, 181–
  82, 182–83, 194 and n.47, 198–99,
  220–27, 293–94; etiquette at symposia,
  213–18; ideological ambiguities, 186–
  87 and n.25, 199–219; invention of
  (Reinsberg), 178–87, 201; Herodotus's
  use of term, 177–78, 220, 226 and
  n.11; names for, 183–84 and nn. 13,
  14, 202 and n.72; simultaneous with
  emergence of coins, 181–82; visual representations of, 199–213, figs. 1–3

(202–4), fig. 4 (208), figs. 5–6 (209–
  10), fig. 7 (212); vocabulary describing,
  224–25. *See also* symposium; *xenia*
hetaira-symposia, 205–7 and n.79, fig. 4
  (208). *See also hetaira*; symposium
hetaireia: in archaic poetry, 182–86, 223;
  organized to resist *dēmos*, 17–18 and
  nn. 45, 46; Persian (in Herodotus), 63,
  65, 70–71 and n.12, 78–79; transgression of (Theognis), 53–55. *See also* symposium; *xenia*
heurēmata (inventions), 250–51 and n.4
Hieron: compared with Kroisos (Herodotus), 135–42; denounced by Diodorus,
  133–34; extolled in epinikia, 131, 134–
  37 and nn. 14, 21, 22, 139
hieros gamos. See sacred marriage
Hipponax, 58–60. *See also Index
  Locorum*
histor, 29, 60, 96–97, 99–100, 111, 118–
  19, 120–21, 123–24 and nn.51, 53,
  129, 143, 148n.52, 164, 165, 166, 167,
  168, 175, 220, 223, 224, 227, 229,
  233, 234, 238, 239, 242, 245, 254,
  295, 296
history: juxtaposed with ethnography
  (Lydians, Herodotus), 165–68. *See also*
  Herodotus
Homer: echoed in Anakreon, 193–94; —
  Herodotus, 225; —Simonides, 225 and
  n.8; embodiment in, 257–60 and nn.12,
  18; exchange in, 14–16 and n.41, 146;
  forms of wealth in, 11, 12; on games,
  249, 254–60 (*Odyssey*), 273, 291–92
  and n.92 (Patroklos in *Iliad*). *See also
  Index Locorum*
homoios/homoioi, 50–51 and n.23, 70,
  71, 96, 118 and n.43, 123–24 and
  n.53, 153 and n.57
Howgego, C. , 8 and n.13, 10 and n.19,
  13n.30, 303 and n.9, 331n.64
Hurwit, J., 272–74
hypothēkai (advice), 139–40

iconography, 201–13; of *astragaloi*
  (statue base), 290, 292–93 and n.94; of
  ballgame, 277 and n.60, 280 and n.68;
  of board game, 262n.26; on coinage,
  293–95 and nn. 97–101, 320–22, 324;
  "full frontal" imagery in, 207; of sex,
  201–5, 207–13; of symposium, 205ff.
  and n.79. *See also* Exekias

ABOUT THE AUTHOR

Leslie Kurke is Professor of Classics at University of California, Berkeley. She is the author of *The Traffic in Praise* (Cornell, 1991) and, with Carol Dougherty, co-edited *Cultural Poetics in Archaic Greece* (Cambridge, 1993).

CPSIA information can be obtained at www.ICGtesting.com
Printed in the USA
BVOW07s2134071014

369908BV00001B/6/A